ISPICS	international standardized profile implementation-conformance statement
JTC1	Joint Technical Committee 1
LAN	local-area network
LAPB	link-access protocol, balanced
LAPD	link-access protocol, D channel
LLC	logical link control
LME	layer-management entity
MAC	medium-access control
MAN	metropolitan area network
MIB	management information base
NET	network-entity title
NIST	National Institute of Standards and Technology
NRZ	nonreturn to zero
NSAP	network service-access point
NT	network termination
OAM	operations, administration, and maintenance
OSI	open systems interconnection
PDU	protocol data unit
PICS	protocol-implementation conformance statement
PIXIT	protocol implementation extra information for testing
PSPDN	packet-switched public data network
QOS	quality of service
ROSE	remote-operations-service element
RPOA	recognized private operating agency
RTSE	reliable-transfer-service element
SAC	single-attachment concentrator
SAP	service-access point
SAPI	service-access point identifier
SAS	single-attachment station
SDH	synchronous digital hierarchy
SDU	service data unit
SMAE	systems-management application entity
SMFA	systems-management functional area
SNPA	subnetwork point of attachment
SONET	synchronous optical network
TDM	time-division multiplexing
TEI	terminal-end-point identifier
TTCN	tree and tabular combined notation
VCC	virtual channel connection
VPC	virtual path connection
WAN	wide area network

Networking Standards

A Guide to OSI, ISDN, LAN, and MAN Standards

Networking Standards

A Guide to OSI, ISDN, LAN, and MAN Standards

William Stallings

ADDISON-WESLEY PUBLISHING COMPANY, INC.
Reading, Massachusetts   Menlo Park, California   New York   Don Mills, Ontario
Wokingham, England   Amsterdam   Bonn   Paris   Milan   Madrid   Sydney   Singapore   Tokyo
Seoul   Taipei   Mexico City   San Juan

Many of the designations used by manufacturers and sellers to distinguish their products are claimed as trademarks. Where those designations appear in this book and Addison-Wesley was aware of a trademark claim, the designations have been printed with initial capital letters.

Figure 4.14 reprinted with permission from *ConneXions,* Volume 3, No. 8, August 1989.
ConneXions-The Interoperability Report® is published monthly by:
Interop Company·
480 San Antonio Road, Suite 100
Mountain View, CA 94040-1219
Phone: (415) 941-3399
Fax: (415) 949-1779
Toll free (in USA): 1-800-INTEROP
E-mail: connexions@interop.com
Free sample issue and list of back issues available upon request.

The publisher offers discounts on this book when ordered in quantity for special sales.

For more information, please contact:
  Corporate & Professional Publishing Group
  Addison-Wesley Publishing Company
  One Jacob Way
  Reading, Massachusetts 01867

Library of Congress Cataloging-in-Publication Data

Stallings, William.
    Networking standards : a guide to OSI, ISDN, LAN, and MAN
standards / William Stallings.
        p.   cm.
    Includes bibliographical references and index.
    ISBN 0-201-56357-6
    1. Computer networks—Standards.   2. Data transmission systems—
Standards.   I. Title.
TK5105.5.S73   1993
004.6'2—dc20   92-30995
                                                                          CIP

0-201-56357-6

1 2 3 4 5 6 7 8 9-MU-96959493

First Printing: January 1993

For my wife Tricia

Contents

Preface

In recent years, there has been an explosion of activity in the design of standards for computer communications and networking and in the implementation of these standards. All this effort has been in the context of the open systems interconnection (OSI) model.

The OSI model has proved its value in the definition of protocols and services for distributed processing among computers, workstations and terminals. In addition, this model has provided the framework for the definition of new network services and technologies, including ISDN, broadband ISDN, the IEEE 802 and FDDI LAN standards, and the IEEE 802.6 MAN standard. More recently, this model has been the foundation for developing standards for interoperable network management and network security facilities.

Despite all this activity, the deployment of OSI products has been slow in coming. But now, a recent emphasis on the standardization of OSI implementation is fast bringing OSI to the commercial marketplace. The OSI conformance testing standards and the international standardized profiles (ISPs) are the long-awaited ingredients that make interoperable OSI products a practical reality.

OBJECTIVES

This book is one of a series by the author that provides a comprehensive treatment of computer-communications standards, presented within the framework of OSI. The series systematically covers all major standards topics, providing the introductory and tutorial text missing from the actual standards. The books function as a primary reference for those who need an understanding of the technology, implementation, design, and application issues that relate to the standards. The books also function as companions to the standards documents for those who need to understand the standards for implementation purposes.

This book covers leading-edge developments in a broad range of standards relating to data communications and telecommunications. Because of the rich variety of standards in this area, no single book can hope to adequately cover all these standards. The book therefore provides an overview of the well-established aspects of OSI, ISDN (integrated services digital network), and LAN standards and focuses on the emerging standards that are the key to practical, interoperable networking at high data rates.

The objectives of the book are as follows:

- To provide a description of the leading-edge standards, in the areas of OSI, ISDN, and LAN/MAN standards: The emphasis is on translating the obscure and often downright unreadable standards documents into a form that a technically minded reader can absorb. This material will serve both as a tutorial, read cover to cover, and as a useful reference that can be repeatedly consulted.

- To present and explain the practical implementation issues that have led to the development of conformance assessment standards and the international standardized profiles and describe the current state of these standards. Again, the emphasis is on providing a readable description of this material, in a tutorial/reference form.

INTENDED AUDIENCE

The book is intended for a broad range of readers interested in computer-communications architecture and protocols:

- *Students and professionals in data processing and data communications:* This book is intended as a basic tutorial and reference source for this exciting area.

- *Computer and communications system customers and managers:* The book provides the reader with an understanding of what features and structure are needed in a communications capability, as well as a knowledge of current and evolving standards. This information provides a means of assessing specific implementations and vendor offerings.

- *Designers and implementers:* The book discusses critical design issues and explores approaches to meeting user requirements.

RELATED MATERIALS

A set of videotape courses prepared by the author covering various topics presented in this book is available from The Media Group, Boston University, 565 Commonwealth Avenue, Boston, Mass. 02215; telephone (617) 353-3227.

ACKNOWLEDGMENTS

Many people reviewed the original proposal for this book. Each chapter was also reviewed by one or more persons active in the relevant standards-making committees for each area. The list includes:

Ramakrishnan, K.K.	Gulbenkian, John	Ellis, Mark
Versteeg, Bill	Lem, Mike	Stang, David
Wright, Gary	Mauceri, Larry	Chlamtac, Imrach

Narayanan, Vish
Nelson, Barbara
Perlman, Radia
Hollis, Lloyd
Chapell, David

Mollenauer, Jim
Emmons, Bud
McNamara, John
Tomlinson, Todd L.
Kappel, Kim

Pierle, Nancy
Faureau, Jean-Phillippe
Partridge, Craig
Stevens, Rich
Taylor, Ed

1
Overview

The basic open systems interconnection (OSI) model has been around for over a decade. The purpose of this model was to provide a framework for developing communication protocol and service standards that would at last allow the true interworking of equipment from many different vendors. The OSI model breaks the overall communications function into seven layers. Within this architecture, standards have been developed at all seven layers, to provide a powerful communications facility for distributed computing. It was hoped that, with the development of these standards, vendors would move quickly to provide standardized communications facilities and users would be able to mix equipment to suit their needs.

Unfortunately, this has not happened. The difficulty of specifying a universal capability far exceeded what anyone expected. Even today, the prospective customer has a very limited set of products and features that are truly standardized. Many vendors have announced, and even delivered, OSI-based products, but OSI has yet to fulfill its promise of providing a universal means for interconnecting diverse systems.

But now, a turning point has arrived, due primarily to two factors.

First, a critical mass of standards has been reached. True interoperative, distributed, standardized processing requires more than the basic protocols at the seven layers. Issues concerned with the choice of networks and the ability to control and manage configurations need to be addressed. Key areas in which standards have been or are being developed to provide the user with a fully functional and flexible set of alternatives include:

- *Internetworking:* Both connectionless and connection-mode internetworking standards have been issued. The vital but vexing issue of routing has also been addressed, and a comprehensive set of options is being developed.
- *WAN (wide area network) alternatives:* WAN standards are keeping pace with changes in technology, giving users standardized alternatives such as frame relay, ATM (asynchronous transfer mode), and SONET (synchronous optical network).
- *LAN and MAN (local area network and metropolitan area network) alternatives:* The continuing evolution of FDDI (fiber distributed data interface) and the progress in 802.6 MAN

1

standards have provided vendors with the guidance they need to produce standardized products and give the user a range of options.

- *Network management and security:* The *sine qua non* for complex networking is effective network management and security. OSI-related standards in this area have reached a level of maturity and functionality that makes standardized network management and security products practical.

Second, a major breakthrough in the way in which standards are specified is at last breaking the logjam and bringing OSI to market. This breakthrough is the development of the international standardized profiles (ISPs), which provide specifications that allow multiple vendors to build products that will work together for specific application areas. They transform OSI from an academic exercise into a practical tool for vendors and customers.

1.1   STANDARDS

Although there is no widely accepted and quoted definition of the term *standard,* the following definition from the 1979 National Policy on Standards for the United States encompasses the essential concept:

> A prescribed set of rules, conditions, or requirements concerning definition of terms; classification of components; specification of materials, performance, or operations; delineation of procedures; or measurement of quantity and quality in describing materials, products, systems, service, or practices. (National Standards Policy Advisory Committee 1979)

1.1.1   The Importance of Standards

It has long been accepted in the telecommunications industry that standards are required to govern the physical, electrical, and procedural characteristics of communication equipment. In the past, this view was not embraced by the computer industry. Whereas communication equipment vendors recognize that their equipment will generally interface to and communicate with other vendors' equipment, computer vendors have traditionally attempted to monopolize their customers. The proliferation of computers and distributed processing has made that an untenable position. Computers from different vendors must communicate with each other, and with the ongoing evolution of protocol standards, customers will no longer accept special-purpose protocol conversion software development.

The key advantages of standardization are as follows:

- A standard assures that there will be a large market for a particular piece of equipment or software. This encourages mass production and, in some cases, the use of very-large-scale integration (VLSI) techniques, resulting in lower costs.
- A standard allows products from multiple vendors to communicate, giving the purchaser more flexibility in equipment selection and use.

The principal disadvantage of standards is that they tend to freeze technology. By the time a standard is developed, subjected to review and compromise, and promulgated, more efficient techniques may have been developed. Nevertheless, the advantages of standards are so great that customers are willing to pay this price.

1.1.2   Standards and Regulation

It is helpful for the reader to distinguish three concepts:

1. Voluntary standards
2. Regulatory standards
3. Regulatory use of voluntary standards

Voluntary standards are developed by standards-making organizations, such as CCITT (International Telegraph and Telephone Consultative Committee) and ISO (International Organization for Standardization). They are voluntary in that the existence of the standard does not compel its use. That is, manufacturers voluntarily implement a product that conforms to a standard if they perceive a benefit to themselves; there is no legal requirement to conform. Such standards are also voluntary in the sense that they are developed by volunteers who are not paid for their efforts by the standards-making organization that administers the process. These volunteers are generally employees of interested organizations, such as manufacturers and government agencies.

The purpose of voluntary standards is to cause the market to prefer a standard solution, as opposed to a nonstandard solution. Voluntary standards work because they are generally developed on the basis of broad consensus and because the customer demand for standard products encourages the implementation of these standards by the vendors.

In contrast, a regulatory standard is developed by a government regulatory agency to meet some public objective, such as economic, health, and safety objectives. These standards have the force of the law behind them and must be complied with by providers in the context in which the regulations apply. Familiar examples of regulatory standards can be found in areas such as fire and health codes. But regulations can apply to a wide variety of products, including those related to computers and communications. For example, the Federal Communications Commission regulates electromagnetic emissions.

A relatively new, or at least newly prevalent, phenomenon is the regulatory use of voluntary standards. A typical example of this is a regulation requiring that the government's purchase of a product be limited to those that conform to some referenced set of voluntary standards. This approach has a number of benefits:

- It reduces the rule-making burden on government agencies.
- It encourages cooperation between government and standards organizations to produce standards of broad applicability.
- It reduces the variety of standards that providers must meet.

1.2   STANDARDS ORGANIZATIONS

Throughout this book, we have made reference to key protocol and communications standards. Various organizations have been involved in the development or promotion of these standards. This section provides a brief description of the most important of these organizations (in the current context). For a more detailed discussion, see Cargill (1989).

1.2.1   International Telegraph and Telephone Consultative Committee (CCITT)

CCITT is a committee of the International Telecommunications Union (ITU), which is itself a United Nations treaty organization. Hence, the members of CCITT are governments. The U.S. representation is housed in the Department of State. The charter of CCITT is "to study and issue recommendations on technical, operating, and tariff questions relating to telegraphy and telephony." Its primary objective is to standardize, to the extent necessary, techniques and operations in telecommunications to achieve end-to-end compatibility of international telecommunication connections, regardless of the countries of origin and destination.

CCITT is organized into 15 study groups that prepare standards, called recommendations by CCITT (Table 1.1).

Work within CCITT is conducted in four-year cycles. Every four years, a plenary assembly is held. The work program for the next four years is established at the assembly in the form of questions submitted by the various study groups, based on requests made to the study groups by their members. The assembly assesses the questions, reviews the scope of the study groups, creates new study groups or abolishes existing ones, and allocates questions to them.

Based on these questions, each study group prepares draft recommendations. Two procedures may be followed for the adoption of a new recommendation. The traditional technique is to submit all proposed recommendations to the next assembly, four years hence. A recommendation is approved if it obtains a majority of the votes. All approved recommendations are then published as a package of "books" once every four years.

In addition to this four-year cycle, a new method for approving recommendations was adopted at the 1988 assembly. The need for a change was dictated by two factors. First, the increasing volume of standards produced by CCITT (Figure 1.1) has made the publication process increasingly cumbersome. Many of the recommendations from the 1988 assembly, which totaled over 16,000 pages, were not finally published until 1990, and some were only published in 1991, nearly

Table 1.1 CCITT Study Groups

Study Group I	Services
Study Group II	Network organization
Study Group III	Tariff and accounting principles
Study Group IV	Maintenance
Study Group V	Protection against electromagnetic effects
Study Group VI	Outside plant
Study Group VII	Data communications networks
Study Group VIII	Terminals for telematic services
Study Group IX	Telegraph networks and telegraph terminal equipment
Study Group X	Languages for telecommunication applications
Study Group XI	Switching and signaling
Study Group XII	Transmission performance of telephone networks and terminals
Study Group XV	Transmission systems and equipment
Study Group XVII	Data transmission over the telephone network
Study Group XVIII	ISDN

Number of
recommendations

Number
of pages

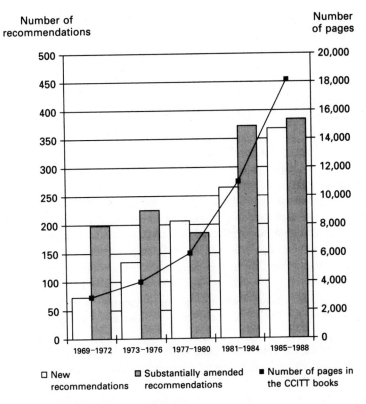

☐ New
recommendations

▨ Substantially amended
recommendations

■ Number of pages in
the CCITT books

Figure 1.1 CCITT Recommendations

three years after approval! Second, with fast-moving areas of technology and user demand, such as broadband ISDN, a four-year gap is simply too long between updates. Accordingly, CCITT adopted a resolution allowing for the approval of recommendations outside the four-year cycle. A study group may submit a proposed recommendation if its members unanimously approve. A vote of all members must be completed within four months. If 70 percent or more of the responding members approve, the recommendation is adopted.

1.2.2   International Organization for Standardization (ISO)

ISO is an international agency for the development of standards on a wide range of subjects. It is a voluntary, nontreaty organization whose members are designated standards bodies of participating nations, plus nonvoting observer organizations. Although ISO is not a governmental body, more than 70 percent of ISO member bodies are governmental standards institutions or organizations incorporated by public law. Most of the remainder have close links with the public administrations in their own countries. The United States member body is the American National Standards Institute (ANSI).

ISO was founded in 1946 and has issued more than 7,000 standards on a broad range of areas. Its purpose is to promote the development of standardization and related activities to facilitate

international exchange of goods and services and to develop cooperation in the sphere of intellec-
tual, scientific, technological, and economic activity. Standards have been issued to cover every-
thing from screw threads to solar energy. One important area of standardization deals with the
open systems interconnection communications architecture and the standards at each layer of the
OSI architecture.

The development of an ISO standard from first proposal to actual publication of the standard
follows a seven-step process. The objective is to ensure that the final result is acceptable to as
many countries as possible. A brief description of the steps follows. (Time limits are the minimum
time in which voting could be accomplished, and amendments require extended time.)

1. A new work item is assigned to the appropriate technical committee and, within that technical
    committee, to the appropriate working group. The working group prepares the technical spec-
    ifications for the proposed standard and publishes these as a *committee draft* (CD). The CD is
    circulated among interested members for balloting and technical comment. At least three months
    are allowed, and there may be iterations. When there is substantial agreement, the CD is sent
    to the administrative arm of ISO, known as the Central Secretariat.

2. The CD is registered at the Central Secretariat within two months of its final approval by the
    technical committee.

3. The Central Secretariat edits the document to ensure conformity with ISO practices; no tech-
    nical changes are made. The edited document is then issued as a *draft international standard*
    (DIS).

4. The DIS is circulated for a six-month balloting period. To be approved, the DIS must receive
    the votes of a majority of the technical committee members and 75 percent of all voting
    members. Revisions may occur to resolve any negative vote. If more than two negative votes
    remain, it is unlikely that the DIS will be published as a final standard.

5. The approved, possibly revised, DIS is returned within three months to the Central Secretariat
    for submission to the ISO Council, which acts as the board of directors of ISO.

6. The DIS is accepted by the council as an *international standard* (IS).

7. The IS is published by ISO.

As can be seen, the process of issuing a standard is a slow one. Certainly, it would be
desirable to issue standards as quickly as the technical details can be worked out, but ISO must
ensure that the standards will receive widespread support.

Within the fields of data communications and information processing, there has traditionally
been a split between the interests of CCITT and ISO. CCITT has primarily been concerned with
data transmission and communication network issues. Roughly, these occupy the lower three layers
of the OSI architecture (see Chapter 2). ISO has traditionally been concerned with computer communications and distributed processing issues, which correspond roughly to layers 4 through 7.
The increasing merger of the fields of data processing and data communications, however, has
resulted in considerable overlap in the areas of concern of these two organizations. Fortunately,
the growth of the overlap has been accompanied by a growth in cooperation, so that competing
standards are not being issued.

1.2.3   International Electrotechnical Commission (IEC)

The IEC, as with ISO, is a voluntary organization composed of national members. The IEC focuses
on the technical aspects of electricity. Each member is supposed to represent all of the electrical

interests of its country—including users, manufacturers, trade associations, government, and academic associations within the country. Frequently, a country's representative to IEC is the same as its representative to ISO. The United States member body is the ANSI.

Procedures for the adoption of new standards are similar to those within ISO.

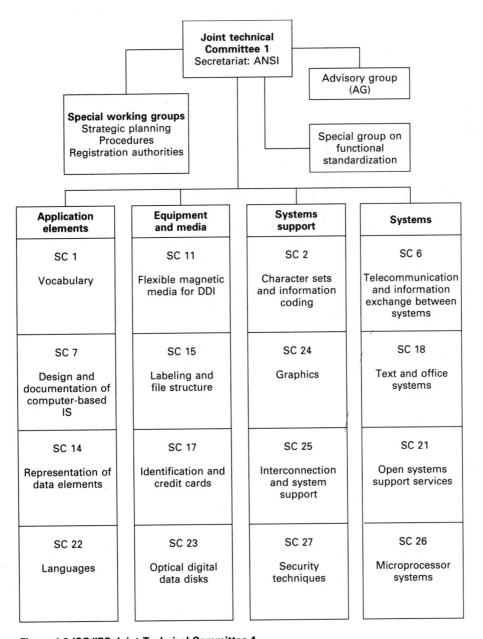

Figure 1.2 ISO/IEC Joint Technical Committee 1

Table 1.2 ISO/IEC Status Acronyms

IS	International standard. Final text of an approved international standard.
DIS	Draft international standard. Essentially stable but occasionally subject to minor change during final balloting.
DP	Draft proposed international standard (obsolete). First formal stage; identified technical direction of the standard but would occasionally have major technical changes.
CD	Committee draft. New designation for a draft proposed international standard.
TR	Technical report. A technical report provides guidance, whereas an IS provides the specification.
DTR	Draft technical report. Equivalent to DIS status.
PDTR	Proposed draft technical report. Equivalent to CD status.
AD	Addendum to a published standard. Adds new material to an existing standard.
DAD	Draft addendum to a published standard.
PDAD	Proposed draft addendum to a published standard.
AM	Amendment to a published standard. Corrects material within an existing standard.
DAM	Draft amendment to a published standard.
PDAM	Proposed draft amendment to a published standard.
WD	Working document.
ISP	A published international standardized profile. Stable. Profiles a group of base standards for product development.
DISP	Draft international standardized profile. Equivalent to DIS status.

1.2.4   Joint Technical Committee 1 (JTC 1)

Just as there is a growing overlap between the telecommunications concerns of CCITT and the information technology interests of ISO, there is a growing overlap between ISO's interests and those of IEC. Accordingly, in 1987, ISO and IEC formed a joint technical committee on information technology. JTC 1 merges the work of ISO Technical Committee 97 on information processing systems with related IEC technical committees. The standards resulting from JTC 1 carry the double logo of ISO and IEC and are published according to the procedures described earlier in this section. Figure 1.2 shows the organization of JTC 1.

The notation used to refer to ISO/IEC documents is:

ISO/IEC {status} {number}

Table 1.2 lists the possible values of the status field.

1.3   AREAS OF STANDARDIZATION

As Figure 1.2 and Table 1.1 suggest, even within the areas of telecommunications and information technology, the range of topics for standardization is very broad, more than can be dealt with in a single volume. In this section, we highlight key areas of standardization and indicate those areas covered in this book.

1.3.1   Communications Architecture

A communications architecture is a structured set of software (and possibly firmware) modules that implement the communications function. A standard for a communications architecture has been adopted jointly by ISO (ISO 7498) and CCITT (X.200), referred to as the open systems interconnection (OSI) reference model. The OSI model, which is a seven-layer structure, provides the following potential benefits:

- The model provides a framework within which standards at each layer can be developed systematically and in parallel. Thus, the standards-making process is more efficient.

- Communications standards assure a large market and therefore promote lower costs through competition and mass production.

- Standards promote interoperability; that is, standards promote the ability for products from different vendors to work together. Interoperability, in turn, gives purchasers more flexibility in equipment selection and promotes distributed applications between and among different organizations.

All international standardization efforts related to networking and all the standards examined in this book are intended to fit within this framework.[1] Because of its central role, OSI is the single most important networking standard. Although the OSI model has been stable for many years, the work required to fill in the details at each layer is ongoing.

1.3.2   Local and Metropolitan Area Networks

One of the most successful areas of networking standardization has been that of local area networks (LANs). LAN standards have been adopted enthusiastically by both vendors and customers, and standards-based LAN products have come to dominate the LAN marketplace.

In the forefront in the development of LAN standards has been the IEEE 802 committee, a standards-making body of the IEEE Computer Society. The 802 committee has been accredited by ANSI to develop draft standards that go on to become ANSI standards. The IEEE 802 documents have achieved international standards status as the ISO 8802 series of standards.

The IEEE standards cover what may now be referred to as LANs of moderate data rates, up to about 20 Mbps. An equally successful set of standards for higher-speed LANs has been developed by an ANSI committee, the ANS X3T9.5 committee. The result is a set of standards referred to as the fiber distributed data interface (FDDI), also adopted by ISO. Work continues in both the 802 and FDDI areas to add more options.

A logical extension of the work on local area networks is that concerned with metropolitan area networks (MANs). Although some of the LAN specifications, notably 802.4 token bus broadband and FDDI, cover designs that are suitable for a metropolitan area network, none of the LAN standards targets that application specifically. The IEEE 802.6 defines a new architecture that provides a system optimized for satisfying MAN requirements.

---

1. A few of the standards discussed in this book predate the OSI model. X.25 is an example. However, these standards have been updated to conform to OSI. In the case of X.25, the most recent version of the standard includes new features and capabilities designed to enable X.25 to support the OSI network service.

1.3.3   Integrated Services Digital Network (ISDN)

The acronym *ISDN* refers to a massive set of standards developed by CCITT that define the characteristics of a digital telecommunications network for voice and data. The focus of the standards is on the externals of the network: interfaces and services. The ISDN standards fall into two categories:

1. *Narrowband ISDN:* The initial version of the ISDN specification is based on the use of a 64-Kbps digital channel as the building block for user services. Recommendations for narrowband ISDN were first issued in 1984, with a more complete set adopted in 1988.

2. *Broadband ISDN (B-ISDN):* The follow-on to narrowband ISDN, B-ISDN, provides data rates in the tens and hundreds of megabits per second. It is intended to support high-speed data applications plus image and video. A brief and preliminary functional description of B-ISDN appeared in the 1988 set of ISDN recommendations. The first detailed set of approved recommendations appeared in 1990, using the new CCITT approval process.

1.3.4   OSI-wide Standards

Much of the work that relates directly to OSI is concerned with the functions and services of a particular layer. There are several areas of concern, however, that span all the layers of the architecture. Perhaps the two most important of these are network management and security.

ISO has developed a set of standards for network management that attempt to cover all the important aspects of this complex task. The standards define a comprehensive set of data-gathering and control tools that can be integrated with the network hardware and software. In addition, the ISO standards include the definition of the form and content of a management information base, which is used to represent and track all the entities in the network that are subject to management.

Similarly, ISO has defined a security architecture, which is based on a definition of security threats, mechanisms for providing security, and a collection of security services.

1.3.5   Conformance Assessment and International Standardized Profiles

Since the publication of the OSI model, computer industry observers and computer users have awaited the arrival of widespread implementation of OSI-related standards. The wait has been far longer than almost anyone would have predicted. Among the problems that have retarded the introduction of standardized products:

- A standard is essentially a prose description of a function, with the attendant opportunity for ambiguity. Thus, well-meaning and competent systems programmers from different organizations, working from the same set of documents, may produce implementations that do not interoperate.

- Standards are made on paper, not in software, leading to implementation problems. This is potentially a more serious problem than the preceding one. In essence, an untested standard may contain logical flaws that are not apparent until after some (perhaps considerable) implementation experience. Not only may two implementations not work together; a single implementation may not work at all!

- A standard typically contains a number of options and a number of unspecified implementation policy alternatives. The result is that two implementations that are fully compliant with the standard may not interoperate because they do not contain a sufficient overlap of options.

One result of all these problems is that the customer is not assured that products from different vendors can be successfully combined in a single distributed system. Another result is that it is difficult for a customer to assess whether a particular implementation meets the requirements.

A number of efforts at overcoming these problems have been initiated, culminating in the development of two key families of standards:

1. *Conformance assessment:* A set of standards have been developed that specify techniques and procedures for assessing an implementation's conformance to a standard. This allows the vendor to obtain confirmation that the vendor's product is in fact standardized.

2. *International standardized profiles (ISPs):* The ISPs define subsets and combinations of base standards that are to be used to provide specific functions or support specific application areas. They also provide a basis for the development of uniform conformance tests.The intent is that ISPs will provide specifications that allow multiple vendors to build products that will work together for specific application areas.

1.3.6 Distributed Applications

The ultimate goal of the entire networking standards effort is to support distributed applications, such as electronic mail, file transfer, distributed transaction processing, remote access, and document transfer. These applications, collectively, account for a considerable number of ISO standards and CCITT recommendations. Because of the range of application-level standards work, a discussion of these standards is beyond the scope of this book. Rather, this book concentrates on the infrastructure of functions and services that support the collection of distributed applications.

1.4 OUTLINE OF THE BOOK

This chapter serves as an introduction to the entire book. A brief synopsis of the remaining chapters follows.

1.4.1 Part 1, "Open Systems Interconnection"

The OSI model is, of course, the framework within which all of the standards are to be discussed. This part provides a summary of the OSI model and then examines the two areas where the most active work is taking place.

Chapter 2, "The OSI Reference Model." This chapter provides an overview of the OSI model. The concepts of service and protocol are explored, and connectionless versus connection-mode operation is examined. A relatively brief discussion of each layer, in terms of functions and services, is provided. The issue of addressing is explored, including the distinction between subnetwork addresses, global internet addresses, and service access points.

Chapter 3, "The OSI Infrastructure: Layers 2 through 5." Layers 2 through 5 include general-purpose protocols and services that form the infrastructure for supporting distributed applications. This chapter examines the key standards at the data link, transport, and session layers. At the network layer, the widely used X.25 standard is summarized. Other protocols and services at the network layer are examined elsewhere, in conjunction with discussions of specific network types.

Chapter 4, "Internetworking." One of the most important facilities required for distributed systems is the ability to interconnect multiple networks. Two key areas of standardization are required for this internetworking:

1. *Internetworking protocol:* A protocol is needed for relaying data units through multiple networks from source to destination. Both connection-mode and connectionless approaches have been standardized.

2. *Routing protocol:* The intermediate systems (ISs) that are used to connect networks must cooperate in relaying data from a source to a destination. These ISs require a protocol to exchange topology and routing information.

Both these areas are explored in Chapter 4.

Chapter 5, "Upper-Layer Architecture." This chapter focuses on the presentation and application layers. It begins with an explanation of presentation-layer concepts. Then, the ISO presentation-layer service and protocol are described. Next, the internal structure of the application layer is examined. Finally, three important general-purpose application-layer facilities are examined: the association control service element, the reliable transfer service element, and the remote operations service element.

1.4.2   Part 2, "Integrated Services Digital Network"

CCITT issued a comprehensive set of standards for ISDN in 1988 and updated these with a set of interim approved recommendations in 1990. This part provides an overview of these standards and then examines the most active areas of standards making.

Chapter 6, "ISDN Overview." This overview begins with a discussion of the body of CCITT standards for ISDN and their structure. A brief survey of each of the major groups of ISDN standards is provided. The ISDN architecture and protocols are then examined.

Chapter 7, "Frame Relay." The most significant technical innovation of the ISDN standards effort is frame relay. This chapter is devoted to a detailed examination of frame-relay services and protocols. The chapter also looks at the congestion-control facilities needed to manage the load on a frame-relay network.

Chapter 8, "Broadband ISDN, Cell Relay, and SONET." This chapter introduces the CCITT standards for broadband ISDN (B-ISDN). The B-ISDN architecture and protocols are then examined. The basic transmission mechanism for B-ISDN is known as the asynchronous transfer mode (ATM), or cell relay. Just as frame relay is the most innovative and interesting aspect of ISDN, cell relay is the major innovation of the B-ISDN standardization effort. The remainder of the chapter is devoted to a discussion of cell relay and related issues. First, the details of the cell-relay mechanism are examined. Then, the way in which B-ISDN services are adapted to operate over cell relay is examined, and a new synchronous digital transmission scheme, known as synchronous optical network (SONET) or synchronous digital hierarchy (SDH), is introduced. Finally, the chapter examines the alternative mechanisms for structuring cell-relay transmission, one of which is the use of SONET/SDH.

1.4.3   Part 3, "Local and Metropolitan Area Networks"

Standards in the area of LAN and MAN are well developed and are examined in this part.

Chapter 9, "ISO 8802 and IEEE 802 Standards." This chapter provides an overall survey of the ISO 8802 family of standards for LANs, including IEEE 802 specifications that are not yet part of ISO 8802. These standards cover logical link control (LLC), CSMA/CD (carrier sense multiple access with collision detection), token bus, and token ring. Appendixes to the chapter provide reference material on LAN technology and LAN addressing.

Chapter 10, "Fiber Distributed Data Interface." In an effort separate from the IEEE 802 work, the ANS X3T9.5 committee has developed a set of standards referred to as fiber distributed data interface (FDDI). The initial set of standards, sometimes referred to as FDDI-I, provides for a LAN optimized to support data traffic. A more recent enhancement, called FDDI-II, includes support for a circuit-switched (isochronous) type of traffic as well as data traffic. Both FDDI-I and FDDI-II are covered in this chapter.

Chapter 11, "MAN Standards." This chapter covers the MAC (medium access control) and physical-layer specifications in IEEE 802.6, which is the MAN standard also known as distributed-queue, dual-bus (DQDB).

1.4.4   Part 4, "Network Management and Security"

As networks and the distributed applications they support grow in scale and complexity, management requirements become increasingly complex and important. This part explores the two areas that are the subject of ongoing standardization efforts: OSI network management and OSI security.

Chapter 12, "OSI Network Management." ISO has issued a set of standards that deal with network management, covering services, protocols, and management information base. This chapter provides an introduction to the overall concepts of standardized network management and examines the architecture and functional areas of OSI network management. Next, the concept of structure of management information and the resulting management information base are introduced. Finally, the chapter examines the network management protocol and services defined by ISO.

Chapter 13, "OSI Security." ISO has also issued standards relating to security. This chapter includes a discussion of security mechanisms and services and their relationship to the OSI architecture. In addition, the authentication facility for association establishment is presented. Finally, the evolving, leading-edge areas of OSI security are summarized.

1.4.5   Part 5, "OSI Implementation"

For the large and growing body of OSI-based standards to result in commercially accepted implementations, two key ingredients are needed. First, the vendor must be able to demonstrate objectively that the offered implementation conforms to the corresponding set of standards. Second, a standardized specification of the set of standards and options required for a particular application area is needed to guide both vendor and customer in the selection of a suite of protocols and options. Both these areas are in the process of standardization and are covered in this part.

Chapter 14, "OSI Conformance Testing." This chapter examines the standards for the conformance testing of OSI-based implementations. It covers the basic methodology of conformance testing, the formal description technique developed for OSI conformance testing, and the conformance test realization and assessment functions.

Chapter 15, "International Standardized Profiles." This chapter begins with a discussion of the purposes of the ISPs. Then, the framework and taxonomy of ISPs are explained. The concepts that comprise a formal ISP document are explained, and the current status of ISP development is examined.

1.4.6 Appendix A, "Digital Signaling"

All the physical-layer protocols discussed in this book include the definition of a technique for encoding binary data into digital signals to optimize the use of the transmission medium. Appendix A provides a summary, which can be used as a reference for readers unfamiliar with these techniques.

Part 1
Open Systems Interconnection

The OSI model is, of course, the framework within which all the standards presented in this book are discussed.

Chapter 2 introduces the OSI model and examines the basic concepts and conventions of OSI. The differences between connection-mode and connectionless-mode operation are examined, and the role of each within the OSI model is presented. Finally, the topic of addressing is examined.

Chapter 3 summarizes the protocol and service standards at OSI layers 2 through 5. These layers are relatively stable and form what might be called the infrastructure of OSI.

The remainder of this part examines the two areas where the most active work is taking place in the development of the OSI model. Chapter 4 is concerned with the issues of internetworking and routing. There are two key areas of standardization here. First are the relaying protocols used for moving data units from source to destination; both connectionless and connection-mode protocols have been defined. Second are the routing protocols used for exchanging information needed in the routing function. This area is less well developed than that of relaying protocols. Work has been done both on protocols between an end system (ES) and an intermediate system (IS) and on protocols between ISs.

Chapter 5 examines some of the important aspects of OSI layers 6 and 7.

2
The OSI Reference Model

2.1 A SIMPLE COMMUNICATIONS ARCHITECTURE

2.1.1 The Need for a Communications Architecture

When computers, terminals, and other data-processing devices exchange data, the procedures involved can be quite complex. Consider, for example, the transfer of a file between two computers attached to a network. These are some of the typical tasks to be performed:

1. The source system must inform the network of the identity of the desired destination system.

2. The source system must determine that the destination system is prepared to receive data.

3. The file-transfer application on the source system must determine that the file-management program on the destination system is prepared to accept and store the file from this particular user.

4. If the file formats used on the two systems are incompatible, one of the two systems must perform a format-translation function.

It is clear that there must be a high degree of cooperation between the two computers. Instead of implementing the logic for this as a single module, the task is broken up into subtasks, each of which is implemented separately. As an example, Figure 2.1 suggests a way in which a file-transfer facility could be implemented. Three modules are used. Tasks 3 and 4 in the preceding list could be performed by a file-transfer module. The two modules on the two systems exchange files and commands. However, rather than requiring the file transfer module to deal with the details of actually transferring data and commands, the file-transfer modules each rely on a communications-service module. This module is responsible for making sure that the file-transfer commands and data are reliably exchanged between systems. Among other things, this module would perform task 2. Now the nature of the exchange between systems is independent of the nature of the network that interconnects them. Therefore, rather than building details of the network interface into the communications-service module, it makes sense to have a third module, the network-access module, that performs task 1 by interacting with the network.

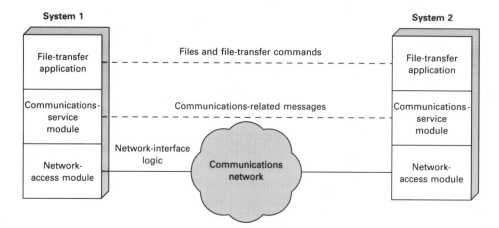

Figure 2.1 A Simplified Architecture for File Transfer

Let us try to summarize the motivation for the three modules in Figure 2.1. The file-transfer module contains all the logic that is unique to the file-transfer application, such as transmitting passwords, file commands, and file records. There is a need to transmit these files and commands reliably. However, the same sorts of reliability requirements are relevant to a variety of applications (e.g., electronic mail, document transfer). Therefore, these requirements are met by a separate communications-service module that can be used by a variety of applications. The communications-service module is concerned with assuring that the two computer systems are active and ready for data transfer and for keeping track of the data that are being exchanged to assure delivery. However, these tasks are independent of the type of network being used. Therefore, the logic for actually dealing with the network is separated out into a separate network-access module. That way, if the network to be used is changed, only the network-access module is affected.

Thus, instead of a single module for performing communications, there is a structured set of modules that implements the communications function. That structure is referred to as a *communications architecture*. In the remainder of this section, we generalize the preceding example to present a simplified communications architecture.

2.1.2   A Three-Layer Model

In very general terms, communications can be said to involve three agents: applications, computers, and networks. The applications that we are concerned with here are distributed applications involving the exchange of data between two computer systems. These applications and others execute on computers that can often support multiple simultaneous applications. Computers are connected to networks, and the data to be exchanged are transferred by the network from one computer to another. Thus, the transfer of data from one application to another involves first getting the data to the computer in which the application resides and then getting it to the intended application within that computer.

With these concepts in mind, it appears natural to organize the communication task into three relatively independent layers:

1. Network-access layer
2. Transport layer
3. Application layer

The *network-access layer* is concerned with the exchange of data between a computer and the network to which it is attached. The sending computer must provide the network with the address of the destination computer, so that the network may route the data to the appropriate destination. The sending computer may wish to invoke certain services, such as priority, that might be provided by the network. The specific software used at this layer depends on the type of network to be used; different standards have been developed for circuit-switching, packet-switching, local area networks, and others. Thus, it makes sense to separate those functions having to do with network access into a separate layer. By doing this, the remainder of the communications software, above the network-access layer, need not be concerned about the specifics of the network to be used. The same higher-layer software should function properly regardless of the particular network to which the computer is attached.

Regardless of the nature of the applications that are exchanging data, there is usually a requirement that data be exchanged reliably. That is, we would like to be assured that all the data arrive at the destination application and that they arrive in the same order in which they were sent. The mechanisms for providing reliability are essentially independent of the nature of the applications. Thus, it makes sense to collect those mechanisms in a common layer shared by all applications, which is referred to as the *transport layer*.

Finally, the *application layer* contains the logic needed to support the various user applications. For each different type of application, such as file transfer, a separate module is needed that is peculiar to that application.

Figures 2.2 and 2.3 illustrate this simple architecture. Figure 2.2 shows three computers connected to a network. Each computer contains software at the network-access and transport layers, as well as software at the application layer for one or more applications. For successful communication, every entity in the overall system must have a unique address. Actually, two levels of addressing are needed. Each computer on the network must have a unique network address; this allows the network to deliver data to the proper computer. Each application on a computer must have an address that is unique within that computer; this allows the transport layer to deliver data to the proper application. These latter addresses are known as *service-access points* (SAPs), connoting the fact that each application is individually accessing the services of the transport layer.

Figure 2.3 indicates the way in which modules at the same level on different computers communicate with each other: by means of a protocol. A protocol is the set of rules or conventions governing the way in which two entities cooperate to exchange data. A protocol specification details the control functions that may be performed, the formats and control codes used to communicate those functions, and the procedures that the two entities must follow.

Let us trace a simple operation. Suppose that an application, associated with SAP 1 at computer A, wishes to send a message to another application, associated with SAP 2 at computer B. The application at A hands the message over to its transport layer with instructions to send it to SAP 2 on computer B. The transport layer hands the message over to the network-access layer, which instructs the network to send the message to computer B. Note that the network need not be told the identity of the destination service-access point. All it needs to know is that the data are intended for computer B.

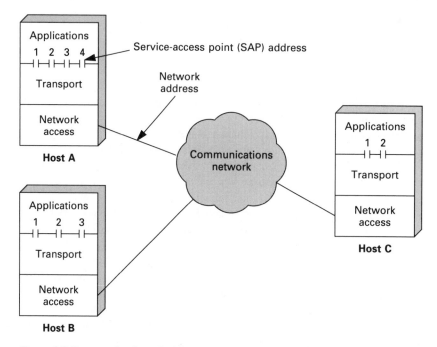

Figure 2.2 Communications Architectures and Networks

To control this operation, control information as well as user data must be transmitted, as suggested in Figure 2.4. Let us say that the sending application generates a block of data and passes this to the transport layer. The transport layer may break this block into two smaller pieces to make it more manageable. To each of these pieces the transport layer appends a transport header, containing protocol-control information. The combination of data from the next higher

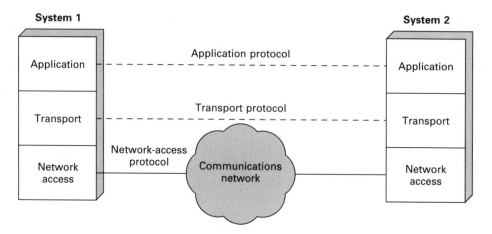

Figure 2.3 Protocols in a Simplified Architecture

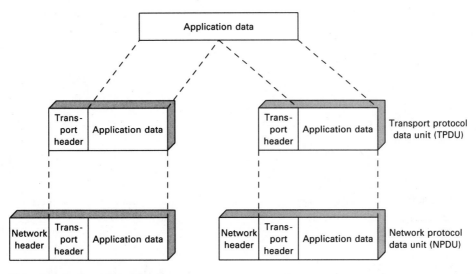

Figure 2.4 Protocol Data Units

layer and control information is known as a protocol data unit (PDU); in this case, it is referred to as a transport protocol data unit (TPDU). The header in each transport PDU contains control information to be used by the peer transport protocol at computer B. Examples of items that may be stored in this header include:

- *Destination SAP:* When the destination transport layer receives the transport protocol data unit, it must know to which SAP the data are to be delivered.
- *Sequence number:* Since the transport protocol is sending a sequence of protocol data units, it numbers them sequentially so that if they arrive out of order, the destination transport entity can reorder them.
- *Error-detection code:* The sending transport entity may calculate and insert an error-detection code so that the receiver can determine whether an error has occurred and discard the protocol data unit.

The next step is for the transport layer to hand each protocol data unit over to the network layer, with instructions to transmit it to the destination computer. To satisfy this request, the network-access protocol must present the data to the network with a request for transmission. As before, this operation requires the use of control information. In this case, the network-access protocol appends a network-access header to the data it receives from the transport layer, creating a network-access PDU. Examples of the items that may be stored in the header include:

- *Destination computer address:* The network must know to which computer on the network the data are to be delivered.
- *Facilities requests:* The network-access protocol might want the network to make use of certain facilities, such as priority.

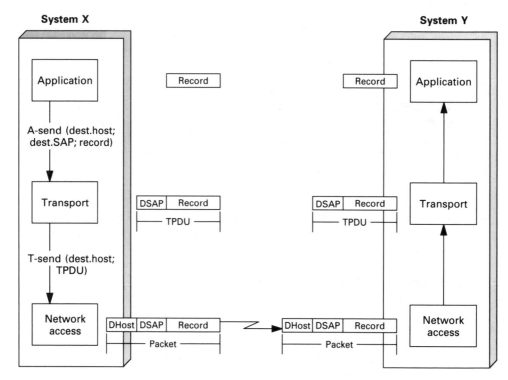

Figure 2.5 Operation of a Communications Architecture

Figure 2.5 puts all these concepts together, showing the interaction between modules to transfer one block of data. Let us say that the file-transfer module in computer X is transferring a file one record at a time to computer Y. Each record is handed over to the transport-layer module. We can picture this action as being in the form of a command or procedure call, A-SEND (application-send). The arguments of this procedure call include the destination computer address, the destination service-access point, and the record. The transport layer appends the destination service-access point and other control information to the record to create a transport PDU. This is then handed down to the network-access layer in a T-SEND command. In this case, the arguments for the command are the destination computer address and the transport protocol data unit. The network-access layer uses this information to construct a network PDU. Suppose the network is an X.25 packet-switching network. In this case, the network protocol data unit is an X.25 data packet. The transport protocol data unit is the data field of the packet, and the packet header includes the virtual circuit number for a virtual circuit connecting X and Y.

The network accepts the data packet from X and delivers it to Y. The network-access module in Y receives the packet, strips off the packet header, and transfers the enclosed transport protocol data unit to Y's transport-layer module. The transport layer examines the transport protocol data unit header and, on the basis of the SAP field in the header, delivers the enclosed record to the appropriate application—in this case, the file-transfer module in Y.

2.2 OSI ARCHITECTURE

As discussed in Chapter 1, standards are needed to promote interoperability among vendor equipment and to encourage economies of scale. Because of the complexity of the communications task, no single standard will suffice. Rather, the functions should be broken down into more manageable parts and organized as a communications architecture. The architecture would then form the framework for standardization.

This line of reasoning led ISO (International Organization for Standardization) in 1977 to establish a subcommittee to develop such an architecture. The result was the open systems interconnection (OSI) reference model. Although the essential elements of the model were in place quickly, the final ISO standard, ISO 7498, was not published until 1984. A technically compatible version was issued by CCITT (International Telegraph and Telephone Consultative Committee) as X.200.

Table 2.1, extracted from ISO 7498, summarizes the purpose of the model. Note that the emphasis is on creating a framework within which standards can be developed. Thus, we can view OSI as a master plan for all networking standards.

2.2.1 The Concept of Open Systems

Open systems interconnection is based on the concept of cooperating distributed applications. In the OSI model, a system consists of a computer, all its software, and any peripheral devices attached to it, including terminals. A distributed application is any activity that involves the

---

Table 2.1 Purpose of the OSI Model Standard

The purpose of this International Standard Reference Model of Open Systems Interconnection is to provide a common basis for the coordination of standards development for the purpose of systems interconnection, while allowing existing standards to be placed into perspective within the overall Reference Model.

The term Open Systems Interconnection (OSI) qualifies standards for the exchange of information among systems that are ''open'' to one another for this purpose by virtue of their mutual use of the applicable standards.

The fact that a system is open does not imply any particular systems implementation, technology or means of interconnection, but refers to the mutual recognition and support of the applicable standards.

It is also the purpose of this International Standard to identify areas for developing or improving standards, and to provide a common reference for maintaining consistency of all related standards. It is not the intent of this International Standard either to serve as an implementation specification, or to be a basis for appraising the conformance of actual implementations, or to provide a sufficient level of detail to define precisely the services and protocols of the interconnection architecture. Rather, this International Standard provides a conceptual and functional framework which allows international teams of experts to work productively and independently on the development of standards for each layer of the Reference Model of OSI.

Source: ISO 7498.

exchange of information between two open systems. Examples of such activities include the following:

- A user at a terminal on one computer is logged on to an application such as transaction processing on another computer.

- A file-management program on one computer transfers a file to a file-management program on another computer.

- A user sends an electronic-mail message to a user on another computer.

- A process-control program sends a control signal to a robot.

OSI is concerned with the exchange of information between a pair of open systems and not with the internal functioning of each individual system. Specifically, it is concerned with the capability of systems to cooperate in exchanging information and accomplishing tasks.

The objective of the OSI effort is to define a set of standards that will enable open systems located anywhere in the world to cooperate by being interconnected through some standardized communications facility and by executing standardized OSI protocols.

An open system may be implemented in any way, provided that it conforms to a minimal set of standards that allows communication to be achieved with other open systems. An open system consists of a number of applications, an operating system, and system software such as a database-management system and a terminal handling package. It also includes the communications software that turns a closed system into an open system. Different manufacturers will implement open systems in different ways in order to achieve a product identity, which will increase their market share or create a new market. However, virtually all manufacturers are now committed to providing communications software that behaves in conformance with OSI in order to provide their customers with the ability to communicate with other open systems.

2.2.2   The Model

A widely accepted structuring technique, and the one chosen by ISO, is layering. The communications functions are partitioned into a hierarchical set of layers. Each layer performs a related subset of the functions required to communicate with another system. It relies on the next lower layer to perform more primitive functions and to conceal the details of those functions. It provides services to the next higher layer. Ideally, the layers should be defined so that changes in one layer do not require changes in the other layers. Thus, we have decomposed one problem into a number of more manageable subproblems.

The task of ISO was to define a set of layers and the services performed by each layer. The partitioning should group functions logically and should have enough layers to make each layer manageably small but not so many layers that the processing overhead imposed by the collection of layers is burdensome. The principles that guided the design effort are summarized in Table 2.2. The resulting reference model has seven layers, which are listed with a brief definition in Table 2.3. Table 2.4 provides ISO's justification for the selection of these layers.

Figure 2.6 illustrates the OSI architecture. Each system contains the seven layers. Communication is between applications in the two computers, labeled application X and application Y in the figure. If application X wishes to send a message to application Y, it invokes the application layer (layer 7). Layer 7 establishes a peer relationship with layer 7 of the target computer, using a

Table 2.2 Principles Used in Defining the OSI Layers

1. Do not create so many layers as to make the system engineering task of describing and integrating the layers more difficult than necessary.
2. Create a boundary at a point where the description of services can be small and the number of interactions across the boundary are minimized.
3. Create separate layers to handle functions that are manifestly different in the process performed or the technology involved.
4. Collect similar functions into the same layer.
5. Select boundaries at a point which past experience has demonstrated to be successful.
6. Create a layer of easily localized functions so that the layer could be totally redesigned and its protocols changed in a major way to take advantage of new advances in architecture, hardware or software technology without changing the services expected from and provided to the adjacent layers.
7. Create a boundary where it may be useful at some point in time to have the corresponding interface standardized.*
8. Create a layer where there is a need for a different level of abstraction in the handling of data, for example morphology, syntax, semantic.
9. Allow changes of functions or protocols to be made within a layer without affecting other layers.
10. Create for each layer boundaries with its upper and lower layer only.

Similar principles have been applied to sublayering:
11. Create further subgrouping and organization of functions to form sublayers within a layer in cases where distinct communication services need it.
12. Create, where needed, two or more sublayers with a common, and therefore minimal functionality to allow interface operation with adjacent layers.
13. Allow by-passing of sublayers.

Source: ISO 7498.

* Advantages and drawbacks of standardizing internal interfaces within open systems are not considered in this international standard. In particular, mention of or reference to principle 7 should not be taken to imply usefulness of standards for such internal interfaces. Also, it is important to note that OSI per se does not require interfaces within open systems to be standardized. Moreover, whenever standards for such interfaces are defined, adherence to such internal interface standards can in no way be considered as a condition of openness.

Table 2.3 The OSI Layers

Layer	Definition
1 Physical	Is concerned with the transmission of an unstructured bit stream over a physical link; involves such parameters as signal voltage swing and bit duration; deals with the mechanical, electrical, and procedural characteristics to establish, maintain, and deactivate the physical link.
2 Data link	Provides for the reliable transfer of data across the physical link; sends blocks of data (frames) with the necessary synchronization, error control, and flow control.

Table 2.3 (*Cont.*)

3	Network	Provides upper layers with independence from the data-transmission and switching technologies used to connect systems; is responsible for establishing, maintaining, and terminating connections across networks.
4	Transport	Provides reliable, transparent transfer of data between end points; provides end-to-end error recovery and flow control.
5	Session	Provides the control structure for communication between applications; establishes, manages, and terminates connections (sessions) between cooperating applications.
6	Presentation	Performs generally useful transformations on data to provide a standardized application interface and common communications services; examples include encryption, text compression, reformatting.
7	Application	Provides services to the users of the OSI environment; examples include transaction server, file-transfer protocol, network management.

Table 2.4 Justification of the OSI Layers

1. It is essential that the architecture permits usage of a realistic variety of physical media for interconnection with different control procedures (for example V.24, V.25, etc.). Application of principles 3, 5, and 8 [Table 2.2] leads to identification of a **Physical Layer** as the lowest layer in the architecture.

2. Some physical communication media (for example telephone line) require specific techniques to be used in order to transmit data between systems despite a relatively high error rate (i.e., an error rate not acceptable for the great majority of applications). These specific techniques are used in data-link control procedures which have been studied and standardized for a number of years. It must also be recognized that new physical communication media (for example fiber optics) will require different data-link control procedures. Application of principles 3, 5, and 8 leads to identification of a **Data Link Layer** on top of the Physical Layer in the architecture.

3. In the open systems architecture, some open systems will act as the final destination of data. Some open systems may act only as intermediate nodes (forwarding data to other systems). Application of principles 3, 5, and 7 leads to identification of a **Network Layer** on top of the data link layer. Network oriented protocols such as routing, for example, will be grouped in this layer. Thus, the Network Layer will provide a connection path (network-connection) between a pair of transport entities; including the case where intermediate nodes are involved.

4. Control of data transportation from source end open system to destination end open system (which is not performed in intermediate nodes) is the last function to be performed in order to provide the totality of the transport service. Thus, the upper layer in the transport service part of the architecture is the **Transport Layer,** on top of the Network Layer. This Transport Layer relieves higher layer entities from any concern with the transportation of data between them.

5. There is a need to organize and synchronize dialogue, and to manage the exchange of data. Application of principles 3 and 4 leads to the identification of a **Session Layer** on top of the Transport Layer.

Table 2.4 (*Cont.*)

6. The remaining set of general interest functions are those related to representation and manipulation of structured data for the benefit of application programs. Application of principles 3 and 4 leads to the identification of a **Presentation Layer** on top of the Session Layer.

7. Finally, there are applications consisting of application processes which perform information processing. An aspect of these application processes and the protocols by which they communicate comprise the **Application Layer** as the highest layer of the architecture.

Source: ISO 7498.

layer-7 protocol (application protocol). This protocol requires services from layer 6, so the two layer-6 entities use a protocol of their own, and so on down to the physical layer, which actually transmits bits over a transmission medium.

Note that there is no direct communication between peer layers except at the physical layer. That is, above the physical layer, each protocol entity sends data down to the next lower layer to get the data across to its peer entity. Even at the physical layer, the OSI model does not stipulate that two systems be directly connected. For example, a packet-switched or circuit-switched network may be used to provide the communication link. This point should become clearer later in the chapter, when we discuss the network layer.

Some useful OSI terminology is illustrated in Figure 2.7. For simplicity, any layer is referred to as the (N) layer, and names of constructs associated with that layer are also preceded by (N). Within a system, there are one or more active entities in each layer. An (N) entity implements functions of the (N) layer and also the protocol for communicating with (N) entities in other systems. An example of an entity is a process in a multiprogrammed or multitasking system. There may be multiple identical (N) entities if this is convenient or efficient for a given system. There might also be differing (N) entities, corresponding to different protocol standards at that level. Each entity communicates with entities in the layers above and below it across an interface. The interface is realized as one or more service-access points. Finally, two (N) entities may communicate across a logical connection provided as a service by the $(N-1)$ layer and known as an $(N-1)$ connection.

2.2.3 Standardization within the OSI Framework

The principal motivation for the development of the OSI model was to provide a framework for standardization. Within the model, one or more protocol standards can be developed at each layer. The model defines in general terms the functions to be performed at that layer and facilitates the standards-making process in two ways:

1. Since the functions of each layer are well defined, standards can be developed independently and simultaneously for each layer. This speeds up the standards-making process.

2. Since the boundaries between layers are well defined, changes in standards in one layer need not affect already-existing software in another layer. This makes it easier to introduce new standards.

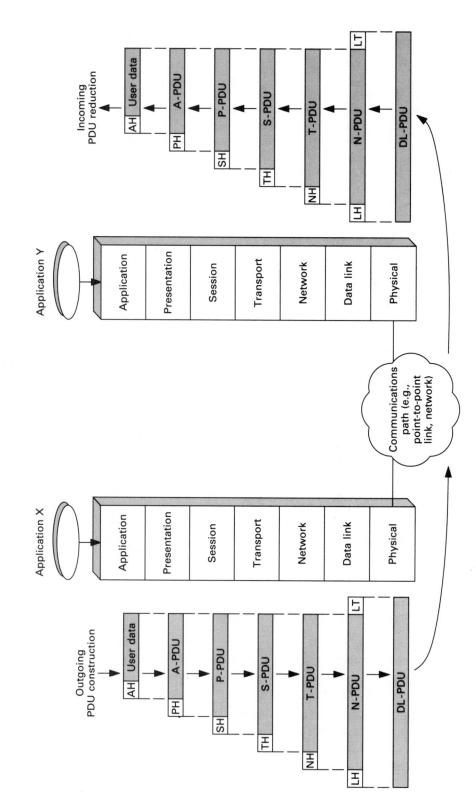

Figure 2.6 The OSI Environment

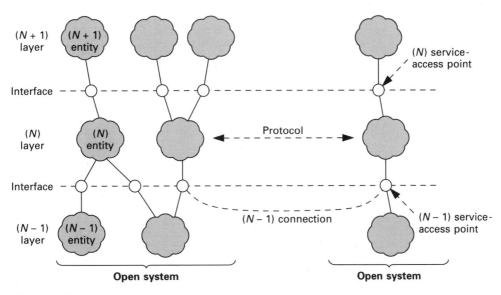

Figure 2.7 The Layer Concept

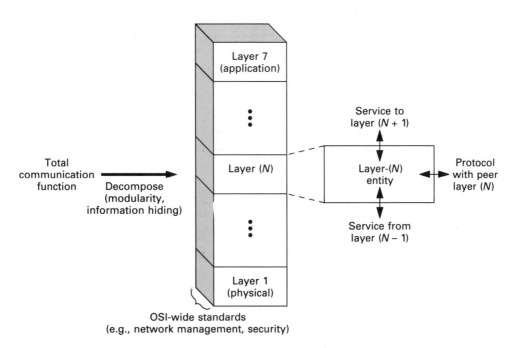

Figure 2.8 The OSI Architecture as a Framework for Standardization

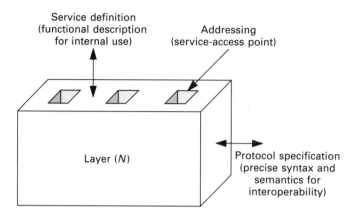

Figure 2.9 Layer-Specific Standards

Figure 2.8 illustrates the use of the OSI model as such a framework. The overall communications function is decomposed into seven distinct layers, using the principles outlined in Table 2.2. These principles essentially amount to using modular design. That is, the overall function is broken up into a number of modules, making the interfaces between modules as simple as possible. In addition, the design principle of information hiding is used: lower layers are concerned with greater levels of detail; upper layers are independent of these details. Within each layer, both the service provided to the next higher layer and the protocol to the peer layer in other systems is provided.

Figure 2.9 shows more specifically the nature of the standardization required at each layer. Three elements are critical:

1. *Protocol specification:* Two entities at the same layer in different systems cooperate and interact by means of a protocol. Since two different open systems are involved, the protocol must be specified precisely. This includes the format of the protocol data units exchanged, the semantics of all fields, and the allowable sequence of PDUs.

2. *Service definition:* In addition to the protocol or protocols that operate at a given layer, standards are needed for the services that each layer provides to the next higher layer. Typically, the definition of services is equivalent to a functional description that specifies *what* services are provided but not *how* the services are to be provided.

3. *Addressing:* Each layer provides services to entities at the next higher layer. These entities are referenced by means of a service-access point (SAP). Thus, a network service-access point (NSAP) indicates a transport entity that is a user of the network service.

The need to provide a precise protocol specification for open systems is self-evident, but items 2 and 3 warrant further comment. With respect to service definitions, the motivation for providing only a functional definition is as follows. First, the interaction between two adjacent layers takes place within the confines of a single open system and is not the concern of any other open system. Thus, as long as peer layers in different systems provide the same services to their next higher layers, the details of how the services are provided may differ from one system to another without loss of interoperability. Second, it will usually be the case that adjacent layers are implemented on the same processor. In that case, it would be desirable to leave the system programmer free to exploit the hardware and operating system to provide an interface that is as efficient as possible.

The final aspect of standardization within a layer, addressing, is explored later in this chapter.

2.2.4 Services

2.2.4.1 Primitives and Parameters

The services between adjacent layers in the OSI architecture are expressed in terms of primitives and parameters. A primitive specifies the function to be performed, and the parameters are used to pass data and control information. The actual form of a primitive is implementation-dependent. An example is a procedure call.

Four types of primitives are used in standards to define the interaction between adjacent layers in the architecture (X.210). These are defined in Table 2.5. The layout of Figure 2.10, part (a), suggests the time ordering of these events. For example, consider the transfer of data from an (N) entity to a peer (N) entity in another system. The following steps occur:

1. The source (N) entity invokes its $(N-1)$ entity with a DATA.request primitive. Associated with the primitive are the parameters needed, such as the data to be transmitted and the destination address.

2. The source $(N-1)$ entity prepares an $(N-1)$ PDU to be sent to its peer $(N-1)$ entity.

3. The destination $(N-1)$ entity delivers the data to the appropriate destination (N) entity via a DATA.indication, which includes the data and source address as parameters.

4. If an acknowledgment is called for, the destination (N) entity issues a DATA.response to its $(N-1)$ entity.

5. The $(N-1)$ entity conveys the acknowledgment in an $(N-1)$ PDU.

6. The acknowledgment is delivered to the source (N) entity as a DATA.confirm.

This sequence of events is referred to as a *confirmed service*, as the initiator receives confirmation that the requested service has had the desired effect at the other end. If only request and indication primitives are involved (corresponding to steps 1 through 3), then the service dialogue is a *nonconfirmed service;* the initiator receives no confirmation that the requested action has taken place (Figure 2.10, part [b]).

Table 2.5 Primitive Types

Request	A primitive issued by a service user to invoke some service and pass the parameters needed to fully specify the requested service
Indication	A primitive issued by a service provider to either: 1. indicate that a procedure has been invoked by the peer service user on the connection and provide the associated parameters 2. notify the service user of a provider-initiated action
Response	A primitive issued by a service user to acknowledge or complete some procedure previously invoked by an indication to that user
Confirm	A primitive issued by a service provider to acknowledge or complete some procedure previously invoked by a request by the service user

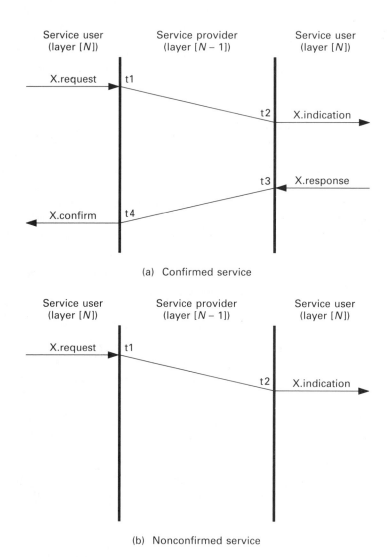

(a) Confirmed service

(b) Nonconfirmed service

Figure 2.10 Time Sequence Diagrams for Service Primitives

2.2.4.2   OSI Service Definition Standards

For layers 1 through 6 of the OSI model, a single service definition has been provided for each layer by CCITT (International Telegraph and Telephone Consultative Committee) (Table 2.6). For the application layer, no single service specification is appropriate for several reasons. First, there are a number of distributed applications supported by OSI, each with its own requirements and characteristics. Second, there is no layer "above" the application layer; therefore, there is no interface across which to define a service specification. Instead, three services that are generally useful to a number of applications have been defined: association control, reliable transfer, and

Table 2.6 OSI Service Definitions

CCITT Recommendation	ISO/IEC Standard
X.211 Physical Service Definition	ISO 10022 Physical Service Definition
X.212 Data Link Service Definition	DIS 8886 Data Link Service Definition
X.213 Network Service Definition	ISO 8348 Network Service Definition
	ISO 8348 AD 1 Connectionless-Mode Transmission
	ISO 8348 AD 2 Network Layer Addressing
	ISO 8348 AD 3 Additional Features of the Network Service
	ISO 8348 DAM 4 Removal of the Preferred Decimal Encoding of the NSAP Address
X.214 Transport Service Definition	ISO 8072 Transport Service Definition
	ISO 8072 AD 1 Connectionless-Mode Transmission
X.215 Session Service Definition	ISO 8326 Basic Connection Oriented Session Service Definition
	ISO 8326 DAD 1 Session Symmetric Synchronization for the Session Service
	ISO 8326 DAD 2 Incorporation of Unlimited User Data
	ISO 8326 DAD 3 Connectionless-Mode Session Service
	ISO 8326 PDAM 4 Additional Synchronization Functionality
X.216 Presentation Service Definition	ISO 8822 Connection Oriented Presentation Service Definition
	ISO 8822 DAD 1 Connectionless-Mode Presentation Service
	ISO 8822 PDAD 2 Support of Session Symmetric Synchronization Service
	ISO 8822 PDAM 3 Registration of Abstract Syntaxes
	ISO 8822 PDAM 5 Additional Session Synchronization Functionality for the Presentation User
X.217 Association Control Service Definition	ISO 8649 Service Definition for the Association Control Service Element
	ISO 8649 DAD 2 Connectionless-Mode ACSE Service
X.218 Reliable Transfer: Model and Service Definition	ISO 9066–1 Reliable Transfer—Part 1: Model and Service Definition
X.219 Remote Operations: Model, Notation and Service Definition	ISO 9072–1 Remote Operations—Part 1: Model, Notation and Service Definition

remote operations. For each of these, a service definition is given indicating the services that may be provided to applications by these general-purpose tools.

Table 2.6 also shows the corresponding ISO documents. In most cases, the material in the two sets of standards is technically equivalent. In the case of ISO, some of the material was added after the initial standard and appears as an addendum. For example, the material in ISO 8348 AD 2 on addressing appears as part of X.213. The principal additional material found in the ISO standards is a set of definitions of connectionless-mode service, which is examined later in this chapter.

2.2.5   Protocols

2.2.5.1   Protocol Data Units

A protocol is concerned with exchanging streams of data between two entities. Usually, the transfer can be characterized as consisting of a sequence of blocks of data of some bounded size, referred to as protocol data units (PDUs). Each PDU contains control information that is used to coordinate the joint operation of the two entities engaged in the protocol. In addition, some of the PDUs contain user data from the next higher layer.

Figure 2.6 (shown earlier) illustrates the use of PDUs in the OSI architecture. When application X has data to send to application Y, it transfers the data to an application entity in the application layer. A header consisting of the protocol-control information for the peer layer-7 entity is appended to the data, forming an application PDU. This PDU is now passed as a unit to layer 6. The presentation entity treats the whole unit as data and appends its own header. This process continues down through layer 2, which generally adds both a header and a trailer, as explained in Chapter 3. This layer-2 PDU is then passed by the physical layer onto the transmission medium as a stream of bits. When the DL-PDU is received by the target system, the reverse process occurs. As the data ascend, each layer strips off the outermost header, acts on the protocol-control information contained therein, and passes the remainder up to the next layer.

2.2.5.2   Segmentation and Reassembly

Figure 2.6 suggests a one-to-one correspondence between PDUs at adjacent layers. This is not necessarily the case. An entity in a layer may segment the PDU it receives from the next higher layer into several parts to accommodate its own requirements. These data units must then be reassembled by the corresponding peer layer on the receiving system before being passed up.

There are a number of reasons for segmentation, depending on the context. For example:

- An intervening communications subnetwork may only accept blocks of data up to a certain size. Thus, the network layer would need to break up a single transport PDU into several network PDUs.

- Error control is more efficient with a smaller PDU size. If an error is detected, only a small amount of data may need to be retransmitted if smaller PDUs are used.

- More equitable access to shared facilities, with shorter average delay, can be provided.

- A smaller PDU size may allow receiving entities to allocate smaller buffers.

There are several disadvantages to segmentation that argue for making PDUs as large as possible:

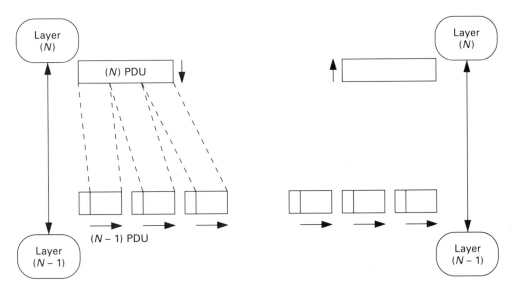

Figure 2.11 Segmentation and Reassembly

- Each PDU contains a fixed minimum of control information. Hence, the smaller the block, the greater the percentage of overhead.
- PDU arrival may generate an interrupt that must be serviced. Smaller blocks result in more interrupts.
- More time is spent processing smaller and more numerous PDUs.

All these factors must be taken into account by the protocol designer in determining minimum and maximum PDU size.

The operation of segmentation and reassembly is illustrated in Figure 2.11. A layer-(*N*) PDU is segmented into three blocks by the (*N* − 1) entity, and an (*N* − 1) header is added to each block to form three (*N* − 1) PDUs. At the receiving system, the (*N* − 1) headers are stripped off, and the (*N*) PDU is reassembled for delivery to the (*N*) entity.

2.2.5.3   OSI Protocol Specification Standards

As with the OSI layer services, there is a set of standards for the basic protocol elements of OSI. For the network layer on down, there are a variety of standards, corresponding to the variety of networks that may be used for interconnection. Above the network layer, a single protocol specification has been provided for each layer by CCITT (Table 2.7). Again, at the application layer, there are protocol specifications for three generally useful application-layer protocols: association control, reliable transfer, and remote operations.

Table 2.7 also shows the corresponding ISO documents. In most cases, the material in the two sets of standards is technically equivalent. Again, the principal difference is that the ISO standards address connectionless-mode operation.

Table 2.7 OSI Protocol Specifications

CCITT Recommendation	ISO/IEC Standard
X.224 Transport Protocol Specification	ISO 8073 Connection Oriented Transport Protocol Specification ISO 8073 AD 1 Network Connection Management Subprotocol ISO 8073 AD 2 Class Four Operation over Connectionless Network Service ISO 8073 DAM 3 PICS Proforma ISO 8073 PDAD 4 Protocol Enhancements
X.225 Session Protocol Specification	ISO 8327 Basic Connection Oriented Session Protocol Specification ISO 8327 DAD 1 Session Symmetric Synchronization for the Session Protocol ISO 8327 DAD 2 Incorporation of Unlimited User Data ISO 8327 PDAM 3 Additional Synchronization Functionality CD 8327–2 Protocol Implementation Conformance Statement (PICS) Proforma
X.226 Presentation Protocol Specification	ISO 8823 Connection Oriented Presentation Protocol Specification ISO 8823 PDAD 2 Support of Session Symmetric Synchronization Service ISO 8823 PDAM 3 Registration of Transfer Syntaxes ISO 8823 PDAM 5 Additional Session Synchronization Functionality for the Presentation User DIS 8823–2 Protocol Implementation Conformance Statement (PICS) Proforma
X.227 Association Control Protocol Specification	ISO 8650 Protocol Specification for the Association Control Service Element ISO 8650 AM 1 Authentication During Association Establishment DIS 8650–2 Protocol Implementation Conformance Statement (PICS) Proforma
X.228 Reliable Transfer: Protocol Specification	ISO 9066–2 Reliable Transfer—Part 2: Protocol Specification
X.229 Remote Operations: Protocol Specification	ISO 9072–2 Remote Operations—Part 2: Protocol Specification

2.3   THE OSI LAYERS

2.3.1   Physical Layer

The physical layer covers the physical interface between devices and the rules by which bits are passed from one to another. The physical layer has four important characteristics:

1. *Mechanical:* Relates to the physical properties of the interface to a transmission medium. Typically, the specification is of a pluggable connector that joins one or more signal conductors, called circuits.
2. *Electrical:* Relates to the representation of bits (e.g., in terms of voltage levels) and the data-transmission rate of bits.
3. *Functional:* Specifies the functions performed by individual circuits of the physical interface between a system and the transmission medium.
4. *Procedural:* Specifies the sequence of events by which bit streams are exchanged across the physical medium.

The physical layer differs from the other OSI layers in that it cannot rely on a lower layer to transmit its PDUs. Rather, it must make use of a transmission medium whose characteristics are not part of the OSI model. There is no physical-layer PDU structure as such; no header of protocol-control information is used. The PDU simply consists of a block or stream of bits.

2.3.2   Data-Link Layer

The data-link layer must deal with the requirements of both the communications facility and the user. Whereas the physical layer provides only a raw bit-stream service, the data-link layer attempts to make the physical link reliable and provides the means to activate, maintain, and deactivate the link. The principal service provided by the data-link layer to higher layers is that of error detection and control. Thus, with a fully functional data-link layer protocol, the next higher layer may assume error-free transmission over the link.

One of the best-known data-link-control protocol standards is HDLC (high-level data-link control), developed by ISO (ISO 4335). It is widely used for point-to-point and multidrop configurations. It is also the ancestor of a number of other data-link-control protocols, including LAPB (link-access protocol, balanced; used in packet-switching networks), LLC (logical link control; used in local area networks), and LAPD (link-access protocol, D channel; used in ISDN).

2.3.3   Network Layer

The network layer provides for the transfer of information between end systems across some sort of communications network. It relieves higher layers of the need to know anything about the underlying data-transmission and switching technologies used to connect systems. At this layer, the computer system engages in a dialogue with the network to specify the destination address and request certain network facilities, such as priority.

There is a spectrum of possibilities for intervening communications facilities to be managed by the network layer. At one extreme, there is a direct point-to-point link between stations. In this case, there may be no need for a network layer because the data-link layer can perform the necessary function of managing the link.

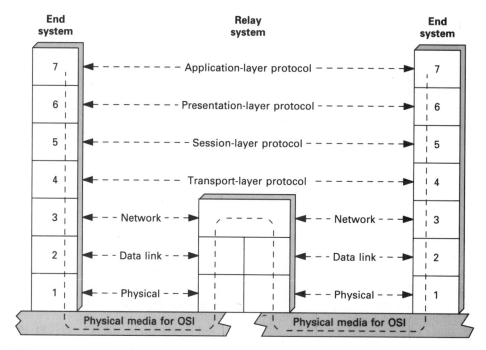

Figure 2.12 The Use of a Relay

Next, the systems could be connected across a single network, such as a circuit-switching or packet-switching network. As an example, the packet level of the X.25 standard is a network-layer standard for this situation. Figure 2.12 shows how the presence of a network is accommodated by the OSI architecture. The lower three layers are concerned with attaching to and communicating with the network. The packets that are created by the end system pass through one or more network nodes that act as relays between the two end systems. The network nodes implement layers 1–3 of the architecture. In the figure, two end systems are connected through a single network node. Layer 3 in the node performs a switching and routing function. Within the node, there are two data-link layers and two physical layers, corresponding to the links to the two end systems. Each data-link (and physical) layer operates independently to provide service to the network layer over its respective link. The upper four layers are "end-to-end" protocols between the attached end systems.

At the other extreme, two end systems might wish to communicate although they are not even connected to the same network. Rather, they are connected to networks that, directly or indirectly, are connected to each other. This case requires the use of some sort of internetworking technique, an approach that is explored in Chapter 4.

2.3.4 Transport Layer

The transport layer provides a mechanism for the exchange of data between end systems. The connection-oriented transport service ensures that data are delivered error-free, in sequence, with no losses or duplications. The transport layer may also be concerned with optimizing the use of network services and providing a requested quality of service to session entities. For example, the session entity may specify acceptable error rates, maximum delay, priority, and security.

The size and complexity of a transport protocol depend on how reliable or unreliable the underlying network and network-layer services are. Accordingly, ISO has developed a family of five transport-protocol standards, each oriented toward a different underlying service.

2.3.5   Session Layer

The lowest four layers of the OSI model provide both the means for the reliable exchange of data and an expedited data service. For many applications, this basic service is insufficient. For example, a remote terminal access application might require a half-duplex dialogue. A transaction-processing application might require checkpoints in the data-transfer stream to permit backup and recovery. A message-processing application might require the ability to interrupt a dialogue in order to prepare a new portion of a message and later resume the dialogue where it was left off.

All these capabilities could be embedded in specific applications at layer 7. However, since these types of dialogue-structuring tools have widespread applicability, it makes sense to organize them into a separate layer: the session layer.

The session layer provides the mechanism for controlling the dialogue between applications in end systems. In many cases, there will be little or no need for session-layer services, but for some applications, such services are used. The key services provided by the session layer include:

- *Dialogue discipline:* This can be two-way simultaneous (full-duplex) or two-way alternate (half-duplex).
- *Grouping:* The flow of data can be marked to define groups of data. For example, if a retail store is transmitting sales data to a regional office, the data can be marked to indicate the end of the sales data for each department. This would signal the host computer to finalize running totals for that department and start new running counts for the next department.
- *Recovery:* The session layer can provide a checkpointing mechanism so that if a failure of some sort occurs between checkpoints, the session entity can retransmit all data since the last checkpoint.

ISO has issued a standard for the session layer that includes, as options, services such as those just described.

2.3.6   Presentation Layer

The presentation layer defines the format of the data to be exchanged between applications and offers application programs a set of data-transformation services. The presentation layer defines the syntax used between application entities and provides for the selection and subsequent modification of the representation used. Examples of specific services that may be performed at this layer include data compression and encryption.

2.3.7   Application Layer

The application layer provides a means for application programs to access the OSI environment. This layer contains management functions and generally useful mechanisms to support distributed applications. In addition, general-purpose applications such as file transfer, electronic mail, and terminal access to remote computers are considered to reside at this layer.

2.4   PERSPECTIVES ON THE OSI MODEL

Figure 2.13 provides a useful perspective on the OSI architecture. The annotation suggests viewing the seven layers in three parts. The lower three layers contain the logic for a computer to interact with a network. The host is attached physically to the network, uses a data-link protocol to reliably communicate with the network, and uses a network protocol to request data exchange with another device on the network and to request network services. The X.25 standard for packet-switching networks encompasses these three layers. Continuing from this perspective, the transport layer provides a reliable end-to-end service regardless of the intervening network facility; in effect, it is the user's liaison to the communications facility. Finally, the upper three layers, taken together, are involved in the exchange of data between end users, making use of a transport service for reliable data transfer. This perspective corresponds to the simple three-layer architecture used earlier in the chapter.

Another way of thinking about the OSI architecture is in terms of how a computer system is configured as an open system in a network of computers. This is suggested in Figure 2.14. In any given computer system, there is typically a connection to a single network facility. This might be a local area network, a wide area X.25 network, or ISDN. The logic for this connection is provided in the lowest three layers of the architecture. If the computer is connected to a single network, then only a single protocol will be needed at each of the lower three layers. Which specific protocols are used will depend on which network is present. The network layer may also include an internetworking capability, allowing the interconnection of devices across multiple networks. For the transport layer, one of five classes of transport protocol will be used, depending on the reliability of the network. A single session-layer protocol is used. Finally, a variety of applications may all be included in the computer. For example, users of the system may wish to have file-transfer, electronic-mail, and document-transfer facilities all available. Each of these facilities includes presentation-layer functionality and so corresponds to the upper two layers of the OSI architecture.

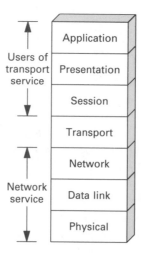

Figure 2.13 A Perspective on the OSI Architecture

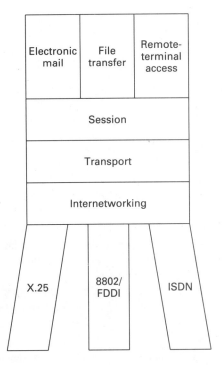

Figure 2.14 Configuration of OSI Protocols

2.5   CONNECTION MODE AND CONNECTIONLESS MODE

At any layer of the OSI architecture, two basic modes of transmission are possible: connection-oriented and connectionless. With the connection mode of transmission, a logical connection is set up between peer entities prior to the exchange of data. This connection allows both sides to maintain state information about the history and current status of the transmission of PDUs between the two sides. In connectionless-mode operation, each data unit transmitted is independent of previous or subsequent data units, and no connection is set up. Table 2.8 contrasts the characteristics of the two modes.

Table 2.8 Characteristics of Connection-Mode and
Connectionless-Mode Transmission

Connection Mode	Connectionless Mode
Clearly distinguishable lifetime	Single-access service
Three-party agreement	Two-party agreement
Negotiation and renegotiation	No negotiation
Connection identifiers	Self-contained data units, with SAPs
Data-unit relationship	Data-unit independence

Table 2.9 Definition of OSI Quality of Service Parameters

(a) Single-transmission-related parameters, connection mode or connectionless mode

---

Parameter	Definition
Transit delay	Average elapsed time between a DATA.request and the corresponding DATA.indication. Desired and maximum acceptable values are specified.
Residual error rate	Equal to $\dfrac{S(L)+S(E)+S(X)}{S}$, where $S(L)$ = lost SDUs $S(E)$ = incorrectly received SDUs $S(X)$ = duplicate SDUs S = total SDUs transferred
Protection	Protection against unauthorized monitoring or manipulation of user information. One of four options may be selected: 1. No protection features 2. Protection against passive monitoring 3. Protection against modification, replay, addition, or deletion 4. Both 2 and 3
Priority	Specifies the relative importance of a connection or connectionless SDU with respect to: 1. The order in which connections have their QOS downgraded or in which connectionless SDUs have their QOS downgraded, if necessary 2. The order in which connections are broken or connectionless SDUs discarded to recover resources, if necessary
Maximum acceptable cost	Composed of communication and end-system resource costs.

(b) Multiple-transmission-related parameters, connection mode or connectionless mode

---

Parameter	Definition
Throughput	Average rate of transfer of SDUs, in octets per second, measured over a sequence of SDUs. Desired target and minimum acceptable values in each direction of transfer are specified.
Transfer-failure probability	Applies to throughput, transit delay, and residual error rate. The quantity is the observed proportion of time that the provider fails to provide the minimum acceptable service.

(c) Connection-mode parameters

Parameter	Definition
Connection-establishment delay	Maximum acceptable delay between a CONNECT.request and the corresponding CONNECT.confirm.

Table 2.9 (*Cont.*)

Connection-establishment-failure probability	Proportion of connection-establishment attempts that fail as a result of provider behavior, such as misconnection, connection refusal, or excessive delay. Connection failures due to user behavior are excluded from the calculation.
Connection-release delay	Maximum acceptable delay between a user-invoked DIS-CONNECT.request and the successful release of the connection at the peer user.
Connection-release-failure probability	Proportion of release requests that are not satisfied within the maximum acceptable delay.
Resilience	Two parameters: (1) probability of a provider-invoked connection release; (2) probability of a provider-invoked connection reset.
Service availability	Fraction of time that a connection is available.
Extended control	Allows user to make use of the resynchronize, abort, activity-interrupt, and activity-discard services when normal flow is congested.
Optimized dialogue transfer	Permits the session protocol to concatenate multiple SSDUs and send them as a unit.

2.5.1 Quality of Service

One concept common to both connection-mode and connectionless-mode transmission is that of quality of service. *Quality of service* (QOS) is the collective name given to a set of parameters associated with data transmission between two (N) service users. They define the quality of the service obtained by two (N) service users during the exchange of data.

A number of QOS parameters have been defined. Not all parameters are appropriate to all layers of the OSI model. Further, some QOS parameters apply to both connection mode and connectionless mode, whereas others are only used with connection-mode service. In the context of connection-mode service, some of the parameters are subject to negotiation at the time of connection setup, as explained later in this section; others are selected or provided by means not specified in the standards. For connectionless service, the QOS parameter values are provided outside the standard. However, when a service user requests data transfer, it may be able to select a QOS parameter value within a predefined range. The parameters are listed and briefly defined in Table 2.9; Table 2.10 shows which parameters are available at each layer.

As Table 2.9 indicates, the QOS parameters can be grouped into three categories:

1. Parameters that deal with the transmission of a single service data unit, in either connection mode or connectionless mode. The parameter value refers to the behavior of a single data transmission.

2. Parameters that deal with the transmission of multiple service data units, in either connection mode or connectionless mode. The parameter value refers to the observed behavior for multiple data units between a pair of (N) service-access points.

Table 2.10 Use of OSI Quality of Service Parameters

	OSI Layer						
	1	**2**	**3**	**4**	**5**	**6**	**7**
Service availability							
Residual error rate	C	C	C	N	N	P	P
Throughput	C	N	N	N	N	P	P
Transit delay	C	C	N	N	N	P	P
Protection	C	N	N	N	N	P	P
Priority		N	N	N	N	P	P
Resilience		C	C	N	C	P	P
Connection-establishment delay			C	N	C	P	P
Connection-release delay			C	N	C	P	P
Connection-establishment-failure probability			C	N	C	P	P
Transfer-failure probability			C	N	C	P	P
Connection-release-failure probability			C	N	C	P	P
Maximum acceptable cost			C				
Extended control					N	P	P
Optimized dialogue transfer					N	P	P

C = configured or selected prior to connection establishment.
N = negotiated on a per-connection basis.
P = parameter passed down to next lower layer.

3. Parameters that are only appropriate for connection-mode service. The parameter value refers to a connection between two (*N*) service-access points.

The values of QOS parameters in connection-mode service may vary with each connection. The values of QOS parameters in connectionless-mode service may vary with each pair of source and destination service-access points.

2.5.2   Connection-Mode Transmission

Connection-mode data transfer is to be preferred (even required) if end systems anticipate a lengthy exchange of data and/or certain details of their protocol must be worked out dynamically. A logical association, or connection, is established between the entities. Three phases occur (Figure 2.15): connection establishment, data transfer, and connection termination. With more sophisticated protocols, there may also be connection-interrupt and recovery phases to cope with errors and other sorts of interruptions.

2.5.2.1   Connection-Mode Service

Since an (*N*) connection is an association established by the (*N*) layer between two (*N* + 1) entities, the functionality of the connection can be defined in terms of the service that the (*N*) layer offers to the (*N* + 1) layer. As mentioned earlier, a service definition has been developed for each layer of the OSI model (Table 2.6). Although these service definitions differ somewhat in detail, they share many similarities.

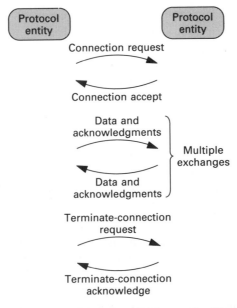

**Figure 2.15 The Phases of a Connection-Mode
Data Transfer**

Table 2.11 shows the basic primitives and parameters that are typical of all the OSI connection-mode service definitions. The first four primitives deal with the *connection-establishment phase*.
The *called address* and *calling address* parameters identify the $(N+1)$ entities that will use the (N)
connection. At most levels, these are expressed as service-access points. The *expedited-data option*
is included to indicate that expedited data will be supported, as explained later in this subsection.
In some cases, *user data* from the $(N+1)$ entity are carried with the connection-establishment

Table 2.11 Connection-Mode Service Primitives

X-CONNECT.request (called address, calling address, expedited data option, quality of service, user data)

X-CONNECT.indication (called address, calling address, expedited data option, quality of
service, user data)

X-CONNECT.response (called address, calling address, expedited data option, quality of service, user data)

X-CONNECT.confirm (called address, calling address, expedited data option, quality of service, user data)

X-DISCONNECT.request (reason, user data)
X-DISCONNECT.indication (reason, user data)

X-DATA.request (user data)
X-DATA.indication (user data)

X-EXPEDITED-DATA.request (user data)
X-EXPEDITED-DATA.indication (user data)

---

dialogue. The remaining parameter shown for the connection-establishment primitives is *quality of service*. As mentioned, this is actually a set of parameters.

For those parameters that are negotiable, the agreement on a particular value actually involves three parties: the two (*N*) service users and the (*N*) service. For example, a particular value of throughput must be agreed to by two transport users, and it must be possible for the transport service to provide that value. The parameters are negotiated as follows:

1. The user initiating the connection request (calling user) sets a proposed value for the parameter in the CONNECT.request primitive. Any defined value for the parameter is allowed.

2a. If the (*N*) service can provide the requested quality of service, then it issues a CON-NECT.indication primitive to the called user with the same value for the parameter.

2b. If the (*N*) service cannot provide the requested quality of service, then:

    ▪ If the parameter includes a range (e.g., desired and minimum acceptable), and if the (*N*) service can provide a service within that range, it issues a CONNECT.indication primitive with a revised range to the called user; otherwise, it issues a DISCONNECT.indication to the calling user, which terminates the connection attempt.

    ▪ For the protection parameter, the (*N*) service issues a DISCONNECT.indication to the calling user.

    ▪ For all other parameters, the (*N*) service issues a CONNECT.indication to the called user with the quality of service that the (*N*) service can provide.

3a. When the called user receives the indication primitive, if it agrees to the indicated value of each primitive, it issues a CONNECT.response with the agreed value. For parameters that are specified by a range, the called user may downgrade the parameter within the range. The (*N*) service conveys the results to the calling user in a CONNECT.confirm, which establishes the connection.

3b. If the called user rejects any of the parameters, it issues a DISCONNECT.request. The (*N*) service then issues a DISCONNECT.indication to the calling user.

Part (a) of Figure 2.16 shows the sequence of events involved in successful connection establishment. Parts (b) and (c) illustrate two ways in which a connection request may be rejected. The called user may refuse the connection, either because of an inability to agree on a quality of service or for other reasons, such as inadequate available resources. The (*N*) service may also refuse the connection. Examples of reasons for this latter event:

▪ The (*N*) service cannot provide an acceptable quality of service.

▪ The local (*N*) protocol entity was unable to set up the connection.

Once a connection is established, the *data-transfer phase* is entered. Ordinary data transfer makes use of DATA.request and DATA.indication primitives (Figure 2.16, part [d]). Note that response and confirm primitives are not used. The reason that there is no need for a confirmation back to the sending user is that the connection-mode service guarantees to deliver all data in the proper order, with no losses. Thus, the user needs no form of acknowledgment.

The other form of data transfer is expedited data, which is used for occasional urgent data. Examples are an interrupt, an alarm, or an abrupt connection termination. The (*N*) service will attempt to deliver the expedited-data unit as rapidly as possible, bypassing ordinary flow-control mechanisms (Figure 2.16, part [e]).

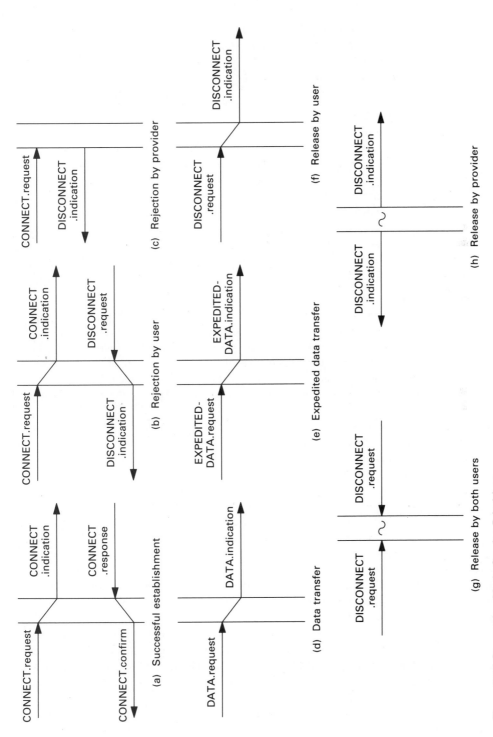

Figure 2.16 Connection-Mode Service Primitives

47

Finally, there are several ways to terminate a connection (Figure 2.16, parts [f], [g], and [h]). Either user may initiate the connection-release process, and the other is informed of the release. Both users may initiate the release process at about the same time. Finally, the (N) service may release the connection and inform the two users. This latter event would be triggered by some error or overflow condition.

2.5.2.2   Connection-Mode Protocol

An (N) connection, provided as a service by the (N) layer to two (N) users, must be supported by a protocol at layer (N). The key characteristic of a connection-mode protocol is that sequencing is used. Each side sequentially numbers the PDUs it sends to the other side. Because each side remembers that it is engaged in a logical connection, it can keep track of both outgoing numbers, which it generates, and incoming numbers, which are generated by the other side. Sequencing supports three main functions:

1.   Ordered delivery

2.   Flow control

3.   Error control

When two protocol entities are in different systems connected by a network, there is a risk that PDUs will not arrive in the order in which they are sent because they may traverse different paths through the network. In connection-oriented protocols, *ordered delivery* is generally required; that is, the PDU sequence must be maintained. For example, if a file is transferred between two systems, we would like to be assured that the records of the received file are in the same order as those of the transmitted file and not shuffled. If each PDU is given a unique number, it is a logically simple task for the receiving entity to reorder received PDUs on the basis of sequence number.

Flow control is a technique for assuring that a transmitting entity does not overwhelm a receiving entity with data. The receiving entity typically allocates a data buffer with some maximum length. When data are received, the receiver must do a certain amount of processing (i.e., examine the header and strip it from the PDU) before passing the data to a higher-layer user. In the absence of flow control, the receiver's buffer may overflow while it is processing old data.

In a connection-oriented protocol, the sequence numbers can be used to provide a flow-control mechanism. Although the details differ somewhat for different protocols, they all involve the same fundamental mechanism. At any given time, the sender is allowed to send PDUs whose numbers are in a contiguous range. Once all of those PDUs are sent, the entity may send no more until it receives permission from the other entity. For example, a protocol entity in one system may have permission to send PDUs numbered 1 through 7. After it sends these, it waits. At some point, it receives a message from the peer protocol entity in the other system indicating that it is now prepared to receive numbers 8 through 15.

Flow control is an example of a protocol function that must be implemented in several layers of the architecture. For example, a network may protect itself from congestion by limiting the flow of data from attached devices, either at the network or at link layers of the architecture. At the same time, the transport protocol in a system may need to restrict the flow of incoming TPDUs to protect its buffer space.

Error control is a function that allows a protocol to recover from lost or damaged PDUs. As with flow control, it is based on the use of sequence numbers. Three mechanisms come into play:

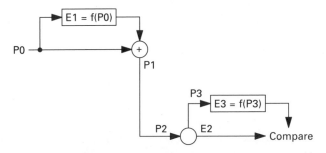

PO = PDU to be transmitted, with a null FCS field
E1 = frame-check sequence (FCS) calculated on P0
P1 = P0 with E1 inserted into the FCS field; transmitted PDU
P2 = received PDU
E2 = received value of FCS field, in P2
P3 = P2 with null FCS field
E3 = FCS calculated on P3

Figure 2.17 Error Detection

1.   Positive acknowledgment

2.   Retransmit after time-out

3.   Error detection

In a connection-mode protocol, each PDU is numbered sequentially. For error control, it is the responsibility of the receiving protocol entity to acknowledge each PDU that it receives; this is done by sending back the sequence number of the received PDU to the other side. If a PDU is lost in transit, then the intended receiver will obviously not acknowledge it. The sending protocol entity notes the time at which it sends each PDU. If a PDU remains unacknowledged after a certain amount of time, the sender assumes that the PDU did not get through and retransmits that PDU.

There is another possibility: the PDU gets through, but the bits have been altered by errors in transit. To cope with this contingency, an error-detection technique is needed, as illustrated in Figure 2.17. The sending entity performs a calculation on the bits of the PDU and inserts the result, known as a frame-check sequence (FCS), as part of the protocol-control information of the PDU. The receiver performs the same calculation and compares the calculated FCS to the result stored in the incoming PDU. If there is a discrepancy, the receiver assumes that an error has occurred and discards the PDU. As before, the sender fails to receive an acknowledgment and retransmits the PDU.

2.5.3   Connectionless-Mode Transmission

With connectionless-mode transmission, no logical connection is set up prior to data-unit exchange. Thus, the overhead of connection setup and connection maintenance is avoided.

2.5.3.1   Connectionless-Mode Service

Again, the functionality of a connectionless-mode (N) service can be defined in terms of the service that the (N) layer offers to the $(N+1)$ layer.

For the connectionless service, there is an *a priori* agreement between $(N+1)$ entities that is unknown to the (N) service and that is sufficient for them to exchange data. A single service access

Table 2.12 Connectionless Service Primitives

X-UNITDATA.request (called address, calling address, quality of service, user data)
X-UNITDATA.indication (called address, calling address, quality of service, user data)

is required to initiate the transmission of a data unit; this access contains all the information required to deliver the data unit to the other side. Because each data unit is handled with a single service access, no negotiation occurs; the parameters and options to be used must be prearranged. From the point of view of the service provider, previous and subsequent data units are unrelated to the current data unit; thus, ordered delivery, flow control, and error control cannot be provided.

Table 2.12 shows the basic primitives and parameters that are typical of all the OSI connectionless-mode service definitions. The service is defined by a single primitive type, UNIT-DATA. The source and destination addresses identify the two users of the service. The quality of service parameter can be used to select a value from a predefined range.

Because no logical connection is set up between end users, there is no opportunity for a negotiation of quality of service. Rather, there must be prior agreement or understanding between the service provider and each user concerning the quality of service available. In the request primitive, the requested quality of service should be within the range that the (N) service provider can accommodate. If, because of changing conditions, the (N) service cannot provide the requested quality of service, then it will nevertheless attempt to deliver the data unit at whatever quality of service is achievable. The quality of service reported in the indication primitive is that actually provided by the network service for this data unit.

2.5.4   Comparison of the Two Modes

The strengths of connection-mode data transmission are easily described. It allows connection-oriented features such as ordered delivery, flow control, and error control. With connection-mode transmission, the two entities can agree on their mutual requirements, such as maximum PDU size and priority, and reserve resources for the exchange. At the network layer, if a connection is set up across a packet-switched network, then the network can design a route to be used for all PDUs and avoid having to make a decision each time. These characteristics are well suited to applications that involve lengthy exchanges of data, such as file transfer and remote access from a terminal to a time-sharing system.

Connectionless service is more appropriate in some contexts. At the network layer, connectionless service is more robust: since each PDU is handled independently, each can follow a different route from source to destination, avoiding changing conditions of congestion and failure. Furthermore, even at transport and above, there is justification for a connectionless service. There are instances in which the overhead of connection establishment and maintenance is unjustified or even counterproductive. Examples include transaction-processing systems and real-time systems.

2.5.5   Relationship between Adjacent Layers

One additional issue that needs to be addressed is the relationship between the mode of transmission service provided by adjacent layers. In principle, the services offered by adjacent layers can conform to one of four alternatives:

1. Both connection mode

2. Both connectionless mode

3. A connection-mode (N) service on top of a connectionless-mode ($N-1$) service

4. A connectionless-mode (N) service on top of a connection-mode ($N-1$) service

2.5.5.1   Connection/Connection

If the (N) service is a connection-mode service, then, as we have seen, the (N) protocol must support connections; that is, the (N) protocol must be a connection-mode protocol. The question then arises as to what services an (N) protocol requires from the ($N-1$) service in order to support connections.

If the ($N-1$) service, like the (N) service, is connection-oriented, then the simplest approach is to map each (N) connection, one to one, onto an ($N-1$) connection (Figure 2.18, part [a]). For

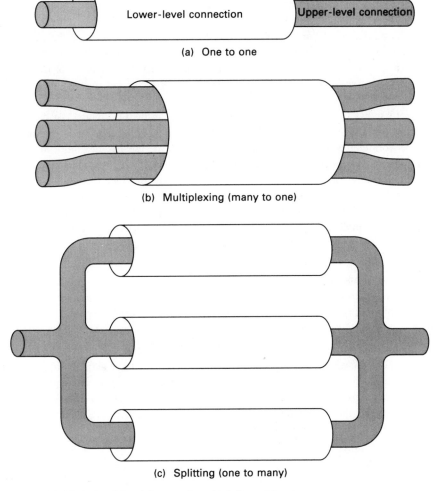

(a) One to one

(b) Multiplexing (many to one)

(c) Splitting (one to many)

Figure 2.18 Relationship of Connections in Adjacent Layers

example, a common network-level protocol, X.25, provides a connection-oriented service in which logical connections are referred to as virtual circuits. For a connection-oriented transport service, the transport protocol will set up a transport connection for each pair of SAPs that wish to exchange data. For each transport connection, a separate virtual circuit could be set up.

The advantage of a one-to-one mapping of (N) connections onto ($N-1$) connections is that it minimizes duplication of effort. Flow control, error control, and parameter negotiation can be done at the lower layer and need not be repeated at the upper layer.

There are alternatives to the one-to-one mapping. A many-to-one relationship, referred to as *multiplexing,* occurs when multiple higher-level connections share a single lower-level connection (Figure 2.18, part [b]). This may be done to make efficient use of the lower-level service. For example, public packet-switched networks generally charge for each virtual circuit that is set up. If several transport connections between the same pair of end systems are multiplexed on a single virtual circuit, a savings results. Also, after the connection is established, each new user does not have to incur the delay of the connection-setup procedure. However, care must be taken. Different (N) connections may require different quality of service, which will influence the parameters used to set up the ($N-1$) connection. Also, if several (N) connections share an ($N-1$) connection, neither the (N) service users nor the (N) protocol has much control over how the ($N-1$) service allocates resources to meet the dynamic data-transfer demands of several (N) connections.

Finally, it is possible for one (N) connection to be divided among multiple ($N-1$) connections, referred to as *splitting* (Figure 2.18, part [c]). This technique may be used to improve reliability, performance, or efficiency.

Table 2.13 shows the use of multiplexing and splitting in the OSI model. At the upper three interfaces, a one-to-one mapping is required. Both multiplexing and splitting of transport connections over network connections are allowed. This provides the greatest flexibility to the transport layer in exploiting the capabilities of the network service and the underlying network facilities available. At the network layer, things are complicated by the fact that the network service may be supplied in a configuration that involves one or multiple real networks, with a variety of characteristics. We defer a discussion of this case until Chapter 4. Data-link connections may be multiplexed over a single physical connection, to make efficient use of the physical link. Also, a data-link connection may be split across multiple physical links, to enhance reliability or performance.

2.5.5.2   Connectionless/Connectionless

The case in which both (N) and ($N-1$) services are connectionless is even more straightforward. The (N) protocol is connectionless. Each (N) SDU is mapped into a single connectionless (N) PDU, which is then handed down to the connectionless ($N-1$) service in a UNITDATA.request.

2.5.5.3   Connection/Connectionless

For the connection/connectionless case, the (N) protocol will need to be sufficiently rich to provide the connection-mode features in spite of a connectionless ($N-1$) service. Thus, the (N) protocol will need to employ sequence numbers, flow control, and error control. All PDUs, including those carrying user data and those carrying just protocol-control information, are contained as user data in the UNITDATA.request primitive used to invoke the ($N-1$) service.

2.5.5.4   Connectionless/Connection

When a connectionless (N) protocol operates over a connection-mode ($N-1$) service, a connection is required prior to the exchange of (N) PDUs. If an ($N-1$) connection already exists between the

Table 2.13 Relationships between Layers at the Interface

	Connection	**Mode**	**SAP**
Application–presentation	1:1	CO–CO CL–CL	#
Presentation–session	1:1	CO–CO CL–CL	1:1
Session–transport	1:1	CO–CO CL–CL	1:1 or (N):1
Transport–network	1:1 or (N):1 or 1:(N)	CO–CO CL–CL CO–CL‡ CL–CO‡	1:1 or (N):1
Network–data link	1:1 or (N):1*†	CO–CO CL–CL CO–CL§ CL–CO§	1:1 or 1:(N)
Data link–physical	1:1 or (N):1 or 1:(N)	‖	1:1 or 1:(N)

*May be provided by subnetwork addresses in tandem.

†May be multiplexed onto a single subnetwork connection.

‡Not fully open system.

§Conversion may be from network service to subnetwork service or from network service to data-link service.

‖Not categorized as connection-mode or connectionless.

#There are no application SAPs.

CL = connectionless mode.
CO = connection-oriented mode.

two end systems, then each connectionless (N) PDU is simply sent in a DATA.request primitive. If no connection exists, then the $(N-1)$ connection must first be set up. Typically, once the connection is set up, it remains in place to handle future connectionless (N) PDUs. If the connection remains idle for an extended period of time, then it can be released.

2.5.5.5 Application to Specific Layers

Although the conversions defined in subsections 2.5.5.3 and 2.5.5.4 could theoretically be performed at any layer, the OSI standard imposes some restrictions, indicated in Table 2.13. First, the physical layer is not classified as either connection-mode or connectionless because it depends in a complex way on the characteristics of the underlying medium. Thus, the data-link protocol must convert between the services offered at the physical layer and the type of data-link service needed. At the network layer, conversion may be provided to support a network service of a given mode over a data-link service of the other mode. Also, we shall see that the network layer may need to deal with one or more subnetworks; if so, the network layer may convert from a subnetwork service of one mode to the opposite mode. Support of these network-layer conversions is required by the OSI standard.

Conversion may also be made at the transport layer, although this capability is not required. The OSI standard points out that if a system only supports a given mode of transport service over a network service of the opposite mode, then that system may not be fully open. The reason is that such a system would be incapable of communicating with a system that does not support such conversion.

To maximize interoperability, conversion above the transport layer is not allowed.

2.6   ADDRESSING

2.6.1   Service-Access Points and Addresses

Consider the following definition from the OSI standard on addressing (ISO 7498–3): "Within an open system, $(N+1)$ entities and (N) entities are bound together at (N) service access points $[(N)$-SAPs]. (N) entities provide service to $(N+1)$ entities via the exchange of service primitives at (N)-SAPs." Thus, an (N) SAP may be considered the address that identifies an (N) entity to an $(N-1)$ entity. In the standard, reference is made to (N) *address* as being a general term that applies to a set of (N) SAPs. However, the standard also states that whether an (N) address refers to one or multiple SAPs is a matter local to that system and is not known to other systems. Thus, for all practical purposes, we can think of a SAP as providing an address for an entity.

Table 2.13 shows the relationship between SAPs at adjacent layers. Presentation SAPs, or PSAPs, are associated with applications. Each PSAP maps into a unique session SAP (SSAP). Multiple SSAPs may be mapped into a single transport SAP (TSAP), and multiple TSAPs may be mapped into a single network SAP (NSAP). Typically, there is a single NSAP for a system, or a small number of NSAPs, and this must fan out to support multiple applications. Thus, the fan-out can occur at the transport or session level.

Below the network level, the situation is reversed. Whereas there is typically a single NSAP, there may be multiple physical links attached to a system, each identified by a physical SAP. Thus, there needs to be a fan-out from the network level down.

2.6.2   Network Addresses

The NSAP occupies a central point in the OSI networking scheme. *NSAP address* is the abstract term used by OSI to refer to points where the service of the network layer is made available to its users. In practical terms, NSAPs can be considered as the addresses of open systems. The OSI standard defines three properties that NSAP addresses must possess:

1. *Global nonambiguity:* An NSAP identifies a unique open system. Synonyms are permitted. That is, an open system may have more than one NSAP address.

2. *Global applicability:* It is possible at any NSAP to identify any other NSAP, in any open system, by means of the NSAP address of the other NSAP.

3. *Route independence:* Network service users cannot derive routing information from NSAP addresses. They cannot control the route chosen by the network service by the choice of synonym, nor can they deduce the route taken by an incoming NSDU from the source or destination NSAP address.

The NSAP must also be contrasted with another sort of address, known as a *subnetwork address*. An open systems environment may consist of multiple networks, with multiple systems on each network. Each network must maintain a unique address for each host attached to that network. This allows the network to route network PDUs through the network and deliver them to the intended destination system. This is referred to as a subnetwork address. The term *subnetwork* is used to identify a physically distinct network that may be part of a complex of interconnected subnetworks to form an open systems environment. This subject is pursued in Chapter 4.

Since the NSAP address uniquely identifies a system, why not use that for the subnetwork address as well? This is not possible since different networks use different addressing schemes, with different formats and address lengths. Thus, there must be a mapping between NSAPs and subnetwork addresses.

2.7 SUMMARY

The communication functionality required for distributed applications is quite complex. This functionality is generally implemented as a structured set of modules. The modules are arranged in a vertical, layered fashion, with each layer providing a particular portion of the needed functionality and relying on the next lower layer for more primitive functions. Such a structure is referred to as a *communications architecture*.

One motivation for the use of this type of structure is that it eases the task of design and implementation. It is standard practice for any large software package to break up the functions into modules that can be designed and implemented separately. After each individual module is designed and implemented, it can be tested. Then the modules can be combined and tested together. This motivation has led computer vendors to develop proprietary layered communications architectures.

A layered architecture can also be used to construct a standardized set of communication protocols. In this case, the advantages of modular design remain. In addition, a layered architecture is particularly well suited to the development of standards. Standards can be developed simultaneously for protocols at each layer of the architecture. This breaks down the work to make it more manageable and speeds up the standards-development process. The open systems interconnection (OSI) architecture is the standard architecture used for this purpose.

The OSI architecture contains seven layers. Each layer provides a portion of the total communications function required for distributed applications. Standards have been developed for each of the layers. Development work still continues, particularly at the top (application) layer, where new distributed applications are still being defined.

APPENDIX 2A   The Origins of OSI

The history of the development of the OSI model is, for some reason, a little-known story. Much of the work on the design of OSI was actually done by a group at Honeywell Information Systems, headed by Mike Canepa, with Charlie Bachman as the principal technical member. This group was chartered, within Honeywell, with advanced product planning and with the design and development of prototype systems.

In the early and middle 70s, the interest of Canepa's group was primarily on database design, and then on distributed database design. By the mid-70s, it became clear that to support database machines, distributed access, and the like, a structured distributed communications architecture would be required. The group studied some of the existing solutions, including IBM's systems network architecture (SNA), the work on protocols being done for ARPANET, and some of the concepts of presentation services being developed for standardized database systems. The result of all of this effort was the development by 1977 of a seven-layer architecture known internally as the distributed systems architecture (DSA).

Meanwhile, in 1977 the British Standards Institute proposed to ISO that a standard architecture was needed to define the communications infrastructure for distributed processing. As a result of this proposal, ISO formed a subcommittee on open systems interconnection (Technical Committee 97, Subcommittee 16). The American National Standards Institute (ANSI) was charged to develop proposals in advance of the first formal meeting of the subcommittee.

Bachman and Canepa participated in these early ANSI meetings and presented their seven-layer model. This model was chosen as the only proposal to be submitted to the ISO subcommittee. When this group met in Washington, DC in March of 1978, the Honeywell team presented their solution. A consensus was reached at that meeting that this layered architecture would satisfy most requirements of Open Systems Interconnection, and had the capacity of being expanded later to meet new requirements. A provisional version of the model was published in March of 1978. The next version, with some minor refinements, was published in June of 1979 and eventually standardized. The resulting OSI model is essentially the same as the DSA model developed in 1977[1].

---

1.   Your author can perhaps be forgiven a personal note. I had the privilege of being a member of Canepa's group in the early 1970s, when the focus was on distributed databases. I subsequently left the group to work on other things, TCP/IP among them. In the early 1980s, I again worked with this group on the design and implementation of OSI-compliant software that spanned a product line from microcomputers to mainframes. Alas, my absence coincided with those exciting years when OSI was invented. Talk about bad timing!

3
The OSI Infrastructure:
Layers 2 through 5

The purpose of this chapter is to look at those elements of OSI that are well developed and can be considered as forming the infrastructure for supporting distributed applications. The chapter provides a survey of layers 2 through 5 of the model. The choice of topics for this chapter is dictated by the following considerations:

- Standards at layer 1 vary considerably from one to another and are specific to a particular interface. Physical-layer standards for various networks are covered in Parts 2 and 3.

- Standards for layer 2 for various networks are also covered in Parts 2 and 3. However, it is useful to present a representative data-link-control standard in some detail in this chapter for several reasons. First, all of the layer-2 standards discussed in this book are based on the same principles and mechanisms. Second, the key mechanisms found in data-link-control protocols are also to be found repeated at layers 3 and 4.

- Layer 3 is the most complex of the OSI layers, and various aspects of this layer are treated in Chapter 4 and in Parts 2 and 3. However, one standard—namely, X.25 level 3—plays a central role in understanding the network layer and is therefore treated here.

- A single transport-service definition and a unified set of transport-protocol specifications comprise the OSI transport layer and are presented here.

- A single session-service definition and a single session-protocol specification comprise the OSI session layer and are presented here.

- The presentation and application layers, together, provide functionality specific to particular distributed applications. Much of this material is beyond the scope of this book. The overall architecture of the presentation and application layers, as well as some of the basic services of these layers, are treated in Chapter 5.

3.1 DATA-LINK LAYER

The bulk of this section is devoted to a presentation of the ISO (International Organization for Standardization) standard HDLC (high-level data-link control), for two reasons:

1. All the other data-link-control standards discussed in this book have evolved from HDLC.

2. Some of the important mechanisms found in HDLC are repeated at the network and transport layers.

3.1.1   HDLC PDU Structure

As with other protocols, HDLC operates by the exchange of protocol data units (PDUs), in this case referred to as data-link PDUs or *frames.*

Figure 3.1 depicts the format of the HDLC frame (ISO 3309), which has the following fields:

- *Flag:* used for synchronization. It appears at the beginning and end of the frame and always contains the pattern 0111110.

- *Address:* indicates the secondary station for this transmission. It is needed in the case of a multidrop line, where a primary may send data to one of a number of secondaries and one of a number of secondaries may send data to the primary.

- *Control:* identifies the purpose and functions of the frame. It is described later in the chapter.

- *Information:* contains the user data to be transmitted.

- *Frame-check sequence:* contains a 16- or 32-bit cyclic redundancy check (CRC), used for error detection. The CRC is a function of the contents of the address, control, and data fields. It is generated by the sender and again by the receiver. If the receiver's calculated result differs from the received CRC field, a transmission error is detected (see Figure 2.17).

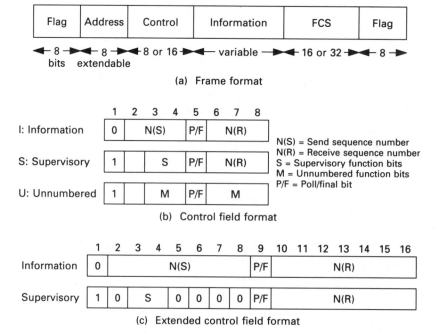

Figure 3.1 HDLC Frame Structure

HDLC defines three types of frames, each with a different control-field format. Information frames (I-frames) carry the user data to be transmitted for the station. Additionally, the information frames contain control information for flow control and error control. The supervisory frames (S-frames) provide another means of exercising flow control and error control. Unnumbered frames (U-frames) provide supplemental link-control functions.

The first 1 or 2 bits of the control field serve to identify the frame type. The remaining bit positions are organized into subfields, as indicated in Figure 3.1, parts (b) and (c). Their use is explained in the next subsection, which discusses HDLC operation. Note that the basic control field for S- and I-frames uses 3-bit sequence numbers. With the appropriate set-mode commands, an extended control field can be used that employs 7-bit sequence numbers.

3.1.2 HDLC Operation

HDLC operation consists of the exchange of I-frames, S-frames, and U-frames between two stations. The various commands and responses defined for these frame types are listed in Table 3.1. In describing HDLC operation, we will discuss these three types of frames.

The operation of HDLC involves three phases. First, one side or the other initializes the data link so that frames may be exchanged in an orderly fashion. During this phase, the options that are to be used are agreed upon. After initialization, the two sides exchange user data and the control information to exercise flow and error control. Finally, one of the two sides signals the termination of the operation.

Table 3.1 HDLC Commands and Responses

Name	Command/response	Description
Information (I)	C/R	Exchange user data
Supervisory (S)		
Receive ready (RR)	C/R	Positive acknowledgment; ready to receive I-frame
Receive not ready (RNR)	C/R	Positive acknowledgment; not ready to receive
Reject (REJ)	C/R	Negative acknowledgment; go back N
Selective reject (SREJ)	C/R	Negative acknowledgment; selective repeat
Unnumbered (U)		
Set normal response/extended mode (SNRM/SNRME)	C	Set mode; extended = 7-bit sequence numbers
Set asynchronous response/ extended mode (SARM/ SARME)	C	Set mode; extended = 7-bit sequence numbers
Set asynchronous balanced/ extended mode (SABM/ SABME)	C	Set mode; extended = 7-bit sequence numbers
Set initialization mode (SIM)	C	Initialize link-control functions in addressed station

Table 3.1 (*Cont.*)

Disconnect (DISC)	C	Terminate logical link connection
Unnumbered Acknowledg- ment (UA)	R	Acknowledge acceptance of one of the set-mode commands
Disconnected mode (DM)	C	Terminate logical link connection
Request disconnect (RD)	R	Request for DISC command
Request initialization mode (RIM)	R	Initialization needed; request for SIM command
Unnumbered information (UI)	C/R	Used to exchange control information
Unnumbered poll (UP)	C	Used to solicit control information
Reset (RSET)	C	Used for recovery; resets $N(R)$, $N(S)$
Exchange identification (XID)	C/R	Used to request/report status
Test (TEST)	C/R	Exchange identical information fields for testing
Frame reject (FRMR)	R	Reports receipt of unacceptable frame

3.1.2.1   Initialization

Initialization may be requested by either side by issuing one of the six set-mode commands. This command serves three purposes:

1. It signals the other side that initialization is requested.

2. It specifies which of the three modes is requested. Normal response mode (NRM) is used on multidrop lines; one station is designated primary, and the others are designated secondaries. A secondary may only transmit data in response to a poll from the primary. Asynchronous balanced mode (ABM) is used on point-to-point lines; either side may initiate data transfer. Asynchronous response mode (ARM) is a rarely used option in which a secondary may initiate data transfer but the primary is still responsible for initialization, error recovery, and logical disconnection.

3. It specifies whether 3- or 7-bit sequence numbers are to be used.

If the other side accepts this request, then the HDLC module on that end transmits an unnumbered acknowledgement (UA) frame back to the initiating side. If the request is rejected, then a disconnected mode (DM) frame is sent.

3.1.2.2   Data Transfer

When the initialization has been requested and accepted, then a logical connection is established. Both sides may begin to send user data in I-frames. The $N(S)$ and $N(R)$ fields in the I-frame provide an efficient technique for both flow control and error control. A station numbers the frames it sends sequentially modulo 8 or 128, depending on whether 3- or 7-bit sequence numbers are used, and places the sequence number in $N(S)$. When a station receives a valid I-frame, it acknowledges that frame with its own I-frame by setting the $N(R)$ field to the number of the next frame it expects to receive. So if it has just received a frame with $N(S) = 5$, it sets $N(R) = 6$ in its next outgoing I-frame. This is known as *piggybacked acknowledgment,* since the acknowledgment rides back on an I-frame. Acknowledgments can also be sent on a supervisory frame, as described later in this subsection.

The use of sequence numbers accomplishes three important functions:

1. *Flow control:* A station is only allowed to send 7 frames (3-bit sequence number) or 127 frames (7-bit sequence number) without an acknowledgment. No more frames may be sent until some of the outstanding frames are acknowledged. Thus, if the receiver is slow to acknowledge, the sender's output is restricted.

2. *Pipelining:* More than one frame may be in transit at a time; this allows more efficient use of links with high propagation delay, such as satellite links.

3. *Error control:* If a frame is received in error, a station can send a negative acknowledgment via a supervisory frame to specify which frame was received in error. This may be done in one of two ways. In the go-back-N approach, the sending station retransmits the rejected frame plus all subsequent frames that have been transmitted since the rejected frame. In the selective-repeat approach, the sending station retransmits only the frame received in error.

There are four types of supervisory frames. The receive-ready (RR) frame is used to acknowledge the last I-frame received by indicating the next I-frame expected. The RR is used when there is no reverse user data traffic (I-frames) to carry an acknowledgment. Receive not ready (RNR) acknowledges an I-frame, as with RR, but also asks the peer entity to suspend transmission of I-frames. When the entity that issued the RNR is again ready, it sends an RR. REJ indicates that the last I-frame received has been rejected and that retransmission of all I-frames beginning with number $N(R)$ is required. Selective reject (SREJ) is used to request retransmission of just a single frame.

3.1.2.3   Disconnect

Either HDLC module can initiate a disconnect, either on its own initiative if there is some sort of fault or at the request of its higher-layer user. HDLC issues a disconnect by sending a disconnect (DISC) frame. The other side must accept the disconnect by replying with a UA.

3.1.2.4   Examples of Operation

In order to enable the reader to better understand HDLC operation, several examples are presented in Figure 3.2. In the example diagrams, each arrow includes a legend that specifies the frame name, the setting of the P/F bit, and where appropriate, the values of $N(R)$ and $N(S)$. The setting of the P or F bit is 1 if the designation is present and 0 if it is absent.

Figure 3.2, part (a), shows the frames involved in link setup and disconnect. The HDLC entity for one side issues an SABM command to the other side and starts a timer. The other side, upon receiving the SABM, returns a UA response and sets local variables and counters to their initial values. The initiating entity receives the UA response, sets its variables and counters, and stops the timer. The logical connection is now active, and both sides may begin transmitting frames. Should the timer expire without a response, the originator will repeat the SABM, as illustrated. This would be repeated until a UA or DM is received or until, after a given number of tries, the entity attempting initiation gives up and reports failure to a management entity. In such a case, higher-layer intervention is necessary. The same figure (Figure 3.2, part [a]) shows the disconnect procedure. One side issues a DISC command, and the other responds with a UA.

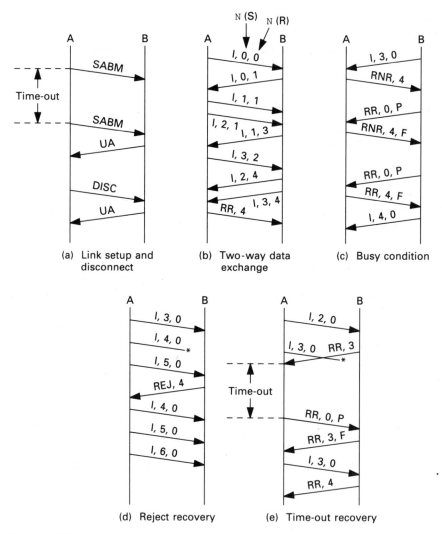

(a) Link setup and disconnect

(b) Two-way data exchange

(c) Busy condition

(d) Reject recovery

(e) Time-out recovery

Figure 3.2 HDLC Operation

Figure 3.2, part (b), illustrates the full-duplex exchange of I-frames. When an entity sends a number of I-frames in a row with no incoming data, then the receive sequence number is simply repeated (e.g., I, 1, 1; I, 2, 1 in the A-to-B direction). When an entity receives a number of I-frames in a row with no outgoing frames, then the receive sequence number in the next outgoing frame must reflect the cumulative activity (e.g., I, 1, 3 in the B-to-A direction). Note that, in addition to I-frames, data exchange may involve supervisory frames.

Figure 3.2, part (c), shows an operation-involving a busy condition. Such a condition may arise because an HDLC entity is not able to process I-frames as fast as they are arriving or the intended user is not able to accept data as fast as they arrive in I-frames. In either case, the entity's receive buffer fills up, and it must halt the incoming flow of I-frames, using an RNR command.

In this example, the station issues an RNR, which requires the other side to halt transmission of I-frames. The station receiving the RNR will usually poll the busy station at some periodic interval by sending an RR with the P bit set. This requires the other side to respond with either an RR or an RNR. When the busy condition has cleared, A returns an RR, and I-frame transmission from B can resume.

An example of error recovery using the REJ command is shown in Figure 3.2, part (d). In this example, A transmits I-frames numbered 3, 4, and 5. Number 4 suffers an error. B detects the error and discards the frame. When B receives I-frame number 5, it discards this frame because it is out of order and sends an REJ with an $N(R)$ of 4. This causes A to initiate retransmission of all I-frames sent, beginning with frame 4. It may continue to send additional frames after the retransmitted frames.

An example of error recovery using a time-out is shown in Figure 3.2, part (e). In this example, A transmits I-frame number 3 as the last in a sequence of I-frames. The frame suffers an error. B detects the error and discards it. However, B cannot send an REJ. This is because there is no way to know whether this was an I-frame. If an error is detected in a frame, all the bits of that frame are suspect, and the receiver has no way to act upon it. A, however, started a timer as the frame was transmitted. This timer has a duration long enough to span the expected response time. When the timer expires, A initiates recovery action. This is usually done by polling the other side with an RR command with the P bit set, to determine the status of the other side. Since the poll demands a response, the entity will receive a frame containing an $N(R)$ field and be able to proceed. In this case, the response indicates that frame 3 was lost. A then retransmits frame 3.

These examples are not exhaustive. However, they should give the reader a good feel for the behavior of HDLC.

3.1.3   Other Data-Link Standards

In addition to HDLC, there are a number of other important data-link standards (Table 3.2). LAPB was issued by CCITT (International Telegraph and Telephone Consultative Committee) as part of its X.25 packet-switching network-interface standard. It is a subset of HDLC that provides only the asynchronous balanced mode and is designed for the point-to-point link between a user system and a packet-switching network node.

Table 3.2 Data-Link-Control Standards

Name	Standard	Application
High-level data-link control (HDLC)	ISO 3309, ISO 4335, ISO 7809	Point-to-point and multipoint links
Link-access procedure, balanced (LAPB)	X.25	Point-to-point link from DTE to packet-switching DCE
Link-access procedure, D channel (LAPD)	I.441	ISDN D-channel data-link control
Logical link control (LLC)	ISO 8802–2	Local area networks
Multilink procedures (MLP)	ISO 7478	Multiple parallel physical circuits

LAPD is part of the I series of CCITT standards for ISDN (integrated services digital network) and is summarized in Chapter 6. The principal difference from HDLC is in the address field.

LLC is part of the ISO 8802 series of standards for local area networks. It, too, is based on HDLC. One major difference from HDLC, again, is in the address field. The other difference is the lack of a CRC field, which, in the case of local area networks, is assigned to a lower layer, the medium-access-control layer. LLC is summarized in Chapter 9.

Finally, MLP is designed to operate over multiple parallel point-to-point links. Over each line, a *single-link procedure,* such as HDLC or LAPB, is used. The MLP operates above the single-link procedure and might be thought of as an upper sublayer of the data-link layer. It provides for load balancing over the multiple links.

3.2   NETWORK LAYER—X.25

3.2.1   CCITT X.25 DTE-DCE Protocol

X.25 was originally issued by CCITT in 1976 and subsequently revised in 1980, 1984, and 1988. The standard, which specifies an interface between a host system and a packet-switched network, refers to user machines as data terminal equipment (DTE) and to a packet-switching network node to which a DTE is attached as data circuit-terminating equipment (DCE). The standard specifically calls out three layers of protocols:

1.   Physical layer
2.   Link layer
3.   Packet layer

The physical layer deals with the physical interface between an attached station (computer, terminal) and the link that attaches that station to the packet-switching node. It makes use of the physical-layer specification in a standard known as X.21, but in many cases, other standards, such as RS-232–C, are substituted. The link layer provides for the reliable transfer of data across the physical link, by transmitting the data as a sequence of frames. The link-layer standard is referred to as LAPB (link-access protocol, balanced). LAPB is a subset of HDLC. The packet layer provides a virtual circuit service and is described briefly in this section.

The three layers of X.25 correspond to the lowest three layers of the OSI model. User data[1] are passed down to X.25 layer 3, which appends control information as a header, creating a network PDU, or *packet.* The entire X.25 packet is then passed down to the LAPB entity, which appends control information at the front and back of the packet, forming an LAPB frame (see Figure 2.6).

3.2.1.1   Virtual Circuit Service

X.25 makes use of the concept of virtual circuit. In this case, this simply means that a logical connection exists between two stations that are exchanging data across the packet-switched network and that the network will deliver packets reliably and in sequence. Normally, this *external virtual circuit* corresponds to an *internal virtual circuit,* which is the actual route that the packets are taking through the network.

---

1.   In the OSI architecture, the transport layer is the user of X.25. However, X.25 can be used in other contexts, in which some other entity would be the user of X.25.

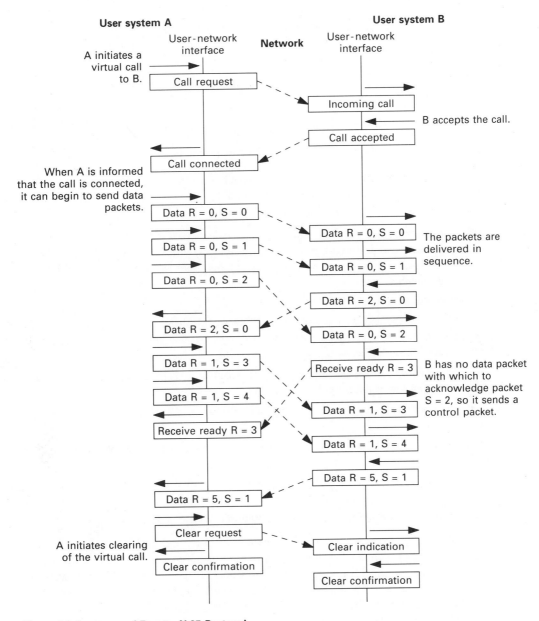

Figure 3.3 Sequence of Events: X.25 Protocol

There are two types of virtual circuit in X.25: virtual call and permanent virtual circuit. A virtual call is a dynamically established virtual circuit using a call-setup and call-clearing procedure. A permanent virtual circuit is a fixed, network-assigned virtual circuit. Data transfer occurs as with virtual calls, but no call setup or clearing is required.

Figure 3.3 shows a typical sequence of events in a virtual call. The left-hand part of the figure shows the packets exchanged between user machine A and the packet-switching node to which it

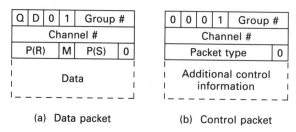

(a) Data packet   (b) Control packet

Figure 3.4 X.25 Layer-3 Packet Formats

attaches; the right-hand part shows the packets exchanged between user machine B and its node. The routing of packets inside the network is not visible to the user.

The sequence of events is as follows:

1. A requests a virtual circuit to B by sending a call request packet to A's DCE. The packet includes the source and destination addresses, as well as the virtual circuit number to be used for this new virtual circuit. Future incoming and outgoing transfers will be identified by this virtual circuit number.

2. The network routes this call request to B's DCE.

3. B's DCE receives the call request and sends an incoming call packet to B. This packet has the same format as the call request packet but a different virtual circuit number, selected by B's DCE from the set of locally unused numbers.

4. B indicates acceptance of the call by sending a call-accepted packet specifying the same virtual circuit number as that of the incoming call packet.

5. A receives a call-connected packet with the same virtual circuit number as that of the call request packet.

6. A and B send data and control packets to each other using their respective virtual circuit numbers.

7. A (or B) sends a clear request packet to terminate the virtual circuit and receives a clear confirmation packet.

8. B (or A) receives a clear indication packet and transmits a clear confirmation packet.

Figure 3.4, part (a), shows the packet format used in X.25 for user data. The data are broken up into blocks of some maximum size, and a 24-bit header is appended to each block to form a *data packet*. The header includes a 12-bit virtual circuit number (expressed as a 4-bit group number and an 8-bit channel number). The P(S) and P(R) fields support the functions of flow control and error control on a virtual circuit basis, as they do on a link basis in HDLC.

Acknowledgment, and hence flow control, may have either local or end-to-end significance, based on the setting of the D bit. When D = 0 (the usual case), acknowledgment is exercised between the DTE and the network. This is used by the local DCE and/or the network to acknowledge receipt of packets and control the flow from the DTE into the network. When D = 1, acknowledgments come from the remote DTE.

3.2.1.2 Packet Sequences

X.25 provides the capability to identify a contiguous sequence of data packets, which is called a *complete packet sequence*. This feature has several uses. We will see in Chapter 4 that it is used in internetworking protocols to allow longer blocks of data to be sent across a network with a smaller packet size restriction without losing the integrity of the block.

To specify this mechanism, X.25 defines two types of packets: A packets and B packets. An *A packet* is one in which the M bit is set to 1, the D bit is set to 0, and the packet is full (equal to the maximum allowable packet length). A *B packet* is any packet that is not an A packet. A complete packet sequence consists of zero or more A packets followed by a B packet. The network may combine this sequence to make one larger packet. The network may also segment a B packet into smaller packets to produce a complete packet sequence.

The way in which the B packet is handled depends on the setting of the M and D bits. If D = 1, an end-to-end acknowledgment is sent by the receiving DTE to the sending DTE. This is, in effect, an acknowledgment of the entire complete packet sequence. If M = 1, there are additional complete packet sequences to follow. This enables the formation of subsequences as part of a larger sequence, so that end-to-end acknowledgment can occur before the end of the larger sequence.

Figure 3.5 shows examples of these concepts. It is the responsibility of the DCEs to reconcile the changes in sequence numbering caused by segmentation and reassembly.

3.2.1.3 Control Information

In addition to transmitting user data, X.25 must transmit control information related to the establishment, maintenance, and termination of virtual circuits. Control information is transmitted in a *control packet* (Figure 3.4, part [b]). Each control packet includes the virtual circuit number; the packet type, which identifies the particular control function; and additional control information related to that function. For example, a call request packet may include the following additional fields:

- Calling DTE address length (4 bits): length of the corresponding address field in 4-bit units.
- Called DTE address length (4 bits): length of the corresponding address field in 4-bit units.
- DTE addresses (variable): the calling and called DTE addresses.
- Facility length: length of the facility field in octets.

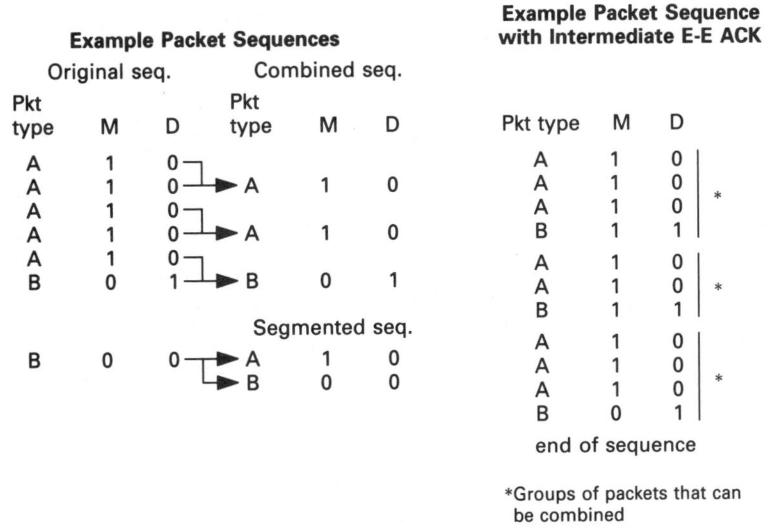

Figure 3.5 X.25 Packet Sequences

- Facilities: a sequence of facility specifications. Each specification consists of an 8-bit facility code and zero or more parameter codes. An example of a facility is reverse charging.

Table 3.3 lists all the X.25 control packets and their parameters. Most of these have already been discussed. A brief description of the remainder follows.

A DTE may send an interrupt packet that bypasses the flow-control procedures for data packets. The interrupt packet is to be delivered to the destination DTE by the network at a higher priority than data packets in transit. An example of the use of this capability is the transmission of a terminal break character.

The reset packets provide a facility for recovering from an error by reinitializing a virtual circuit. This means that the sequence numbers on both ends are set to 0. Any data or interrupt packets in transit are lost. A reset can be triggered by a number of error conditions, including loss of a packet, sequence-number error, congestion, or loss of the network's internal logical connection. In the latter case, the two DCEs must rebuild the internal logical connection to support the still-existing X.25 DTE-DTE virtual circuit.

A more serious error condition is dealt with by a restart, which terminates all active virtual calls. An example of a condition warranting restart is temporary loss of access to the network.

The diagnostic packet provides a means to signal certain error conditions that do not warrant reinitialization. The registration packets are used to invoke and confirm X.25 facilities.

3.2.2   ISO X.25 DTE-DTE Protocol

X.25 was developed as a protocol across the interface between a user system (DTE) and a packet-switching network (DCE); the architecture implied is shown in Figure 2.12. There are configurations, however, where two DTEs are connected without any intermediate relay systems at layer 3. One example is a direct point-to-point link between systems. Another example is a local area network, in which the intervening network essentially operates at layer 2. This latter architecture will be examined in Part 3.

Although X.25 was designed for the DTE-DCE application, it has a number of features that are appealing in the DTE-DTE context for supporting the connection-mode network service. In particular, it is a connection-oriented protocol that provides for multiple logical connections, sequencing, flow control, and error control. Thus, ISO has issued a standard (ISO 8208) that encompasses the use of the X.25 logic in both DTE-DCE mode and DTE-DTE mode. The DTE-DTE mode is substantially the same as the DTE-DCE mode. This subsection summarizes the DTE-DTE mode; for greater detail, see Kessler (1988).

To explain the operation of the DTE-DTE mode, it is important to note that a number of packets in X.25 have two names or, more precisely, two interpretations. That is, a number of packet type codes (Figure 3.4, part [b]) have two interpretations, one in the DTE-DCE direction and one in the DCE-DTE direction. The correspondences are as follows:

Type Code	DTE → DCE Packet	DCE → DTE Packet
0000101	Call request	Incoming call
0000111	Call accepted	Call connected
0001001	Clear request	Clear indication
0001101	Reset request	Reset indication
1111101	Restart request	Restart indication
1111001	Registration request	Registration confirmation

Table 3.3 X.25 Control-Packet Types and Parameters

Packet Type	Direction	Parameters
Call request	DTE → DCE	Calling DTE address, called DTE address, facilities, call user data
Incoming call	DCE → DTE	Calling DTE address, called DTE address, facilities, call user data
Call accepted	DTE → DCE	Calling DTE address, called DTE address, facilities, call user data
Call connected	DCE → DTE	Calling DTE address, called DTE address, facilities, call user data
Clear request	DTE → DCE	Clearing cause, diagnostic code, calling DTE address, called DTE address, facilities, clear user data
Clear indication	DCE → DTE	Clearing cause, diagnostic code, calling DTE address, called DTE address, facilities, clear user data
Clear confirmation	DTE → DCE DCE → DTE	Calling DTE address, called DTE address, facilities
Interrupt	DTE → DCE DCE → DTE	Interrupt user data
Interrupt confirmation	DTE → DCE DCE → DTE	—
RR	DTE → DCE DCE → DTE	$P(R)$
RNR	DTE → DCE DCE → DTE	$P(R)$
REJ	DTE → DCE	$P(R)$
Reset request	DTE → DCE	Resetting cause, diagnostic code
Reset indication	DCE → DTE	Resetting cause, diagnostic code
Reset confirmation	DTE → DCE DCE → DTE	—
Restart request	DTE → DCE	Restarting cause, diagnostic code
Restart indication	DCE → DTE	Restarting cause, diagnostic code
Restart confirmation	DTE → DCE DCE → DTE	—
Diagnostic	DCE → DTE	Diagnostic code, diagnostic explanation
Registration request	DTE → DCE	DTE address, DCE address, registration
Registration confirmation	DCE → DTE	Cause, diagnostic, DTE address, DCE address, registration

Figure 3.6, part (a), shows the X.25 connection-setup sequence. The calling DTE issues a call request packet to its DCE. This triggers activity inside the packet-switching network (outside the scope of X.25) and results in the issuance of an incoming call packet to the called DTE. This latter packet is identical to the call request packet, including the packet type code and all the parameters, with one exception. The only change is that the virtual circuit number is changed to one that is

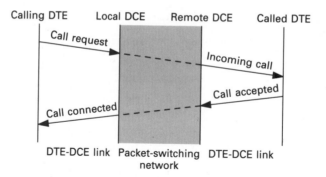

DTE-DCE link   Packet-switching   DTE-DCE link
network

(a) Call setup across a DTE-DCE interface with intervening
packet-switching network (X.25 and ISO 8208)

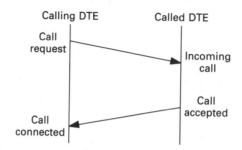

(b) Call setup across a DTE-DTE interface (ISO 8208)

Figure 3.6 Call-Setup Procedures Between DTEs

locally chosen. Similarly, the call-accepted and call-connected packets are identical except for the virtual circuit number.

From the point of view of the DTEs, the activity can be described as follows:

1. The calling DTE issues a call request with a virtual circuit number assigned by the calling DTE.

2. The called DTE receives an incoming call with the virtual circuit number already defined (by the called DCE).

3. The called DTE issues a call accepted with the same virtual circuit number as the incoming call.

4. The calling DTE receives a call connected with the same virtual circuit number as the call request.

The connection-setup sequence for the DTE-DTE interface is illustrated in Figure 3.6, part (b). The preceding description applies equally well in this case. The only difference is that the locally significant virtual circuit numbers at the two DTEs are the same.

3.3   TRANSPORT PROTOCOL

3.3.1   ISO Connection-Mode Transport-Protocol Family

The complexity of a connection-mode transport protocol depends on the level of service provided by the network layer and underlying communications facility. If the network service is connection-mode and reliable, then the transport protocol can be quite streamlined, whereas a connectionless, unreliable network service will require an elaborate transport protocol.

ISO has defined three types of network service, which are used in specifying transport-protocol standards:

1. *Type A:* connection-mode network service with acceptable residual error rate and acceptable rate of signaled failures

2. *Type B:* connection-mode network service with acceptable residual error rate but unacceptable rate of signaled failures

3. *Type C:* network service, either connectionless or connection-mode, with residual error rate not acceptable to the transport-service user

In this context, an error is defined as a lost, duplicated, or misordered network protocol data unit. If the error is caught and corrected by the network service in a fashion that is transparent to the transport entity, then the transport entity is not informed and need take no action. If the network service detects an error, cannot recover, and signals the transport layer, then this is known as a signaled failure. An example would be the notification by X.25 that a reset has occurred. The transport protocol would then require mechanisms for error recovery. Finally, a residual error is one that is not corrected by the network service and regarding which the transport layer is not notified. In this case, the transport protocol requires mechanisms for both error detection and recovery.

To account for differences among underlying network services, ISO has defined a family of five classes of transport protocols, all of which provide the same transport service. The advantage of this approach is that the minimum transport capability required for a particular network environment can be implemented. The five classes are listed in Table 3.4, and their relationship to the three types of network service is shown in Table 3.5.

The simplest class of transport protocol, *class 0,* is intended for use with a highly reliable connection-oriented network (type A). Transport connections are mapped one-to-one onto network connections (e.g., X.25 virtual circuits). Because the network service is reliable, the transport protocol does not require mechanisms for error detection and correction. Furthermore, because each transport connection has its own dedicated network connection, there is no need for sequence numbers and flow-control mechanisms at the transport level; this is handled at the network level.

The class-0 protocol can be enhanced in two independent ways: signaled error recovery and connection multiplexing. The first enhancement yields the *class-1* protocol, which is capable of dealing with type-B networks. In this case, if any PDUs are lost on the network connection, the transport protocol is notified. The two peer transport protocols then cooperate to retransmit the lost PDUs.

The second enhancement, connection multiplexing, yields the *class-2* protocol. This protocol is limited to use with type-A networks but allows multiple transport connections to be multiplexed

Table 3.4 The ISO Transport-Protocol Family

Class	Name	Description
0	Simple	Simple connection establishment and data transfer
1	Basic error recovery	Recovery from network-signaled errors
2	Multiplexed	Multiple transport connections on single network connection; flow control
3	Error recovery	Multiplexed connections; recovery from network-signaled errors
4	Error detection and recovery	Detection and recovery from lost, duplicated, or out-of-sequence data

over a single network connection. Flow control on a per-transport-connection basis is provided by the transport connection.

If both enhancements are present, we have a *class-3* protocol, which provides for connection multiplexing over type-B networks.

Finally, the *class-4* protocol assumes that the underlying network service is unreliable (type C). The service may be either connection-mode or connectionless, but it does not guarantee to signal the occurrence of errors. Thus, the class-4 protocol must include elaborate mechanisms to deal with the loss, duplication, or misordering of PDUs. Because this class provides the fullest set of transport-protocol mechanisms, it is examined in detail in the following subsection.

Table 3.5 Relationship Between Transport-Protocol Class and Network Service Type

	Network Service Type		
	Type A (Virtually no errors occur.)	**Type B (Transport protocol is notified of any errors.)**	**Type C (Errors occur without notification.)**
One transport connection per network connection	Class 0	Class 1	Class 4
Multiple transport connections per network connection	Class 2	Class 3	Class 4
Connectionless network service	—	—	Class 4

3.3.2   Class-4 Transport-Protocol Mechanisms

The class-4 transport protocol is faced with two fundamental flaws in the network service: transport PDUs (TPDUs) are occasionally lost; and TPDUs may arrive out of sequence due to variable transit delays. As we shall see, elaborate mechanisms are required to cope with these two interrelated network deficiencies.

The three key transport-protocol mechanisms are:

1. Connection establishment

2. Error control

3. Flow control

3.3.2.1   Connection Establishment

Connection establishment is accomplished by an exchange of TPDUs. The side wishing to initiate a connection sends a connection request (CR). The transport-protocol entity on the called side responds with a connection confirm (CC). This exchange serves to establish a connection. At the same time, the exchange is used to declare or negotiate certain characteristics of the connection:

- *Class:* The initiator (CR) proposes a preferred protocol class and any number of alternative classes. The responder (CC) selects the class.

- *Normal or extended format:* The initiator may propose the use of extended format (31-bit sequence numbers). The responder may accept this or select normal format (7-bit sequence numbers).

- *TPDU size:* The initiator proposes a maximum size, and the responder may accept this value or set the maximum size at some lower value.

- *Checksum:* The initiator may propose that, in class 4, no error-detecting code (checksum) be used. The responder may accept this or require the use of a checksum.

- *Expedited-data service:* The initiator may propose that expedited-data service be supported. The responder may accept or reject.

- *Quality of service parameters:* The initiator proposes values for throughput, transit delay, priority, and residual error rate (see Table 2.10). The responder may accept these values or set lesser values.

As with other transport-protocol mechanisms, connection establishment must take into account the unreliability of the network service. Suppose that transport-entity A issues a CR to transport-entity B. It expects to get a CC back, confirming the connection. Two things can go wrong: A's CR can be lost, or B's answering CC can be lost. Both cases can be handled by using a retransmission timer. If A issues a CR and does not receive a responding CC within the retransmission time, it reissues the CR.

This gives rise, potentially, to duplication. If A's first CR is lost, of course, then there is no duplication. But if A's first CR is successfully delivered and B's responding CC is lost, then B will receive two CRs from A. Further, if B's CC is not lost but simply delayed, then B will receive two CRs from A, and A will receive two CCs from B. All of this means that A and B must simply ignore duplicate CRs and CCs once a connection is established.

Now, consider that a duplicate CR may survive past the termination of the connection. In this case, B receives a CR from A after the connection for which the CR was issued has already been used and terminated. B assumes that this is a fresh request and responds with a CC. B now assumes that there is an open connection with A, whereas A will simply ignore the CC as being a duplicate. The result is that B is hung up on a half-open connection.

Although unlikely, even more complicated problems can arise. Again, suppose that an obsolete CR from A arrives at B and that B responds with a CC. Meanwhile, A has decided to open a new connection with B and sends a new CR. B discards this as a duplicate. In this case, A has sent a CR and received a CC, so both sides know there is a connection. The problem is that B responded to the wrong CR, and so there is no guarantee that the transport-connection characteristics have been negotiated properly.

Similarly, it is possible for a CC to survive beyond the end of the life of a connection, arrive in the midst of a new connection establishment, and interfere with the intended negotiation process.

The way out of all these problems is to provide some sort of unique identification for the transport connection and to provide for explicit acknowledgment of the CC. The procedure is known as a *three-way handshake*. With this strategy, both transport entities hesitate during connection establishment to assure that both the CR and the CC are acknowledged before declaring the connection open.

Figure 3.7, part (a), illustrates normal three-way-handshake operations. The CR includes a source reference (src-ref), which identifies the transport connection to the initiating transport entity. The CC includes a src-ref that identifies the transport connection to the responding transport entity and a dst-ref, which is the identifier assigned by the initiating transport entity. The initiating transport entity acknowledges the CC in its first data TPDU, which includes a dst-ref, which is the identifier assigned by the responding transport entity. Subsequently, all data TPDUs and other TPDUs sent over the connection will include a dst-ref field, which is the identifier assigned by the other side. Thus, the identifiers serve the same function as the X.25 virtual circuit numbers, and as in X.25, each side has its own identifier for the connection.

Figure 3.7, part (b), shows a situation in which an obsolete CR arrives at B after the close of the relevant connection. B assumes that this is a fresh request and responds with a CC. When A receives this message, it realizes that it has not requested a connection and therefore sends a disconnect request (DR), which signals B that the connection is to be aborted. Note that the dst-ref in the DR is essential so that an old, duplicate DR does not abort a legitimate connection establishment.

The final example (Figure 3.7, part [c]) shows a case in which an old CC arrives in the middle of a new connection establishment. Because of the use of reference numbers, this event causes no mischief.

3.3.2.2 Error Control

To cope with the loss, duplication, and misordering of data TPDUs, each data TPDU (DT) is labeled with a unique sequence number, and the DTs must be explicitly acknowledged with an acknowledgment (AK) TPDU. For efficiency, one AK per DT is not required. Rather, a cumulative acknowledgment can be used. Thus, one side may receive DTs numbered 1, 2, and 3 and then send back an AK with the sequence number 4, indicating that the next expected DT is number 4.

If a DT is lost in transit, no AK will be sent. To cope with this situation, there is a timer associated with each transmitted DT. If the timer expires before the DT is acknowledged, the sender will retransmit the DT. A certain amount of judgment is needed in setting the value of the

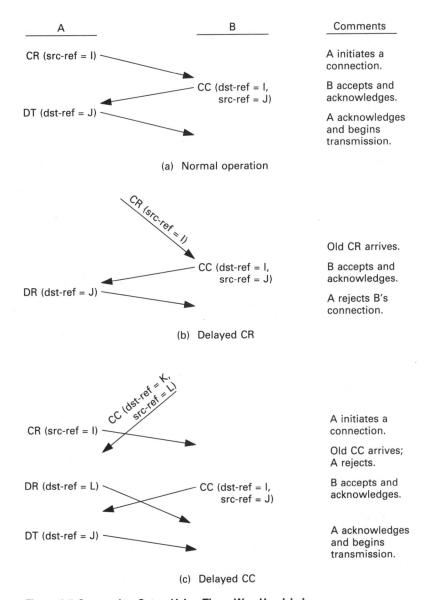

(a) Normal operation

(b) Delayed CR

(c) Delayed CC

Figure 3.7 Connection Setup Using Three-Way Handshake

timer. If the value is high, the protocol is sluggish in responding to errors. If the value is low, then a DT may be retransmitted even though an AK is en route from the other side.

If a DT is retransmitted even though an AK is on the way, or if an AK itself is lost in the network, then a transport entity may receive duplicate copies of a DT. There are two cases of interest:

1. A duplicate is received prior to the close of the connection.
2. A duplicate is received after the close of the connection.

Because of the use of sequence numbers, the first case should cause no confusion: the receiver will simply discard all copies of a DT with the same sequence number except the first one that it receives. However, the receiver should acknowledge the second DT, since its acknowledgment to the first DT may have been lost. Also, the sequence-number space must be long enough so as not to "cycle" in less than the maximum possible TPDU lifetime.

Figure 3.8 illustrates the reason for this latter requirement. For this example, a 3-bit sequence number is used, so the sequence space is of length 8. A transmits DTs numbered 0, 1, and 2 and awaits acknowledgment. For some reason, DT 0 is excessively delayed. B has received 1 and 2 but not 0. Thus, B does not send back any acknowledgments. A eventually times out and retransmits DT 0. When the duplicate DT 0 arrives, B acknowledges 0, 1, and 2. Meanwhile, A has timed out again and retransmits 1, which B acknowledges with another AK 3. Things now seem to have sorted themselves out, and data transfer continues. When the sequence space is exhausted, A cycles back to sequence number 0 and continues. Alas, the old DT 0 makes a belated appearance and is accepted by B before the new DT 0 arrives.

It should be clear that the untimely emergence of the old DT would have caused no difficulty if the sequence numbers had not yet returned to 0. The problem is, how big must the sequence-number space be? This depends, among other things, on whether the network enforces a maximum packet lifetime and on the rate at which TPDUs are being transmitted. The ISO transport protocol calls for the use of 7-bit sequence numbers as the default, which should be plenty for most applications, and 31-bit sequence numbers as an option. The latter should be more than enough for any application.

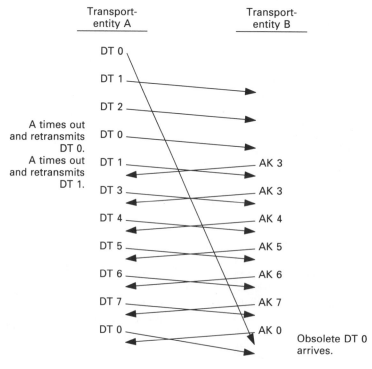

Figure 3.8 Example of Incorrect Duplicate Detection

A different problem is posed by DTs that continue to rattle around after a transport connection is closed. If a subsequent connection is opened between the same two entities, a DT from the old connection could arrive and be accepted on the new connection. Similarly, a delayed AK could enter a new connection and cause problems. To prevent these problems, the standard dictates the use of reference numbers. Each connection is assigned a reference number by both parties. Reference numbers so assigned are *frozen* and may not be used again for future connections for an amount of time sufficient to assure that no old TPDUs will reappear.

3.3.2.3   Flow Control

The flow-control technique used in the ISO transport protocol is known as a *credit-allocation* technique. At any time on a given transport connection, each transport entity is only allowed to transmit DTs corresponding to a *window* of sequence numbers. Each time a DT is sent, the window is narrowed by 1. From time to time, the receiver will issue a credit, allowing the sender to widen the window by the granted amount. Credit allocation and acknowledgment are independent of each other. Thus, a DT may be acknowledged without granting new credit and vice versa.

Credit allocation is granted in an acknowledgment TPDU, which contains both a sequence-number field and a credit field. Let us represent an acknowledgment TPDU as AK (N, M), where N is the sequence number, which acknowledges receipt of all DTs up through $N-1$, and M is the credit allocation, which allows DTs numbered N through $N+M-1$ to be transmitted. Figure 3.9 illustrates the protocol. For simplicity, we show data flow in one direction only and assumed the use of 3-bit sequence numbers. Initially, through the connection-establishment process, A is granted a credit allocation of 7, beginning with DT 0. The window is represented in the diagram as the shaded portion of a circle that includes all the sequence numbers. A advances the trailing edge of its window each time it transmits and advances the leading edge only when it is granted credit.

This mechanism is quite powerful. Consider that the last AK issued by B was AK (N, M). Then:

- To increase or decrease credit to A when no additional DT has arrived, B can issue AK (N, X), where $X \neq M$.
- To acknowledge an additional DT without increasing credit, B can issue AK $(N+1, M-1)$.

The credit-allocation scheme is robust in the face of an unreliable network service. If an AK is lost, little harm is done. Future AKs to future DTs will resynchronize the protocol. Furthermore, if no new AKs are forthcoming, the sender times out and retransmits a DT, which triggers a new AK. However, it is still possible for a deadlock to occur. Suppose B sends an AK $(N, 0)$, temporarily closing the window. Subsequently, B sends AK (N, M), but this TPDU is lost. A is awaiting the opportunity to send data, and B thinks it has granted that opportunity. To overcome this problem, a window timer is used. This timer is reset with each outgoing AK. If the timer expires, the transport entity is required to send an AK, even if it duplicates a previous one. This breaks the deadlock and also acts to assure the other end that the protocol entity is still active.

3.3.3   Protocol Formats

The ISO protocol makes use of ten types of transport-protocol data units:

1. Connection request (CR)
2. Connection confirm (CC)

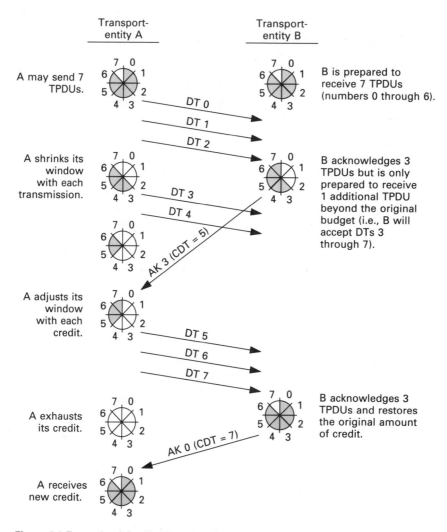

Figure 3.9 Example of Credit-Allocation Mechanism

3.   Disconnect request (DR)

4.   Disconnect confirm (DC)

5.   Data TPDU (DT)

6.   Expedited data (ED)

7.   Acknowledgment (AK)

8.   Expedited acknowledgment (EA)

9.   Reject (RJ)

10. TPDU error (ER)

The use of most of these TPDUs should be self-explanatory. CR and CC are used to establish a transport connection and negotiate its parameters. If the called transport entity chooses to reject the connection, it does so with a DR. DR is also used with DC to terminate an existing connection. Data is sent in DTs and acknowledged in AKs. The RJ is used to reject a DT and force its retransmission. Expedited data are sent in EDs and acknowledged in EAs. Sequence numbers are used with EDs, but only one ED may be outstanding at a time. Finally, ER is used when a TPDU is rejected because of an invalid value in one of the fields.

Each TPDU consists of three parts: a fixed header, a variable header, and a data field. The latter two optionally may not be present in a TPDU. The fixed header contains the frequently occurring parameters, and the variable header contains optional or infrequently occurring parameters. Table 3.6 defines all the fixed- and variable-header fields; Tables 3.7 and 3.8 indicate which parameters are used with each type of TPDU.

3.4 SESSION LAYER

The session layer provides the mechanisms for controlling the dialogue between applications in end systems. To support a dialogue, the session layer creates a logical connection, called a session connection, that maps one-to-one onto a transport connection. The session connection provides numerous services that impose structure on the dialogue between applications that takes place over a reliable transport connection.

Table 3.6 ISO Transport PDU Fields—Fixed-Header Fields

Length indicator (8 bits)
Length of the header (fixed plus variable), excluding the LI field, in octets.

TPDU code (4 bits)
Type of TPDU.

Credit (4 or 16 bits)
Flow-control credit allocation.

Source reference (16 bits)
Number used by a transport entity to uniquely identify a connection in its own system.

Destination reference (16 bits)
Number used by a transport entity to uniquely identify a connection in the peer system.

Class (4 bits)
Protocol class.

Option (4 bits)
Specifies the use of normal (7-bit sequence number, 4-bit credit) or extended (31-bit sequence number, 16-bit credit) flow-control fields.

Reason (8 bits)
Reason for requesting a disconnect or rejecting a connection request.

EOT (1 bit)
Used when a block of user data has been segmented into multiple DTs. It is set to 1 on the last DT.

TPDU-NR (7 or 31 bits)
Send sequence number of a DT.

EDTPDU-NR (7 bits)
Send sequence number of an ED.

YR-TU-NR (7 or 31 bits)
The next expected DT sequence number.

YR-EDTU-NR (7 or 31 bits)
The next expected ED sequence number.

Cause (8 bits)
Reason for rejection of a TPDU.

Table 3.6 (*Cont.*)

Variable Header Fields

Calling TSAP ID

Service access point that identifies the calling transport user.

Called TSAP ID

Service access point that identifies the called transport user.

TPDU Size (8 bits)

Maximum TPDU size in octets. The range of options is from 128 to 8192 in powers of 2.

Version Number (8 bits)

Version of protocol to be used. This accommodates future revisions to the standard.

Security Parameter

User-defined.

Checksum (16 bits)

Result of checksum algorithm for entire TPDU. The checksum is used only for Class 4 and, within that class, it is mandatory for all CRs, and for all TPDUs if the checksum option is selected.

Additional Option Selection (8 bits)

Used to specify the use or nonuse of certain options, including network expedited data in Class 1, acknowledgment in Class 1, checksum in Class 4, and transport expedited data service.

Alternative Protocol Class

Specifies whether only the requested protocol class is acceptable, or that some other class is also acceptable.

Acknowledge Time (16 bits)

An estimate of the time taken by the transport entity to acknowledge a DT. This helps the other side to select a value for its retransmission timer.

Throughput (96 or 192 bits)

Specifies the user's throughput requirements in octets per second. Eight values are specified: target and minimum acceptable values for both maximum throughput and average throughput, in both the calling-called and the called-calling directions.

Residual error rate (24 bits)

Expresses the target and minimum rate of unreported user data loss.

Priority (16 bits)

Priority of this connection.

Transit Delay (64 bits)

Specifies the user's delay requirements in milliseconds. Four values are specified: target and minimum acceptable delay in both directions.

Reassignment Time (16 bits)

Amount of time an entity will persist in attempts to reconnect after a network connection is broken.

Additional Information

Related to the clearing of the connection. User defined.

Subsequence Number (16 bits)

Sequence number assigned to each AK, used to assure that AKs with the same YR-TU-NR are processed in correct sequence.

Flow Control Confirmation (64 bits)

Echoes parameter values in the last AK received. It contains the values of YR-TU-NR, CDT, and subsequence number fields.

Invalid TPDU

The bit pattern of the rejected TPDU up to and including the octet that caused the rejection.

3.4.1 Session Service

The connection-mode session service is defined in ISO 8326 and in X.215. Table 3.9 summarizes the services provided and lists the relevant session-service primitives and parameters.

The types of service provided enable users to:

Table 3.7 ISO Transport-Protocol Fixed-Header Parameters

	CR	CC	DR	DC	DT	ED	AK	EA	RJ	ER
Length indicator	X	X	X	X	X	X	X	X	X	X
TPDU Code	X	X	X	X	X	X	X	X	X	X
Credit	X	X					X		X	
Source reference	X	X	X	X						
Destination reference		X	X	X	2, 3, 4	X	X	X	X	X
Class	X	X								
Option	X	X								
Reason			X							
EOT					X	X				
TPDU-NR					X					
EDTPDU-NR						X				
YR-TU-NR							X			
YR-EDTU-NR								X		
Cause										X

2, 3, 4 = classes 2, 3, and 4 only.

Table 3.8 ISO Transport-Protocol Variable-Header Parameters

	CR	CC	DR	DC	DT	ED	AK	EA	RJ	ER
Calling TSAP ID	X	X								
Called TSAP ID	X	X								
TPDU size	X	X								
Version number	X	X								
Security parameter	X	X								
Checksum	4	4	4	4	4	4	4	4	4	
Additional option selection	X	X								
Alternative protocol class	X	X								
Acknowledge time	4	4								
Throughput	X	X								
Residual error rate	X	X								
Priority	X	X								
Transmit delay	X	X								
Reassignment time	1, 3	1, 3								
Additional information				X						
Subsequence number							4			
Flow-control information							4			
Invalid TPDU										X

4 = class 4 only.

1, 3 = classes 1 and 3 only.

Table 3.9 ISO Session Service

Primitive and Parameters	Description
Session Connection-Establishment Phase	
S-CONNECT.request (identifier, calling SSAP, called SSAP, quality of service, requirements, serial number, token, data) S-CONNECT.indication (identifier, calling SSAP, called SSAP, quality of service, requirements, serial number, token, data) S-CONNECT.response (identifier, responding SSAP, result, quality of service, requirements, serial number, token, data) S-CONNECT.confirm (identifier, responding SSAP, result, quality of service, requirements, serial number, token, data)	Used to establish a connection between two session users. Allows users to negotiate tokens and parameters to be used for the connection.
Data-Transfer Phase	
Data-Transfer-Related	
S-DATA.request (data) S-DATA.indication (data)	Allows the transfer of normal SSDUs over a session connection, in either half-duplex or full-duplex mode.
S-EXPEDITED-DATA.request (data) S-EXPEDITED-DATA.indication (data)	Allows the transfer of expedited SSDUs containing up to 14 octets of user data over a session connection, free from the token and flow-control constraints of the other data-transfer services.
S-TYPED-DATA.request (data) S-TYPED-DATA.indication (data)	Allows the transfer of SSDUs over a session connection, independent of the assignment of the data token. Thus, data may be sent against the normal flow in half-duplex mode.
S-CAPABILITY-DATA.request (data) S-CAPABILITY-DATA.indication (data) S-CAPABILITY-DATA.response (data) S-CAPABILITY-DATA.confirm (data)	Used when activity services are available. Allows users to exchange data while not within an activity.
Activity-Related	
S-ACTIVITY-START.request (activity ID, data) S-ACTIVITY-START.indication (activity ID, data)	Used to indicate that a new activity is entered.
S-ACTIVITY-INTERRUPT.request (reason, data) S-ACTIVITY-INTERRUPT.indication (reason ID, data) S-ACTIVITY-INTERRUPT.response (data) S-ACTIVITY-INTERRUPT.confirm (data)	Allows an activity to be abnormally terminated with the implication that the work accomplished thus far is not to be discarded and may be resumed later.

Table 3.9 (*Cont.*)

Primitive and Parameters	Description
Data-Transfer Phase	
S-ACTIVITY-RESUME.request (activity ID, old activity ID, serial number, old session connection ID, data) S-ACTIVITY-RESUME.indication (activity ID, old activity ID, serial number, old session connection ID, data)	Used to indicate that a previously interrupted activity is reentered.
S-ACTIVITY-DISCARD.request (reason, data) S-ACTIVITY-DISCARD.indication (reason ID, data) S-ACTIVITY-DISCARD.response (data) S-ACTIVITY-DISCARD.confirm (data)	Allows an activity to be abnormally terminated with the implication that the work accomplished thus far is to be discarded.
S-ACTIVITY-END.request (serial number, data) S-ACTIVITY-END.indication (serial number, data)	Used to end an activity.
Session Connection-Release Phase	
S-RELEASE.request (data) S-RELEASE.indication (data) S-RELEASE.response (result, data) S-RELEASE.confirm (result, data)	Allows the session connection to be released after all in-transit data have been delivered and accepted by both users. If the negotiated-release option is selected during connection setup, the user receiving a release request may refuse the release and continue the session.
S-U-ABORT.request (data) S-U-ABORT.indication (data)	Releases a session in a way that will terminate any outstanding service requests. This service will cause the loss of undelivered SSDUs.
S-P-ABORT.indication (reason)	Used by the session-service provider to indicate the release of a connection for internal reasons. This service will cause the loss of undelivered SSDUs.
Token-Management-Related	
S-TOKEN-GIVE.request (tokens, data) S-TOKEN-GIVE.indication (tokens, data)	Use to surrender one or more specific tokens to the other user.
S-TOKEN-PLEASE.request (tokens, data) S-TOKEN-PLEASE.indication (tokens, data)	Allows a user to request a token currently assigned to the other user. Thus, this service is only used for a particular token when the other user possesses that token.
S-CONTROL-GIVE.request (data)	Allows a user to surrender all avail-

Table 3.9 (*Cont.*)

Primitive and Parameters	Description
Session Connection-Release Phase	
S-CONTROL-GIVE.indication (data)	able tokens to the other user. This service is part of the activity-management service.
Synchronization-Related	
S-SYNC-MINOR.request (type, serial number, data)	Allows the user to define minor sync points in the flow of SSDUs. The requester may request explicit confirmation that the minor sync point has been received by the other user.
S-SYNC-MINOR.indication (type, serial number, data)	
S-SYNC-MINOR.response (serial number, data)	
S-SYNC-MINOR.confirm (serial number, data)	
S-SYNC-MAJOR.request (serial number, data)	Allows the user to define major sync points in the flow of SSDUs, which completely separates the flow before and after each major sync point.
S-SYNC-MAJOR.indication (serial number, data)	
S-SYNC-MAJOR.response (serial number, data)	
S-SYNC-MAJOR.confirm (serial number, data)	
S-RESYNCHRONIZE.request (type, serial number, tokens, data)	Used to set the session connection to a previous synchronization point but no further back than the last major sync point. The state of the connection at that point is restored.
S-RESYNCHRONIZE.indication (type, serial number, tokens, data)	
S-RESYNCHRONIZE.response (serial number, tokens, data)	
S-RESYNCHRONIZE.confirm (serial number, tokens, data)	
Exception-Reporting-Related	
S-P-EXCEPTION-REPORT.indication (reason)	Notifies the user of exception conditions or session-protocol errors.
S-U-EXCEPTION-REPORT.request (reason, data)	Allows a user to report an exception condition when the data token is assigned to the other user.
S-U-EXCEPTION-REPORT.indication (reason, data)	

- Establish a connection with another session-service user, exchange data with that user, and release the connection in an orderly manner
- Establish synchronization (sync) points within the dialogue and, in the event of errors, resume the dialogue from an agreed sync point
- Interrupt a dialogue and resume it later from a prearranged sync point
- Negotiate for the use of tokens to exchange data, synchronize and release the connection, and arrange for data exchange to be half-duplex or full-duplex

In addition to providing for the establishment, maintenance, and termination of session connections, the session service provides a variety of ways of structuring the dialogue that takes place over those connections. The simplest of these facilities is the ability to choose two-way simultaneous (full-duplex) or two-way alternate (half-duplex) operation.

The session service also provides an optional facility for labeling the data stream with synchronization points, which serves two purposes. Sync points can be used to clearly isolate a portion of the dialogue, and they can be used in error recovery.

3.4.1.1   Synchronization Points

Two types of sync points are defined: major and minor. The relationship between these two is illustrated in Figure 3.10, part (a). *Major sync points* are used to structure the exchange of data into *dialogue units*. All data within a dialogue unit are completely separated from all data before and after it. After defining a major sync point, the user may not send more data until that sync point is acknowledged by the destination user. For recovery purposes, it is not possible to back up beyond the last major sync point.

Thus, the two purposes mentioned above are achieved:

1. Since the completion of one dialogue unit must be acknowledged before the next begins, the dialogue unit can be used by the session user to define application-oriented functions. For example, if a sequence of files is to be transferred, each file could be segregated into a separate dialogue unit. The sender could then be assured that a particular file had been received and accepted before attempting to send another file.

2. The dialogue unit defines the limit of recovery. For example, in a transaction-processing application, each transaction could be equated with a dialogue unit. When a transaction is complete and acknowledged, each side can purge any recovery information that had been saved for the purpose of permitting backup to the beginning of that transaction.

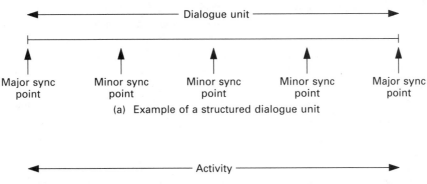

(a) Example of a structured dialogue unit

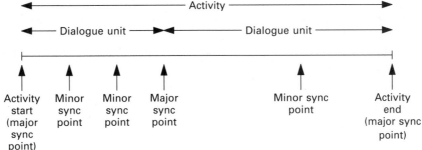

(b) Example of a structured activity

Figure 3.10 Session Interaction Structure

Minor sync points are used to structure the exchange of data within a dialogue. They provide more flexibility for recovery. A session user may define one or more minor sync points within a dialogue unit and need not wait for acknowledgment before proceeding. At any point, it is possible to resynchronize the dialogue to any previous minor sync point within the current dialogue unit or, of course, to resynchronize to the beginning of the dialogue unit (the most recent major sync point). This permits the session user to make a trade-off: with frequent sync points, backup and recovery can be speeded up at the expense of saving frequent checkpoints.

In the session-service standard, it is not the responsibility of the session layer to save any data that have already been transmitted. The session service will simply mark the data stream as requested with a sequentially assigned serial number. When resynchronization occurs, the session service decrements the serial number back to the point of resynchronization. To retransmit data that had previously been transmitted, the session user must have saved that data and must present it to the session service again.

3.4.1.2   Activities

One additional level of structuring is available as an option that may be selected when setting up the session: the activity option. An activity is defined as a logical unit of work, consisting of one or more dialogue units (Figure 3.10, part [b]). The key feature of the activity is that it can be interrupted and later resumed. For example, if an activity (such as a very long database transfer) is taking place and one machine or the other needs to interrupt the process (to go down for maintenance or to handle a higher-priority task), then the session service stops the activity. The session service remembers the last serial number used (for a major or minor sync point), so that the activity may be resumed later at the same sync point. Again, it is the responsibility of the session user to save any other context information that is needed for resumption.

The relationship between activities and session connections is not fixed. As indicated in Figure 3.11, part (a), it is possible to have a one-to-one correspondence. In this case, a new activity begins a new session connection, and when the activity is completed, the session connection is terminated. It is also possible to perform multiple activities in sequence over a single session connection (Figure 3.11, part [b]). This approach may be desirable if session establishment is time- or resource-consuming. If two session users know they will engage in a series of activities, it makes sense to maintain the session connection. Finally, a single activity can span multiple session connections (Figure 3.11, part [c]). If an activity is interrupted and is not expected to be resumed immediately, it makes sense to break the connection, freeing up resources, and begin a new connection at some point in the future when the users are prepared to resume their activity.

Figure 3.11 also illustrates the use of capability data. If two users select the activity option, then, normally, data may be exchanged only when an activity is in progress. Capability data is a mechanism whereby such users can exchange a small amount of data over a session connection when no activity is in progress. For example, this feature could be used to transmit control information without going through the overhead of setting up an activity.

3.4.1.3   Session Tokens

A session token is an attribute of a session connection that is dynamically assigned to one user at a time and that grants the user exclusive rights to invoke certain services. Put another way, certain services can only be invoked by the current token holder.

The token mechanism is used in the session service to structure the dialogue. The session service provides mechanisms by which a token can initially be assigned to one of the two users

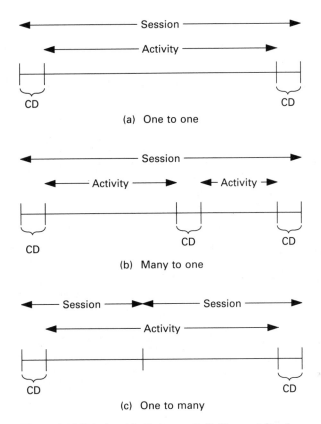

Figure 3.11 Relationship Between Activities and Sessions

engaged in a session and subsequently passed from one user to the other. Four tokens are defined, as follows:

1. *Data token:* used to manage a half-duplex connection
2. *Synchronize-minor token:* used to govern the setting of minor sync points
3. *Major/activity token:* used to govern the setting of major sync points and to manage the activity structure
4. *Release token:* used to govern the release of connections

Three services are associated with the token mechanism: (1) the give-token service allows a user to pass a token to the other user of a session connection; (2) the please-token service allows a user who does not possess a token to request it; (3) the give-control service is used to pass all tokens from one user to the other.

Figure 3.12 shows the use of the data token to provide the half-duplex mode of operation. In this example, the token is initially possessed by user A, who is free to transmit data. User B may not transmit normal data but may transmit a small amount of what is referred to as typed data. An example of typed data would be the transmission of a break character from a terminal to halt the

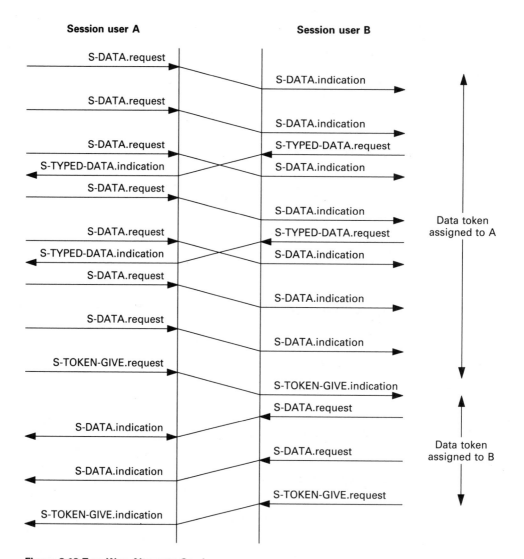

Figure 3.12 Two-Way Alternate Service

flow of data from an application. User B may request the data token at any time, but the token is relinquished only at user A's discretion.

Each of the tokens is always in one of the following two states:

1. *Not available:* All four tokens are optional, so their use must be negotiated during connection establishment. In the case of the data and release tokens, their unavailability means that the corresponding services (normal data transfer, connection release) are always available to both users. In the case of the synchronize-minor and major/activity tokens, their unavailability means that the corresponding services (synchronization, activities) are unavailable to both users.

Table 3.10 The Use of ISO Session Tokens

Function	Tokens Required			
	Data	Minor Sync	Major Sync	Release
Transfer SSDU (half-duplex)	M	—	—	—
Transfer capability data	I	I	M	—
Set minor sync point	I	M	—	—
Set major sync point	I	I	M	—
Start activity	I	I	M	—
Resume activity	I	I	M	—
Interrupt activity	—	—	M	—
Discard activity	—	—	M	—
End activity	I	I	M	—
Release connection	I	I	I	I

M = mandatory (token must be available and assigned to user to perform function).

I = if available (if token is available, it must be assigned to user to perform function).

— = which side owns token when function is performed is irrevelant.

2. *Available:* An available token is assigned to one of the two users, who then has the exclusive right to use the associated service.

Table 3.10 shows which tokens a user must possess to perform which functions. Note that, with the exception of the release service, each service listed in the table requires the use of a particular token and may require the use of additional tokens if they are available. These restrictions appear reasonable. For example, in the case of half-duplex operation, only the holder of the data token can set sync points.

3.4.1.4 Connection-Establishment Phase

For the connection-establishment phase, the S-CONNECT primitives are used (Table 3.9). This phase involves negotiating the characteristics of the session connection. The negotiation results either in the failure to establish a session connection or in a three-party agreement (i.e., between the two session users and the session service) on those characteristics. The following items are negotiated:

- *Quality of service:* This negotiation follows the pattern described in section 2.5 and includes the parameters listed in Table 2.11 and defined in Table 2.9. For the most part, these parameters are passed down to the transport service.

- *Requirements:* a list of functional units that may be requested. These are summarized later in this subsection. One side proposes the list in the request primitive; only those that appear in the response primitive are provided.

- *Serial number:* When synchronization services are to be employed, this is the proposed initial serial number.

- *Token:* a list of the available tokens and the side to which each is initially assigned.

3.4.1.5 Data-Transfer Phase

During the data-transfer phase, the users pass data to the session provider in session-service data units (SSDUs) and observe the discipline imposed by the tokens. For example, if there is a data token, the connection is half-duplex, and the users must take turns sending data. If synchronization and resynchronization are allowed, then the holder of the appropriate tokens can set major and minor sync points.

Each sync point has an associated serial number that is unique within a given session connection. Major sync points are consecutively numbered in step with minor sync points, facilitating resynchronization by the service provider.

When requesting resynchronization, the user indicates the value to be assigned to the serial number by selecting one of the following options (Figure 3.13):

- *Abandon:* any unused value greater than the current serial number
- *Restart:* any value equal to a past acknowledged major or minor sync point serial number and greater than or equal to the serial number that identifies the last acknowledged major sync point
- *Set:* any value

The restart option is used for recovery to a previous point in the dialogue. However, it is up to the session user to perform any data retransmission or other recovery function; the session service merely changes the value of the serial number and reassigns the tokens to the previous state. The set and abandon options are used where recovery is not desired but the current dialogue is to be aborted without dropping the connection. Again, the semantics of these options is up to the individual session user.

3.4.1.6   Connection-Release Phase

The connection-release service is orderly. That is, release is performed cooperatively between the two session users of the connection. All in-transit data are delivered and accepted prior to the release. If the negotiated-release option was selected, then the user receiving a release indication may refuse the release and continue the session connection without loss of data.

3.4.1.7   Session Functional Units

As the reader might be able to gather, the session service tries to be all things to all people. The result is that a full-blown implementation of the session standard is not only complex but unnecessary for virtually all applications. Thus, it is likely that only subsets of the session service will be provided by particular implementations. The standard anticipates this and tries to impose some order by introducing the concept of session functional units. The services supported by each of these functional units are indicated in Table 3.11. Note that when a functional unit implies the availability of a token, services concerned with the management of that token are provided in order

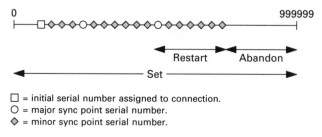

□ = initial serial number assigned to connection.
○ = major sync point serial number.
◇ = minor sync point serial number.

Figure 3.13 Synchronization Serial-Number Assignment

Table 3.11 Session Functional Units

Functional Unit	Service(s)	Token Use
Kernel (non-negotiable)	Session connection	—
	Normal data transfer	
	Orderly release	
	U-abort	
	P-abort	
Negotiated release	Orderly release	Release token
	Give tokens	
	Please tokens	
Half-duplex	Give tokens	Data token
	Please tokens	
Duplex	No additional services	—
Expedited data	Expedited-data transfer	—
Typed data	Typed-data transfer	—
Capability-data exchange	Capability-data exchange	—
Minor synchronize	Minor synchronization point	Synchronize-minor token
	Give tokens	
	Please tokens	
Major synchronize	Major synchronization point	Major/activity token
	Give tokens	
	Please tokens	
Resynchronize	Resynchronize	—
Exceptions	Provider exception reporting	—
	User exception reporting	
Activity management	Activity start	Major/activity token
	Activity resume	
	Activity interrupt	
	Activity discard	
	Activity end	
	Give tokens	
	Please tokens	
	Give control	

to enable the request and transfer of the available token; the tokens involved are also indicated in the table.

Each functional unit is a logical grouping of services. The definition of functional units allows the following:

- Higher-layer entities (applications, presentation entities) may specify which functional units they require. This alerts the session service that it need not attempt to provide other functional units. Furthermore, if the session service is unable to provide the requested functional units, this can be reported to the session user.

- During the session connection-establishment phase, the two session entities negotiate the use of functional units, using the requirements parameter in the S-CONNECT primitive.

The minimum requirement is support of the kernel functional unit, which provides the basic session services required to establish a session connection, transfer normal data, and release the session connection.

There are a few restrictions on the selection of functional units:

- It is not possible to select both the half-duplex and duplex functional units. Clearly, only one mode of operation at a time is possible.

- The capability-data-exchange functional unit can only be selected when the activity-management functional unit has been selected. The reverse is not true; that is, it is not necessary to select the capability-data-exchange functional unit if the activity-management functional unit has been selected.

- The exceptions functional unit can only be selected when the half-duplex functional unit has been selected.

3.4.2   Session Protocol

In the CCITT 1988 set of recommendations, the OSI session service definition occupies 82 pages, whereas the OSI session protocol specification occupies 143 pages. This is a clue to the observer that the session protocol, in its full glory, may be quite a bear to implement. However, for the present purposes, we are principally concerned with explaining the functionality of the session protocol and its relationship to the session service above and the transport service below. From that point of view, happily, things are reasonably straightforward.

It is the job of the session protocol to bridge the gap between the services provided by the transport layer and those required by the session user. In essence, the transport layer provides three services:

1. Establishment, maintenance, and release of a transport connection with certain quality of service characteristics
2. Reliable transfer of data
3. Reliable transfer of expedited data

The session service, as we have seen, provides a variety of services relating to the management and structuring of the exchange of data. Hence, it is the job of the session protocol to provide these structuring mechanisms on top of these transport services. In one sense, it appears that the session-protocol standard is far more elaborate than the transport-protocol standard. For example, the transport protocol includes 10 types of TPDUs, whereas the session protocol includes 36 types of SPDUs. One reason for this complexity is that the session-protocol standard has resulted from the merger of various ISO and CCITT endeavors and is anything but cleanly designed.

In another sense, however, this appearance of complexity is misleading. In the transport protocol, elaborate mechanisms are needed to deal with the unreliability and variable-delay problems that are faced. The session protocol is provided with a rather straightforward service. The complexity is in the session service, with its many session-service primitives and its abundance of rules for how these primitives are to be used to provide the rich set of session services. The session protocol basically provides a rather straightforward mapping of session-service primitives into session-protocol data units and makes use of the comparatively simple, reliable interface to the transport layer to exchange these primitives.

3.4.2.1 Protocol Data Units and Mechanisms

As with most protocols, the session protocol is best explained by focusing on the collection of PDUs that are used. These are listed in Table 3.12, with an explanation of the parameters in Table 3.13. For the most part, these SPDUs represent a one-to-one mapping with session-service primitive pairs (Table 3.14). That is, for each request-indication or response-confirm pair (see Figure 2.10), a single SPDU is used to convey the information. There are two classes of exceptions to this rule:

1. In some cases, more than one possible SPDU exists, to reflect more than one possible response to a service request. These cases are:

   - S-CONNECT.response → S-CONNECT.confirm: the accept and refuse SPDUs indicate acceptance or refusal of a connection request, respectively.
   - S-RELEASE.response → S-RELEASE.confirm: the disconnect and not finished SPDUs indicate acceptance or refusal of an orderly release request, respectively.

2. If the transport protocol imposes a maximum size on the data that it will accept in a single transport-service request (maximum TSDU size), then it may be necessary for the session

Table 3.12 Session-Protocol Data Units, Parameters, and Functions

SPDU	Parameters	Function
Connect	Connection ID, protocol options, maximum TSDU size, version number, initial serial number, token setting, user requirements, calling SSAP, called SSAP, user data, data overflow	Initiate session connection
Accept	Connection ID, protocol options, maximum TSDU size, version number, initial serial number, token setting, token, user requirements, calling SSAP, responding SSAP, enclosure item, user data	Establish session connection
Overflow accept	Maximum TSDU size, version number	Request remainder of the S-CONNECT.request user data
Connect data overflow	Enclosure item, user data	Send subsequent segments of the S-CONNECT.request user data
Refuse	Connection ID, transport disconnect, user requirements, version number, enclosure item, reason	Reject connection request
Finish	Transport disconnect, enclosure item, user data	Initiate orderly release
Disconnect	Enclosure item, user data	Acknowledge orderly release
Not finished	Enclosure item, user data	Reject orderly release

Table 3.12 (*Cont.*)

SPDU	Parameters	Function
Abort	Transport disconnect, error code, enclosure item, user data	Abnormal connection release
Abort accept	—	Acknowledge abort
Data transfer	Enclosure item, user data	Transfer normal data
Expedited	User data	Transfer expedited data
Typed data	Enclosure item, user data	Transfer typed data
Capability data	Enclosure item, user data	Transfer capability data
Capability-data ACK	Enclosure item, user data	Acknowledge capability data
Give tokens	Token, enclosure item, user data	Transfer tokens
Please tokens	Token, enclosure item, user data	Request token assignment
Give-tokens confirm	Enclosure item, user data	Transfer all tokens
Give-tokens ACK	—	Acknowledge all tokens
Minor sync point	Confirm-required flag, serial number, enclosure item, user data	Define minor sync point
Minor sync ACK	Serial number, enclosure item, user data	Acknowledge minor sync point
Major sync point	End-of-activity flag, serial number, enclosure item, user data	Define major sync point
Major sync ACK	Serial number, enclosure item, user data	Acknowledge major sync point
Resynchronize	Token settings, resync type, serial number, enclosure item, user data	Resynchronize
Resynchronize ACK	Token settings, serial number, enclosure item, user data	Acknowledge resynchronize
Prepare	Type	Notify type SPDU is coming
Exception report	SPDU bit pattern	Protocol error detected
Exception data	Reason, enclosure item, user data	Put protocol in error state
Activity start	Activity ID, enclosure item, user data	Signal beginning of activity
Activity resume	Connection ID, old activity ID, new activity ID, serial number, enclosure item, user data	Signal resumption of activity
Activity interrupt	Reason, enclosure item, user data	Interrupt activity
Activity-interrupt ACK	Enclosure item, user data	Acknowledge interrupt
Activity discard	Reason, enclosure item, user data	Cancel activity
Activity-discard ACK	Enclosure item, user data	Acknowledge cancellation
Activity end	Serial number, enclosure item, user data	Signal activity end
Activity-end ACK	Serial number, enclosure item, user data	Acknowledge activity end

Table 3.13 Session-Protocol Parameters

Connection ID

Enables SS users to identify this specific session connection. The value consists of portions defined by the calling and called SS users.

Protocol options

Indicates whether or not the initiator is able to receive extended concatenated SPDUs. Certain SPDUs may be concatenated and transmitted as a single unit by the transport layer. Basic concatenation allows two SPDUs to be concatenated. Extended concatenation allows more than two SPDUs to be concatenated.

Maximum TSDU size

The maximum transport-service data-unit size. This is the maximum size of an SPDU or a concatenation of SPDUs.

Version number

Indicates which versions of this protocol are supported. Version 1 limits the size of user data to 512 octets. Version 2 imposes no restrictions on the length of user data.

Initial serial number

Required if minor synchronize, major synchronize, or resynchronize functional unit is proposed.

Token setting

Initial token position for each token available on this connection.

User requirements

List of functional units to be supported on this connection.

Calling SSAP

Identifies the calling session user.

Called SSAP

Identifies the called session user.

User data

Session user data.

Data overflow

This flag is present if more than 10,240 octets of user data are to be transmitted with the session connection establishment. The first 10,240 octets are sent in the connect SPDU; the remainder are sent in one or more connect data-overflow SPDUs.

Token

Identifies tokens being passed or requested.

Responding SSAP

Identifies the session user that actually responds to a connection request.

Enclosure item

Used when a session-service data unit is segmented into more than one SPDU. This parameter indicates whether the SPDU that contains it is the beginning, an intermediate, or the ending SPDU in the sequence.

Transport disconnect

Used in the finish SPDU to indicate whether or not the transport connection is to be retained after the termination of the associated session connection.

Error code

Contains an implementation-defined value related to a protocol error.

Table 3.14 Relationship between Session-Service (SS) Primitives and Session-Protocol Data Units (SPDUs)

SS Primitive →	SPDU →	SS Primitive
S-CONNECT.request	CONNECT and (0 or 1) OVERFLOW ACCEPT and (0 or more) CONNECT DATA OVERFLOW	S-CONNECT.indication
S-CONNECT.response	ACCEPT or REFUSE	S-CONNECT.confirm
S-DATA.request	DATA TRANSFER	S-DATA.response
S-EXPEDITED-DATA.request	EXPEDITED DATA	S-EXPEDITED-DATA.indication
S-TYPED-DATA.request	TYPED DATA	S-TYPED-DATA.indication

Table 3.14 (*Cont.*)

SS Primitive →	SPDU →	SS Primitive
S-CAPABILITY-DATA.request	CAPABILITY DATA	S-CAPABILITY-DATA.indication
S-CAPABILITY-DATA.response	CAPABILITY-DATA ACK	S-CAPABILITY-DATA.confirm
S-TOKEN-GIVE.request	GIVE TOKENS	S-TOKEN-GIVE.indication
S-TOKEN-PLEASE.request	PLEASE TOKENS	S-TOKEN-PLEASE.indication
S-CONTROL-GIVE.request	GIVE-TOKENS CONFIRM	S-CONTROL-GIVE.indication
S-SYNC-MINOR.request	MINOR SYNC POINT	S-SYNC-MINOR.indication
S-SYNC-MINOR.response	MINOR SYNC ACK	S-SYNC-MINOR.confirm
S-SYNC-MAJOR.request	MAJOR SYNC POINT	S-SYNC-MAJOR.indication
S-SYNC-MAJOR.response	MAJOR SYNC ACK	S-SYNC-MAJOR.confirm
S-RESYNCHRONIZE.request	RESYNCHRONIZE	S-RESYNCHRONIZE.indication
S-RESYNCHRONIZE.response	RESYNCHRONIZE ACK	S-RESYNCHRONIZE.confirm
S-U-EXCEPTION-REPORT.request	EXCEPTION DATA	S-U-EXCEPTION-REPORT.indication
S-ACTIVITY-START.request	ACTIVITY START	S-ACTIVITY-START.indication
S-ACTIVITY-RESUME.request	ACTIVITY RESUME	S-ACTIVITY-RESUME.indication
S-ACTIVITY-INTERRUPT.request	ACTIVITY INTERRUPT	S-ACTIVITY-INTERRUPT.indication
S-ACTIVITY-INTERRUPT.response	ACTIVITY-INTERRUPT ACK	S-ACTIVITY-INTERRUPT.confirm
S-ACTIVITY-DISCARD.request	ACTIVITY DISCARD	S-ACTIVITY-DISCARD.indication
S-ACTIVITY-DISCARD.response	ACTIVITY-DISCARD ACK	S-ACTIVITY-DISCARD.confirm
S-ACTIVITY-END.request	ACTIVITY END	S-ACTIVITY-END.indication
S-ACTIVITY-END.response	ACTIVITY-END ACK	S-ACTIVITY-END.confirm
S-RELEASE.request	FINISH	S-RELEASE.indication
S-RELEASE.response	DISCONNECT or NOT FINISHED	S-RELEASE.confirm
S-U-ABORT.request	ABORT	S-U-ABORT.indication

protocol to segment session data into smaller blocks for transmission. This, in turn, leads to two cases:

a. For the following SPDUs, multiple SPDUs of the same type are used to carry the session data:

- Refuse
- Finish
- Disconnect
- Not finished
- Abort
- Data transfer
- Typed data
- Capability data
- Resynchronize
- Resynchronize ACK
- Exception data
- Activity start
- Activity resume
- Activity interrupt

- Capability-data ACK
- Give tokens
- Please tokens
- Give-tokens confirm
- Minor sync point
- Minor sync ACK
- Major sync point
- Major sync ACK
- Activity-interrupt ACK
- Activity discard
- Activity-discard ACK
- Activity end
- Activity-end ACK

b. If the S-CONNECT.request primitive, because it includes user data, is too large to be contained in a connect SPDU, then the connect SPDU includes a data-overflow parameter indicating that more user data are to follow. The called session-protocol entity returns an overflow-accept SPDU, and the calling session protocol entity sends as many connect data-overflow SPDUs as are necessary to transfer the user data. Only when all of the data have been transferred will the called entity issue an accept SPDU to complete the session connection establishment.

Ignoring these complications, the most complex relationship between session-service primitives and SPDUs occurs at connection-establishment time. Figure 3.14 depicts the possible sequence of events. A request for a connection by a user triggers a connect SPDU by the user's session-protocol entity (Figure 3.14, part [a]). The SPDU contains those parameters that were contained in the S-CONNECT.request and that need to be communicated to the other user. These include connection ID, serial number, token selection, requirements parameters, calling and called SSAP, and finally, those quality of service parameters that are negotiated between the users (extended control and optimized dialogue), referred to as protocol options. This information is transmitted via the SPDU to the other session-protocol entity, which delivers the connection request and associated parameters in an S-CONNECT.indication primitive. The user accepts the connection

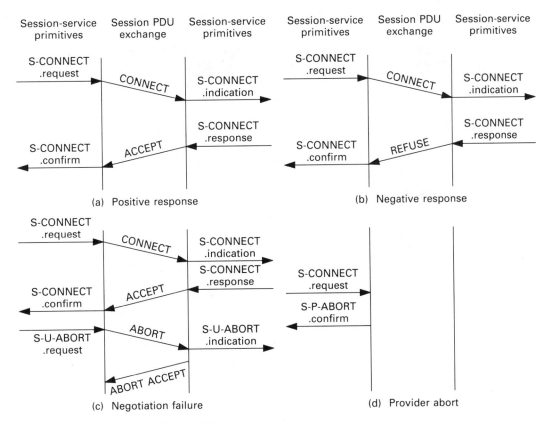

Figure 3.14 Session Connection Establishment

and negotiates the parameters with a respond primitive, which triggers the transmission of an accept SPDU back to the other side, where a confirm primitive is generated.

A session user may refuse a connection because of congestion, unavailability of the desired application, or other reasons (Figure 3.14, part [b]). This is reported to the session-protocol entity with a response primitive in which the result parameter indicates the reason for refusal. The session protocol then sends a refuse SPDU back to the calling side, which sends a confirm primitive to the calling user, indicating that the connection is refused and specifying the reason.

A third alternative sequence is that the called session user accepts the connection request but proposes session parameters (e.g., no use of synchronization) unacceptable to the calling user (Figure 3.14, part [c]). In this case, the calling user will abort the connection as soon as it is confirmed, and the called user will be informed. Note in Figure 3.14, part (c), that both an abort and an abort-accept SPDU are used. The latter is needed so that the session-protocol entity that initiated the abort knows that the other side is ready for a new session connection and that the transport connection can now be resumed, if desired.

Finally, a session provider can refuse to establish a connection because of inability to set up a transport connection, inability to provide the desired quality of service, or some other reason (Figure 3.14, part [d]). In this case, no SPDUs are employed, since the action is purely local.

Most of the other SPDUs are self-explanatory. However, some additional comments will be useful. In the case of the data-transfer SPDU, each SSDU received from a session user is typically encapsulated with a session header and transmitted as a single SPDU. If, however, there is a size restriction on data units to be presented to the transport layer, as indicated in the connect and accept SPDUs, then the session entity may need to segment the user's data and send them out in two or more data-transfer SPDUs. In this latter case, the enclosure-item parameter is used to indicate whether or not a data-transfer SPDU is the last one of a group that carries a single SSDU. The receiving session entity will buffer the user data from incoming SPDUs until the last one in a group is received and then transfer all the data to the user in an S-DATA.indication primitive.

The prepare SPDU is only used when the transport expedited-flow option is available. It notifies the recipient session-protocol entity of the imminent arrival of a certain SPDU. The SPDUs that may be so signaled include resynchronize, activity interrupt, activity discard, and activity end. In some cases, this alert will allow the session entity to discard some incoming SPDUs that arrive prior to the anticipated SPDU. In all cases, it is useful as a means of preparing the recipient for the occurrence of an important event.

3.4.2.2   Transport Connections

Session connections must be mapped into transport connections by the session-protocol entity. As indicated in Table 2.13, a transport connection, at any one time, must be dedicated to at most one session connection. When a session connection is terminated, the session-protocol entity that initially set up the corresponding transport connection has the option of terminating that connection or not. If the transport connection is retained, then it may be used to support a new session connection, provided that it meets the required quality of service.

If a transport connection provides expedited service, then abort, abort-accept, expedited-data, and prepare SPDUs are sent using this service. If this service is not available, the abort and abort-accept SPDUs are sent using normal transport data-transfer service, and the expedited-data and prepare SPDUs cannot be sent.

4
Internetworking

OSI (open systems interconnection) layer 3, the network layer,[1] must implement two key functions to support the provision of the network service. The network layer must first determine the end-to-end path over which data are to travel (*routing*) and then actually convey the data over the path (*relaying*). When a single network is used to interconnect devices, these functions are typically not visible to the network-layer protocol but are relegated to lower layers and to the internal operation of the network itself. However, in the quite common situation in which a number of networks are interconnected, the routing and relaying functions are often performed by network-layer entities.

It is well to define some of the commonly used terms relating to the interconnection of networks, or internetworking. An interconnected set of networks, from a user's point of view, may appear simply as a larger network. However, if each of the constituent networks retains its identity and special mechanisms are needed for communicating across multiple networks, then the entire configuration is often referred to as an *internet* and each of the constituent networks as a *subnetwork*.

Each constituent subnetwork in an internet supports communication among the devices attached to that subnetwork. In addition, subnetworks are connected by devices referred to in the ISO documents as *intermediate systems* (ISs).[2] ISs provide a communications path and perform the necessary relaying and routing functions so that data can be exchanged between devices attached to different subnetworks in the internet.

Two types of ISs of particular interest are bridges and routers. The differences between them have to do with the types of protocols used for the internetworking logic. In essence, a bridge

---

1. The reader will by now have observed the abundance of acronyms in use when discussing OSI, and a list is provided at the end of the book for reference. The reader should be warned, however, that nowhere are these acronyms used with such abandon as in the network layer. Furthermore, there seems to be an oversupply of *N*s and *S*s in the network-layer-related acronyms, confusing the casual reader. The author uses these not only to save space but also—and this is the important point—because the standards consistently use acronyms instead of the full terms. The standards are incomprehensible unless the reader knows the acronyms. To understand all is to forgive all.

2. The term *gateway* is sometimes used to refer to an IS or to a particular kind of IS. Because of the lack of consistency in the use of this term, we will avoid it.

operates at layer 2 of the open systems interconnection seven-layer architecture and acts as a relay of frames between like subnetworks. A router operates at layer 3 of the OSI architecture and routes packets between potentially different subnetworks. Both the bridge and the router assume that the same upper-layer protocols are in use. This chapter is concerned with layer-3 internetworking and will be confined to the router.

The examination begins with a discussion of the principles underlying various approaches to internetworking. The remainder of the chapter is devoted to a discussion of standards related to relaying and routing. The relaying function involves the use of the same protocol by both the end systems and the routers that are traversed. Thus, the discussion of relaying focuses on these protocols plus the relaying functions performed by the routers. The router function involves the cooperative effort of the routers and the end systems to develop and maintain a model of the topology and behavior of the internet in order to make optimal routing decisions. This effort involves protocols that are not used to convey user data end-to-end but only to support this cooperative effort. The latter part of the chapter is devoted to these routing protocols.

4.1 PRINCIPLES OF INTERNETWORKING

4.1.1 OSI Network Service

The key to understanding the OSI approach to internetworking is the OSI network service. The essential characteristics of the network service, as listed in the defining documents (ISO 8348, X.213), are:

- *Independence of the underlying communications facility:* Network users need not be aware of the details of the subnetwork facilities used.

- *End-to-end transfer:* All routing and relaying are performed by the network-service provider and are not of concern to the network-service user.

- *Transparency:* The network service does not restrict the content, format, or coding of user data.

- *Quality of service selection:* The network-service user has some ability to request a given quality of service.

- *User addressing:* A system of addressing (NSAP addressing) is used that allows network-service users to refer unambiguously to one another.

Figure 4.1 depicts the OSI network-service concept. The network service provided to layer 4 is defined by a set of network-service primitives and parameters. The network-service provider consists of the protocols and functions within and below the network layer in the two systems and in the subnetworks and ISs that connect the two end systems.

This model provides a point of view for developing an internetworking strategy. The essential requirement for internetworking is that the two communicating end users are presented with the same network service; that is, they employ the same set of network-service primitives and parameters. The network-service provider must be organized in such a way as to preserve this network service between the two end systems and across all of the intervening subnetworks. Two types of

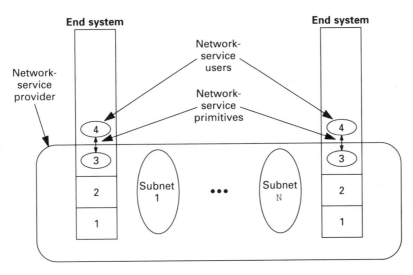

Figure 4.1 Network-Service Concepts

network service have been defined: a connection-mode network service (CONS) and a connection-less-mode network service (CLSN). Thus, internetworking strategies are needed for each service. Before examining these strategies, we provide a brief overview of the two services.

4.1.1.1   Connection-Mode Network Service

Table 4.1 defines the connection-mode network service. Much of this has already been covered in the general discussion of connection-mode service primitives (Table 2.11). The first four primitives deal with connection establishment. In addition to specifying the calling and called addresses, the user can request that certain services be provided for the requested connection:

- *Receipt confirmation:* Ordinarily, the network service will not confirm that data have been delivered to the other side; it is assumed that the data are delivered. However, the user may request that explicit confirmation be provided. If this parameter is accepted by the network-service provider and the remote-network user, then data primitives issued for this connection can request confirmation through the use of the confirmation-request parameter of the N-DATA.request primitive.

- *Expedited data:* The user may request an expedited-data service. If the network-service provider accepts this request, then expedited data may be issued with the N-EXPEDITED-DATA.request primitive.

- *Quality of service:* The two network-service users and the network-service provider may negotiate the use of the quality of service parameters listed in Table 2.9.

The N-DISCONNECT primitives provide for abrupt connection termination and are also used for connection rejection. The N-DATA-ACKNOWLEDGE primitives are used to acknowledge an N-DATA transmission when the confirmation-request option is selected.

Table 4.1 ISO Connection-Mode Network-Service Primitives

N-CONNECT.request (called address, calling address, receipt-confirmation selection, expedited-data selection, quality of service, NS-user data)

N-CONNECT.indication (called address, calling address, receipt-confirmation selection, expedited-data selection, quality of service, NS-user data)

N-CONNECT.response (responding address, receipt-confirmation selection, expedited-data selection, quality of service, NS-user data)

N-CONNECT.confirm (responding address, receipt-confirmation selection, expedited-data selection, quality of service, NS-user data)

N-DISCONNECT.request (reason, NS-user data, responding address)

N-DISCONNECT.indication (originator, reason, NS-user data, responding address)

N-DATA.request (NS-user data, confirmation request)

N-DATA.indication (NS-user data, confirmation request)

N-DATA-ACKNOWLEDGE.request

N-DATA-ACKNOWLEDGE.indication

N-EXPEDITED-DATA.request (NS-user data)

N-EXPEDITED-DATA.indication (NS-user data)

N-RESET.request (reason)

N-RESET.indication (originator, reason)

N-RESET.response

N-RESET.confirm

The N-RESET primitives may be employed by the network-service user to resynchronize the use of a network connection or by the network-service provider to report the loss of user data that it cannot recover. In either case, outstanding service data units on the network connection may be lost; it is up to higher layers of software to recover the lost data.

4.1.1.2 Connectionless-Mode Network Service

The ISO (International Organization for Standardization) connectionless service, defined in ISO 8348 AD 1, provides for the connectionless exchange of user data. The service provider may perform any or all of the following actions:

- Discard data units
- Duplicate data units
- Deliver data units in a different order than the order in which they were presented by the user

In addition, the service provider may support service characteristics beyond those attributed to the basic connectionless-mode network service:

- Objects will be discarded only after a stated time.
- Objects must be discarded no later than a stated time.
- Objects will be discarded only if more than a certain number of objects are in the queue.
- Objects will not be discarded.

Table 4.2 ISO Connectionless-Mode Network-Service Primitives

N-UNITDATA.request (source address, destination address, quality of service, NS-user data)
N-UNITDATA.indication (source address, destination address, quality of service, NS-user data)

- The order of the objects in the queue will not be changed.
- Objects will not be duplicated.

The exact nature of the service provided is based on some *a priori* arrangement and is not subject to negotiation by means of the network service itself. The same is true of the quality of service.

The service is defined by a single primitive type, N-UNITDATA (Table 4.2).

4.1.1.3 Protocol Support

In some layers of the OSI reference model, it is possible to provide a single protocol specification that dictates how a layer service is to be supported. This is true, for example, at the transport and session layers. At the network layer, this is not possible, for two reasons:

1. The network service must operate over a wide variety of real network technologies, each with its own access procedures and delivery protocols.

2. In an internetworking environment, a variety of subnetwork technologies and interconnection strategies must be accommodated.

The response of ISO to this dilemma is ISO 8880, which is a three-part standard that specifies various combinations of standardized protocols that can be used to support the two OSI network services (CONS and CLNS). The strategy developed by ISO is simple and effective: mandate a single end-to-end protocol to support each of the two network services regardless of the mix of subnetworks in the internet. In some cases, this approach may not be the most efficient, but its strength is that it promotes ease of internetworking.

ISO 8880-2 specifies the protocols that are to be used to support the connection-mode network service over a variety of subnetworks. These are illustrated in Figure 4.2, part (a). In all cases, the recommended end-to-end protocol that directly supports the CONS is ISO 8208. Recall from Chapter 3 that this protocol is an extension of X.25 that allows both DTE-DTE and DTE-DCE modes of operation. In effect, every type of subnetwork is converted into an X.25 subnetwork, and the virtual circuit capability is used to provide network connections.

ISO 8880-3 specifies the protocols that are to be used to support the connectionless-mode network service over a variety of subnetworks (Figure 4.2, part [b]). In all cases, the recommended end-to-end protocol that directly supports the CLNS is ISO 8473. This protocol can be used across a single subnetwork. However, the protocol was specifically designed to provide a connectionless internetworking capability that would ride on top of a variety of subnetwork protocols.

4.1.2 Internal Organization of the Network Layer

A consideration of the OSI network-service definitions leads to the conclusion that there must be two internetworking strategies: one to support the connection-mode network service and one to support the connectionless-mode network service. ISO 8880 indicates that, in both cases, a single

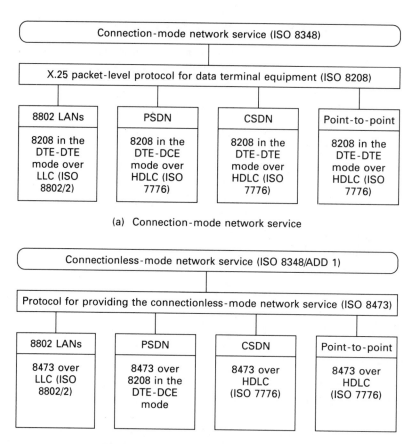

(a) Connection-mode network service

(b) Connectionless-mode network service

Figure 4.2 Protocols to Provide and Support the OSI Network Service (ISO 8880)

end-to-end protocol will be used to provide the corresponding network service. Before examining how this strategy can be implemented over a variety of subnetwork types, it is necessary to understand the internal organization of the network layer.

Because of the complexity of the network-layer task, and to provide a framework for developing internetworking strategies, ISO has developed a model of the network layer that, like the overall OSI model, consists of a structured set of layers. The network-layer model, referred to as the internal organization of the network layer (IONL), specifies a three-sublayer architecture (ISO 8648). The IONL model describes the types of protocols and different strategies that might be used for OSI interconnection of *real-world* networks. Like the OSI model, the IONL model does not standardize specific protocols or services. Rather, it provides a framework within which network-level protocols can be developed and standardized.

The IONL considers a number of strategies by which network-layer services may be provided. These may be grouped into three general strategies:

1. If two end systems are connected through a single subnetwork, then the DTE-DCE protocol used for subnetwork attachment is used to support the network service. If the service offered

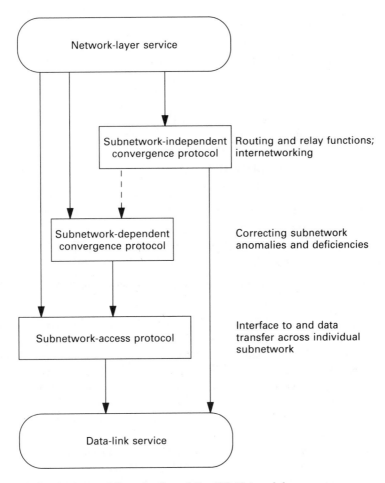

Figure 4.3 Internal Organization of the ISO Network Layer

by the subnetwork is insufficient, then it is enhanced by means of a protocol above the level of the DTE-DCE protocol.

2. If two end systems are connected by means of multiple subnetworks, then a hop-by-hop strategy can be used. The service available from each subnetwork (each hop) is used and, if necessary, enhanced individually to the level of the OSI network service to be provided. As the reader will see, this strategy is used to support the connection-mode network service.

3. If two end systems are connected by means of multiple subnetworks, then an internetwork-protocol approach can be used. The internetworking protocol is an end-to-end protocol that sits on top of the subnetwork protocol at each hop and provides a uniform set of functions across all subnetworks. As the reader will see, this strategy is used to support the connection-less-mode network service.

To support these strategies, a three-sublayer model has been developed by ISO (Figure 4.3). At each sublayer, there may be a protocol that fulfills a particular role:

- Subnetwork-access protocol (SNAcP)
- Subnetwork-dependent convergence protocol (SNDCP)
- Subnetwork-independent convergence protocol (SNICP)

In a given situation, it may not be necessary to use all three protocols. In many cases, there will be only one or two protocols at the network layer. However, it is useful to organize the network layer into these three sublayers to understand the requirements for providing the network service and the protocols needed to satisfy these requirements.

The SNAcP is the protocol that operates between a network entity in the subnetwork and a network entity in the end system (a DTE-DCE protocol). The SNAcP entity in the end system directly makes use of the services of the subnetwork and performs three key functions:

1. *Data transfer:* NPDUs are presented to the subnetwork for transfer to another end system or an intermediate system (IS, or router).

2. *Connection management:* If a connection-oriented subnetwork service is available and required, the connection is established and maintained.

3. *Quality of service selection:* The end system requests the required quality of service from the network.

All information (e.g., quality of service, flow control) needed to provide the OSI network service is carried in the appropriate fields of the SNAcP PDUs. An example of SNAcP is the X.25 packet-level protocol (ISO 8208). Another example is the logical link control (LLC) protocol for local area networks. In this latter case, there is no DCE as such, since the network is a passive, broadcast network, with no switching involved. Nevertheless, LLC can be viewed as the access protocol for the network.

Above the level of the SNAcP, ISO defines two types of convergence protocols. A convergence protocol operates on top of a subnetwork service and utilizes it. Some of the information needed to provide the OSI network service is transferred as transparent user data at the SNAcP level and is handled at the convergence-protocol level. This is analogous to the relationship that exists between adjacent layers of the OSI model. For example, the session layer provides functions and features for session users that supplement the services of the transport layer. The session protocol enhances the transport connection to produce a session connection that provides greater service than the transport connection alone.

The SNDCP is defined for, and requires beneath it, a particular type of subnetwork. Such a protocol can be used to enhance an SNAcP to provide a particular network service to transport entities. An example of an SNDCP is found in the provision of the OSI connection-mode network service over a subnetwork that employs the 1980 version of CCITT X.25. The 1980 version is still in use on a number of networks but does not provide all the facilities required by the OSI network service. The deficiencies in 1980 X.25 are primarily the absence of elements in the protocol for conveying some of the parameter information needed to support OSI network connection establishment and release (e.g., complete NSAP addresses, quality of service parameters, and reason codes). ISO has defined an SNDCP (ISO 8878) that makes use of 1980 X.25 as far as possible and carries the rest of the required information as user data in X.25 packets. To support connection establishment, the convergence protocol defines two different procedures. Over a subnetwork where the fast-select facility is available, that facility is used to convey as user data the parameter information not accommodated by fields in the X.25 call-setup packet. Where fast select is not available, or where more than 128 octets are needed to carry the remaining parameter information, the SNDCP uses X.25 data packets with the Q bit set to 1, transferred immediately following the virtual call establishment. To provide connection release, the SNDCP makes use of clear request and clear confirmation packets and in some circumstances must precede the virtual call clearing procedure with a transfer of parameter information by means of a data packet with the Q bit set to 1.

An SNICP is intended for use over a wide variety of different subnetwork types and thus is defined to require a minimal subnetwork service underneath. The ISO connectionless internetworking protocol, explored in section 4.3, is an example.

Figure 4.3 shows the protocol architecture and the interaction of the various sublayers of the network layer. One or more network-layer protocols are needed to support the network service over the data-link service. If internetworking is not involved, the network service can often be provided by just an SNAcP. If the SNAcP is inadequate, it is supplemented by an SNDCP. In the case of internetworking, an SNICP is needed, which may operate directly over the data-link service (in the case of a point-to-point link or a LAN) or over an SNAcP. Rarely, all three sublayers are needed. Figure 4.4 shows specific protocols and facilities related to the network layer.

4.1.3   Architectural Approaches

Having looked at the network service to be supported and the way in which the network layer may be structured, we are now in a position to consider the protocol architecture for internetworking. Two general strategies have been standardized, one to support CONS and one to support CLNS.

4.1.3.1   Connection-Mode Operation

In connection-mode operation, it is assumed that it is possible to establish a logical network connection (e.g., virtual circuit) between any two DTEs attached to the same subnetwork. The connection-mode approach is as follows:

1.   An intermediate system (IS) is used to connect two or more subnetworks; each IS appears as a DTE to each of the subnetworks to which it is attached.

2.   When DTE A wishes to exchange data with DTE B, a logical connection is set up between them. This logical connection consists of the concatenation of a sequence of logical connections across subnetworks. The sequence is such that it forms a path from DTE A to DTE B.

3.   The individual subnetwork logical connections are spliced together by ISs. For example, in Figure 4.5, part (a), there is a logical connection from DTE A to IS I across subnetwork 1 and another logical connection from IS I to IS M across subnetwork 2. Any traffic arriving at IS I on the first logical connection is retransmitted on the second logical connection and vice versa.

Several points can be made about this form of operation. First, this approach is suited to providing support for a connection-mode network service. From the point of view of network users in DTEs A and B, a logical network connection is established between them that provides all the features of a logical connection across a single network.

Second, this approach assumes there is a connection-mode capability available from each subnet and that these capabilities are equivalent. This may not always be the case. For example, an IEEE 802 local area network provides a service defined by the logical link control. Two of the options with LLC provide only connectionless service. Even the connection-mode option of LLC does not provide all the services and capabilities required of the CONS (e.g., receipt confirmation,

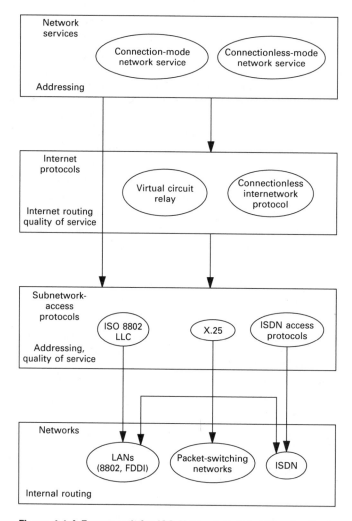

Figure 4.4 A Framework for ISO Network-Related Standardization

expedited data, user data in connection request). Therefore, in this case, the subnetwork service must be enhanced. An example of how this would be done is for the ISs to implement X.25 on top of LLC across the LAN. Thus, there are two versions of the connection-mode internetwork operation:

1. *Interconnection of subnetworks whose respective SNAcPs support all elements of the OSI network service:* In this case, a single network-layer protocol is used between the end systems and ISs attached to each such subnetwork to provide the CONS. As Figure 4.2 indicates, it is assumed that ISO 8208 is used as the single network-layer protocol.

2. *Hop-by-hop harmonization:* The subnetwork service of each subnetwork that does not support all of the elements of CONS is "harmonized" such that its service is identical to CONS. This

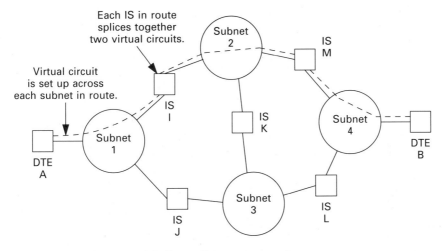

Each IS in route
splices together
two virtual circuits.

Virtual circuit
is set up across
each subnet in route.

(a) Connection-mode operation

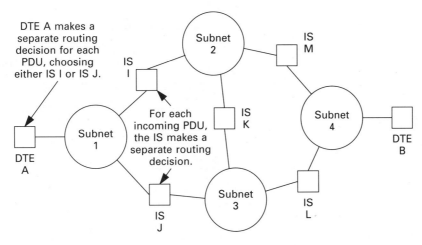

DTE A makes a
separate routing
decision for each
PDU, choosing
either IS I or IS J.

For each
incoming PDU,
the IS makes a
separate routing
decision.

(b) Connectionless-mode operation

Figure 4.5 Internetworking Approaches

requires the operation of a protocol on top of the access protocol for the subnetwork (e.g.,
ISO 8208 on top of ISO 8802/2 LLC). As in the previous case, it is assumed that ISO 8208
is used on all end systems and ISs.

The first method is the simplest and is illustrated in Figure 4.6. In this example, it is assumed
that one of the subnetworks is a LAN in which all DTEs attached to the LAN use the 1988 X.25
packet-level protocol (PLP); thus, this may be considered to be the SNAcP for the LAN. In this
case, there is no need for an SNDCP or SNICP.

The hop-by-hop harmonization method is illustrated in Figure 4.7. With this method, at least
some of the subnetworks use an SNAcP that does not fully support CONS. Thus, a protocol acting

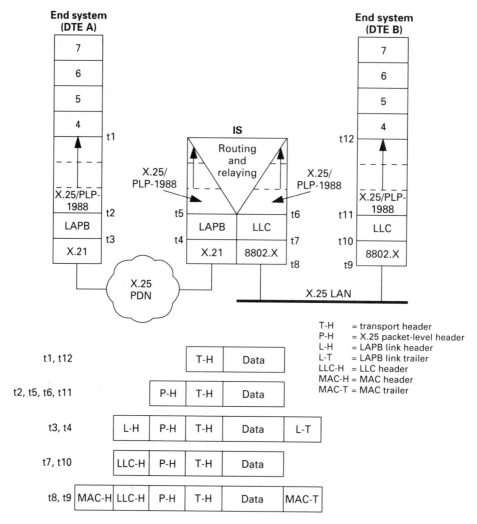

Figure 4.6 Sample Scenario for Interconnecting Subnetworks That Support All the Elements of the OSI Connection-Mode Network Service

in the SNDCP role is required to enhance the "deficient" SNAcP to provide all the elements of the CONS. In this example, the SNDCP defined in ISO 8878 is used to enhance the 1980 version of X.25. The ISDN subnetwork already employs the 1988 version and need not be enhanced.

For both approaches, access to all subnetworks, either inherently or by enhancement, is by means of the same network-layer protocol. The intermediate systems operate at layer 3. As was mentioned, layer-3 ISs are commonly referred to as routers. A connection-oriented router performs the following key functions:

- *Relaying:* Data units arriving from one subnetwork via the network-layer protocol are relayed (retransmitted) on another subnetwork. Traffic is over logical connections that are spliced together at the routers.

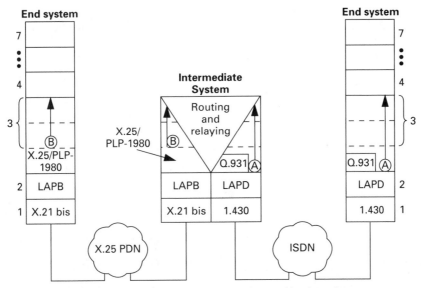

Source: F. Burg and N. Iorio, "Networking of Networks: Interworking According to OSI," IEEE Journal on Selected Areas in Communications (September 1989) © 1989 IEEE.

Ⓐ = X.25/PLP-1984

Ⓑ = SNDCP for X.25/PLP-1980

Figure 4.7 Sample Scenario for Hop-by-Hop Harmonization Method

- *Routing:* When an end-to-end logical connection, consisting of a sequence of logical connections, is to be set up, each router in the sequence must make a routing decision that determines the next hop in the sequence.

Thus, at layer 3, a relaying operation is performed. It is assumed that all the end systems share common protocols at layer 4 (transport) and above for successful end-to-end communication. The connection-oriented approach is examined in sections 4.2 and 4.4.

4.1.3.2 Connectionless-Mode Operation

Figure 4.5, part (b), illustrates the connectionless mode of operation. Whereas connection-mode operation corresponds to the virtual circuit mechanism of a packet-switching network, connectionless-mode operation corresponds to the datagram mechanism of a packet-switching network. Each network-protocol data unit is treated independently and routed from source DTE to destination DTE through a series of ISs and subnetworks. For each data unit transmitted by A, A makes a decision as to which IS should receive the data unit. The data unit hops across the internet from one IS to the next until it reaches the destination subnetwork. At each IS, a routing decision is made (independently for each data unit) concerning the next hop. Thus, different data units may travel different routes between source and destination DTE.

Figure 4.8 gives an example of the protocol architecture for connectionless-mode operation. All DTEs and all ISs share a common network-layer protocol referred to in ISO 8648 as an internetworking protocol and commonly known as the connectionless network protocol (CLNP). The

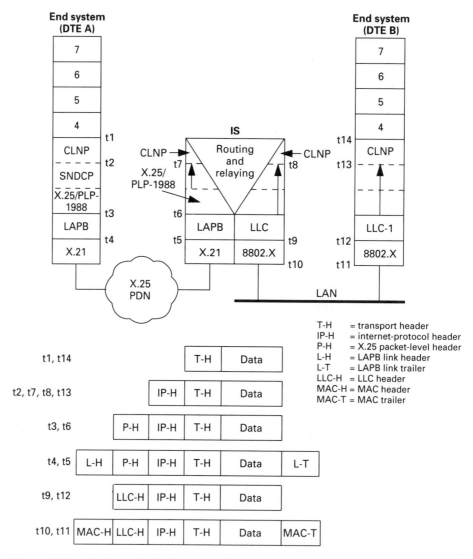

Figure 4.8 Sample Scenario for Internetworking-Protocol Approach

ISO standard for CLNP is ISO 8473. This protocol fulfills the function of an SNICP. The basic strategy is that, wherever required, a function/protocol acting in the SNDCP role is used such that the basic service provided by the subnetwork's SNAcP is altered to provide the underlying service required by the SNICP.

In the example presented here, no SNDCP is needed to enhance LLC type 1, which is a connectionless protocol for operation across a LAN. For the X.25 public data network (PDN), an SNDCP is required to provide a connectionless service on top of the connection-oriented X.25.

The connectionless internet-protocol approach is examined in sections 4.3 and 4.5.

4.1.4   Addressing

In order to transfer data from one DTE to another DTE, there must be some way of uniquely identifying the destination DTE. Thus, we must be able to associate a unique identifier, or address, with each DTE. This address will allow DTEs and ISs to perform the routing function properly.

In the OSI environment, this unique address is typically equated to a *network-service-access point* (*NSAP*). An NSAP uniquely identifies a DTE within the internet. A DTE may have more than one NSAP, but each is unique to that particular system. A network-layer address may also refer to the network-protocol entity itself. This latter is appropriate in an intermediate system, which does not support upper layers via an NSAP. In the case of an IS, the network-layer address is called a *network entity title* (*NET*).

Both NSAPs and NETs provide an unambiguous global internet address. Frequently, this address is in the form of (network, host), where the network portion of the address identifies a particular subnetwork and the host portion identifies a particular DTE attached to that subnetwork.

Figure 4.9 suggests that another level of addressing may be needed. Each subnetwork must maintain a unique address for each DTE attached to that subnetwork. This allows the subnetwork to route data units through the subnetwork and deliver them to the intended DTE. Such an address can be referred to as a *subnetwork point of attachment* (*SNPA*) address.

It would appear convenient for the host portion of the global address to be identical to the SNPA for that DTE. Unfortunately, this may not always be practical. Different networks use different addressing formats and different address lengths. Furthermore, a station may enjoy more than one attachment point into the same network. Accordingly, we must assume that the host

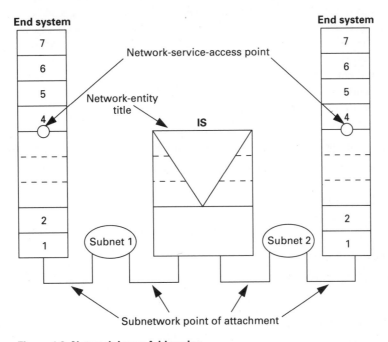

Figure 4.9 Network-Layer Addressing

portion of the NSAP and the SNPA differ. In this case, the internetworking facility must translate from the global address to the locally significant address to route data units.

4.2   CONNECTION-MODE RELAYING

ISO standard TR 10029 specifies the architecture and functioning of a connection-mode internetworking facility, using ISO 8208 (X.25) as the network-layer protocol. This section starts with an examination of the protocol architecture of this approach and then considers the functions that must be performed by the routers.

4.2.1   Protocol Architecture for Connection-Oriented Internetworking

We use Figure 4.6 to illustrate the protocol activity for transferring data from DTE A, attached to a packet-switching network; through a router; to DTE B, attached to a LAN that has been enhanced with the use of X.25. The lower portion of the figure shows the format of the data unit being processed at various points during the transfer.

To begin, from the network layer's point of view, data are presented to the network layer by the transport layer (t_1). The data are in the form of a data unit consisting of a transport-protocol header and data from the transport-layer user. This block of data is received by the packet-level protocol of X.25, which appends a packet header (t_2) to form an X.25 packet. The header will include the virtual circuit number of the virtual circuit that connects host A to the router. The packet is handed down to the data-link-layer protocol (LAPB), which appends a link header and trailer (t_3) and transmits the resulting frame to the DCE to which it attaches. The packet is transferred across the network and through another DCE to the router, which appears as just another DTE to the network. Eventually, we reach the packet level at t_5 in the router. At this point, the packet is relayed onto the LAN. This will involve going through the LAN-protocol layers (logical link control, medium-access control) on transmission and reception. Note that on this hop, an X.25 virtual circuit is set up on top of LLC.

Several points are worth noting:

- There is no encapsulation by the router. The same layer-3 header format is reused.

- There is no true end-to-end protocol. Each hop constitutes a single virtual circuit controlled by X.25.

- Because of the 12-bit virtual circuit number field in X.25, the router can handle a maximum of 4,096 connections.

4.2.2   Operation of an X.25 Router

The operation of the X.25 router can be described by considering the following areas:

- Virtual call setup
- Data and interrupt transfer
- Virtual call clearing

- Reset
- Restart

4.2.2.1   Virtual Call Setup

Let us consider the configuration of Figure 4.6 and suppose that DTE A wishes to set up a logical network connection to DTE B. The process begins when the transport layer issues a request to the network layer for a virtual circuit to DTE B. This request is mapped into a call request packet. It is at this point that we see the distinction between global addresses and SNPAs. The request from the transport layer will refer to the global internet address. It will be conveyed as an optional user facility known as called address extension in the call request packet. In addition, the call request packet includes as a parameter called DTE address; this parameter appears in the packet header. In this case, the called DTE address is the SNPA for the router on the X.25 PDN.

What has happened is this. The network-service user has requested a logical connection to DTE B. This request passes down to the network-level entity in A, which is an X.25 packet-level module. The network entity makes a routing decision that the connection can be set up through the router. So the X.25 protocol sets up a virtual circuit to the router, using the call request packet. The called DTE address parameter of the call request packet is used by the local DCE to set up a virtual circuit to the remote DCE, which then issues an incoming call packet to the router.

When an incoming call packet arrives at a DTE, it will normally accept or reject the connection promptly. If the connection is accepted, a call-accepted packet is issued. In the case of the router, however, this activity must be deferred until it can be determined whether the virtual call can be set up all the way to DTE B. Therefore, upon receipt of the call request packet, the router performs the following tasks:

1. It makes a routing decision on the basis of the called address parameter. This parameter was generated as part of the transport request primitive in A and carried in the call user data field of the incoming call packet. In this case, there is no need for a hop to another router. Rather, the destination DTE is B, which is attached to a subnetwork to which this router is attached.

2. It selects a free virtual circuit number on the LAN side and associates it with the virtual circuit number of the incoming call on the packet-switching network side.

3. It issues a call request packet onto the LAN with the SNPA of B in the called DTE address field. A match is made of optional user facilities.

4. If DTE B accepts the call, the router will soon receive a call-connected packet on the virtual circuit across the LAN. It then transmits a call-accepted packet on the logical channel corresponding to the original incoming call packet on the packet-switching network side.

4.2.2.2   Data and Interrupt Transfer

Once the virtual call is set up, the router performs a mapping function between the virtual circuit numbers on the two sides. Incoming data packets on one virtual circuit are relayed and retransmitted on the other virtual circuit. The router may need to perform segmentation if the maximum packet size on the incoming virtual circuit is greater than that on the outgoing virtual circuit. A packet is segmented by dividing it into two or more smaller packets forming a complete packet sequence, using the M bit.

When a DTE receives an interrupt packet, it responds with an interrupt-confirmation packet. The originating DTE may not send another interrupt packet until it receives a confirmation to the outstanding one. Since this confirmation is end-to-end, the router must obey the following procedure:

1. When an interrupt packet is received on one virtual circuit, an interrupt packet is transmitted on the matching virtual circuit.

2. When an interrupt-confirmation packet is received back on the second virtual circuit, the router transmits an interrupt-confirmation packet on the first virtual circuit.

4.2.2.3   Virtual Call Clearing

The virtual call clearing process is not a cooperative function between DTEs. Rather, either DTE may clear the virtual circuit; the other side is merely informed that the clearing has occurred. Accordingly, the router behaves as follows: when a clear indication packet is received on a virtual circuit, the router issues a clear confirmation packet on that virtual circuit and a clear request packet on the matching virtual circuit.

4.2.2.4   Reset

A reset may be initiated by either a DTE or a router. In the former case, the router will receive a reset indication packet on a virtual circuit. It will respond by issuing a DTE reset confirmation on that virtual circuit and a reset request on the matching virtual circuit.

If the router needs to reset a virtual call, it issues a reset request on both of the virtual circuits that are part of that virtual call.

4.2.2.5   Restart

When a router receives a restart indication on the interface to one subnetwork, it responds as follows:

1. The router issues a DTE restart confirmation on that interface.

2. For each virtual circuit that had existed on that interface, the router issues a clear request packet on the matching virtual circuit on the other subnetwork interface.

Similarly, a router may itself initiate a restart by issuing a restart request packet on one subnetwork interface. It must then also issue a clear request packet on the other interface for each virtual circuit that was destroyed by the restart.

4.3   CONNECTIONLESS-MODE RELAYING

ISO 8473 defines a connectionless network protocol (CLNP) that is to be used as the internetworking protocol to support the connectionless-mode network service. This section starts by examining the protocol architecture of this approach and then looks at the functions that must be performed by the routers and the format of the CLNP PDU.

4.3.1   Protocol Architecture for Connectionless Internetworking

Figure 4.8 illustrates the protocol activity for transferring data from DTE A, attached to a packet-switching network; through a router; to DTE B, attached to a LAN. The lower portion of the figure shows the format of the data unit being processed at various points during the transfer.

To begin, from the network layer's point of view, data are presented to the network layer by the transport layer (t_1). The data are in the form of a data unit consisting of a transport-protocol header and data from the transport-layer user. This block of data is received by the connectionless network protocol and encapsulated in an internet-protocol data unit (t_2), referred to as a *datagram,* or CLNP PDU, with a header specifying the global internet address of B (B's NSAP). At this point, the CLNP module in DTE A recognizes that the destination is on another network. Therefore, the datagram must be forwarded to a router for subsequent delivery—in this case, the router shown in the example figure. The datagram is encapsulated in the X.25 packet (t_3) and link (t_4) fields and transmitted to the router. The packet header will include the virtual circuit number of the virtual circuit that connects DTE A to the router.

The packet then travels through the X.25 PDN to the router. The router strips off the X.25 fields to expose the CLNP datagram. The router reads the destination NSAP address in the header and makes a routing decision. There are three possibilities:

1. The destination DTE is attached directly to one of the networks to which the router is attached. In this case, the router can deliver the datagram directly to the destination.

2. To reach the destination, one or more additional routers must be traversed. In this case, the router must make a routing decision and forward the datagram to the appropriate next router on the path.

3. The router does not know the destination address and must discard the datagram.

In this example, the destination DTE is connected to the same 8802 LAN as the router. Thus, the router wraps the datagram in the appropriate LLC and MAC (medium-access control) headers and trailers and submits the resulting frame to the LAN for delivery. In doing this, the router must translate between DTE B's global NSAP address and its SNPA address. The latter address is used by the LAN for delivery.

At any point along an internet path, before a router transmits data, it may need to segment the datagram to accommodate a smaller maximum packet size limitation on the outgoing network. Each segment becomes an independent CLNP datagram. Each new datagram is wrapped in a lower-layer packet for transmission. The router then queues each packet for transmission. It may also enforce a maximum queue length size for each network to which it attaches to avoid having a slow network penalize a faster one. In any case, once the queue limit is reached, additional datagrams are simply discarded.

At the destination, if segmentation has occurred, the CLNP module in the destination station buffers the incoming data until the original data field is reassembled. It then passes this block of data (NSDU) to a higher layer. The higher layer (i.e., transport) is responsible for proper sequencing of a stream of datagrams and for end-to-end error control and flow control.

4.3.2 CLNP Functions

Table 4.3 lists the functions that are provided by the ISO connectionless internetwork protocol. These are grouped into three types. Type-1 functions are mandatory; these must be supported by any implementation of the protocol. Most of these functions are always utilized. Two of the type-1 functions, which relate to error handling, must be implemented, but they are only provided when selected by the sending network-service user. The remaining functions are considered less important than the type-1 functions and may or may not be supported. This allows the network-service

Table 4.3 ISO 8473 CLNP Functions

TYPE 1—Mandatory

PDU composition
Construct PDU header in response to an N-UNITDATA.request.

PDU decomposition
Remove and analyze header to generate an N-UNITDATA.indication.

Header format analysis
Determines whether full protocol or subset is employed. Determines whether destination has been reached or PDU must be forwarded.

PDU lifetime control
Enforces maximum PDU lifetime.

Route PDU
Determines the network entity to which PDU should be forwarded and the underlying service that must be used to reach that network entity.

Forward PDU
Forward PDU using subnetwork-access protocol.

Segmentation
Segment PDU when required by subnetwork service used for forwarding.

Reassembly
Reconstruct initial PDU from segments.

Discard PDU
Discard PDU when one of a list of designated conditions is met.

TYPE 2—Optional/Discard

Security
Indicates the provision of protection services (e.g., data-origin authentication, data confidentiality, data integrity of a single NSDU).

Complete source routing
List of network entities to be visited in path from source to destination. The entities must be visited in the designated order, and no other entities may be visited.

Complete source recording
Path taken by PDU is recorded as it traverses the internet. Record consists of a

TYPE 1—Mandatory and Selectable

Error reporting
An attempt to return an error-report PDU to the source network entity when a PDU is discarded.

PDU header error detection
Uses a checksum computed on the entire PDU header. The checksum is verified at each point at which the PDU header is processed and modified each time the header is modified.

TYPE 3—Optional/Ignore

Partial source routing
List of network entities to be visited in path from source to destination. The entities must be visited in the designated order. However, a PDU may take any path to arrive at the next entity on the list, including a path that visits other network entities.

Partial route recording
Path taken by PDU is recorded as it traverses the internet. Record consists of a list of all network entities visited. When intermediate reassembly of segments that followed different paths occurs, the route recorded in any one of the segments may be placed in the reassembled PDU.

Priority
Provides a means whereby the resources of network entities, such as outgoing transmission queues and buffers, can be used preferentially to process higher-priority PDUs ahead of lower-priority PDUs.

Quality of service maintenance
Provides information to network entities along the route that may be used to make routing decisions and subnetwork service requests to provide a requested quality of service.

Congestion notification
Intermediate systems may inform the destination network entity of congestion. This information is provided to the network-service user.

Table 4.3 (*Cont.*)

TYPE 1—Mandatory	TYPE 1—Mandatory and Selectable
list of all network entities visited. Prohibits intermediate reassembly of segments that followed different paths.	**Padding** Allows space to be reserved in the PDU header for aligning the data field to a boundary convenient for the originating network entity.

provider the flexibility to deploy reduced versions of the protocol for efficiency or resource conservation. Type-2 functions are those optional functions that, if requested, are considered essential to the successful delivery of a PDU. Thus, if an intermediate system receives a PDU that includes a request for a type-2 function not supported by that intermediate system, then the PDU is discarded. Finally, type-3 functions are those optional functions that, if requested, are considered desirable but not essential. Thus, if an intermediate system receives a PDU that requests a type-3 function not supported by that intermediate system, then the PDU is processed exactly as though the function had not been selected.

Although most of the functions in Table 4.3 are self-explanatory, a few warrant further elaboration in the following subsections.

4.3.2.1 PDU Lifetime Control

The PDU lifetime-control function addresses two concerns:

1. Because of a flaw in the routing algorithm or unusual fluctuations in internet load, it might be possible for a PDU to remain in the internet for an undesirably long period of time, consuming router and subnetwork resources.

2. It is generally easier for the transport protocol to deal with a lost PDU than an excessively delayed PDU.

The PDU lifetime is expressed as a multiple of 500 ms. It is determined and placed in the outgoing PDU by the source DTE, either based on internal network-layer concerns or specified by the network-service user. Each router that the PDU visits decrements this field by 1 for each 500 ms of estimated delay for that hop.

4.3.2.2 Segmentation and Reassembly

The segmentation and reassembly algorithm makes use of four parameters, each of which is either contained in the CLNP PDU or can be derived from other fields in the CLNP PDU:

1. Data unit identifier (ID)

2. Data length

3. Segment offset

4. More segments (MS) flag

The ID is a sequence number that uniquely identifies a DTE-originated PDU. The data length is the length of the user data field in octets, and the segment offset is the position of a segment of user data in the data field of the original PDU, in multiples of 64 bits.

The source DTE creates a PDU with a data length equal to the NSDU received from the transport layer, with segment offset = 0 and MS set to 0 (false). To segment a PDU, a CLNP module in a router performs the following tasks:

1. It creates two new PDUs and copies the header fields of the incoming PDU into both.

2. It divides the incoming user data field into two approximately equal portions along a 64-bit boundary, placing one portion in each new PDU. The first portion must be a multiple of 64 bits.

3. It sets the data length of the first new PDU to the length of the inserted data and sets MS to 1 (true). The segment offset is unchanged.

4. It sets the data length of the second new PDU to the length of the inserted data and adds the length of the first data portion divided by 8 to the segment offset field. The MS field remains the same.

The procedure can easily be generalized to an n-way split. Here is an example of a two-way split:

Original PDU	**First Segment**	**Second Segment**
Data length = 472	Data length = 240	Data length = 232
Segment offset = 0	Segment offset = 0	Segment offset = 30
MS = 0	MS = 1	MS = 0

To reassemble a PDU, there must be sufficient buffer space at the reassembly point. As segments with the same ID arrive, their data fields are inserted in the proper position in the buffer until the entire data field is reassembled.

4.3.2.3   Error Reporting

The network-service provider does not guarantee successful delivery of every datagram. A PDU may be discarded by a router for a number of reasons, including lifetime expiration, congestion, and header error detection. In the latter case, error reporting is not possible because the source address field may have been damaged.

If error reporting has been selected for a given PDU, then a router that discards that PDU will generate an error-report PDU. This PDU is transmitted back to the originating DTE, using the same CLNP protocol. Thus, there is no guarantee that the error report will get through.

4.3.3   CLNP Formats

Two PDU formats are defined in ISO 8473: data PDUs and error-report PDUs (Figure 4.10).

4.3.3.1   Data PDU

The data PDU (Figure 4.10, part [a]) consists of four parts. The fixed part is always present and is of fixed length. It contains the following fields:

▪ *Protocol identifier:* set to 10000001 to identify this network-layer protocol as ISO 8473.

▪ *Length indicator:* length of the header in octets.

▪ *Version:* included to allow evolution of the protocol.

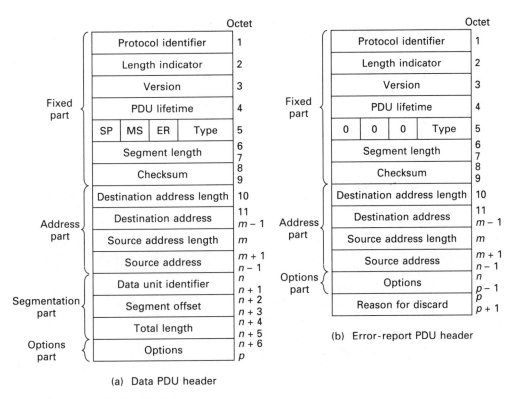

(a) Data PDU header

(b) Error-report PDU header

Figure 4.10 ISO CLNP Header Formats

- *PDU lifetime:* expressed as a multiple of 500 ms.

- *Flags:* three 1-bit flags. SP indicates whether segmentation is permitted. MS is used in segmentation, as described earlier. ER indicates whether an error report is desired by the source station if this PDU is discarded.

- *Type:* indicates whether this is a data or an error-report PDU.

- *Segment length:* total length of this PDU, including header and data field, in octets.

- *Checksum:* result of a checksum algorithm computed on the header. The algorithm, originally specified in Fletcher (1982), is simpler and therefore easier to implement than a CRC (cyclic redundancy check).[3] Since some header fields may change (e.g., PDU lifetime, segmentation-related fields); this value is reverified and recomputed at each router.

The address part of the header is variable-length and is always present. Since the NSAP values are not of fixed length, an address length field precedes both the source and destination addresses.

If the SP flag is set to 1, then the header includes a segmentation part, with the following fields:

---

3. A description can be found in Stallings (1991).

- *Data unit identifier:* intended to uniquely identify the PDU. Thus, the originating DTE must assign values that are unique for the PDU's destination and for the maximum time that the PDU may remain in the internet.

- *Segment offset:* indicates where in the initial PDU this segment's data field belongs.

- *Total length:* specifies the total length of the original PDU, including header and data field.

Finally, the header may include an optional part, used to convey optional parameters. Each option is encoded in three fields: parameter code, parameter length, and parameter value. The parameters that may be specified include padding, security, source routing, recording of route, quality of service, and priority.

4.3.3.2 Error-Report PDU

The error-report PDU (Figure 4.10, part [b]) has substantially the same format as the data PDU. The fixed part contains the same fields. In the case of the error-report PDU, the three flags are set to 0; there is no segmentation of error reports, and if an error report is discarded, this does not generate another error report. In the address part, the source address specifies the originator of the error report, and the destination address specifies the originator of the discarded PDU. Because an error-report PDU cannot be segmented, there is no segmentation part in its header. The options part of the error-report header is determined by the options that are present in the corresponding data PDU. If the system generating the error report does not support an option found in the corresponding data PDU, then that option will not be placed in the header.

The last field in the header contains a code that indicates the reason for the discard of the corresponding PDU. The body of the error-report PDU contains the entire header of the discarded data PDU and may contain some or all of its data field.

4.4   END SYSTEM TO INTERMEDIATE SYSTEM ROUTING

The two key functions of internetworking are relaying and routing. In examining the relaying function, we (and ISO) have found it fruitful to break the problem down into two distinct requirements: support of connection-mode network service (CONS), requiring a connection-mode protocol, and support of connectionless-mode network service (CLNS), requiring a connectionless-mode protocol. This same distinction between connection mode and connectionless exists in dealing with the function of routing. Indeed, the routing function can be summarized as follows:

- When support is provided for CONS, the routing function uses the same X.25 protocol as the relaying function to exchange routing commands and information.

- When support is provided for CLNS, the routing function uses a protocol to exchange routing commands and information that is similar in format and operation to the connectionless network protocol, ISO 8473, used for the relaying function.

However, there is another way to partition the problem that is more useful from the point of view of both allocating routing functions properly and effective standardization. This is to partition the routing function into:

- Routing between end systems (ESs) and intermediate systems (ISs)
- Routing between ISs

The reason for the partition is that there are fundamental differences between what an ES must know to route a packet and what an IS must know. In the case of an ES, it must first know whether the destination ES is on the same subnet. If so, then a data NPDU can be delivered directly using the subnetwork-access protocol. If not, then the ES must forward the NPDU to an IS attached to the same subnetwork. If there is more than one such IS, it is simply a matter of choosing one. The IS forwards NPDUs on behalf of other systems and needs to have some idea of the overall topology of the network in order to make a global routing decision.

Accordingly, ISO has developed standards for two types of routing protocols: ES-IS protocols and IS-IS protocols. ISO TR 9575 lists three technical advantages to this approach:

1. The more difficult and complicated procedures can be placed in the ISs, which are dedicated to the internetworking function, minimizing overhead in the ESs.

2. A specialized ES-IS protocol can be made independent of the IS-IS routing procedures. This allows multiple IS-IS procedures to be used, if necessary, without burdening the ESs.

3. Many subnetworks are of a broadcast nature; the ES-IS protocol can exploit this feature, where it exists, to improve efficiency.

This section examines ES-IS routing protocols; section 4.5 deals with IS-IS routing protocols.

4.4.1   Principles of ES-IS Routing

The ES-IS protocol is designed to solve the basic routing problems associated with ESs on a subnetwork. These are:

-   When an ES is presented with an NSDU from a higher layer, with a destination NSAP, it must first decide whether the destination ES is on the same subnetwork as itself. If so, then it can deliver the user data by using the subnetwork-access protocol (SNAcP) and providing that protocol with the subnetwork point of attachment (SNPA) address of the destination ES. However, direct examination of the NSAP may not reveal the identity of the destination subnetwork. Therefore, the ES needs a method for discovering the existence and SNPA of other ESs on the same subnetwork.

-   If the destination ES is not on the same subnetwork, then the ES must forward the user data to an IS for routing through the internet. It does this, again, by using the SNAcP and providing that protocol with the SNPA of an IS attached to this subnetwork. Therefore, the ES needs a method for discovering the existence and SNPA of at least one IS on the same subnetwork.

-   If there is more than one IS on the subnetwork, then the ES should send each NPDU to that IS which can most efficiently deliver the NPDU to the destination. Therefore, the ES needs a method for deciding which IS to use for any particular destination ES.

-   For ISs, we have seen that the final stage of relaying occurs when the IS is connected to the same subnetwork as the destination ES. Hence, when an NPDU is forwarded to an IS, the IS must first decide whether the destination ES is on one of the subnetworks to which the IS is directly attached. If so, then it can deliver the NPDU by using the subnetwork-access protocol and providing that protocol with the subnetwork point of attachment address of the destination ES. However, direct examination of the NSAP may not reveal the identity of the destination subnetwork. Therefore, the IS needs a method for discovering the existence and SNPA of these ESs.

To address these problems, the ES-IS protocol provides ESs and ISs with two types of information: configuration information and route-redirection information. Configuration information deals with the existence of ESs and ISs attached to a particular subnetwork. The information includes the NSAP or NET of the system and its SNPA address. Configuration information permits ESs to discover the existence and reachability of other ESs and of ISs; it also permits ISs to discover the existence and reachability of ESs. This information is provided dynamically by the protocol, eliminating the need for manual insertion of the information. Route-redirection information is supplied to an ES to indicate a preferred IS to be used for a particular remote NSAP. The delivery of this information is triggered by an ES attempt to forward data through a less-preferred IS.

We mentioned at the beginning of this section that routing protocols may be connection-mode or connectionless-mode. This is true of both ES-IS and IS-IS protocols. For the ES-IS requirement, ISO has defined a connectionless-mode protocol in ISO 9542 and a connection-mode protocol in ISO 10030. Each of these protocols will be examined in turn. But first, it will be useful to draw a distinction among several related concepts.

Table 4.4 shows how the two ES-IS protocols relate to the various types of subnetworks and the service they provide. Two general types of subnetworks are identified for the ES-IS protocol:[4] broadcast subnetworks and general-topology subnetworks. The key difference between the two is the cost of sending an NPDU to a large subset of the systems on the subnetwork. For the broadcast subnetwork, a single NPDU is transmitted and can be received by all systems (broadcast transmission) or by a defined subset (multicast transmission); an example is a local area network. For a general-topology network, a separate NPDU must be transmitted for each destination. For the connectionless ES-IS protocol, it is important to be able to send configuration information simultaneously to many systems on the subnetwork. Accordingly, the configuration information function is normally not provided for general-topology networks.[5]

There is, however, an additional proviso that must be made. Not only must a subnetwork be capable of broadcast transmission, but it must make that capability available to attached systems. An example when this is not the case is a LAN on which all the systems employ the X.25 DTE-DTE protocol (Figure 4.6). In this case, unless it is possible to bypass the X.25 layer, the ES-IS protocol will not have access to the broadcast capability. Thus, when the subnetwork provides a connection-mode service, the configuration function of the connectionless ES-IS protocol is normally not provided, whether or not the underlying subnetwork technology is broadcast. In addition, for the connectionless ES-IS protocol, some form of SNDCP must be used in dealing with a subnetwork that provides the connection-mode network service.

In the case of the connection-mode ES-IS protocol, we will see that both configuration and route-redirection functions are performed regardless of subnetwork technology or service. In the case of a connectionless subnetwork service, an SNDCP is needed.

---

4. Actually, there is a third type: point-to-point networks, consisting of a single ES and a single IS. This is a trivial case, which presents no special problems.

5. It is, unfortunately, more complicated than it seems. At one point in ISO 9542 (Section 5.4.3.1, p. 6), it is stated that "on a general topology subnetwork the configuration information is not employed." Elsewhere in the same standard (Section 5.3.1, p. 4), we have: "where a subnetwork does not inherently support broadcast, a convergence function may be used to provide *n*-way transmission." Presumably, this latter approach, which supports the configuration function, would be more likely to be taken for subnetworks with a relatively small number of attached systems.

Table 4.4 Relationship Among ES-IS Mode, Subnetwork Service, and Subnetwork Type

Subnet Service	Subnetwork Type	Example Subnetwork Protocol	ES-IS Protocol Mode	
			Connectionless ES-IS Protocol (ISO 9542)	Connection-Mode ES-IS Protocol (ISO 10030)
Connectionless subnetwork service	Broadcast	LLC 1	Full ES-IS protocol	SNDCP to provide X.25; full ES-IS protocol, plus dynamic SNARE (subnetwork address-resolution entity) address acquisition
	General topology	CLNP (ISO 8473) used as SNICP	Only route-redirection function	SNDCP to provide X.25; full ES-IS protocol
Connection-mode subnetwork service	Broadcast	X.25 DTE-DTE	SNDCP to provide connectionless service; only route-redirection function	Full ES-IS protocol
	General topology	X.25 DTE-DCE	SNDCP to provide connectionless service; only route-redirection function	Full ES-IS protocol

A final note before proceeding. In discussing the various operations involved, we need to be clear about the distinction between the internetworking protocol that is providing the end-to-end network service and the subnetwork-access protocol that is being used over a particular subnetwork. As we have seen, the internetworking protocol is ISO 8473, the CLNP, for connectionless-mode operation, and X.25 for connection-mode operation. The SNAcP can be any of a variety of subnetwork protocols. To maintain the distinction between PDUs of the internetworking protocol and PDUs of the SNAcP, ISO refers to the former as NPDUs and the latter as SNPDUs.

4.4.2   Connectionless-Mode ES-IS Protocol

The connectionless ES-IS protocol is defined in ISO 9542. The protocol is best explained by looking first at its PDU formats. Then the configuration and route redirection functions are examined.

4.4.2.1   PDU Formats

Figure 4.11 shows the formats of the three types of PDUs defined for ISO 9542. All share a fixed part consisting of the following fields:

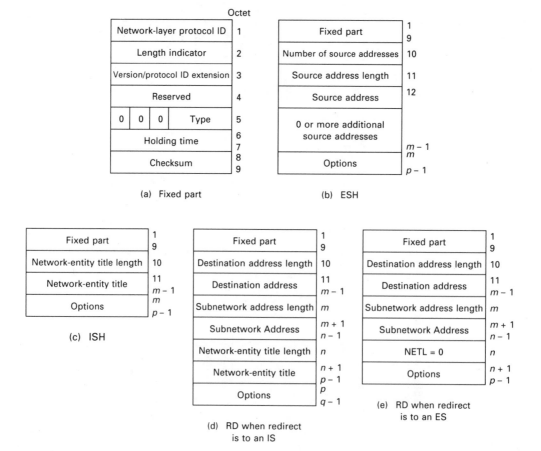

Figure 4.11 ISO 9542 ES-IS PDU Formats

Table 4.5 Optional Parameters in ISO 9542

Option	PDU	Description
Security	RD	Security of data PDU that caused the RD to be issued
	ESH, ISH	Security information concerning the ES or IS that issued this PDU
Quality of service maintenance	RD	QOS of data PDU that caused the RD to be issued
Priority	RD	Priority of data PDU that caused the RD to be issued
	ESH, ISH	Priority information concerning the ES or IS that issued this PDU
Address mask	RD	Set of NSAPs for which this RD is valid
SNPA mask	RD	SNPA information related to the address mask
Suggested ES configuration timer	ISH	Value that an IS would like the receiving ESs to use as their local configuration timer

- *Network-layer protocol identifier:* set to 10000010 to identify this network-layer protocol as ISO 9542.
- *Length indicator:* length of the PDU in octets. Since the PDUs all consist entirely of header, with no data field, this is also the length of the header.
- *Version/protocol identifier extension:* included to allow evolution of the protocol.
- *Type:* identifies the type of PDU (ESH, ISH, RD).
- *Holding time:* specifies the maximum time for the receiving network entity to retain the configuration/routing information contained in this PDU.
- *Checksum:* result of a checksum algorithm computed on the entire header. It is the same Fletcher checksum used in the CLNP (ISO 8473).

This fixed part is almost identical to that in CLNP. As with CLNP, ISO 9542 is connectionless, with no flow control or error control. If a PDU is received with a checksum or syntactic error, it is simply discarded.

Following the fixed part of the header is an addressing parameters part. The contents of this part depend on the PDU type, as explained in the following subsection.

Finally, each PDU may contain an options part, consisting of one or more parameters encoded as (parameter code, length, value). Table 4.5 lists the optional parameters.

4.4.2.2 Configuration Functions

The configuration functions of ISO 9542 include the following:

- An ES learns the NET and SNPA of each IS on the subnet by means of an ES-IS exchange.
- An IS learns the NSAP and SNPA of each ES on the subnet by means of an ES-IS exchange.

- An ES learns the NSAP and SNPA of other ESs on the subnet by means of an ES-ES exchange.

These functions are accomplished by means of the ES hello (ESH) and IS hello (ISH) PDUs.

The ESH is broadcast to all ISs periodically by each ES on the subnetwork. It includes a list of all NSAPs (usually one but sometimes multiple) that are valid for that ES. On receipt of an ESH, the IS stores the associated addressing information. In the absence of an update, this information is retained only for the amount of time specified in the holding timer and then discarded. The ES sets the holding-time parameter to twice the value of its configuration timer. The configuration timer is a local timer (i.e., maintained independently by each system) that determines how often the ES issues an ESH. By setting the holding timer to twice this value, the loss of an occasional ESH (remember, this is a connectionless protocol) will not result in loss of configuration information.

The ISH is broadcast to all ESs periodically by each IS on the subnetwork. It identifies the IS by its NET address. The reader will note that in both the ESH and ISH, there is no SNPA address information, yet this information is needed by the recipient. However, this information is supplied by the subnetwork service. When a data unit is delivered by a subnetwork service, it is accompanied by the subnetwork source and destination SNPAs.

There are several additional ways in which ESH and ISH PDUs can be used. First, consider the case in which an ES has no knowledge of any IS on its subnetwork. This could happen if the holding timer on all incoming ISHs have expired or if the system has only recently been initialized. In this case, if a network entity receives data from a higher layer, with a destination NSAP, there are two possibilities: (1) the destination system is on the same subnet—in which case, the ES can deliver it directly; (2) the destination system is on another subnet—in which case, the ES cannot deliver the data since it knows no IS to use for forwarding. To decide which case applies, the following steps occur:

1. The ES constructs the NPDU that it needs to send using the internetworking protocol. Typically, this protocol will be the CLNP (ISO 8473).

2. The resulting NPDU is then passed down to the SNAcP level for transmission, and the SNAcP level is instructed to send the data with a multicast address of all ESs on the subnetwork. That is, the SNPA address in the SNPDU will be the multicast SNPA for all ESs on this subnetwork.

3a. If an ES receives such an SNPDU and finds that the enclosed NPDU is addressed to one of its NSAPs, it responds with an ESH PDU directed only to the ES that sent the original NPDU. This allows the originating ES to update its configuration information to include information about the responding ES.

3b. If no such return ESH is received within a reasonable period of time, the originating ES simply gives up and reports failure to the higher layer.

A final use of ESH and ISH PDUs is for configuration notification. They are used to transmit configuration information quickly to a system that has newly become available, in order to allow that system to build up its routing information base as soon as possible. The procedure is as follows. If an ES receives an ISH from an IS that has just become available, it sends an ESH to that IS with the SNPA of that IS as the destination address in the SNPDU. Similarly, if an IS receives an ESH from an ES that has just become available, it sends an ISH to that ES with the SNPA of that ES as the destination address in the SNPDU.

4.4.2.3   Route-Redirection Functions

Redirection information is provided by ISs in the form of RD PDUs. When an IS receives an NPDU for forwarding, it will attempt to forward the NPDU according to the rules of the CLNP. Two cases lead to the use of the RD:

1. If the NPDU is forwarded to another IS on the same subnetwork as the originating ES, then it is clear that resources could have been saved if the ES had simply forwarded the NPDU directly to the other IS. Therefore, *after* forwarding the original NPDU, the IS sends an RD to the originating ES (Figure 4.11, part [d]) that instructs the ES to forward all future NPDUs intended for that NSAP to the other IS. The NET and SNPA of the other IS are supplied to the ES.

2. If the destination system is on the same subnetwork over which the NPDU arrived, then it is clear that resources could have been saved if the originating ES had simply forwarded the NPDU directly to the destination ES. Therefore, *after* forwarding the original NPDU, the IS sends an RD to the originating ES (Figure 4.11, part [e]) informing the ES that it can directly address the destination ES. The NSAP and SNPA of the destination ES are supplied to the originating ES.

4.4.2.4   Examples

At this point, it may be useful to present a few examples to enable the reader to get a feel for the action of the protocol. These are based on examples in Hagens (1989), where Figure 4.12 appears. In the examples, capital letters refer to NSAP and NET addresses, and lowercase letters refer to corresponding SNPA addresses.

Example 1: Suppose ES A has an NPDU to send to ES C. ES A is aware of IS X and knows its SNPA because it receives periodic ISH PDUs from it. Therefore, ES A transfers the NPDU inside an SNPDU to IS X at SNPA x. IS X recovers the NPDU and forwards it to the destination.

Example 2a: ES A has an NPDU to send to ES B. As before, ES A is aware of IS X and transfers the NPDU to IS X for delivery. IS X delivers the NPDU to ES B. It then sends an RD

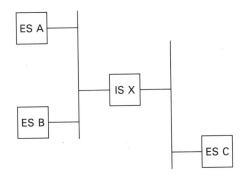

**Figure 4.12 Network Configuration for
Connectionless ES-IS Protocol
Examples**

PDU to ES A, indicating that ES B may be reached directly via SNPA b. ES A sends subsequent NPDUs directly to ES B.

Example 2b: Same scenario as 2a; in this case, though, ES A knows that the ES with NSAP B is on the same subnetwork but does not know its SNPA address. ES A has three choices. As in 2a, it could send the NPDU to IS X and receive a redirect. Alternatively, it could multicast the NPDU to all ESs, as explained earlier in this section, and learn the SNPA for future use via a return ESH. Finally, ES A could eavesdrop on other ESHs on the network. If it heard an ESH from ES B, it would know B's SNPA and could then transmit the NPDU directly.

4.4.3   Connection-Mode ES-IS Protocol

The connection-mode ES-IS protocol is defined in ISO 10030. It assumes the use of X.25 as the connection-mode internetworking protocol. Hence, it assumes that X.25 is available across each subnetwork, either as an SNAcP or as an SNDCP.

As with ISO 9542, ISO 10030 specifies both configuration and route-redirection functions. The fact that both the internetworking protocol and the ES-IS routing protocol are connection-mode has led to a very different approach for ISO 10030, compared to ISO 9542. Specifically, it is felt to be impractical to allow ES-IS routing connections to be set up for all possible ES-IS pairs. Rather, the standard defines a specialized entity on the subnetwork whose task it is to disseminate configuration and redirection information to ESs. This entity is referred to as a subnetwork address-resolution entity (SNARE).

The routing protocol in fact takes place between ESs and the SNARE. The interaction between the SNARE and ISs, if required, is not covered by the standard. It is assumed that somehow, perhaps by manual configuration or perhaps by a dynamic SNARE-IS protocol, the SNARE is aware of the routing information that the ESs require. Thus, ISO 10030 should more accurately be referred to as an ES-SNARE protocol. Furthermore, there is an interesting characteristic of the use of this protocol in conjunction with X.25. Recall from the discussion of connection-mode relaying that the internetworking protocol is not an additional protocol on top of X.25 but uses X.25 directly. Thus, the first step is to set up a virtual circuit from the calling DTE to another DTE on the same subnetwork. This is true whether the called DTE is another ES or an IS. The procedure is the same in both cases. Thus, for ISO 10030, the ES is concerned with the SNPA of the called DTE but not with the distinction between an ES and an IS.

4.4.3.1   PDU Formats

In 10030, the PDUs are carried in the user data field of an X.25 data packet or an X.25 control packet. In the case of PDUs carried in X.25 data packets, multiple data packets may be required to transmit a single PDU. In that case, each PDU is transmitted as a complete packet sequence using the M bit, as described in Chapter 3. Table 4.6 lists the PDUs defined for ISO 10030, and Figure 4.13 shows their formats. All share a fixed part consisting of the following fields:

- *Network-layer protocol identifier:* set to 10001010 to identify this network-layer protocol as ISO 10030
- *Version number:* included to allow evolution of the protocol
- *Type:* identifies one of 11 different PDUs

The remaining fields on the PDU, if any, depend on the PDU type, as explained in the following subsection.

Table 4.6 ISO 10030 Protocol Data Units

PDU	Direction	Enclosed in	Description
ECQ (end-system configuration query)	ES → SNARE	X.25 data packet	Request for information concerning an NSAP
ENC (end-system notification complete)	ES → SNARE	X.25 data packet	Indicates end of a sequence of ESHs
ESC (end-system connect)	ES → SNARE	X.25 call request/incoming call packet	ES request to connect to a SNARE
ESH (end-system hello)	ES → SNARE	X.25 data packet	Notifies SNARE of NSAP at this SNPA
RD (redirect)	SNARE → ES	X.25 clear request/clear indication packet	Provides redirection information to the ES
SCC (SNARE configuration complete)	SNARE → ES	X.25 data packet	Indicates end of sequence of SCRs; or indicates no information is available for requested NSAP
SCR (SNARE configuration response)	SNARE → ES	X.25 data packet	Response to ECQ; indicates SNPA through which NSAP may be reached
SHL (SNARE hello)	SNARE → ES	LLC 1 data frame	Broadcast to provide SNARE SNPA to ESs
SNC (SNARE notification complete)	SNARE → ES	X.25 call-accepted/call-connected packet	Positive acknowledgment of an ESC
SRH (SNARE request hello)	ES → SNARE	LLC 1 data frame	Broadcast to obtain SNARE SNAP
SRN (SNARE-received notification)	SNARE → ES	X.25 data packet	Positive acknowledgment of a sequence of ESHs followed by ENC

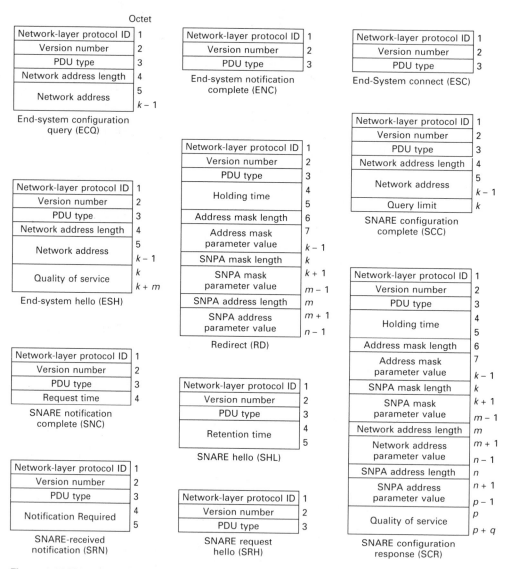

Figure 4.13 ISO 10030 ES-IS PDU Formats

4.4.3.2   Configuration Functions

There are two configuration functions:

1.   ESs notify the SNARE of their existence and reachability (NSAP and SNPA).

2.   The SNARE provides each ES with the SNPA to be used in setting up a virtual circuit to a destination NSAP.

In what follows, it is assumed that the ESs already know the SNPA of the SNARE, a point to which we return at the end of this section.

Both the configuration functions are performed in a two-phase process over a virtual circuit between an ES and the SNARE. The process is as follows:

1. Using X.25, the ES issues a call request packet to the SNARE to set up the virtual circuit. The user data field contains an end-system connect (ESC) PDU, which alerts the SNARE that this virtual circuit is to be used for ISO 10030.

2. If the call is accepted, a call-connected packet is returned to the ES. The packet contains a SNARE notification complete (SNC) PDU, which includes a request time parameter. This parameter indicates how long the SNARE will wait for requests from an ES over this connection or that it will wait an unlimited time. Thus, the connection, once set up, may stay in existence for some considerable time.

3. *Phase 1—configuration notification:* Using X.25 data-packet sequences, the ES transmits one ES hello (ESH) PDU for each NSAP reachable through its SNPA. Each ESH includes a quality of service (QOS) parameter that specifies the range of QOS that can be supported over virtual circuits to this NSAP. When the ES has transmitted all its NSAP information, it issues an ES notification complete (ENC) PDU. The SNARE will acknowledge receipt of all configuration information with a SNARE received notification (SRN) PDU. This PDU may contain a notification-required parameter indicating when the next configuration notification should be sent.

4. *Phase 2—configuration collection:* The ES may now request information about remote NSAPs. For each NSAP, the ES issues an ES configuration query (ECQ) PDU. In response, it may receive one or more SNARE configuration response (SCR) PDUs. Each SCR identifies an SNPA via which the NSAP may be reached and the associated potential QOS. It also includes a holding time indicating how long this information may be retained. As with ISO 9542, address masking may be used to indicate sets of addresses. After transmission of all SCRs (or immediately if it has no information about suitable SNPAs), the SNARE transmits a SNARE configuration complete (SCC) PDU. The query-limit field indicates whether another query request is allowed. If so, the phase 2 procedures may be repeated for an additional NSAP.

5. If the query-limit field indicates that no more query requests are allowed, the ES clears the call using normal X.25 virtual call clearing procedures. Otherwise, the ES may retain the virtual circuit for future use or may choose to clear the call at this time.

4.4.3.3   Redirection Functions

The redirection function is triggered by the ES. If an ES wishes to set up a virtual call to a particular NSAP and does not know the SNPA to use, the ES follows the normal X.25 call-establishment procedures but uses the SNPA of the SNARE as the called DTE address.

The redirection procedures are best explained by looking first at the operation of the SNARE and then at the operation of the calling ES.

When the SNARE receives an incoming call packet, it examines the user data field, if any. If there is no user data field, or if there is but the first octet is not the ISO 10030 protocol identifier (10001010), then the SNARE proceeds to perform the redirection function. There are five possibilities:

Table 4.7 X.25 Call-Redirection and Call-Deflection Optional User Facilities

	Where Implemented	Description
Call deflection	DTE	The originally called DTE, after receiving an incoming call packet, deflects the call. The originally called DTE issues a clear request packet that contains the address of the alternative DTE. The network issues an incoming call packet to the alternative DTE. The resulting call-accepted packet or clear indication packet delivered to the calling DTE will contain the called address of the alternative DTE.
Call redirection	DCE	The DCE redirects a call destined to the originally called DTE. No incoming call packet is delivered to the originally called DTE. The network issues an incoming call packet to the alternative DTE. The resulting call-accepted packet or clear indication packet delivered to the calling DTE will contain the called address of the alternative DTE.

1. If the SNARE does not have information concerning the called NSAP, it issues a clear request with a diagnostic code parameter of 232 (indicating SNARE rejection).

2. If the SNARE is prepared to act as an IS, it may do so. It would then accept the call and perform the relaying functions outlined in section 4.2.

3. If the X.25 call-deflection facility is available (see Table 4.7), the SNARE may use it to deflect the call to the appropriate SNPA. This will result in an attempt by the network to set up the virtual call from the calling ES to the DTE with that SNPA.

4. If the SNARE function is integrated with the subnetwork (i.e., the SNARE function is embedded in a DCE), and if the X.25 call-redirection facility is available (see Table 4.7), the SNARE may use it to redirect the call to the appropriate SNPA. This will result in an attempt by the network to set up the virtual call from the calling ES to the DTE with that SNPA.

5. If none of the above options is selected, the SNARE will reject the incoming call request by issuing an X.25 clear request packet with a diagnostic code parameter of 230 (indicating SNARE redirection) and transmit a redirect (RD) PDU in the user data field of the packet. The PDU contains the SNPA by which the destination ES may be reached, as well as a holding time indicating how long this information should be considered valid.

Now, let us consider how the originating ES will act in each of the preceding circumstances:

1. If the SNARE has no information, then the connection attempt fails.

2. In this case, with the SNARE acting as a relay, connection establishment proceeds without any further action on the part of the originating ES. The connection will be established or rejected according to X.25 procedures by the called ES.

3. If the call is deflected and successfully set up, the originating ES will receive an X.25 call-connected packet from the responding DTE with a parameter indicating that the call was deflected. Since the call is now set up, the ES can proceed with data transfer using X.25. In addition, the ES may record the SNPA (called DTE address) to which the call was eventually established and use this as configuration information for subsequent connections. If the call is deflected and rejected, the originating ES will receive an X.25 clear indication packet with no user data field, and the connection attempt fails.

4. From the point of view of the calling ES, this case is identical to case 3, except that, for a successful call, the call-connected packet contains a parameter indicating that the call was redirected.

5. If the calling ES receives a clear indication packet containing an RD PDU in the user data field, the ES retries the call using the SNPA in the RD PDU.

4.4.3.4 Obtaining SNARE SNPA Addresses

In order to use the ISO 10030 ES-IS protocol, an ES needs to know at least one SNPA address that can be used to access a SNARE. In general, this address is preconfigured in the ES. However, if the subnetwork is an ISO 8802 broadcast network, and if the ES network-layer entity has access to the connectionless link protocol (LLC 1) for 8802 LANs, then it is possible for the ES to dynamically discover a SNARE SNPA.

There are two ways in which an ES may discover a SNARE SNPA over an LLC 1 LAN. The first way is for the SNARE to broadcast its address in a SNARE hello (SHL) PDU. The PDU is transmitted in an LLC 1 frame with a multicast destination address whose value means "all ES network-layer entities" on the subnetwork. If an ES receives such an SHL, it can record the information for future use.

The second method can be used if an ES wishes to discover a SNARE SNPA address and has not received an SHL. The ES may transmit a SNARE request hello (SRH) PDU inside an LLC 1 frame with a multicast destination address of "all X.25 SNAREs." If a SNARE receives such an SRH, it responds by broadcasting an SHL PDU.

4.5 INTERMEDIATE SYSTEM TO INTERMEDIATE SYSTEM ROUTING

The ISs in an internet perform much the same function as packet-switching nodes (PSNs) in a packet-switching network. As with the nodes of a packet-switching network, the ISs of an internet need to make routing decisions based on knowledge of the topology and conditions of the internet. In simple internets, a fixed routing scheme is possible. However, in more complex internets, a degree of dynamic cooperation is needed among the ISs. In particular, the ISs must avoid portions of the network that have failed and should avoid portions of the network that are congested. In order to make such dynamic routing decisions, ISs exchange routing information using a special protocol for that purpose. Information is needed about the status of the internet, with respect to which networks can be reached by which routes and the delay characteristics of various routes.

In considering the routing function of ISs, it is important to distinguish two concepts:

1. *Routing information:* information about the topology and delays of the internet
2. *Routing algorithm:* the algorithm used to make a routing decision for a particular datagram, based on current routing information

An IS-IS protocol can be used for the purpose of exchanging routing information. The routing algorithm is performed within an IS based on the information that it maintains about the internet.

As of this writing, only a connectionless-mode IS-IS protocol has been defined (in ISO 10589), and the remainder of this section is devoted to it.

4.5.1   Routing Environment

In order to make the complexity of large internets more manageable, ISO has defined a multilevel, hierarchical routing environment. At the top level, an internet can be divided into a number of *routing domains*. A domain is a large-scale portion of an internet, generally organized along geographical or organizational lines. For example, all of the local area networks at a site, such as a military base or campus, could be linked by ISs to form a routing domain. This complex might be linked through a wide area network to other routing domains. Domains can be further subdivided into *areas*. McConnell (1991) and Hagens (1989) list a number of advantages of this hierarchical approach:

- It minimizes the amount of information exchanged by ISs, thus simplifying the operation of ISs at all levels.
- It allows different routing optimizations within each level of the hierarchy.
- It protects the entire routing environment from inaccurate information generated by any intermediate system.
- It permits the construction of ''fire walls'' between different portions (areas, domains), which would provide access control and other mechanisms to protect and secure the environment.
- It simplifies routing-protocol evolution, since ISs at one level need not know the protocol or topology at other levels.

Four levels of routing can be defined:

1. *Level-0 routing:* routing of traffic between ESs and ISs on the same subnet
2. *Level-1 routing:* routing of traffic between ISs within the same area
3. *Level-2 routing:* routing of traffic between different areas within the same routing domain
4. *Level-3 routing:* routing of traffic between different domains

Level-0 routing is covered by ES-IS routing protocols, as described in section 4.4. Levels 1 and 2 are covered by the IS-IS routing protocols, discussed in this section. Currently, there is no standard for level-3 routing. At this level, the gross topology will generally be rather simple, and static routing based on manual configuration will usually suffice.

Figure 4.14 illustrates the routing hierarchy. Level-1 ISs know the topology in their area (by means of the level-1 IS-IS interchange), including all ESs and ISs in their area. However, level-1 ISs do not know the identity of ISs or ESs outside their area. Level-1 ISs forward all traffic for ESs outside their area to a level-2 IS in their area.

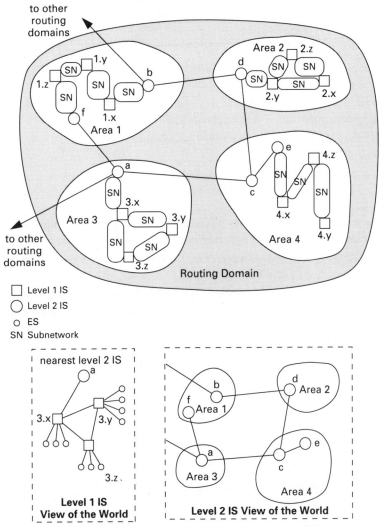

Reprinted with permission from *ConneXions,* Volume 3, No. 8, August 1989.

Figure 4.14 Routing Hierarchy

Level-2 ISs form a backbone that connects the level-1 areas within a routing domain. All the level-2 ISs in a routing domain are connected at level 2. That is, any level-2 IS can reach any other level-2 IS by going through level-2 ISs only (without visiting any level-1 ISs). Level-2 ISs know the level-2 topology and know which addresses are reachable via each level-2 IS in their routing domain. Each level-2 IS is also a level-1 IS in a particular area; this allows for final delivery of NPDUs. Thus, the obligation of a level-2 IS is to forward NPDUs to the destination area. The final level-2 IS on the path will also be a level-1 IS in the destination area and can forward the NPDU to other level-1 ISs in the area to reach the destination subnet and ultimately the destination ES. Assume that ES A receives user data from the transport layer and constructs an ISO 8473 NPDU with a destination NSAP indicating ES B. Then:

1. If ES B is on the same subnetwork as ES A, ES A delivers the NPDU directly (routing information may be preconfigured or obtained via ES-IS protocol ISO 9542).

2. Otherwise, ES A delivers the NPDU to a level-1 IS on the same subnetwork for internetwork routing (routing information may be obtained via ES-IS protocol ISO 9542).

3. The IS examines the NSAP in the NPDU to determine whether ES B is in the same area as this IS. If so:

   a. The IS makes a routing decision to forward the NPDU through zero or more additional level-1 ISs to reach ES B's subnetwork (routing information may be obtained via level-1 IS-IS protocol ISO 10589).

   b. The final IS on the path shares a subnetwork with ES B and delivers the NPDU directly (routing information may be obtained via ES-IS protocol ISO 9542).

4. If the condition in step 3 does not prevail, then the IS forwards the NPDU through zero or more additional level-1 ISs to reach a level-1 IS in this area that also acts as a level-2 IS (routing information may be obtained via level-1 IS-IS protocol ISO 10589).

5. The level-2 IS examines the NSAP in the NPDU to determine the destination area. It then forwards the NPDU through one or more level-2 ISs to a level-2 IS that is in the destination area (routing information may be obtained via level-2 IS-IS protocol ISO 10589).

6. Once the NPDU reaches a level-2 IS in the target area, that IS acts as a level-1 IS and performs step 3.

4.5.2   Routing Algorithm

Recall in the discussion of the CLNP (ISO 8473) that one of the functions of an IS is to make a routing decision in order to forward the NPDU on its next hop. This routing decision is based on the IS's having information about the topology of the internet and the cost associated with alternative paths through the internet. In discussing any routing algorithm, the following aspects must be considered:

- Information required
- Routing metric
- Path calculation
- Information-exchange discipline

4.5.2.1   Information Required

Three types of information are required by an IS to perform the routing function: topology, NSAP reachability, and hop cost. The *topology information* required will depend on the role of the IS (Figure 4.14). For topology information, a level-1 IS only needs to know the existence of the other level-1 ISs in its area and at least one level-2 IS in its area, as well as the way in which these ISs are interconnected. Similarly, a level-2 IS only needs to know the identity of the other level-2 ISs in its routing domain and the way in which these are interconnected. In either case, the topology can be abstracted into a graph consisting of nodes connected by edges. Each node is an IS, and each edge is either a point-to-point link or a subnetwork.

The second type of information needed by the IS is *NSAP reachability*. In the case of a level-1 IS, it needs to know, for each ES (identified by an NSAP) in its area, the identity of the subnet that contains that ES. In the case of a level-2 IS, it needs to know, for each ES, the area that contains that ES and a level-2 IS that is in that area.

Finally, for either level-1 or level-2 routing, each "hop" must be assigned a *cost* in each direction. In the case of level-1 routing, a hop is a subnetwork or point-to-point link connecting ISs. For level-2 routing, a hop is a point-to-point link between level-2 ISs.

4.5.2.2   Routing Metric
The cost associated with each hop, in each direction, is generally referred to as a routing metric. The routing metrics used in ISO 10589 are arranged in four levels and defined in such a way that a lower value indicates a more optimum (lower-cost) choice. In order, the routing metrics are:

1. *Default:* assigned by routing administrators to satisfy any administrative policies. The default metric is understood by every IS in the domain. Each hop has a positive integer value assigned to it. The values may be assigned arbitrarily, but the intent is that the metric should be a function of throughput or capacity: higher values indicate lower capacity.

2. *Delay:* a measure of the transit time or delay through a particular hop. This is made up of propagation delay plus queueing delay at the IS and is measured dynamically by each IS for each hop element to which it is connected.

3. *Expense:* related to the monetary cost of moving internet traffic through a particular subnet.

4. *Error:* a measure of the probability of error over this hop.

Routing metrics are applied in a cumulative fashion, so that the cost of a particular hop is equal to the sum of all applicable metrics.

4.5.2.3   Path Calculation
The hop costs are used as input to the path-calculation routine. Each IS maintains an information base containing the topology and hop costs of each link for the level of interest (level-1 area, level-2 routing domain). This information is used to perform what is referred to as a *least-cost routing algorithm,* which can be simply stated as follows:

> Given a network of nodes connected by bidirectional links, where each link has a cost associated with it in each direction, define the cost of a path between two nodes as the sum of the costs of the links traversed. For each pair of nodes, find the path with the least cost.

The algorithm used in ISO 10589 was originally proposed by Dijkstra (1959).[6] It enables each IS to find the least-cost route to every other IS of interest.

4.5.2.4   Information-Exchange Discipline
The validity of the algorithm will, of course, depend on the validity of the information used as input. The routing information may change over time. An IS or a subnetwork failure can alter the topology, and some of the costs, especially delay, are variable. Thus, some sort of information-

---

6.   A description can be found in Stallings (1991).

exchange discipline is needed to govern the frequency with which ISs exchange routing information. One such discipline is ISO 10589.

4.5.3   ISO 10589 Strategy

Having presented the requirements for the routing algorithm, we can now summarize the strategy used in ISO 10589 to enable each IS to acquire the routing information it needs. We then look in more detail at the functions of ISO 10589 and the PDUs that support those functions. The general strategy has the following elements:

1. Each IS generates and maintains information about its local environment, consisting of:

    - The identity of each of its IS neighbors and the cost to reach each neighbor, using some or all of the routing metrics
    - The identity of each of its ES neighbors

    Thus, there must be some type of discovery function by which each IS learns of its neighbors.

2. The information generated in point 1 is referred to as link-status information. Each IS broadcasts this information to all peer ISs using the ISO 10589 protocol.

3. Based on points 1 and 2, each IS can maintain the following information:

    - The topology of its area or routing domain, consisting of a set of ISs and the links connecting them
    - The cost of each link in each direction
    - A list of ESs that are neighbors of each IS

    This information is sufficient to make a routing decision for each NPDU.

4.5.4   ISO 10589 Functions

Having described the routing environment and the concept of a routing algorithm, we are now in a position to describe the key functions of ISO 10589, which are:

- Discovery
- Information exchange
- Pseudonode/designated-IS definition
- Synchronization
- Partitioning

4.5.4.1   Discovery

The IS makes use of the ES-IS protocol (ISO 9542) to determine the network-layer addresses (and on broadcast subnetworks, the SNPA) and the identities (ES or IS) of all adjacent neighbors. This information is used to create link-state PDUs, discussed later in the section.

Although ISO 9542 allows an IS to identify that it has IS neighbors by the receipt of an ISO 9542 ISH PDU, there is no provision in ISO 9542 for indicating whether the neighbor is a level-1 or level-2 IS. ISs convey this information through the exchange of IS-IS hello PDUs. There are three types:

1. *Level-1 LAN IS-IS hello PDU:* used by level-1 ISs on broadcast LANs. The PDU is multicast to all ISs on the same broadcast subnetwork.

2. *Level-2 LAN IS-IS hello PDU:* used by level-2 ISs on broadcast LANs. The PDU is multicast to all ISs on the same broadcast subnetwork.

3. *Point-to-point IS-IS hello PDU:* used on nonbroadcast media, such as point-to-point links and general-topology subnetworks.

4.5.4.2 Information Exchange

Each IS has the responsibility of transmitting its link-state information to all other peer ISs: a level-1 IS must get this information to all level-1 ISs in the same area, and a level-2 IS must get this information to all level-2 ISs within the same routing domain. The information is transmitted in a link-state PDU (LSP) and includes the characteristics of all links (hops) to which the reporting IS is attached and the identity of all neighbor ESs. The details of the LSP information are provided later in the chapter. A new LSP is sent periodically (when a timer expires) or when the connectivity or status of an IS changes.

Since the point of distributing LSPs is to enable each IS to build up a picture of the topology of its area or domain, how can an IS know where and how to deliver the LSPs? There appears to be a circular dilemma: an IS needs to know the topology in order to directly address its LSPs to each other IS, and the IS learns the topology from LSPs. The way out of this dilemma is flooding: the LSP is sent by the source IS to every one of its neighbor ISs. At each IS, an incoming LSP is retransmitted on all outgoing links except for the link from which it arrived. Eventually, all ISs will receive a copy of the LSP.

Flooding solves the delivery problem but raises some new problems that must be solved:

- How is the flooding stopped? That is, how can the indefinite retransmission of an LSP by every IS that receives it be prevented?

- How can obsolescence be prevented? That is, if an IS fails, how will other ISs know that the last LSP they received from the failed IS is obsolete?

- How can currency be ensured? Since LSPs are being transmitted in a connectionless fashion, an older LSP may arrive after a younger LSP from the same source.

Let us examine each of these problems in turn. First, flooding is easily controlled, since each IS stores a copy of each LSP that it receives. Each LSP includes a sequence number so that two different LSPs from the same source can be distinguished. When an IS receives an LSP from a given source, it checks to see whether it already has a copy of that particular LSP (same source, same sequence number). If so, it does not retransmit the incoming LSP. The result is that each LSP traverses each link in the topology only once.

Next, consider the problem of obsolescence. Each LSP includes a parameter called remaining lifetime, which is set to some default maximum value by the source IS. The parameter is decremented each time the LSP is retransmitted by an IS. Once an IS stores an LSP in its database, it periodically decrements the lifetime parameter until it reaches zero. If the parameter of an LSP reaches zero (no new LSP from the same source arrives in time), the LSP is purged from the database.

Finally, an IS can determine which of two LSPs from the same source is the more recent on the basis of the sequence number. When an IS is initialized, it issues its first LSP with a sequence number of 1 and increments the sequence number for each subsequent LSP that it creates. With a 32-bit sequence number, it is unlikely that all the sequence numbers will be used up. However, if an IS reaches the maximum sequence number ($2^{32} - 1$), the routing function at the IS is disabled for a period sufficient to ensure that all the prior LSPs issued by this IS have expired. The IS then begins again with a sequence number of 1.

4.5.4.3   Pseudonode/Designated-IS Definition

An opportunity for limiting the amount of routing overhead associated with the IS-IS protocol exists in the case of a broadcast LAN that has multiple level-1 ISs attached to it. Without special treatment, we have the following situation:

- Each IS on the subnetwork would transmit link-status reports (LSPs) to every other IS on the subnetwork.

- Each IS would report the same identical list of ESs on the subnetwork, resulting in substantial duplication.

Figure 4.15, part (a), illustrates the problem. It shows a broadcast LAN with four level-1 ISs and four ESs. Figure 4.15, part (b), shows the logical topology that is created by the routing protocol. Each IS recognizes a link to every other IS, and each IS recognizes that all of the ESs are directly reachable through itself. In general, for N ISs on a subnetwork, there are $(N \times [N-1])$ IS-IS links defined and N lists of the ESs maintained.

To avoid this situation, the LAN is represented by a *pseudonode*. Each IS on the subnetwork reports that it has a link to the pseudonode rather than a link to all the other ISs on the subnetwork. One of the ISs is declared to be the *designated IS* and represents the pseudonode. All the other ISs report a link to the designated IS, while the designated IS reports a link to all the other ISs and to all the ESs. Thus, the designated IS broadcasts all routing updates on behalf of the community of ISs sharing the same subnetwork, thereby avoiding duplicate traffic and taking advantage of the broadcast nature of the subnetwork.

Figure 4.15, part (c), shows the resulting logical topology, which is a star rather than a mesh, with N links. The number of IS-IS links has been reduced to $(2 \times [N-1])$, and the number of lists of the ESs has been reduced to one.

4.5.4.4   Synchronization

Sequence-numbers PDUs are used to synchronize the database information and ensure that all ISs have a consistent view of the network topology. Synchronization serves to terminate the flooding of LSPs and to distinguish old LSPs from new ones. Four types of PDUs are used in the synchronization process:

1. *Level-1 complete-sequence-numbers PDU:* A designated level-1 IS will broadcast this PDU over a broadcast subnet periodically. It contains the ID of the sending system as well as the start and ending LSP sequence numbers in its database. This PDU is viewed by all other level-1 ISs sharing the same subnetwork, to determine whether they and the sending IS have synchronized LSP databases. If a recipient detects that the transmitter is out of date, the recipient IS multicasts the newer information in a link-state PDU. If not all LSP information fits into a single PDU, multiple PDUs are used to convey the entire range.

2. *Level-2 complete-sequence-numbers PDU:* as above, for level-2 ISs.

3. *Level-1 partial-sequence-numbers PDU:* If a level-1 IS, upon receipt of a complete-sequence-numbers PDU, detects that the transmitter has information that is more up-to-date, the recipient issues a partial-sequence-numbers PDU containing a list of the link-state records that are not current. When the designated system receives a partial-sequence-numbers PDU, it supplies the missing information in a link-state PDU.

4. *Level-2 partial-sequence-numbers PDU:* as above, for level-2 ISs.

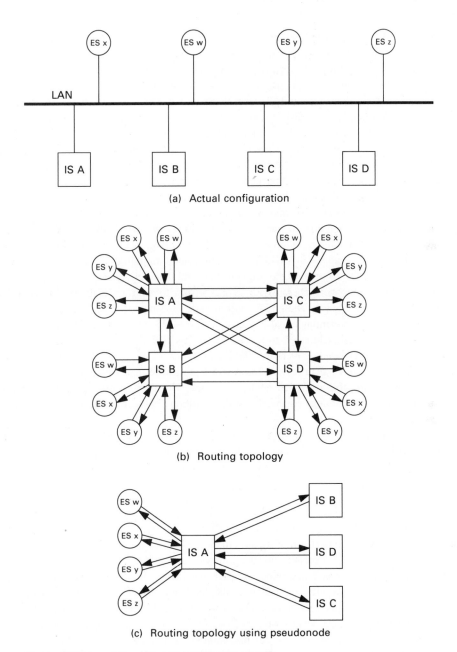

(a) Actual configuration

(b) Routing topology

(c) Routing topology using pseudonode

Figure 4.15 Use of Pseudonode and Designated IS

4.5.4.5   Partitioning

The failure of a level-1 IS or a subnetwork can result in the partition of an area. For example, if the link (subnetwork) between 1.y and 1.x in Figure 4.14 is broken, then level-1 IS 1.y could not deliver an NPDU to 1.x even though a physical path exists (via level-2 ISs). The reason is that since 1.x is part of the same area as 1.y, 1.x is precluded from using a level-2 IS for delivery. In addition, some NPDUs coming from outside the area will be discarded because they enter the wrong partition. This situation is referred to as a *level-1 partition*.

The responsibility for repairing a level-1 partition is assigned to level-2 ISs. A level-2 IS discovers a partition when it obtains inconsistent information from (1) level-1 ISs telling which level-2 ISs are attached to an area and (2) level-2 ISs telling which level-1 areas can be reached. The first sort of information is available, since every level-2 IS must also function as a level-1 IS in its area. The partition is repaired by the establishment of a virtual level-1 link. This link is virtual in the sense that it appears to the level-1 ISs in the partitioned area that a new link between level-1 ISs has been created. This new link reestablishes connectivity between the partitions. In fact, the link makes use of the level-2 backbone to relay NPDUs from one partition in an area to the other. The mechanism for establishing the link is encapsulation: any traffic between level-1 ISs is encapsulated in a CLNP PDU and routed through the level-2 network.

As an example, let us return to the case of a break in the link between 1.x and 1.y. The level-2 ISs b and f discover the partition and set up a virtual link. All traffic arriving at b destined for the other partition is wrapped in a CLNP PDU and routed through d, c, and a to f. Level-2 IS f strips off the CLNP PDU to recover the original PDU and then delivers it. For example, suppose an ES attached to a subnetwork shared with IS 2.z wishes to send a CLNP PDU to an ES that shares a subnetwork with IS 1.z. The NPDU will initially be routed to level-2 IS b, since it is the shortest path to that area (assuming equal link costs). Level-2 IS b will proceed to wrap the NPDU in an enclosing CLNP PDU addressed to level-2 IS f. This NPDU backtracks to f, which decapsulates the enclosed NPDU and delivers it to IS 1.z.

Notice that no ISs other than level-2 ISs b and f are aware that a partition exists in area 1. Clearly, there is considerable overhead in this approach. However, it does provide a temporary patch for a partition. The strategy assumes that the partition can be repaired in a relatively short period of time.

A partition can also occur at level 2. For example, if the link between level-2 ISs c and d went down, traffic from area 3 could not reach area 2 even though there is a physical path available through area 1. The current version of the standard does not contain any mechanism for repairing level-2 partitions.

4.5.5   IS Operation

Figure 4.16 is a block diagram that reflects the functions performed by an IS that uses ISO 10589. There are four key processes: decision, updating, forwarding, and receiving.

The *decision process* calculates routes to each destination in the area (level 1) or routing domain (level 2) for this IS. The process uses the link-state database as input (9) to the path-calculation algorithm and produces/updates (10) a forwarding database. The forwarding database indicates the next hop for each destination.

The *updating process* is responsible for maintaining the link-state database and for providing link-state information to other systems. Incoming link-state PDUs (6) provide the information needed to keep the database current. The updating process also issues LSPs (7) to other ISs.

The *forwarding process* supplies and manages the buffers necessary to support NPDU relaying to all destinations. It receives (5) ISO 8473 (CLNP) PDUs to be forwarded from the receiving process. Using the forwarding database (11), it makes a forwarding decision and sends (12) the NPDU down to the subnetwork-dependent protocol for transmission. If an error occurs, ISO 8473

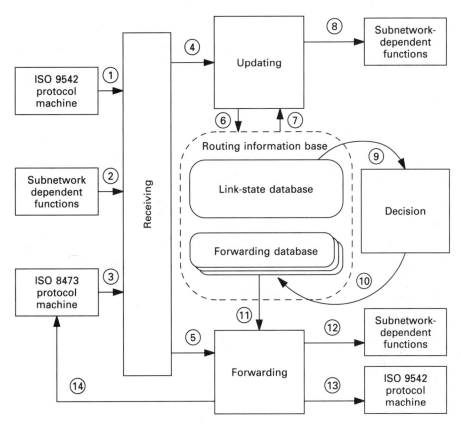

Figure 4.16 Model of IS Defined by ISO 10589

is used to issue an error NPDU. If redirection is indicated, ISO 9542 (ES-IS) is used to issue (13) a redirect PDU.

The *receiving process* obtains inputs from a variety of sources. Routing information is derived from the ES-IS protocol (1). IS-IS PDUs are delivered from the subnetwork-dependent protocol (2). NPDUs for forwarding are delivered via ISO 8473 (3).

4.5.6 IS-IS Protocol Data Units

Figure 4.17 depicts the format of the nine PDUs that make up the ISO 10589 protocol. All of the PDUs begin with the same seven fixed-length fields:

1. *Intradomain-routing-protocol discriminator:* a constant unique to ISO 10589
2. *Length indicator:* length of the fixed portion of the header in octets
3. *Version/protocol ID extension:* included to allow evolution of the protocol
4. *ID length:* length of the ID field of NSAP addresses and NETs used in this routing domain
5. *PDU type:* identifies one of nine different PDUs

6. *Version:* version number of ISO 10589; redundant with version/protocol ID extension field

7. *Reserved:* for future use

After these fields, each of the PDU formats includes some more fixed-length fields, followed by a number of variable-length fields. Each of the variable-length fields is represented by three subfields: code, length, and value.

4.5.6.1   IS-IS Hello PDUs

As described earlier, the three IS-IS hello PDUs allow for ISs to discover the type (level 1 or 2) of neighboring ISs. The fixed part of the level-1 and level-2 LAN IS-IS PDUs, in addition to the common part already described, consists of the following fields:

- *Reserved/circuit type:* indicates whether the IS will use this hop for level-1 traffic only, level-2 traffic only, or both level-1 and level-2 traffic.

- *Source ID:* the identifier of the transmitting IS.

- *Holding time:* holding timer to be used for this IS. If this IS is not heard from in that time, the receiving IS purges this IS from its database.

- *PDU length:* length of the PDU in octets.

- *Priority:* priority for being designated intermediate system.

- *LAN ID:* identifies the designated intermediate system.

The variable part of the level-1 and level-2 LAN IS-IS PDUs consists of the following fields:

- *Area addresses:* the set of area addresses for this IS.

- *IS neighbors:* the set of ISs that are recognized as neighbors.

- *Padding:* used to pad out the PDU to a standardized length.

- *Authentication information:* a password used to authenticate the originator of the PDU. This optional parameter can be used to assure the security of the routing function.

The point-to-point IS-IS hello PDU has a similar format to the LAN IS-IS hello PDUs. In the fixed portion of the header, the priority and LAN ID fields, which deal with the designated intermediate system, are not needed. Instead, a local circuit ID field gives the identification of the point-to-point link.

4.5.6.2   Link-State PDUs

Link-state PDUs are used for transmitting link-state information. The fixed part of the level-1 and level-2 link-state PDUs, in addition to the common part already described, consists of the following fields:

- *PDU length:* length of the PDU in octets

- *Remaining lifetime:* number of seconds before this LSP is considered expired

- *LSP ID:* the identifier of the source of this LSP

- *Sequence number:* sequence number of this LSP

- *Checksum:* checksum of the LSP's contents from LSP ID to the end

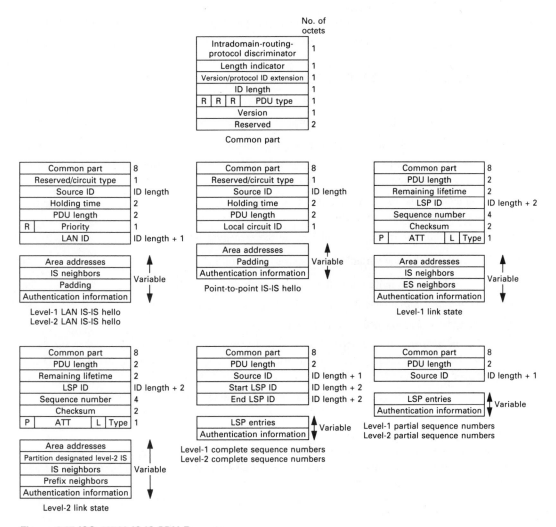

Figure 4.17 ISO 10589 IS-IS PDU Formats

- *P:* indicates whether the issuing IS supports the partition-repair optional function
- *ATT:* indicates which of the following routing metrics are being used: default, delay, expense, error
- *L:* indicates whether the LSP database is overloaded
- *Type:* indicates whether this is a level-1 or level-2 IS

For level-1 LSPs, the variable part consists of the following fields:

- *Area addresses:* as indicated in the preceding subsection.
- *IS neighbors:* list of IS and pseudonode neighbors. For each neighbor, the value of each of the four metrics and the neighbor's ID are included.
- *ES neighbors:* list of ES neighbors. For each neighbor, the value of each of the four metrics and the neighbor's ID are included.
- *Authentication information:* as indicated in the preceding subsection.

For level-2 LSPs, the variable part consists of the following fields:

- *Area addresses:* as indicated in the preceding subsection.
- *Partition designated level-2 IS:* ID of the designated IS for the partition.
- *IS neighbors:* as indicated in the preceding subsection.
- *Prefix neighbors:* list of reachable address-prefix neighbors; these are neighbors in the same area. For each neighbor, the value of each of the four metrics and the neighbor's ID are included.
- *Authentication information:* as indicated in the preceding subsection.

4.5.6.3   Sequence-Numbers PDUs

Sequence-numbers PDUs are used in the synchronization of link-state databases. The fixed part of the level-1 and level-2 complete-sequence-numbers PDUs, in addition to the common part already described, consists of the following fields:

- *PDU length:* length of the PDU in octets
- *Source ID:* the identifier of the transmitting IS
- *Start LSP ID:* ID of the first LSP in the range covered by this PDU
- *End LSP ID:* ID of the last LSP in the range covered by this PDU

For complete-sequence-numbers PDUs, the variable part consists of the following fields:

- *LSP entries:* a list of LSP entries, in ascending ID order. Each entry includes the LSP ID, remaining lifetime, LSP sequence number, and a checksum.
- *Authentication information:* as indicated in subsection 4.5.6.1.

The partial-sequence-numbers PDUs have the same format as the complete-sequence-numbers PDUs, except that they do not include start and end LSP IDs.

4.6 SUMMARY

When a configuration consists of more than one network, some form of internetworking architecture is needed to provide full connectivity. The key components of an internetwork architecture are:

- Subnetworks: Each individual network in the configuration is referred to as a subnetwork. The collection of subnetworks is referred to as an internet. The individual subnetworks may have different topologies, access control schemes, and performance and reliability characteristics.
- End systems: Each end system attaches to one or more subnetworks and provides end-user services.
- Intermediate systems: The subnetworks are connected by means of intermediate systems, which are responsible for forwarding data across the internet from one end system to another.

Two key functions are required of an internet:

- *Relaying:* Data are transmitted as packets from a source end system through one or more subnetworks and intermediate systems to a destination end system. Each intermediate system is responsible for relaying packets that it receives that are destined for an end system. For this purpose, a network-layer protocol is needed to provide the necessary protocol control information for relaying.
- *Routing:* Each source end system and each intermediate system must make a routing decision that specifies the next hop on the journey from source to destination. For this purpose, a routing protocol is needed that will enable end systems and intermediate systems to exchange routing information.

For both the relaying and routing protocols, connection-oriented and connectionless approaches have been pursued by the standards committees.

5
Upper-Layer Architecture

The presentation and application layers, together, provide functionality specific to particular distributed applications. Much of this material is beyond the scope of this book. The overall architecture of the presentation and application layers, as well as some of the basic services of these layers, are treated in this chapter. Throughout the chapter, we focus on connection-mode services and protocols. Although connectionless versions of all the services and protocols have been developed, these are relatively straightforward and have so far enjoyed little use.

5.1   PRESENTATION LAYER

We begin with a basic discussion of presentation-layer concepts, after which the presentation service and protocol are examined.

5.1.1   Presentation-Layer Concepts

Before looking at the details of the ISO (International Organization for Standardization) standards for the presentation layer, it is useful to examine some of the fundamental concepts that apply at this layer. Figure 5.1, which shows the placement of the presentation layer, and Table 5.1, which defines some key terms, summarize the concepts to be discussed.

As we cross the boundary from the session layer to the presentation layer, there is a significant change in the way in which data are viewed. For the session service and below, the user data parameter of a service primitive is specified as a sequence of octets. This binary value can be directly assembled into service data units (SDUs) for passing between layers and into protocol data units (PDUs) for passing between protocol entities within a layer. The application layer, however, is concerned with a user's view of data. In general, that view is one of a structured set of information, such as text in a document, a personnel file, an integrated database, or a visual display of image information. The user is primarily concerned with the semantics of data. The presentation layer must provide a representation of these data that can be converted to binary values; that is, it must be concerned with the syntax of the data.

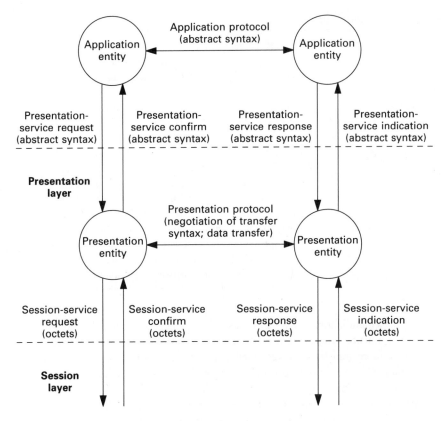

Figure 5.1 The Role of the Presentation Service

The approach taken in the OSI (open systems interconnection) architecture to support application data is as follows. At the application layer, information is represented in an abstract syntax that deals with data types and data values. The abstract syntax formally specifies data independently from any specific representation. Thus, an abstract syntax has many similarities to the datatype-definition aspects of conventional programming languages such as Pascal, C, and Ada and to grammars such as Backus-Naur Form (BNF). Application protocols describe their PDUs in terms of an abstract syntax.

The presentation layer communicates with the application layer in terms of this abstract syntax. The actual details of this communication are implementation-dependent and thus beyond the scope of the relevant standards. The presentation layer translates between the abstract syntax of the application layer and a transfer syntax that describes the data values in a binary form, suitable for interaction with the session service. For example, an abstract syntax may include a data type of character; the transfer syntax could specify ASCII (American Standard Code for Information Interchange) or EBCDIC (Extended Binary-Coded Decimal Interchange Code) encoding.

The transfer syntax thus defines the representation of the data to be exchanged between presentation entities. The translation from the abstract syntax to the transfer syntax is accomplished by means of encoding rules that specify the representation of each data value of each data type.

Table 5.1 Presentation-Layer Terms

Abstract syntax	Describes the generic structure of data independent of any encoding technique used to represent the data. The syntax allows data types to be defined and values of those types to be specified.
Data type	A named set of values. A type may be simple, which is defined by specifying the set of its values, or structured, which is defined in terms of other types.
Encoding	The complete sequence of octets used to represent a data value.
Encoding rules	A specification of the mapping from one syntax to another. Specifically, encoding rules determine algorithmically, for any set of data values defined in an abstract syntax, the representation of those values in a transfer syntax.
Presentation context	A combination of abstract syntax and transfer syntax that can be used for the transfer of data using the presentation service.
Transfer syntax	The way in which data are actually represented in terms of bit patterns while in transit between presentation entities.

Before a presentation connection can be used to exchange data, the two presentation entities must agree on a transfer syntax. Each entity knows the abstract syntax of its user, and each has available one or more transfer syntaxes suitable for encoding. It is simply a matter of the two presentation entities' agreeing on a particular transfer syntax to use. The combination of abstract and transfer syntaxes being used for the exchange is referred to as the presentation context.

This approach for the exchange of application data solves the two problems that relate to data representation in a distributed, heterogeneous environment:

1.   There is a common representation for the exchange of data between differing systems.

2.   Internal to a system, an application uses some particular representation of data. The abstract/transfer-syntax scheme automatically resolves differences in representation between cooperating application entities.

The ISO standards make no assumptions about the way in which abstract or transfer syntaxes are specified. The presentation service is general-purpose and is intended to support all application protocols and any appropriate syntax.

The fundamental requirement for selection of a transfer syntax is that it support the corresponding abstract syntax. In addition, the transfer syntax may have other attributes that are not related to the abstract syntaxes that it can support. For example, an abstract syntax could be supported by any one of four transfer syntaxes, which are the same in all respects except that one provides data compression, one provides encryption, one provides both, and one provides neither. The choice of which transfer syntax to use would depend on cost and security considerations.

5.1.2   Presentation Service

The OSI presentation service is defined in ISO 8822 and X.216. It provides two general categories of service: presentation-related and session-related. Presentation-related services deal with the representation of application data in such a way that two application entities can successfully exchange

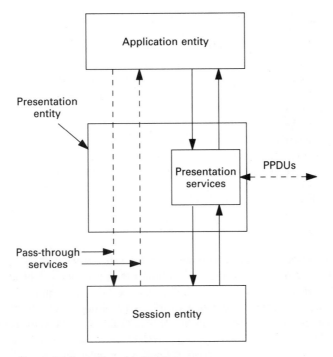

Figure 5.2 Pass-Through Services

data even if they use different local representations for that data. For this purpose, the presentation layer has two functions that it carries out on behalf of presentation-service users:

1. *Negotiation of transfer syntaxes:* For any given type of user data, a transfer syntax is negotiated that is usable by each presentation entity for transformation to/from its user's data representation.

2. *Transformation:* Data provided by the user are transformed into the transfer-syntax representation for transmission; data received for delivery to the user are transformed from the transfer-syntax representation to the user's representation.

In addition to these presentation services, application entities require the services provided by the session layer for dialogue management. Because of the layered architecture of OSI, applications do not have direct access to session services. Thus, session-related service requests must be passed through the presentation layer to the session service (Figure 5.2), a point elaborated on in the following discussion.

At any time during the life of a presentation connection, the presentation entity is dealing with one or more presentation contexts. Each context specifies the abstract syntax of the user's data and the transfer syntax to be used in transmitting that data. Two categories of contexts are employed. The defined-context set consists of presentation contexts that have been defined by agreement between the two presentation users and the presentation-service provider. The default context is a presentation context that is always known to the presentation provider and is used when the defined-context set is empty. It is also used for special circumstances, such as the transmission of

Table 5.2 Session and Presentation Functional Units

Session Functional Units	Presentation Functional Units
Negotiated release	Presentation kernel
Half-duplex	Context management
Duplex	Context restoration
Expedited data	
Typed data	
Capability-data exchange	
Minor synchronization	
Major synchronization	
Resynchronize	
Exceptions	
Activity management	

expedited data. At the presentation-service interface, the value of the user data parameter is structured as a list of typed data values; the type identifies the presentation context applicable to the data value and the syntactic description of the data value within that context.

As with the session service, presentation services are grouped into functional units for the purpose of negotiation at connection-establishment time (Table 5.2). Most of these are identical to those defined for the session service. These are provided so that, at connection-establishment time, a presentation user may request and negotiate the use of particular session services.

There are three presentation-related functional units. The *presentation-kernel functional unit* is always available and supports information transfer on whatever session functional-unit services are selected. If two applications are using a common representation for all data to be exchanged, then only the presentation kernel is needed, and the presentation layer is essentially a null service that merely passes requests and responses down to the session service and passes session indications and confirms up to the presentation user.

If two applications do not share a common representation, then the presentation layer performs the necessary transformation. If only the kernel functional unit is selected, then only the default context and the contexts negotiated as part of the defined-context set at the time of connection establishment may be used. If the *context-management functional unit* is selected, it is possible to change the defined-context set during the course of a presentation connection. Both additions to and deletions from the context set are permitted.

The *context-restoration functional unit* deals with the interaction between context management and session synchronization. If changes are made to the defined-context set during the life of a connection and resynchronization occurs, then it becomes necessary to determine the state of the defined-context set after resynchronization. In general, it would be desirable to make the defined-context set conform to the change in dialogue that has taken place. How this is done is illustrated in Figure 5.3 (compare this with Figure 3.13) and can be summarized as follows, based on the resynchronization option selected:

- *Abandon:* The defined-context set remains the same. Thus, the current dialogue is being abandoned, but the two sides remember the most recent context agreement between them.

- *Restart:* A restart moves the dialogue back to a previously defined synchronization point. The defined-context set is set equal to the value it had when that synchronization point was origi-

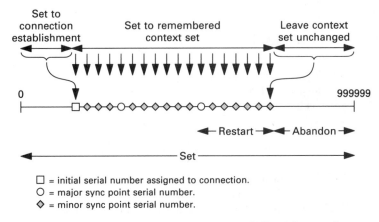

Figure 5.3 Effect of Resynchronization on the Defined-Context Set

nally defined. This is an appropriate action, as a restart is used to recover to a known point in the dialogue.

■ *Set:* If the serial number for the set option falls into the range of the restart or abandon option, then the action previously indicated for the corresponding option is taken. If the serial number is for some other known synchronization point, then the defined-context set is restored to that point. Otherwise, the defined-context set is restored to the value negotiated at connection-establishment time.

Table 5.3 lists the primitives and parameters of the presentation service. Note that all presentation primitives correspond to session-service primitives of the same name, with the exception of the P-ALTER-CONTEXT primitives. The presentation-service parameters have the same meanings as the corresponding session-service parameters, with the additional parameters noted in the following discussion. The presentation primitives are grouped into five facilities, which are discussed in turn.

Table 5.3 Presentation-Service Primitives and Parameters

Connection-Establishment Facility

P-CONNECT.request (calling presentation address, called presentation address, presentation-context-definition list, default-context name, quality of service, presentation requirements, mode, session requirements, serial number, token, session-connection identifier, data)

P-CONNECT.indication (calling presentation address, called presentation address, presentation-context-definition list, presentation-context-definition result list, default-context name, quality of service, presentation requirements, mode, session requirements, serial number, token, session-connection identifier, data)

P-CONNECT.response/confirm (responding presentation address, presentation-context-definition list, default-context result, quality of service, presentation requirements, session requirements, serial number, token, session-connection identifier, result, data)

Table 5.3 (*Cont.*)

Connection-Termination Facility

P-RELEASE.request/indication (data)
P-RELEASE.response/confirm (result, data)
P-U-ABORT.request/indication (data)
P-P-ABORT.indication (provider reason)

Context-Management Facility

P-ALTER-CONTEXT.request (presentation-context-addition list, presentation-context-deletion list, data)
P-ALTER-CONTEXT.indication (presentation-context-addition list, presentation-context-deletion list, presentation-context-addition result list, data)
P-ALTER-CONTEXT.response/confirm (presentation-context-addition result list, presentation-context-deletion result list, data)

Information-Transfer Facility

P-DATA.request/indication (data)
P-TYPED-DATA.request/indication (data)
P-EXPEDITED-DATA.request/indication (data)
P-CAPABILITY-DATA.request/indication/response/confirm (data)

Dialogue-Control Facility

P-TOKEN-GIVE.request/indication (tokens)
P-TOKEN-PLEASE.request/indication (tokens, data)
P-CONTROL-GIVE.request/indication
P-SYNC-MINOR.request/indication (type, serial number, data)
P-SYNC-MINOR.response/confirm (serial number, data)
P-SYNC-MAJOR.request/indication (serial number, data)
P-SYNC-MAJOR.response/confirm (data)
P-RESYNCHRONIZE.request (type, serial number, tokens, data)
P-RESYNCHRONIZE.indication (type, serial number, tokens, presentation-context-identification list, data)
P-RESYNCHRONIZE.response (serial number, tokens, data)
P-RESYNCHRONIZE.confirm (serial number, tokens, presentation-context-identification list, data)
P-U-EXCEPTION-REPORT.request/indication (reason, data)
P-P-EXCEPTION-REPORT.indication (reason)
P-ACTIVITY-START.request/indication (activity ID, data)
P-ACTIVITY-RESUME.request/indication (activity ID, old activity ID, serial number, old session-connection ID, data)
P-ACTIVITY-END.request/indication (serial number, data)
P-ACTIVITY-END.response/confirm (data)
P-ACTIVITY-INTERRUPT.request/indication (reason)
P-ACTIVITY-INTERRUPT.response/confirm
P-ACTIVITY-DISCARD.request/indication (reason)
P-ACTIVITY-DISCARD.response/confirm

5.1.2.1   Connection-Establishment Facility

A presentation connection is established using the P-CONNECT primitive. Connection establishment results in the establishment, on a one-to-one basis, of a session connection whose lifetime is identical to that of the supported presentation connection. Many of the parameters in the P-CONNECT.request primitive, such as quality of service and session requirement, are passed down unchanged to the session layer for use in setting up the session connection. The new parameters are as follows:

- *Context-definition list:* a list of the presentation contexts to be placed in the initial defined-context set. Each entry in the list consists of an identifier, by which the context will be known, and an abstract syntax name, which specifies the syntax used by the application. It is up to the service provider to determine the transfer syntax to be used for each context.

- *Context-definition result list:* contains an entry for each item in the context-definition list, indicating acceptance or rejection.

- *Default-context name:* supplied by the user if it wishes to identify explicitly the abstract syntax supported by the default context for future reference. If the parameter is not included, then there has been some prior arrangement regarding the definition of the default context.

- *Default-context result:* has the value agreed or refused.

- *Presentation requirements:* used to select the context-management and/or context-restoration functional units.

- *Mode:* has the value normal or X.410-1984. In the latter case, there are a few restrictions that limit the presentation service to that defined in the 1984 version of X.410.

5.1.2.2   Connection-Termination Facility

P-RELEASE provides access to the S-RELEASE session service. Similarly, P-U-ABORT and P-P-ABORT are passed down to the session S-U-ABORT service. In the case of P-U-ABORT, a context-identifier list is provided to specify the contexts that are used in the user data parameter.

5.1.2.3   Context-Management Facility

The context-management facility allows changes to be made to the defined-context list. The requester provides a list of contexts to be added and a list of contexts to be deleted. The service provider delivers these to the other user, together with an indication of which proposed new contexts it can support. The user can either accept or reject each proposed change. Based on the provider's ability to support new contexts plus the response of the other user, the service provider confirms to the requesting user the resulting additions and deletions to the defined-context set.

5.1.2.4   Information-Transfer Facility

The information-transfer facility provides the user with access to the information-transfer facility of the session layer. In the case of data, typed data, and capability data, the data parameter is passed between application entities using the defined-context set or in the default context if the defined-context set is empty. In the case of expedited data, the data are passed using the default context. This convention is used because it is possible for an expedited-data request to overtake an alter-context request. Hence, the two sides may not agree on the defined-context set at the time of arrival of the expedited data.

5.1.2.5   Dialogue-Control Facility

All the primitives in this facility provide access to the corresponding session-layer primitives. There is no added value, and none of the services of the session layer is lost.

In the case of the resynchronization service, care must be taken to deal correctly with the interaction between context management and synchronization. If changes are made to the defined-context set during the lifetime of a connection and resynchronization occurs, then it becomes necessary to determine the state of the defined-context set after the resynchronization. In general, the defined-context set must be restored to a state appropriate to the change in the synchronization.

5.1.3   Presentation Protocol

The OSI presentation protocol is defined in ISO 8823 and X.226. We begin by looking at the presentation PDUs and then we examine the protocol support for each of the five presentation facilities.

5.1.3.1   Presentation-Protocol Data Units

The PDUs for the presentation protocol are listed in Table 5.4. Two aspects of this list are noteworthy. First, the list is not very long. Second, many of the parameters are identical to parameters found in a corresponding session-service primitive; these parameters pass through to the session service. These two aspects are manifestations of the same underlying concept: that there is a tight linkage between the presentation layer and the session layer. We have already referred to this linkage in discussing the presentation service (Figure 5.2). Let us explore this linkage further.

Below the presentation layer, there is a direct relationship between layer-(N) service primitives and layer-(N) PDUs. Consider Figure 3.14, part (a). An S-CONNECT.request triggers the transmission of a connect SPDU, which triggers an S-CONNECT.indication; in the other direction, an S-CONNECT.response triggers an accept SPDU, which triggers an S-CONNECT.confirm. In general, a confirmed session service causes the exchange of two SPDUs, and a nonconfirmed service causes the transmission of a single SPDU. Each SPDU becomes user data in a transport-level data or expedited-data TPDU. A similar set of statements can be made about lower layers. In some cases, more PDUs are exchanged for a given service (e.g., transport-level retransmission of lost TPDUs), but the principles remain the same:

- Each (N)-layer service is implemented by the exchange of layer-(N) PDUs.
- Each layer-(N) PDU becomes user data and is encapsulated in a layer ($N-1$) data or expedited-data PDU.

At the presentation layer (and as the reader will see, also at the application layer), these principles do not apply. Not every presentation service requires presentation PDUs, and some parameters in some presentation service primitives do not appear as user data in SPDUs. To explain the motivation for these differences, consider two presentation services: connection establishment and token passing.

As protocols for the upper three layers of the OSI model were being developed, it became evident that for the negotiation of connection options to work well, it would be useful to negotiate and establish the session, presentation, and application connections simultaneously and subsequently terminate the three connections simultaneously. This, of course, dictates a strict one-to-one relationship, with coextensive lifetimes for the three connection types. This process is known

Table 5.4 Presentation-Protocol Data Units and Parameters

PPDU	Parameters Carried in PPDU (SS User Data)	Parameters Passed Down as Parameters in Session-Service Primitive
Connect (CP)	Mode, protocol version, calling presentation selector, called presentation selector, presentation-context-definition list, default-context name, presentation requirements, user session requirements, user data	Calling session address, called session address, quality of service, revised session requirements, serial number, token assignment, session-connection ID
Connect accept (CPA)	Protocol version, responding presentation selector, presentation-context-definition result list, default-context result, provider reason, user data	Responding session address, quality of service, session requirements, session-connection ID
Connect reject (CPR)	Protocol version, responding presentation selector, presentation-context-definition result list, default-context result, provider reason, user data	Responding session address, quality of service, session requirements, session-connection ID
Abnormal-release user (ARU)	Presentation-context identifier list, user data	—
Abnormal-release provider (ARP)	Provider reason, event identifier	—
Alter context (AC)	Presentation-context-addition list, presentation-context-deletion list, user data	—
Alter-context ACK (ACA)	Presentation-context-addition result list, presentation-context-deletion result list, user data	—
Typed data (TTD)	User data	—
Data (TD)	User data	—
Expedited data (TE)	User data	—
Capability-data ACK (TCC)	User data	—
Resynchronize (RS)	Presentation-context-identifier list, user data	Type, serial number, tokens
Resynchronize ACK (RSA)	Presentation-context-identifier list, user data	Serial number, tokens

Table 5.5 Connection Establishment Through Two Layers

Layer-by-Layer Approach

1. In System A, the (Na) layer performs the following functions:
   a. It receives a connection request from $(Na + 1)$ with service parameters:
      $$CX - (Na + 1) (PAR/1 . . . PAR/P)$$
   b. (Na) processes these parameters and defines the class of services it has to negotiate with the layer (Nb) in system B.
   c. (Na) issues a connection request to $(Na - 1)$ with service parameters:
      $$CX - (Na) (PAR'/1 . . . PAR'/J)$$
   d. (Na) receives a connection confirm from $(Na - 1)$.
   e. (Na) creates a connect PDU and issues it in a data request to $(Na - 1)$ on the (N) connection that has been established to (Nb).
   f. (Na) receives a connect Ack PDU in a data indication from $(Na - 1)$ and issues a connection confirm to $(Na + 1)$.
2. In System B, the (Nb) layer performs the following functions:
   a. It receives a connection indication from $(Nb - 1)$ with service parameters:
      $$CX - (Na) (PAR'/1 . . . PAR'/J)$$
   b. If (Nb) can respond positively, it issues a connection response to $(Nb - 1)$.
   c. (Nb) receives a connect PDU as a data indication from $(Nb - 1)$ on the (N) connection that has been established to (Na).
   d. (Nb) issues a connection indication to $(Nb + 1)$, passing the connection-request parameters from the PDU to $(Nb + 1)$.
   e. If $(Nb + 1)$ responds positively with a connect response, (Nb) creates a connect ACK PDU and issues it in a data request on the (N) connection that has been established to $(Na.)$

Embedding Approach

1. In System A, the (Na) layer performs the following functions:
   a. It receives a connection request from $(Na + 1)$ with service parameters:
      $$CX - (Na + 1) (PAR/1 . . . PAR/P)$$
   b. (Na) processes these parameters and defines the class of services it has to negotiate with layer (Nb) in system B.
   c. (Na) issues a connection request to $(Na - 1)$ with service parameters:
      $$CX - (Na) (PAR'/1 . . . PAR'/J)(DATA - [Na])$$
      $$DATA - (Na) = CX - (Na + 1) (PAR/1 . . . PAR/P)$$
   d. (Na) receives a connection confirm from $(Na - 1)$.
   e. (Na) issues a connection confirm to $(Na + 1)$.
2. In System B, the (Nb) layer performs the following functions:
   a. It receives a connection indication from $(Nb - 1)$ with service parameters:
      $$CX - (Na) (PAR'/1 . . . PAR'/J)$$
   b. If (Nb) can respond positively, it issues a connection indication to $(Nb + 1)$, passing the user data portion of the connection indication from $(Nb - 1)$ to $(Nb + 1)$.
   c. If $(Nb + 1)$ responds positively with a connect response, (Nb) issues a connection response to $(Nb - 1)$.

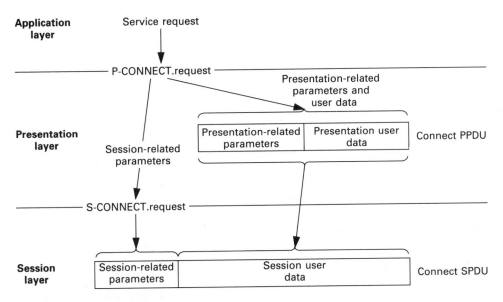

Figure 5.4 Connect-Request Embedding

as embedding, as the connection-request and response PDUs of the three upper layers are carried one inside the other. Embedding is briefly referenced in the basic OSI document (ISO 7498) and is treated in detail in ISO document SC 21 N5217.[1] Table 5.5, which contrasts a layer-by-layer approach to connection establishment with embedding, is based on that latter document. In the layer-by-layer approach, before an (N) connection can be established, an $(N-1)$ connection is established, and the connection exchange at the (N) level is carried on by an exchange of data PDUs over the $(N-1)$ connection. In the embedding approach, the connection-request PDU of the (N) level is carried as user data in the connection-request PDU of the $(N-1)$ level.

Figure 5.4 shows how the connect PPDU is embedded in the connect SPDU. Embedding allows for connection establishment at the application level with the minimum number of PDU exchanges. Without embedding, a session connection must be established even when it turns out that a presentation connection cannot be established (e.g., lack of agreement on a transfer syntax). These unnecessary connections would then be released, requiring additional PDU exchanges. Furthermore, the responding application entity could not specify values for negotiating presentation services, because the information needed for such a decision (i.e., the information in the connection-indication primitive) would not be available until after the session and presentation connections had been established.

Now consider the P-TOKEN-GIVE service. The presentation layer has nothing to do with this service. It does not add any value to the corresponding session service or impose any conditions on its use. Thus, when a P-TOKEN-GIVE.request is issued by a presentation user, the presentation entity simply invokes an S-TOKEN-GIVE.request, with no user data (PPDU) parameter. The S-TOKEN-GIVE triggers the transmission of a give-token SPDU. When this is received by the

---

1.   Approved Commentaries on the Basic Reference Model for OSI.

Table 5.6 Relationship Among Presentation Primitives, Presentation PDUs, and Session Primitives

Presentation Primitives	Presentation PDUs	Session Primitives
P-CONNECT	CP, CPA, CR	S-CONNECT
P-RELEASE	—	S-RELEASE
P-U-ABORT	ARU	S-U-ABORT
P-P-ABORT	ARP	S-U-ABORT
P-P-ABORT	—	S-P-ABORT
P-ALTER-CONTEXT	AC, ACA	S-TYPED-DATA
P-TYPED-DATA	TTD	S-TYPED-DATA
P-DATA	TD	S-DATA
P-EXPEDITED-DATA	TE	S-EXPEDITED-DATA
P-CAPABILITY-DATA	TC, TCC	S-CAPABILITY-DATA
P-TOKEN-GIVE	—	S-TOKEN-GIVE
P-TOKEN-PLEASE	—	S-TOKEN-PLEASE
P-CONTROL-GIVE	—	S-CONTROL-GIVE
P-SYNC-MINOR	—	S-SYNC-MINOR
P-SYNC-MAJOR	—	S-SYNC-MAJOR
P-RESYNCHRONIZE	—	S-RESYNCHRONIZE
P-RESYNCHRONIZE	RS, RSA	S-RESYNCHRONIZE
P-U-EXCEPTION-REPORT	—	S-U-EXCEPTION-REPORT
P-P-EXCEPTION-REPORT	—	S-U-EXCEPTION-REPORT
P-ACTIVITY-START	—	S-ACTIVITY-START
P-ACTIVITY-RESUME	—	S-ACTIVITY-RESUME
P-ACTIVITY-END	—	S-ACTIVITY-END
P-ACTIVITY-INTERRUPT	—	S-ACTIVITY-INTERRUPT
P-ACTIVITY-DISCARD	—	S-ACTIVITY-DISCARD

other session entity, it issues an S-TOKEN-GIVE.indication to the receiving presentation entity, which issues a P-TOKEN-GIVE.indication to the receiving presentation user. Thus, in the data exchanged between systems, there is no presentation header.

Table 5.4 indicates those presentation-level parameters that are passed through to the session service and are therefore not included in any PPDU header. Table 5.6 shows the relationship between presentation-service primitives, PPDUs, and session-service primitives.

5.1.3.2   Connection-Establishment Facility

As has been mentioned, connection-related PPDUs are embedded the user data field in connection-related SPDUs. Figure 5.5 illustrates the sequence, highlighting the negotiation of syntaxes:

1.   A presentation user issues a P-CONNECT.request primitive that includes, as the presentation-context-definition list parameter, a list of abstract syntaxes that are requested for use.

2.   For each abstract syntax requested by its user that it can support, the presentation entity selects one or more transfer syntaxes that it can use for that abstract syntax. The resulting list of abstract syntaxes and transfer syntaxes is encoded in a CP PDU as the presentation-context-

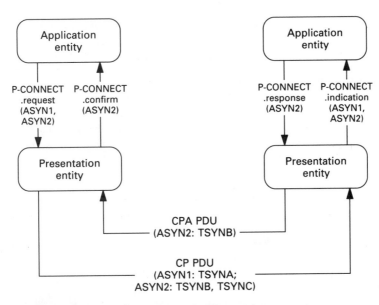

Figure 5.5 Establishing a Presentation Connection

definition list parameter. The CP PDU is sent to the peer presentation entity by issuing it as user data to the session service via an S-CONNECT.request.

3. When the responding presentation entity receives the CP PDU (via an S.CONNECT.indication), it issues a P-CONNECT.indication to the target presentation user. The indication includes a list of all the requested abstract syntaxes that the responding presentation entity can support.

4. The responding presentation user issues a P-CONNECT.response that includes a list of those requested abstract syntaxes that it is prepared to support.

5. For each selected abstract syntax, the responding presentation entity selects a transfer syntax from among those proposed by the requesting presentation entity. It then issues a CPA PDU via an S-CONNECT.response.

6. The requesting presentation entity receives the CPA PDU via an S-CONNECT.confirm and issues a P-CONNECT.confirm to the requesting presentation user.

5.1.3.3   Connection-Termination Facility

Orderly release of the connection is a session function. When the session connection is released, the presentation connection is automatically released. Hence, there are no PPDUs for this service.

When a presentation user aborts a connection, it may wish to pass some user-defined data, and this requires the context and user data parameters in the ARU PPDU. Two other possibilities for connection abortion exist:

1. One of the two presentation entities may initiate the abort. In this case, the entity sends an ARP PPDU to the other presentation entity. Each presentation entity issues a P-P-ABORT.indication to its user. Note that the ARP is issued using an S-U-ABORT primitive, since it is a session-service user that initiates the abort.

2.   The session-service provider aborts the session connection, which causes the simultaneous abort of the presentation connection. In this case, each presentation entity receives an S-P-ABORT.indication, with no embedded PPDU, and issues a P-P-ABORT.indication to its user.

5.1.3.4   Context-Management Facility

The P-ALTER-CONTEXT service is a confirmed service. Hence, two PPDUs are involved: AC and ACA. This is a service that has nothing to do with the session service, and therefore, there is no corresponding SPDU as a vehicle. Furthermore, it is desired that this facility not depend on data-token control. Accordingly, the AC and ACA PPDUs are transmitted as typed session data, allowing them to bypass token control.

5.1.3.5   Information-Transfer Facility

The four types of data (normal, typed, expedited, and capability) are transferred using the corresponding session service. In each case, the only parameter is the presentation user data.

5.1.3.6   Dialogue-Control Facility

All the services in this facility are essentially session services. With the exception of the P-RESYNCHRONIZE service, none of the services in this facility requires that the presentation entities exchange data.

If the context-restoration functional unit has been selected, then there is the possible need to restore a defined-context set to a previous value. Accordingly, the presentation entity will remember the value of the defined-context set at the time of each minor and major synchronization service. However, this function does not require the exchange of PPDUs.

The P-RESYNCHRONIZE request and response primitives are handled in one of three ways:

1.   If neither the context-management nor the context-restoration functional unit is selected, then the presentation entity issues an S-RESYNCHRONIZE request or response.

2.   If context management is selected but context restoration is not, then the presentation entity issues an RS or RSA PPDU in the user data parameter of an S-RESYNCHRONIZE request or response. The context-identifier-list parameter refers to the current defined-context set.

3.   If both context management and context restoration are selected, then the presentation entity issues an RS or RSA PPDU with the context-identifier-list parameter set to the appropriate restored defined-context set.

The reception of an S-RESYNCHRONIZE indication or confirm is handled in the corresponding manner. A P-SYNCHRONIZE indication or confirm is issued, and context restoration, if required, is performed.

It should be clear why the RS and RSA PPDUs are not needed for case 1 and why they are needed for case 3. It is perhaps less obvious that they are also needed for case 2, as case 2 does not allow the restoration of a previous defined context set. The problem that case 2 addresses is this: Suppose that one presentation entity attempts to alter the context at about the same time that the other attempts to resynchronize the connection. The scenario of Figure 5.6 could occur. User A issues a P-ALTER-CONTEXT.request. User B receives the indication and issues a response that accepts the alteration. At this point, user B assumes that the new defined-context set is in force. User B now issues a P-RESYNCHRONIZE.request, which triggers an S-RESYNCHRON-IZE.request. The session-protocol entity will issue a resynchronize SPDU, which will be carried by a data TPDU. But recall from section 3.4 that the session-protocol entity may also issue a

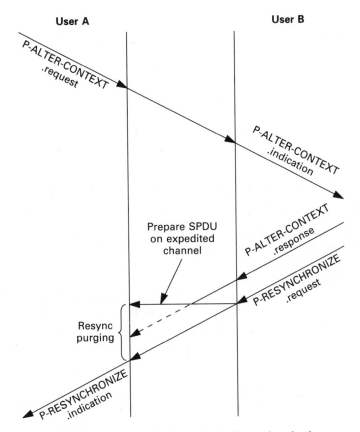

Figure 5.6 Loss of Defined-Context Set by Resynchronization

prepare SPDU, which is carried by an expedited-data TPDU. If the expedited-data TPDU overtakes the TPDU that is carrying the ACA PPDU, then the latter TPDU is discarded, and the ACA never gets through. Hence, user A never receives a P-ALTER-CONTEXT.confirm and assumes that the defined-context set has not been altered. This would leave the two presentation entities with different opinions on the contexts of the defined-context set. To avoid this possibility, the resynchronization activity results in the exchange of RS and RSA primitives to enforce agreement.

5.2 ABSTRACT SYNTAX NOTATION ONE

Abstract Syntax Notation One (ASN.1) is a formal language developed and standardized by CCITT (X.208) and ISO (IS0 8824). ASN.1 is important for several reasons. First, it can be used to define abstract syntaxes of application data, as discussed in section 5.1. Although any formal language could be used for this purpose, in practice, ASN.1 is likely to be used almost exclusively. In addition, ASN.1 is used to define the structure of application and presentation PDUs. Finally, ASN.1 is used to define the management information base for OSI network management (see Chapter 12).

ASN.1 is a formalism for defining data structures and their values. Thus, there are two key aspects to ASN.1: (1) the data types that can be defined using ASN.1 and (2) conventions for describing a structure consisting of data types. Each of these two aspects is considered in turn.

5.2.1 Data Types

ASN.1 refers to four classes of types:

1. *Universal:* generally useful, application-independent types and construction mechanisms. These are defined in the standard and are listed in Table 5.7.
2. *Applicationwide:* relevant to a particular application. These are defined in other standards.
3. *Context-specific:* also relevant to a particular application but applicable in a limited context.
4. *Private:* types defined by users and not covered by any standard.

Each type is distinguished by a tag, which specifies the class of type and identifies the particular type within the class. For example, UNIVERSAL 4 refers to octetstring, which is of class UNIVERSAL and has identifier 4 within the class.

Data types in the UNIVERSAL class can be grouped into several categories, as indicated in Table 5.7. A *simple type* is one defined by directly specifying the set of its values. These may be thought of as the atomic types; all other types are built up from the simple types. The Boolean type is straightforward. The integer type is the set of positive and negative integers and zero. In addition, individual integer values can be assigned names to indicate a specific meaning. The

Table 5.7 Universal-Class Tag Assignments

Tag	Type	Set of Values
	Simple Types	
UNIVERSAL 1	Boolean	TRUE or FALSE.
UNIVERSAL 2	Integer	The positive and negative whole numbers, including zero.
UNIVERSAL 3	Bitstring	A sequence of zero or more bits.
UNIVERSAL 4	Octetstring	A sequence of zero or more octets.
UNIVERSAL 9	Real	Real numbers.
UNIVERSAL 10	Enumerated	An explicit list of integer values that an instance of a data type may take.
	Object Types	
UNIVERSAL 6	Object identifier	The set of values associated with information objects allocated by this standard.
UNIVERSAL 7	Object descriptor	Each value is human-readable text providing a brief description of an information object.
	Constructor Types	
UNIVERSAL 16	Sequence and sequence-of	Sequence: defined by referencing a fixed, ordered list of types. Each value is an ordered list of values, one from each component type.

Table 5.7 (*Cont.*)

Tag	Type	Set of Values
UNIVERSAL 17	Set and set-of	Sequence-of: defined by referencing a single existing type. Each value is an ordered list of zero or more values of the existing type. Set: defined by referencing a fixed, unordered list of types, some of which may be declared optional. Each value is an unordered list of values, one from each component type. Set-of: defined by referencing a single existing type. Each value is an unordered list of zero or more values of the existing type.

Character-String Types

Tag	Type	Set of Values
UNIVERSAL 18	Numericstring	Digits 0 through 9, space.
UNIVERSAL 19	Printablestring	Printable characters.
UNIVERSAL 20	Teletexstring	Character set defined by CCITT Recommendation T.61.
UNIVERSAL 21	Videotexstring	Set of alphabetic and graphical characters defined by CCITT Recommendations T.100 and T.101.
UNIVERSAL 22	IA5string	International alphabet five (equivalent to ASCII).
UNIVERSAL 25	Graphicstring	Character set defined by ISO 8824.
UNIVERSAL 26	Visiblestring	Character set defined by ISO 646 (equivalent to ASCII).
UNIVERSAL 27	Generalstring	General character string.

Miscellaneous Types

Tag	Type	Set of Values
UNIVERSAL 5	Null	The single value NULL. Commonly used where several alternatives are possible but none of them applies.
UNIVERSAL 8	External	A type defined in some external document. It need not be one of the valid ASN.1 types.
UNIVERSAL 23	UTCtime	Consists of the date, specified with a two-digit year, a two-digit month, and a two-digit day; followed by the time, specified in hours, minutes, and optionally seconds; followed by an optional specification of the local time differential from universal time.
UNIVERSAL 24	Generalizedtime	Consists of the date, specified with a four-digit year, a two-digit month, and a two-digit day; followed by the time, specified in hours, minutes, and optionally seconds; followed by an optional specification of the local time differential from universal time.
UNIVERSAL 11–15	Reserved	Reserved for addenda to the ASN.1 standard.
UNIVERSAL 28–	Reserved	Reserved for addenda to the ASN.1 standard.

bitstring is an ordered set of zero or more bits; individual bits can be assigned names. The actual value of a bitstring can be specified as a string of either binary or hexadecimal digits. Similarly, an octetstring can be specified as a string of either binary or hexadecimal digits. The real data type consists of numbers expressed in scientific notation (mantissa, base, exponent); base 2 or base 10 may be used. Finally, the enumerated type consists of an explicitly enumerated list of integers, together with an associated name for each integer. The same functionality can be achieved with the integer type by naming some of the integer values; however, because of the utility of this feature, a separate type has been defined.

Object types are used to name and describe information objects. Examples of information objects are standards documents, abstract and transfer syntaxes, and data structures. In general, an information object is a class of information (e.g., a file format) rather than an instance of such a class (e.g., an individual file). The object identifier is a unique identifier for a particular object. Its value consists of a sequence of integers. The set of defined objects has a tree structure, with the root of the tree being the object referring to the ASN.1 standard. Starting with the root of the object-identifier tree, each object-identifier component value identifies a branch in the tree. The object descriptor is a human-readable description of an information object.

ASN.1 provides several *constructor types* for building complex data types from simple data types. The sequence and sequence-of types are used to define an ordered list of values of one or more other data types. This is analogous to the record structure found in many programming languages, such as COBOL. A sequence consists of an ordered list of elements, each specifying a type and, optionally, a name. A sequence may consist of a fixed number of elements, possibly of more than one type, or a fixed number of elements, some of which are optional. In the latter case, all elements, including the optional ones, must be of distinct types. A sequence-of consists of a variable number of elements, all of one type. A set is similar to a sequence, except that the order of the elements is not significant; the elements may be arranged in any order when they are encoded into a specific representation. As with a sequence, a set may consist of a fixed number of elements, possibly of more than one type, or a fixed number of elements, some of which are optional. A set-of is an unordered, variable number of elements, all of one type.

ASN.1 defines a number of built-in *character-string types*. The values of each of these types consist of a sequence of zero or more characters from a standardized character set.

Some other, *miscellaneous types* have also been defined in the universal class. The null type is used in places in a structure where a value may or may not be present. The null type is simply the alternative of no value being present at that position in the structure. An external type is one whose values are unspecified in the ASN.1 standard; it is defined in some other document or standard and can be defined using any well-specified notation. UTCtime and generalizedtime are two different formats for expressing time. In both cases, either a universal or local time may be specified.

5.2.2 Structure Definition

ASN.1 is a language that can be used to define data structures. A structure definition is in the form of a named module. The name of the module can then be used to reference the structure. For example, the module name can be used as an abstract-syntax name; an application can pass this name to the presentation service to specify the abstract syntax of the APDUs that the application wishes to exchange with a peer application entity.

Figure 5.7 defines the syntax for ASN.1 in Backus-Naur Form (BNF). The easiest way to describe the syntax is by example.

Figure 5.8, taken from the ASN.1 standard, is an example that defines the structure of a personnel record. Part (a) of the figure depicts the personnel record informally by giving an example of a specific record.

In part (b), we see the formal description of the data structure. In the notation, a structure definition has the form:

```
ModuleDefinition ::= modulereference DEFINITIONS "::=" BEGIN ModuleBody END
ModuleBody ::= AssignmentList | empty
AssignmentList ::= Assignment | AssignmentList Assignment
Assignment ::= Typeassignment | Valueassignment
Typeassignment ::= typereference "::=" Type
Valueassignment ::= valuereference Type "::=" Value
Type ::= BuiltinType | DefinedType
BuiltinType ::= BooleanType | IntegerType | BitStringType | OctetStringType | NullType |
                SequenceType | SequenceOfType | SetType | SetOfType | ChoiceType |
                SelectionType | TaggedType | AnyType | ObjectIdentifierType |
                CharacterStringType | UsefulType | EnumeratedType | RealType
Value ::= BuiltinValue | DefinedValue
BuiltinType ::= BooleanValue | IntegerValue | BitStringValue | OctetStringValue | NullValue |
                SequenceValue | SequenceOfValue | SetValue | SetOfValue | ChoiceValue |
                SelectionValue | TaggedValue | AnyValue | ObjectIdentifierValue |
                CharacterStringValue | EnumeratedValue | RealValue
DefinedValue ::= Externalvaluereference | valuereference
BooleanType ::= BOOLEAN
BooleanValue ::= TRUE | FALSE
IntegerType ::= INTERGER | INTEGER {NamedNumberList}
NamedNumberList ::= NamedNumber | NamedNumberList, NamedNumber
NamedNumber ::= identifier(SignedNumber) | identifier(DefinedValue)
SignedNumber ::= number | -number
IntegerValue ::= SignedNumber | identifier
BitStringType ::= BIT STRING | BIT STRING{NamedBitList}
NamedBitList ::= NamedBit | NamedBitList, NamedBit
NamedBit ::= identifier(number) | identifier(DefinedValue)
BitStringValue ::= bstring | hstring | {IdentifierList} | { }
IdentifierList ::= Identifier | IdentifierList, identifier
OctetStringType ::= OCTETSTRING
OctetStringValue ::= bstring | hstring
NullType ::= NULL
NullValue ::= NULL
SequenceType ::= SEQUENCE {ElementTypeList} | SEQUENCE { }
ElementTypeList ::= ElementType | ElementTypeList, ElementType
ElementType ::= NamedType | NamedTypeOPTIONAL | NamedType DEFAULT Value |
                COMPONENTS OF Type
NamedType ::= identifierType | Type | SelectionType
SequenceValue ::= {ElementValueList } | { }
ElementValueList ::= NamedValue | ElementValueList, NamedValue
SequenceOfType ::= SEQUENCE OF Type | SEQUENCE
SequenceOfValue ::= {ValueList} | { }
SetType ::= SET{ElementTypeList} | SET{ }
SetValue ::= {ElementValueList} | { }
SetOfType ::= SET OF Type | SET
SetOfValue ::= {ValueList} | { }
```

Figure 5.7 BNF Grammar for ASN.1

```
ChoiceType ::= CHOICE {AlternativeTypeList}
AlternativeTypeList ::= NamedType | AlternativeTypeList, NamedType
ChoiceValue ::= NamedValue
SelectionType ::= identifier < Type
SelectionValue ::= NamedValue
TaggedType ::= Tag Type | Tag IMPLICIT Type
Tag ::= [Class ClassNumber]
ClassNumber ::= number | DefinedValue
Class ::= UNIVERSAL | APPLICATION | PRIVATE | empty
TaggedValue ::= Value
AnyType ::= ANY | ANY DEFINED BY identifier
AnyValue ::= Type Value
ObjectIdentifierType ::= OBJECT IDENTIFIER
ObjectIdentifierValue ::= {ObjIdComponentList} | {DefinedValue ObjIdComponentList}
ObjIdComponentList ::= ObjIdComponent | ObjIdComponent ObjIdComponentList
ObjIdComponent ::= NameForm | NumberForm | NameAndNumberForm
NameForm ::= identifier
NumberForm ::= number | DefinedValue
NameAndNumberForm ::= identifier(NumberForm)
CharacterStringType ::= typereference
CharacterStringValue ::= cstring
UsefulType ::= typereference
EnumeratedType ::= ENUMERATED {Enumeration}
Enumeration ::= NamedNumber | NamedNumber, Enumeration
EnumerationValue ::= identifier
RealType ::= REAL
RealValue ::= NumericRealValue | SpecialRealValue
NumericRealValue ::= {Mantissa, Base, Exponent} | 0
Mantissa ::= SignedNumber
Base ::= 2 | 10
Exponent ::= SignedNumber
SpecialRealValue ::= PLUS-INFINITY | MINUS-INFINITY
```

Figure 5.7 BNF Grammar for ASN.1 (continued)

$$<type\ name> :: = <type\ definition>$$

A simple example is:

$$SerialNumber :: = INTEGER$$

There are no simple types defined in the example. A similar construction is:

$$EmployeeNumber :: = [APPLICATION\ 2]\ IMPLICIT\ INTEGER$$

This definition makes use of the universal type integer, but the user has chosen to give the type a new tag. The use of the term *[APPLICATION 2]* gives the tag (class and ID) for this new type. The designation *IMPLICIT* has to do with the representation of values in the transfer syntax. With that term present, values of this type will be encoded only with the tag APPLICATION 2. If the designation were not present, then the values would be encoded with both the APPLICATION and UNIVERSAL tags. The use of the implicit option results in a more compact representation. In some applications, compactness may be less important than other considerations, such as the ability to carry out type checking. In the latter case, explicit tagging can be used by omitting the word *IMPLICIT*.

```
Name:                John P Smith
Title:               Director
Employee Number:     51
Date of Hire:        17 September 1971
Name of Spouse:      Mary T Smith
Number of Children:  2


Child Information
     Name:           Ralph T Smith
     Date of Birth:  11 November 1957

Child Information:
     Name:           Susan B Jones
     Date of Birth:  17 July 1959
```

(a) Informal description of personnel record

```
PersonnelRecord ::= [APPLICATION 0] IMPLICIT SET {
        Name,
        title [0] VisibleString,
        number EmployeeNumber,
        dateOfHire [1] Date,
        nameOfSpouse [2] Name,
        children [3] IMPLICIT SEQUENCE OF ChildInformation DEFAULT {} }


ChildInformation ::= SET {
        Name,
        dateOfBirth [0] Date }

Name ::= [APPLICATION 1] IMPLICIT SEQUENCE {
        givenName VisibleString,
        initial VisibleString,
        familyName VisibleString }

EmployeeNumber ::= [APPLICATION 2] IMPLICIT INTEGER

Date ::= [APPLICATION 3] IMPLICIT VisibleString -- YYYYMMDD
```

(b) ASN.1 description of the record structure

```
{                     {givenName "John", initial "P", familyName "Smith"},
     title            "Director"
     number           51
     dateOfHire       "19710917"
     nameOfSpouse     {givenName "Mary", initial "T", familyName "Smith"},
     children
     { {              {givenName "Ralph", initial "T", familyName "Smith"},
       dateOfBirth    "19571111" },
       {              {givenName "Susan", initial "B", familyName "Jones"},
       dateOfBirth    "19590717" } } }
```

(c) ASN.1 description of a record value

Figure 5.8 Example of the Use of ASN.1

```
Remote_Operations_APDUs DEFINITIONS ::= BEGIN

ROSEapdus ::= CHOICE {roiv-apdu [1] IMPLICIT ROIVapdu,
                      rors-apdu [2] IMPLICIT RORSapdu,
                      roer-apdu [3] IMPLICIT ROERapdu,
                      rorj-apdu [4] IMPLICIT RORJapdu}

ROERapdu ::= SEQUENCE {InvokeID InvokedIDType,
                       linked-ID IMPLICIT InvokedIDType OPTIONAL,
                       operation-value OPERATION,
                       argument ANY DEFINED BY operation-value OPTIONAL}

InvokedIDType ::= INTEGER

RORSapdu ::= SEQUENCE {InvokeID InvokedIDType,
                       SEQUENCE {operation-value OPERATION,
                                 result ANY DEFINED BY operation-value
                                 }OPTIONAL}
ROSEapdu ::= SEQUENCE {InvokeID InvokedIDType,
                       error-value ERROR,
                       parameter ANY DEFINED BY error-value OPTIONAL}

RORJapdu ::= SEQUENCE {InvokeID CHOICE {InvokedIDTYPE, NULL},
                       problem CHOICE {[0] IMPLICIT GeneralProblem,
                                       [1] IMPLICIT InvokeProblem,
                                       [2] IMPLICIT ReturnResultProblem,
                                       [3] IMPLICIT ReturnErrorProblem}}

GeneralProblem ::= INTEGER {unrecognizedAPDU (0),
                            mistypedAPDU (1),
                            badlyStructuredAPDU (2)}

InvokeProblem ::= INTEGER {duplicateInvocation (0),
                           unrecognizedOperation (1),
                           mistypedArgument (2),
                           resourceLimitation (3),
                           initiatorReleasing (4),
                           unrecognizedLinkedID (5),
                           linkedResponseUnexpected (6),
                           unexpectedChildOperation (7)}

ReturnResultProblem ::= INTEGER {unrecognizedInvocation
(0),                             resultResponseUnexpected (1),
                                 mistypedResult (2)}

ReturnErrorProblem ::= INTEGER {unrecognizedInvocation (0),
                                errorResponseUnexpected (1),
                                unrecognizedError (2),
                                unexpectedError (3),
                                mistypedParameter (4)}

END
```

Figure 5.9 ASN.1 Abstract-Syntax Specification of ROSE Protocol

The definition of the date type is similar to that of employeenumber. In this case, the type is a character string consisting of characters defined in ISO 646, which is equivalent to ASCII. The double hyphen indicates that the rest of the line is a comment; the format of the date type will not be checked other than to determine that the value is an ISO 646 character string.

The type of name is the sequence type. In this case, each of the three elements in the sequence is named. Childinformation is of the SET type. Note that no name is given to the first element of the set but that the second element is given the name dateofbirth. The second element is the data type date, defined elsewhere. This data type is used in two different locations, here and in the definition of personnelrecord. In each location, the data type is given a name and a context-specific tag—[0] and [1], respectively.

Finally, the overall structure, personnelrecord, is defined as a set with five elements. Associated with the last element is a default value of a null sequence, to be used if no value is supplied.

Figure 5.8, part (c), is an example of a particular value for the personnel record, expressed in the abstract syntax.

As another example, consider the ASN.1 specification of the format of the protocol data units for the ROSE protocol (described in section 5.6). The specification from the standard is reproduced in Figure 5.9.

One new construct in this example is the CHOICE type, which is used to describe a variable selected from a collection. Thus, any instance of the type ROSEapdus, will be one of four alternative types. Note that each of the choices is labeled with a name. In the definition of RORJapdu, the CHOICE construct is used without the benefit of names.

The ROIVapdu definition is a sequence of four elements. This APDU is used to invoke a remote operation and always includes an integer that identifies the type of APDU (invokeID) and an integer that indicates the operation invoked (OPERATION). This latter data type is defined externally. In addition, there are two optional elements to the definition. The linked-ID element is used to link this invocation to a previous one. Finally, the operation may include an argument. This definition also includes the use of the type ANY, which is the union of all defined types. A variable declared to be of type ANY may contain any value. The additional qualifier DEFINED BY provides a pointer to the semantics for this type.

The RORSapdu is used to report the result of an invoked operation. This definition gives an example of a recursive use of a structuring element. In this case, the APDU consists of a sequence of two elements, the second of which is itself a sequence of two elements. The reason that the entire structure is not defined as a simple sequence of three elements is that the last two elements, taken as a pair, are optional: either both are present or both are absent.

5.3 APPLICATION LAYER

At each layer (N) of the OSI model, from layer 2 through 6, the following statements are true:

- An (N) entity within the (N) layer provides service for a user through an (N) SAP.

- An (N) connection is set up between two peer (N) entities in different open systems to support communication between two (N) users. The connection links the respective (N) SAPs of the two users. Alternatively, a connectionless mode of communication is supported between the two (N) users.

- The two peer (N) entities in different open systems support communication between two (N) users by means of an (N) protocol.

The application layer differs from the other OSI layers in the following ways:

- As the top layer of the OSI model, the application layer does not provide service to a user at a higher OSI layer. Rather, it provides service to a user outside the OSI architecture. No ASAP is used.

- An application entity is made up of a collection of application-service entities (ASEs). A single logical connection, called an application association, is set up to support communication between two application users. This connection is used by all the application service entities supporting an application service.

- There is a separate application-level protocol between each pair of peer ASEs that make up an application entity.

The services of an application-layer entity are provided not to a higher OSI layer but to an application process. An application process is a set of resources, including processing resources, within an open system that may be used to perform a particular information-processing activity. The following examples of application processes are provided in ISO 7498:

- A person operating a banking terminal is a manual application process.

- A FORTRAN program executing in a computer center and accessing a remote database is a computerized application process; the remote-database-management system server is also an application process.

- A process-control program executing in a dedicated computer attached to some industrial equipment and linked into a plant control system is a physical application process.

Application processes in different open systems that wish to exchange information do so by means of the application layer. An application entity is incorporated as part of the application process. ISO 7498 states that the application entity consists of "the aspects of an application process pertinent to OSI." SC 21 N 5217[2] elaborates this concept by stating that the cooperation of application processes residing in different systems is modeled as cooperation of application entities expressed in an application protocol. The application entities are concerned with the interconnection aspects of cooperation.

Figure 5.10, based on concepts in ISO 9545, illustrates the structure of the application layer. The application entity that provides the interconnection functions for an application process is made up of a number of ASEs. An ASE is an indivisible component of an application entity. It is a combination of application communication functions that is defined for purposes of OSI service and protocol specification.

This modular approach facilitates the process of standardization. Some ASEs are of general use. For example, the association-control-service element (ACSE) is used to set up an application association between two application entities. The remote-operations-service element (ROSE) facilitates request-response interactions. Other ASEs are specific to a particular application. For example, the file transfer, access, and management (FTAM) service is provided by a single ASE.

---

2. Approved Commentaries on the Basic Reference Model for OSI.

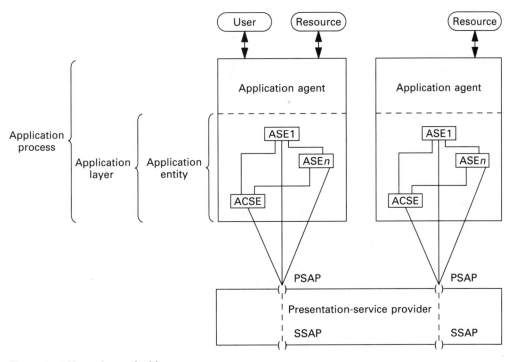

Figure 5.10 Upper-Layer Architecture

Other examples of specific-purpose ASEs are message exchange, job transfer, and virtual terminal access. ISO and CCITT have developed and are continuing to develop general-purpose and special-purpose ASE standards.

It should be emphasized that the ASEs do not form sublayers of the application layer, such as was found in the network layer. As Figure 5.10 indicates, an application entity consists of a collection of ASEs. The ACSE is always present, together with other general-purpose and special-purpose ASEs. Each ASE engages in a protocol with its peer ASE in an application entity in a remote system. Each ASE may rely on the services of other ASEs within its entity and/or the presentation service. Each application entity is unambiguously identified by means of a presentation-service-access point (PSAP), which is, in turn, mapped one-to-one onto an SSAP. If connection-oriented service is provided, a single application association is mapped onto a single presentation connection.

5.4   ASSOCIATION-CONTROL-SERVICE ELEMENT

One set of services that is a common requirement of almost all applications is that of establishing, maintaining, and terminating connections. Accordingly, service (ISO 8649, X.217) and protocol (ISO 8650, X.227) standards for an association-control-service element (ACSE) have been developed.

Table 5.8 Application-Layer Terms (ISO 7498, ISO 8649, ISO 9545)

Application association
　　A cooperative relationship between two application entities formed by the exchange of application-protocol control information through their use of presentation services.

Application context
　　A set of rules shared in common by two application-entity invocations in order to enable their cooperative operation. An application association has only one application context.

Application-entity invocation
　　A specific utilization of part or all of the capabilities of a given application entity in support of the communication requirements of an application-process invocation.

Application-process invocation
　　A specific utilization of part or all of the capabilities of a given application process in support of a specific occasion of information processing.

Application process
　　A set of resources, including processing resources within a real open system, that may be used to perform a particular information-processing activity.

Application-service element
　　A part of an application entity that provides an OSI environment capability, using underlying services where appropriate.

Application entity
　　The aspects of an application process pertinent to OSI.

5.4.1 Basic Concepts

Two concepts are essential to an understanding of the association-control facility: application association and application context, which are defined in Table 5.8. The concept of *application association* needs to be contrasted with that of presentation connection. The application association and the presentation connection are actually two different aspects of the same thing—namely, the relationship that exists between two application entities that are performing a shared task. From the point of view of the connection mechanisms needed to support information exchange, the relationship is a presentation connection. The presentation connection provides a "pipe" for the transfer of abstract data values with no constraints on the way these values are used. From the point of view of the information exchange itself, the relationship is an application association, which supports agreed procedures and shared semantics for the use of the corresponding presentation connection.

　　The application association supports the meaningful cooperative exchange between application entities within a defined *application context*. An application context is a mutually agreeable relationship between application entities in different open systems. The relationship exists for a period of time during which a cooperative task is performed. The relationship includes an agreement as to which application-service elements will be employed and the options and procedures related to those ASEs.

5.4.2   Association-Control Service

Table 5.9 lists the primitives and parameters for the ACSE service. The purpose of this service is to provide for the establishment and termination of application associations. Note that many of the parameters provided by a user are not used directly by the application association service but are mapped directly into parameters for the presentation or session service.

The A-ASSOCIATE service is used to set up an application association. A one-to-one correspondence exists between an application association and a presentation connection and, therefore, between an application association and a session connection. The A-ASSOCIATE primitives are supported by the P-CONNECT primitives (see Table 5.3). The added value of the association-control service is represented by those parameters that are carried in APDUs and not mapped onto the lower layers:

- Application-context name
- Calling, called, and responding application-process (AP) titles
- Calling, called, and responding application-entity (AE) qualifiers
- Calling, called, and responding AP invocation-identifier
- Calling, called, and responding AE invocation-identifier
- User information
- Result, result source
- Diagnostic

Application-context names identify the context; the responder may propose a different application context than the requester. The result of this negotiation is not defined in the standard but is application-specific. Names may be assigned to application contexts by standards organizations as part of the application-layer standards.

The next four entries on the preceding list are parameters that unambiguously identify application processes, application entities, and the invocations of application processes and entities (see Table 5.8).

Either the requester or the accepter may optionally include user information. Its meaning depends on the application context that accompanies the primitive.

The result parameter indicates the result of using the A-ASSOCIATE service and takes one of the following values:

- Accepted
- Rejected (permanent)
- Rejected (transient)

If the association is accepted, then an application association is created simultaneously with the underlying presentation and session connections.

The result-source parameter indicates that the result is provided by either the responding ACSE user, ACSE, or the presentation-service provider.

The diagnostic parameter is only used if the result parameter has the value rejected (permanent) or rejected (transient). If the result-source parameter has the value ACSE service provider, then the diagnostic parameter takes on one of the following values:

Table 5.9 Association-Control-Service Primitives and Parameters

Primitive	Parameters Carried in APDU	Parameters Mapped Directly to Presentation Service	Parameters Mapped Directly to Session Service
A-ASSOCIATE.request	Application-context name, calling AP title, calling AE qualifier, calling AP invocation-identifier, calling AE invocation-identifier, called AP title, called AE qualifier, called AP invocation-identifier, called AE invocation-identifier, user information	Mode, calling presentation address, called presentation address, presentation-context definition list, default presentation-context name, presentation requirements	Quality of service, session requirements, serial number, token assignment, session-connection identifier
A-ASSOCIATE.indication	Application-context name, calling AP title, calling AE qualifier, calling AP invocation-identifier, calling AE invocation-identifier, called AP title, called AE qualifier, called AP invocation-identifier, called AE invocation-identifier, user information	Mode, calling presentation address, called presentation address, presentation-context definition list, presentation-context-definition result list, default presentation-context name, presentation requirements	Quality of service, session requirements, serial number, token assignment, session-connection identifier
A-ASSOCIATE.response	Application-context name, responding AP title, responding AE qualifier, responding AP invocation-identifier, responding AE invocation-identifier, user information, result, diagnostic	Responding presentation address, presentation-context-definition result list, default presentation-context result, presentation requirements	Quality of service, session requirements, serial number, token assignment, session-connection identifier
A-ASSOCIATE.confirm	Application-context name, responding AP title, responding AE qualifier, responding AP invocation-identifier, responding AE invocation-identifier, user information, result, result source, diagnostic	Responding presentation address, presentation-context-definition result list, default presentation-context result, presentation requirements	Quality of service, session requirements, serial number, token assignment, session-connection identifier
A-RELEASE.request/indication	Reason, user information	—	—
A-RELEASE.response/confirm	Reason, user information, result	—	—
A-ABORT.request	User information	—	—
A-ABORT.indication	Abort source, user information	—	—
A-P-ABORT.indication		Provider reason	—

- No reason given
- No common ACSE version

If the result-source parameter has the value ACSE service user, then the diagnostic parameter takes on one of the following values:

- No reason given
- Application-context name not supported
- Calling AP title not recognized
- Calling AE qualifier not recognized
- Calling AP invocation-identifier not recognized
- Calling AE invocation-identifier not recognized
- Called AP title not recognized
- Called AE qualifier not recognized
- Called AP invocation-identifier not recognized
- Called AE invocation-identifier not recognized

Of the A-ASSOCIATE parameters, only the application-context name, the result, and the result-source parameters are mandatory. The others may be assumed to be set by prior agreement to simplify implementation.

The A-RELEASE service is used for the orderly release of an association. If the session negotiated-release functional unit was selected for the association, the responder may respond negatively, thus causing the unsuccessful completion of the release service and the continuation of the association. For the request and indication primitives, the reason parameter takes on one of the following values: normal, urgent, or user-defined. For the response and confirm primitives, it takes on one of the following values: normal, not finished, or user-defined. The result parameter indicates acceptance or rejection of the release request. If the release is successful, then the application association is released simultaneously with the underlying presentation and session connections.

The A-ABORT and A-P-ABORT services cause the termination of the application association simultaneously with the underlying presentation and session connections. With A-ABORT, the abort-source parameter indicates that the abort was initiated by either the ACSE or the other service user. With A-P-ABORT, the provider-reason parameter is mapped directly from the P-P-ABORT service.

5.4.3 Association-Control Protocol

Table 5.10 lists the application-protocol data units (APDUs) for the association-control protocol, together with their parameters. In keeping with the listing in the standards document, this table shows only those parameters that are actually part of the APDU and passed down to the presentation layer as presentation-service user data. In contrast, Table 5.4 lists PPDU parameters plus parameters that are passed directly to the session layer. There seems to be no particular significance to this stylistic change.

Table 5.11 shows how application-service primitives are mapped into presentation-service primitives via the APDUs. As with the presentation service, we see the tight coupling from the

Table 5.10 Association-Control Protocol Data Units and Parameters

APDU	Parameters
A-ASSOCIATE-REQUEST (AARQ)	Protocol version, application-context name, calling AP title, calling AE qualifier, calling AP invocation-identifier, calling AE invocation-identifier, called AP title, called AE qualifier, called AP invocation-identifier, called AE invocation-identifier, implementation information, user information
A-ASSOCIATE-RESPONSE (AARE)	Protocol version, application-context name, responding AP title, responding AE qualifier, responding AP invocation-identifier, responding AE invocation-identifier, result, result-source diagnostic, implementation information, user information
A-RELEASE-REQUEST (RLRQ)	Reason, user information
A-RELEASE-RESPONSE (RLRE)	Reason, user information
A-ABORT (ABRT)	Abort source, user information

application service down to the presentation service. For example, Figure 5.11 expands Figure 5.4 to show the interrelationship between application, presentation, and session in the setting up of a connection between entities.

As with PPDUs, the format of APDUs is defined using ASN.1.

5.5   RELIABLE-TRANSFER-SERVICE ELEMENT

Many, indeed most, applications require a reliable, connection-oriented data-exchange service. Such a service involves the selection of some of the session-service features, as mediated by the presentation service, and the use of the association-control-service element (ACSE). To avoid burdening each individual application with the complexity of invoking these services, the reliable-transfer-service element (RTSE) was developed. When RTSE is used by an application, the application does not access ACSE or the presentation service; instead, it uses a rather simplified inter-

Table 5.11 Relationship Among Application Association Primitives, Application Association APDUs, and Presentation Primitives

Application Primitives	APDUs	Presentation Primitives
A-ASSOCIATE.request/indication	AARQ	P-CONNECT.request/indication
A-ASSOCIATE.response/confirm	AARE	P-CONNECT.response/confirm
A-RELEASE.request/indication	RLRQ	P-RELEASE.request/indication
A-RELEASE.response/confirm	RLRE	P-RELEASE.response/confirm
A-ABORT.request/indication	ABRT	P-U-ABORT.request/indication
A-P-ABORT.indication	—	P-P-ABORT.indication

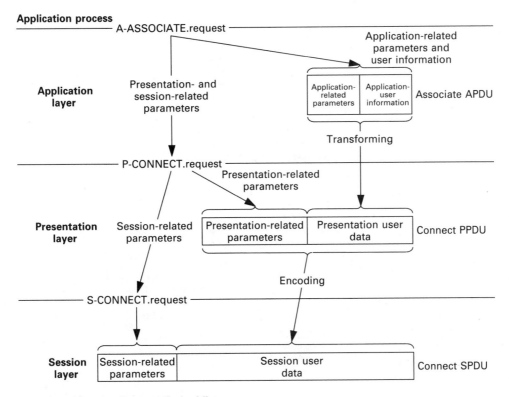

Figure 5.11 Connect-Request Embedding

face to RTSE and depends on RTSE to employ the services of ACSE, presentation, and session to provide reliable data delivery. The relationship is shown in Figure 5.12.

The term *reliable* here means far more than just that data are reliably delivered over an existing connection. RTSE provides an application-independent mechanism to recover from communications and end-system failure. It does so by exploiting the activity and synchronization facilities of the session service.

RTSE operates on the following principle: information is exchanged between application entities (AEs) using RTSE in the form of APDUs. It is the task of RTSE to ensure that each APDU is completely transferred between AEs exactly once or that the sending AE is warned of an exception.

5.5.1   Reliable-Transfer Service

The reliable-transfer service is defined in X.218 and ISO 9066-1. Table 5.12 lists the RTSE primitives and their parameters, and Figure 5.13 illustrates the operation of each.

5.5.1.1   RT-OPEN Service

The RT-OPEN service is a confirmed service that enables an RTSE user to request the establishment of an application association with another AE. Table 5.13 shows the parameters for each of

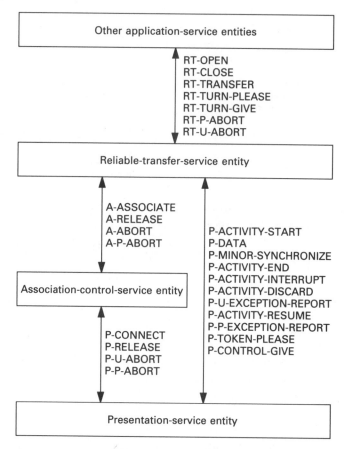

Figure 5.12 Relationship of RTSE to ACSE, Presentation Service, and Other ASEs

the four RT-OPEN-service primitives. As can be seen, most of the parameters are simply passed down to either ACSE or the presentation service. Only three parameters are unique to the RT-OPEN service and are carried in an RTSE APDU:

1. *Dialogue mode:* The type of use of the application association is either monologue or two-way-alternate. In the former case, user data are passed in only one direction. In the latter case, the two AEs may take turns sending user data.

2. *Initial turn:* indicates whether the RTSE user that is to have the turn initially is the association initiator or the association responder. For monologue mode, the user with the initial turn is the only user that may transmit data over this association.

3. *User data:* the user data associated with establishing the application association.

It is important to note that the monologue dialogue mode does not mean that all data transfer is in one direction only. Clearly, for reliable transfer, acknowledgments at lower OSI layers will

Table 5.12 Reliable-Transfer-Service Primitives and Parameters

Primitives	Parameters Used by RTSE Protocol	Parameters Passed through to ACSE	Parameters Passed through to Presentation Service
RT-OPEN.request	Dialogue mode, initial turn, user data	See Table 5.13.	See Table 5.13.
RT-OPEN.indication	Dialogue mode, initial turn, user data	See Table 5.13.	See Table 5.13.
RT-OPEN.response	User data	See Table 5.13.	See Table 5.13.
RT-OPEN.confirm	User data	See Table 5.13.	See Table 5.13.
RT-CLOSE.request/indication/response/confirm	—	Reason, user data	—
RT-TRANSFER.request	APDU, transfer time	—	—
RT-TRANSFER.indication	APDU	—	—
RT-TRANSFER.confirm	APDU, result	—	—
RT-TURN-PLEASE.request/indication	Priority	—	—
RT-TURN-GIVE.request/indication	—	—	—
RT-P-ABORT.indication	—	—	—
RT-U-ABORT.request/indication	User data	—	—

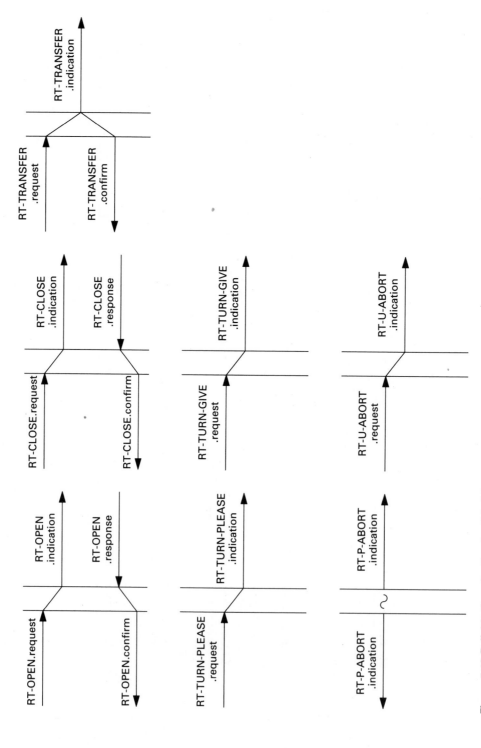

Figure 5.13 Reliable-Transfer-Service Primitives

Table 5.13 RT-OPEN-Service Parameters

Parameter	Request	Indication	Response	Confirm
Dialogue mode	M	M (=)		
Initial turn	MS	MS (=)		
User data	U	C (=)	U	C (=)
Mode	P	P		
Application-context name	A	A	A	A
Calling AP title	A	A		
Calling AP invocation-identifier	A	A		
Calling AE qualifier	A	A		
Calling AE invocation-identifier	A	A		
Called AP title	A	A		
Called AP invocation-identifier	A	A		
Called AE qualifier	A	A		
Called AE invocation-identifier	A	A		
Responding AP title			A	A
Responding AP invocation-identifier			A	A
Responding AE qualifier			A	A
Responding AE invocation-identifier			A	A
Result			A	A
Result source				A
Diagnostic			A	A
Calling presentation address	P	P		
Called presentation address	P	P		
Responding presentation address			P	P
Presentation-context-definition list	P	P	P	
Presentation-context-definition result list		P	P	P
Default presentation-context name	P	P		
Default presentation-context result		P	P	P

M = mandatory.

MS = mandatory, used for setting token parameter for session service.

U = user option.

C = conditional.

(=) = meter value is equal to the value to its left in the table.

A = passed through to ACSE.

P = passed through to presentation service.

need to flow in the opposite direction. In fact, both RTSE dialogue modes are supported over a two-way-alternate session connection.

The RT-OPEN service makes use of the ACSE A-ASSOCIATE service for establishing the application association.

5.5.1.2 RT-TRANSFER Service

The RT-TRANSFER service enables an RTSE user that possesses the turn to request the reliable transfer of an APDU over a previously established application association. It may do so only when there is no outstanding RT-TRANSFER.confirm primitive.

Figure 5.13 indicates the functionality of this service, which differs from the usual confirmed and unconfirmed services. In this case, there are only three primitives. The RT-TRANS-FER.confirm primitive includes a result parameter that signifies that the APDU has been secured by the receiving RTSE provider (positive confirm) or that the requested transfer of an APDU could not be completed within the specified transfer time (negative confirm). The transfer time is supplied by the requester of the service in the RT-TRANSFER.request primitive.

Note that the way in which this service is defined enforces a discipline that only a single APDU may be transferred at a time. The sender must await confirmation before requesting another transfer. Once the confirmation is received, the requester is assured that the APDU is secured even if a system crash or communication failure occurs.

The RT-TRANSFER service makes use of the following presentation services: P-ACTIVITY START, P-DATA, P-MINOR-SYNCHRONIZE, and P-ACTIVITY-END. The transfer mechanism is discussed in subsection 5.5.2, "Reliable-Transfer Protocol."

5.5.1.3   RT-CLOSE Service

The RT-CLOSE service is a confirmed service that enables the association-initiating RTSE user to request the release of an established application. It may do so only if it possesses the turn and there is no outstanding RT-TRANSFER.confirm primitive. The release is without loss of information in transit.

The RT-CLOSE service makes use of the ACSE A-RELEASE service for releasing the application association.

5.5.1.4   RT-TURN-PLEASE Service

The RT-TURN-PLEASE service is a nonconfirmed service that enables the RTSE user that does not possess the turn to request the turn. The turn may be requested by either user in order to enable it to transfer APDUs, and it may be requested by the association initiator in order to release the association.

The request conveys the priority of the action to be taken. A priority of zero, the highest priority, is used to request the turn for association release. A range of other priorities may be associated with the transfer of APDUs; these are application-dependent. The receiving user employs the priority as guidance concerning when to relinquish the turn.

The RT-TURN-PLEASE service makes use of the P-TOKEN-PLEASE presentation service.

5.5.1.5   RT-TURN-GIVE Service

The RT-TURN-GIVE service is a nonconfirmed service that enables the RTSE user that possesses the turn to relinquish the turn to its peer. It may do so only if there is no outstanding RT-TRANS-FER.confirm primitive.

The RT-TURN-GIVE service makes use of the P-CONTROL-GIVE presentation service.

5.5.1.6   RT-P-ABORT Service

The RT-P-ABORT service provides an indication to the RTSE user that the application association cannot be maintained. That is, the association has been lost and cannot be recovered. This service is initiated by the provider. For the side whose user has the turn, RTSE will first issue a negative RT-TRANSFER.confirm if there is an outstanding APDU. For the side whose user does not have the turn, RTSE will first delete any partially received APDUs prior to issuing the RT-P-ABORT.indication.

The RT-P-ABORT service makes use of the ACSE A-ABORT service.

5.5.1.7   RT-U-ABORT Service

The RT-U-ABORT service is an unconfirmed service that enables an RTSE user to abort the application association. The abort may be requested by either the user with the turn or the user without the turn.

The RT-U-ABORT service makes use of the ACSE A-ABORT service.

5.5.2   Reliable-Transfer Protocol

The reliable-transfer protocol, specified in X.228 and ISO 9066-2, provides a relatively straightforward mapping of RTSE service primitives to RTSE APDUs. Table 5.14 lists the APDUs, their parameters, and their relationship to RTSE service primitives.

The RTSE protocol consists of the elements of procedure listed in Table 5.15.

5.5.2.1   Association Establishment and Release

The procedure for establishing and releasing an association is straightforward. When an RTSE user issues an RT-OPEN.request, the RTSE-protocol entity issues an RTORQ APDU to the other side via the A-ASSOCIATE service. The APDU carries the dialogue-mode and user data parameters from the initiating RTSE user to the responding RTSE user. The turn parameter from the RT-OPEN.request is used to set the token-assignment parameter in the A-ASSOCIATE.request primitive. In addition, the following parameters are generated by the sending RTSE-protocol entity and used by the receiving RTSE-protocol entity:

- *Checkpoint size:* allows the negotiation of the maximum amount of data that may be sent between two minor synchronization points. A value of zero invites the responding protocol entity to select the size.

- *Window size:* allows negotiation of the maximum number of outstanding minor synchronization points before data transfer shall be suspended.

The relevance of these two parameters will become clear in the discussion of user data transfer, in the following subsection.

Upon receipt of the RTORQ, the receiving RTSE entity issues an RT-OPEN.indication to its user. If it receives a positive response, it issues an RTOAC. If it receives a negative response, it issues an RTORJ. The ultimate result is a positive or negative RT-OPEN.confirm issued to the requesting user.

The association-release operation does not involve any RTSE APDUs. RTSE simply uses the A-RELEASE service to support the RT-CLOSE service.

5.5.2.2   User Data Transfer

Recall that the RTSE service enforces the discipline that only a single RTSE user APDU at a time may be transferred. Each such transfer is managed as a session activity. Once the activity is started, using the P-ACTIVITY-START service, there are two transfer options:

1. If checkpointing is not allowed, the RTSE user data are transferred as a single RTTR APDU using the P-DATA service.

2. If checkpointing is allowed, the RTSE user data are transferred in segments in a series of RTTR APDUs, the maximum size of each being the negotiated checkpoint size. The initiator follows each RTTR with a minor synchronization point. The responder must acknowledge

Table 5.14 RTSE Service Primitives and APDUs

(a) Use of ACSE

RTSE Service Primitive	RTSE APDU	APDU Parameters Used by Protocol Entities	APDU Parameters to/from RTSE Users	ACSE Service Primitive
RT-OPEN.request/indication	RTORQ	Checkpoint size, window size	Dialogue mode, user data	A-ASSOCIATE.request/indication
RT-OPEN.response/confirm	RTOAC	Checkpoint size, window size	User data	A-ASSOCIATE.response/confirm
RT-OPEN.response/confirm	RTORJ	Refuse reason	User data	A-ASSOCIATE.response/confirm
RT-CLOSE.request/indication	—	—	—	A-RELEASE.request/indication
RT-CLOSE.response/confirm	—	—	—	A-RELEASE.response/confirm
Association recovery	RTORQ	Checkpoint size, window size, session-connection identifier	Dialogue mode	A-ASSOCIATE.request/indication
	RTOAC	Checkpoint size, window size, session-connection identifier	Dialogue mode	A-ASSOCIATE.response/confirm
	RTORJ	Refuse reason	—	A-ASSOCIATE.response/confirm
Association abort	RTAB	Abort reason, reflected parameter	—	A-ABORT.request/indication
Association-provider abort	—	—	—	A-P-ABORT.indication
RT-P-ABORT.indication	RTAB	Abort reason	—	A-ABORT.request/indication
RT-U-ABORT.request/indication	RTAB	Abort reason	User data	A-ABORT.request/indication

(b) Use of presentation service

RTSE Service Primitive	RTSE APDU	APDU Parameters to/from RTSE Users	ACSE Service Primitive
RT-TRANSFER. request	—	—	P-ACTIVITY-START.request/indication
	RTTR	User data part	P-DATA.request/indication
	—	—	P-MINOR-SYNCHRONIZE.request/indication/response/confirm
RT-TRANSFER.indication/confirm	—	—	P-ACTIVITY-END.request/indication/response/confirm
RT-TURN-PLEASE.request/indication	RTTP	Priority	P-TOKEN-PLEASE.request/indication
RT-TURN-GIVE.request/indication	—	—	P-CONTROL-GIVE.request/indication
User exception report	—	—	P-U-EXCEPTION-REPORT.request/indication
Provider exception report	—	—	P-P-EXCEPTION-REPORT.indication
Transfer interrupt	—	—	P-ACTIVITY-INTERRUPT.request/indication/response/confirm
Transfer discard	—	—	P-ACTIVITY-DISCARD.request/indication/response/confirm
Transfer resumption	—	—	P-ACTIVITY-RESUME.request/indication

Table 5.15 RTSE Protocol Elements of Procedure

a. Association establishment
b. Association release
c. Transfer
d. Turn-please
e. Turn-give
f. Error reporting
    1. User exception report
    2. Provider exception report
g. Error handling
    1. Transfer interrupt
    2. Transfer discard
    3. Association abort
    4. Association-provider abort
h. Error recovery
    1. Transfer resumption (for recovery from g.1 or after successful h.3)
    2. Transfer retry (for recovery from g.2)
    3. Association recovery (for recovery from g.3 or g.4)
i. Abort
    1. Transfer abort (recovery from g.1, g.2, g.3, g.4 not possible)
    2. Provider retry (recovery from g.1, g.2, g.3, g.4 not possible)
    3. User abort

each minor synchronization point as soon as it has secured the corresponding RTTR. Meanwhile, the initiator may continue to send RTTRs while waiting for sync point acknowledgments up to the agreed window size. Thus, if the window size is three, the initiator may have up to three outstanding RTTRs.

Once the responding RTSE entity has secured the entire RTSE user data and notified the requesting RTSE, the requesting RTSE ends the activity.

5.5.2.3 Turn Management

In response to an RT-TURN-PLEASE.request, an RTSE uses the P-TOKEN-PLEASE service to request the tokens, and therefore to request the turn. The request includes an RTTP APDU, which carries the priority of the request.

When an RTSE user decides to pass the turn to its peer by using the RT-TURN-GIVE service, the RTSE entity employs the P-CONTROL-GIVE service to pass the turn by passing possession of the tokens.

5.5.2.4 Error Management

Error management consists of a set of procedures performed by the RTSE-protocol entity that are transparent to the RTSE user. The only time that this activity is visible to the user is if the recovery from an error fails, necessitating an abort of the association that is reported to the RTSE user.

Table 5.15 lists the various elements of error management, and Table 5.14 shows the relationship of these elements to RTSE APDUs and lower-level services.

5.5.2.5   Abort

Abort procedures are performed when a successful recovery from one of the error-handling procedures is not possible.

If the RTSE entity fails in its attempt to deliver a user APDU, it issues an RT-TRANS-FER.confirm primitive with a result value of "APDU not transferred." It then issues an RT-P-ABORT to its user to abort the association with the other RTSE user.

An RTSE user may also initiate an abort by using the RT-U-ABORT service.

5.6   REMOTE-OPERATIONS-SERVICE ELEMENT

Though not as universally employed as the ACSE, the remote-operations-service element (ROSE) is one of the most widely used of the general-purpose application-service entities. For example, it will be seen in Chapter 12 that the common management information protocol (CMIP) makes use of ROSE. ROSE is intended to support interactive types of applications, which are characterized by a request by one application for another application to perform some operation. In the programming field, a common example of this mechanism is the remote-procedure call.

5.6.1   Principles

The basic service provided by ROSE is the facility for invoking an operation on a remote open system. The application entity (AE) invoking the operation issues a request to the peer AE, specifying a particular operation to be performed. The other AE attempts to perform the operation and may report the outcome of the attempt. The interchange between the two entities is carried out in the context of an application association.

5.6.1.1   Operation Class

Operations invoked by one application entity (*the invoker*) are performed by the other application entity (*the performer*). The interaction between two entities that results in an operation's being attempted is characterized by an operation class, which is agreed between the two entities for each separate invocation. The operation class is defined by two characteristics of the interchange: the reporting behavior of the AE attempting the operation and whether the interchange is synchronous or asynchronous (Table 5.16).

The performing AE may observe one of four types of reporting behavior:

1. Always report a result, whether it is success or failure.

2. Only report a failure.

3. Only report a success.

4. Do not report the result.

If a result, success or failure, is always reported, then the invoking AE has the option of waiting for a report before continuing or not. With synchronous operation, the invoker requires a reply from the performer before invoking another operation. With asynchronous operation, the invoker may continue to invoke further operations without awaiting a reply.

Table 5.16 ROSE Operation Classes

		Operation Mode	
		Synchronous	**Asynchronous**
Reporting Mode	If success, return result reply. If failure, return error reply.	Operation class 1	Operation class 2
	If success, no reply. If failure, return error reply.	—	Operation class 3
	If success, return result reply. If failure, no reply.	—	Operation class 4
	If success, no reply. If failure, no reply.	—	Operation class 5

5.6.1.2 Association Class

ROSE may be used by two application entities that share an application association to invoke one or more operations. The AE that initiates an application association (by issuing an A-ASSOCI-ATE.request to ACSE) is called the *association initiator,* while the AE that responds to the request is called the *association responder.* The two AEs must agree on one of three association classes that will hold for the life of the association:

Association class 1:   Only the association initiator can invoke operations.
Association class 2:   Only the association responder can invoke operations.
Association class 3:   Both the association initiator and the association responder
                        can invoke operations.

The association class is an attribute of an application context, and must be selected at the time that the association is set up using ACSE.

When association class 3 is selected, it is possible to group operations into a set of linked operations, which is formed by one parent operation and one or more child operations. The sequence is as follows:

1. One AE invokes an operation on the peer AE, referred to as the parent operation.

2. The performer of the parent operation may invoke zero, one, or more child operations during the execution of the parent operation. Thus, each of these child operations is performed by the AE that is the invoker of the corresponding parent operation.

3 . Each child operation may, in turn, function as a parent operation to trigger zero, one, or more child operations in a recursive fashion.

Figure 5.14 illustrates the concept of linked operations.

5.6.2 Remote-Operations-Service Definition

The remote-operations service is defined in X.219 and ISO 9072-1. Table 5.17 lists the remote-operations-service primitives and parameters.

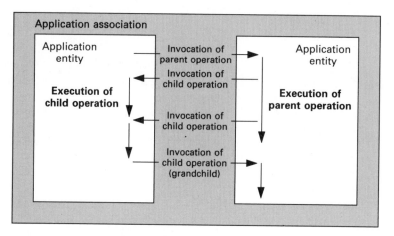

Figure 5.14 Linked Operations

The RO-INVOKE primitive is used by the invoker to request an operation of the performer. The parameters of this primitive are:

- *Operation value:* identifies the operation to be performed. The identity and nature of the operation are beyond the scope of ROSE and must be agreed between the two application entities.

- *Operation class:* indicates one of the five operation classes (Table 5.16).

- *Argument:* the argument or list of arguments that accompany the operation. Again, the nature of these arguments is beyond the scope of ROSE.

- *Invoke ID:* identifies the request of an RO-INVOKE service and is subsequently used to correlate this request with the corresponding replies. This parameter is needed for asynchronous operation.

- *Linked ID:* if this parameter is present, the invoked operation is a child operation and the parameter is the invoke ID of the linked parent operation.

Table 5.17 Remote-Operations-Service Primitives and Parameters

RO-INVOKE.request (operation value, operation class, argument, invoke ID, linked ID, priority)

RO-INVOKE.indication (operation value, argument, invoke ID, linked ID)

RO-RESULT.request (operation value, result, invoke ID, priority)
RO-RESULT.indication (operation value, result, invoke ID)

RO-ERROR.request (error value, error parameter, invoke ID, priority)
RO-ERROR.indication (error value, error parameter, invoke ID)

RO-REJECT-U.request (reject reason, invoke ID, priority)
RO-REJECT-U.indication (reject reason, invoke ID)

RO-REJECT-P.indication (invoke ID, returned parameters, reject reason)

- *Priority:* identifies the priority of the transfer of the corresponding APDU relative to other APDUs to be exchanged between the AEs.

The RO-RESULT primitives are used to provide a reply in the event of a successful operation. The result parameter provides information concerning a successfully performed operation and is beyond the scope of ROSE.

The RO-ERROR primitives are used to provide a reply in the event of an unsuccessfully performed operation. The error-value parameter indicates the type of error, and error parameter provides additional information about the error. Both parameters are beyond the scope of ROSE.

The RO-REJECT-U service is used by a ROSE user to reject a request (RO-INVOKE) if the user has detected a problem. It may also be used to reject a reply (RO-RESULT, RO-ERROR). Table 5.18 lists the values of the reject-reason parameter.

Table 5.18 Values of the Reject-Reason Parameter for the Remote-Operations Service

(a) ROSE user reject of an RO-INVOKE

Parameter Value	Interpretation
Duplication invocation	Invoke ID parameter is inconsistent or conflicts with outstanding IDs.
Unrecognized operation	Operation is not one of those agreed between the ROSE users.
Mistyped argument	Type of the operation argument is not that agreed between the ROSE users.
Resource limitation	Performer is unable to perform the invoked operation due to resource limitation.
Initiator releasing	Association initiator is not willing to perform the invoked operation because it is about to attempt to release the application association.
Unrecognized linked ID	No operation is in progress with an invoke ID equal to the specified linked ID.
Linked response unexpected	Invoked operation referred to by the linked ID is not a parent operation.
Unexpected child operation	Invoked child operation is not one that the invoked parent operation referred to by the linked ID allows.

(b) ROSE user reject of an RO-RESULT

Parameter Value	Interpretation
Unrecognized invocation	No operation with the specified invoke ID is in progress.
Result response unexpected	Invoked operation does not report a result.
Mistyped result	Type of the result parameter is not that agreed between the ROSE users.

Table 5.18 (*Cont.*)

(c) ROSE user reject of an RO-ERROR

Parameter Value	Interpretation
Unrecognized invocation	No operation with the specified invoke ID is in progress.
Error response unexpected	Invoked operation does not report a failure.
Unrecognized error	Reported error is not one of those agreed between the ROSE users.
Unexpected error	Reported error is not one that the invoked operation may report.
Mistyped parameter	Type of the error parameter is not that agreed between the ROSE users.

(d) ROSE provider reject of an APDU

Parameter Value	Interpretation
Unrecognized APDU	Type of the APDU is not one of the four defined for the ROSE protocol.
Mistyped APDU	Structure of the APDU does not conform to the ROSE protocol.
Badly structured APDU	Structure of the APDU does not conform to the standard notation and encoding.

5.6.3 Remote-Operations Protocol

The remote-operations protocol, specified in X.229 and ISO 9072-2, provides a relatively straightforward mapping of ROSE-service primitives to ROSE APDUs. Table 5.19 lists the APDUs, their parameters, and their relationship to ROSE-service primitives.

ROSE has two options for transferring APDUs: the P-DATA presentation service can be used, or alternatively, the reliable-transfer-service element (RTSE) can be used.

5.7 SUMMARY

The presentation layer is concerned with the syntax of information exchanged between applications. At this layer, a general-purpose presentation service and protocol are provided to enable application-level users to define and manage contexts for the exchange of information. Each context defines the syntax that is used in the exchange. A useful tool for defining syntax, and one that is enjoying widespread use in OSI standards, is abstract syntax notation one (ASN.1). ASN.1 is a language that is used for specifying the syntax of information to be exchanged and the protocol data units used in the exchange.

The application layer contains applications that are directly useful to end users in the accomplishment of distributed functions, such as file transfer, electronic mail, and remote terminal access. In addition, a number of general-purpose application service elements have been defined. These elements are modules that implement commonly used functions and that are used by other

Table 5.19 Remote-Operations Protocol Data Units

APDU	Parameters	ROSE-Service Primitives
RO-INVOKE (ROIV)	Invoke ID, linked ID, operation value, argument	RO-INVOKE.request/indication
RO-RESULT (RORS)	Invoke ID, operation value, result	RO-RESULT.request/indication
RO-ERROR (ROER)	Invoke ID, error value, error parameter	RO-ERROR.request/indication
RO-REJECT (RORJ)	Invoke ID, problem	RO-REJECT-P.request/indication RO-REJECT-U.indication

applications. Three of the most important application-service elements that have been standardized are:

- *Association-control-service element (ACSE)*: This service is used to establish, maintain, and terminate application-level associations between applications.

- *Reliable-transfer-service element (RTSE)*: This service provides a simplified interface for applications that require a generic reliable exchange mechanism. RTSE takes care of all of the details of invoking ACSE and presentation services on behalf of users, and provides a data-exchange service that is reliable both in terms of data delivery and in terms of recovery from communications and end-system failure.

- *Remote-operations-service element (ROSE)*: This service supports interactive types of applications, which are characterized by a request by one application triggering an action by another application and a response by that application giving the result of the action.

Part 2
Integrated Services
Digital Network

Perhaps the most important development in the computer-communications industry over the remainder of this decade will be the evolution of the integrated services digital network (ISDN) and broadband ISDN.

This part begins with an overview of the original ISDN design, now sometimes referred to as narrowband ISDN. Although narrowband ISDN is important, it does not represent a major advance in networking technology. Rather, it constitutes a packaging and standardization of preexisting digital wide area networking services and facilities. Chapter 6 summarizes the standards developed for narrowband ISDN.

Chapter 7 is devoted to perhaps the most important aspect of narrowband ISDN: frame relay. Although frame relay is being used in contexts other than ISDN, it is within the context of ISDN that the standards for frame relay are being developed. As a replacement for traditional X.25 packet switching, frame relay represents a major advance in wide area network support for high-speed data transport.

Chapter 8 examines broadband ISDN and its most important aspect: cell relay, or asynchronous transfer mode (ATM). The chapter also looks at a related set of standards, known as SONET (synchronous optical network) or SDH (synchronous digital hierarchy).

6
ISDN Overview

Rapid advances in computer and communication technologies have resulted in the increasing merger of these two fields. The lines have blurred among computing, switching, and digital transmission equipment, and the same digital techniques are being used for data, voice, and image transmission. Merging and evolving technologies—coupled with increasing demands for efficient and timely collection, processing, and dissemination of information—are leading to the development of integrated systems that transmit and process all types of data. The ultimate goal of this evolution is something its proponents—some of the most powerful forces in the computing and telecommunications industries—call the integrated services digital network (ISDN).

The ISDN is intended to be a worldwide public telecommunications network to replace existing public telecommunications networks and deliver a wide variety of services. The ISDN is defined by the standardization of user interfaces and will be implemented as a set of digital switches and paths supporting a broad range of traffic types and providing value-added processing services. In practice, there will be multiple networks, implemented within national boundaries, but from the user's point of view, there will be a single, uniformly accessible, worldwide network.

The impact of ISDN on both users and vendors will be profound. To control the evolution and impact of ISDN, a massive effort at standardization is under way. Although ISDN standards are still evolving, both the technology and the emerging implementation strategy are well understood.

Despite the fact that ISDN has yet to achieve the universal deployment hoped for, it is already in its second generation. The first generation, sometimes referred to as *narrowband ISDN,* is based on the use of a 64-Kbps channel as the basic unit of switching and has a circuit-switching orientation. The major technical contribution of the narrowband ISDN effort has been frame relay. The second generation, referred to as *broadband ISDN* (BISDN), supports very high data rates (hundreds of megabits per second) and has a packet-switching orientation. The major technical contribution of the broadband ISDN effort has been asynchronous transfer mode (ATM), also known as cell relay.

This chapter provides an overview of narrowband ISDN. The following two chapters treat frame relay and broadband ISDN, respectively.

6.1   ISDN STANDARDS

The development of ISDN is governed by a set of recommendations issued by CCITT, called the I series of recommendations.[1] These recommendations, or standards, were first issued in 1984. A more complete set was issued in 1988.

6.1.1   The 1988 I-Series Recommendations

The bulk of the description of ISDN is contained in the I series of recommendations, with some related topics covered in other recommendations. The characterization of ISDN contained in these recommendations is centered on three main areas:

1. The standardization of services offered to users, so as to enable services to be internationally compatible

2. The standardization of user-network interfaces, so as to enable terminal equipment to be portable and to assist in achieving the first objective on this list

3. The standardization of ISDN capabilities to the degree necessary to allow user-network and network-network interworking and thus achieve the first and second objectives

A list of the 1988 I-series recommendations, together with a brief description of each recommendation, is provided in Appendix 6A. Figure 6.1 illustrates the relationship among the various I-series standards. The 1984 set contained recommendations in series I.100 through I.400. Some updates and expansions occurred in these series in the 1985–1988 study period. The I.500 and I.600 series were left for further study in 1984, and a preliminary set of specifications was ready for 1988, with additional work to be done in the 1989–1992 study period.

6.1.1.1   I.100 Series—General Concepts

The I.100 series serves as a broad introduction to ISDN. The general structure of the ISDN recommendations is presented as well as a glossary of terms. I.120 provides an overall description of ISDN and the expected evolution of ISDNs. I.130 introduces terminology and concepts that are used in the I.200 series to specify services.

6.1.1.2   I.200 Series—Service Aspects

The I.200 series is, in a sense, the most important part of the CCITT ISDN recommendations. Here, the services to be provided to users are specified. This may be looked on as a set of requirements that the ISDN must satisfy. In the ISDN glossary (I.112), the term *service* is defined as, "That which is offered by an Administration or recognized private operating agency (RPOA) to its customers in order to satisfy a specific telecommunication requirement." Although this is a very general definition, the term *service* has come to have a very specific meaning in CCITT, a meaning that is somewhat different from the use of that term in an OSI (open systems interconnection) context. For CCITT, a standardized service is characterized by Cerni (1984) as follows:

■   Complete, guaranteed end-to-end compatibility

■   CCITT-standardized terminals, including procedures

---

1.   Some recommendations have two designations. For example, I.450 is also designated as Q.930. When such standards are referenced in this book, both designations are supplied (e.g., I.450/Q.930).

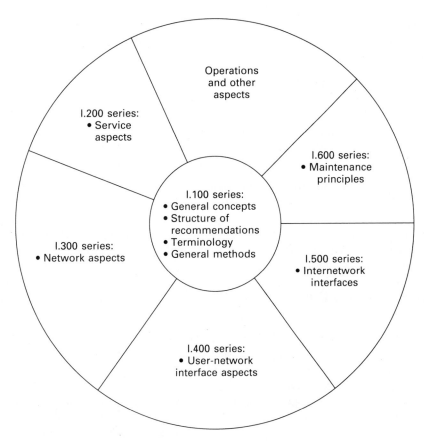

Figure 6.1 I-Series Recommendations

- A listing of the service subscribers in an international directory
- CCITT-standardized testing and maintenance procedures
- Charging and accounting rules

6.1.1.3   I.300 Series—Network Aspects

Whereas the I.200 series focuses on the user, in terms of the services provided to the user, the I.300 series focuses on the network, in terms of how the network goes about providing those services. A protocol reference model is presented that, while based on the seven-layer OSI model, attempts to account for the complexity of a connection that may involve two or more users (e.g., a conference call) plus a related common-channel signaling dialogue. Issues such as numbering and addressing are covered. There is also a discussion of ISDN connection types.

6.1.1.4   I.400 Series—User-Network Aspects

The I.400 series deals with the interface between the user and the network. Three major topics are addressed:

1. *Physical configurations:* the issue of how ISDN functions are configured into equipment. The standards specify functional groupings and define reference points between those groupings.

2. *Transmission rates:* the data rates and combinations of data rates to be offered to the user.

3. *Protocol specifications:* the protocols at OSI layers 1 through 3 that specify the user-network interaction.

6.1.1.5   I.500 Series—Internetwork Interfaces

ISDN will support services that are also provided on older circuit-switched and packet-switched networks. Thus, it is necessary to provide interworking between an ISDN and other types of networks to allow communications between terminals belonging to equivalent services offered through different networks. The I.500 series deals with the various network issues that arise in attempting to define interfaces between ISDN and other types of networks.

6.1.1.6   I.600 Series—Maintenance Principles

The I.600 series provides guidance for maintenance of the ISDN subscriber installation, the network portion of the ISDN basic-access, primary-access, and higher-data-rate services. Maintenance principles and functions are related to the reference configuration and general architecture of ISDN. A key function that is identified in the series is loopback. In general, loopback testing is used for failure localization and verification.

6.1.2   Ongoing Work and the Interim 1990 Recommendations

With the publication of the 1988 set of ISDN recommendations, much of the work on ISDN was complete. The focus for the 1989–1992 study period has shifted to broadband ISDN. However, a number of details on ISDN remain to be resolved, and these were assigned to various working groups for the 1989–1992 study period.

Because of the pace of change of technology and the rapidity with which new products and services are being introduced into the telecommunications arena, CCITT is finding that the traditional four-year cycle is inadequate. This is especially so in the case of broadband ISDN. However, even in the ordinary ISDN area, there is a desire to produce results outside of the normal four-year schedule. Accordingly, a number of the CCITT working groups published interim new recommendations and interim revisions to existing recommendations in 1990. Those that relate to ISDN (as opposed to BISDN) are listed in Appendix 6B.

6.2   ISDN SERVICES

The I.200 series of CCITT recommendations, referred to as *service capabilities,* provides a classification and method of description of the telecommunication services supported by ISDN. These recommendations encompass existing services and define additional ones. The purpose of the recommendations is to provide a unifying framework for viewing these services and to set forth the user requirements for ISDN. The series, however, does not impose implementation or configuration guidelines. That is, the way in which the services are to be provided is left open. For example, the description of a teletex service does not presuppose which organization (user, private network, public network, information-service provider, etc.) provides the various elements that make up a complete teletex service.

Three types of services are defined by CCITT: bearer services, teleservices, and supplementary services. *Bearer services* provide the means to convey information (speech, data, video, etc.)

between users in real time and without alteration of the content of the message. These services correspond to the lower three layers of the OSI model. *Teleservices* combine the transportation function with the information-processing function. They employ bearer services to transport data and, in addition, provide a set of higher-layer functions, which correspond to OSI layers 4 through 7. Whereas bearer services define requirements for, and are provided by, network functions, teleservices include terminal as well as network capabilities. Examples of teleservices are telephony, teletex, videotex, and message handling. Both bearer services and teleservices may be enhanced by *supplementary services*. A supplementary service is one that may be used in conjunction with one or more of the bearer services or teleservices. It cannot be used alone. An example is reverse charging. This can be used to reverse charges on a circuit-switched call or a packet-switched virtual call. Reverse charging can also be used with a teleservice, such as the message-handling service, to create a "collect message."

In each of these three categories (bearer, teleservice, supplementary), there are a number of specific services defined by CCITT. To characterize, and differentiate, these various services, a collection of *attributes* has been defined. Each service is characterized by specific values assigned to each descriptive attribute. This method makes it easy to precisely define a service and to compare different services.

Table 6.1 lists the attributes that have so far been defined by CCITT (in I.140). A distinction is made between a communication and a connection. These terms are defined as follows in I.112:

Communication: The transfer of information according to agreed conventions.

Connection: A concatenation of transmission channels or telecommunication circuits, switching and other functional units set up to provide for the transfer of signals between two or more points in a telecommunication network, to support a single communication.

Thus, a communication is a user-oriented concept, and a connection is a network-oriented concept. Those attributes that refer to communication are used to characterize ISDN service, whereas those attributes that refer to connections are used to characterize ISDN connections.

6.2.1   Bearer Services

So far, a total of 11 different bearer services have been defined by CCITT; these are listed in Table 6.2.

The first four defined services provide for the capability of 64-Kbps data transfer. This data rate is the fundamental building block of ISDN services. The first of these—known as *64-Kbps, unrestricted, 8-kHz structured*—is the most general-purpose service at that data rate. The term *unrestricted* means that the information is transferred without alteration; this is also known as a transparent bearer service. Users may employ this service for any application that requires a data rate of 64 Kbps.

The term *8-kHz structured* means that, in addition to bit transmission, a structure is transferred between customers. When one user transmits information to another user, the transmission is accompanied by 8-kHz timing information, which delimits the data in 8-bit units. This 8-kHz structural integrity implies that octets are preserved within the corresponding time interval; that is, an octet is never split across a time-interval boundary. This applies in particular to speech, which requires the 8-kHz structure in addition to the 64-Kbps information flow so as to enable the octets,

Table 6.1 Service and Network Attributes

Service Attributes		Network Attributes	
Bearer services		**Connection types**	
1	Information-transfer mode	1	Information-transfer mode
2	Information-transfer rate	2	Information-transfer rate
3	Information-transfer capability	3	Information-transfer susceptance
4	Structure	4	Establishment of connection
5	Establishment of communication	5	Symmetry
6	Symmetry	6	Connection configuration
7	Communication configuration	7	Structure
8	Access channel and rate	8	Channel (rate)
9-1	Signaling-access protocol layer 1	9	Connection-control protocol
9-2	Signaling-access protocol layer 2	10	Information-transfer coding/protocol
9-3	Signaling-access protocol layer 3	11	Network performance
9-4	Information-access protocol layer 1	12	Network interworking
9-5	Information-access protocol layer 2	13	Operations and management
9-6	Information-access protocol layer 3	**Connection elements**	
10	Supplementary services provided	1 through 13, as for "Connection types"	
11	Quality of service		
12	Interworking possibilities		
13	Operational and commercial		
Teleservices			
1 through 9-6, as for "Bearer services"			
10	Type of user information		
11	Layer-4 protocol		
12	Layer-5 protocol		
13	Layer-6 protocol		
14	Layer-7 protocol		
15	Supplementary services provided		
16	Quality of service		
17	Interworking possibilities		
18	Operational and commercial		

formed by speech encoding, to be recognized at the receiving side. In text transmission, character boundaries are preserved. Thus, there is no need for the user to provide an in-band, user-to-user synchronization scheme.

The service referred to as *64-Kbps, 8-kHz structured, usable for speech information transfer* defines a specific structure for the digital signal—namely, pulse code modulation (PCM), as defined in CCITT Recommendation G.711. Because the network may assume that the encoded data are speech, it may use processing techniques appropriate for speech, such as analog transmission, echo cancelation, and low-bit-rate voice encoding. Because these transformations may not be precisely reversible, bit integrity is not guaranteed. However, the received signal should produce a high-quality reproduction of the transmitted voice signal. In other respects, this service is the same

Table 6.2 ISDN Bearer Services (I.230)

Circuit-Mode Bearer Services	Packet-Mode Bearer Services
64-Kbps, unrestricted, 8-kHz structured	Virtual call and permanent virtual circuit
64-Kbps, 8-kHz structured, usable for speech information transfer	Connectionless (further study)
64-Kbps, 8-kHz structured, usable for 3.1-kHz audio information transfer	User signaling (further study)
Alternate speech/64-kbps, unrestricted, 8-kHz structured	
2×64-Kbps, unrestricted, 8-kHz structured	
384-Kbps, unrestricted, 8-kHz structured	
1,536-Kbps, unrestricted, 8-kHz structured	
1,920-Kbps, unrestricted, 8-kHz structured	

as the unrestricted service. The restriction to speech allows the use of processing techniques in the network that may optimize the transmission. Furthermore, the network may perform conversions between digital encoding laws. For example, the G.711 standard specifies two versions of the PCM algorithm: μ law and A law. The former is used in North America and Japan; the latter is used in the rest of the world. Thus, the voice signal on a connection that crosses these geographic boundaries is automatically converted.

The service referred to as *64-Kbps, 8-kHz structured, usable for 3.1-kHz audio information transfer* assumes that digitized audio information is being transmitted. This permits routing over analog circuits using codes, as in the previous service. However, other forms of processing peculiar to speech signals are prohibited. For example, a form of multiplexing known as time-assigned speech interpolation (TASI) exploits the bursty character of speech to multiplex speech channels. With TASI, 30 speech calls can be squeezed into a T1 24-channel system with no noticeable degradation. However, this technique is not appropriate for nonspeech signals that happen to occupy the voice frequency band, such as digital data that have been passed through a voice-grade modem.

The next service—*alternate speech/64-Kbps, unrestricted, 8-kHz structured*—involves the alternate transfer of speech and unrestricted. There is a requirement for a short (as yet undefined) changeover time when the user requests a change from one service to the alternate service.

The next circuit-mode bearer service is *2 × 64-Kbps, unrestricted, 8-kHz structured*. This service provides for the use of two 64-Kbps channels that bear some relationship to each other. The details of this service remain to be worked out.

The next three services provide for high-speed digital transfer, at rates of *384, 1,536, and 1,920 Kbps*. These services could be used for a variety of applications, including video, private networking between PBXs, and links between other networks.

The remaining services are of the packet-switching types. The *virtual call and permanent virtual circuit* service is the traditional packet-network interface allowing both types of virtual circuits; the user attaches to ISDN in the same manner as attaching to a packet-switched network, using X.25. The *connectionless* service provides for a datagram style of packet service. This service might be provided to support applications such as telemetry, alarm, and transaction services, which do not need the connection-oriented service. The access protocol would differ from X.25 and is a subject for further study. The final packet-mode bearer service, *user signaling,* provides for user-to-user control signaling in a packetized manner. The protocol for this signaling is a subject for further study.

More bearer services, especially at higher data rates, will be defined in the future. However, this mix of services so far defined provides the capability of meeting a wide variety of user requirements and is sufficient for initial implementations of ISDN.

6.2.2   Teleservices

The area of teleservices is significantly less well developed than that of bearer services. Teleservices are intended to cover a wide variety of user applications over ISDN. The list of services so far defined in I.212 is shown in Table 6.3. In general, teleservices cover applications that are in the nature of terminal-service applications, most of which have been defined by CCITT. This can

Table 6.3 ISDN Teleservices

Telephony

Provides 3.1-kHz speech communication. The digital signal follows the agreed encoding laws for speech, and the network may use digital signal-processing techniques, such as echo cancelation. User information is provided over a B channel; signaling is provided over the D channel.

Teletex

Provides end-to-end text communication using standardized character sets, presentation formats, and communication protocols. The high-layer attributes are based on those of the CCITT standardized teletex service (F.200). User information is provided over a B channel; signaling is provided over the D channel.

Telefax

Provides end-to-end facsimile communication using standardized picture coding, resolution, and communication protocols. The high-layer attributes are based on the facsimile Group 4 Recommendations of CCITT. User information is provided over a B channel; signaling is provided over the D channel.

Mixed mode

Provides combined text and facsimile communication (mixed mode) for end-to-end transfer of documents containing mixed information consisting of text and fixed images. The high-layer attributes are based on the CCITT recommendation for the teletex service and facsimile Group 4, mixed mode (F.200, Annex C). User information is provided over a B channel; signaling is provided over the D channel.

Videotex

An enhancement of the existing videotex service with retrieval and mailbox functions for text (alpha) and graphic (mosaic, geometric, photographic) information.

Telex

Provides interactive text communication. The digital signal follows the internationally agreed recommendations for telex above the ISDN physical layer. User information is transferred over circuit- or packet-mode bearer channels; signaling is provided over the D channel.

be contrasted with what might be considered computer-to-computer applications. These latter applications have mostly been defined by ISO and include file transfer and document architecture.

One service conspicuously absent from Table 6.3 is the message-handling service (MHS), defined by the X.400 series of recommendations. This is one of the most important and widely available of the CCITT-defined teleservices and will be included in future revisions to I.212.

6.2.3 Supplementary Services

As was mentioned, supplementary services are always associated with a bearer service or teleservice. Each service is defined, and could be implemented, in a manner independent from the bearer services and teleservices with which it might be used. This allows each supplementary service to be used in a uniform fashion, regardless of the bearer service or teleservice that it supports. For example, the methods for requesting and authorizing reverse charging should be the same for a circuit-switched call or an MHS message.

Table 6.4 lists the supplementary services that have been defined so far. All of these originated in the telephone world. However, most of them can also be applied to packet-mode bearer services and to some teleservices.

Table 6.4 ISDN Supplementary Services (I.250)

Number Identification

Direct-dialing-in
Enables a user to call directly to another user on an ISDN-compatible PBX or Centrex, without attendant intervention, or to call a terminal on a passive bus selectively.

Multiple subscriber number
Allows multiple ISDN numbers to be assigned to a single interface (e.g., multiple telephone numbers at the same residence).

Calling-line-identification presentation
Service offered to the called party that provides the ISDN number of the calling party.

Calling-line-identification restriction
Service offered to the calling party to restrict presentation of the calling party's ISDN number to the called party.

Connected-line-identification presentation
Service offered to the calling party that provides the ISDN number of the party to whom the caller is connected.

Connected-line-identification restriction
Service offered to the connected party to restrict presentation of the connected party's ISDN number to the calling party.

Malicious-calls identification
For further study.

Subaddressing
For further study.

Call Offering

Call transfer
Enables a user to transfer an established call to a third party. This service is different from the call-forwarding service, since, in this case, the call to be transferred must have an established end-to-end connection prior to the transfer.

Table 6.4 (*Cont.*)

Call forwarding busy

Permits a served user to have the network send incoming calls (or just those associated with a specified basic service) addressed to the served user's ISDN number to another number when this user's line is busy. The served user's originating service is unaffected.

Call forwarding no reply

Permits a served user to have the network send incoming calls (or just those associated with a specified basic service) addressed to the served user's ISDN number to another number when there is no answer on this user's line. The served user's originating service is unaffected.

Call forwarding unconditional

Permits a served user to have the network send all incoming calls (or just those associated with a specified basic service) addressed to the served user's ISDN number to another number. The served user's originating service is unaffected.

Call deflection

For further study.

Line hunting

Enables incoming calls to a specific ISDN number (or numbers) to be distributed over a group of interfaces or terminals.

Call Completion

Call waiting

Enables a piece of terminal equipment that is already active in a communication to notify its user of an incoming call. The user then has the choice of accepting, rejecting, or ignoring the waiting call.

Call hold

Allows a user to interrupt communications on an existing call and then subsequently reestablish the connection.

Completion of calls to busy subscribers

For further study.

Multiparty

Conference calling

Allows multiple users to simultaneously communicate with one another.

Three-party service

Allows a subscriber to hold an existing call and make a call to a third party. The following arrangements may then be possible: the ability to switch between the two calls, the introduction of a common speech path between the three parties, and the connection of the other two parties.

Community of Interest

Closed user group

Allows a group of users to intercommunicate only among themselves, or as required, one or more users may be provided with incoming/outgoing access to users outside the group.

Private-numbering plan

For further study.

Charging

Credit-card calling

For further study.

Table 6.4 (*Cont.*)

Advice of charge

Provides the user paying for a call with usage-based charging information. This service may be provided at call-setup time, during the call, and/or at the completion of the call.

Reserve charging

For further study.

Additional-Information Transfer

User-to-user signaling

Allows an ISDN user to send/receive a limited amount of information to/from another ISDN user over the signaling channel in association with a call to the other ISDN user.

6.3   ISDN TRANSMISSION STRUCTURE

6.3.1   Network Architecture

Figure 6.2, based on a figure in CCITT Recommendation I.325, is an architectural depiction of ISDN. The ISDN supports a completely new physical connector for users, a digital subscriber loop, and a variety of transmission services.

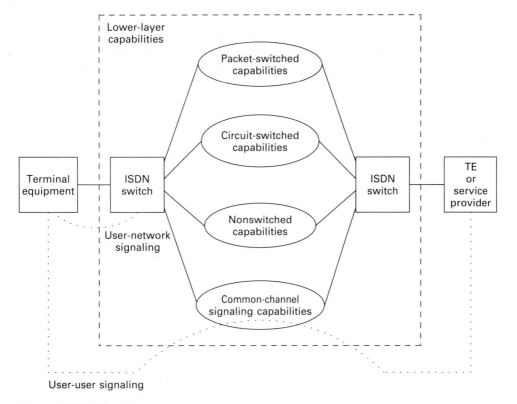

Figure 6.2 ISDN Architecture

The common physical interface provides a standardized means of attaching to the network. The same interface is usable for telephones, computer terminals, and videotex terminals. Protocols are required to define the exchange of control information between user devices and the network. Provision must be made for high-speed interfaces to, for example, a digital PBX or a LAN.

The subscriber loop provides the physical signal path from subscriber to ISDN central office. This loop must support full-duplex digital transmission. Initially, much of the subscriber-loop plant will be twisted-pair. As the network evolves and grows, optical fiber will increasingly be used.

The ISDN central office connects the numerous subscriber loops to the digital network. This provides access to a variety of lower-layer (OSI layers 1–3) transmission functions, including circuit-switched, packet-switched, and dedicated facilities. In addition, common-channel signaling, used to control the network and provide call management, will be accessible to the user. This signaling will allow user-network control dialogue. The use of these control-signaling protocols for user-to-user dialogue is a subject for further study within CCITT. By and large, these lower-layer functions will be implemented within the ISDN. In some countries with a competitive climate, some of these lower-layer functions (e.g., packet switching) may be provided by separate networks that may be reached by a subscriber through ISDN.

There will also be higher-layer (OSI layers 4–7) functions, to support applications such as teletex, facsimile, and transaction processing. These functions may be implemented within ISDN or provided by separate networks, or a mixture of the two.

6.3.2   ISDN Channels

The digital pipe between the central office and the ISDN subscriber will be used to carry a number of communication channels. The capacity of the pipe, and therefore the number of channels carried, may vary from user to user. The transmission structure of any access link is constructed from the following types of channels:

- *B channel:* 64 Kbps
- *D channel:* 16 or 64 Kbps
- *H0 channel:* 384 Kbps
- *H11 channel:* 1.536 Mbps
- *H12 channel:* 1.92 Mbps

The *B channel* is the basic user channel. It can be used to carry digital data, digitized voice, or a mixture of lower-rate traffic, including digital data and digitized voice encoded at a fraction of 64 Kbps. In the case of mixed traffic, all traffic of the B channel must be destined for the same end point; that is, the elemental unit of circuit switching is the B channel. If a B channel consists of two or more subchannels, all subchannels must be carried over the same circuit between the same subscribers. Three kinds of connections can be set up over a B channel:

1. *Circuit-switched:* This is equivalent to switched digital service, available today. The user places a call, and a circuit-switched connection is established with another network user.

2. *Packet-switched:* The user is connected to a packet-switching node, and data are exchanged with other users via X.25 or frame relay.

3. *Semipermanent:* This is a connection to another user set up by prior arrangement and not requiring a call-establishment protocol. It is equivalent to a leased line.

The designation of 64 Kbps as the standard user-channel rate highlights the fundamental disadvantage of standardization. The rate was chosen as the most effective for digitized voice, yet the technology has progressed to the point at which 32 Kbps or even less will produce equally satisfactory voice reproduction. To be effective, a standard must freeze the technology at some defined point. By the time the standard is approved, however, it may already be obsolete.

The *D channel* serves two main purposes. First, it carries signaling information to control circuit-switched calls on associated B channels at the user interface. That is, if a user wishes to place a call on a B channel, a control message is sent to the ISDN central office on the D channel requesting the connection. The D channel is used to set up calls on all the B channels at the customer's interface. This technique is known as *common-channel signaling,* as the D channel is a common channel for providing control signals for all the other channels. Common-channel signaling allows the other (B) channels to be used more efficiently.

In addition to its use for control signaling, the D channel may be used for packet switching or low-speed telemetry. The three types of traffic share the D channel by means of statistical multiplexing.

H channels (H0, H11, H12) are provided for user information at higher bit rates. The user may use such a channel as a high-speed trunk or subdivide the channel according to the user's own TDM (time-division multiplexing) scheme. Examples of applications include fast facsimile, video, high-speed data, high-quality audio, and multiplexed information streams at lower data rates.

These channel types are grouped into transmission structures that are offered as a package to the user. The best-defined structures at this time are the basic-channel structure (basic access) and the primary-channel structure (primary access).

Basic access consists of two full-duplex 64-Kbps B channels and a full-duplex 16-Kbps D channel. The total bit rate, by simple arithmetic, is 144 Kbps. However, framing, synchronization, and other overhead bits bring the total bit rate on a basic-access link to 192 Kbps. The basic service is intended to meet the needs of most individual users, including residential subscribers and very small offices. It allows the simultaneous use of voice and several data applications, such as packet-switched access, a link to a central alarm service, facsimile, teletex, and so on. These services could be accessed through a single multifunction terminal or several separate terminals. In either case, a single physical interface is provided. Most existing twisted-pair local loops can support this interface.

In some cases, one or both of the B channels are not needed. This results in a B + D or D interface rather than the 2B + D interface. However, to simplify the network implementation, the data rate at the interface remains at 192 Kbps. Nevertheless, for those subscribers with more modest transmission requirements, there may be a cost savings in using a reduced basic interface.

Primary access is intended for users with greater capacity requirements, such as offices with a digital PBX or a LAN. Because of differences in the digital-transmission hierarchies used in different countries, it was not possible to get agreement on a single data rate. The United States, Canada, and Japan make use of a transmission structure based on 1.544 Mbps; this corresponds to the T-1 transmission facility of AT&T. In Europe, 2.048 Mbps is the standard rate. Both of these data rates are provided as a primary interface service. Typically, the channel structure for the 1.544-Mbps rate will be 23 B channels plus one 64-Kbps D channel and, for the 2.048-Mbps rate, 30 B channels plus one 64-Kbps D channel. Again, it is possible for a customer with lesser requirements to employ fewer B channels—in which case, the channel structure is $nB + D$, where n ranges from 1 to 23 or from 1 to 30 for the two primary services. Also, a customer with high-data-rate demands may be provided with more than one primary physical interface. In this case, a single D channel on one of the interfaces may suffice for all signaling needs, and the other inter-faces may consist solely of B channels (24B or 31B).

The primary interface may also be used to support H channels. Some of these structures include a 64-Kbps D channel for control signaling. When no D channel is present, it is assumed that a D channel on another primary interface at the same subscriber location will provide any required signaling. The following structures are recognized:

- *Primary-rate-interface H0 channel structures:* This interface supports multiple 384-Kbps H0 channels. The structures are 3H0 + D and 4H0 for the 1.544-Mbps interface and 5H0 + D for the 2.048-Mbps interface.

- *Primary-rate-interface H11 and H12 channel structures:* The H11 channel structure consists of one 1,536-Kbps H11 channel. The H12 channel structure consists of one 1,920-Kbps H12 channel and one D channel.

- *Primary-rate-interface structures for mixtures of B and H0 channels:* This interface consists of zero or one D channel plus any possible combination of B and H0 channels up to the capacity of the physical interface (e.g., 3H0 + 5B + D and 3H0 + 6B for the 1.544-Mbps interface).

6.4 ISDN REFERENCE POINTS AND FUNCTIONAL GROUPINGS

In defining standards for user access to ISDN and for the user interfaces to ISDN, some consideration needs to be given to the likely configurations of user premises equipment. The first step is to group functions that may exist on the user's premises in ways that suggest actual physical configurations. Figure 6.3 shows the CCITT approach to this task, using:

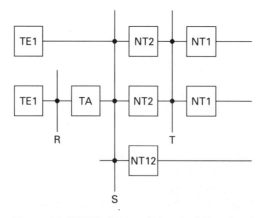

Figure 6.3 ISDN Reference Points and Functional Groupings

- *Functional groupings:* certain finite arrangements of physical equipment or combinations of equipment

- *Reference points:* conceptual points used to separate groups of functions

The architecture on the subscriber's premises is broken up functionally into groupings separated by reference points. This permits interface standards to be developed at each reference point, which effectively organizes the standards work and offers guidance to the equipment providers. Once stable interface standards exist, technical improvements on either side of an interface can be made without impact on adjacent functional groupings. Finally, with stable interfaces, the subscriber is free to procure equipment from different suppliers for the various functional groupings, so long as the equipment conforms to the relevant interface standards.

Let us first consider the functional groupings. *Network termination 1* (NT1) includes functions that may be regarded as belonging to OSI layer 1—that is, functions associated with the physical and electrical termination of the ISDN on the user's premises. The NT1 may be controlled by the ISDN provider and forms a boundary to the network. This boundary isolates the user from the transmission technology of the subscriber loop and presents a new physical connector interface for user-device attachment. In addition, the NT1 will perform line-maintenance functions such as loop-back testing and performance monitoring. The NT1 supports multiple channels (e.g., 2B + D); at the physical level, the bit streams of these channels are multiplexed together, using synchronous time-division multiplexing. Finally, the NT1 interface might support multiple devices in a multi-drop arrangement. For example, a residential interface might include a telephone, a personal computer, and an alarm system, all attached to a single NT1 interface via a multidrop line.

Network termination 2 (NT2) is an intelligent device that may provide, depending on the requirement, up through OSI layer-3 functionality. NT2 can perform switching and concentration functions. Examples of NT2 are a digital PBX, a terminal controller, and a LAN-to-ISDN bridge or router. An example of a switching function is the construction of a private network using semipermanent circuits among a number of sites. Each site could include a PBX that acts as a circuit switch or a host computer that acts as a packet switch. The concentration function simply means that multiple devices—attached to a digital PBX, LAN, or terminal controller—may transmit data across ISDN.

Network termination 1, 2 (NT12) is a single piece of equipment that contains the combined functions of NT1 and NT2. This points out one of the regulatory issues associated with ISDN interface development. In many countries, the ISDN provider will own the NT12 and provide full service to the user. In the United States, there is a need for a network termination with a limited number of functions to permit competitive provision of user-premises equipment. Hence, the user-premises network functions are split into NT1 and NT2.

Terminal equipment refers to subscriber equipment that makes use of ISDN. Two types are defined. *Terminal equipment type 1* (TE1) refers to devices that support the standard ISDN interface. Examples are digital telephones, integrated voice/data terminals, and digital facsimile equipment. *Terminal equipment type 2* (TE2) encompasses existing non-ISDN equipment. Examples are terminals with a physical interface such as EIA-232 and host computers with an X.25 interface. Such equipment requires a *terminal adapter* (TA) to plug into an ISDN interface.

The definitions of the functional groupings also define, by implication, the reference points. *Reference point T* (terminal) corresponds to a minimal ISDN network termination at the customer's premises. It separates the network provider's equipment from the user's equipment. *Reference point S* (system) corresponds to the interface of individual ISDN terminals. It separates user terminal equipment from network-related communications functions. *Reference point R* (rate) corresponds to a non-ISDN interface between user equipment that is not ISDN-compatible and adapter equipment. Typically, the interface at the R reference point will comply with an X-series or V-series CCITT recommendation.

6.5   ISDN PROTOCOLS

We begin this section with a discussion of the overall ISDN protocol architecture and then look at the types of connections that this architecture supports. The remainder of the section examines each of the three layers of the architecture in turn.

6.5.1   ISDN Protocol Architecture

The development of standards for ISDN includes, of course, the development of protocols for interaction between ISDN users and the network and for interaction between two ISDN users. It would be desirable to fit these new ISDN protocols into the OSI framework, and to a great extent, this has been done. However, there are certain requirements for ISDN that are not met within the current structure of OSI. Examples of these are:

- *Multiple related protocols:* The primary example of this is the use of a protocol on the D channel to set up, maintain, and terminate a connection on a B channel.

- *Multimedia calls:* ISDN allows a call to be set up that permits information flow consisting of multiple types, such as voice, data, facsimile, and control signals.

- *Multipoint connections:* ISDN allows conference calls.

These and other functions are not directly addressed in the current OSI specification. However, the basic seven-layer framework appears valid even in the ISDN context, and the issue is more one of specific functionality at the various layers. The issue of the exact relationship between ISDN and OSI remains one for further study.

Figure 6.4 suggests the relationship between OSI and ISDN. As a network, ISDN is essentially unconcerned with user layers 4–7. These are end-to-end layers employed by the user for the exchange of information. Network access is concerned only with layers 1–3. Layer 1, defined in I.430 and I.431, defines the physical interface for basic and primary access, respectively. Since the B and D channels are multiplexed over the same physical interface, these standards apply to both types of channels. Above this layer, the protocol structure differs for the two channels.

For the D channel, a new data-link-layer standard, LAPD (link-access protocol, D channel), has been defined. This standard is based on HDLC (high-level data-link control), modified to meet ISDN requirements. All transmission on the D channel is in the form of LAPD frames that are exchanged between the subscriber equipment and an ISDN switching element. Three applications are supported: control signaling, packet switching, and telemetry. For *control signaling,* a call-control protocol has been defined (I.451/Q.931). This protocol is used to establish, maintain, and terminate connections on B channels. Thus, it is a protocol between the user and the network. Above layer 3, there is the possibility for higher-layer functions associated with user-to-user control signaling. These are a subject for further study. The D channel can also be used to provide *packet-*

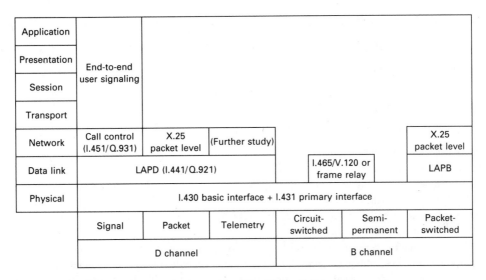

Figure 6.4 ISDN Protocol Architecture at the User-Network Interface

switching services to the subscriber. In this case, the X.25 level-3 protocol is used, and X.25 packets are transmitted in LAPD frames. The X.25 level-3 protocol is used to establish virtual circuits on the D channel to other users and to exchange packetized data. The final application area, *telemetry,* is a subject for further study.

The B channel can be used for circuit switching, semipermanent circuits, and packet switching. For *circuit switching,* a circuit is set up on a B channel on demand. The D-channel call-control protocol is used for this purpose. Once the circuit is set up, it may be used for data transfer between the users.

A *semipermanent circuit* is a B-channel circuit that is set up by prior agreement between the connected users and the network. As with a circuit-switched connection, it provides a transparent data path between end systems.

With either a circuit-switched connection or a semipermanent circuit, it appears to the connected stations that they have a direct full-duplex link with each other. They are free to use their own formats, protocols, and frame synchronization. Hence, from the point of view of ISDN, layers 2–7 are neither visible nor specified. In addition, however, CCITT has standardized I.465/V.120, which does provide a common link-control functionality for ISDN subscribers.

In the case of *packet switching,* a circuit-switched connection is set up on a B channel between the user and a packet-switched node using the D-channel control protocol. Once the circuit is set up on the B channel, the user may employ X.25 levels 2 and 3 to establish a virtual circuit to another user over that channel and exchange packetized data. As an alternative, the recently defined frame-relay service may be used. Frame relay can also be used over H channels.

Some of the protocols shown in Figure 6.4 are summarized in the remainder of this section. The following subsection looks at the way in which packet-switched and circuit-switched connections are set up. Next, the control signaling protocol and then LAPD are examined. Finally, the physical-layer specifications are reviewed. Because of its importance, frame relay is discussed in depth in Chapter 7.

6.5.2   ISDN Connections

ISDN provides four types of service for end-to-end communication:

1. Circuit-switched calls over a B channel

2. Semipermanent connections over a B channel

3. Packet-switched calls over a B channel

4. Packet-switched calls over the D channel

6.5.2.1   Circuit-Switched Calls

The network configuration and protocols for circuit switching involve both the B and D channels. The B channel is used for the transparent exchange of user data. The communicating users may employ any protocols they wish for end-to-end communication. The D channel is used to exchange control information between the user and the network for call establishment and termination, as well as access to network facilities.

The B channel is serviced by an NT1 or NT2 using only layer-1 functions. The end users may employ any protocol, although generally layer 3 will be null. On the D channel, a three-layer network-access protocol is used, as explained later in the chapter. Finally, the process of establishing a circuit through ISDN involves the cooperation of switches internal to ISDN to set up the connection. These switches interact using signaling system number 7.

6.5.2.2   Semipermanent Connections

A semipermanent connection between agreed points may be provided for an indefinite period of time after subscription, for a fixed period, or for agreed periods during a day, week, or other interval. As with circuit-switched connections, only layer-1 functionality is provided by the network interface. The call-control protocol is not needed, since the connection already exists.

6.5.2.3   Packet-Switched Calls over a B Channel

The ISDN must also permit user access to packet-switched services for data traffic (e.g., interactive) that is best serviced by packet switching. There are two possibilities for implementing this service: either the packet-switching capability is furnished by a separate network, referred to as a packet-switched public data network (PSPDN), or the packet-switching capability is integrated into ISDN. In the former case, the service is provided over a B channel. In the latter case, the service may be provided over a B or D channel. This subsection examines the use of a B channel for packet switching; the following subsection examines the use of a D channel for this purpose.

When the packet-switching service is provided by a separate PSPDN, the access to that service is via a B channel. Both the user and the PSPDN must therefore be connected as subscribers to the ISDN. In the case of the PSPDN, one or more of the packet-switching network nodes, referred to as packet handlers, are connected to ISDN. Each such node can be thought of as a traditional X.25 DCE (data circuit-terminating equipment) supplemented by the logic needed to access ISDN. That is, the ISDN subscriber assumes the role of an X.25 DTE (data terminal equipment), the node in the PSPDN to which it is connected functions as an X.25 DCE, and the ISDN simply provides the connection from DTE to DCE. Any ISDN subscriber can then communicate, via X.25, with any user connected to the PSPDN, including:

- Users with a direct, permanent connection to the PSPDN

- Users of the ISDN that currently enjoy a connection, through the ISDN, to the PSPDN

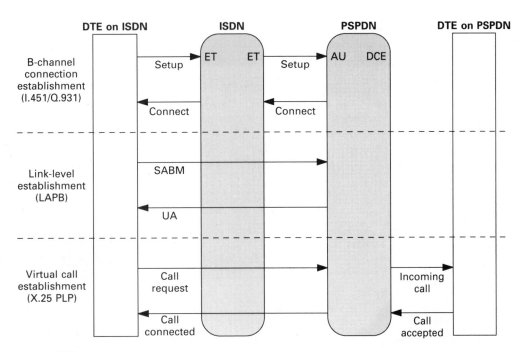

AU = ISDN access unit.
SABM = set asynchronous balanced mode.
UA = unnumbered acknowledgment.

Figure 6.5 Virtual Call Setup

The connection between the user (via a B channel) and the packet handler with which it communicates may be either semipermanent or circuit-switched. In the former case, the connection is always there, and the user may freely invoke X.25 to set up a virtual circuit to another user. In the latter case, the D channel is involved, and the following sequence of steps occurs (Figure 6.5):

1. The user requests, via the D-channel call-control protocol (I.451/Q.931), a circuit-switched connection on a B channel to a packet handler.

2. The connection is set up by ISDN, and the user is notified via the D-channel call-control protocol.

3. The user sets up a virtual circuit to another user via the X.25 call-establishment procedure on the B channel (described in section 3.2). This requires that a data-link connection, using LAPB, first be set up between the user and the packet handler.

4. The user terminates the virtual circuit using X.25 on the B channel.

5. After one or more virtual calls on the B channel, the user is done and signals via the D channel to terminate the circuit-switched connection to the packet-switching node.

6. The connection is terminated by ISDN.

Figure 6.6 shows the configuration involved in providing this service. In the figure, the user is shown to employ a DTE device that expects an interface to an X.25 DCE. Hence, a terminal

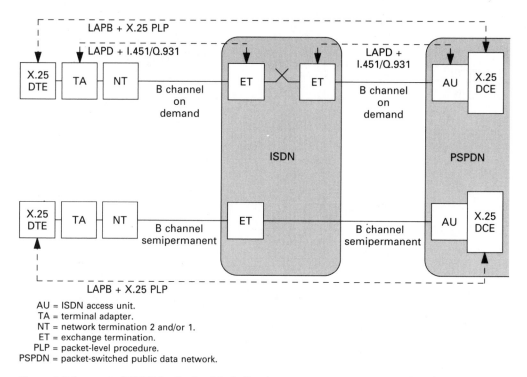

AU = ISDN access unit.
TA = terminal adapter.
NT = network termination 2 and/or 1.
ET = exchange termination.
PLP = packet-level procedure.
PSPDN = packet-switched public data network.

Figure 6.6 Access to PSPDN for Packet-Mode Service

adapter is required. Alternatively, the X.25 capability can be an integrated function of an ISDN TE1 device, dispensing with the need for a separate TA.

When the packet-switching service is provided by ISDN, the packet-handling function is provided within the ISDN, either by separate equipment or as part of the exchange equipment. The user may connect to a packet handler by either a B channel or the D channel. On a B channel, the connection to the packet handler may be either switched or semipermanent, and the same procedures described in the preceding list apply for switched connections. In this case, rather than establishing a B-channel connection to another ISDN subscriber that is a PSPDN packet handler, the connection is to an internal element of ISDN that is a packet handler.

6.5.2.4 Packet-Switched Calls over a D Channel

When the packet-switching service is provided internally to the ISDN, it can also be accessed on the *D channel*. For D-channel access, ISDN provides a semipermanent connection to a packet-switching node within the ISDN. The user employs the X.25 level-3 protocol, as is done in the case of a B-channel virtual call. Here, the level-3 protocol is carried by LAPD frames. Since the D channel is also used for control signaling, some means is needed to distinguish between X.25 packet traffic and ISDN control traffic. This is accomplished by means of the link-layer addressing scheme, as explained later in the chapter.

Figure 6.7 shows the configuration for providing packet switching within ISDN. The packet-switching service provided internally to the ISDN over the B and D channels is logically provided

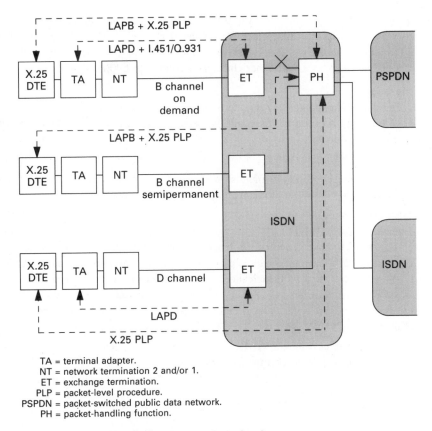

TA = terminal adapter.
NT = network termination 2 and/or 1.
ET = exchange termination.
PLP = packet-level procedure.
PSPDN = packet-switched public data network.
PH = packet-handling function.

Figure 6.7 Access to ISDN for Packet-Mode Service

by a single packet-switching network. Thus, virtual calls can be set up between two D-channel users, between two B-channel users, and between a B-channel user and a D-channel user. In addition, it will be typical to provide access to X.25 users on other ISDNs and PSPDNs by appropriate interworking procedures. One common approach is the use of X.75, which specifies an interworking scheme between two public X.25 networks.

6.5.3   ISDN Call-Control Protocol

The ISDN specification for call control is contained in three recommendations:

1. *I.450/Q.930:* a general description of the layer-3 interface for call control

2. *I.451/Q.931:* a specification of the call-control protocol

3. *I.452/Q.932:* additional procedures for the control of ISDN supplementary services

In what follows, we will simply refer to the protocol specified in these three documents as I.451/Q.931. This protocol specifies procedures for establishing connections on the B channels that share the same interface to ISDN as the D channel. It also provides user-to-user control signaling over the D channel. In OSI terms, I.451/Q.931 is a layer-3, or network-layer, protocol. This protocol relies on LAPD to transmit messages over the D channel. Each I.451/Q.931 message is encapsulated in a link-layer frame. This link-layer frame is transmitted on the D channel, which is multiplexed at the physical layer with other channels according to I.430 or I.431.

6.5.3.1   Messages

The process of establishing, controlling, and terminating a call occurs as a result of control-signaling messages exchanged between the user and the network over a D channel. A common format is used for all messages defined in I.451/Q.931, as illustrated in Figure 6.8, part (a). Three fields are common to all messages:

1. *Protocol discriminator:* used to distinguish messages for user-network call control from other message types. Other signaling protocols may share the D channel.

2. *Call reference:* identifies the B-channel call to which this message refers. As with X.25 virtual circuit numbers, it has only local significance. The call-reference field comprises three sub-fields. The *length* subfield specifies the length of the remainder of the field in octets. This length is 1 octet for a basic-rate interface and 2 octets for a primary-rate interface. The *flag* indicates which end of the LAPD logical connection initiated the call. The *call-reference value* is the number assigned to this call. A call-reference value of zero is referred to as the *global call reference;* a message with a global call reference refers to all call references currently in use at this interface.

3. *Message type:* identifies which I.451/Q.931 message is being sent. The contents of the remainder of the message depend on the message type.

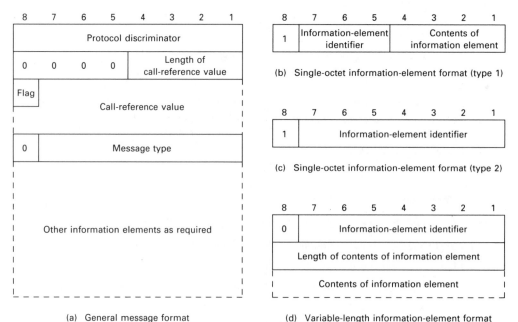

(a) General message format

(b) Single-octet information-element format (type 1)

(c) Single-octet information-element format (type 2)

(d) Variable-length information-element format

Figure 6.8 I.451/Q.931 Formats

Following these three common fields, the remainder of the message consists of a sequence of zero or more information elements, or parameters. These contain additional information to be conveyed with the message. Thus, the message type specifies a command or response, and the details are provided by the information elements. Some information elements must always be included with a given message (mandatory), and others are optional (additional). Three formats for information elements are used, as indicated in Figure 6.8, parts (b) through (d).

I.451/Q.931 messages can be grouped along two dimensions: the application they support and the functions they perform. Messages apply to one of four applications:

1. *Circuit-mode connection control:* refers to the functions needed to set up, maintain, and clear a circuit-switched connection on a B channel. This function corresponds to call control in existing circuit-switching telecommunications networks.

2. *Packet-mode access-connection control:* refers to the functions needed to set up a circuit-switched connection (called an access connection in this context) to an ISDN packet-switching node; this connects the user to the packet-switching network furnished by the ISDN provider.

3. *User-to-user signaling not associated with circuit-switched calls:* allows two users to communicate without setting up a circuit-switched connection. A temporary signaling connection is established and cleared in a manner similar to the control of a circuit-switched connection. Signaling takes place over the D channel and thus does not consume B-channel resources.

4. *Messages used with the global call reference:* refers to the functions that enable user or network to return one or more channels to an idle condition.

In addition, messages perform functions in one of four categories:

1. *Call establishment:* used to set up a call initially. This group includes messages between the calling terminal and the network and between the network and the called terminal. These messages support the following services: set up a B-channel call in response to a user request; provide particular network facilities for this call; inform the calling user of the progress of the call-establishment process.

2. *Call information:* sent between user and network once a call has been set up but prior to the disestablishment (termination) phase. One of the messages in this group allows the network to relay, without modification, information between the two users of the call. The nature of this information is beyond the scope of the standard, but it is assumed that it is control-signaling information that cannot or should not be sent directly over the B-channel circuit. The remainder of the messages in this group allow users to request the suspension and later resumption of a call. When a call is suspended, the network remembers the identity of the called parties and the network facilities supporting the call but deactivates the call so that no additional charges are incurred and so that the corresponding B channel is freed up. Presumably, resuming a call is quicker and cheaper than originating a new call.

3. *Call clearing:* sent between user and network in order to terminate a call.

4. *Miscellaneous:* may be sent between user and network at various stages of the call. Some may be sent during call setup; others may be sent even though no calls exist. The primary function of these messages is to negotiate network features (supplementary services).

Table 6.5 I.451/Q.931 Messages for Circuit-Mode Connection Control

Message	Significance	Direction	Function
Call-Establishment Messages			
ALERTING	Global	Both	Indicates that the user alerting has begun
CALL PROCEEDING	Local	Both	Indicates that call establishment has been initiated
CONNECT	Global	Both	Indicates call acceptance by the called TE
CONNECT ACKNOWLEDGE	Local	Both	Indicates that the user has been awarded the call
PROGRESS	Global	Both	Reports the progress of a call
SETUP	Global	Both	Initiates call establishment
SETUP ACKNOWLEDGE	Local	Both	Indicates that call establishment has been initiated but requests more information
Call-Information-Phase Messages			
RESUME	Local	$u \rightarrow n$	Requests resumption of a previously suspended call
RESUME ACKNOWLEDGE	Local	$n \rightarrow u$	Indicates that the requested call has been reestablished
RESUME REJECT	Local	$n \rightarrow u$	Indicates failure to resume a suspended call
SUSPEND	Local	$u \rightarrow n$	Requests suspension of a call
SUSPEND ACKNOWLEDGE	Local	$n \rightarrow u$	Indicates that the call has been suspended
SUSPEND REJECT	Local	$n \rightarrow u$	Indicates failure of a requested call suspension
USER INFORMATION	Access	Both	Transfers information from one user to another
Call-Clearing Messages			
DISCONNECT	Global	Both	Sent by a user to request connection clearing; sent by the network to indicate connection clearing
RELEASE	Local	Both	Indicates intent to release channel and call reference
RELEASE COMPLETE	Local	Both	Indicates release of channel and call reference
Miscellaneous Messages			
CONGESTION CONTROL	Local	Both	Sets or releases flow control on USER INFORMATION messages
FACILITY	Local	Both	Requests or acknowledges a supplementary service

Table 6.5 (*Cont.*)

Message	Significance	Direction	Function
	Miscellaneous Messages		
INFORMATION	Local	Both	Provides additional information
NOTIFY	Access	Both	Indicates information pertaining to a call
STATUS	Local	Both	Sent in response to a STATUS ENQUIRY or at any time to report an error
STATUS ENQUIRY	Local	Both	Solicits a STATUS message

6.5.3.2 Circuit-Mode Connection Control

Table 6.5 lists and briefly defines the messages used for circuit-mode connection control. Each entry includes an indication of the direction of the message:

- Only user to network (u → n)
- Only network to user (n → u)
- Both directions (both)

Each entry also specifies whether the message has:

- *Local significance:* relevant only in the originating or terminating access to the network by the user (i.e., the user-network interface for the user that originated the call or the user that accepted the call)
- *Access significance:* relevant in the originating and terminating access but not in the network
- *Global significance:* relevant in the originating and terminating access and in the network

Figure 6.9 is an example of the use of I.451/Q.931 to set up a B-channel circuit-switched telephone call. Although the example involves the placement of a telephone call, the sequence would be similar for a computer-to-computer or terminal-to-computer data call.

The process begins when a calling subscriber lifts the handset. The ISDN-compatible telephone ensures that the D channel is active before itself generating a dial tone (not shown). When the subscriber keys in the called number (not shown), the telephone set accumulates the digits, and when all are keyed in, sends a SETUP message over the D channel to the exchange. The SETUP message includes the destination number; a channel identification, which specifies which B channel is to be used; and any requested network services or facilities (e.g., reverse charging).

The SETUP message triggers two activities at the local exchange. First, using internal control signaling, the local exchange sends a message through the network that results in designating a route for the requested call and allocating resources for that call. Second, the exchange sends back a CALL PROC message indicating that call setup is under way. The exchange may also request more information from the caller (via SETUP ACK and INFO). When the internal control message reaches the remote exchange, it sends a SETUP message to the called telephone. The called telephone accepts the call by sending an ALERT message to the network and generating a ringing

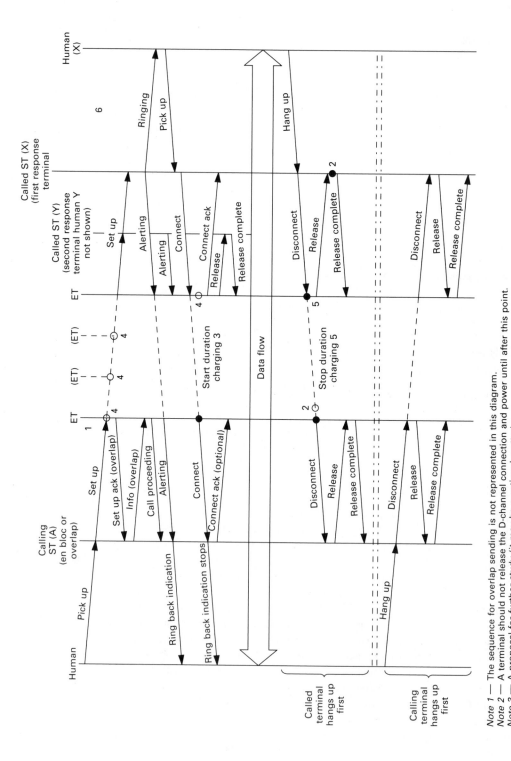

Note 1 — The sequence for overlap sending is not represented in this diagram.
Note 2 — A terminal should not release the D-channel connection and power until after this point.
Note 3 — A proposal for further study (it may be a national matter).
Note 4 — Proposed switch-through points and the sequence in which they occur.
Note 5 — Proposed network release points and sequence.
Note 6 — The interactions between the human and the terminal are shown for illustration only.

Figure 6.9 Procedure for a Simple Circuit-Switched Call (Example)

tone. The ALERT message is transmitted all the way back to the calling telephone set. When the called party lifts the handset, the telephone sends a CONN message to the network. The local exchange sends a CONN ACK message to its subscriber and forwards the CONN message to the calling exchange; it, in turn, forwards it to the calling telephone. The B-channel circuit is now available for the called and calling telephones.

Because the call-setup process makes use of common-channel signaling, other channels are undisturbed, and the fact that all the B channels are engaged does not prevent the D-channel dialogue. For example, even if all of a user's channels are assigned to circuits, an incoming call request will be presented to the user via the D channel; the user can, if desired, put a call in progress on hold in order to use the corresponding B channel for the new call.

Once the circuit is set up, full-duplex 64-Kbps data streams are exchanged via the B channel between the two end users. Additional signaling messages, such as call-information-phase messages, may be transmitted during this period.

Call termination begins when one of the telephone users hangs up. This causes a DISC message to be sent from the telephone to the exchange. The exchange responds with an REL message, and when the telephone sends REL COM, the B channel is released. The complementary action takes place at the other telephone-network interface.

6.5.3.3 Packet-Mode Access-Connection Control

Table 6.6 lists and briefly defines the messages used for packet-mode access-connection control. As can be seen, these are a subset of the messages used for circuit-mode connection control.

6.5.3.4 User-to-User Signaling Not Associated with Circuit-Switched Calls

Table 6.7 lists and briefly defines the messages used for user-to-user signaling not associated with circuit-switched calls. This feature allows users to communicate information without setting up a circuit-switched connection. A temporary signaling connection is established and cleared in a manner similar to the control of a circuit-switched call. The information exchanged is end-to-end, and no service descriptions for these connections are currently provided.

6.5.3.5 Global Call Reference

Table 6.8 lists and briefly defines the messages used for global call reference; these are messages that refer to all the calls that are currently defined. Only three messages are used. The STATUS message is the same as that used in other contexts to report an error condition. The RESTART and RESTART ACKNOWLEDGE messages, employed only for global call reference, are used to return a given channel or all channels to a predefined state after a fault condition.

6.5.3.6 Supplementary-Services Control

Recommendation I.452/Q.932, first issued in the 1988 CCITT recommendations, defines the generic procedures applicable for the control of supplementary services. These procedures may be associated with a particular call or outside any existing call.

I.452/Q.932 identifies three major methods by which supplementary services may be controlled:

1. Keypad protocol
2. Feature-key-management protocol
3. Functional protocol

Table 6.6 I.451/Q.931 Messages for Packet-Mode Access-Connection Control

Message	Significance	Direction	Function
Access-Connection-Establishment Messages			
ALERTING	Local	u → n	Indicates that user alerting has begun
CALL PROCEEDING	Local	Both	Indicates that access-connection establishment has been initiated
CONNECT	Local	Both	Indicates access-connection acceptance by the called TE
CONNECT ACKNOWLEDGE	Local	Both	Indicates that the user has been awarded the access connection
PROGRESS	Local	u → n	Reports progress of an access connection in the event of interworking with a private network
SETUP	Local	Both	Initiates access-connection establishment
Access-Connection-Clearing Messages			
DISCONNECT	Local	Both	Sent by a user to request connection clearing; sent by the network to indicate connection clearing
RELEASE	Local	Both	Indicates intent to release channel and call reference
RELEASE COMPLETE	Local	Both	Indicates release of channel and call reference
Miscellaneous Messages			
STATUS	Local	Both	Sent in response to a STATUS ENQUIRY or at any time to report an error
STATUS ENQUIRY	Local	Both	Solicits a STATUS message

The first two methods are appropriate for stimulus terminals, where individual keystrokes (keypad) or button pressing (feature-key management) are used to trigger service operation. These methods emulate the behavior of a keypad or an analog phone set (one digit = one message) and allow an early implementation with minimal changes to switch software.

The functional protocol allows more sophisticated use of supplementary services for functional terminals. It is based on the use of a FACILITY message for carrying explicit supplementary-service requests. The following cases have been defined:

- The invocation of supplementary services during the establishment of a call
- The invocation of supplementary services during the clearing of a call
- The invocation of call-related supplementary services during the active state of a call

Table 6.7 I.451/Q.931 Messages for User-to-User Signaling Not Associated with Circuit-Switched Calls

Message	Significance	Direction	Function
Call-Establishment Messages			
ALERTING	Global	Both	Indicates that user alerting has begun
CALL PROCEEDING	Local	Both	Indicates that call establishment has been initiated
CONNECT	Global	Both	Indicates call acceptance by the called TE
CONNECT ACKNOWLEDGE	Local	Both	Indicates that the user has been awarded the call
SETUP	Global	Both	Initiates call establishment
SETUP ACKNOWLEDGE	Local	Both	Indicates that call establishment has been initiated but requests more information
Call-Information-Phase Messages			
USER INFORMATION	Access	Both	Transfers information from one user to another
Call-Clearing Messages			
RELEASE	Local	Both	Indicates intent to release channel and call reference
RELEASE COMPLETE	Local	Both	Indicates release of channel and call reference
Miscellaneous Messages			
CONGESTION CONTROL	Local	Both	Sets or releases flow control on USER INFORMATION messages
INFORMATION	Local	Both	Provides additional information
STATUS	Local	Both	Sent in response to a STATUS ENQUIRY or at any time to report an error
STATUS ENQUIRY	Local	Both	Solicits a STATUS message

Table 6.8 I.451/Q.931 Messages Used with the Global Call Reference

Message	Significance	Direction	Function
RESTART	Local	Both	Requests that the recipient restart the indicated channel(s) or interface
RESTART ACKNOWLEDGE	Local	Both	Indicates that the requested restart is complete
STATUS	Local	Both	Reports an error condition

- The invocation or registration of supplementary services independent from an active call
- The invocation of multiple, different supplementary services within a single message
- The invocation of supplementary services related to different calls
- Cancellation of invoked supplementary services and notification to the initiator of the supplementary service

The methods described in I.452/Q.932 are still evolving and are the subject of ongoing study.

6.5.4   LAPD

All traffic over the D channel employs a link-layer protocol known as LAPD (link-access protocol, D channel). As usual, we examine both the services and the protocol of this layer.

6.5.4.1   LAPD Services

The LAPD standard provides two forms of service to LAPD users: the unacknowledged information-transfer service and the acknowledged information-transfer service. The *unacknowledged information-transfer service* simply provides for the transfer of frames containing user data with no acknowledgment. The service does not guarantee that data presented by one user will be delivered to another user, nor does it inform the sender if the delivery attempt fails, nor does it provide any flow-control or error-control mechanism. This service supports both point-to-point (deliver to one user) and broadcast (deliver to a number of users). It allows for fast data transfer and is useful for management procedures such as alarm messages and messages that need to be broadcast to multiple users.

The *acknowledged information-transfer service* is the more common one and is similar to the service offered by LAPB (link-access procedures, balanced) and HDLC (high-level data-link control). With this service, a logical connection is established between two LAPD users prior to the exchange of data.

6.5.4.2   LAPD Protocol

The LAPD protocol is based on HDLC. Both user information and protocol-control information and parameters are transmitted in frames. Corresponding to the two types of service offered by LAPD, there are two types of operation:

1. *Unacknowledged operation:* Layer-3 information is transferred in unnumbered frames. Error detection is used to discard damaged frames, but there is no error control or flow control.

2. *Acknowledged operation:* Layer-3 information is transferred in frames that include sequence numbers and are acknowledged. Error-control and flow-control procedures are included in the protocol. This type is also referred to in the standard as multiple-frame operation.

These two types of operation may coexist on a single D channel. With the acknowledged operation, it is possible to simultaneously support multiple logical LAPD connections.

Both types of operation make use of the frame format illustrated in Figure 6.10. This format is identical to that of HDLC (Figure 3.1), with the exception of the address field.

To explain the address field, we need to consider that LAPD has to deal with two levels of multiplexing. First, at a subscriber site, there may be multiple user devices sharing the same physical interface. Second, within each user device, there may be multiple types of traffic: specifically, packet-switched data and control signaling. To accommodate these levels of multiplexing,

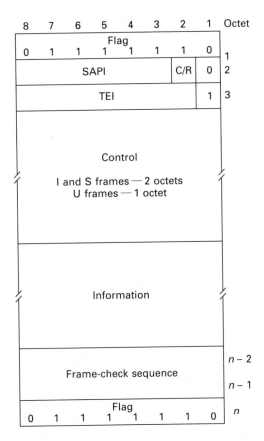

Figure 6.10 LAPD Frame

LAPD employs a two-part address, consisting of a terminal-end-point identifier (TEI) and a service-access-point identifier (SAPI).

Typically, each user device is given a unique *terminal-end-point identifier*. It is also possible for a single device to be assigned more than one TEI. This might be the case for a terminal concentrator. TEI assignment either occurs automatically when the equipment first connects to the interface or is done manually by the user. In the latter case, care must be taken that multiple pieces of equipment attached to the same interface do not have the same TEI. The advantage of the automatic procedure is that it allows the user to change, add, or delete equipment at will without prior notification to the network administration. Without this feature, the network would be obliged to manage a database for each subscriber, which would need to be updated manually. Table 6.9, part (a), shows the assignment of TEI numbers.

The *service-access-point identifier* identifies a layer-3 user of LAPD and thus corresponds to a layer-3 protocol entity within a user device. Four specific values have been assigned, as shown in Table 6.9, part (b). An SAPI of 0 is used for call-control procedures for managing B-channel circuits; the value 16 is reserved for packet-mode communication on the D channel using X.25 level 3; and the value 63 is used for the exchange of layer-2 management information. The most

Table 6.9 SAPI and TEI Assignments

(a) TEI assignments

TEI Value	User Type
0–63	Nonautomatic TEI assignment user equipment
64–126	Automatic TEI assignment user equipment
127	Used during automatic TEI assignment

(b) SAPI assignments

SAPI Value	Related Protocol or Management Entity
0	Call-control procedures
1	Reserved for packet-mode communication using I.451 call-control procedures
16	Packet communication conforming to X.25 level 3
32–62	Frame-relay communication
63	Layer-2 management procedures
All others	Reserved for future standardization

recent assignment, made in 1988, is the value 1 for packet-mode communication using I.451/ Q.931. This could be employed for user-user signaling. Finally, values in the range 32 to 62 have tentatively been reserved to support frame-relay connections, as described in Chapter 7.

For acknowledged operation, LAPD follows essentially the same procedures described for HDLC in Chapter 3. For unacknowledged operation, the user information (UI) frame is employed to transmit user data. When an LAPD user wishes to send data, it passes the data to its LAPD entity, which passes the data in the information field of a UI frame. When this frame is received, the information field is passed up to the destination user. No acknowledgment is returned to the other side. However, error detection is performed, and erroneous frames are discarded.

6.5.5 Physical Layer

The ISDN physical layer is presented to the user at either reference point S or T (Figure 6.3).

The electrical specification depends on the specific interface. For the basic-access interface, pseudoternary coding is used.[2] With pseudoternary, the line signal may take one of three levels. This is not as efficient as a two-level code, but it is reasonably simple and inexpensive. At the relatively modest data rate of the basic-access interface, this is a suitable code.

For the higher-speed primary-access interface, a more efficient coding scheme is needed. For the 1.544-Mbps data rate, the B8ZS code is used, whereas for the 2.048-Mbps data rate, the HDB3 code is used.[3] There is no particular advantage of one over the other; the specification reflects historical usage.

The functional specification for the physical layer includes the following functions:

- Encoding of digital data for transmission across the interface
- Full-duplex transmission of B-channel data

---

2. See Appendix A for an explanation of pseudoternary coding.

3. See Appendix A.

- Full-duplex transmission of D-channel data
- Multiplexing of channels to form a basic- or primary-access transmission structure
- Activation and deactivation of the physical circuit
- Power feeding from network termination to the terminal
- Terminal identification
- Faulty-terminal isolation
- D-channel contention access

The last function is needed when there is a multipoint configuration for basic access; this is described in the following subsection.

The nature of the physical interface and functionality differs for basic and primary user-network interfaces. Each interface is examined in turn.

6.5.5.1   Basic-Rate User-Network Interface

The basic user-network interface has three key aspects:

1. Line coding
2. Framing for multiplexing
3. Contention resolution for multidrop configurations

At the interface between the subscriber and the network terminating equipment (T or S reference point), digital data are exchanged using full-duplex transmission. A separate physical line is used for the transmission in each direction. The *line-coding* specification for the interface dictates the use of a pseudoternary coding scheme.[4] Binary 1 is represented by the absence of voltage; binary 0 is represented by a positive or negative pulse of 750 mV ± 10 percent. The data rate is 192 Kbps.

The basic-access structure consists of two full-duplex 64-Kbps B channels and one full-duplex 16-Kbps D channel. Figure 6.11 shows the *frame structure* for basic access.

Each frame of 48 bits includes 16 bits from each of the two B channels and 4 bits from the D channel. The remaining bits have the following interpretation. Let us first consider the frame structure in the TE-to-NT direction. Each frame begins with a framing bit (F), which is always transmitted as a positive pulse. This is followed by a DC-balancing bit (L), which is set to a negative pulse to balance the voltage. The F-L pattern thus acts to synchronize the receiver on the beginning of the frame. The specification dictates that, following these first two bit positions, the first occurrence of a 0 bit will be encoded as a negative pulse. After that, the pseudoternary rules are observed. The next 8 bits (B1) are from the first B channel. This is followed by another DC-balancing bit (L). Next comes a bit from the D channel, followed by its balancing bit. This is followed by the auxiliary framing bit (F_a), which is set to 0 unless it is to be used in a multiframe structure. There follows another balancing bit (L), 8 bits (B2) from the second B channel, and another balancing bit (L). This is followed by bits from the D channel, first B channel, D channel again, second B channel, and the D channel yet again, with each group of channel bits followed by a balancing bit.

---

4.   See Appendix A.

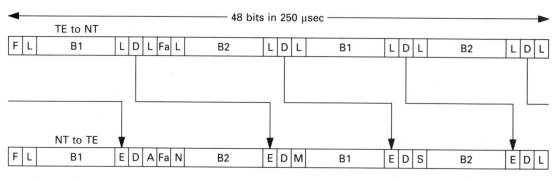

F = framing bit.
L = DC-balancing bit.
E = D-channel echo bit.
A = activation bit.
Fa = auxiliary framing bit.
N = set to opposite of Fa.
M = multiframing bit.

B1 = B-channel bits (16 per frame).
B2 = B-channel bits (16 per frame).
D = D-channel bits (4 per frame).
S = spare bits.

Figure 6.11 Frame Structure at Reference Points S and T for Basic-Rate Access

The frame structure for transmission in the NT-to-TE direction is similar to the frame structure for transmission in the TE-to-NT direction. The following new bits replace some of the DC-balancing bits. The D-channel echo bit (E) is a retransmission by the NT of the most recently received D bit from the TE; the purpose of this echo is explained later in this subsection. The activation bit (A) is used to activate or deactivate a TE, allowing the device to come on line or, when there is no activity, to be placed in low-power-consumption mode. The N bit is normally set to binary 1. The N and M bits may be used for multiframing. The S bit is reserved for other future standardization requirements.

The *contention-resolution* function is required when multiple TE1 terminals share a single physical line (i.e., a multipoint line). There are three types of traffic to consider:

1. *B-channel traffic:* No additional functionality is needed to control access to the two B channels, since each channel is dedicated to a particular TE at any given time.

2. *D-channel traffic:* The D channel is available for use by all the devices for both control signaling and packet transmission, so the potential for contention exists. There are two subcases:

   a. Incoming traffic: The LAPD addressing scheme is sufficient to sort out the proper destination for each data unit.

   b. Outgoing traffic: Access must be regulated so that only one device at a time transmits. This is the purpose of the contention-resolution algorithm.

The contention-resolution algorithm regulates transmission over the D channel so that signaling information is given priority (priority class 1) over all other types of information (priority class 2). The D-channel contention-resolution algorithm has the following elements:

1. When a subscriber device has no LAPD frames to transmit, it transmits a series of binary 1s on the D channel. Using the pseudoternary encoding scheme, this corresponds to the absence of line signal.

2. The NT, on receipt of a D-channel bit, reflects back the binary value as a D-channel echo bit.

3. When a terminal is ready to transmit an LAPD frame, it listens to the stream of incoming D-channel echo bits. If it detects a string of 1 bits of length equal to a threshold value X_i, where i = the priority class for this LAPD frame, it may transmit. Otherwise, the terminal must assume that some other terminal is transmitting and wait.

4. It may happen that several terminals are monitoring the echo stream and begin to transmit at the same time, causing a collision. To overcome this condition, a transmitting TE monitors the echo bits and compares them to its transmitted bits. If a discrepancy is detected, the terminal ceases to transmit and returns to a listen state.

The electrical characteristics of the interface (i.e., 1 bit = absence of signal) are such that any user equipment transmitting a 0 bit will override user equipment transmitting a 1 bit at the same instant. This arrangement ensures that one device will be guaranteed successful completion of its transmission.

The priority mechanism is based on the threshold value X_i. Signaling information is given priority over packet information. Within each of these two priority classes, a station begins at normal priority and is then reduced to lower priority after a transmission. It remains at the lower priority until all other terminals have had an opportunity to transmit. The values of X_i are as follows:

- Signaling information:
  Normal priority $X_1 = 8$
  Lower priority $X_1 = 9$
- Packet information:
  Normal priority $X_2 = 10$
  Lower priority $X_2 = 11$

6.5.5.2 Primary-Rate User-Network Interface

The primary interface, like the basic interface, multiplexes multiple channels across a single transmission medium. In the case of the primary interface, only a point-to-point configuration is allowed. Typically, the interface exists at the T reference point, with a digital PBX or other concentration device controlling multiple TEs and providing a synchronous TDM (time-division multiplexing) facility for access to ISDN. Two data rates are defined for the primary interface: 1.544 Mbps and 2.048 Mbps.

The *ISDN interface at 1.544 Mbps* is based on the North American DS-1 transmission structure, which is used on the T1 transmission service. Figure 6.12, part (a), illustrates the frame format for this data rate. The bit stream is structured into repetitive 193-bit frames. Each frame consists of 24 8-bit time slots and a framing bit; the framing bit is used for synchronization and other management purposes. The same time slot repeated over multiple frames constitutes a channel. At a data rate of 1.544 Mbps, frames repeat at a rate of 1 every 125 μsec, or 8,000 frames per second. Thus, each channel supports 64 Kbps. Typically, the transmission structure is used to support 23 B channels and 1 D channel. As discussed earlier in the chapter, other assignments can be made, including 24 B channels and various combinations of H channels.

The line coding for the 1.544-Mbps interface is AMI (alternate mark inversion) using B8ZS.

The *ISDN interface at 2.048 Mbps* is based on the European transmission structure of the same data rate. Figure 6.12, part (b), illustrates the frame format for this data rate. The bit stream is structured into repetitive 256-bit frames. Each frame consists of 32 8-bit time slots. The first

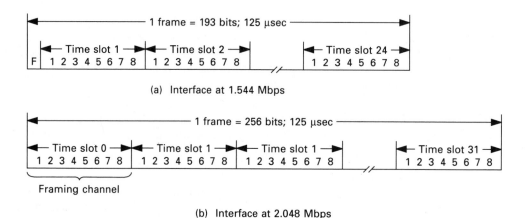

(a) Interface at 1.544 Mbps

(b) Interface at 2.048 Mbps

Figure 6.12 Primary-Access Frame Formats

time slot is used for framing and synchronization purposes; the remaining 31 time slots support user channels. At a data rate of 2.048 Mbps, frames repeat at a rate of 1 every 125 μsec, or 800 frames per second. Thus, each channel supports 64 Kbps. Typically, the transmission structure is used to support 30 B channels and 1 D channel. As discussed earlier, other assignments can be made, such as 31 B channels and various combinations of H channels.

The line coding for the 2.048-Mbps interface is AMI using HDB3.

6.6   SUMMARY

The term *integrated services digital network* (ISDN) refers to a set of recommendations from CCITT that specify the characteristics of a digital voice and data service provided by a digital wide-area network.

The ISDN service is based on the concept of providing a set of channels at a single interface. The B channel, at 64 Kbps, is the principal channel used for circuit switching, packet switching, and dedicated (leased) circuits. The D channel is used for control signaling (call setup) and may also carry some data. For residential users and small businesses, a basic access service of two B channels and one D channel is adequate. For customers with digital PBX or LAN installations, a primary access service of either 23 B channels or 30 B channels and one D channel can be used.

The protocol architecture of ISDN corresponds to the lowest three layers of the OSI model. The physical layer specifies a basic access rate of 192 Kbps and a primary access rate of 1.544 or 2.048 Mbps. At the data-link layer, the LAPD protocol provides a user-to-network protocol over the D channel. At the network layer, a call-control protocol that makes use of LAPD enables the user to request B-channel connections.

APPENDIX 6A   1988 CCITT Recommendations on ISDN

Number	Title	Description
I.110	Preamble and General Structure of the I-Series Recommendations	Provides a broad outline of the structure of the I-series recommendations and their relationships to other recommendations.
I.111	Relationship with Other Recommendations Relevant to ISDNs	Lists other recommendations relevant to ISDNs and/or used in developing the I-series recommendations.
I.112	Vocabulary of Terms for ISDNs	Defines terms considered essential to the understanding and application of the principles of an ISDN.
I.113	Vocabulary of Terms for Broadband Aspects of ISDN	Defines terms considered essential to the understanding and application of the principles of BISDN.
I.120	Integrated Services Digital Networks	Defines the principles used to develop ISDNs; describes the evolutionary path to be taken.
I.121	Broadband Aspects of ISDN	Serves as a guideline for evolving recommendations on BISDN during the study period 1989–1992. Includes principles, service aspects, and basic architectural model.
I.122	Framework for Providing Additional Packet Mode Bearer Services	Establishes an architectural framework that allows for the description of additional packet-mode services. Also provides a general description of interworking requirements between I.122-based services and I.462 (X.31)–based services or PSPDNs.
I.130	Method for the Characterization of Telecommunication Services Supported by an ISDN and Network Capabilities of an ISDN	Defines an attribute method for characterizing ISDN services and capabilities. Describes the methodology to be used to ensure compatibility among all ISDN recommendations.
I.140	Attribute Technique for the Characterization of Telecommunication Services Supported by an ISDN and Network Capabilities of an ISDN	Introduces the attribute technique, describes attributes, and lists attribute values. Attributes characterize services and network capabilities of an ISDN. Serves as a library of all attributes and attribute values used in other I-series recommendations.
I.141	ISDN Network Charging Capabilities Attributes	Discusses the method for identifying the network-charging capabilities and provides a list of attributes.
I.200	Guidance to the I.200 Series of Recommendations	General introduction to the I.200 series.

APPENDIX 6A   *(Cont.)*

Number	Title	Description
I.210	Principles of Telecommunication Services Supported by an ISDN and the Means to Describe Them	Provides classification and a descriptive method for the telecommunication services to be supported by an ISDN as defined in I.130. Gives a basis for defining network capabilities required by ISDNs.
I.220	Common Dynamic Description of Basic Telecommunication Services	Diagrams provide the dynamic description of basic telecommunication services. Provides terminology for user-network interactions.
I.221	Common Specific Characteristics of Services	Identifies and describes specific characteristics of services that are common to individual services and also form a relationship between services.
I.230	Definition of Bearer Service Categories	Defines a recommended set of bearer-service categories that may be supported by an ISDN, together with an overall provision.
I.231	Circuit Mode Bearer Service Categories	Identifies eight bearer-service categories and defines their attributes, values, and dynamic descriptions.
I.232	Packet Mode Bearer Service Categories	Describes a recommended set of packet-mode bearer-service categories and their provision in ISDN.
I.240	Definition of Teleservices	Defines a recommended set of teleservices supported by an ISDN.
I.241	Teleservices Supported by an ISDN	Contains service descriptions for telephony, teletex, telefax 4, mixed mode, videotex, and telex.
I.250	Definition of Supplementary Services	Defines supplementary services to be used in association with basic bearer services and basic teleservices.
I.251	Number Identification Supplementary Services	Describes supplementary number-identification services.
I.252	Call Offering Supplementary Services	Describes and defines call-offering supplementary services.
I.253	Call Completion Supplementary Services	Describes call-completion supplementary services.
I.254	Multiparty Supplementary Services	Describes multiparty supplementary services.
I.255	Community of Interest Supplementary Services	Describes community-of-interest supplementary services.
I.256	Charging Supplementary Services	Describes charging supplementary services.

APPENDIX 6A   *(Cont.)*

Number	Title	Description
I.257	Additional Information Transfer	Describes additional-information-transfer services.
I.310	ISDN—Network Functional Principles	Outlines of the functional principles of the network aspects of ISDNs.
I.320	ISDN Protocol Reference Model	Describes the reference model used to model the information flow within ISDN.
I.324	ISDN Network Architecture	Describes the components and capabilities of the basic architectural model of an ISDN.
I.325	Reference Configurations for ISDN Connection Types	Describes the development of reference configurations for ISDN connection types and what form reference configurations should take. Gives specific reference configurations for 64 Kbps, packet, and broadband classes.
I.326	Reference Configurations for Relative Network Resource Requirements	Evaluates relative network resource requirements. Describes minimum requirements for international transit connection elements.
I.330	ISDN Numbering and Addressing Principles	Provides the concepts, principles, and requirements of the ISDN numbering plan.
I.331	Number Plan for the ISDN Era	The ISDN numbering plan and addressing principles.
I.332	Numbering Principles for Interworking between ISDNs and Dedicated Networks with Different Numbering Plans	Represents a framework by which progress on numbering-plan interworking in study groups may be coordinated.
I.333	Terminal Selection in ISDN	Defines terminal selection and outlines selection procedures and responsibilities.
I.334	Principles Relating ISDN Numbers/Subaddresses to the OSI Reference Model Network Layer Addresses	Specifies concepts and terminology relating ISDN numbers and subaddresses to one another and to OSI reference model network-layer addresses.
I.335	ISDN Routing Principles	Describes the basic routing principles defining the relationship between ISDN telecommunication services and ISDN network capabilities.
I.340	ISDN Connection Types	Describes the set of connection types to be used to support ISDN services.
I.350	General Aspects of Quality of Service and Network Performance in Digital	Defines, describes, and states the purpose of quality of service and network performance and how these concepts are applied

APPENDIX 6A   *(Cont.)*

Number	Title	Description
	Networks, Including ISDN	in digital networks, including ISDN.
I.351	Recommendations in Other Series Concerning Network Performance Objectives that Apply at Reference Point T of an ISDN	Simply a reference to G.821 and G.822.
I.352	Network Performance Objectives for Connection Processing Delays in an ISDN	Provides network performance objectives and values for connection-processing delays that can be used as design objectives in network planning and system design.
I.410	General Aspects and Principles Relating to ISDN User-Network Interfaces	Provides the general aspects and principles to be used in defining the user-network interfaces of ISDNs. Elaborates the concept of having a limited set of such interfaces.
I.411	ISDN User-Network Interfaces—Reference Configurations	Defines the various reference configurations to be found at the ISDN user-network interface.
I.412	ISDN User-Network Interfaces—Interface Structures and Access Capabilities	Defines limited sets of channel types and interface structures for ISDN.
I.420	Basic User-Network Interface	Simply a list of I.400-series recommendations that specify the basic user-network interface.
I.421	Primary Rate User-Network Interface	Simply a list of I.400-series recommendations that specify the primary user-network interface.
I.430	Basic User-Network Interface—Layer 1 Specification	Defines the layer-1 characteristics of the basic user-network interface to be applied at the S or T reference point.
I.431	Primary Rate User-Network Interface—Layer 1 Specification	Defines the layer-1 characteristics of the primary user-network interface to be applied at the S or T reference point.
I.440	ISDN User-Network Interface Data Link Layer—General Aspects	A cross-reference to Q.920, which provides a service definition of the ISDN LAPD data-link layer.
I.441	ISDN User-Network Interface Data Link Layer Specification	A cross-reference to Q.921, which provides a specification of the LAPD protocol.

APPENDIX 6A *(Cont.)*

Number	Title	Description
I.450	ISDN User-Network Interface Layer 3—General Aspects	A cross-reference to Q.930, which provides a definition of the ISDN layer-3 signaling service.
I.451	ISDN User-Network Interface Layer 3 Specification for Basic Call Control	A cross-reference to Q.931, which provides a specification of the ISDN layer-3 user-network signaling protocol.
I.452	Generic Procedures for the Control of ISDN Supplementary Services	Defines the generic procedures applicable for the control of supplementary services at the user-network interface.
I.460	Multiplexing, Rate Adaptation, and Support of Existing Interfaces	A description of how ISDN will support older terminals by means of rate adaptation. Defines methods for multiplexing multiple lower-rate information streams onto a 64-Kbps channel.
I.461	Support of X.21, X.21 *bis,* and X.20 *bis* Based DTEs by an ISDN	Covers the connection of X.21, X.21 *bis,* and X.20 *bis* terminals to an ISDN operating in accordance with circuit-switched or leased-circuit service.
I.462	Support of Packet Mode Terminal Equipment by an ISDN	Defines the aspects of the packet-mode services provided to ISDN users in accordance with ISDN bearer services.
I.463	Support of DTEs with V-Series Type Interfaces by an ISDN	A description of the functions needed to support synchronous V-series terminals on an ISDN.
I.464	Multiplexing, Rate Adaptation, and Support of Existing Interfaces for Restricted 64 kbit/s Transfer Capability	A description of the method of supporting data rates of less than 64 Kbps on an ISDN.
I.465	Support by an ISDN of DTEs with V-Series Type Interfaces with Provisions for Statistical Multiplexing	A cross-reference to V.120, which covers the connection to ISDN of terminals with interfaces for V-series modems.
I.470	Relationship of Terminal Functions to ISDN	Provides direction to the potential functional requirements that may be necessary for any specific terminal to be compatible with ISDN.
I.500	General Structure of ISDN Interworking Recommendations	Explains the organization of the I.500 series of recommendations.

APPENDIX 6A   *(Cont.)*

Number	Title	Description
I.510	Definitions and General Principles of ISDN Interworking	Establishes the definitions and general principles for interworking between ISDNs, between ISDNs and other networks, and internal to an ISDN.
I.511	ISDN-to-ISDN Layer 1 Internetwork Interface	Defines the layer-1 aspects of the ISDN interworking, including reference configurations and interworking functions.
I.515	Parameter Exchange for ISDN Interworking	Provides parameter-exchange principles and functional descriptions for ISDN interworking.
I.520	General Arrangements for Network Interworking between ISDNs	Identifies the general arrangements for ISDN–ISDN interworking and defines the functions and other requirements for the ISDN–ISDN interface.
I.530	Network Interworking between an ISDN and a PSTN	Identifies the interworking functions and requirements to support interworking between an ISDN and a PSTN (public switched telephone network).
I.540	General Arrangements for Interworking between CSPDNs and ISDNs for the Provision of Data Transmission	Describes the general arrangements for interworking between CSPDNs (circuit-switched public data networks) and ISDNs.
I.550	General Arrangements for Interworking between PSPDNs and ISDNs for the Provision of Data Transmission	Describes the general arrangements for interworking between PSPDNs and ISDNs.
I.560	Requirements to Be Met in Providing the Telex Service within the ISDN	Outlines configuration models for the integration of the telex service into ISDN.
I.601	General Maintenance Principles of ISDN Subscriber Access and Subscriber Installation	Outlines general aspects and principles relating to reference configuration and general architecture.
I.602	Application of Maintenance Principles to ISDN Subscriber Installation	Presents the possible elementary functions for the maintenance of the subscriber installation.
I.603	Application of Maintenance Principles to ISDN Basic Accesses	Covers the maintenance part of the ISDN subscriber basic access, controlled by the network.
I.604	Application of Maintenance	Describes the minimum functions required to

APPENDIX 6A *(Cont.)*

Number	Title	Description
	Principles to ISDN Primary Rate Accesses	maintain the subscriber primary access.
I.605	Application of Maintenance Principles to Static Multiplexed ISDN Basic Accesses	Cover the maintenance of the static multiplexed basic-rate access and describes the operations and maintenance aspects of the V_4 interface, defined in Q.512.

APPENDIX 6B   1990 CCITT Interim Recommendations on ISDN

Number	Title	Description
I.2xy	ISDN Frame Mode Bearer Services	Describes the frame-mode bearer services for the order-preserving bidirectional transfer of LAPD frames from one S or T reference point to another. The two services are frame-relay bearer service and frame-switching bearer service.
I.320	ISDN Protocol Reference Model	Revised version of I.320, which now includes a discussion of protocol blocks.
I.324	ISDN Network Architecture	Revised version of I.324, which now includes the aspects of private networks.
I.325	Reference Configurations for ISDN Connection Types	Revised version of I.325, which now includes the aspects of private networks and definitions of network fabric, portions, and boundaries.
I.333	Terminal Selection in ISDN	Revised version.
I.351	Recommendations in Other Series Concerning Network Performance Objectives that Apply at Reference Point T of an ISDN	This revised recommendation now describes the relationships among the 14 existing or planned ISDN performance-related recommendations.
I.352	Network Performance Objectives for Connection Processing Delays in an ISDN	Revised version of I.352, which now includes consideration of national and international network fabrics.
I.35a	Availability Performance for 64 kbit/s ISDN Connection Types	Specifies service availability performance parameters for circuit-mode and packet-mode ISDN bearer services.
I.35e	Reference Events for Defining ISDN Performance Parameters	Defines the performance model, consistent with I.325, to be used in the ISDN performance description.

APPENDIX 6B   *(Cont.)*

Number	Title	Description
I.35p	Network Performance Objectives for Packet-Mode Communication in an ISDN	Defines speed, accuracy, and dependability performance parameters and performance objectives for packet-mode information transfer in an ISDN.
I.3xx	Congestion Management for the Frame Relaying Bearer Service	Describes the user-plane congestion-management strategy and mechanisms for the frame-relaying bearer service. It covers both network and end-user mechanisms and responsibilities to avoid or recover from periods of congestion.
I.464	Multiplexing, Rate Adaptation, and Support of Existing Interfaces for Restricted 64 kbit/s Transfer Capability	Adds an appendix to I.464 that describes an HDLC-based approach to rate adaptation.
I.515	Parameter Exchange for ISDN Interworking	Addition to I.515 that describes optional out-of-band protocol-selection procedures for use by multiprotocol terminal adapters.
I.520	General Arrangements for Network Interworking between ISDNs	Minor revision to Table 4 of I.520.
I.530	Network Interworking between an ISDN and a PSTN	Amendments to I.530 to include packet-mode interworking and the special requirements for the 7-kHz audio bearer service.
I.5xz	FMBS Interworking	Provides the guidelines and functional requirements across interfaces for interworking between the two frame-mode bearer services (FMBSs) and other services.

7
Frame Relay

The 1988 I.122 Recommendation, entitled Framework for Providing Additional Packet Mode Bearer Services, introduced a new form of packet transmission that has become one of the most significant contributions of the ISDN (integrated services digital network) work reflected in the 1988 standards. This new technique is now generally referred to as *frame-mode bearer service* (FMBS), or *frame relay*. The former term emphasizes the service being offered to the user, whereas the latter emphasizes the protocol that implements the service.

Since 1988, significant progress has been made on frame relay. In 1990, CCITT published two interim recommendations:

1. I.2xy: ISDN Frame Mode Bearer Services
2. I.3xx: Congestion Management for the Frame Relaying Bearer Service

The work on frame relay is more developed in the United States, where ANSI (American National Standards Institute) has issued three standards:

1. ANSI T1.606: Architectural Framework and Service Description for Frame-Relaying Bearer Service (1990)
2. ANSI T1.617: Signalling Specification for Frame Relay Bearer Service (1991)
3. ANSI T1.618: Core Aspects of Frame Protocol for Use with Frame Relay Bearer Service (1991)

It is anticipated that the final CCITT recommendations will be closely aligned with the current ANSI standards. This chapter draws on all of these documents, using the ANSI specifications for details not provided by CCITT.

7.1 MOTIVATION

The traditional approach to packet switching, as discussed in Chapter 3, is X.25. The following are several key features of the X.25 approach:

- Call-control packets, used for setting up and clearing virtual circuits, are carried on the same channel and the same virtual circuit as data packets. In effect, in-band signaling is used.

243

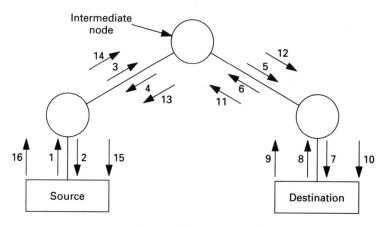

(a) Packet-switching network

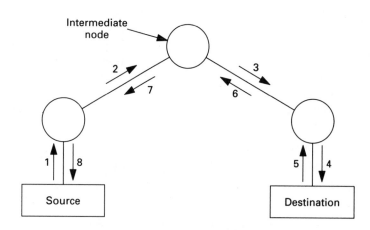

(b) Frame-relay network

**Figure 7.1 Packet Switching versus Frame Relay:
Source Sending, Destination Responding**

- Multiplexing of virtual circuits takes place at layer 3.
- Both layer 2 and layer 3 include flow-control and error-control mechanisms.

This approach results in considerable overhead. Figure 7.1, part (a), indicates the flow of data-link frames required for the transmission of a single data packet from source end system to destination end system and the return of an acknowledgment packet. At each hop through the network, the data-link control protocol involves the exchange of a data frame and an acknowledgment frame. Furthermore, at each intermediate node, state tables must be maintained for each virtual circuit to deal with the call-management and flow-control/error-control aspects of the X.25 protocol.

All this overhead may be justified when there is a significant probability of error on any of the links in the network. This approach may not be the most appropriate for ISDN. On the one hand, ISDN employs reliable digital transmission technology over high-quality, reliable transmission links, many of which are optical fiber. On the other hand, with ISDN, high data rates can be achieved, especially with the use of H channels. In this environment, the overhead of X.25 is not only unnecessary but degrades the effective utilization of the high data rates available with ISDN.

Frame relaying is designed to eliminate as much as possible of the overhead of X.25. The key respects in which frame relaying differs from a conventional X.25 packet-switching service are:

- Call-control signaling is carried on a separate logical connection from user data. Thus, intermediate nodes need not maintain state tables or process messages relating to call control on an individual per-connection basis.

- Multiplexing and switching of logical connections takes place at layer 2 instead of layer 3, eliminating one entire layer of processing.

- There is no hop-by-hop flow control and error control. End-to-end flow control and error control are the responsibility of a higher layer, if they are employed at all.

Figure 7.1, part (b), indicates the operation of frame relay, in which a single user data frame is sent from source to destination, and an acknowledgment, generated at a higher layer, is carried back in a frame.

Let us consider the advantages and disadvantages of this approach. The principal potential disadvantage of frame relaying, compared to X.25, is that we have lost the ability to do link-by-link flow and error control. (Although frame relay does not provide end-to-end flow and error control, these are easily provided at a higher layer.) In X.25, multiple virtual circuits are carried on a single physical link, and LAPB (link-access protocol, balanced) is available at the link level for providing reliable transmission from the source to the packet-switching network and from the packet-switching network to the destination. In addition, at each hop through the network, the link control protocol can be used for reliability. With the use of frame relaying, this hop-by-hop link control is lost. However, with the increasing reliability of transmission and switching facilities, this is not a major disadvantage.

The advantage of frame relaying is that we have streamlined the communications process. The protocol functionality required at the user-network interface is reduced, as is the internal network processing. As a result, lower delay and higher throughput can be expected. Preliminary results indicate a reduction in frame-processing time of an order of magnitude (Bush 1989), and the CCITT recommendation (I.2xy) indicates that frame relay is to be used at access speeds up to 2 Mbps. Thus, we can expect to see frame relaying supplant X.25 as ISDN matures.

ANSI standard T1.606 lists four examples of applications that would benefit from the frame-relay service used over a high-speed H channel:

1. *Block-interactive data applications:* An example of a block-interactive application would be high-resolution graphics (e.g., high-resolution videotex, CAD/CAM). The pertinent characteristics of this type of application are low delays and high throughput.

2. *File transfer:* The file-transfer application is intended to cater to large file-transfer requirements. Transit delay is not as critical for this application as it is, for example, for the first application. High throughput might be necessary in order to produce reasonable transfer times for large files.

3. *Multiplexed low bit rate:* The multiplexed low-bit-rate application exploits the multiplexing capability of the frame-relaying service in order to provide an economical access arrangement

for a large group of low-bit-rate applications. An example of one such low-bit-rate application is given in point 4. The low-bit-rate sources may be multiplexed onto a channel by an NT (network termination) function.

4. *Character-interactive traffic:* An example of a character-interactive traffic application is text editing. The main characteristics of this type of application are short frames, low delays, and low throughput.

Frame relay can be viewed as a streamlined version of X.25, which accomplishes the key functions of X.25 using only two layers. Another way of viewing frame relay is that it is an enhanced version of I.465/V.120. That latter standard allows for multiple logical connections to be multiplexed on a single circuit between two subscribers. Frame relay supports not only multiplexing but switching: multiple logical connections from one subscriber over one channel can be set up to multiple subscribers across the network.

7.2 FRAME-RELAY ARCHITECTURE

Figure 7.2 depicts the protocol architecture for frame relay. As in other areas of ISDN, we need to consider two separate planes of operation: a control (C) plane, which is involved in the establishment and termination of logical connections, and a user (U) plane, which is responsible for the transfer of user data between subscribers. Thus, C-plane protocols are between a subscriber and the network, whereas U-plane protocols provide end-to-end functionality.

For the actual transfer of information between end users, the U-plane protocol is Q.922. Q.922 is a new recommendation, issued for the first time on an interim basis in 1991, that is an enhanced

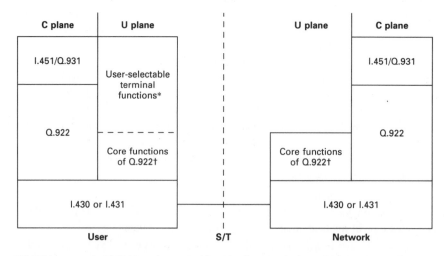

*Q.922 is one protocol that may be used, although other standard or proprietary protocols may also be used. Additional requirements may be placed on terminals, depending on the congestion control and throughput enforcement used. One mechanism that can satisfy the congestion-control requirements is for the terminal to implement a dynamic window algorithm.
†Additional functions may be needed for throughput monitoring and enforcement.

Figure 7.2 Frame-Relay-Protocol Architecture

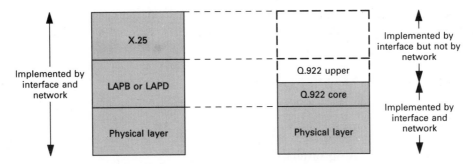

Figure 7.3 A Comparison of X.25 and Frame-Relay-Protocol Stacks

version of LAPD (link-access protocol, D channel; I.441/Q.921). Only the core functions of Q.922 are used for frame relay:

- Frame delimiting, alignment, and transparency

- Frame multiplexing/demultiplexing using the address field

- Inspection of the frame to ensure that it consists of an integer number of octets prior to zero-bit insertion or following zero-bit extraction

- Inspection of the frame to ensure that it is neither too long nor too short

- Detection of transmission errors

- Congestion-control functions

The last function listed is new to Q.922 and is discussed in a later section of the chapter. The remaining functions listed are also core functions of I.441/Q.921.

The core functions of Q.922 in the U plane constitute a sublayer of the data-link layer. This provides the bare service of transferring data-link frames from one subscriber to another, with no flow control or error control. Above this, the user may choose to select additional data-link or network-layer end-to-end functions. These are not part of the ISDN service. Based on the core functions, ISDN offers frame relaying as a connection-oriented link-layer service with the following properties:

- Preservation of the order of frame transfer from one edge of the network to the other

- Nonduplication of frames

- A small probability of frame loss

In the control plane, Q.922 is used to provide a reliable data-link control service, with error control and flow control, for the delivery of I.451/Q.931 messages.

As can be seen, this architecture reduces to the bare minimum the amount of work accomplished by the network. User data are transmitted in frames with virtually no processing by the intermediate network nodes, other than to check for errors and to route based on connection number. A frame in error is simply discarded, leaving error recovery to higher layers.

Figure 7.3 compares the protocol architecture of frame relay to that of X.25. The packet-handling functions of X.25 operate at layer 3 of the OSI (open systems interconnection) model. At layer 2, either LAPB or LAPD is used, depending on whether the protocol is operating on a B channel or a D channel. Figure 7.4 illustrates the functional difference between X.25 and frame relay. As can be seen, the processing burden on the network is considerably higher for X.25 than for frame relay.

7.3   FRAME-RELAY CALL CONTROL

This section examines the various approaches for setting up frame relay connections, and then describes the protocol used for connection control.

7.3.1   Call-Control Alternatives

The call-control protocol for frame relay must deal with a number of alternatives. First, let us examine the provision of frame-handling services. For frame-relay operation, a user is not connected directly to another ISDN user but rather to a frame handler in the network, just as, for X.25, an ISDN user is connected to a packet handler. There are two cases to be considered (Figure 7.5):

1. *Case A:* The local exchange does not provide the frame-handling capability. In this case, switched access must be provided from the TE to the frame handler elsewhere in the network. This can be either a demand connection or a semipermanent connection. In either case, the frame-relay service is provided over a B or an H channel.

2. *Case B:* The local exchange does provide the frame-handling capability. In this case, the frame-relay service may be provided on a B or an H channel or on the D channel. For B- or H-channel service, a demand connection must be used to dedicate a B or an H channel to frame relay, unless a semipermanent assignment already exists. For D-channel service, this point has not been finally specified, but it appears that both a demand service and a semipermanent service via the D channel may be options.

All of the preceding considerations have to do with the connection between the subscriber and the frame handler, which we refer to as the *access connection.* Once this connection exists, it is possible to multiplex multiple logical connections, referred to as *frame-relay connections,* over this access connection. Such logical connections may be either on-demand or semipermanent.

Table 7.1 summarizes these call-control alternatives. First, consider the establishment of an access connection. If the connection is semipermanent, then no call-control protocol is required. If the connection is to be set up on demand, then there are two alternatives:

1. *Case A:* The connection is to be set up on a B or an H channel. The normal ISDN call-control protocol, I.451/Q.931, is used on the D channel to set up the access connection. This is the same strategy used to support X.25 on a B channel.

2. *Case B:* If the connection is to be set up on a B or an H channel, then the normal ISDN call-control protocol, I.451/Q.931, is used on the D channel to set up the access connection. If the D channel is to be used and the access connection is on-demand rather than semipermanent (for X.25, the connection is always semipermanent), then, again, I.451/Q.931 is used on the D channel to set up the access connection.

Now, consider the establishment of a frame-relay connection. For this purpose, an access connection must already exist. For a semipermanent frame-relay connection, no call-control pro-

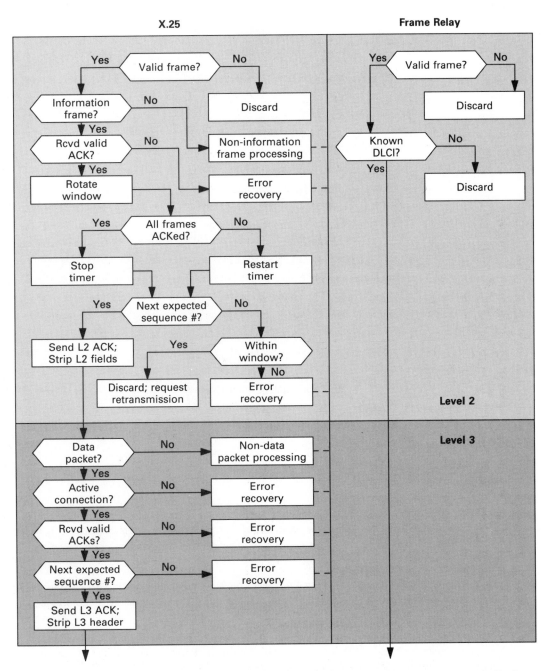

Source: T. Jones, K. Rehbehn, and E. Jennings, *The Buyer's Guide to Frame Relay Networking* (Herndon, Va.: Netrix Corporation, 1991).

Figure 7.4 Simplified Model of X.25 and Frame-Relay Processing

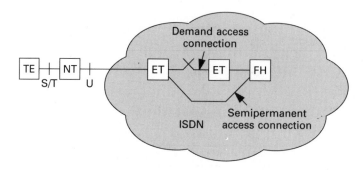

(a) Case A: switched access

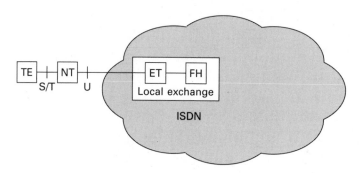

(b) Case B: integrated access

TE = terminal equipment.
NT = network termination.
ET = exchange termination.
FH = frame handler.

Figure 7.5 Frame-Relay Access Modes

tocol is required; note that this requires the existence of a semipermanent access connection. If the frame-relay connection is to be set up on demand over an existing access connection, there are, again, two alternatives:

1. *Case A:* It is possible to use call-control messages on frame-relay connection DLCI (data-link connection identifier) = 0. As with I.465/V.120, these messages are carried in the information field of the data-link frame.

2. *Case B:* Alternatively—again, as with I.465/V.120—it is possible to use the same call-control messages embedded in LAPD frames on the D channel. For this purpose, SAPI (service-access-point identifier) = 0 is used, as for I.451/Q.931 messages.

In either case, the call-control messages are actually a subset of the messages used in I.451/Q.931, with some new parameters tailored to the frame-relay application.

Table 7.1 Connection Establishment for Frame-Relay Services

		Access Connection/Frame-Relay Connection		
		Demand/Demand	**Semipermanent/ Demand**	**Semipermanent/ Semipermanent**
Case A: switched access to frame handler	**Establishment of access connection**	I.451/Q.931 on D channel to set up connection on B or H channel	Semipermanent	
	Establishment of frame-relay connection	In-channel frame-relay messages on B or H channel, DLCI = 0		Semipermanent
Case B: integrated access to frame handler	**Establishment of access connection**	I.451/Q.931 on D channel to set up connection on D, B, or H channel	Semipermanent	
	Establishment of frame-relay connection	Frame-relay messages on D channel, SAPI = 0		Semipermanent

7.3.2 Call-Control Protocol

The call-control protocol involves the exchange of messages between the user and a frame handler over a previously created connection. The messages are transmitted in one of two ways:

1. *Case A:* Messages are transmitted in frame-relay frames over the same channel (B or H) as the frame-relay connection, using the same frame structure, with a data-link connection identifier of DLCI = 0.
2. *Case B:* Messages are transmitted in LAPD frames with SAPI = 0 over the D channel.

In either case, the set of messages is a subset of those used in I.451/Q.931. For frame relay, however, these messages are used to set up and manage logical frame-relay connections rather than actual circuits. Accordingly, some of the parameters used for frame-relay call control differ from those used in I.451/Q.931.

The set of messages used for frame-relay call control is, in fact, identical with those used for packet-mode access-connection control. These were listed, with brief definitions, in Table 6.6. Tables 7.2 through 7.4 show the parameters used with these messages for frame-relay call control. Parameters are designated as mandatory (M) or optional (O). Table 7.5 provides a brief definition of these parameters.

Several of the parameters are new and warrant further elaboration in the following subsections.

Table 7.2 Parameters for Frame-Relay Call-Establishment Messages

	Alerting	Call Proceeding	Connect	Connect Acknowledge	Progress	Setup
Protocol discriminator	M	M	M	M	M	M
Call reference	M	M	M	M	M	M
Message type	M	M	M	M	M	M
Channel identification	O	O	O			O
Data-link connection identifier	O	O	O			O
Progress indicator	O	O	O		M	O
Display	O	O	O	O	O	O
User-user	O		O			O
End-to-end transit delay			O			O
Link-layer core parameters			O			O
Link-layer protocol parameters			O			O
Connected number			O			
Connected subaddress			O			
Low-layer compatibility			O			O
Cause					O	
Bearer capability						M
Network-specific facilities						O
Calling party number						O
Calling party subaddress						O
Called party subaddress						O
Transit-network selection						O
Repeat indicator						O
High-layer compatibility						O

7.3.2.1 Bearer Capability

The bearer-capability parameter is used in the SETUP message to request a bearer service, as specified in I.122, to be provided by the network (Figure 7.6). Unlike many of the messages parameters, which are passed through from source to destination, this one is used by the network in establishing the connection.

Table 7.3 Parameters for Frame-Relay Call-Clearing Messages

	Disconnect	Release	Release Complete
Protocol discriminator	M	M	M
Call reference	M	M	M
Message type	M	M	M
Cause	M	O	O
Display	O	O	O
Connected number	O	O	O
Connected subaddress	O	O	O
User-user	O	O	O

The format of this parameter conforms to the general bearer-capability parameter in Q.931. In the current version of the standard, only one value is allowed in each field; all other values are reserved for future use.

Octet 3 includes an indication of whether or not the bearer capability is a CCITT standard. If it is, then the information-transfer-capability field specifies unrestricted digital information. Octet 4 indicates that the transfer mode is frame-mode. The remainder of the octet is normally used in Q.931 to specify a transfer rate; this subfield is reserved for current use. Octet 6 specifies the use of the core aspects of Q.922.

7.3.2.2 Link-Layer Core Parameters

The link-layer core parameters information element indicates requested parameters related to the core data-link service. This information is exchanged between each end user and the network. The format of this information element is shown in Figure 7.7. Note that each parameter consists of a parameter-identifier field followed by 1 or more octets of parameter value. The following parameters are included:

- *Maximum frame size:* the maximum size of a frame in octets, determined independently in each direction. The default value is 262 octets for the D channel and 4,096 octets for the B and H channels. The two end users may negotiate a smaller maximum size.

- *Requested/agreed throughput:* the average number of frame-relay information field bits transferred per second. The value is expressed in the form $A \times 10^B$ bps, where A is the multiplier and B is the magnitude.

Table 7.4 Parameters for Miscellaneous Frame-Relay Messages

	Status	Status Enquiry
Protocol discriminator	M	M
Call reference	M	M
Message type	M	M
Cause	M	
Call state	M	
Display	O	O

Table 7.5 Parameters for Frame-Relay Messages

Bearer capability

Indicates provision, by the network, of one of the bearer capabilities defined in I.231 and I.232. Contains detailed information on protocol options at each layer to construct the desired service.

Call Reference

Identifies the B-channel call to which this message refers. As with X.25 virtual circuit numbers, it has only local significance. The call-reference field comprises three subfields. The length subfield specifies the length of the remainder of the field in octets. This length is 1 octet for a basic-rate interface and 2 octets for a primary-rate interface. The flag indicates which end of the LAPD logical connection initiated the call.

Call state

Describes the current status of a call, such as active, detached, or disconnect request.

Called/calling party number

Identifies the subnetwork address of the called or calling party.

Called/calling party subaddress

Identifies the subaddress of the called or calling party.

Cause

Used to describe the reason for generating certain messages, to provide diagnostic information in the event of procedural errors, and to indicate the location of the cause originator. The location is specified in terms of which network originated the cause.

Channel identification

Identifies the channel/subchannel within the interface (e.g., which B channel).

Connected number/connected subaddress

Indicates the connected user to the calling user, according to OSI network-service requirements.

Data-link connection identifier

Identifies the logical connection that is the subject of the message. The DLCI allows multiple logical connections to be multiplexed over the same channel.

Display

Supplies additional information coded in IA5 (International Alphabet 5, also known as ASCII) characters. Intended for display on a user terminal.

End-to-end transit delay

Used to request and indicate the nominal maximum permissible transit delay applicable on a per-call basis. The end-to-end delay is the time it takes to send a frame containing user data from one end user to another, including the total frame-relay processing time in the end-user systems.

High Layer Compatibility

Supplies the type terminal that is on the user side of an S/T interface. The network transports this information transparently end-to-end.

Link Layer Core Parameters

Indicates requested parameters related to the core data-link service. This information is exchanged between each end user and the network.

Link Layer Protocol Parameters

Indicates requested parameters related to the end-to-end data-link service. This information is exchanged between a pair of end users and is carried transparently by the network.

Table 7.4 (*Cont.*)

Low Layer Compatibility

Used for compatibility checking. Includes information transfer capability, information transfer rate, and protocol identification at layers 1 through 3.

Message Type

Identifies which message is being sent. The contents of the remainder of the message depend on the message type.

Network-Specific Facilities

Allows the specification of facilities peculiar to a particular network.

Progress Indicator

Describes an event that has occurred during the life of a call.

Protocol Discriminator

Used to distinguish messages for user-network call control from other message types. Other sorts of protocols may share the D channel.

Repeat Indicator

Indicates that one possibility should be selected from repeated information elements.

Transit Network Selection

Identity of a network that connection should use to get to final destination. This parameter may be repeated within a message to select a sequence of networks through which a call must pass.

User-User Information

Used to transfer information between ISDN users that should not be interpreted by the network(s).

- *Minimum acceptable throughput:* the lowest throughput value that the calling user is willing to accept for the call. If the network or the called user is unable to sustain this throughput, the call is cleared.
- *Burst size:* the maximum amount by which the cumulative frames can exceed the value allowed by the mean throughput at any time.
- *Maximum frame-rate value:* the maximum number of frames per second that may be sent in one direction across the user-network interface.

8	7	6	5	4	3	2	1	Octet
Bearer-capability								
0	0	0	0	0	1	0	0	1
Information-element identifier								
Length of the bearer-capability contents								2
1 Ext.	Coding standard	Information-transfer capability						3
1 Ext.	Transfer mode	0	0	0	0	0		4 *
		Reserved						
1 Ext.	1 0 Layer-2 ident.	User information layer-2 protocol						6

*Octets 4a and 5 are omitted. The configuration is assumed to be point-to-point, and the method of establishment is on-demand.

Figure 7.6 Bearer-Capability Information Element

8	7	6	5	4	3	2	1	Octet
Link-layer core parameters / Information-element identifier								
0	1	0	0	1	0	0	0	1
Length of link-layer core parameters contents								2
Outgoing maximum frame size								3
0	0	0	0	1	0	0	1	
0 Ext.	Outgoing maximum frame size							3a *
1 Ext.	Outgoing maximum frame size (cont.)							3b
Incoming maximum frame size								4
0	0	0	0	1	0	1	0	
0 Ext.	Incoming maximum frame size							4a *
1 Ext.	Incoming maximum frame size (cont.)							4b
Requested/agreed throughput								5
0	0	0	0	1	0	1	1	
0 Ext.	Outgoing magnitude			Outgoing multiplier				5a
0/1 Ext.	Outgoing multiplier (cont.)							5b
0 Ext.	Incoming magnitude			Incoming multiplier				5c
1 Ext.	Incoming multiplier (cont.)							5d
Minimum acceptable throughput								6 †
0	0	0	0	1	1	0	0	
0 Ext.	Outgoing magnitude			Outgoing multiplier				6a
0/1 Ext.	Outgoing multiplier (cont.)							6b
0 Ext.	Incoming magnitude			Incoming multiplier				6c
1 Ext.	Incoming multiplier (cont.)							6d
Outgoing burst size								7
0	0	0	0	1	1	0	1	
0 Ext.	Outgoing-burst-size value							7a
1 Ext.	Outgoing-burst-size value (cont.)							7b
Incoming burst size								8
0	0	0	0	1	1	1	0	
0 Ext.	Incoming-burst-size value							8a
1 Ext.	Incoming-burst-size value (cont.)							8b
Outgoing maximum frame rate								9
0	0	0	0	1	1	1		
1 Ext.	Outgoing-maximum-frame-rate value							9a
Incoming maximum frame rate								10
0	0	0	1	0	0	0		
1 Ext.	Incoming-maximum-frame-rate value							10a

Notes: The terms *incoming* and *outgoing* are defined with respect to the calling user. All the parameters are optional and position-independent. If certain parameters are not included, the network default value will be used.

*The size of a frame is the number of octets after the address field and before the FCS field in the frame. The count is done either before zero-bit insertion or following zero-bit extraction.

†Included only in the SETUP message.

Figure 7.7 Link-Layer Core Parameters Information Element

7.3.2.3 Link-Layer-Protocol Parameters

The link-layer-protocol parameters information element indicates requested parameters related to the end-to-end data-link service. This information is exchanged between a pair of end users and is carried transparently by the network. The format of this information element is shown in Figure 7.8. The following parameters are included:

8	7	6	5	4	3	2	1	Octet
0	1	Link-layer-protocol parameters 0 0 1 0 0 Information-element identifier					1	1
Length of link-layer-protocol parameters contents								2
0 Ext.	0	Forward-window identifier 0 0 0 0				1	0	3
1 Ext.	Forward-window value							3a
0 Ext.	0	Backward-window identifier 0 0 0				1	1	4
1 Ext.	Backward-window value							4a
0 Ext.	0	Forward-acknowledgment-timer identifier 0 0 0 1				1	0	5 *
0 Ext.	Forward-acknowledgment-timer value							5a
1 Ext.	Forward-acknowledgment-timer value (cont.)							5b
0 Ext.	0	Backward-acknowledgment-timer identifier 0 0 0 1				1	1	6
0 Ext.	Backward-acknowledgment-timer value							6a
1 Ext.	Backward-acknowledgment-timer value (cont.)							6b
0 Ext.	0	Mode of operation 0 0 1			0	0	0	7 †
1 Ext.	Spare						Mode indication	7a

*In the case of frame-relay bearer service, layer-2 elements of procedures are end-to-end. The acknowledgment-timer value should be based on per-call cumulative transit delay. If included by the originating user, it will be based on the maximum end-to-end transit delay. The terminating user can adjust the value based on the cumulative transit delay.
†Mode of operation is only included when the LLC (logical link control) octet 6 "user information layer-2 protocol" is coded with one of the codepoints: CCITT Rec. X.25 link layer, CCITT Rec. X.25 multilink, extended LAPB for half-duplex operation (T71), and CCITT Rec. X.75 Single Link Procedure (SLP).

Figure 7.8 Link-Layer-Protocol Parameters Information Element

(a) Frame format

Flag	Address	Information	FCS	Flag
1 octet	2–4	Variable	2	1

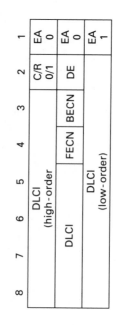

(b) Address field — 2 octets (default)

(c) Address field — 3 octets

(d) Address field — 4 octets

8	7	6	5	4	3	2	1

DLCI (high-order)

| | FECN | BECN | C/R 0/1 | EA 0 |
| DLCI (low-order) | | | DE | EA 1 |

DLCI (low-order)

	DLCI					C/R 0/1	EA 0
	FECN	BECN	DE	EA 0
				EA 1

C/R = command/response; use is application-specific.
EA = address-field extension.
DE = discard-eligibility indicator.
BECN = backward explicit congestion notification.
FECN = forward explicit congestion notification.
DLCI = data-link connection identifier.

Figure 7.9 Frame-Relay Formats

258

- *Window value:* the maximum size of the sliding-window flow-control window; may take on a value from 1 to 127

- *Acknowledgment-timer value:* the amount of time that a sender will wait for acknowledgment before retransmission, expressed in units of tenths of a second

- *Mode of operation:* indicates whether 3-bit or 7-bit sequence numbers will be used

7.4   USER DATA TRANSFER

The operation of frame relay for user data transfer is best explained by beginning with the frame format, illustrated in Figure 7.9, part (a). The format is similar to that of LAPD and LAPB, with one obvious omission: there is no control field. This has the following implications:

- There is only one frame type, used for carrying user data. There are no control frames.

- It is not possible to use in-band signaling; a logical connection can only carry user data.

- It is not possible to perform flow control and error control, since there are no sequence numbers.

The flag and frame-check sequence (FCS) fields function as in LAPD and LAPB. The information field carries higher-layer data. If the user elects to implement additional data-link control functions end-to-end, then a data-link frame can be carried in this field. Specifically, a common selection will be to use enhanced LAPD, as defined in Q.922, to perform functions above the core functions of Q.922. Thus, the entire LAPD frame would be carried in the information field. Note that the protocol implemented in this fashion is strictly between the end subscribers and is transparent to ISDN.

The address field has a default length of 2 octets and may be extended to 3 or 4 octets. It carries a data-link connection identifier (DLCI) of 10, 17, or 24 bits. The DLCI serves the same function as the virtual circuit number in X.25: it allows multiple logical frame-relay connections to be multiplexed over a single channel. As in X.25, the connection identifier has only local significance: each end of the logical connection assigns its own DLCI from the pool of locally unused numbers, and the network must map from one to the other. The alternative, using the same DLCI on both ends, would require some sort of global management of DLCI values.

For D-channel frame relay, a 2-octet address field is assumed, and the DLCI values are limited to the range 480–1,007. This is equivalent to an SAPI (service-access-point identifier) of 32–62. Thus, frame-relay frames can be multiplexed with LAPD frames on the D channel, and the two types of frames are distinguished on the basis of bits 8 to 3 in the first octet of the address field.

The length of the address field, and hence of the DLCI, is determined by the address-field extension (EA) bits. The C/R bit is application-specific and not used by the standard frame-relay protocol. The remaining bits in the address field have to do with congestion control and are discussed in section 7.6.

7.5   NETWORK FUNCTION

The frame-relaying function performed by ISDN, or any network that supports frame relaying, consists of the routing of frames with the format of Figure 7.9, part (a), based on their DLCI values.

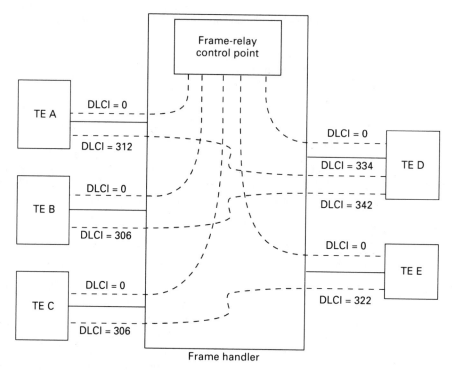

Figure 7.10 Frame-Handler Operation

Figure 7.10 suggests the operation of a frame handler in a situation in which a number of users are directly connected to the same frame handler over different physical channels. The operation could just as well involve relaying a frame through two or more frame handlers. In this figure, the decision-making logic is shown conceptually as a separate module, the frame-relay control point. This module is responsible for making routing decisions.

Typically, routing is controlled by entries in a connection table based on DLCI that map incoming frames on one channel to another. The frame handler switches a frame from an incoming channel to an outgoing channel based on the appropriate entry in the connection table and translates the DLCI in the frame before transmission. For example, incoming frames from TE B on logical connection 306 are retransmitted to TE D on logical connection 342. This technique has been referred to as chained-link path routing (Lai 1988). The figure also shows the multiplexing function: multiple logical connections to TE D are multiplexed over the same physical channel.

Note also that all the TEs have a logical connection to the frame-relay control point with a value of DLCI = 0. These connections are reserved for in-channel call control, to be used when I.451/Q.931 on the D channel is not used for frame-relay call control.

As part of the frame-relay function, the FCS of each incoming frame is checked. When an error is detected, the frame is simply discarded. It is the responsibility of the end users to institute error recovery above the frame-relay protocol.

Figure 7.11 is another view of the protocols involved in frame relay, this time from the point of view of the individual frame-relay connections. There is a common physical layer and frame-

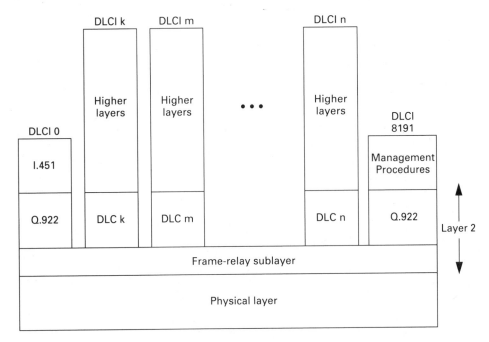

Figure 7.11 Multiplexing at the Frame-Relay Sublayer

relay sublayer. An optional layer-2 data-link control protocol may be included above the frame-relay sublayer. This selection is application-dependent and may differ for different frame-relay connections (DLC i). If frame-relay call-control messages are carried in frame-relay frames, these are carried on DLCI 0, which provides a frame-relay connection between the user and the frame handler. DLCI 8191 is dedicated to management procedures.

7.6 CONGESTION CONTROL

7.6.1 Background

A frame-relay network is a form of packet-switching network in which the "packets" are layer-2 frames. As in any packet-switching network, one of the key areas in the design of a frame-relay network is congestion control. To understand the issue involved in congestion control, we need to look at some results from queueing theory. In essence, a frame-relay network is a network of queues. At each frame handler, there is a queue of frames for each outgoing link. If the rate at which frames arrive and queue up exceeds the rate at which frames can be transmitted, the queue size grows without bound and the delay experienced by a frame goes to infinity. Even if the frame-arrival rate is less than the frame-transmission rate, queue length will grow dramatically as the arrival rate approaches the transmission rate. As a rule of thumb, when the line for which frames are queueing becomes more than 80 percent utilized, the queue length grows at an alarming rate.

Consider the queueing situation at a single frame handler, such as is illustrated in Figure 7.12. Any given frame handler has a number of transmission links attached to it: one or more to other

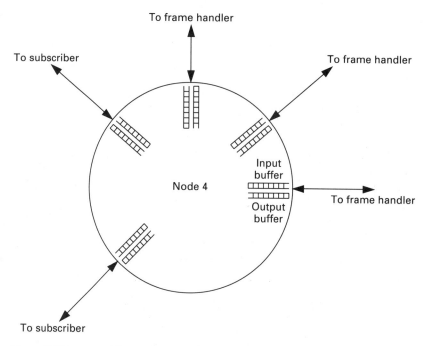

Figure 7.12 Input and Ouput Queues of a Frame Handler

frame handlers and zero or more to ISDN subscribers. On each link, frames arrive and depart. We can consider that there are two buffers at each link: one to accept arriving frames and one to hold frames that are waiting to depart. In practice, there might be two fixed-size buffers associated with each link, or there might be a pool of memory available for all buffering activities. In the latter case, we can think of each link as having two variable-size buffers associated with it, subject to the constraint that the sum of all buffer sizes is a constant.

In any case, as frames arrive, they are stored in the input buffer of the corresponding link. The frame handler examines each incoming frame to make a routing decision and then moves the frame to the appropriate output buffer. Frames queued up for output are transmitted as rapidly as possible. Now, if frames arrive too fast for the frame handler to process them (make routing decisions) or faster than frames can be cleared from the outgoing buffers, then eventually, frames will arrive for which no memory is available.

When such a saturation point is reached, one of two general strategies can be adopted. The first such strategy is to simply discard any incoming frame for which there is no available buffer space. This approach is self-defeating, since the discarded frames will have to be retransmitted, adding to network congestion. The other alternative is to use some mechanism that restricts the rate at which new frames are inserted into the network. This latter approach is referred to as congestion control.

Figure 7.13 shows the effect of congestion in general terms. Figure 7.13, part (a), plots the throughput of a network (number of frames delivered to a destination station per unit of time) versus the offered load (number of frames transmitted by all subscribers), whereas Figure 7.13,

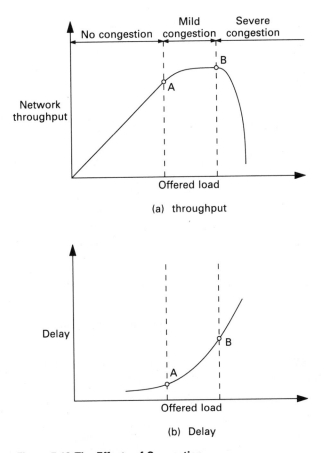

(a) throughput

(b) Delay

Figure 7.13 The Effects of Congestion

part (b), plots the average delay from entry to exit across the network. At light loads, throughput—and hence, network utilization—increase as the offered load increases. As the load continues to increase, a point is reached (point A in the plot) beyond which the throughput of the network increases at a rate slower than the rate at which the offered load is increased. This is due to network entry into a mild congestion state. In this region, the network continues to cope with the load, although with increased delays.

As the load on the network increases, the queue lengths of the various frame handlers grow. Eventually, a point is reached (point B in the plot) beyond which throughput actually drops with increased offered load. The reason for this is that the buffers at each frame handler are of finite size. When the buffers at a frame handler become full, it must discard frames. Thus, the sources must retransmit the discarded frames in addition to new frames. This only exacerbates the situation: as more and more frames are retransmitted, the load on the system grows, and more buffers become saturated. While the system is trying desperately to clear the backlog, users are pumping old and new frames into the system. Even successfully delivered frames may be retransmitted because it took too long, at a higher layer (e.g., the transport layer), to acknowledge them: the sender assumes the frame did not get through. Under these circumstances, the effective capacity of the system is virtually zero.

It is clear that these catastrophic events must be avoided, which is the task of congestion control. The object of all congestion-control techniques is to limit queue lengths at the frame handlers so as to avoid throughput collapse.

7.6.2   Frame Relay and Congestion Control

CCITT, in I.3xx, defines the objectives for frame-relay congestion control as follows:

- Minimize frame discard
- Maintain, with high probability and minimum variance, the agreed-upon quality of service
- Minimize the possibility of one end user's monopolizing network resources at the expense of other end users
- Be simple to implement and place little overhead on either end users or the network
- Create minimal additional network traffic
- Distribute network resources fairly among end users
- Limit the spread of congestion to other networks and elements within the network
- Operate effectively regardless of the traffic flow in either direction between end users
- Have minimum interaction with or impact on other systems in the frame-relaying network
- Minimize the variance in quality of service delivered to individual frame-relay connections during congestion (e.g., individual logical connections should not experience sudden degradation when congestion approaches or has occurred)

The challenge of congestion control is particularly acute for a frame-relay network because of the limited tools available to the frame handlers. The frame-relay protocol has been streamlined in order to maximize throughput and efficiency. A consequence of this is that a frame handler cannot control the flow of frames coming from a subscriber or an adjacent frame handler using the typical sliding-window flow-control protocol, such as is found in LAPD.

Congestion control is the joint responsibility of the network and the end users. The network (i.e., the collection of frame handlers) is in the best position to monitor the degree of congestion, whereas the end users are in the best position to control congestion by limiting the flow of traffic. With the preceding in mind, we can consider two general congestion-control strategies: congestion avoidance and congestion recovery.

Congestion-avoidance procedures are used at the onset of congestion to minimize the effect on the network. Thus, these procedures would be initiated at or prior to point A in Figure 7.13, to prevent congestion from progressing to point B. Near point A, there would be little evidence available to end users that congestion is increasing. Thus, there must be some *explicit signaling* mechanism from the network that will trigger the congestion avoidance.

Congestion-recovery procedures are used to prevent network collapse in the face of severe congestion. These procedures are typically initiated when the network has begun to drop frames due to congestion. Such dropped frames will be reported by some higher layer of software (e.g., Q.922) and serve as an *implicit signaling* mechanism. Congestion-recovery procedures operate around point B and within the region of severe congestion, as shown in Figure 7.13.

CCITT and ANSI consider congestion avoidance with explicit signaling and congestion recovery with implicit signaling to be complementary forms of congestion control in the frame-relaying bearer service.

7.6.3 Congestion Avoidance with Explicit Signaling

For explicit signaling, 2 bits in the address field of each frame are provided. Either bit may be set by any frame handler that detects congestion. If a frame handler receives a frame in which one or both of these bits are set, it must not clear the bits before forwarding the frame. Thus, the bits constitute signals from the network to the end user. The 2 bits are:

1. *Backward explicit congestion notification (BECN)*: notifies the user that congestion-avoidance procedures should be initiated where applicable for traffic in the direction opposite to that of the received frame. It indicates that the frames the user transmits on this logical connection may encounter congested resources.

2. *Forward explicit congestion notification (FECN)*: notifies the user that congestion-avoidance procedures should be initiated where applicable for traffic in the same direction as the received frame. It indicates that this frame, on this logical connection, has encountered congested resources.

Let us consider how these bits are employed by the network and the user. First, for the *network response,* it is necessary for each frame handler to monitor its queueing behavior. If queue lengths begin to grow to a dangerous level, then either FECN or BECN bits, or a combination, should be set to try to reduce the flow of frames through that frame handler. The choice of FECN or BECN may be determined by whether the end users on a given logical connection are prepared to respond to one or the other of these bits. This may be determined at configuration time. In any case, the frame handler has some choice as to which logical connections should be alerted to congestion. If congestion is becoming quite serious, all logical connections through a frame handler might be notified. In the early stages of congestion, the frame handler might just notify users for those connections that are generating the most traffic.

In an appendix to ANSI T1.606, a procedure for monitoring queue lengths is suggested. The frame handler monitors the size of each of its queues. A cycle begins when the outgoing circuit goes from idle (queue empty) to busy (nonzero queue size, including the current frame). The average queue size over the previous cycle and the current cycle is calculated. If the average size exceeds a threshold value, then the circuit is in a state of incipient congestion, and the congestion-avoidance bits should be set on some or all logical connections that use that circuit. By averaging over two cycles instead of just monitoring current queue length, the system avoids reacting to temporary surges that would not necessarily produce congestion.

The average queue length may be computed by determining the area (product of queue size and time interval) over the two cycles and dividing by the time of the two cycles. This algorithm is illustrated in Figure 7.14.

The *user response* is determined by the receipt of BECN or FECN signals. The simplest procedure is the response to a BECN signal: the user simply reduces the rate at which frames are transmitted until the signal ceases. The response to an FECN is more complex, since it requires the user to notify its peer user on this connection to restrict its flow of frames. The core functions used in the frame-relay protocol do not support this notification. Therefore, it must be done at a

---

The algorithm employs the following variables:

t = current time
t_i = time of the ith arrival or departure event
f_{qi} = number of frames in the system after the event
T_0 = time at the beginning of the previous cycle
T_1 = time at the beginning of the current cycle

The algorithm consists of the three components:

1. Queue-length update:
   beginning with $q0 := 0$,
   if the ith event is an arrival event, $q_i := q_{i-1} + 1$
   if the ith event is a departure event, $q_i := q_{i-1} - 1$

2. Queue-area (integral) update:

   area of the previous cycle $= \sum_{t_i \varepsilon [T_0, T_1)} q_{i-1}(t_i - t_{i-1})$

   area of the current cycle $= \sum_{t_i \varepsilon [T_1, t)} q_{i-1}(t_i - t_{i-1})$

3. Average-queue-length update:

   average queue length over the two cycles

   $$= \frac{\text{area of the two cycles}}{\text{time of the two cycles}} = \frac{\text{area of the two cycles}}{t - T_0}$$

Figure 7.14 Queue-Length Averaging Algorithm

higher layer, such as the transport layer. The flow control could also be accomplished by Q.922 or some other link control protocol implemented above the frame-relay sublayer (Figure 7.11). Q.922 is particularly useful, since it includes an enhancement to LAPD that permits the user to adjust the window size.

7.6.4   Congestion Recovery with Implicit Signaling

Implicit signaling occurs when the network discards a frame and this fact is detected by the end user at a higher layer, such as Q.922. When this happens, the end-user software may deduce that congestion exists. For example, in a data-link control protocol such as Q.922, when a frame is dropped because of buffer overflow in the network, the following frame will generate a REJECT frame from the receiving end point. Thus, a higher-layer procedure can be used to provide flow control to recover from congestion.

The ANSI standard suggests that a user that is capable of varying the flow-control window size use this mechanism in response to implicit signaling. Let us assume that the layer-2 window size, W, can vary between the parameters W_{min} and W_{max} and is initially set to W_{max}. In general, we would like to reduce W as congestion increases to gradually throttle the transmission of frames. Three classes of adaptive window schemes, based on response to the receipt of a REJECT frame, have been suggested (Chen and Rege 1989; Doshi and Nguyen 1988):

1.1 Set $W = \max [W - 1, W_{\min}]$.

1.2 Set $W = W_{\min}$.

1.3 Set $W = \max [\alpha W, W_{\min}]$, where $0 < \alpha < 1$.

Successful transmissions (measured by receipt of acknowledgments) may indicate that the congestion has gone away and window size should be increased. Two possible approaches are:

2.1 Set $W = \min [W + 1, W_{\max}]$ after N consecutive successful transmissions.

2.2 Set $W = \min [W + 1, W_{\max}]$ after W consecutive successful transmissions.

A study reported by Chen and Rege (1989) suggests that the use of strategy 1.3 with $\alpha = 0.5$ plus strategy 2.2 provides good performance over a wide range of network parameters and traffic patterns.

So far, we have talked about the user role in congestion recovery. The network role, of course, is to discard frames as necessary. One bit in the address field of each frame can be used to provide guidance—*discard eligibility (DE)*, which indicates a request that a frame be discarded in preference to other frames in which this bit is not set when it is necessary to discard frames.

The DE capability makes it possible for the user to temporarily send more frames than it is allowed to on average. In this case, the user sets the DE bit on the excess frames. The network will forward these frames if it has the capacity to do so.

The DE bit can also be set by a frame handler. The network can monitor the influx of frames from the user and employ the DE bit to protect the network with flexible "fire walls." That is, if the frame handler to which the user is directly connected decides that the input is potentially excessive, it sets the DE bit on each frame and then forwards it further into the network.

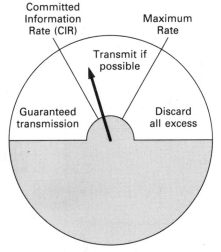

Source: T. Jones, K. Rehbehn, and E. Jennings,
The Buyer's Guide to Frame Relay Networking
(Herndon, Va.: Netrix Corporation, 1991).

Figure 7.15 Operation of the CIR

The DE bit can be used in such a way as to provide guidance for the discard decision and at the same time serve as a tool for providing a guaranteed level of service. This tool can be used on a per-logical-connection basis to ensure that heavy users can get the throughput they need without penalizing lighter users. The mechanism works as follows: Each user can negotiate a *committed information rate (CIR)* (in bits per second) at connection-setup time. The requested CIR represents the user's estimate of its "normal" traffic during a busy period; the granted CIR, which is less than or equal to the requested CIR, is the network's commitment to deliver data at that rate in the absence of errors. The frame handler to which the user's station attaches then performs a metering function (Figure 7.15). If the user is sending data at less than the CIR, the incoming frame handler does not alter the DE bit. If the rate exceeds the CIR, the incoming frame handler will set the DE bit on the excess frames and then forward them; such frames may either get through or be discarded if congestion is encountered. Finally, a maximum rate is defined, such that any frames above the maximum are discarded at the entry frame handler.

This procedure, in theory, could be exercised on a continuous basis. In practice, the practical approach is for the frame handler to measure traffic over each logical connection for a time interval Tc, which is set by the network. Accordingly, two additional parameters may be negotiated. The *committed burst size (Bc)* is the maximum amount of data that the network commits to deliver over a logical connection during an interval Tc. The *excess burst size (Be)* is the maximum amount of data by which a user can exceed Bc during an interval Tc; these data are delivered with lower probability than the data within Bc.

The ANSI specification suggests the use of a leaky-bucket algorithm for monitoring flow (illustrated in Figure 7.16). The frame handler records the cumulative amount of data sent by each user in a counter, C. The counter is decremented at a rate of Bc every Tc time units. Of course, the counter is not allowed to become negative, so the actual assignment is C ← MIN [C,,Bc]. Whenever the counter value exceeds Bc but is less than Bc + Be, incoming data are in excess of the committed burst size and are forwarded with the DE bit set. If the counter reaches Bc + Be, all incoming frames are discarded until the counter has been decremented.

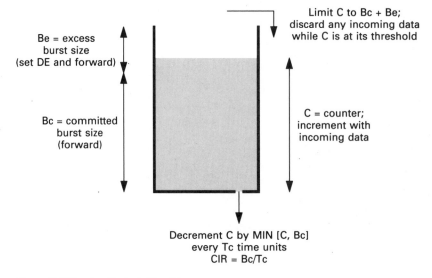

Figure 7.16 Leaky-Bucket Algorithm

7.7   SUMMARY

Frame relay was developed as an alternative to X.25 and provides a streamlined packet-switching interface and mechanism. By reducing the considerable overhead associated with X.25, frame relay provides a means for exploiting the high data rates available on contemporary networks. Although the standards for frame relay are being developed in the context of ISDN, frame relay is enjoying widespread acceptance in a number of non-ISDN environments.

The frame relay specification covers two major areas: call control and data transfer. Frame relay connections may be permanent, in which case call control is not required. For switched frame relay connections, a separate call-control connection is used, providing efficient out-of-band signaling.

The data-transfer portion of the frame-relay specification calls for a two-layer protocol architecture, the physical and data-link layers. End-system addressing and connection multiplexing are done at layer 2, eliminating one layer of processing.

Because of the simplicity of the frame-relay protocol, there are no mechanisms for traditional data-link error and flow control. Thus, a frame-relay network is vulnerable to congestion. To compensate for this, simple congestion avoidance and congestion recovery mechanisms are built into the protocol.

8
Broadband ISDN, Cell Relay, and SONET

In 1988, as part of its I series of recommendations on ISDN (integrated services digital network), CCITT issued the first two recommendations relating to BISDN (broadband ISDN): I.113, Vocabulary of Terms for Broadband Aspects of ISDN, and I.121, Broadband Aspects of ISDN. These documents represent the level of consensus reached among the participants concerning the nature of the future BISDN as of late 1988. They provide a preliminary description and a basis for future standardization and development work. Some of the important notions developed in these documents are presented in Table 8.1.

With both demand (user interest) and supply (the technology for high-speed networking) evolving rapidly, the usual four-year cycle would have been fatal to hopes of developing a standardized high-speed network utility. To head off the possibility of a fragmentation of effort and a proliferation of nonstandard products and services, CCITT has issued an interim set of 1990 draft recommendations on BISDN. The set of thirteen documents (Appendix 8A) provides, for the first time, a detailed and specific master plan for the broadband revolution. Although much work remains to be done, the 1990 standards are sufficient to allow field trials to follow within a few years of the issue date (Day 1991). This chapter provides an overview of this master plan.

We begin this chapter with an overview of BISDN architecture and protocols. Next is an examination of the details of the ATM protocol and formats. Then, the requirement for mapping various applications onto ATM is examined, with a consideration of the ATM-adaptation layer (AAL). The remaining aspect of ATM to examine is the manner in which ATM cells are actually packaged for transmission across the user-network interface. Before addressing this topic, however, we need to look at one of the alternative transmission structures to be used: SONET/SDH (synchronous optical network/synchronous digital hierarchy).

8.1 BROADBAND ISDN ARCHITECTURE

The BISDN will differ from a narrowband ISDN in a number of ways. To meet the requirement for high-resolution video, an upper-channel rate on the order of 150 Mbps is needed. To simultaneously support one or more interactive services and distributive services, a total subscriber line

Table 8.1 Noteworthy Statements in I.113 and I.121

Broadband: A service or system requiring transmission channels capable of supporting rates greater than the primary rate.

The term B-ISDN is used for convenience in order to refer to and emphasize the broadband aspects of ISDN. The intent, however, is that there be one comprehensive notion of an ISDN which provides broadband and other ISDN services.

Asynchronous transfer mode (ATM) is the target transfer mode solution for implementing a B-ISDN. It will influence the standardization of digital hierarchies and multiplexing structures, switching and interfaces for broadband signals.

B-ISDN will be based on the concepts developed for ISDN and may evolve by progressively incorporating additional functions and services (e.g., high quality video applications).

The reference configuration defined in I.411 is considered sufficiently general to be applicable not only for a basic access and a primary rate access but also to a broadband access. Both reference points S and T are valid for broadband accesses.

rate of about 600 Mbps is needed. In terms of today's installed telephone plant, this is a stupendous data rate to sustain. The only appropriate technology for widespread support of such data rates is optical fiber. Hence, the introduction of BISDN depends on the pace of introduction of fiber subscriber loops.

Internal to the network, there is the issue of the switching technique to be used. The switching facility has to be capable of handling a wide range of different bit rates and traffic parameters (e.g., burstiness). Despite the increasing power of digital circuit-switching hardware and the increasing use of optical-fiber trunking, it is difficult to handle the large and diverse requirements of BISDN with circuit-switching technology. For this reason, there is increasing interest in some type of fast packet switching as the basic switching technique for BISDN. This form of switching readily supports a new user-network interface protocol known as asynchronous transfer mode (ATM), which is examined in detail later in this chapter.

8.1.1 Functional Architecture

Figure 8.1 depicts the functional architecture of BISDN (compare this with Figure 6.2). As with narrowband ISDN, control of BISDN is based on common-channel signaling. Within the network, common-channel signalling will be enhanced to support the expanded capabilities of a higher-speed network. Similarly, the user-network control-signaling protocol will be an enhanced version of I.451/Q.931.

BISDN must, of course, support all the 64-Kbps transmission services, both circuit-switching and packet-switching, that are supported by narrowband ISDN. This protects the user's investment and facilitates migration from narrowband to broadband ISDN. In addition, broadband capabilities are provided for higher-data-rate transmission services. At the user-network interface, these capabilities will be provided with the connection-oriented ATM facility.

8.1.2 User-Network Interface

The reference configuration defined in I.411 is considered general enough to be used for BISDN. Figure 8.2, which is almost identical to Figure 6.3, shows the reference configuration for BISDN. In order to clearly illustrate the broadband aspects, the notations for reference points and functional

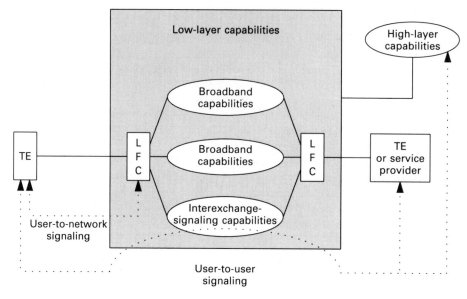

LFC = local function capabilites.
TE = terminal equipment.

Figure 8.1 BISDN Architecture

groupings are appended with the letter B (e.g., B-NT1, T_B). The broadband functional groups are equivalent to the functional groups defined in I.411. Interfaces at the R reference point may or may not have broadband capabilities.

8.1.3   Transmission Structure

In terms of data rates available to BISDN subscribers, three new transmission services are defined. The first of these consists of a full-duplex 155.52-Mbps service. The second service defined is asymmetrical, providing transmission from the subscriber to the network at 155.52 Mbps and in the other direction at 622.08 Mbps. And the highest-capacity service yet defined is a full-duplex 622.08-Mbps service.

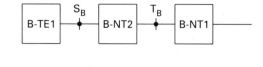

Figure 8.2 BISDN Reference Configurations

A data rate of 155.52 Mbps can certainly support all the narrowband ISDN services. That is, it readily supports one or more basic- or primary-rate interfaces. In addition, it can support most of the BISDN services. At that rate, one or several video channels can be supported, depending on the video resolution and the coding technique used. Thus, the full-duplex 155.52-Mbps service will probably be the most common BISDN service.

The higher data rate of 622.08 Mbps is needed to handle multiple video distribution, such as might be required when a business conducts multiple simultaneous videoconferences. This data rate makes sense in the network-to-subscriber direction. The typical subscriber will not initiate distribution services and thus would still be able to use the lower, 155.52-Mbps, service. The full-duplex 622.08-Mbps service would be appropriate for a video distribution provider.

The 1988 document (I.121) discussed the need for a 150-Mbps and 600-Mbps data-rate service. The specific rates chosen for the 1990 documents were designed to be compatible with defined digital-transmission services.

The 1988 document also included a list of specific channel data rates to be supported within these services. The 1990 documents drop all reference to channel rates. This allows the user and the network to negotiate any channel capacity that can fit in the available capacity provided by the network. Thus, BISDN becomes considerably more flexible and can be tailored precisely to a wide variety of applications.

8.2 BROADBAND ISDN PROTOCOLS

The protocol architecture for BISDN introduces some new elements not found in the ISDN architecture, as depicted in Figure 8.3. For BISDN, it is assumed that the transfer of information across the user-network interface will employ what is referred to as asynchronous transfer mode (ATM). ATM is, in essence, a form of packet transmission across the user-network interface in the same way that X.25 is a form of packet transmission across the user-network interface. One difference between X.25 and ATM is that X.25 includes control signaling on the same channel as data transfer, whereas ATM makes use of common-channel signaling. Another difference is that X.25 packets may be of varying length, whereas ATM packets are of fixed size, referred to as cells.

The decision to use ATM for BISDN is a remarkable one. This implies that BISDN will be a packet-based network, certainly at the interface and almost certainly in terms of its internal switch-

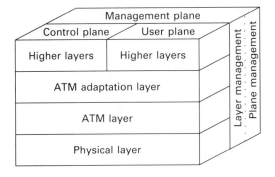

Figure 8.3 BISDN Protocol Reference Model

Table 8.2 Functions of the BISDN Layers

	Higher-Layer Functions		Higher Layers	
	Convergence	CS	AAL	
	Segmentation and reassembly	SAR		
	Generic flow control Cell-header generation/extraction Cell VPI/VCI (virtual path identifier/virtual channel identifier) translation Cell multiplex and demultiplex	ATM		
Layer Management	Cell-rate decoupling HEC (header-error control) header-sequence generation/verification Cell delineation Transmission-frame adaptation Transmission-frame generation/recovery	TC	Physical layer	
	Bit timing Physical medium	PM		

CS = convergence sublayer.
SAR = segmentation-and-reassembly sublayer.
AAL = ATM-adaptation layer.
ATM = asynchronous transfer mode.
TC = transmission-control sublayer.
PM = physical-medium sublayer.

ing. Although the recommendation also states that BISDN will support circuit-mode applications, this will be done over a packet-based transport mechanism. Thus, ISDN, which began as an evolution from the circuit-switching telephone network, will transform itself into a packet-switching network as it takes on broadband services.

Two layers of the BISDN protocol architecture relate to ATM functions. There is an ATM layer common to all services that provides packet-transfer capabilities and an ATM-adaptation layer (AAL) that is service-dependent. The AAL maps higher-layer information into ATM cells to be transported over BISDN, then collects information from ATM cells for delivery to higher layers. The use of ATM creates the need for an adaptation layer to support information-transfer protocols not based on ATM. Two examples listed in I.121 are PCM (pulse code modulation) voice and LAPD (link-access protocol, D channel). PCM voice is an application that produces a stream of bits from a voice signal. To employ this application over ATM, it is necessary to assemble PCM bits into packets (called cells in the recommendation) for transmission and to read them out on reception in such a way as to produce a smooth, constant flow of bits to the receiver. For LAPD, LAPD frames must be mapped into ATM packets, which will probably mean segmenting one LAPD frame into a number of packets on transmission and reassembling the frame from packets on reception. By allowing the use of LAPD over ATM, all the existing ISDN applications and control-signaling protocols can be used on BISDN.

The protocol reference model makes reference to three separate planes:

1. *User plane:* provides for user information transfer, along with associated controls (e.g., flow control, error control)

2. *Control plane:* performs call-control and connection-control functions

3. *Management plane:* includes plane management, which performs management functions related to a system as a whole and provides coordination between all the planes, and layer management, which performs management functions related to resources and parameters residing in its protocol entities

The 1988 I.121 Recommendation contains the protocol reference model depicted in Figure 8.3 but provides virtually no detail on the functions to be performed at each layer. The 1990 documents include a more detailed description of the functions to be performed, as illustrated in Table 8.2. These functions are explored later in this chapter.

8.3 ASYNCHRONOUS TRANSFER MODE

We begin this section with a discussion of the design considerations that led to the choice of ATM for broadband ISDN. The remainder of the section is concerned with the details of the ATM specification.

8.3.1 The Choice of Cell Relay for Broadband ISDN

Figure 8.4 depicts a spectrum of switching techniques available to transport information across a network. The two extreme ends of the spectrum represent the two traditional switching techniques: circuit switching and packet switching; the remaining techniques are of more recent vintage. In general, the techniques toward the left end of the line provide transmission with little or no variability and with minimal processing demands on attached stations, whereas techniques toward the right end provide increased flexibility to handle varying bit rates and unpredictable traffic at the expense of increased processing complexity.

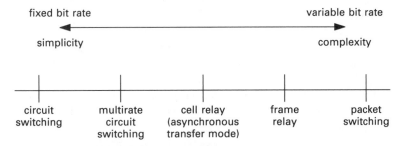

Source: Reproduced with permission from *Asynchronous Transfer Mode: Solution for Broadband ISDN* by Martin de Prycker published in 1991 by Ellis Horwood, Chichester.

Figure 8.4 Spectrum of Switching Techniques

8.3.1.1   Circuit Switching

Circuit switching, the traditional technique used for telephone networks, is the basic technology for narrowband ISDN. The essence of circuit switching is the establishment of a fixed-capacity circuit for the complete duration of a connection. To accommodate different data-rate requirements and/or multiple users at an end point, a number of circuits can be multiplexed in a fixed, synchronous time-division-multiplexing (TDM) structure.

When the standards work on broadband ISDN began in the mid-1980s, it was generally assumed by most participants that some form of synchronous time-division-multiplexing technique would be used, as is the case with the basic- and primary-rate access methods for ISDN. Under this approach, the interface structure that was proposed was:

$$j \times H4 + k \times H2 + l \times H1 + m \times H0 + n \times B + D$$

where D, B, H0, and H1 (H11 or H12) are narrowband ISDN channels and H2 and H4 are new BISDN fixed-rate channels. H2 would be in the range of 30 to 45 Mbps and H4 in the range of 120 to 140 Mbps.

Although the synchronous-TDM approach is a natural extension of narrowband ISDN, it does not provide the best model for BISDN. The synchronous approach has two basic disadvantages. First, it does not provide a flexible interface for meeting a variety of needs. At the high data rates offered by BISDN, there could be a wide variety of applications, and many different data rates, that need to be switched. One or two fixed-rate channel types do not provide a structure that can easily accommodate this requirement. Furthermore, many data (as opposed to voice or video) applications are bursty in nature and can more efficiently be handled with some sort of packet-switching approach.

The second disadvantage of the synchronous approach for high-speed transmission is that the use of multiple high data rates (e.g., a number of H2 and H4 channels) complicates the switching system. It would require switches that can handle data streams of multiple high data rates. This is in contrast to narrowband ISDN, which has just the 64-Kbps data stream to switch.

Thus, synchronous TDM has been rejected. However, it is still possible to multiplex several ATM streams using synchronous-TDM techniques to achieve transmission interfaces that exceed the rate of operation of ATM switches and multiplexers. We examine this topic in section 8.6.

8.3.1.2   Multirate Circuit Switching

An enhancement of the traditional synchronous-TDM approach has been investigated that seeks to provide more flexibility (Prycker 1991). This technique is known as multirate circuit switching. The transmission technique for multirate circuit switching is the same as that for pure circuit switching. The enhancement provided by multirate circuit switching is the ability to construct a connection consisting of multiple, synchronized circuits. For example, the video codecs developed for narrowband ISDN, and standardized by Recommendation H.261, can operate at bit rates that are multiples of the 64-Kbps B-channel circuit rate.

The multirate circuit-switching approach does provide some increased level of flexibility at the cost of increased switching and access complexity, and it does support a variety of applications that require different sustained data rates. However, it still does not provide an efficient means of supporting bursty traffic.

8.3.1.3   Packet Switching

The long-haul circuit-switched telecommunications network was originally designed to handle voice traffic, and the majority of traffic on these networks continues to be voice. A key characteristic of circuit-switched networks is that resources within the network are dedicated to a particular call. For voice connections, the resulting circuit will enjoy a high percentage of utilization, since, most of the time, one party or the other is talking. However, as the circuit-switched network began to be used increasingly for data connections, two shortcomings became apparent:

1. In a typical terminal-to-host data connection, the line is idle much of the time. Thus, with data connections, a circuit-switched approach is inefficient.

2. In a circuit-switched network, the connection provides for transmission at a constant data rate. Thus, each of the two devices that are connected must transmit and receive at the same data rate as the other. This limits the utility of the network in interconnecting a variety of host computers and terminals.

Traditional packet switching, based on X.25, overcomes these shortcomings. However, X.25 is itself limited in two areas. First, because of the considerable overhead in the protocol, it is difficult to implement an X.25-based network to support applications that require high data rates. Second, because of the variable delay in delivering packets, X.25 is not suitable for applications such as voice that require a constant bit rate.

8.3.1.4   Frame Relay

Packet switching was developed at a time when digital long-distance transmission facilities exhibited a relatively high error rate compared to today's facilities. As a result, there is a considerable amount of overhead built into packet-switching schemes to compensate for errors. The overhead includes extra bits added to each packet to enhance redundancy and additional processing at the end stations and the intermediate network nodes to detect and recover from errors.

With modern, high-speed telecommunications systems, this overhead is unnecessary and counterproductive. It is unnecessary because the rate of errors has been dramatically lowered and any remaining errors can easily be caught by logic in the end systems that operates above the level of the packet-switching logic. It is counterproductive because the overhead involved soaks up a significant fraction of the high capacity provided by the network.

To take advantage of the high data rates and low error rates of contemporary networking facilities, frame relay was developed. Whereas the original packet-switching networks were designed with a data rate to the end user of about 64 Kbps, frame-relay networks are designed to operate at user data rates of up to 2 Mbps. The key to achieving these high data rates is to strip out most of the overhead involved with error control.

8.3.1.5   Cell Relay

Cell relay, also known as asynchronous transfer mode, is, in a sense, a culmination of all the developments in circuit switching and packet switching over the past 20 years. One useful way to view cell relay is as an evolution from frame relay. Both frame relay and ATM take advantage of the reliability and fidelity of modern digital facilities to provide faster packet switching than X.25. Like frame relay and X.25, cell relay allows multiple logical connections to be multiplexed over a single physical interface. As with frame relay, there is no link-by-link error control or flow control with cell relay. The most obvious difference between cell relay and frame relay is that frame relay uses variable-length packets, called frames, and cell relay uses fixed-length packets, called cells. As with frame relay, cell relay provides minimum overhead for error control, depending on the inherent reliability of the transmission system and on higher layers of logic to catch and correct remaining errors. By using a fixed packet length, the processing overhead is reduced even further for cell relay compared to frame relay. The result is that cell relay is designed to work in the range of tens and hundreds of megabits per second, compared to the 2 Mbps of frame relay.

Another way to view cell relay is as an evolution from multirate circuit switching. With multirate circuit switching, only fixed-data-rate channels are available to the end system. Cell relay allows the definition of virtual channels with data rates that are dynamically defined at the time that the virtual channel is created. By using small, fixed-size cells, cell relay is so efficient that it can offer a constant-data-rate channel even though it is using a packet-switching technique. Thus, cell relay extends multirate circuit switching to allow multiple channels with the data rate of each channel dynamically set on demand.

With cell relay, a key design issue is the size of the cell. The choice of cell size is governed by a trade-off among factors such as overall network delay, transmission efficiency, and network complexity. Depending on the weighting given to the various factors, a payload value for cell relay of between 32 and 64 octets is derived (Prycker 1991). Within the CCITT deliberations, representatives from Europe favored a 64-octet payload, whereas the United States and Japan favored a 32-octet payload. Splitting the difference, a compromise value of 48 octets was selected, and that is the value in the standard.

8.3.2   Overview of ATM

Figure 8.5 shows the overall hierarchy of function in an ATM-based network. This hierarchy is seen from the point of view of the internal network functions needed to support ATM as well as the user-network functions. The ATM layer consists of virtual channel and virtual path levels; these are discussed in the next subsection.

The physical layer can be divided into three functional levels:

1. *Transmission path level:* extends between network elements that assemble and disassemble the payload of a transmission system. For end-to-end communication, the payload is end-user information. For user-to-network communication, the payload may be signaling information. Cell-delineation and header-error-control functions are required at the end points of each transmission path.

	Higher layers		
ATM layer	Virtual channel level		
	Virtual path level		
Physical layer	Transmission path level		
	Digital section level		
	Regenerator section level		

Figure 8.5 ATM Transport Hierarchy

2. *Digital section level:* extends between network elements that assemble and disassemble a continuous bit or byte stream. This refers to the exchanges or signal-transfer points in a network that are involved in switching data streams.

3. *Regenerator section level:* a portion of a digital section. An example of this level is a repeater that is used to simply regenerate the digital signal along a transmission path that is too long to be used without such regeneration; no switching is involved.

8.3.3   Virtual Channels and Virtual Paths

Logical connections in ATM are referred to as virtual channel connections (VCCs). A VCC is analogous to a virtual circuit in X.25 or a frame-relay logical connection. It is the basic unit of switching in BISDN. A VCC is set up between two end users through the network, and a variable-rate, full-duplex flow of fixed-size cells is exchanged over the connection. VCCs are also used for user-network exchange (control signaling) and network-network exchange (network management and routing).

For ATM, a second sublayer of processing has been introduced that deals with the concept of virtual path (Figure 8.6). A virtual path connection (VPC) is a bundle of VCCs that have the same end points. Thus, all the cells flowing over all the VCCs in a single VPC are switched together.

The virtual path concept was developed in response to a trend in high-speed networking in which the control cost of the network is becoming an increasingly higher proportion of the overall network cost (Burg and Dorman 1991). The virtual path technique helps contain the control cost by grouping connections sharing common paths through the network into a single unit. Network-management actions can then be applied to a small number of groups of connections instead of to a large number of individual connections.

Several advantages can be listed for the use of VPCs:

- *Simplified network architecture:* Network transport functions can be separated into those related to an individual logical connection (VCC) and those related to a group of logical connections (VPC).

- *Increased network performance and reliability:* The network deals with fewer, aggregated entities.

- *Reduced processing and short connection-setup time:* Much of the work is done when the VPC is set up. By reserving capacity on a VPC in anticipation of later call arrivals, new virtual channel connections can be established by executing simple control functions at the end points of the VPC; no call processing is required at transit nodes. Thus, the addition of new VCCs to an existing VPC involves minimal processing.

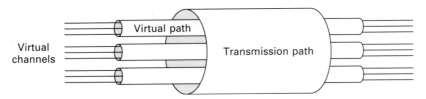

Figure 8.6 ATM Connection Relationships

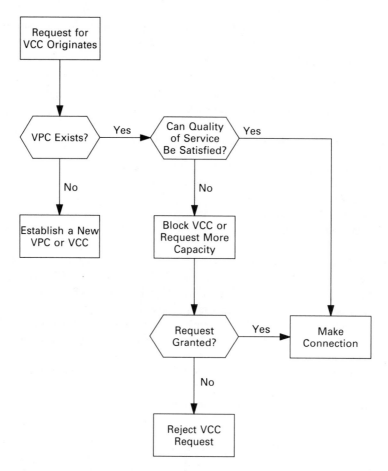

Source: J. Burg and D. Dorman, "Broadband ISDN Resource Management: The Role of Virtual Paths," *IEEE Communications Magazine* (September 1991).

Figure 8.7 Call Establishment Using Virtual Paths

- *Enhanced network services:* The VPC is used internally to the network but is also visible to the end user. Thus, the user may define closed user groups or closed networks of virtual channel bundles.

Figure 8.7 suggests in a general way the call-establishment process using VCCs and VPCs. The process of setting up a VPC is decoupled from the process of setting up an individual VCC:

- The VPC control mechanisms include calculating routes, allocating capacity, and storing connection state information.

- For an individual VCC setup, control involves checking that there is a VPC to the required destination node with sufficient available capacity to support the VCC and with the appropriate quality of service, and then storing the required state information (VCC/VPC mapping).

Table 8.3 Virtual Path/Virtual Connection Terminology

Virtual channel (VC)	A generic term used to describe unidirectional transport of ATM cells associated by a common unique identifier value.
Virtual channel link	A means of unidirectional transport of ATM cells between a point where a VCI value is assigned and the point where that value is translated or terminated.
Virtual channel identifier (VCI)	Identifies a particular VC link for a given VPC.
Virtual channel connection (VCC)	A concatenation of VC links that extends between two points where the adaptation layer is accessed. VCCs are provided for the purpose of user-user, user-network, or network-network information transfer. Cell-sequence integrity is preserved for cells belonging to the same VCC.
Virtual path	A generic term for a bundle of VC links; all the VC links in a bundle have the same end points.
Virtual path link	A group of VC links, identified by a common value of VPI, between a point where a VPI value is assigned and the point where that value is translated or terminated.
Virtual path identifier (VPI)	Identifies a particular VP link.
Virtual path connection (VPC)	A concatenation of VP links that extends between the point where the VCI values are assigned and the point where those values are translated or removed—i.e., extending the length of a bundle of VC links that share the same VPI. VPCs are provided for the purpose of user-user, user-network, or network-network information transfer.

The terminology of virtual paths and virtual channels used in the standard is a bit confusing and is summarized in Table 8.3. Whereas most of the ISDN and BISDN concepts that we deal with in this book relate only to the user-network interface, the concepts of virtual path and virtual channel are defined in the CCITT recommendations with reference to both the user-network interface and the internal network operation.

Figure 8.8 may help to clarify the relationship among the various terms. A virtual channel connection provides end-to-end transfer of ATM cells between ATM users (usually, the ATM-adaptation layer). Each end point associates a unique virtual channel identifier with each VCC; as with X.25, the two end points may employ different VCIs for the same VCC. In addition, within the network, there may be a number of points at which VCCs are switched, and at those points, the VCI may be changed. Thus, a VCC consists of a concatenation of one or more virtual channel links, with the VCI remaining constant for the extent of the VC link and changing at the VC switch points.

Between an end point and a VC switch point, or between two VC switch points, a virtual path connection provides a route for all VC links that share the two VPC end points. Again, at this level, there may be internal switching, such that a VPC passes through one or more VP switch points, with the virtual path identifier changing at each such point. Thus, a VPC consists of a concatenation of one or more virtual path links.

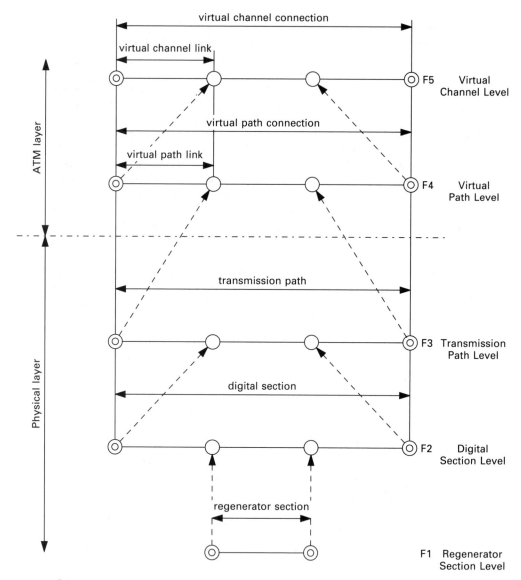

Figure 8.8 Hierarchical Layer-to-Layer Relationship

Figure 8.9 shows the concepts of VC and VP switching. VP switches terminate VP links. A VP switch translates incoming VPIs to the corresponding outgoing VPIs according to the destination of the VPC; VCI values remain unchanged. VC switches terminate VC links and necessarily VP links. A VC switch must therefore switch both virtual paths and virtual channels, so both VPI and VCI translation are performed.

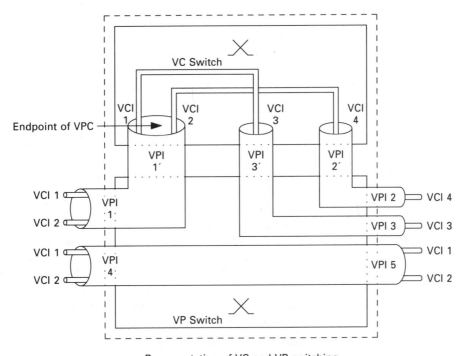

Representation of VC and VP switching

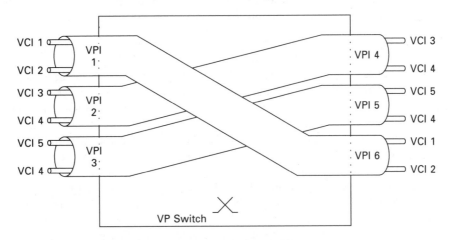

Representation of VP switching

Figure 8.9 Representation of the VP and VC Switching Hierarchy

8.3.3.1 Virtual Channel Connection Uses

The end points of a VCC may be end users, network entities, or an end user and a network entity. In all cases, cell-sequence integrity is preserved within a VCC—that is, cells are delivered in the same order in which they are sent. Let us consider examples of the three uses of a VCC:

1. *Between end users:* can be employed to carry end-to-end user data; can also be employed to carry control signaling between end users, as explained later in this subsection. A VPC between end users provides them with an overall capacity; the VCC organization of the VPC is up to the two end users, provided the set of VCCs does not exceed the VPC capacity.

2. *Between an end user and a network entity:* employed for user-to-network control signaling, as discussed later in this subsection. A user-to-network VPC can be employed to aggregate traffic from an end user to a network exchange or network server.

3. *Between two network entities:* used for network traffic-management and routing functions. A network-to-network VPC can be used to define a common route for the exchange of network-management information.

8.3.3.2   Virtual Path/Virtual Channel Characteristics

As yet, many of the details of the virtual path/virtual channel concept have not been worked out. Interim Recommendation I.150 lists the following as characteristics of virtual channel connections:

- *Quality of service:* A user of a VCC is provided with a quality of service specified by parameters such as cell-loss ratio (ratio of cells lost to cells transmitted) and cell-delay variation.

- *Switched and semipermanent virtual channel connections:* Both switched connections, which require call-control signaling, and dedicated channels can be provided.

- *Cell-sequence integrity:* The sequence of transmitted cells within a VCC is preserved.

- *Traffic-parameter negotiation and usage monitoring:* Traffic parameters can be negotiated between a user and the network for each VCC. The input of cells to the VCC is monitored by the network to ensure that the negotiated parameters are not violated.

The types of traffic parameters that can be negotiated would include average rate, peak rate, burstiness, and peak duration. The network may need a number of strategies to deal with congestion and to manage existing and requested VCCs. At the crudest level, the network may simply deny new requests for VCCs to prevent congestion. Additionally, cells may be discarded if negotiated parameters are violated or if congestion becomes severe. In an extreme situation, existing connections might be terminated.

I.150 also lists characteristics of VPCs. The first four listed characteristics are identical to those listed above for VCCs. That is, quality of service, switched and semipermanent VPCs, cell-sequence integrity, and traffic-parameter negotiation and usage monitoring are all characteristics of a VPC as well. There are a number of reasons for this duplication. First, this provides some flexibility in how the network manages the requirements placed upon it. Second, the network service must be concerned with the overall requirements for a VPC, and within a VPC, may negotiate the establishment of VCCs with given characteristics. Finally, once a VPC is set up, it is possible for the end users to negotiate the creation of new VCCs. The VPC characteristics impose a discipline on the choices the end users may make.

In addition, a fifth characteristic is listed for VPCs:

- *Virtual channel identifier restriction within a VPC:* One or more virtual channel identifiers, or numbers, may not be available to the user of the VPC but may be reserved for network use. Examples would be VCCs used for network management.

8.3.3.3 Control Signaling

In narrowband ISDN, the D channel is provided for control signaling of calls on B and H channels. In BISDN, with its ATM interface, there is no simple fixed-rate structure of H, B, and D channels. Thus, a more flexible arrangement for control signaling is needed. The requirement is further complicated by the need for the establishment and release of two types of entities: VCCs and VPCs.

For VCCs, I.150 specifies four methods for providing an establishment/release facility. One or a combination of these methods will be used in any particular network:

1. *Semipermanent VCCs* may be employed for user-to-user exchange. In this case, no control signaling is required.

2. If there is no preestablished call-control signaling channel, then one must be set up. For that purpose, a control-signaling exchange must take place between the user and the network on some channel. Hence, we need a permanent channel, probably of low data rate, that can be employed to set up VCCs that can be used for call control. Such a channel is called a *meta-signaling channel*, since the channel is used to set up signaling channels.

3. The metasignaling channel can be employed to set up a VCC between the user and the network for call-control signaling. This *user-to-network signaling virtual channel* can then be used to set up VCCs to carry user data.

4. The metasignaling channel can also be employed to set up a *user-to-user signaling virtual channel*. Such a channel must be set up within a preestablished VPC. It can then be employed to allow the two end users, without network intervention, to establish and release user-to-user VCCs to carry user data.

For VPCs, three methods are defined in I.150 for providing an establishment/release facility:

1. A VPC can be established on a *semipermanent* basis by prior agreement. In this case, no control signaling is required.

2. VPC establishment/release may be *customer-controlled*. In this case, the customer uses a signaling VCC to request the VPC from the network.

3. VPC establishment/release may be *network-controlled*. In this case, the network establishes a VPC for its own convenience. The path may be network-to-network, user-to-network, or user-to-user.

8.3.4 ATM Cells

The asynchronous transfer mode makes use of fixed-size cells, consisting of a 5-octet header and a 48-octet information field (Figure 8.10, part [a]). In the 1988 document (I.121), the header fields and header size were undefined, and it had not yet been decided to use fixed-size cells. The definitive decision to use fixed-size cells is documented in the 1990 interim recommendations.

There are several advantages to the use of small, fixed-size cells. First, the use of small cells may reduce queueing delay for a high-priority cell, since it waits less if it arrives slightly behind a lower-priority cell that has gained access to a resource (e.g., the transmitter). Second, it appears that fixed-size cells can be switched more efficiently, which is important for the very high data rates of ATM. For a discussion of these issues, see Parekh and Sohraby (1988).

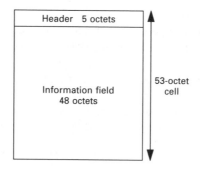

(a) Overall cell structure

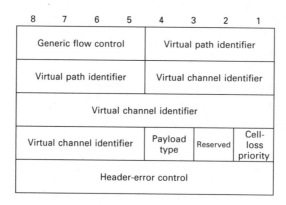

(b) Header format at user-network interface

(c) Header format at network-node interface

Figure 8.10 ATM Cell Format

Figure 8.10, part (b), shows the header format at the user-network interface (S or T reference point). Figure 8.10, part (c), shows the cell-header format internal to the network. The generic flow-control (GFC) field, which performs end-to-end functions, is not retained. Instead, the virtual path identifier field is expanded from 8 to 12 bits. This allows support for an expanded number of VPCs internal to the network, to include those supporting subscribers and those required for network management.

8.3.4.1   Generic Flow Control

The generic flow-control field does not appear in the cell header internal to the network but only at the user-network interface. Hence, it can be used for control of cell flow only at the local user-network interface. Although the details of its application are a subject for further study, two general functions are under consideration: flow control across a T interface and medium-access control across an S or a T interface (see Figure 8.2).

The field could be used to assist the customer in controlling the flow of traffic for different qualities of service. One candidate for the use of this field is a multiple-priority-level indicator to control the flow of information in a service-dependent manner. In any case, the GFC mechanism is used to alleviate short-term overload conditions in the network.

As with the basic-rate interface to ISDN, multiple terminals may share a single access link to BISDN. The GFC mechanism supports both point-to-point and point-to-multipoint configurations. In the former case, the GFC can be used to control the flow from an individual TE. In the latter case, the GFC can only provide aggregate flow control. However, the GFC might also be used for some sort of medium-access control when multiple terminals share a common-bus medium attachment at the user-network interface.

I.150 lists as a requirement for the GFC mechanism that all terminals be able to get access to their assured capacities. This includes all constant-bit-rate (CBR) terminals as well as the variable-bit-rate (VBR) terminals that have an element of guaranteed capacity.

8.3.4.2   Virtual Path and Virtual Channel Identifiers

The virtual path identifier (VPI) constitutes a routing field for the network. It is 8 bits at the user-network interface and 12 bits at the network-network interface, allowing for more virtual paths to be supported within the network.

The virtual channel identifier (VCI) is used for routing to and from the end user. Thus, it functions much as a service-access point.

8.3.4.3   Payload Type

The payload-type field indicates the type of information in the information field. A value of 00 indicates user information; that is, information from the next higher layer. Other values are a subject for further study. Presumably, network-management and maintenance values will be assigned. This field allows the insertion of network-management cells onto a user's VCC without impacting the user's data. Thus, it could provide in-band control information.

8.3.4.4   Cell-Loss Priority

The cell-loss priority (CLP) is used to provide guidance to the network in the event of congestion. A value of 0 indicates a cell of relatively higher priority, which should not be discarded unless no other alternative is available. A value of 1 indicates a cell that is subject to discard within the network. The user might employ this field so that extra information may be inserted into the network, with a CLP of 1, and delivered to the destination if the network is not congested. The

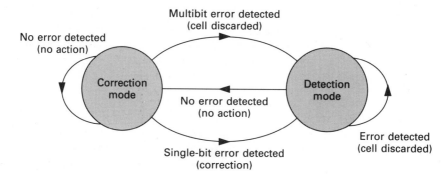

Figure 8.11 HEC Operation at the Receiver

network might set this field to 1 for any data cell that is in violation of a traffic agreement. In this case, the switch that does the setting realizes that the cell exceeds the agreed traffic parameters but that that switch is capable of handling the cell. At a later point in the network, if congestion is encountered, this cell has been marked for discard in preference to cells that fall within agreed traffic limits.

8.3.4.5   Header-Error Control

Each ATM cell includes an 8-bit header-error-control field (HEC), which is calculated based on the remaining 32 bits of the header. The polynomial used to generate the code is $X^8 + X^2 + X + 1$. In most existing protocols that include an error-control field, such as LAPD (link-access protocol, D channel) and LAPB (link-access protocol, balanced), the data that serve as input to the error-code calculation are in general much longer than the size of the resulting error code. This allows for error detection. In the case of ATM, the input to the calculation is only 32 bits, compared to 8 bits for the code. The fact that that input is relatively short allows the code to be used not only for error detection but, in some cases, for actual error correction. This is because there is sufficient redundancy in the code to recover from certain error patterns.

Figure 8.11 depicts the operation of the HEC algorithm at the receiver. At initialization, the receiver's error-correction algorithm is in the default mode for single-bit error correction. As each cell is received, the HEC calculation and comparison are performed. As long as no errors are detected, the receiver remains in error-correction mode. When an error is detected, the receiver will correct the error if it is a single-bit error, or it will detect that a multibit error has occurred. In either case, the receiver now moves to the detection mode. In this mode, no attempt is made to correct errors. The reason for this change is to recognize that a noise burst or other event might cause a sequence of errors. The receiver remains in detection mode as long as erroneous cells are received. When a header is examined and found not to be in error, the receiver switches back to correction mode. The flowchart in Figure 8.12 shows the consequence of errors in the cell header.

The error-protection function provides both recovery from single-bit header errors and a low probability of the delivery of cells with erroneous headers under bursty error conditions. The error characteristics of fiber-based transmission systems appear to be a mix of single-bit errors and relatively large burst errors (Prycker 1991). For some transmission systems, the error-correction capability, which is more time-consuming, might not be invoked.

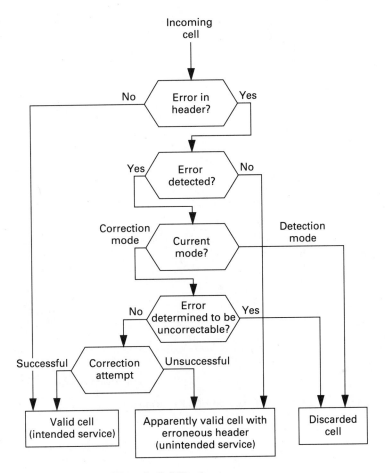

Figure 8.12 Effect of Error in Cell Header

Figure 8.13, from I.432, indicates how random bit errors impact the probability of the occurrence of discarded cells and valid cells with erroneous headers.

8.3.4.6 Preassigned Cell-Header Values

Cells reserved for the use of the physical layer have preassigned values reserved for the whole header; these values are not to be used by the ATM layer. The assigned values cover octets 1 through 4 of the cell header; the HEC field is calculated in the usual fashion, since the HEC function is a physical-layer rather than an ATM-layer function.

Figure 8.14 shows the general format of preassigned cell-header values. Bits 5 through 28 of the cell header are set to 0; all other header bits can be used by assigned cells. There are actually two types of preassigned cells: those that are reserved for use by the physical layer and those that are currently unassigned. The least-significant bit of octet 4 distinguishes between these two types; this bit is therefore not available for use in the cell-loss-priority (CLP) mechanism. Of course,

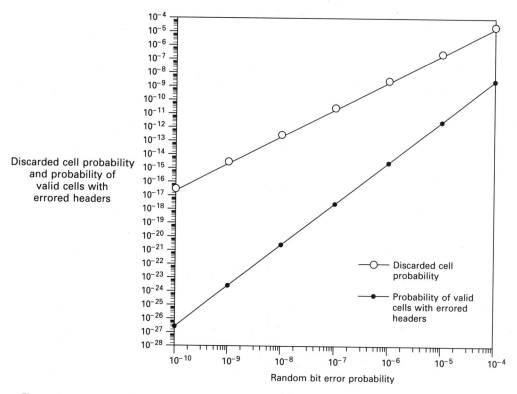

Discarded cell probability and probability of valid cells with errored headers

Random bit error probability

Figure 8.13 Impact of Random Bit Errors on HEC Performance

since the CLP function is an ATM-layer and not a physical-layer function, the CLP bit is not needed for physical-layer cells.

Several specific preassigned physical-layer cell-header values have been defined. Some of these relate to operations, administration, and maintenance (OAM) functions, which are discussed in section 8.6. Another assignment is for the idle cell. When there are no ATM or OAM cells available for transmission, an idle cell is inserted in order to adapt the rate of valid ATM cells to

	Octet 1	Octet 2	Octet 3	Octet 4
Reserved for use of the physical layer	PPPP0000	00000000	00000000	0000PPP1
Unassigned cell identification	AAAA0000	00000000	00000000	0000AAA0

Notes: A indicates that the bit is available for use by the ATM layer. P indicates that the bit is available for use by the physical layer. Values assigned to these latter bits have no meaning with respect to the fields occupying the corresponding bit positions of the ATM layer.

Figure 8.14 Preassigned Cell-Header Values at the User Network Interface (Excluding the HEC Field)

Octet 1	Octet 2	Octet 3	Octet 4	Octet 5
00000000	00000000	00000000	00000001	valid HEC code

Figure 8.15 Idle-Cell Header

the payload capacity of the transmission system. Such cells can be discarded at the receiving end or at some intermediate point for purposes of traffic-flow control. Idle cells are identified by a preassigned cell-header value (Figure 8.15). Each octet of an idle cell is filled with 01101010.

8.3.5   Operations, Administration, and Maintenance Functions

Recommendation I.610 describes functions for maintaining the physical layer and the ATM layer at the user-network interface. Maintenance is defined in Recommendation M.60 as, ''The combination of all technical and corresponding administrative actions, including supervision actions, intended to retain an item in, or restore it to, a state in which it can perform a required function.''

Table 8.4 lists the five phases or types of actions that are used by CCITT in specifying an OAM capability. The last phase, fault localization, has not been addressed for BISDN and is a subject for further study.

Table 8.4 OAM Actions (I.610)

Name	Action	Result
Performance monitoring	Normal functioning of the managed entity is monitored by continuous or periodic checking of functions.	Maintenance-event information is produced.
Defect and failure detection	Malfunctions or predicted malfunctions are detected by continuous or periodic checking.	Maintenance-event information or various alarms are produced.
System protection	The effect of the failure of a managed entity is minimized by blocking or changeover to other entities.	The failed entity is excluded from operation.
Failure or performance information	Failure information is given to other management entities.	Alarm indications are given to other management planes. A response to a status-report request is also given.
Fault localization	Determination of a failed entity is made by an internal or external test system if failure information is insufficient.	

Table 8.5 OAM Functions of the ATM Layer

Level	Function	Defect/Failure Detection
Virtual path	Monitoring of path availability	Path not available
	Performance monitoring	Degraded performance
Virtual channel	Performance monitoring	Degraded performance

OAM functions are implemented as bidirectional information flows that are defined on five hierarchical levels, associated with the ATM and physical layers. Figure 8.8 shows the relationship between the flows, labeled F1 through F5, and the hierarchical structure of the BISDN protocol reference model.[1] As an example of an OAM flow, cited in Handel and Huber (1991), two end points could monitor a VPC by means of a loopback test. During the monitoring phase, each cell received at one end point could be repeated back to the sender.

Table 8.5 lists the OAM functions of the ATM layer. Monitoring of availability is done at the virtual path level, and monitoring of performance is done at the virtual path and virtual channel levels. These OAM flows are provided by cells dedicated to ATM-layer OAM functions. The implementation of these cells is a subject for further study. One possibility mentioned in I.610 is that the ATM-layer OAM cells could be identified by the payload-type field in the cell header and by VPI/VCI.

OAM functions of the physical layer are examined in section 8.6.

8.4   ATM-ADAPTATION LAYER

This section examines the AAL services and protocols that have been specified for BISDN.

8.4.1   AAL Services

The 1988 recommendation briefly mentions the ATM-adaptation layer (AAL) and points out its functions of mapping information into cells and performing segmentation and reassembly. The 1990 documents provide greater detail regarding the functions and services of this layer. In the area of services, four classes of service are defined (Table 8.6). The classification is based on whether a timing relationship must be maintained between source and destination, whether the application requires a constant bit rate, and whether the transfer is connection-oriented or connectionless. An example of a class-A service is circuit emulation. In this case, a constant bit rate, which requires the maintenance of a timing relationship, is used, and the transfer is connection-oriented. An example of a class-B service is variable-bit-rate video, such as might be used in a teleconference. Here, the application is connection-oriented and timing is important, but the bit rate varies depending on the amount of activity in the scene. Classes C and D correspond to data-transfer applications. In both cases, the bit rate may vary, and no particular timing relationship is required; differences in data rate are handled by the end systems using buffers. The data transfer may be either connection-oriented (class C) or connectionless (class D).

---

1.   For cell-based transmission, flows F1 through F5 apply; for SDH-based transmission, only flows F3 through F5 apply. These forms of transmission are explained in section 8.6.

Table 8.6 Service Classification for AAL

	Class A	Class B	Class C	Class D
Timing relation between source and destination	Required		Not required	
Bit rate	Constant	Variable		
Connection mode	Connection-oriented			Connectionless

8.4.2 AAL Protocols

To support these various classes of service, a set of protocols at the AAL level is defined. In the 1990 version, a preliminary definition is provided, which is primarily functional. However, the document does include some detail concerning header formats and procedures. The details of the AAL protocols remain to be worked out. An overview of the preliminary specification is provided in the remainder of this subsection.

The AAL layer is organized in two logical sublayers: the convergence sublayer (CS) and the segmentation-and-reassembly sublayer (SAR). The convergence sublayer provides the functions needed to support specific applications using AAL. Each AAL user attaches to AAL at a service-access point (SAP), which is simply the address of the application. This sublayer is thus service-dependent.

The segmentation-and-reassembly sublayer is responsible for packaging information received from CS into cells for transmission and unpacking the information at the other end. As we have seen, at the ATM layer, each cell consists of a 5-octet header and a 48-octet information field. Thus, SAR must pack any SAR headers and trailers plus CS information into 48-octet blocks.

Four AAL protocols have been defined by CCITT, one to support each of the four classes of service. The type-1 protocol supports class A, type 2 supports class B, and so on. Table 8.7 lists the currently defined functional details regarding the four types.

Figure 8.16 shows the format of the protocol data units (PDUs) at the SAR level for the four types; the PDU fields are defined in Table 8.8. PDUs for the CS level are not specified, since these are application-dependent. For type-1 operation, we are dealing with a constant-bit-rate source. In this case, the only responsibility of the SAR protocol is to pack the bits into cells for transmission and unpack them at reception. Each block is accompanied by a sequence number so that erroneous PDUs can be tracked. The sequence-number-protection field is an error code for error detection and possibly correction on the sequence-number field.

The remainder of the protocol types (2 through 4) deal with variable-bit-rate information. Type 2 is intended for analog applications, such as video and audio, that require timing information but do not require a constant bit rate. Again, a sequence number is provided. In addition, an information-type field and a length-indicator field are used to allow the segmentation and reassembly of bursts of information from higher levels. The IT field indicates whether this is the beginning, continuation, or end of a block from the application. If this is the last segment, the LI field indicates how many octets of information are included. This field is needed because each cell is of fixed size; therefore, the last cell is likely to be only partially filled. Note that segmentation and reassembly are also done in the type-1 protocol. However, since type 1 supports constant-bit-rate applications, there is no concept of bursts of information and therefore no need to mark begin-

Table 8.7 ATM-Adaptation-Layer Protocol Types

	Services Provided	Overall Functions	SAR Functions	CS Functions
Type 1	Transfer of SDUs with constant bit rate (CBR) Transfer of timing information between source and destination Indication of lost or erroneous information not recovered by type 1	Segmentation and reassembly Handling of cell-delay variation Handling of lost and misinserted cells Source clock frequency recovery at destination Monitoring and handling of PCI bit errors Monitoring of user information for bit errors and possible corrective action	For further study	Forward error correction for high-quality video and audio For some services, clock recovery at the receiver For services requiring explicit time indication, insertion of a time-stamp pattern Handling of lost and misinserted cells
Type 2	Transfer of SDUs with variable bit rate (VBR) Transfer of timing information between source and destination	Segmentation and reassembly Handling of cell-delay variation Handling of lost and misinserted cells	For further study	Forward error correction for high-quality video and audio For some services, clock recovery at the receiver

	Service Features	Functions
	Indication of lost or erroneous information not recovered by type 2	Source clock frequency recovery at destination
		Monitoring and handling of header and trailer bit errors
		Monitoring of user information for bit errors and possible corrective action
		Handling of lost and misinserted cells
Type 3	Message-mode service	Segmentation and reassembly
	Streaming-mode service	Error detection
	Assured operation	Multiplexing
	Nonassured operation	For further study
Type 4	Message-mode service	Segmentation and reassembly
	Streaming-mode service	Error detection
	Assured operation	Multiplexing
	Nonassured operation	Higher-layer PDU delineation and transparency
		Mapping between AAL SAPs and ATM-layer connections
		Error detection and handling
		Message segmentation and reassembly
		Identification of information
		Buffer-allocation size

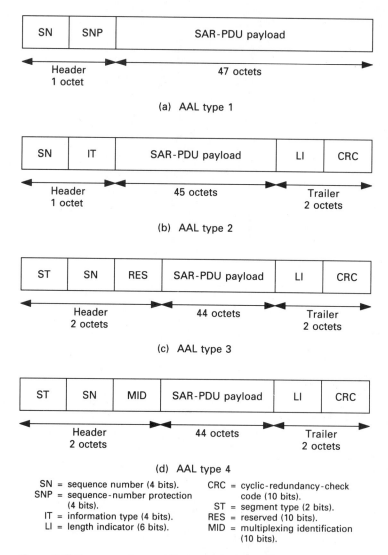

SN	SNP	SAR-PDU payload

Header
1 octet ← → 47 octets

(a) AAL type 1

SN	IT	SAR-PDU payload	LI	CRC

Header
1 octet ← → 45 octets ← Trailer
2 octets

(b) AAL type 2

ST	SN	RES	SAR-PDU payload	LI	CRC

Header
2 octets ← 44 octets → Trailer
2 octets

(c) AAL type 3

ST	SN	MID	SAR-PDU payload	LI	CRC

Header
2 octets ← 44 octets → Trailer
2 octets

(d) AAL type 4

SN = sequence number (4 bits).
SNP = sequence-number protection
       (4 bits).
 IT = information type (4 bits).
 LI = length indicator (6 bits).

CRC = cyclic-redundancy-check
       code (10 bits).
 ST = segment type (2 bits).
RES = reserved (10 bits).
MID = multiplexing identification
       (10 bits).

Figure 8.16 Segmentation and Reassembly Protocol Data Units

ning, middle, and end; there is simply a constant stream of bits to be packaged into cells. The information-type field can also be used to indicate whether the information is the video or audio component of a video signal.

Type-3 and type-4 protocols are intended for data-transmission applications, so that the information received from a higher layer will be in the form of protocol data units or blocks of data. Type 3 provides a connection-oriented service. The reserved field can be used for multiplexing purposes. This would allow multiple user sessions to be multiplexed on a single ATM connection. All the user sessions would need to have the same quality of service parameters as the underlying ATM connection.

Table 8.8 AAL Segmentation-and-Reassembly PDU Parameters

Cyclic-redundancy-check code (10 bits)

Used to detect errors and correct up to two correlated bit errors in the SAR PDU. The generating polynomial is $X^{10} + X^9 + X^5 + X^4 + X + 1$.

Information type (4 bits)

Used in type-2 operation to indicate beginning of message, continuation of message, or end of message and also a component of the video or audio signal.

Length indicator (6 bits)

Indicates the number of octets of the CS PDU that are included in the SAR PDU payload.

Multiplexing identification (10 bits)

Provides for the multiplexing and demultiplexing of multiple CS PDUs concurrently over a single ATM connection. All SAR PDUs of a given CS PDU will have the same MID value.

Segment type (2 bits)

Used in type-3 and type-4 operation to indicate beginning of message, continuation of message, end of message, or single-segment message.

Sequence number (4 bits)

Used to detect lost or misinserted cells.

Sequence-number protection (4 bits)

May be used to provide error-detection and error-correction capabilities for the sequence-number field. For further study.

Type 4 provides a connectionless service. In this case, the concept of multiplexing takes on a different meaning than for type-3 operation. For type 4, if a single PDU at the CS level is divided into multiple PDUs at the SAR level, then all the resulting SAR PDUs will have the same multiplexing identification value. Thus, information from more than one CS PDU can be interleaved over a single ATM connection without confusion.

For both type-3 and type-4 operation, two modes of service are defined:

1. *Message-mode service:* used for framed data. Thus, any of the OSI-related protocols and applications would fit into this category. In particular, LAPD or frame relay would be message-mode. A single block of data from the layer above AAL is transferred in one or more cells.

2. *Streaming-mode service:* used for low-speed continuous data with low delay requirements. The data are presented to AAL in fixed-size blocks, which may be as small as 1 octet. One block is transferred per cell.

Figure 8.17 gives an example of how the message-mode service could be implemented by AAL. The convergence sublayer accepts a block of information from a user and creates a CS protocol data unit. The PDU includes a header and trailer with protocol-control information and padding to make the PDU an integral multiple of 32 bits. This is then passed down to the SAR sublayer. The SAR sublayer accepts a CS PDU from the CS sublayer and segments it into N 44-octet SAR-PDU payloads; (see Figure 8.16c and d); thus, the last payload may have some unused portion.

For streaming-mode service, a CS PDU may contain one or more blocks from the AAL user (Figure 8.18). This is in contrast to the message-mode service, where there is a one-to-one rela-

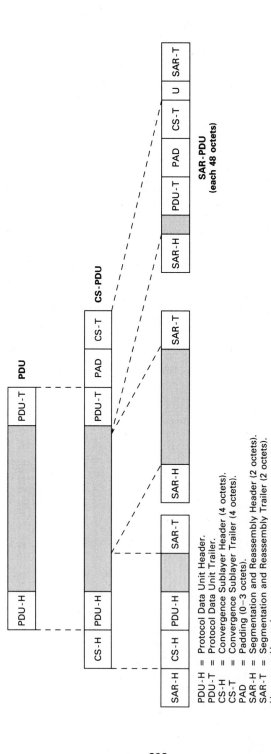

PDU-H = Protocol Data Unit Header.
PDU-T = Protocol Data Unit Trailer.
CS-H = Convergence Sublayer Header (4 octets).
CS-T = Convergence Sublayer Trailer (4 octets).
PAD = Padding (0–3 octets).
SAR-H = Segmentation and Reassembly Header (2 octets).
SAR-T = Segmentation and Reassembly Trailer (2 octets).
U = Unused.

Source: J. Bae and T. Suda, "Survey of Traffic Control Schemes and Protocols in ATM Networks," *Proceedings of the IEEE* (February 1991). © 1991 IEEE.

Figure 8.17 Example of ATM-Adaptation Layer (Message-Mode Service)

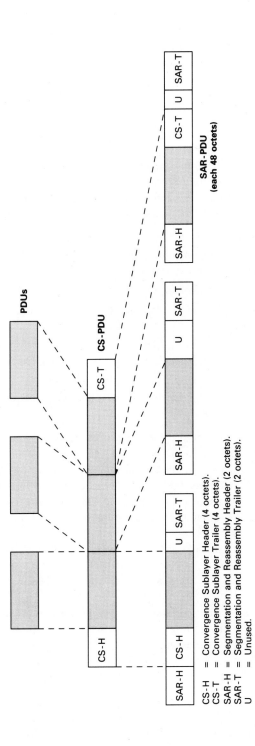

CS-H = Convergence Sublayer Header (4 octets).
CS-T = Convergence Sublayer Trailer (4 octets).
SAR-H = Segmentation and Reassembly Header (2 octets).
SAR-T = Segmentation and Reassembly Trailer (2 octets).
U = Unused.

Source: J. Bae and T. Suda, "Survey of Traffic Control Schemes and Protocols in ATM Networks," *Proceedings of the IEEE* (February 1991). © 1991 IEEE.

Figure 8.18 Example of ATM-Adaptation Layer (Streaming-Mode Service)

tionship. Furthermore, each block from the user ultimately travels in its own cell. Therefore—unlike in message-mode service, where only the last segment may contain an unused portion—in streaming-mode service, any segment can have some unused portion.

8.5   SONET/SDH

SONET (synchronous optical network) is an optical transmission interface originally proposed by BellCore and standardized by ANSI (American National Standards Institute). A compatible version, referred to as synchronous digital hierarchy (SDH), has been published by CCITT in Recommendations G.707, G.708, and G.709.[2] SONET is intended to provide a specification for taking advantage of the high-speed digital-transmission capability of optical fiber.

The SONET standard addresses the following specific issues (Bellamy 1991):

- It establishes a standard multiplexing format using any number of 51.84-Mbps signals as building blocks. Because each building block can carry a DS3 signal, a standard rate is defined for any high-bandwidth transmission system that might be developed.

- It establishes an optical-signal standard for interconnecting equipment from different suppliers.

- It establishes extensive operations, administration, and maintenance (OAM) capabilities as part of the standard.

- It defines a synchronous-multiplexing format for carrying lower-level digital signals (DS1, DS2, CCITT standards). The synchronous structure greatly simplifies the interface to digital switches, digital cross-connect switches, and add-drop multiplexers.

- It establishes a flexible architecture capable of accommodating future applications such as broadband ISDN with a variety of transmission rates.

Three key requirements have driven the development of SONET. First was the need to push multiplexing standards beyond the existing DS3 (44.736 Mbps) level. With the increasing use of optical transmission systems, a number of vendors have introduced their own proprietary schemes of combining anywhere from two to twelve DS3s into an optical signal. In addition, the European schemes, based on the CCITT hierarchy, are incompatible with North American schemes. SONET provides a standardized hierarchy of multiplexed digital-transmission rates that accommodates existing North American and CCITT rates.

A second requirement was to provide economic access to small amounts of traffic within the bulk payload of an optical signal. For this purpose, SONET introduces a new approach to time-division multiplexing. We address this issue later in this section, when we examine the SONET frame format.

A third requirement is to prepare for future sophisticated service offerings, such as virtual private networking, time-of-day bandwidth allocation, and support of the broadband ISDN ATM transmission technique. To meet this requirement, a major increase in network-management capabilities within the synchronous time-division signal was needed.

In this section, we provide an overview of SONET/SDH that shows how these requirements have been met.

---

2.   In what follows, we will use the term *SONET* to refer to both specifications. Where differences exist, these will be addressed.

Table 8.9 SONET/SDH Signal Hierarchy

SONET Designation	CCITT Designation	Data Rate (Mbps)
STS-1/OC-1	—	51.84
STS-3/OC-3	STM-1	155.52
STS-9/OC-9	STM-3	466.56
STS-12/OC-12	STM-4	622.08
STS-18/OC-18	STM-6	933.12
STS-24/OC-24	STM-8	1,244.16
STS-36/OC-36	STM-12	1,866.24
STS-48/OC-48	STM-16	2,488.32

8.5.1 Signal Hierarchy

The SONET specification defines a hierarchy of standardized digital data rates (Table 8.9). The lowest level, referred to as STS-1 (synchronous transport signal level 1) or OC-1 (optical carrier level 1),[3] is 51.84 Mbps. This rate can be used to carry a single DS3 signal or a group of lower-rate signals, such as DS1, DS1C, DS2, plus CCITT rates (e.g., 2.048 Mbps).

Multiple STS-1 signals can be combined to form an STS-N signal. The signal is created by interleaving bytes from N STS-1 signals that are mutually synchronized.

For the CCITT synchronous digital hierarchy, the lowest rate is 155.52 Mbps, which is designated STM-1 (synchronous transfer mode level 1). This corresponds to SONET STS-3. The reason for the discrepancy is that STM-1 is the lowest-rate signal that can accommodate a CCITT level-4 signal (139.264 Mbps).

8.5.2 System Hierarchy

SONET capabilities have been mapped into a four-layer hierarchy (Figure 8.19, part [a]):

1. *Photonic:* This is the physical layer. It includes a specification of the type of optical fiber that may be used and details such as the required minimum powers and dispersion characteristics of the transmitting lasers and the required sensitivity of the receivers. This layer is also responsible for converting STS (electrical) signals to OC (optical) signals.

2. *Section:* This layer creates the basic SONET frames. Transmission functions include framing, scrambling, and error monitoring.

3. *Line:* This layer is responsible for synchronization, multiplexing of data onto the SONET frames, and protection switching.

4. *Path:* This layer is responsible for end-to-end transport of data at the appropriate signaling speed.

Figure 8.19, part (b), shows the physical realization of the logical layers. A section is the basic physical building block and represents a single run of optical cable between two optical-fiber transmitter/receivers. For shorter distances, the cable may run directly between two end units. For

---

3. An OC-N rate is the optical equivalent of an STS-N electrical signal. End-user devices transmit and receive electrical signals; these must be converted to and from optical signals for transmission over optical fiber.

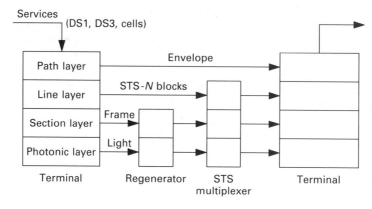

(a) Logical hierarchy

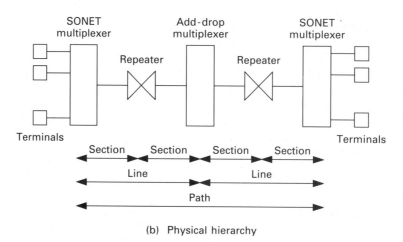

(b) Physical hierarchy

Figure 8.19 SONET System Hierarchy

longer distances, regenerating repeaters are needed. The repeater is a simple device that accepts a digital stream of data on one side and regenerates and repeats each bit out the other side. Issues of synchronization and timing need to be addressed. A line is a sequence of one or more sections such that the internal signal or channel structure of the signal remains constant. End points and intermediate switches/multiplexers that may add or drop channels terminate a line. Finally, a path connects two end terminals; it corresponds to an end-to-end circuit. Data are assembled at the beginning of a path and are not accessed or modified until they are disassembled at the other end of the path.

8.5.3   Frame Format

The basic SONET building block is the STS-1 frame, which consists of 810 octets and is transmitted once every 125 μs, for an overall data rate of 51.84 Mbps (Figure 8.20, part [a]). The frame can logically be viewed as a matrix of nine rows of 90 octets each, with transmission being one row at a time, from left to right and top to bottom.

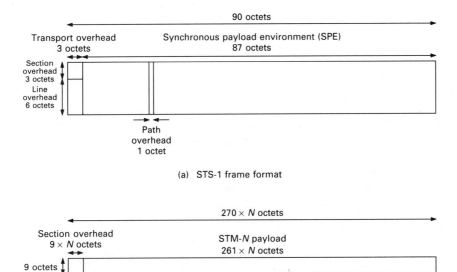

(a) STS-1 frame format

(b) STM-*N* frame format

Figure 8.20 SONET/SDH Frame Formats

	Framing	Framing	STS-ID		Trace
	A1	A2	C1		J1
Section overhead	BIP-8	Orderwire	User		BIP-8
	B1	E1	F1		B3
	Data com	Data com	Data com		Signal label
	D1	D2	D3		C2
	Pointer	Pointer	Pointer action		Path status
	H1	H2	H3		G1
	BIP-8	APS	APS		User
	B2	K1	K2		F2
Line overhead	Data com	Data com	Data com		Multiframe
	D4	D5	D6		H4
	Data com	Data com	Data com		Growth
	D7	D8	D9		Z3
	Data com	Data com	Data com		Growth
	D10	D11	D12		Z4
	Growth	Growth	Orderwire		Growth
	Z1	Z2	E2		Z5

(a) Section overhead   (b) Path overhead

Figure 8.21 SONET STS-1 Overhead Octets

Table 8.10 STS-1 Overhead Bits

Section Overhead

A1, A2: Framing bytes = F6,28 hex; used to synchronize the beginning of the frame.

C1: STS-1 ID identifies the STS-1 number (1 to *N*) for each STS-1 within an STS-*N* multiplex.

B1: Bit-interleaved parity byte providing even parity over previous STS-*N* frame after scrambling; the *i*th bit of this octet contains the even parity value calculated from the *i*th bit position of all octets in the previous frame.

E1: Section-level 64-Kbps PCM orderwire; optional 64-Kbps voice channel to be used between section-terminating equipment, hubs, and remote terminals.

F1: 64-Kbps channel set aside for user purposes.

D1–D3: 192-Kbps data communications channel for alarms, maintenance, control, and administration between sections.

Line Overhead

H1–H3: Pointer bytes used in frame alignment and frequency adjustment of payload data.

B2: Bit-interleaved parity byte for line-level error monitoring.

K1, K2: Two bytes allocated for signaling between line-level automatic-protection switching equipment; uses a bit-oriented protocol that provides for error protection and management of the SONET optical link.

D4–D12: 576-Kbps data communications channel for alarms, maintenance, control, monitoring, and administration at the line level.

Z1, Z2: Reserved for future use.

E2: 64-Kbps PCM voice channel for line-level orderwire.

Path Overhead

J1: 64-Kbps channel used to repetitively send a 64-octet fixed-length string so a receiving terminal can continuously verify the integrity of a path; the contents of the message are user-programmable.

B3: Bit-interleaved parity byte at the path level, calculated over all bits of the previous SPE.

C2: STS path signal label to designate equipped versus unequipped STS signals. Unequipped means that the line connection is complete but there are no path data to send. For equipped signals, the label can indicate the specific STS payload mapping that might be needed in receiving terminals to interpret the payloads.

G1: Status byte sent from path-terminating equipment back to path-originating equipment to convey the status of terminating equipment and path error performance.

F2: 64-Kbps channel for path user.

H4: Multiframe indicator for payloads needing frames that are longer than a single STS frame; multiframe indicators are used when packing lower-rate channels (virtual tributaries) into the SPE.

Z3–Z5: Reserved for future use.

The first three columns (3 octets × 9 rows = 27 octets) of the frame are devoted to overhead octets, with 9 octets being devoted to section-related overhead and 18 octets to line overhead. Figure 8.21, part (a), shows the arrangement of overhead octets, and Table 8.10 defines the various fields.

The remainder of the frame is payload, which is provided by the path layer. The payload includes a column of path overhead, which is not necessarily in the first available column position; the line overhead contains a pointer that indicates where the path overhead starts. Figure 8.21, part (b), shows the arrangement of path overhead octets, and Table 8.10 defines these.

Figure 8.20, part (b), shows the general format for higher-rate frames, using the CCITT designation.

8.5.4 Pointer Adjustment

In conventional circuit-switched networks, most multiplexers and telephone-company channel banks require the demultiplexing and remultiplexing of the entire signal just to access a piece of information that is addressed to a node. For example, consider that T-1 multiplexer B receives data on a single T-1 circuit from T-1 multiplexer A and passes the data on to multiplexer C. In the signal received, a single DS0 channel (64 Kbps) is addressed to node B. The rest will pass on to node C and farther on into the network. To remove that single DS0 channel, B must demultiplex every bit of the 1.544-Mbps signal, remove the data, and remultiplex every bit. A few proprietary T-1 multiplexers provide drop-and-insert capability, meaning that only part of the signal has to be demultiplexed and remultiplexed, but this equipment will not communicate with that of other vendors.

SONET offers a standard drop-and-insert capability, and it applies not just to 64-Kbps channels but to higher data rates as well. SONET makes use of a set of pointers that locates channels

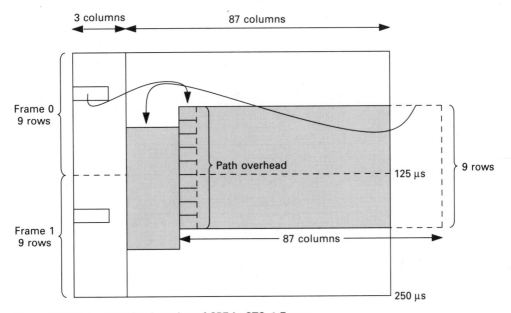

Figure 8.22 Representative Location of SPE in STS-1 Frame

within a payload and the entire payload within a frame, so that information can be accessed, inserted, and removed with a simple adjustment of pointers. Pointer information is contained in the path overhead that refers to the multiplex structure of the channels contained within the payload. A pointer in the line overhead serves a similar function for the entire payload. We examine the use of this latter pointer in the remainder of this section.

The synchronous payload environment (SPE) of an STS-1 frame can float with respect to the frame. The actual payload (87 columns × 9 rows) can straddle two frames (Figure 8.22). The H1 and H2 octets in the line overhead indicate the start of the payload.

Because even the best atomic timing sources can differ by small amounts, SONET is faced with coping with the resulting timing differences. Each node must recalculate the pointer to alert the next receiving node of the exact location of the start of the payload. Thus, the payload is

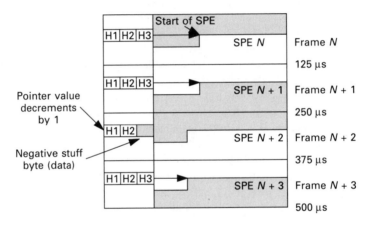

(a) Negative pointer adjustment

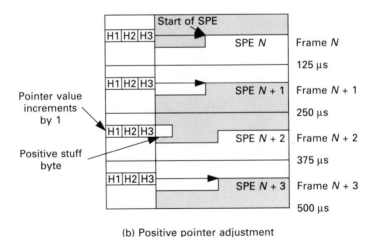

(b) Positive pointer adjustment

Figure 8.23 STS-1 Pointer Adjustment

allowed to slip through an STS-1 frame, increasing or decreasing the pointer value at intervals by one byte position.

If the payload rate is higher than the local STS frame rate, the pointer is decreased by 1 octet position so that the next payload will begin 1 octet sooner than the earlier payload. To prevent the loss of an octet on the payload that is thus squeezed, the H3 octet is used to hold the extra octet for that one frame (Figure 8.23, part [a]). Similarly, if the payload rate lags the frame rate, the insertion of the next payload is delayed by 1 octet. In this case, the octet in the SPE that follows the H3 octet is left empty to allow for the movement of the payload (Figure 8.23, part [b]).

8.6   TRANSMISSION OF ATM CELLS

The 1990 interim recommendations for BISDN specify that ATM cells are to be transmitted at a rate of 155.52 Mbps or 622.08 Mbps. As with ISDN, we need to specify the transmission structure that will be used to carry this payload. For 622.08 Mbps, the matter has been left for further study. For the 155.52-Mbps interface, two approaches are defined in I.413 as a cell-based physical layer and an SDH-based physical layer. We examine each of these approaches in turn.

8.6.1   Cell-Based Physical Layer

For the cell-based physical layer, no framing is imposed. The interface structure consists of a continuous stream of 53-octet cells (Figure 8.24).

8.6.1.1   Synchronization

Since there is no external frame imposed in the cell-based approach, some form of synchronization is needed. Synchronization is achieved on the basis of the header-error-control (HEC) field in the cell header. The procedure is as follows (Figure 8.25):

1. In the HUNT state, a cell-delineation algorithm is performed bit by bit to determine whether the HEC coding law is observed (i.e., match between received HEC and calculated HEC). Once a match is achieved, it is assumed that one header has been found, and the method enters the PRESYNC state.

2. In the PRESYNC state, a cell structure is now assumed. The cell-delineation algorithm is performed cell by cell until the encoding law has been confirmed Δ times consecutively.

3. In the SYNC state, the HEC is used for error detection and correction (see Figure 8.11). Cell delineation is assumed to be lost if the HEC coding law is recognized as incorrect α times consecutively.

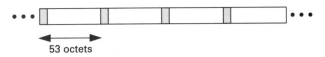

Figure 8.24 Cell-Based Physical Interface for ATM Cell Transmission

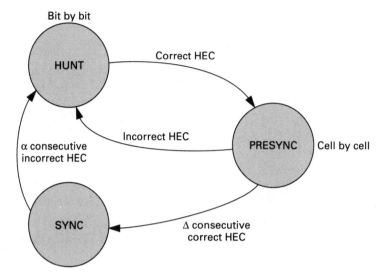

Figure 8.25 Cell-Delineation-State Diagram

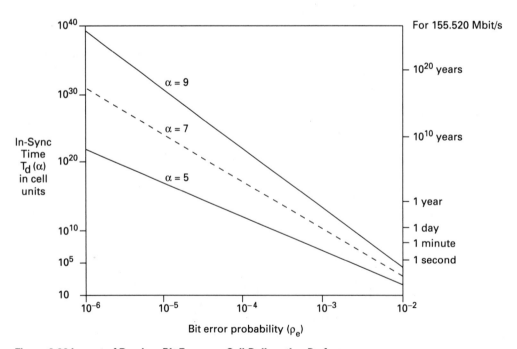

Figure 8.26 Impact of Random Bit Errors on Cell-Delineation Performance

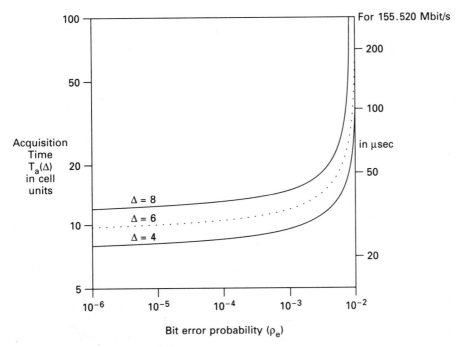

Figure 8.27 Acquisition Time versus Bit-Error Probability

The values of α and Δ are design parameters. Greater values of Δ result in longer delays in establishing synchronization but greater robustness against false delineation. Greater values of α result in longer delays in recognizing a misalignment but greater robustness against false misalignment. Figures 8.26 and 8.27 show the impact of random bit errors on cell-delineation performance for various values of α and Δ. The first figure shows the average amount of time that the receiver will maintain synchronization in the face of errors, with α as a parameter. The second figure shows the average amount of time to acquire synchronization as a function of error rate, with Δ as a parameter.

Finally, ATM cells are used to convey operations, administration, and maintenance (OAM) information. A virtual path identifier of 0 and a virtual channel identifier of 9 identify OAM cells.

The advantage of using a cell-based transmission scheme is the simplified interface that results when both transmission and transfer-mode functions are based on a common structure.

8.6.1.2   OAM Functions

Table 8.11 provides an overview of OAM functions for the cell-based physical layer. The OAM cells are identified by preassigned cell-header values, one for each level of information flow (Figure 8.28).

8.6.2   SDH-Based Physical Layer

The SDH-based physical layer imposes a structure on the ATM cell stream.

Table 8.11 OAM Functions of the Cell-Based Physical Layer

Level	Function	Defect/Failure Detection
Regenerator section	Physical-layer OAM (PLOAM) cell recognition	Loss of PLOAM cell recognition
Digital section	PLOAM cell recognition	Loss of PLOAM cell recognition
	Section-error monitoring	Degraded error performance
	Section-error reporting	Degraded error performance
Transmission path	Customer-network (CN) status monitoring	CN alarm-indication signal
	Cell delineation	Loss of cell synchronization
	Header-error detection/correction	Uncorrectable header
	Header-error performance monitoring	Degraded header-error performance
	Cell-rate decoupling	Failure of insertion and suppression of idle cells

8.6.2.1   Framing

For the SDH-based physical layer, framing is imposed using the STM-1 (STS-3) frame. Figure 8.29 shows the payload portion of an STM-1 frame. This payload may be offset from the beginning of the frame, as indicated by the pointer in the section overhead of the frame. As can be seen, the payload consists of a 9-octet path overhead portion and the remainder, which contains ATM cells. Since the payload capacity (2,340 octets) is not an integer multiple of the cell length (53 octets), a cell may cross a payload boundary.

The H4 octet in the path overhead is set at the sending side to indicate the next occurrence of a cell boundary. That is, the value in the H4 field indicates the number of octets to the first cell boundary following the H4 octet. The permissible range of values is 0 to 52.

The advantages of the SDH-based approach include the following (Minzer 1989):

- It can be used to carry either ATM-based or STM-based payloads, making it possible to initially deploy a high-capacity fiber-based transmission infrastructure for a variety of circuit-switched and dedicated applications and then readily migrate to the support of BISDN.

OAM cell type	Octet 1	Octet 2	Octet 3	Octet 4	Octet 5
F1	00000000	00000000	00000000	00000011	Valid HEC code
F2	00000000	00000000	00000000	00000101	Valid HEC code
F3	00000000	00000000	00000000	00001001	Valid HEC code

Figure 8.28 Physical-Layer OAM Cell Headers

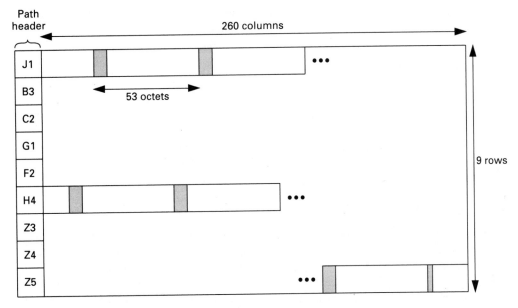

Figure 8.29 STM-1 Payload for SDH-Based ATM Cell Transmission

- Some specific connection can be circuit-switched using an SDH channel. For example, a connection carrying constant-bit-rate video traffic can be mapped into its own exclusive payload envelope of the STM-1 signal, which can be circuit-switched. This may be more efficient than ATM switching.

- Using SDH synchronous-multiplexing techniques, several ATM streams can be combined to build interfaces with higher bit rates than those supported by the ATM layer at a particular

Table 8.12 OAM Functions of the SDH-Based Physical Layer

Level	Function	Defect/Failure Detection
Regenerator section	Frame alignment	Loss of frame
	Section-error monitoring	Degraded error performance
Digital section	Frame alignment	Loss of frame
	Section-error monitoring	Degraded error performance
	Section-error reporting	Degraded error performance
Transmission path	Customer-network (CN) status monitoring	CN alarm-indication signal
	Cell delineation	Loss of cell synchronization
	VC-4 offset	Loss of AU-4 pointer
	Path-error monitoring	Degraded error performance
	Path-error reporting	Degraded error performance
	Cell-rate decoupling	Failure of insertion and suppression of idle cells

site. For example, four separate ATM streams, each with a bit rate of 155 Mbps (STM-1), can be combined to build a 622-Mbps (STM-4) interface. This arrangement may be more cost-effective than one using a single 622-Mbps ATM stream.

8.6.2.2   OAM Functions

With the SDH frame structure, OAM information is carried in the overhead octets of the frame. Flows F1 and F2 are carried on bytes in the section overhead. Flow F3 is carried in the path overhead. Part of the F3 flow could also be carried in physical-layer OAM cells as part of the ATM cell stream; this is a matter for further study.

Table 8.12 provides an overview of OAM functions of the SDH-based physical layer. The VC-4 offset function refers to the placement of the ATM payload within the STM-1 frame.

8.7   SUMMARY

Although ISDN is only just beginning to become widely available, plans are already in motion for a much more significant introduction: the broadband ISDN (BISDN). BISDN will rely heavily on optical fiber technology to bring a wide range of voice, data, image, and video services to customers.

Broadband ISDN uses fundamentally the same user-interface architecture and the same protocol architecure as ISDN. The major difference is that BISDN supports very high data rates at the user interface. To support these data rates, a new data-transfer mechanism is defined, known as asynchronous transfer mode (ATM), or cell relay.

As with frame relay, ATM is a streamlined packet transfer interface. ATM makes use of fixed-size packets, called cells. By using packets of fixed size and fixed format, even greater efficiencies can be achieved with ATM compared to frame relay. To accommodate a variety of link-layer and network-layer protocols as well as circuit-switched types of traffic, an ATM adaptation layer (AAL) is defined. The AAL maps various kinds of traffic into streams of cells.

Related to the development of BISDN is the development of a new family of synchronous time-division multiplexing-transmission specifications, referred to as SONET or SDH. SONET/SDH may be used independently of BISDN to provide high-speed synchronous data transfer. In addition, SONET/SDH may be used as a backbone transport mechanism within BISDN or any ATM network to support the transmission of the ATM cell stream.

APPENDIX 8A   1990 CCITT Interim Recommendations on ISDN

Number	Title	Description
I.113	Vocabulary of Terms for Broadband Aspects of ISDN	Defines terms considered essential to the understanding and application of the principles of BISDN.
I.121	Broadband Aspects of ISDN	States the basic principles of BISDN and indicates the evolution of ISDN required to support advanced services and applications.
I.150	B-ISDN ATM Functional Characteristics	Summarizes the functions of the ATM layer.
I.211	B-ISDN Service Aspects	Serves as a guideline for evolving recommendations on BISDN services. Includes a classification of BISDN services and a consideration of necessary network aspects.
I.311	B-ISDN General Network Aspects	Describes networking techniques, signaling principles, traffic control, and resources management for BISDN. Introduces the concepts of transmission path, virtual path, and virtual channel.
I.321	B-ISDN Protocol Reference Model and Its Application	Describes additions to the ISDN protocol reference model needed to accommodate BISDN services and functions.
I.327	B-ISDN Functional Architecture	Describes additions to the ISDN functional architecture needed to accommodate BISDN services and functions.
I.361	B-ISDN ATM Layer Specification	Describes the ATM layer, including cell structure, cell coding, and ATM protocol.
I.362	B-ISDN ATM Adaptation Layer (AAL) Functional Description	Provides a service classification for AAL and indicates the relationship between AAL services and AAL protocols.
I.363	B-ISDN ATM Adaptation Layer (AAL) Specification	Describes the interactions between the AAL and the next higher layer, the AAL and the ATM layer, and AAL peer-to-peer operations.
I.413	B-ISDN User-Network Interface	Gives the reference configuration for the BISDN user-network interface and examples of physical realizations.
I.432	B-ISDN User-Network Interface Physical Layer Specification	Defines the physical-layer interface for BISDN. Includes physical-medium specification, timing and framing aspects, and header-error control.
I.610	OAM Principles of B-ISDN Access	Describes the minimum functions required to maintain the physical layer and the ATM layer of the customer access.

Part 3
Local and Metropolitan Area Networks

One of the most successful areas of standardization is that of local and metropolitan area networks (LANs and MANs). Both customers and vendors have enthusiastically supported these standardization efforts, and standardized products dominate the marketplace.

Chapter 9 looks at those LAN standards that are the best established: the IEEE 802 LAN standards. Each of the four major standards (logical link control, CSMA/CD [carrier sense multiple access with collision detection], token bus, and token ring) is surveyed.

Chapter 10 is devoted to the fiber-distributed data interface (FDDI). The chapter covers the original FDDI set of standards as well as the enhancement, FDDI-II, designed to support both packet-switching and circuit-switching types of traffic.

Finally, Chapter 11 examines the newest standard in this area: the IEEE 802.6 MAN standard.

9
ISO 8802 and
IEEE 802 Standards

Much of the work on the development of standards for local area networks (LANs) has been done through IEEE (the Institute of Electrical and Electronics Engineers), which is accredited by ANSI (the American National Standards Institute) to develop American National Standards. Within the IEEE Computer Society, a committee known as IEEE 802 was organized and has developed standards for LANs with data rates ranging from 1 Mbps to 20 Mbps. All of these standards are labeled as ANSI/IEEE Std 802.x. As the work has progressed in ANSI, it has been submitted to ISO (the International Organization for Standardization) for standardization, and a series of international standards, labeled ISO 8802-x, has been issued. The international standards lag somewhat behind the ANSI standards, but it has so far proved to be the case that all of the 802 standards eventually become 8802 standards. This chapter focuses on the current version of the 802 standards.

9.1 OVERVIEW

The key to the development of the LAN market is the availability of a low-cost interface. The cost of connecting equipment to a LAN must be much less than the cost of the equipment alone. This requirement, plus the complexity of the LAN logic, dictates a solution based on the use of chips and very-large-scale integration (VLSI). However, chip manufacturers will be reluctant to commit the necessary resources unless there is a high-volume market. A widely accepted LAN standard assures that volume and also enables equipment from a variety of manufacturers to intercommunicate. This is the rationale of the IEEE 802 committee.

The committee issued a set of four standards, which were subsequently adopted in 1985 by ANSI as American National Standards. These standards were subsequently revised and reissued as international standards by ISO in 1987, with the designation ISO 8802.

The committee characterized its work in this way:

The LANs described herein are distinguished from other types of data networks in that they are optimized for a moderate size geographic area such as a single office building, a ware-

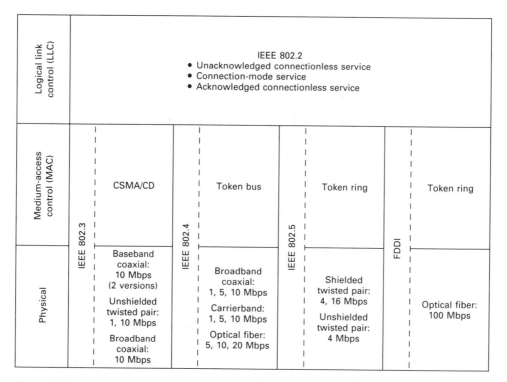

Figure 9.1 Local Area Network Standards

house, or a campus. The IEEE 802 LAN is a shared medium peer-to-peer communications network that broadcasts information for all stations to receive. As a consequence, it does not inherently provide privacy. The LAN enables stations to communicate directly using a common physical medium on a point-to-point basis without any intermediate switching node being required. There is always need for an access sublayer in order to arbitrate the access to the shared medium. The network is generally owned, used, and operated by a single organization. This is in contrast to Wide Area Networks (WANs) that interconnect communication facilities in different parts of a country or are used as a public utility. These LANs are also different from networks, such as backplane buses, that are optimized for the interconnection of devices on a desk top or components within a single piece of equipment. (IEEE 1990, p. 9)

Two conclusions were quickly reached. First, the task of communication across the local network is sufficiently complex that it needs to be broken up into more manageable subtasks. Second, no single technical approach will satisfy all requirements.

The second conclusion was reached reluctantly when it became apparent that no single standard would satisfy all committee participants. There was support for various topologies, access methods, and transmission media. The committee's response was to standardize all serious proposals rather than attempt to settle on just one. Figure 9.1 illustrates the results.

9.1.1   LAN-Protocol Reference Model

Figure 9.2 relates the LAN standards to the OSI (open systems interconnection) architecture. The work on LAN standards has resulted, in effect, in a communications architecture for LAN communication. Fortunately, this architecture was designed to be a subset of the OSI architecture.

Working from the bottom up, the lowest layer corresponds to the *physical layer* of the OSI model and includes such functions as:

- Encoding/decoding of signals
- Preamble generation/removal (for synchronization)
- Bit transmission/reception

In addition, the physical layer of the 802 model includes a specification of the transmission medium. Generally, this is considered "below" the lowest layer of the OSI model. However, the choice of transmission medium is critical in LAN design, and so a specification of the medium is included.

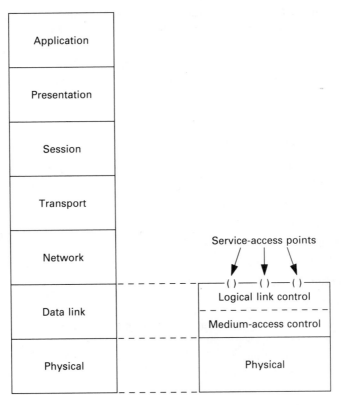

**Figure 9.2 Relationship of IEEE 802 Reference Model to OSI
Model**

Above the physical layer are the functions associated with providing service to LAN users. These include:

- Providing one or more service-access points (SAPs)

- On transmission, assembling data into a frame with address and CRC (cyclic redundancy check) fields

- On reception, disassembling the frame and performing address-recognition and CRC validation

- Governing access to the LAN transmission medium

These are functions typically associated with OSI layer 2. The first function, and related functions, are grouped into a *logical link control* (*LLC*) layer. The last three functions are treated as a separate layer, called *medium-access control* (*MAC*). This is done for the following reasons:

- The logic required to manage access to a multiple-source, multiple-destination link is not found in traditional layer-2 data-link control.

- For the same LLC, several MAC options may be provided.

Figure 9.1 illustrates the results.[1] Note that the physical and MAC layers are treated as a unit for the purposes of developing standards. This is because of the intimate relationship between the MAC protocol on the one hand and the topology and transmission medium on the other.

9.1.2 Organization of IEEE 802

The work of the IEEE 802 committee is currently organized into the following subcommittees:

- 802.1: Higher Layer Interface
- 802.2: Logical Link Control
- 802.3: CSMA/CD Networks
- 802.4: Token Bus Networks
- 802.5: Token Ring Networks
- 802.6: Metropolitan Area Networks
- 802.7: Broadband Technical Advisory Group
- 802.8: Fiber Optic Technical Advisory Group
- 802.9: Integrated Voice and Data LAN Interface
- 802.10: Standard for Interoperable LAN Security
- 802.11: Wireless LAN

The Higher Layer Interface subcommittee deals with issues related to network architecture, internetworking, and network management for LANs.

Work has been completed on LLC, CSMA/CD, token-bus, and token-ring standards, which are described in this chapter, and work on new options and features continues in each subcommittee.

---

1. The figure also shows how the fiber-distributed data interface standard fits into the model. (FDDI is discussed in Chapter 10.)

The work on metropolitan area networks (MANs) has only recently solidified into standards. This important topic is dealt with in Chapter 11.

The purpose of 802.7 and 802.8 is to provide technical guidance to the other subcommittees on broadband and optical-fiber technology, respectively. The Broadband Technical Advisory Group has produced a recommended-practices document for broadband cabling systems. The Fiber Optic Technical Advisory Group is investigating the use of optical fiber as an alternative transmission medium for 802.3, 802.4, and 802.5. It is also considering installation recommendations and a tutorial on fiber-optic standards and related information.

The Integrated Voice and Data (IVD) LAN Interface Working Group was chartered in 1986. It is developing an architecture and an interface standard for desktop devices designed for connection to 802 LANs and to integrated services digital networks (ISDNs), utilizing twisted-pair wiring to carry both voice and data.

The Standard for Interoperable LAN Security Working Group, formed in 1988, addresses such issues as secure data exchange, encryption-key management, security aspects of network management, and the application of the OSI security architecture to LANs.

The most recent addition to the 802 structure is the Wireless LAN Working Group. This group, begun in 1990, is developing standards for radio-frequency LANs.

9.2 LOGICAL LINK CONTROL

This section provides an overview of the three types of LLC service and the protocols that support these services.

9.2.1 LLC Services

Logical link control (LLC) provides services to users through LLC service-access points (LSAPs). The LLC standard specifies three forms of service to LLC users:

1. Unacknowledged connectionless service
2. Connection-mode service
3. Acknowledged connectionless service

As usual, these services, which are discussed in the following subsections, are defined in terms of primitives and parameters (Table 9.1).

9.2.1.1 Unacknowledged Connectionless Service

The unacknowledged connectionless service exhibits the same characteristics as any OSI connectionless-mode service that we have discussed. It provides no flow control or error control and does not guarantee the delivery of data in the order in which they were sent.

This service provides for only two primitives across the interface between the next higher layer and LLC. DL-UNITDATA.request is used to pass a block of data down to LLC for transmission. DL-UNITDATA.indication is used to pass a block of data up to the destination user from LLC upon reception. The source address and destination address parameters specify the local and remote LLC users, respectively. Each of these parameters is actually a combination of LLC service-access point and the MAC address. The data parameter is the block of data transmitted

Table 9.1 Logical Link Control Primitives

Unacknowledged Connectionless Service

DL-UNITDATA.request (source address, destination address, data, priority)
DL-UNITDATA.indication (source address, destination address, data, priority)

Connection-Mode Service

DL-CONNECT.request (source address, destination address, priority)
DL-CONNECT.indication (source address, destination address, priority)
DL-CONNECT.response (source address, destination address, priority)
DL-CONNECT.confirm (source address, destination address, priority)

DL-DATA.request (source address, destination address, data)
DL-DATA.indication (source address, destination address, data)

DL-DISCONNECT.request (source address, destination address)
DL-DISCONNECT.indication (source address, destination address, reason)

DL-RESET.request (source address, destination address)
DL-RESET.indication (source address, destination address, reason)
DL-RESET.response (source address, destination address)
DL-RESET.confirm (source address, destination address)

DL-CONNECTION-FLOWCONTROL.request (source address, destination address, amount)
DL-CONNECTION-FLOWCONTROL.indication (source address, destination address, amount)

Acknowledged Connectionless Service

DL-DATA-ACK.request (source address, destination address, data, priority, service class)
DL-DATA-ACK.indication (source address, destination address, data, priority, service class)
DL-DATA-ACK-STATUS.indication (source address, destination address, priority, service class, status)

DL-REPLY.request (source address, destination address, data, priority, service class)
DL-REPLY.indication (source address, destination address, data, priority, service class)
DL-REPLY-STATUS.indication (source address, destination address, data, priority, service class, status)

DL-REPLY-UPDATE.request (source address, data)
DL-REPLY-UPDATE-STATUS.indication (source address, status)

---

from one LLC user to another. The priority parameter specifies the desired parameter. This (together with the MAC portion of the address) is passed down through the LLC entity to the MAC entity, which has the responsibility of implementing a priority mechanism. Token bus (IEEE 802.4) and token ring (IEEE 802.5, FDDI) are capable of this, but the 802.3 CSMA/CD system is not.

9.2.1.2   Connection-Mode Service

The connection-mode LLC service is quite similar to the connection-mode network service (compare Table 9.1 with Table 4.1). The first four primitives listed for the service in Table 9.1 deal with connection establishment. In addition to specifying the source and destination addresses, the user can indicate a priority level to be provided for the requested connection.

The DL-DISCONNECT primitives provide for abrupt connection termination and are also used for connection rejection.

The DL-RESET primitives may be employed by the LLC service user to resynchronize the use of an LLC connection or by the LLC service provider to report the loss of user data that it cannot recover. In either case, outstanding service data units on the LLC connection may be lost; it is up to higher layers to recover the lost data.

Finally, the two flow-control primitives regulate the flow of data across the LSAP, which can be controlled in either direction. This is a local flow-control mechanism that specifies the amount of data that may be passed across the LSAP.

9.2.1.3   Acknowledged Connectionless Service

The acknowledged connectionless service provides a mechanism by which a user can send a unit of data and receive an acknowledgment that the data were delivered, without the necessity of setting up a connection. There are actually two related but independent services. The DL-DATA-ACK service is a guaranteed-delivery service, in which data are sent from an originating LLC user and acknowledged. The DL-REPLY service is essentially a poll with a guaranteed response; it enables a user to request a previously prepared data unit from another user or to exchange data units with another user.

The DL-DATA-ACK service includes DL-DATA-ACK.request and DL-DATA-ACK.indication, with meanings analogous to those for the unacknowledged connectionless service. The service-class parameter specifies whether or not an acknowledgment capability in the MAC layer is to be used for the data-unit transmission. So far, only the 802.4 standard supports this capability. The DL-DATA-ACK-STATUS.indication provides acknowledgment to the sending user; it includes a status parameter that indicates whether or not the data unit was successfully received by the peer LLC entity.

The DL-REPLY primitives provide a data-exchange service. This service allows a user to request that data be returned from a remote station or that data units be exchanged with a remote station. Associated with these primitives are the DL-REPLY-UPDATE primitives, which allow a user to pass data to LLC to be held and then sent out at a later time when requested to do so (by means of a DL-REPLY primitive) by some other station.

9.2.2   LLC Protocol

The basic LLC protocol is modeled after HDLC (high-level data-link control) and has similar functions and formats. The differences between the two protocols can be summarized as follows:

- LLC only makes use of the asynchronous balanced mode of operation of HDLC, to support connection-mode LLC service. The other HDLC modes are not employed.

- LLC supports a connectionless service using the unnumbered information PDU.

- LLC permits multiplexing by the use of LSAPs.

- LLC supports an acknowledged connectionless service by using two new unnumbered PDUs.

9.2.2.1   LLC Types and Classes

Three LLC protocols (referred to as types of operation) are defined in the standard, one for each of the three forms of service:

1.   Type-1 operation supports unacknowledged connectionless service.

2.   Type-2 operation supports connection-mode service.

3.   Type-3 operation supports acknowledged connectionless service.

Table 9.2 LLC Classes

		Class of LLC			
		I	**II**	**III**	**IV**
Types of	1	X	X	X	X
Operation	2		X		X
Supported	3			X	X

It is possible for a single system on the LAN (referred to as a station) to support more than one form of service and hence employ more than one of the types of protocols. The combination of services supported is indicated by the station class. Table 9.2 shows the allowable station classes. Note that all allowable classes support type 1. This ensures that all stations on a LAN will have a common service mode that can be used for management operations.

If a station supports more than one mode of service, then individual LSAPs may be activated for one or more of the available services. This is a configuration function beyond the scope of the standard.

9.2.2.2   LLC Protocol Data Units

All three LLC protocols employ the same PDU format (Figure 9.3), which consists of four fields. The DSAP and SSAP fields each contain a 7-bit address.[2] One bit of the DSAP indicates whether this is an individual or a group address. One bit of the SSAP indicates whether this is a command or response PDU.

The format of the LLC control field is identical to that of HDLC (Figure 3.1), using extended (7-bit) sequence numbers.

Table 9.3 lists the PDUs used in all three LLC protocols.

9.2.2.3   Type-1 Operation

For type-1 operation, the UI PDU is used to transfer user data. There is no acknowledgment, flow control, or error control. However, there is error detection and discard at the MAC level.

The remaining two type-1 PDUs are intended to support management functions associated with all three types of operation. Both PDUs are used in the following fashion. An LLC entity may issue a command (C/R bit=0) XID or TEST. The receiving LLC entity issues a corresponding XID or TEST in response.

The XID PDU is used to exchange two types of information: types of operation supported and window size. If the DSAP and SSAP fields are null (all 0s), then the information field indicates which LLC class (Table 9.2) is provided by the sending LLC entity.[3] If the XID includes specific DSAP and SSAP addresses, then the information field indicates which types of operation may be provided for that particular SSAP. For an SAP that supports type-2 operation, and for a particular connection (identified by the SSAP, DSAP pair), the information field also includes the receive window size used in the sliding-window flow-control mechanism.

---

2.   See Appendix 9A for a discussion of LAN addresses.

3.   The identity of the sending end system is known because its MAC address is included in the MAC frame.

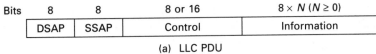

Bits   8   8   8 or 16 $8 \times N \ (N \geq 0)$

| DSAP | SSAP | Control | Information |

(a) LLC PDU

| I/G | 7-bit destination service-access point | C/R | 7-bit source service-access point |

I/G = 0: individual DSAP   C/R = 0: command
I/G = 1: group DSAP   C/R = 1: response

(b) LLC address fields

Figure 9.3 LLC Protocol Data Unit Formats

Table 9.3 LLC Protocol Data Units

Name	Function	Description
(a) Unacknowledged connectionless service		
Unnumbered (U)		
UI (unnumbered information)	C	Exchange user data
XID (exchange identification)	C/R	Type of operation and window-size information
Test	C/R	Loopback test
(b) Connection-mode service		
Information (I)	C/R	Exchange user data
Supervisory (S)		
RR (receive ready)	C/R	Positive acknowledgment; ready to receive I PDU
RNR (receive not ready)	C/R	Positive acknowledgment; not ready to receive
REJ (reject)	C/R	Negative acknowledgment; go back N
Unnumbered		
SABME (set asynchronous balanced mode extended)	C	Connection request
DISC (disconnect)	C	Terminate connection
UA (unnumbered acknowledgment)	R	Acknowledge unnumbered command
DM (disconnected mode)	R	Connection rejection
FRMR (frame reject)	R	Reports receipt of unacceptable frame
(c) Acknowledged connectionless service		
Unnumbered		
AC (acknowledged connectionless) information	C/R	Exchange user information

The TEST PDU is used to conduct a loopback test of the transmission path between two LLC entities. Upon receipt of a TEST command PDU, the addressed LLC entity issues a TEST response PDU as soon as possible.

9.2.2.4   Type-2 Operation

With type-2 operation, a data-link connection is established between two LLC SAPs prior to data exchange. Connection establishment is attempted by the type-2 protocol in response to a DL-CONNECT.request from a user. The LLC entity issues an SABME[4] PDU to request a logical connection with the other LLC entity. If the connection is accepted by the LLC user designated by the DSAP, then the destination LLC entity returns a UA PDU. The connection is henceforth uniquely identified by the pair of user SAPs. If the destination LLC user rejects the connection request, its LLC entity returns a DM PDU.

Once the connection is established, data are exchanged using information PDUs, as in HDLC. The information PDUs include send and receive sequence numbers, for sequencing and flow control. The supervisory PDUs are used, as in HDLC, for flow control and error control.

Either LLC entity can request a reset, either on its own initiative or in response to a user's DL-RESET.request. An LLC entity requests a reset on a particular connection simply by issuing a SABME using the appropriate SSAP and DSAP. The remote LLC user has the choice of accepting the reset, which causes its LLC entity to reply with a UA, or rejecting it, which causes its LLC entity to reply with a DM. When a reset occurs, both LLC entities reset their send and receive sequence numbers to zero.

Either LLC entity can terminate a logical LLC connection by issuing a DISC PDU.

9.2.2.5   Type-3 Operation

With type-3 operation, each transmitted PDU is acknowledged. A new (not found in HDLC) un-numbered PDU, the acknowledged connectionless (AC) information PDU is defined. User data are sent in AC command PDUs and must be acknowledged using an AC response PDU. To guard against lost PDUs, a 1-bit sequence number is used. The sender alternates the use of 0 and 1 in its AC command PDU, and the receiver responds with an AC PDU whose number is the opposite of that of the corresponding command. Only one PDU in each direction may be outstanding at any time.

For the DL-DATA-ACK service, the P/F bit is always set to 0. The AC command PDU contains user data, and the AC response PDU does not. For the DL-REPLY service, the P/F bit is always set to 1. The AC command may or may not contain user data. The AC response contains user data if data are available; otherwise, it does not, and this signals the other side that the reply has failed.

9.3   CSMA/CD

The IEEE 802.3 standard is based on the Ethernet specification. The standard states that it is intended for use in commercial and light-industrial environments. Use in home or heavy-industrial

---

4.   This stands for set asynchronous balanced mode extended. It is used in HDLC to choose ABM and to select extended sequence numbers of 7 bits. Both ABM and 7-bit sequence numbers are mandatory in type-2 operation.

environments, although not precluded, is not considered within the scope of the standard. The IEEE 802.3 standard, as with 802.4 and 802.5, defines both a medium-access-control layer and a physical layer.

9.3.1   IEEE 802.3 Medium-Access Control

The medium-access control protocol for IEEE 802.3 is carrier sense multiple access with collision detection (CSMA/CD). The original baseband version of this technique was developed by Xerox as part of the Ethernet LAN. The original broadband version was developed by MITRE as part of its MITREnet LAN.

9.3.1.1   MAC Protocol

With CSMA/CD, a station wishing to transmit first listens to the medium to determine whether another transmission is in progress (carrier sense). If the medium is idle, the station may transmit. It could happen that two or more stations attempt to transmit at about the same time. If this occurs, there will be a collision; the data from both transmissions will be garbled and not received successfully. Thus, a procedure is needed that specifies what a station should do if the medium is found to be busy and what it should do if a collision occurs:

1. If the medium is idle, transmit; otherwise, go to step 2.

2. If the medium is busy, continue to listen until the channel is idle, then transmit immediately.

3. If a collision is detected during transmission, transmit a brief jamming signal to assure that all stations know that there has been a collision and then cease transmission.

4. After transmitting the jamming signal, wait a random amount of time, then attempt to transmit again (repeat from step 1).

The preceding procedure raises several timing issues, all of which depend on a single parameter called the *slot time*. This parameter describes four important aspects of collision handling:

1. It is an upper bound on the time it takes to detect a collision and hence on the amount of wasted bandwidth.

2. It is an upper bound on the acquisition time (i.e., the time beyond which the transmission will not suffer a collision).

3. It is an upper bound on the length of a frame fragment generated by a collision.

4. It is the scheduling quantum for retransmission.

To fulfill all these functions, the slot time is defined to be larger than the sum of the physical-layer round-trip propagation time (twice the time it takes for a signal to travel from one end of the medium to the other) and the MAC-layer jam time.

Figure 9.4 illustrates the slot time for a baseband bus,[5] showing the worst case of two stations that are as far apart as possible. For clarity, the transmission time for a frame is normalized to 1. In this example, the propagation time is half the frame-transmission time. As can be seen, the amount of time it takes to detect a collision is twice the one-way propagation delay. For broadband bus, the wait is even longer. Figure 9.5 shows operation on a dual-cable system. With broadband

---

5. See Appendix 9B for a discussion of LAN topology.

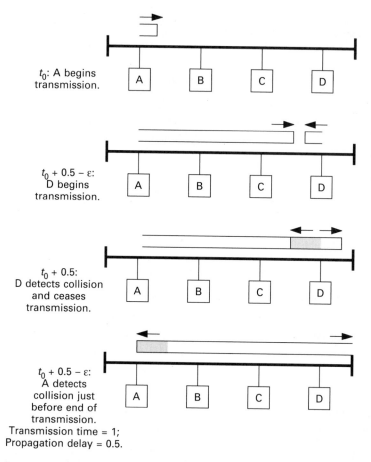

Figure 9.4 CSMA/CD Operation on Baseband Bus

bus, the worst case is two stations close together and as far as possible from the headend. In this case, the time required to detect a collision is four times the propagation delay from the station to the headend.

Both figures indicate the use of frames long enough to allow collision detection before the end of transmission. The 802.3 standard requires that all frames be at least this long, to avoid the possibility that a station will transmit a frame and be unaware of a collision.

The slot time also comes into play in the retransmission algorithm. Consider that if a collision occurs and the two stations involved pause an equal amount of time and then try again, there will be another collision. To avoid this, each station backs off a random amount of time taken from a uniform probability distribution. Furthermore, it should be observed that collisions generate additional LAN traffic. As the medium becomes busier, it is important not to clog the network with retransmissions, which lead to more collisions, which lead to more retransmissions, and so on. Accordingly, when a station experiences repeated collisions, it backs off for longer periods of time to compensate for the extra load on the network.

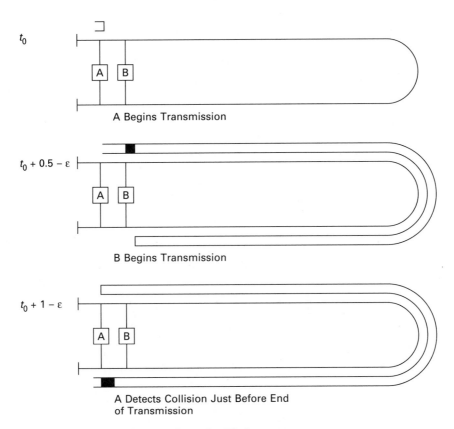

t_0

A Begins Transmission

$t_0 + 0.5 - \varepsilon$

B Begins Transmission

$t_0 + 1 - \varepsilon$

A Detects Collision Just Before End
of Transmission

Figure 9.5 Broadband Collision-Detection Timing

The rule, known as *truncated binary exponential backoff,* is as follows. The backoff delay is an integral number of time slots. The number of time slots to delay before the nth retransmission attempt is chosen as a uniformly distributed random integer r in the range $0 < r < 2^k$, where $k = $ min$(n, 10)$. After a user-defined number of attempts, the MAC entity assumes that some problem exists, gives up, and reports failure to LLC. More formally:

$$\begin{aligned}
&while \text{ attempts} < \text{backOffLimit} \\
&\quad \text{k} := \text{Min(attempts, 10)} \\
&\quad \text{r} := \text{Random}(0, 2^k) \\
&\quad \text{delay} := r \times \text{slotTime}
\end{aligned}$$

9.3.1.2   MAC Frame

Figure 9.6 depicts the frame[6] format for the 802.3 protocol. It consists of the following fields:

- *Preamble:* a 7-octet pattern of alternating 0s and 1s used by the receiver to establish bit synchronization.

---

6.   The MAC-level PDU is generally referred to as a *frame.*

Table 9.4 IEEE 802.3 Physical-Layer Medium Alternatives

Parameter	10BASE5	10BASE2	1BASE5	10BASET	10BROAD36
Transmission medium	Coaxial cable (50 ohm)	Coaxial cable (50 ohm)	Unshielded twisted pair	Unshielded twisted pair	Coaxial cable (75 ohm)
Signaling technique	Baseband (Manchester)	Baseband (Manchester)	Baseband (Manchester)	Baseband (Manchester)	Broadband (DPSK [differential phase-shift keying])
Data rate (Mbps)	10	10	1	10	10
Maximum segment length (m)	500	185	500	100	1,800
Network span (m)	2,500	925	2,500	500	3,600
Nodes per segment	100	30	—	—	—
Cable diameter (mm)	10	5	0.4–0.6	0.4–0.6	0.4–1.0

Octets	7	1	2 or 6	2 or 6	2	≥ 0	≥ 0	4
	Preamble	SFD	DA	SA	Length	LLC data	Pad	FCS

SFD = start-frame delimiter.   SA = source address.
DA = destination address.   FCS = frame-check sequence.

Figure 9.6 IEEE 802.3 Frame Format

- *Start-frame delimiter:* the sequence 10101011, which indicates the actual start of the frame and enables the receiver to locate the first bit of the rest of the frame.

- *Destination address:* specifies the station(s) for which the frame is intended. It may be a unique physical address, a group address, or a global address. The choice of 16- or 48-bit address length is an implementation decision and must be the same for all stations on a particular LAN.

- *Source address:* specifies the station that sent the frame.

- *Length:* length of the LLC data field.

- *LLC data:* data unit supplied by LLC.

- *Pad:* octets added to ensure that the frame is long enough for proper CD operation.

- *Frame-check sequence:* a 32-bit cyclic-redundancy check, based on all fields except preamble, SFD, and FCS.

9.3.2 IEEE 802.3 Physical-Layer Specifications

A variety of physical media and topologies have been defined for IEEE 802.3, to meet a variety of application requirements. To distinguish implementations using these alternatives, the following notation is used in the standard:

<data rate in Mbps><medium type><maximum segment length (× 100 m)>

The defined alternatives are:

- 10BASE5
- 10BASE2
- 1BASE5
- 10BASET[7]
- 10BROAD36

Table 9.4 summarizes the key characteristics of each specification. We examine these in turn in the following subsections.

9.3.2.1 Medium-Access Unit

The IEEE 802.3 standard anticipates that it may be desirable to locate stations some distance from their actual attachment point to the medium. A common configuration would place a minimum of electronics at the point of attachment to the medium and the bulk of the hardware and software at

---

7.   *10BASET* does not quite follow the notation; *T* stands for "twisted pair."

the station. That portion which is colocated with the tap is referred to in the standard as the *medium-attachment unit (MAU)*.

The specification assumes that the MAU performs the following functions:

- It transmits signals on the medium.

- It receives signals from the medium.

- It recognizes the presence of a signal on the medium.

- It recognizes a collision.

When the MAU is not physically integrated with the remainder of the 802.3 logic, the two are joined by a set of twisted-pair cables referred to as the *attachment-unit interface (AUI)*. There is one twisted pair for transmission in each direction and several pairs for control signals.

9.3.2.2 10BASE5 Medium Specification

The original 802.3 medium specification (and the only one included in the original 1985 IEEE/ANSI standard), 10BASE5 is based on Ethernet. It specifies the use of 50-ohm coaxial cable, a special-purpose coaxial cable that is generally used for baseband-bus LANs in preference to the more common CATV 75-ohm cable. For digital signals, the 50-ohm cable suffers less-intense reflections from the insertion capacitance of the taps and provides better immunity against low-frequency noise.

The data rate for 10BASE5 is 10 Mbps, using Manchester digital signaling.[8] With these parameters, the maximum length of a cable segment is set at 500 meters. The length of the network can be extended by the use of repeaters. In essence, a repeater consists of two MAUs joined together and connected to two different segments of cable. A repeater passes digital signals in both directions between the two segments that it connects, amplifying and regenerating the signals as they pass through. A repeater is transparent to the MAC level; because it does no buffering, it does not isolate one segment from another. So if, for example, two stations on different segments attempt to transmit at the same time, their transmissions will collide. To avoid looping, only one path of segments and repeaters is allowed between any two stations. The standard allows a maximum of four repeaters in the path between any two stations, extending the effective length of the medium to 2.5 km. Figure 9.7 is an example of a LAN with three segments and two repeaters.

In a baseband system, a collision should produce substantially higher voltage swings than those produced by a single transmitter. Accordingly, the standard specifies that a transmitting MAU will detect a collision if the signal on the cable exceeds the maximum that could be produced by the transmitter alone.

9.3.2.3 10BASE2 Medium Specification

To provide a lower-cost system than 10BASE5 for personal-computer LANs, 10BASE2 was added. As with 10BASE5, this specification uses 50-ohm coaxial cable and Manchester signaling at a data rate of 10 Mbps. The key difference is that 10BASE2 uses a thinner cable. This cable, employed in products such as public-address systems, is more flexible, which makes it easier to bend around corners and bring to a workstation cabinet rather than installing the cable in the wall and having to provide a drop cable to the station.

---

8. See Appendix A for a discussion of digital signaling.

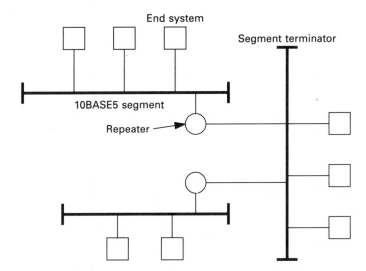

Figure 9.7 10BASE5 Configuration with Three Segments

The use of thinner cable results in cost savings in two ways. First, the thinner cable is cheaper. Second, the electronics is simpler, since there is no need for transmitters and receivers between the station and the cable across a drop cable. That is, the MAU is integrated with the station, and there is no attachment-unit interface. On the other hand, the thinner cable supports fewer taps over a shorter distance than the 10BASE5 cable.

Because they have the same data rate, it is possible to mix 10BASE5 and 10BASE2 segments in the same network, by using a repeater that conforms to 10BASE5 on one side and 10BASE2 on the other side. The only restriction is that a 10BASE2 segment should not be used to bridge two 10BASE5 segments because a ''backbone'' segment should be as resistant to noise as the segments it connects.

9.3.2.4   1BASE5 Medium Specification

The 1BASE5 specification, which is intended to provide a very-low-cost system, supports a significantly lower data rate than the other 802.3 versions at a correspondingly lower cost. It calls for the use of unshielded twisted-pair wire and Manchester signaling at a data rate of 1 Mbps.

The intended configuration of 1BASE5 is a star-shaped topology. Figure 9.8 shows the simplest example. The central element of the star is an active element, referred to as the *hub*. Each station is connected to the hub by two twisted pairs (transmit and receive). The hub acts as a repeater: when a single station transmits, the hub repeats the signal, on the outgoing line to each station.

Note that although this scheme is physically a star, it is logically a bus: a transmission from any one station is received by all other stations, and if two stations transmit at the same time, there will be a collision. When a collision occurs, the hub detects activity on more than one input and hence detects the collision. It then generates a collision-presence (CP) signal, which it broadcasts instead of the originally transmitted signals.

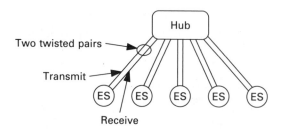

Figure 9.8 Single-Hub 1BASE5

The maximum station-to-hub distance is 250 m. Thus, the maximum end-to-end distance for two stations attached to the same hub is 500 m. The standard does not specify a maximum number of stations to be connected to a given hub; this is an implementation decision.

With a 250-m radius, a 1BASE5 LAN can be laid out with the hub in a wiring closet and individual stations scattered in various offices. This approach has a number of advantages:

■ It lends itself to prewiring of the building. The layout is regular and conforms to normal installation practices in office buildings. Furthermore, most existing buildings are prewired with excess unshielded twisted pair.

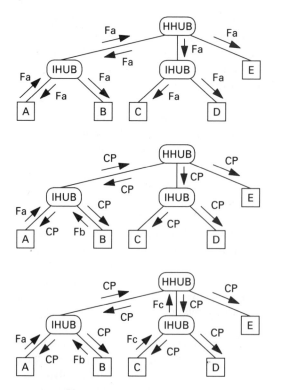

Figure 9.9 Operation of 1BASE5

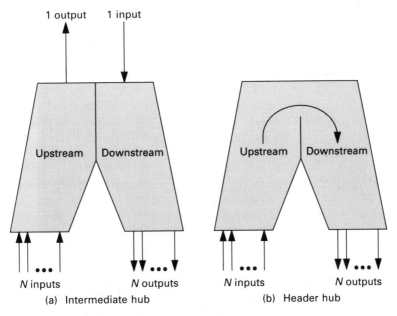

1 output   1 input

Upstream Downstream   Upstream Downstream

N inputs   N outputs   N inputs   N outputs

(a) Intermediate hub   (b) Header hub

Figure 9.10 1BASE5 Intermediate and Header Hubs

- The system can easily be expanded simply by patching additional cables into the network at the wiring closet.
- Servicing and maintenance are easier. Diagnosis of problems can be performed from centralized points. Faults can be isolated easily by patching cables out of the network.

Up to five levels of hubs can be cascaded in a hierarchical configuration. Figure 9.9 illustrates a two-level configuration. There is one *header hub* (HHUB) and one or more *intermediate hubs* (IHUBs). Each hub may have a mixture of stations and other hubs attached to it from below. The maximum distance between adjacent hubs is 250 m. Hence, the maximum span of the network (five levels) is 2,500 m. This layout fits well with building wiring practices. Typically, there is a wiring closet on each floor of an office building, and a hub can be placed in each one. Each hub could service the stations on its floor.

Figure 9.10 shows an abstract representation of the intermediate and header hubs. The header hub performs all the functions described previously for a single-hub configuration. In addition, the header hub may receive a CP signal from one of its subordinate hubs (upstream). This signal is broadcast on all of its output (downstream) lines. In the case of an intermediate hub, any incoming signal from below is repeated upward to the next higher level. If an intermediate hub detects a collision among upstream inputs or if it receives a CP signal from one of its subordinate hubs, it signals collision presence on its upstream output. Any data or CP signal from above is repeated on all lower-level outgoing lines.

Figure 9.9 gives examples of the operation of a multiple-hub 1BASE5 network. In the first example, a frame (Fa) transmitted from station A propagates up to HHUB and is eventually received by all stations in the network. In the second example, a collision is detected by A's IHUB. The collision-presence signal propagates up to HHUB and is rebroadcast down to all hubs and stations. The third example shows the result of a three-way collision.

9.3.2.5   10BASET Medium Specification

The attraction of the 1BASE5 specification is that it allows the use of inexpensive unshielded-twisted-pair wire, which is ordinary telephone wire. Such wire is often found prewired in office buildings as excess telephone cable and can be used for LANs. Of course, the disadvantage of this specification is the rather low data rate of 1 Mbps. By sacrificing some distance, it is possible to develop a 10-Mbps LAN using the unshielded-twisted-pair medium. Such an approach is specified in the latest physical-medium addition to the 802.3 family, the 10BASET specification.

As with the 1BASE5 specification, the 10BASET specification defines a star-shaped topology. The details of this topology differ slightly from those of 1BASE5. In both cases, a simple system consists of a number of stations connected to a central point. In both cases, stations are connected to the central point via two twisted pairs. The central point accepts input on any one line and repeats it on all the other lines. In the case of the 10BASET specification, the central point is referred to as a multiport repeater.

Stations attach to the multiport repeater via a point-to-point link. Ordinarily, the link consists of two unshielded twisted pairs. The data rate is 10 Mbps using Manchester encoding. Because of the high data rate and the poor transmission qualities of unshielded-twisted-pair wire, the length of a link is limited to 100 m. As an alternative, an optical-fiber link may be used. In this case, the maximum length is 500 m.

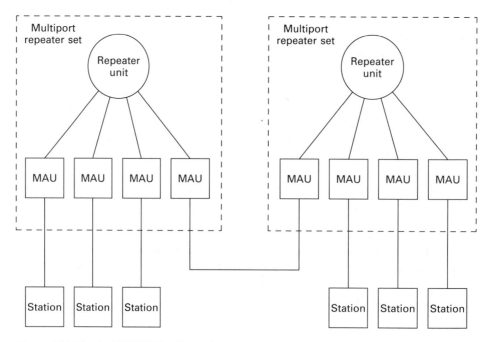

Figure 9.11 Simple 10BASET Configuration

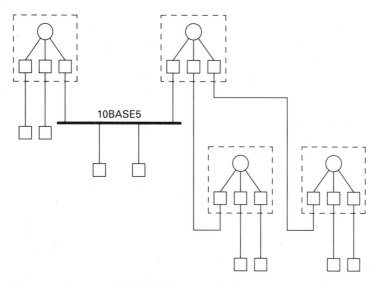

Figure 9.12 Mixed 10BASET, 10BASE5 Configuration

The distinction between a 1BASE5 hub and a 10BASET multiport repeater becomes clear when we consider a multistar arrangement. Figure 9.11 shows a sample configuration for 10BASET. Note that the connection between one repeater and the next is a link that appears the same as an ordinary station link. In fact, the repeater makes no distinction between a station and another repeater. Recall that in the 1BASE5 system, there is a distinction between intermediate hubs and a header hub and that the handling of data signals and collision-presence signals differs for the two types of hubs. In the 10BASET system, all multiport repeaters function in the same manner and indeed function in the same manner as an ordinary repeater on a 10BASE5 or 10BASE2 system:

- A valid signal appearing on any input is repeated on all other links.
- If two inputs occur simultaneously, causing a collision, a collision-enforcement signal is transmitted on all links.
- If a collision-enforcement signal is detected on any input, it is repeated on all other links.

One advantage of the use of repeaters and the use of a data rate of 10 Mbps is that the 10BASET system can be mixed with 10BASE2 and 10BASE5 systems. All that is required is that

Table 9.5 Allowable Connections to a 10BASET Multiport Repeater

Transmission Medium	Number of Attached Devices	Maximum Length (m)
Two unshielded twisted pairs	2	100
Two optical-fiber cables	2	500
Coaxial cable (10BASE5)	30	185
Coaxial cable (10BASE2)	100	500

the medium-attachment unit (MAU) conform to the appropriate specification. Figure 9.12 shows a configuration containing four 10BASET systems and one 10BASE5 system.

Table 9.5 summarizes the allowable connections. The maximum transmission path permitted between any two stations is five segments and four repeater sets. A segment is either a point-to-point link segment or a coaxial-cable 10BASE5 or 10BASE2 segment. The maximum number of coaxial-cable segments in a path is three.

9.3.2.6   10BROAD36 Medium Specification

The 10BROAD36 specification is the only 802.3 specification for broadband. The medium employed is the standard 75-ohm CATV coaxial cable. Either a dual-cable or split-cable configuration is allowed.[9] The maximum length of an individual segment, emanating from the headend, is 1,800 m; this results in a maximum end-to-end span of 3,600 m. A data rate of 10 Mbps is provided.

Before each MAC frame is transmitted, it goes through a scrambling algorithm.[10] This gives the data a pseudorandom nature that helps the receiver extract bit-timing information. It also improves the spectral characteristics of the signal, giving it a more uniform power distribution, as opposed to the potentially strong discrete spectral lines in nonscrambled data. The scrambled data are then modulated onto an analog carrier using differential phase-shift keying (DPSK). In ordinary PSK, a binary 0 is represented by a carrier with a particular phase, and a binary 1 is represented by a carrier with the opposite phase (180-degree difference). DPSK makes use of differential encoding, in which a change of phase occurs when a 0 occurs, and there is no change of phase when a 1 occurs. The advantage of differential encoding is that it is easier for the receiver to detect a change in phase than to determine the phase itself.

The characteristics of the modulation process are specified so that the resulting 10-Mbps signal fits into a 14-MHz bandwidth.

For broadband collision detection, we can take advantage of the fact that there is a delay between a station's transmission and its reception of its own transmission. In essence, the station does a bit-by-bit comparison of the transmitted and received scrambled bits up through the last bit of the source address. A mismatch indicates a collision.

A station detecting a collision generates a constant-amplitude signal, known as the *collision-enforcement signal,* on a dedicated band to notify all stations on the network. This collision enforcement is necessary because signals from different stations on the broadband cable system may be received at different power levels. As an example of the problem, consider that A and B are transmitting and that A's signals are received by both A and B at a significantly higher power level than B's signals. At both modems, the frame from A is demodulated error-free; the overlapping signal from B appears as a small amount of noise. A does not detect the collision and therefore assumes that its frame reached the destination. B detects the collision by means of the bit-by-bit comparison and uses the collision-enforcement signal to notify A.

Each 14-MHz data channel is provided with a dedicated 4-MHz collision-enforcement channel. Thus, on a dual-cable system, each channel requires 18 MHz, and on a split-cable system, each channel requires 36 MHz.

---

9.   See Appendix 9B for a discussion of baseband and broadband technology.

10.   A discussion of scrambling can be found in Stallings (1992).

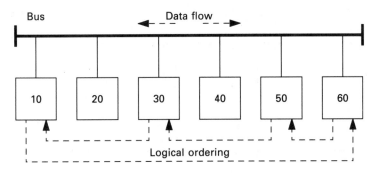

Figure 9.13 Token Bus

9.4   TOKEN BUS

The IEEE 802.4 standard is designed to be applicable not only in office environments but also in factory and other industrial environments as well as in military environments. The standard makes use of the bus and tree topologies.

9.4.1   IEEE 802.4 Medium-Access Control

9.4.1.1   MAC Protocol

The medium-access control protocol for IEEE 802.4 is token bus. For token bus, the stations on the bus or tree form a logical ring; that is, the stations are assigned logical positions in an ordered sequence, with the last member of the sequence followed by the first. Each station knows the identity of the station preceding and following it. The physical ordering of the stations on the bus is irrelevant to and independent of the logical ordering.

A control frame known as the *token* regulates the right of access. The token contains a destination address. The station possessing the token is granted control of the medium for a specified time. The station may transmit one or more frames and may poll stations and receive responses. When the station is finished or time has expired, it passes the token to the next station in logical sequence. This station now has permission to transmit. Hence, normal operation consists of alternating data-transfer and token-transfer phases. In addition, non–token-using stations are allowed on the bus. These stations can only respond to polls or requests for acknowledgment.

Figure 9.13 shows an example.[11] At any given time, a certain number of stations are active on the network and may receive frames. A certain number of these stations are part of the logical ring. The ordering within the logical ring is as follows: Each participating station knows the address of its predecessor (the station from which it receives the token), referred to as the previous station (PS), and it knows its successor (the station to which it sends the token), referred to as the next station (NS). The PS and NS addresses are dynamically determined to maintain a single

---

11.   The figure shows the numerical addresses in physical order on the bus; this is not required in the standard.

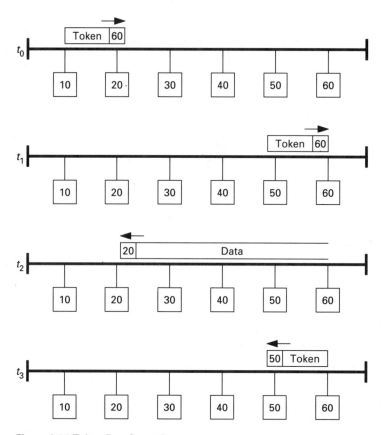

Figure 9.14 Token-Bus Operation

logical ring, in a manner described later in this section. The logical ring is created and maintained in such a way that the stations are logically ordered in numerically descending order of MAC address, except that the station with the lowest address is followed by the station with the highest address. In this example, stations 60, 50, 30, and 10, in that order, are part of the logical ring. Station 60 will pass the token to station 50, which passes it to station 30, which passes to station 10, which passes it to station 60.

Figure 9.14 shows a portion of the operation of this configuration. At t_0, station 10 passes the token. Since the current ordering dictates that the next station in logical sequence is station 60, the destination address portion of the token transmitted by station 10 is 60. The token is seen by all the other stations on the LAN, but it is ignored by all but station 60, whose address matches that in the token (t_1). Once station 60 has received the token, it is free to transmit a data frame. In this example, it transmits a data frame addressed to station 20 (t_2). Note that station 20 need not be part of the logical ring to receive frames. However, it cannot initiate any transmissions of its own. Once station 60 has completed its data transmission, it then issues a token addressed to the next station on the logical ring—in this case, station 50 (t_3).

This scheme requires considerable maintenance. These functions, at a minimum, must be performed by one or more stations:

- *Addition to ring:* Periodically, nonparticipating stations must be granted the opportunity to join the logical ring.

- *Deletion from ring:* A station can remove itself from the logical ring.

- *Ring initialization:* When the network is started, some cooperative procedure is needed to sort out who goes first, who goes second, and so on.

- *Token recovery:* If the token is lost, due to a transmission error or station failure, some means of recovery is needed.

The remainder of this subsection briefly describes the approach taken for these functions in the 802.4 standard.

To accomplish *addition to ring,* each station in the logical ring has the responsibility of periodically granting an opportunity for a new station to enter the ring. There are two variations on this process, depending on a station's position in the logical ring. First, consider a station other than the one with the lowest address (e.g., any station other than 10 in Figure 9.13). While holding the token, the station issues a *solicit-successor* frame, inviting stations with an address between itself and the next station in logical sequence to demand entrance. The transmitting station then waits for one response window (equal to twice the end-to-end propagation delay of the medium). One of four events can occur:

1. *No response:* The station passes the token to its successor as usual.

2. *One response:* One station issues a *set-successor* frame. The token holder sets its successor station to be the responding station and transmits the token to it; the requester sets its linkages accordingly and proceeds.

3. *Multiple responses:* If more than one station demands to enter the ring, the token holder will detect a garbled response. This conflict is resolved by an address-based contention scheme. The token holder transmits a *resolve-contention* frame and waits four response windows. Each demander can respond in one of these windows based on the first 2 bits of its address. If a demander hears anything before its window comes up, it refrains from demanding. If the token holder receives a valid set-successor frame, it proceeds as in step 2. Otherwise, it tries again, and only those stations that responded the first time are allowed to respond this time, based on the second pair of bits in their address. This process continues until a valid set-successor frame is received, no response is received, or the end of the address bits is reached. In the latter two cases, the token holder gives up and passes the token.

4. *Invalid response:* If the token holder receives a frame other than set-successor, it assumes that some other station thinks it holds the token. To avoid conflict, the station reverts to a listen state.

Now consider the case of the station in the logical ring with the lowest address (e.g., station 10 in Figure 9.13). In this case, the procedure begins with the station's sending a *solicit-successor-2* frame and waiting two response windows. Stations with an address lower than that of the token holder may respond with a set-successor frame in the first response window. Stations with an address higher than that of the token holder's current successor must wait for one response window. If they hear nothing, they may then respond; otherwise, they may not respond to this invitation. The remainder of the procedure follows the sequence listed earlier.

Deletion of a station is a much simpler process than addition. If a station wishes to drop out of the logical ring, it waits until it receives the token and then sends a set-successor frame to its predecessor containing the address of its successor. This causes the predecessor station to update its NS variable. The token holder then sends the token as usual to its successor. On the next token rotation, the former predecessor of the exited station sends the token to the former successor of the exited station. Every time that a station receives a token, it updates its PS variable to equal the MAC address of the sending station. Thus, the exited station is spliced out of the logical ring. For example, in Figure 9–13, station 50 can exit the ring by sending a set-successor frame to station 60 with an address of 30. The next time that station 60 gets the token, it will pass it on to station 30.

If a LAN has just been activated, or if the token has been lost, there will be no activity, since there is no token. When one or more stations detect a lack of activity whose duration is longer than a time-out value, *ring initialization* is triggered. A detecting station will issue a *claim-token* frame. Contending claimants are resolved as follows: Any station issuing a claim-token frame pads the data field to be 0, 2, 4, or 6 times the length that would be transmitted in one response window, based on the first 2 bits of its address. After transmitting, a claimant listens to the medium and, if it hears anything, drops its claim (some other station has transmitted a longer claim-token frame). Otherwise, it tries again, using the second pair of its address bits. When all address bits have been used, a station that succeeds on the last iteration considers itself the token holder. The ring can now be rebuilt by the station-addition process described earlier.

The need for *token recovery* becomes evident during the token-passing process. When the current token holder (A) issues a token frame, its successor (B) should, upon receipt, immediately issue a data or token frame. Therefore, after sending a token, A will listen for one slot time to make sure that its successor is active. The following sequence of events occurs:

1. If B is active, A will hear a valid frame and revert to listener mode.

2. If A does not hear a valid frame, it reissues the token to B a second time.

3. If A still does not hear a valid frame after two tries, it assumes that B has failed and issues a *who-follows* frame asking for the identity of the station that follows B. A should get back a set-successor frame from B's successor. If it does, A updates its NS variable and issues a token (back to step 1).

4. If A gets no response to its who-follows frame, it tries a second time.

5. If A gets no response to its second who-follows frame, it issues a solicit-successor frame with the full address range (every station is invited to respond). If this process succeeds, a two-station ring is established.

6. If two attempts of step 5 fail, A assumes that some major fault has occurred—e.g., all other stations have left the logical ring, the medium has failed, or A's own receiver has failed. At this point, if A has any more data to send, it sends those data and tries passing the token again. It then ceases transmission and listens to the bus.

9.4.1.2   Token-Bus Priority

As an option, 802.4 allows for the use of *classes of service* that provide a mechanism of prioritizing access to the bus. Four classes of service are defined, in descending order of priority: 6, 4, 2, 0. Any station may have data to send in one or more of these classes. The object is to allocate bus capacity to the higher-priority frames and only send lower-priority frames when there is sufficient capacity. To explain the algorithm, let us define the following variables:

THT = token-holding time—the maximum time that a station can hold the token to transmit class-6 data

$TRTi$ = token-rotation time for class i ($i = 4, 2, 0$)—the maximum time that a token can take to circulate and still permit class-i transmission

When a station receives the token, it can transmit classes of data according to the following rules (Figure 9.15). First, the station may transmit class-6 data for a time THT. Hence, for an N-station ring, during one circulation of the token, the maximum amount of time available for class-6 transmission is $N \times THT$. Next, after transmitting class-6 data, or if there were no class-6

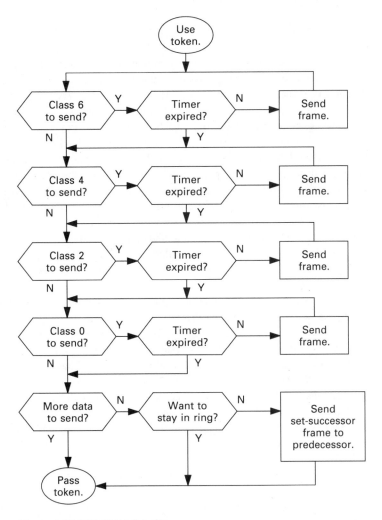

Figure 9.15 IEEE 802.4 Priority

data to transmit, the station may transmit class-4 data only if the amount of time for the last circulation of the token (including any class-6 data just sent) is less than TRT4. Class-2 and class-0 data are then handled in the same way as class 4.

This scheme, within limits, gives preference to frames of higher priority. Specifically, it guarantees that class-6 data may have a certain portion of the capacity, with any excess capacity utilized for classes 4, 2, and 0 in descending order of preference. Two cases are possible. If $N \times THT$ is greater than MAX[TRT4, TRT2, TRT0], the maximum possible token-circulation time is $N \times THT$, and class-6 data may occupy the entire cycle to the exclusion of the other classes. If $N \times THT$ is less than MAX[TRT4, TRT2, TRT0], the maximum circulation time is MAX[TRT4, TRT2, TRT0], and class-6 data are guaranteed $N \times THT$ amount of that time. This analysis ignores the time it takes to transmit the token and any other overhead, such as the reaction time at a station upon receipt of a token. However, these overhead quantities will generally be small compared to data-transmission time.

Figure 9.16, which is adapted from one in Jayasumana (1987), illustrates the average behavior of the 802.4 capacity-allocation scheme. That is, the plots ignore temporary load fluctuations, instead depicting the steady-state performance. For convenience, we assume that TRT4 > TRT2 > TRT0 and that the load generated in each class of data is the same.

Figure 9.16, part (a), depicts the first case ($N \times THT$ > TRT4). At very low loads, the token-circulation time is very short, and all the data offered in all four classes are transmitted. As the load increases, the average token-circulation time reaches TRT0. There is then a range, as indicated in the figure, in which the load continues to increase but the token-circulation time remains at TRT0. In this range, the other classes of data increase their throughput at the expense of class-0 data, whose throughput declines. At some point, the load is such that the token-circulation time equals TRT0, but the amount of transmission in classes 2, 4, and 6 uses up all of that time and no class-0 data can be transmitted. A further increase in offered load results in a renewed increase in the token-circulation time. The same pattern repeats for class-2 and class-4 data. There is a period when the load increases at a constant token circulation time of TRT2, and during that period, class-2 data are gradually crowded out. Class-4 data are similarly crowded out at a higher level of load. Finally, a situation is reached in which only class-6 data are being transmitted, and the token-circulation time stabilizes at $N \times THT$.

For the second case just mentioned ($N \times THT$ < TRT4), we need to examine two subcases. Figure 9.16, part (b), shows the case in which (TRT4/2) < ($N \times THT$) < TRT4. As before, with increasing load, class-0 and class-2 traffic are eliminated, and the token-circulation time increases. At some point, the increasing load drives the token-circulation time to TRT4. Using our simple example, when this point is reached, approximately half of the load is class-4 data and the other half is class-6. But since $N \times THT$ > (TRT4/2), if the load on the network continues to increase, the portion of the load that is class-6 traffic will also increase. This will cause a corresponding decrease in class-4 traffic. Eventually, a point is reached at which all of the allowable class-6 traffic is being handled during each token circulation. This will take an amount of time $N \times THT$ and still leave some time remaining for class-4 data. Thereafter, the total token-circulation time remains stable at TRT4.

Finally, Figure 9.16, part (c), shows the case in which $N \times THT$ < (TRT4/2). As before, increasing load eliminates class-0 and class-2 traffic. A point is reached at which the token-circulation time is $2 \times N \times THT$, with half of the traffic being class-4 and half being class-6. This is a maximum throughput per token circulation for class 6. However, the amount of class-4 data can continue to increase until the token-circulation time is TRT4.

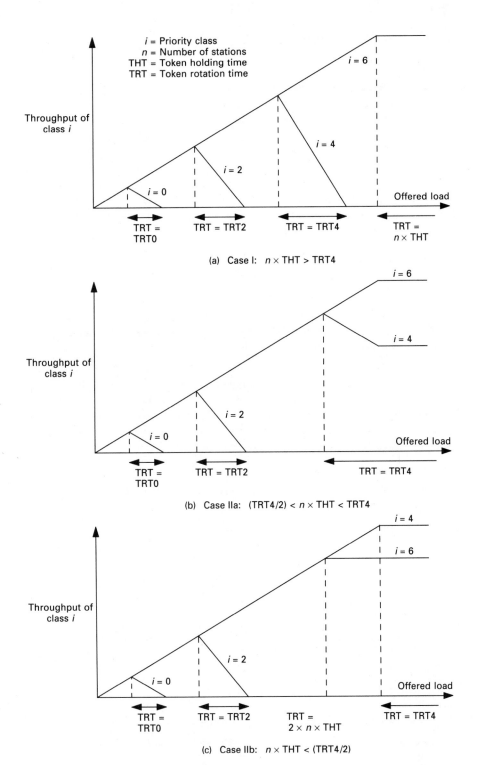

(a) Case I: $n \times$ THT > TRT4

(b) Case IIa: (TRT4/2) < $n \times$ THT < TRT4

(c) Case IIb: $n \times$ THT < (TRT4/2)

Source: A. Jayasumana, "Performance Analysis of Token Bus Priority Schemes," *Proceedings, INFOCOM '87* (1987): 405.

Figure 9.16 Throughput of Token-Bus Priority Classes

9.4.1.3   Request-with-Response Mechanism

An additional facility, known as the request-with-response mechanism, is defined as an option in 802.4. The mechanism is, in essence, an acknowledged connectionless mechanism and works as follows. When a station holds the token, it may temporarily delegate its right to transmit to another station by sending a *request-with-response* data frame instead of a normal data frame. A station hearing such a frame addressed to itself copies the incoming data and responds with a *response* data frame. The station that responds is not required to be a member of the logical ring. If a valid response is not forthcoming, the station requesting the response will try a number of times, up to some predefined maximum, to elicit the response. Whether or not a response is received, the station that issued the request retains the token.

9.4.1.4   MAC Frame

Figure 9.17 depicts the frame format for the 802.4 protocol. It consists of the following fields:

- *Preamble:* a pattern of 1 or more octets used by the receiver to establish bit synchronization.

- *Start delimiter:* indicates start of frame. The SD consists of signaling patterns that are distinguishable from data. It is coded NN0NN000, where *N* is a nondata symbol. The actual form of a nondata symbol depends on the signal encoding on the medium.

- *Frame control:* The first 2 bits indicate whether this is a control frame or an LLC data frame. Control frames are used to manage the token-bus protocol; one example is the token. For a control frame, the remaining 6 bits of the FC field indicate the identity of the control frame. For a frame containing LLC data, 3 bits of the FC field indicate whether this is a request-with-no-response frame (the default case), a request-with-response frame, or a response frame.

- *Destination address:* as with 802.3.

- *Source address:* as with 802.3.

- *Data unit:* contains an LLC data unit or information related to a control operation.

- *Frame-check sequence:* as with 802.3.

- *End delimiter:* indicates end of frame.

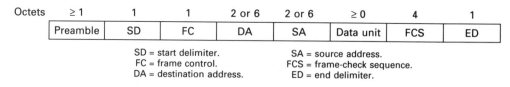

Octets	≥ 1	1	1	2 or 6	2 or 6	≥ 0	4	1
	Preamble	SD	FC	DA	SA	Data unit	FCS	ED

SD = start delimiter.   SA = source address.
FC = frame control.   FCS = frame-check sequence.
DA = destination address.   ED = end delimiter.

(a) Frame

0	0	C	C	C	C	C	C

CCCCCC = type of control frame.

(b) Frame-control field for control frame

0	1	M	M	M	P	P	P

MMM = request with no response,
        request with response, or response.
PPP = priority bits.

(c) Frame-control field for data frame

Figure 9.17 IEEE 802.4 Frame Format

9.4.2   IEEE 802.4 Physical-Layer Specifications

The 802.4 standard specifies four alternative physical media, whose characteristics are listed in Table 9.6 and discussed in the balance of this subsection.

Two of the alternatives use an analog transmission scheme known as carrierband. In contrast to broadband, with carrierband, the entire spectrum of the cable is devoted to a single transmission path for the analog signals; frequency-division multiplexing is not used. Typically, a carrierband LAN has the following characteristics: Bidirectional transmission, using a bus topology, is employed. Hence, there can be no amplifiers, and there is no need for a headend. Although the entire spectrum is used, most of the signal energy is concentrated at relatively low frequencies. This is an advantage, because attenuation is less at lower frequencies.

Because the cable is dedicated to a single task, it is not necessary to take care that the modem output be confined to a narrow bandwidth. Energy can spread over the entire spectrum. As a result, the electronics are simple and relatively inexpensive.

9.4.2.1   Phase-Continuous Carrierband

The lowest-cost alternative provided in 802.4 is the 1-Mbps phase-continuous carrierband, which uses a form of frequency-shift keying (FSK) in which the transition between signaling frequencies is accomplished by a continuous change of frequency, as opposed to the discontinuous replacement of one frequency by another. This type of FSK results in a tighter bandwidth and improved transmission and reception efficiency. To further improve reception, the digital data to be transmitted are first encoded using Manchester encoding. The high and low levels of the Manchester code are then passed through a modem at 6.25 MHz and 3.75 MHz, respectively.

This specification is intended to provide a low-cost system that can be installed with flexible or semirigid cable. A variety of older cables, already installed in buildings, can be used.

9.4.2.2   Phase-Coherent Carrierband

The other carrierband technique standardized by 802.4 is phase-coherent FSK, at data rates of 5 and 10 Mbps. This is a form of FSK in which the two signaling frequencies are integrally related to the data rate. The scheme is called phase-coherent because the zero crossing points are in phase at the beginning and end of each bit time.

A binary 1 is represented by a frequency equal to the data rate, and a binary 0 is represented by a frequency equal to twice the data rate. Thus, for the 5-Mbps data rate, the two frequencies are 5 MHz and 10 MHz, and for the 10-Mbps data rate, the two frequencies are 10 MHz and 20 MHz.

The phase-coherent scheme is intermediate in expense between a phase-continuous system and a broadband system. When implemented with semirigid coaxial cable, this system may be converted to broadband by making relatively simple hardware changes.

9.4.2.3   Broadband

The broadband specification allows for data rates of 1, 5, and 10 Mbps, with bandwidths of 1.5, 6, and 12 MHz, respectively. The standard recommends the use of a single-cable system with a headend frequency translator. Dual cable is also permitted.

The modulation scheme used for the broadband specification is known as duobinary AM/PSK modulation. In this scheme, data are precoded and signaled as pulses in which both the amplitude and the phase may vary. The nature of the encoding is such that receivers can demodulate the

Table 9.6 IEEE 802.4 Physical-Layer Medium Alternatives

Parameter	Phase-Continuous Carrierband	Phase-Coherent Carrierband		Broadband			Optical Fiber
Data rate (Mbps)	1	5	10	1	5	10	5,10,20
Bandwidth	N.A.	N.A.	N.A.	1.5 MHz	6 MHz	12 MHz	270 nm
Center frequency	5 MHz	7.5 MHz	15 MHz	—	—	—	800–910 nm
Modulation	Manchester/phase-continuous FSK	Phase-coherent FSK		Multilevel duobinary AM/PSK			On-off
Topology	Omnidirectional bus	Omnidirectional bus		Directional bus (tree)			Active or passive star
Transmission medium	Coaxial cable (75 ohm)	Coaxial cable (75 ohm)		Coaxial cable (75 ohm)			Optical fiber
Scrambling	No	No		Yes			No

modulated signal without having to recover the phase of the signal. In essence, the PSK component of the modulation is used to reduce the signal bandwidth, not to carry data.

As with the 802.3 10BROAD36 specification, the 802.4 broadband specification includes the use of scrambling.

9.4.2.4   Optical Fiber

The most recent addition to the IEEE 802.4 physical-layer standard is an optical-fiber specification. Three data rates are specified: 5, 10, and 20 Mbps. In keeping with standard practice for optical-fiber systems, the bandwidth and carrier are specified in terms of wavelength instead of frequency. For all three data rates, the bandwidth is 270 nm, and the center wavelength is between 800 and 910 nm.

The encoding technique used for 802.4 optical fiber is a form of amplitude-shift keying (ASK) known as intensity modulation. Normally, with intensity modulation, a binary 1 is encoded as a pulse of light, and a binary 0 is encoded as the absence of light. Because a long string of 0s or 1s could result in loss of synchronization, the approach in 802.4 is to first encode the binary data to guarantee the presence of transitions and then to present the encoded data to the optical source for transmission. The precoding technique that is used is Manchester. Thus, a binary 0 is transmitted as a pulse of light (H) followed by the absence of a pulse (L), in uniform time slots; and a binary 1 is transmitted as the absence of a pulse (L) followed by a pulse (H). Note that this doubles the effective signaling rate. The data rates of 5, 10, and 20 Mbps therefore require optical-signaling rates of 10, 20, and 40 Mbaud (1 baud = one signal element per second).

The 802.4 optical-fiber specification can be used with any topology that is logically a bus. That is, a transmission from any one station is received by all other stations, and if two stations transmit at the same time, a collision occurs. At the present time, a simple bus system is impractical because of the high cost of low-loss optical taps. Instead, the standard recommends the use of active or passive stars.

For both the active and passive stars, each station attaches to a central node via two optical fibers, one for transmission in each direction. The active star operates in the same fashion as the star topologies used for 802.3. That is, a transmission on any one input fiber to the central node is retransmitted on all output fibers.

The passive-star system is based on the use of a passive-star coupler, which is fabricated by fusing together a number of optical fibers. The transmit fibers from all of the stations enter the coupler on one side, and all the receive fibers exit on the other side. Any light input to one of the fibers on one side of the coupler will be equally divided among, and output through, all the fibers on the other side.

9.5   TOKEN RING

The IEEE 802.5 standard states that the token ring is intended for use in commercial and light-industrial environments. Use in home or heavy-industrial environments, although not precluded, is not considered within the scope of the standard. These environments are identical to those specified for IEEE 802.3.

9.5.1   IEEE 802.5 Medium-Access Control

9.5.1.1   MAC Protocol

The token-ring technique is based on the use of a small frame, called a *token*, that circulates when all stations are idle. A station wishing to transmit must wait until it detects a token passing by. It then seizes the token by changing 1 bit in the token, which transforms it from a token to a start-of-frame sequence for a data frame. The station then appends and transmits the remainder of the fields needed to construct a data frame.

When a station seizes a token and begins to transmit a data frame, there is no token on the ring, so other stations wishing to transmit must wait. The frame on the ring will make a round trip and be absorbed by the transmitting station. The transmitting station will insert a new token on the ring when both of the following conditions have been met:

- The station has completed transmission of its frame.

- The leading edge of the transmitted frame has returned to the station (after a complete circulation of the ring).

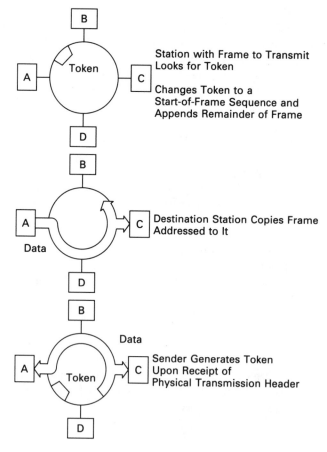

Figure 9.18 Token-Ring Operation

Once the new token has been inserted on the ring, the next station downstream with data to send will be able to seize the token and transmit. Figure 9.18 illustrates the technique.

Note that under lightly loaded conditions, there is some inefficiency with token ring, since a station must wait for the token to come around before transmitting. However, under heavy loads, which is when it matters, the ring functions in a round-robin fashion, which is both efficient and fair. To see this, consider the configuration in Figure 9.18. After station A transmits, it releases a token. The first station with an opportunity to transmit is D. If D transmits, it then releases a token and C has the next opportunity, and so on.

9.5.1.2   MAC Frame

Figure 9.19 depicts the frame format for the 802.5 protocol. It consists of the following fields:

- *Starting delimiter:* indicates start of frame. The SD consists of signaling patterns that are distinguishable from data. It is coded JK0JK000, where *J* and *K* are nondata symbols. The actual form of a nondata symbol depends on the signal encoding on the medium.

- *Access control:* has the format PPPTMRRR, where PPP and RRR are 3-bit priority and reservation variables and M is the monitor bit; their use is explained later in this subsection. T indicates whether this is a token or data frame. In the case of a token frame, the only remaining field is ED.

- *Frame control:* indicates whether this is an LLC data frame. If not, bits in this field control operation of the token-ring MAC protocol.

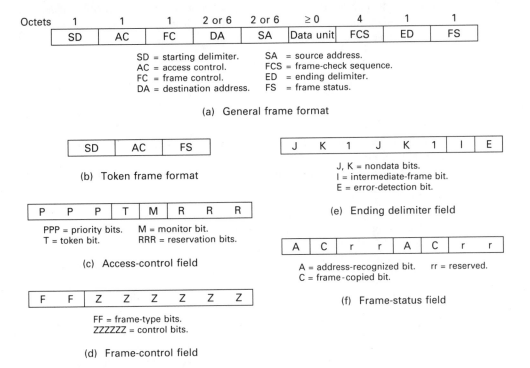

Figure 9.19 IEEE 802.5 Frame Format

- *Destination address:* as with 802.3.

- *Source address:* as with 802.3.

- *Data unit:* contains an LLC data unit.

- *Frame-check sequence:* as with 802.3.

- *Ending delimiter:* contains the error-detection bit (E), which is set if any repeater detects an error, and the intermediate-frame bit (I), which is used to indicate that this is a frame other than the final one of a multiple-frame transmission.

- *Frame status:* contains the address-recognized (A) and frame-copied (C) bits, whose use is explained later in this subsection. Because the A and C bits are outside the scope of the FCS, they are duplicated to provide a redundancy check to detect erroneous settings.

We can now restate the token-ring algorithm for the case when a single priority is used. In this case, the priority and reservation bits are set to 0. A station wishing to transmit waits until a token goes by, as indicated by a token bit of 0 in the AC field. The station seizes the token by setting the token bit to 1. The SD and AC fields of the received token now function as the first two fields of the outgoing frame. The station transmits one or more frames, continuing until either its supply of frames is exhausted or a token-holding timer expires. When the AC field of the last transmitted frame returns, the station sets the token bit to 0 and appends an ED field, resulting in the insertion of a new token on the ring.

Stations in the receive mode listen to the ring. Each station can check passing frames for errors and set the E bit to 1 if an error is detected. If a station detects its own MAC address, it sets the A bit to 1; it may also copy the frame, setting the C bit to 1. This allows the originating station to differentiate three results of a frame transmission:

1. Destination station nonexistent or not active (A = 0, C = 0).
2. Destination station exists but frame not copied (A = 1, C = 0).
3. Frame received (A = 1, C = 1).

9.5.1.3   Token-Ring Priority

The 802.5 standard includes a specification for an optional priority mechanism. Eight levels of priority are supported by providing two 3-bit fields in each data frame and token: a priority field and a reservation field. To explain the algorithm, let us define the following variables:

P_f = priority of frame to be transmitted by a station
P_s = service priority: priority of the current token
P_r = value of P_s as contained in the last token received by this station
R_s = reservation value in the current token
R_r = highest reservation value in the frames received by this station during the last token rotation

The scheme works as follows:

1. A station wishing to transmit must wait for a token with $P_s \leq P_f$.

2. While waiting, a station may reserve a future token at its priority level(P_f). If a data frame goes by, and if the reservation field is less than its priority ($R_s < P_f$), then the station may set the reservation field of the frame to its priority ($R_s \leftarrow P_f$). If a token frame goes by, and if

$(R_s < P_f$ and $P_f < P_s)$, then the station sets the reservation field of the frame to its priority $(R_s \leftarrow P_f)$. This has the effect of preempting any lower-priority reservation.

3. When a station seizes a token, it sets the token bit to 1 to start a data frame, sets the reservation field of the data frame to 0, and leaves the priority field unchanged (the same as that of the incoming token frame).

4. Following transmission of one or more data frames, a station issues a new token with the priority and reservation fields set as indicated in Table 9.7.

The effect of the preceding steps is to sort the competing claims and allow the waiting transmission of highest priority to seize the token as soon as possible. A moment's reflection reveals that, as stated, the algorithm has a ratchet effect on priority, driving it to the highest used level and keeping it there. To avoid this, a station that raises the priority (issues a token that has a higher

Table 9.7 Actions Performed by the Token Holder to Implement the Priority Scheme

Conditions	Actions
Frame available AND $P_s \leq P_f$	Send frame
(Frame not available OR THT expired) AND $P_r \geq$ MAX $[R_r, P_f]$	Send token with: $P_s \leftarrow P_f$ $R_s \leftarrow$ MAX $[R_r, P_f]$
(Frame not available OR THT expired) AND $P_r <$ MAX $[R_r, P_f]$ AND $P_r > S_x$	Send token with: $P_s \leftarrow$ MAX $[R_r, P_f]$ $R_s \leftarrow 0$ Push $S_r \leftarrow P_r$ Push $S_x \leftarrow P_s$
(Frame not available OR THT expired) AND $P_r <$ MAX $[R_r, P_f]$ AND $P_r = S_x$	Send token with: $P_s \leftarrow$ MAX $[R_r, P_f]$ $R_s \leftarrow 0$ Pop S_x Push $S_x \leftarrow P_s$
(Frame not available OR Frame available and $P_f < S_x$) AND $P_s = S_x$ AND $R_r > S_r$	Send token with: $P_s \leftarrow R_r$ $R_s \leftarrow 0$ Pop S_x Push $S_x \leftarrow P_s$
(Frame not available OR Frame available and $P_f < S_x$) AND $P_s = S_x$ AND $R_r \leq S_r$	Send token with: $P_s \leftarrow R_r$ $R_s \leftarrow 0$ Pop S_r Pop S_x

Source: A. Valenzano, C. DeMartini, and L. Ciminiera, *MAP and TOP Communications: Standards and Applications* (Wokingham, England.: Addison-Wesley, 1992). Reprinted with permission of the publisher.

priority than the token that it received) has the responsibility of later lowering the priority to its previous level. Therefore, a station that raises the priority must remember both the old and the new priorities and downgrade the priority of the token at the appropriate time. In essence, each station is responsible for assuring that no token circulates indefinitely because its priority is too high. By remembering the priority of earlier transmissions, a station can detect this condition and downgrade the priority to a previous, lower priority or reservation.

To implement the downgrading mechanism, two stacks are maintained by each station, one for reservations and one for priorities:

$$S_x = \text{stack used to store new values of token priority}$$
$$S_r = \text{stack used to store old values of token priority}$$

The reason that stacks rather than scalar variables are required is that the priority can be raised a number of times by one or more stations. The successive raises must be unwound in the reverse order.

To summarize: A station having a higher-priority frame to transmit than the current frame can reserve the next token for its priority level as the frame passes by. When the next token is issued, it will be at the reserved priority level. Stations of lower priority cannot seize the token, so it passes to the reserving station or to an intermediate station with data to send having a priority level equal to or higher than the reserved priority level. The station that upgraded the priority level is responsible for downgrading it to its former level when all higher-priority stations are finished. When that station sees a token at the higher priority, it can assume that there is no more higher-priority traffic waiting, and it downgrades the token before passing it on.

Figure 9.20 is an example. The following events occur:

(A) A is transmitting a data frame to B at priority 0. When the frame has completed a circuit of the ring and returns to A, A will issue a token frame. However, as the data frame passes D, D makes a reservation at priority 3 by setting the reservation field to 3.

(B) A issues a token with the priority field set to 3.

(C) If neither B nor C has data of priority 3 or greater to send, it cannot seize the token. The token circulates to D, which seizes the token and issues a data frame.

(D) After D's data frame returns to D, D issues a new token at the same priority as the token that it received: priority 3.

(E) A sees a token at the priority level that it used when last issuing a token. It therefore seizes the token even if it has no data to send.

(F) A issues a token at the previous priority level: priority 0.

Note that, after A has issued a priority-3 token, any station with data of priority 3 or greater may seize the token. Suppose that, at this point, station C now has priority-4 data to send. C will seize the token, transmit its data frame, and reissue a priority-3 token, which is then seized by D. By the time that a priority-3 token arrives at A, all intervening stations with data of priority 3 or greater to send will have had the opportunity. It is therefore now appropriate for A to downgrade the token.

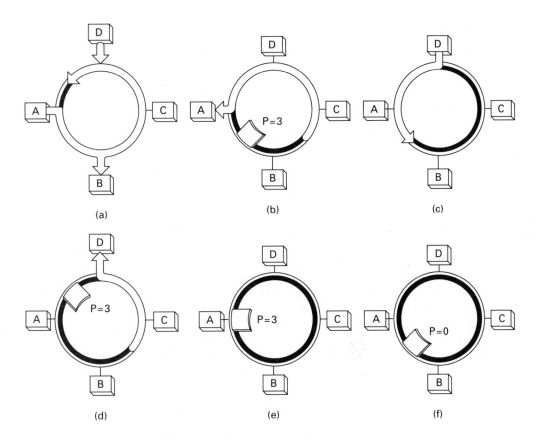

Figure 9.20 Token-Ring Priority Scheme

9.5.1.4   Token Maintenance

To overcome various error conditions, one station is designated as the active monitor. The active monitor periodically issues an active-monitor-present control frame to assure other stations that there is an active monitor on the ring. To detect a lost-token condition, the monitor uses a valid-frame timer that is greater than the time required to completely traverse the ring. The timer is reset after every valid token or data frame. If the time expires, the monitor issues a priority-0 token. To detect a persistently circulating data frame, the monitor sets the monitor bit to 1 on any passing data frame the first time it goes by. If it sees a data frame with the monitor bit already set, it knows that the transmitting station failed to absorb the frame. The monitor absorbs the frame and transmits a priority-0 token. The same strategy is used to detect a failure in the priority mechanism: no token should circulate completely around the ring at a constant non-0 priority level. Finally, if the active monitor detects evidence of another active monitor, it immediately goes into standby-monitor status.

All the active stations on the ring cooperate to provide each station with a continuous update on the identity of its upstream neighbor. Each station periodically issues a standby-monitor-present

Table 9.8 IEEE 802.5 Physical-Layer Medium Specification

Transmission medium	Shielded twisted pair	Unshielded twisted pair
Data rate (Mbps)	4 or 16	4
Maximum number of repeaters	250	250
Maximum length between repeaters	Not specified	Not specified

(SMP) frame. Its downstream neighbor absorbs this frame; notes its sending address; and after a pause, sends its own SMP frame. The absence of SMP frames can be used in fault isolation.

9.5.1.5 Early Token Release

When a station issues a frame, if the bit length of the ring is less than that of the frame, the leading edge of the transmitted frame will return to the transmitting station before it has completed transmission; in this case, the station may issue a token as soon as it has finished frame transmission. If the frame is shorter than the bit length of the ring, then after a station has completed transmission of a frame, it must wait until the leading edge of the frame returns before issuing a token. In this latter case, some of the potential capacity of the ring is unused.

To allow for more efficient ring utilization, an early-token-release (ETR) option has been added to the 802.5 standard. ETR allows a transmitting station to release a token as soon as it completes frame transmission, whether or not the frame header has returned to the station. The priority used for a token released prior to receipt of the previous frame header is the priority of the most recently received frame.

One effect of ETR is that access delay for priority traffic may increase when the ring is heavily loaded with short frames. Since a station must issue a token before it can read the reservation bits of the frame that it just transmitted, the station will not respond to reservations. Thus, the priority mechanism is at least partially disabled.

Stations that implement ETR are compatible and interoperable with those that do not.

9.5.2 IEEE 802.5 Physical-Layer Specification

The 802.5 standard (Table 9.8) specifies the use of shielded-twisted-pair wire with data rates of 4 and 16 Mbps.[12] Differential Manchester encoding is used. A recent addition to the standard is the use of unshielded-twisted-pair wire at 4 Mbps.

9.6 SUMMARY

The LAN marketplace exhibits wide variety, making the job of selection difficult. Fortunately, there is a way of structuring the various options available so that an intelligent strategy can be developed: the standards for LANs. Although a number of products remain on the market that are

---

12. In the latest edition of the IEEE standard (1989), it states: "The previously specified 1 Mbps mode of operation is not covered by this standard. Users and implementers of 1 Mbps should refer to ANSI/IEEE Std 802.5-1985, under which it is allowed."

proprietary and nonstandard, there has been overwhelming acceptance of standards by both vendors and customers. In addition, the set of standards that has been developed is rich enough to allow the customer to select a LAN or number of LANs that is tailored to the specific requirements of the organization.

The LAN standards are organized on the basis of logical link control, medium-access control, and physical specifications. Logical link control specifies the mechanisms for addressing stations across the medium and for controlling the exchange of data between two users. Three services are provided as alternatives for attached devices using logical link control: unacknowledged connectionless service, connection-mode service, and acknowledged connectionless service.

The medium-access control specification depends on the topology chosen. For bus and tree topologies, the alternatives are CSMA/CD and token bus. The CSMA/CD technique was originally used on Ethernet and is perhaps the most common access technique in use. Token bus was intended for factory applications, although it can also be used in the office environment. For the ring topology, the token ring technique is used.

Three families of standards have been developed for LANs based on the medium-access control technique and the physical LAN involved. The IEEE 802.3 standards employ CSMA/CD. They are used on baseband bus, broadband bus/tree, and unshielded twisted pair. In the latter case, the configuration is physically a star but logically a bus. The IEEE 802.4 standard employs token bus, and is used on broadband and carrierband bus/tree systems. An optical-fiber option has also been specified. IEEE 802.5 is the token ring, using shielded or unshielded twisted pair.

APPENDIX 9A   LAN Addressing

The IEEE 802 standards employ two levels of addressing. User data to be sent are passed down to LLC, which appends a header. This header contains control information that is used to manage the protocol between the local LLC entity and the remote LLC entity. The combination of user data and LLC header is referred to as an LLC *protocol data unit* (PDU). After the sending LLC has prepared a PDU, the PDU is then passed as a block of data down to the MAC entity. The MAC entity appends both a header and a trailer, to manage the MAC protocol. The result is a MAC-level PDU. To avoid confusion with an LLC-level PDU, the MAC-level PDU is typically referred to as a *frame*.

Now, the MAC header must contain a destination address that uniquely identifies a station on the local network. This is needed since each station on the local network will read the destination address field to determine whether it should capture the MAC frame. When a MAC frame is captured, the MAC entity strips off the MAC header and trailer and passes the resulting LLC PDU up to the LLC entity. The LLC header must contain a destination SAP address so the LLC can determine to which station the data are to be delivered. Hence, two levels of addressing are needed:

1. *MAC address:* identifies a station on the local network
2. *LLC address (LSAP):* identifies an LLC user

The MAC address is associated with a physical attachment point on the network. The LSAP is associated with a particular user within a station. In some cases, the LSAP corresponds to a host process. Another case relates to a common type of attached equipment, referred to as a network-

Table 9.9 Local Network Addressing

MAC Address	LLC User Address (Service-Access Point)
Individual	Individual
Individual	Group
Individual	Global
Group	Global
Global	Global
Group	Individual
Group	Group
Global	Individual
Global	Group

interface unit (NIU). Often, an NIU is used as a terminal concentration device. In this case, each terminal port on the NIU has a unique LSAP.

So far, we have discussed the use of addresses that identify unique entities. In addition to these *individual addresses,* group addresses are employed. A *group address* specifies a collection of one or more entities. For example, one might wish to send a message to all terminal users attached to a particular NIU or all terminal users on the entire LAN. Two types of group addresses are used. A *global address* refers to all entities within some context; this is also referred to as an all-stations address. A *group address* refers to some subset of entities within some context.

Table 9.9 depicts the possible combinations. The first five combinations are straightforward. A specific user can be addressed. A group of users or all users at a specific station can be addressed. And all users on some stations or all users on all stations can be addressed.

The last four combinations in the table are less obvious. It should be clear that LLC addresses are unique only within a single station. It is only the LLC entity within a station that examines the LLC header and determines the user. However, it is possible to assign LLC addresses uniquely across all stations; this is undesirable, for two reasons:

1. The total number of users on all stations would be limited by the LSAP field length in the LLC header.

2. Central management of LSAP assignment would be required, no matter how large and heterogeneous the user population.

On the other hand, it may be desirable to assign the same LSAP value to entities in different stations. For example, a station-management entity in a station may always be given an LSAP value of 1, to facilitate network management. Or a group of management and control entities within a station may always be given the same group LSAP address. When such a convention is followed, it then becomes possible to address data to one LSAP address or a group LSAP address in a group of stations or all stations.

9A.1 LSAP FORMAT

The 802.2 standard specifies the use of an 8-bit LSAP field. The formats for the source and destination LSAP fields in an LLC PDU are shown in Figure 9.3, part (b).

Several address values have meanings assigned in the standard:

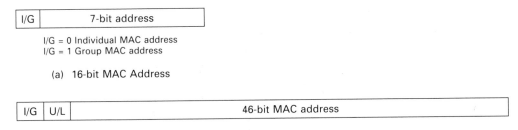

(a) 16-bit MAC Address

(b) 48-bit MAC Address

Figure 9.21 MAC Address Formats

- An address of all 0s in the DSAP or SSAP field is predefined to be the null address. The null LSAP designates the LLC that is associated with the underlying MAC service and is not used to identify any LLC user; thus, this LSAP may be used for information directed to the LLC entity.

- An address of all 1s in the DSAP field is predefined to be the global address; this address designates all DSAPs actively being served by the underlying MAC address.

- The addresses 01000000 and 11000000 are designated as the individual and group addresses, respectively, for an LLC sublayer management function at the station.

9A.2 MAC ADDRESS FORMAT

The MAC address field format used in the 802 LAN and MAN standards (802.3, 802.4, 802.5, 802.6) and in FDDI follows the same formatting rules for all of these standards. The address may be either 16 or 48 bits in length; the formats are shown in Figure 9.21. For a destination MAC address, the first bit is set to 0 or 1 to indicate an individual or a group address, respectively. A group address of all 1s is a global address for all active stations on the LAN or MAN. All other group addresses designate a logical user group defined at configuration time or by a higher-layer convention.

For 48-bit addresses, the second bit is set to 1 to indicate a locally administered address and to 0 to indicate a universally administered address. A locally administered address is set up by the LAN or MAN manager and has significance only for the purposes of that environment. A universally administered address is one assigned by the IEEE Standards Office on behalf of ISO. The concept of a universal address is based on the idea that all potential members of a communication environment need to have a unique identifier, in order to coexist and communicate with other members. The advantage of a universal address is that a station with such an address can be attached to any LAN in the world with an assurance that its address is unique.

APPENDIX 9B   LAN Topology and Transmission Techniques

In the context of a communication network, the term *topology* refers to the way in which the end points, or stations, attached to the network are interconnected. The common topologies for LANs are bus, tree, ring, and star (Figure 9.22).

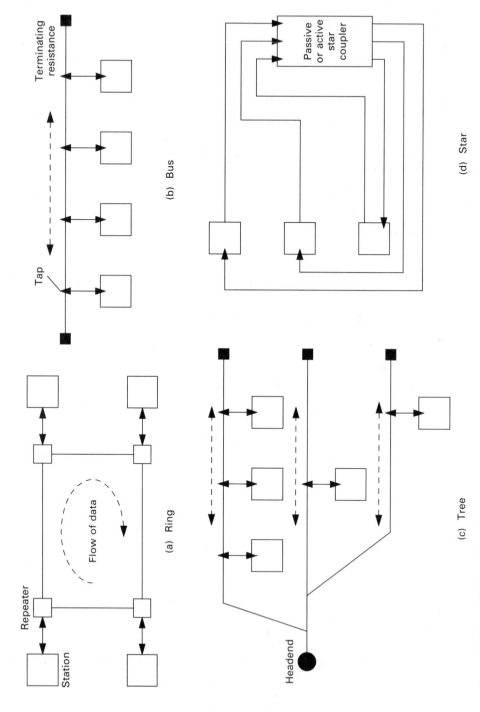

Figure 9.22 Local Network Topologies

9B.1   RING TOPOLOGY

In the ring topology, the network consists of a set of repeaters joined by point-to-point links in a closed loop. Hence, each repeater participates in two links on the ring. The repeater is a comparatively simple device, capable of receiving data on one link and transmitting them, bit by bit, on the other link as fast as the data are received, with no buffering at the repeater. The links are unidirectional; that is, data are transmitted in one direction only, and all links are oriented in same way. Thus, data circulate around the ring in one direction (clockwise or counterclockwise).

Each station attaches to the network at a repeater. Data are transmitted in frames inserted onto the ring by the stations. Each frame contains source and destination address fields as well as other control information and user data. As a frame circulates, the destination station copies the data into a local buffer. Typically, the frame continues to circulate until it returns to the source station, where it is absorbed, removing it from the ring.

Since multiple devices share the ring, some form of medium-access logic is needed to control the order and timing of frame transmissions.

9B.2   BUS AND TREE TOPOLOGY

Both bus and tree topologies are characterized by the use of a multipoint medium. With the bus topology, all stations attach, through appropriate interfacing hardware, directly to a linear transmission medium, or bus. A transmission from any station propagates the length of the medium in both directions and can be received by all other stations.

The tree topology is a generalization of the bus topology. The transmission medium is a branching cable with no closed loops. The tree layout begins at a point known as the headend. One or more cables start at the headend, and each of these may have branches. The branches, in turn, may have additional branches to allow quite complex layouts. Again, a transmission from any station propagates throughout the medium, can be received by all other stations, and is absorbed at the endpoints.

As with the ring, transmission is in the form of frames containing addresses and user data. Each station monitors the medium and copies frames addressed to itself. Because all stations share a common transmission link, only one station can successfully transmit at a time, and some form of medium-access-control technique is needed to regulate access.

9B.3   BUS AND TREE TRANSMISSION TECHNIQUES

The distinction between bus and tree systems is based on the distinction between two different transmission techniques for LANs: baseband and broadband. Baseband transmission requires the use of a bus topology; broadband can employ bus or tree topology.

9B.3.1   Baseband Bus

A baseband bus uses digital signaling; that is, the binary data to be transmitted are inserted onto the cable as a sequence of voltage pulses, usually using Manchester or differential Manchester encoding (see Appendix A). The nature of digital signals is such that the entire frequency spectrum of the cable is consumed. Hence, it is not possible to have multiple channels (frequency-division multiplexing) on the cable. Transmission is bidirectional. That is, a signal inserted at any point on the medium propagates in both directions to the ends, where it is absorbed (Figure 9.23, part [a]). The digital signaling requires a bus topology. Unlike analog signals, digital signals cannot easily be propagated through the branching points required for a tree topology. Baseband-bus LAN systems can extend only a limited distance, about 1 km at most. This is because the attenuation of the signal, which is most pronounced at higher frequencies, causes a blurring of the pulses and a weakening of the signal to the extent that communication over larger distances is impractical.

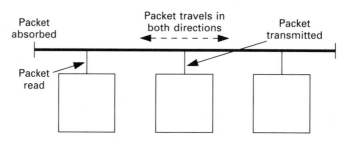

(a) Bidirectional (baseband, single-channel broadband).

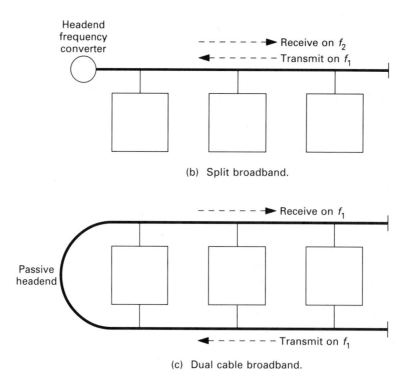

(b) Split broadband.

(c) Dual cable broadband.

Figure 9.23 Baseband and Broadband Transmission Techniques

9B.3.2 Broadband Bus and Tree

In the context of LANs, the term *broadband* refers to the use of analog signaling with frequency-division multiplexing. The frequency spectrum of the cable can be divided into channels or sections of bandwidth. Separate channels can support separate and independent data traffic, television, and radio signals. Broadband components allow splitting and joining operations; hence, both bus and tree topologies are possible. Much greater distances—some tens of kilometers—are possible with broadband compared to baseband. This is because the analog signals that carry the digital data can propagate greater distances before noise and attenuation damage the data.

Unlike baseband, broadband is inherently a unidirectional signaling technique; signals inserted onto the medium can propagate in only one direction. The primary reason for this is that it is not feasible to build amplifiers that will pass signals of one frequency in both directions. This unidirectional property means that only those stations "downstream" from a transmitting station can receive its signals. How, then, can full connectivity be achieved?

Clearly, two data paths are needed. These paths are joined at the headend (Figure 9.22, part [c]). For the bus topology, the headend is simply one end of the bus. For the tree topology, the headend is the root of a branching tree. All stations transmit on one path toward the headend (inbound). Signals arriving at the headend are then propagated along a second data path away from the headend (outbound). All stations receive on the outbound path.

Physically, two alternative configurations are used to implement the inbound and outbound paths (Figure 9.23, parts [b] and [c]). On a *dual-cable* configuration, the inbound and outbound paths are separate cables, with the headend simply a passive connector between the two. Stations send and receive on the same frequency. On a *split* configuration, the inbound and outbound paths are different frequencies on the same cable. Bidirectional amplifiers pass lower frequencies inbound and higher frequencies outbound. The headend contains a device, known as a frequency converter, for translating inbound frequencies to outbound frequencies.

9B.4 STAR TOPOLOGY

In the star LAN topology, each station attaches to a central node, referred to as the star coupler, via two point-to-point links, one for transmission in each direction. A transmission from any one station enters the central node and is retransmitted on all the outgoing links. Thus, although the arrangement is physically a star, it is logically a bus: a transmission from any station is received by all other stations, and only one station at a time may successfully transmit. Thus, the medium-access-control techniques used for the star topology are the same as for bus and tree.

There are two ways of implementing the star coupler. In the case of the *passive-star coupler*, there is an electromagnetic linkage in the coupler so that any incoming transmission is physically passed to all the outgoing links. In the case of optical fiber, this coupling is achieved by fusing together a number of fibers, so that incoming light is automatically split among all the outgoing fibers. In the case of coaxial cable or twisted pair, transformer coupling is used to split the incoming signal.

The other type of star coupler is the *active-star coupler*. In this case, there is digital logic in the central node that acts as a repeater. As bits arrive on any input line, they are automatically regenerated and repeated on all outgoing lines. If multiple input signals arrive simultaneously, a collision signal is transmitted on all outgoing lines.

10
Fiber Distributed
Data Interface

The accredited standards committee ASC X3T9.5 is responsible for the development of the fiber distributed data interface (FDDI) LAN standards and their follow-on, the standards for FDDI-II. The bulk of the FDDI work has been standardized both by ANSI (the American National Standards Institute) and in the ISO (International Organization for Standardization) 9314 series. Work on FDDI-II is still ongoing. This chapter examines both these specifications.

10.1 SCOPE OF THE FDDI STANDARD

As with the IEEE (Institute of Electrical and Electronics Engineers) 802.3, 802.4, and 802.5 standards, the FDDI standard encompasses both the MAC (medium-access control) and physical layers and supports the use of IEEE 802.3 logical link control (LLC). Figure 10.1 depicts the overall FDDI-protocol architecture, which, below the LLC level, consists of four parts:

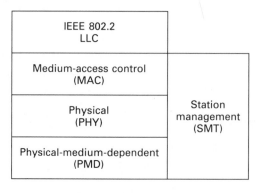

Figure 10.1 FDDI-Protocol Architecture

364

1. *Medium-access control:* As with the 802 standards, the FDDI MAC layer is the portion of the data-link layer that regulates access to the LAN medium.

2. *Physical:* This is the medium-independent portion of the physical layer, which includes the encoding of digital data.

3. *Physical-layer-medium-dependent:* characterizes the medium-dependent aspects of the physical layer.

4. *Station management:* provides the control necessary at the station level to manage the processes underway in the various FDDI layers.

Both the FDDI and FDDI-II standards make use of a ring LAN topology with optical-fiber medium, operating at 100 Mbps. We turn first to FDDI.

10.2   FDDI MAC PROTOCOL

The FDDI MAC protocol is a token ring protocol, similar to the IEEE 802.5 specification. There are several differences that are designed to accommodate the higher data rate (100 Mbps) of FDDI. The protocol is best explained after an examination of the frame format.

10.2.1   MAC Frame

Figure 10.2 depicts the frame formats for the FDDI protocol. The standard defines the contents of these formats in terms of symbols, with each data symbol corresponding to 4 data bits. Symbols are used because, at the physical layer, data are encoded in 4-bit chunks. However, MAC entities must in fact deal with individual bits, so the discussion that follows sometimes refers to 4-bit symbols and sometimes to bits. A frame other than a token frame consists of the following fields:

- *Preamble:* synchronizes the frame with each station's clock. The originator of the frame uses a field of 16 idle symbols; subsequent repeating stations may change the length of the field consistent with clocking requirements. The idle symbol is a nondata fill pattern. The actual form of a nondata symbol depends on the signal encoding on the medium.

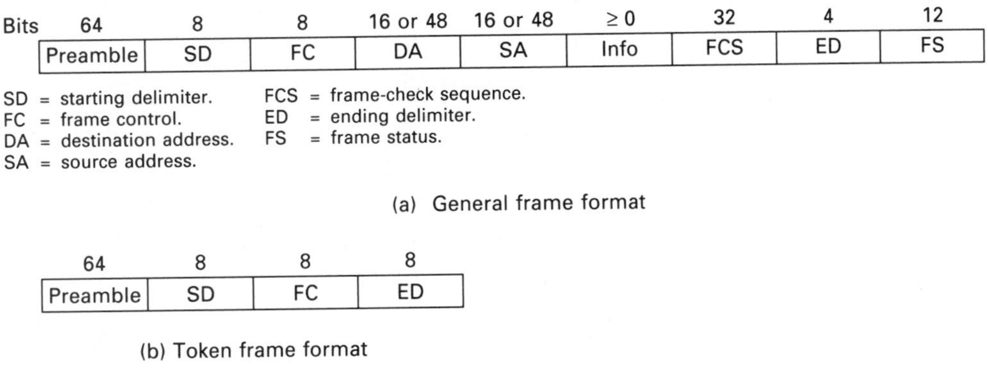

Bits	64	8	8	16 or 48	16 or 48	≥ 0	32	4	12
	Preamble	SD	FC	DA	SA	Info	FCS	ED	FS

SD = starting delimiter.   FCS = frame-check sequence.
FC = frame control.   ED = ending delimiter.
DA = destination address.   FS = frame status.
SA = source address.

(a) General frame format

64	8	8	8
Preamble	SD	FC	ED

(b) Token frame format

Figure 10.2 FDDI Frame Formats

- *Starting delimiter:* indicates start of frame. It is coded as JK, where *J* and *K* are nondata symbols.
- *Frame control:* has the bit format CLFFZZZZ, where C indicates whether this is a synchronous or an asynchronous frame (explained later in this section); L indicates the use of 16- or 48-bit addresses; FF indicates whether this is an LLC, a MAC control, or a reserved frame. For a control frame, the remaining 4 bits indicate the type of control frame. Table 10.1 lists the formats defined in the standard. Some of these are self-explanatory; others will be explained as the discussion proceeds.
- *Destination address:* specifies the station(s) for which the frame is intended. It may be a unique physical address, a multicast group address, or a broadcast address. The ring may contain a mixture of 16- and 48-bit address lengths.
- *Source address:* specifies the station that sent the frame.

Table 10.1 FDDI Frame-Control Field

Type	CLFF ZZZZ	Description
Void	0X00 0000	Logically not a frame; ignored
Nonrestricted token	1000 0000	For synchronous and nonrestricted asynchronous transmission
Restricted token	1100 0000	For synchronous and restricted asynchronous transmission
MAC Frames		
MAC	1L00 0001 to 1L00 1111	Range of values reserved for MAC control frames
Beacon	1L00 0010	Indicated serious ring failure
Claim	1L00 0011	Used to determine which station creates a new token and initializes the ring
Station-Management Frames		
Station management	0L00 0001 to 0L00 1111	Range of values reserved for station-management frames
Next-station addressing	0L00 1111	Used in station management
LLC Frames		
Asynchronous	0L01 rPPP	Asynchronous transmission at priority PPP
Synchronous	1L01 rrrr	Synchronous transmission
Reserved Frames		
Reserved for implementer	CL10 r000 to CL10 r111	Implementation-dependent
Reserved for future standardization	CL11 rrrr	To be used in future version of standard

- *Information:* contains an LLC data unit or information related to a control operation.
- *Frame-check sequence:* a 32-bit cyclic-redundancy check, based on the FC, DA, SA, and information fields.
- *Ending delimiter:* contains a nondata symbol (T) and marks the end of the frame, except for the FS field.
- *Frame status:* contains the error-detected (E), address-recognized (A), and frame-copied (F) indicators. Each indicator is represented by a symbol, which is R for ''reset'' or ''false'' and S for ''set'' or ''true.''

A token frame consists of the following fields:

- *Preamble:* as for the general frame format
- *Starting delimiter:* as for the general frame format
- *Frame control:* has the bit format 10000000 or 11000000 to indicate that this is a token
- *Ending delimiter:* contains a pair of nondata symbols (T) that terminate the token frame

10.2.2 MAC Protocol

The basic (without capacity allocation) FDDI MAC protocol is fundamentally the same as IEEE 802.5. There are two key differences:

1. In FDDI, a station waiting for a token seizes the token by aborting (failing to repeat) the token transmission as soon as the token frame is recognized. After the captured token is completely received, the station begins transmitting one or more data frames. The 802.5 technique of flipping a bit to convert a token to the start of a data frame was considered impractical because of the high data rate of FDDI.

2. In FDDI, a station that has been transmitting data frames releases a new token as soon as it completes data-frame transmission, even if it has not begun to receive its own transmission. This is the same technique as the early-token-release option of 802.5. Again, because of the high data rate, it would be too inefficient to require the station to wait for its frame to return, as in normal 802.5 operation.

Figure 10.3 gives an example of ring operation. After station A has seized the token, it transmits frame F1 and immediately transmits a new token. F1 is addressed to station C, which copies it as it circulates past. The frame eventually returns to A, which absorbs it. Meanwhile, B seizes the token issued by A and transmits F2, followed by a token. This action could be repeated any number of times, so that at any one time, there may be multiple frames circulating the ring. Each station is responsible for absorbing its own frames based on the source address field.

A further word should be said about the frame-status field. Each station can check passing bits for errors and can set the E indicator if an error is detected. If a station detects its own address, it sets the A indicator; it may also copy the frame, setting the C indicator. This allows the originating station, when it absorbs a frame that it previously transmitted, to differentiate three conditions:

1. Station nonexistent/nonactive
2. Station active but frame not copied
3. Frame copied

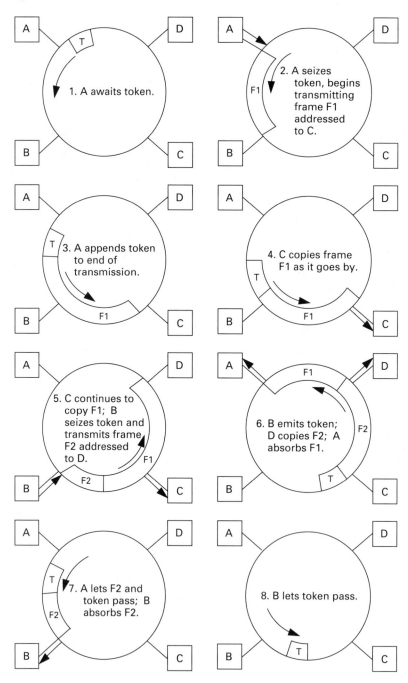

Figure 10.3 Example of FDDI Token-Ring Operation

When a frame is absorbed, the status indicators (E, A, C) in the FS field may be examined to determine the result of the transmission. However, if an error or a failure-to-receive condition is discovered, the MAC-protocol entity does not attempt to retransmit the frame but reports the condition to LLC. It is the responsibility of LLC or some higher-layer protocol to take corrective action.

10.2.3   Capacity Allocation

As with IEEE 802.4 and 802.5, FDDI provides a capacity-allocation scheme.

10.2.3.1   Requirements

The priority scheme used in 802.5 will not work in FDDI, because a station will often issue a token before its own transmitted frame returns. Hence, the use of a reservation field is not effective. Furthermore, the FDDI standard is intended to provide for greater control over the capacity of the network than 802.5 to meet the requirements for a high-speed LAN. Specifically, the FDDI capacity-allocation scheme seeks to accommodate the following requirements:

- Support for a mixture of stream and bursty traffic
- Support for multiframe dialogue

With respect to the first requirement, a high-capacity LAN would be expected to support a large number of devices or to act as a backbone for a number of other LANs. In either case, the LAN would be expected to support a wide variety of traffic types. For example, some of the stations may generate short, bursty traffic with modest throughput requirements but with a need for a short delay time. Other stations may generate long streams of traffic that require high throughput, but they may be able to tolerate moderate delays prior to the start of transmission.

With respect to the second requirement, there may sometimes be a need to dedicate a fixed fraction or all of the capacity of the LAN to a single application. This permits a long sequence of data frames and acknowledgments to be interchanged. An example of the utility of this feature is a read or write to a high-performance disk. Without the ability to maintain a constant high-data-rate flow over the LAN, only one sector of the disk could be accessed per revolution—an unacceptable performance.

10.2.3.2   Synchronous Traffic

To accommodate the first requirement, FDDI defines two types of traffic: synchronous and asynchronous. Each station is allocated a portion of the total capacity (the portion may be zero); the frames that it transmits during this time are referred to as synchronous frames. Any capacity that is not allocated or that is allocated but not used is available for the transmission of additional frames, referred to as asynchronous frames.

The scheme works as follows. A *target token-rotation time (TTRT)* is defined; each station stores the same value for TTRT. Some or all stations may be provided a *synchronous allocation* (SA_i), which may vary among stations. The allocations must be such that:

$$\text{DMax} + \text{FMax} + \text{TokenTime} + \sum SA_i \leq \text{TTRT}$$

where

SA_i	= synchronous allocation for station i
DMax	= propagation time for one complete circuit of the ring

FMax   = time required to transmit a maximum-length frame (4,500 octets)

TokenTime = time required to transmit a token

The assignment of values for SA_i is by means of a station management (SMT) protocol involving the exchange of SMT frames. The protocol assures that the preceding equation is satisfied. Initially, each station has a zero allocation, and it must request a change in the allocation. Support for synchronous allocation is optional; a station that does not support synchronous allocation may only transmit asynchronous traffic.

All stations have the same value of TTRT and a separately assigned value of SA_i. In addition, several variables that are required for the operation of the capacity-allocation algorithm are maintained at each station:

- Token-rotation timer (TRT)

- Token-holding timer (THT)

- Late counter (LC)

Each station is initialized with TRT set equal to TTRT and LC set to 0.[1] When the timer is enabled, TRT begins to count down. If a token is received before TRT expires, TRT is reset to TTRT. If TRT counts down to 0 before a token is received, then LC is incremented to 1 and TRT is reset to TTRT and again begins to count down. If TRT expires a second time before receiving a token, LC is incremented to 2, the token is considered lost, and a claim process (described later in this section) is initiated. Thus, LC records the number of times, if any, that TRT has expired since the token was last received at that station. The token is considered to arrive early if TRT has not expired since the station received the token; that is, if LC = 0.

When a station receives the token, its actions will depend on whether the token is early or late. If the token is early, the station saves the remaining time from TRT in THT, resets TRT, and enables TRT:

THT ← TRT

TRT ← TTRT

Enable TRT

The station can then transmit according to the following rules:

1. It may transmit synchronous frames for a time SA_i.

2. After it has transmitted synchronous frames, or if there were no synchronous frames to transmit, THT is enabled. The station may begin transmission of asynchronous frames as long as THT > 0.

If a station receives a token and the token is late, then LC is set to 0, and TRT continues to run. The station can then transmit synchronous frames for a time SA_i. The station may not transmit any asynchronous frames.

This scheme is designed to assure that the time between successive sightings of a token is on the order of TTRT or less. Of this time, a given amount is always available for synchronous traffic,

---

1. All timer values in the standard are negative numbers, with counters counting up to 0. For clarity, the discussion uses positive numbers.

and any excess capacity is available for asynchronous traffic. Because of random fluctuations in traffic, the actual token-circulation time may exceed TTRT, as demonstrated later in this subsection.

The FDDI algorithm is similar to the 802.4 algorithm with only two classes of data, 6 and 4. Synchronous data correspond to class 6, and the value of SA_i in FDDI corresponds to the token-holding time in 802.4. TTRT corresponds to TRT4. Since the sum of the SA_i (all the synchronous allocations) must be less than or equal to TTRT, the FDDI restrictions correspond to case IIa in Figure 9.16.

Figure 10.4 illustrates the use of the station variables in FDDI by displaying the values of TRT, THT, and LC for a particular station. In this example, taken from McCool (1988), the TTRT is 100 ms (milliseconds). The station's synchronous capacity allocation, SA_i, is 30 ms. The following events occur:

A. A token arrives early. The station has no frames to send. TRT is set to TTRT (100 ms) and begins to count down. The station allows the token to go by.

B. The token returns 60 ms later. Since TRT = 40 and LC = 0, the token is early. The station sets THT ← TRT and TRT ← TTRT, so that THT = 40 and TRT = 100. TRT is immediately enabled. The station has synchronous data to transmit and begins to do so.

C. After 30 ms, the station has consumed its synchronous allocation. It has asynchronous data to transmit, so it enables THT and begins transmitting.

D. THT expires, and the station must cease transmission of asynchronous frames. The station issues a token.

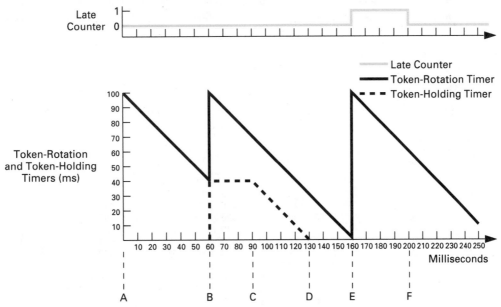

Source: J. McCool, "FDDI: Getting to Know the Inside of the Ring," *Data Communications* (Mar. 1988).

Figure 10.4 FDDI Capacity-Allocation Example

E.   TRT expires. The station increments LC to 1 and resets TRT to 100.

F.   The token arrives. Since LC is 1, the token is late, and no asynchronous data may be transmitted. At this point, the station also has no synchronous data to transmit. LC is reset to 0, and the token is allowed to go by.

Figure 10.5 provides a simplified example of a four-station ring. The following assumptions are made:

- Traffic consists of fixed-length frames.

- TTRT = 100 frame times.

- SA_i = 20 frame times for each station.

- Each station is always prepared to send its full synchronous allocation plus as many asynchronous frames as possible.

- The total overhead during one complete token circulation is 4 frame times (1 frame time per station).

One row of the lower portion of the figure corresponds to one circulation of the token. For each station, the token-arrival time is shown, followed by the value of TRT at the time of arrival, followed by the number of synchronous and asynchronous frames transmitted while the station holds the token.

The example begins after a period during which no data frames have been sent, so that the token has been circulating as rapidly as possible (4 frame times). Thus, when station 1 receives the token at time 4, it measures a circulation time of 4 (its TRT = 96). It is therefore able to send not only its 20 synchronous frames but also 96 asynchronous frames; recall that THT is not enabled until after the station has sent its synchronous frames. Station 2 experiences a circulation time of

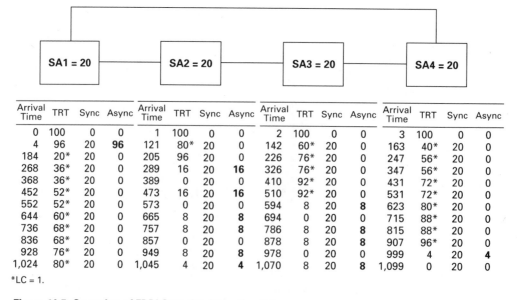

Arrival Time	TRT	Sync	Async	Arrival Time	TRT	Sync	Async	Arrival Time	TRT	Sync	Async	Arrival Time	TRT	Sync	Async
0	100	0	0	1	100	0	0	2	100	0	0	3	100	0	0
4	96	20	96	121	80*	20	0	142	60*	20	0	163	40*	20	0
184	20*	20	0	205	96	20	0	226	76*	20	0	247	56*	20	0
268	36*	20	0	289	16	20	16	326	76*	20	0	347	56*	20	0
368	36*	20	0	389	0	20	0	410	92*	20	0	431	72*	20	0
452	52*	20	0	473	16	20	16	510	92*	20	0	531	72*	20	0
552	52*	20	0	573	0	20	0	594	8	20	8	623	80*	20	0
644	60*	20	0	665	8	20	8	694	0	20	0	715	88*	20	0
736	68*	20	0	757	8	20	8	786	8	20	8	815	88*	20	0
836	68*	20	0	857	0	20	0	878	8	20	8	907	96*	20	0
928	76*	20	0	949	8	20	8	978	0	20	0	999	4	20	4
1,024	80*	20	0	1,045	4	20	4	1,070	8	20	8	1,099	0	20	0

*LC = 1.

Figure 10.5 Operation of FDDI Capacity-Allocation Scheme

120 (20 frames + 96 frames + 4 overhead frames) but is nevertheless entitled to transmit its 20 synchronous frames. Note that if each station continues to transmit its maximum allowable synchronous frames, then the circulation time surges to 180 (at time 184) but soon stabilizes at approximately 100. With a total synchronous utilization of 80 and an overhead of 4 frame times, there is an average capacity of 16 frame times available for asynchronous transmission. Note that if all stations always have a full backlog of asynchronous traffic, the opportunity to transmit asynchronous frames is distributed among them.

This example demonstrates that the synchronous allocation does not always provide a guaranteed fraction of capacity $SA_i/TTRT$. Rather, the fraction of capacity available to a station for synchronous transmission during any token circulation is SA_i/τ, where τ is the actual circulation time. As we have seen, τ can exceed TTRT. It can be shown that τ tends, in the steady state, to TTRT and has an upper bound of $2 \times TTRT$ (Johnson 1987).

10.2.3.3 Asynchronous Traffic

Asynchronous traffic can be further subdivided into eight levels of priority. Each station has a set of eight threshold values, $T\_Pr(1), \ldots, T\_Pr(8)$, such that $T\_Pr(i) =$ the maximum time that a token can take to circulate and still permit priority-i frames to be transmitted. Rule 2 in the preceding subsection is revised as follows:

2. After the station has transmitted synchronous frames, or if there were no synchronous frames to transmit, THT is enabled and begins to run from its set value. The station may transmit asynchronous data of priority i only so long as $THT > T\_Pr(i)$. The maximum value of any of the $T\_Pr(i)$ values must be no greater than TTRT.

This scheme is essentially the one used in the 802.4 token-bus standard.

The preceding rules satisfy the requirement for support for both stream and bursty traffic and, with the use of priorities, provide a great deal of flexibility. In addition, FDDI provides a mechanism that satisfies the requirements for dedicated multiframe traffic mentioned earlier. When a station wishes to enter an extended dialogue, it may gain control of all the unallocated (asynchronous) capacity on the ring by using a restricted token. The station captures a nonrestricted token, transmits the first frame of the dialogue to the destination station, and then issues a restricted token. Only the station that received the last frame may transmit asynchronous frames using the restricted token. The two stations may then exchange data frames and restricted tokens for an extended period, during which no other station may transmit asynchronous frames. The standard assumes that restricted transmission is predetermined not to violate the TTRT limitation, and it does not mandate the use of THT during this mode. Synchronous frames may be transmitted by any station upon capture of either type of token.

Figure 10.6 depicts the complete FDDI capacity-allocation scheme, and Figure 10.7 summarizes the relationship among the various types of traffic.

10.2.4 Ring Monitoring

The responsibility for monitoring the functioning of the token-ring algorithm is distributed among all stations on the ring. Each station monitors the ring for invalid conditions requiring ring initialization. Invalid conditions include an extended period of inactivity or incorrect activity (e.g., a persistent data frame). To detect the latter condition, each station keeps track of how long it has been since it last saw a valid token. If this time exceeds $2 \times TTRT$, an error condition is assumed.

Three processes are involved in error detection and correction:

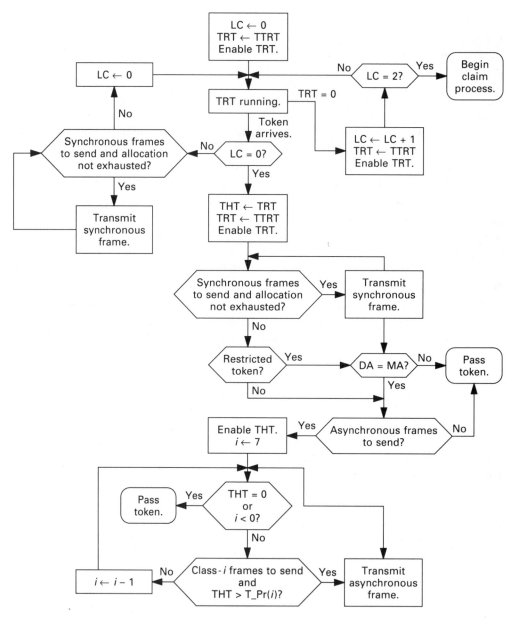

Figure 10.6 FDDI Capacity-Allocation Scheme

1. Claim-token process
2. Initialization process
3. Beacon process

Two MAC control frames are used: the Beacon frame and the claim frame (Table 10.1).

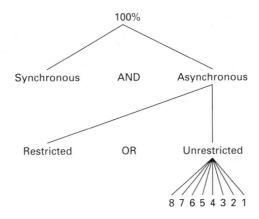

Figure 10.7 FDDI Capacity Allocation

10.2.4.1 Claim-Token Process

A station will detect the need for initialization of the ring by observing the lack of a token; as explained earlier in this section, this event occurs when the station sets LC to 2. Any station detecting a lost token initiates the claim-token process by issuing a sequence of claim frames. The purpose of the claim-token process is to negotiate the value to be assigned to TTRT and to resolve contention among stations attempting to initialize the ring. Each claiming station sends a continuous stream of claim frames. The information field of the claim frame contains the station's bid for the value of TTRT. Each claiming station inspects incoming claim frames and either defers (ceases to transmit its own claim frames and just repeats incoming frames) or not (continues to transmit its own claim frames and absorbs incoming frames), according to the following arbitration hierarchy:

- The frame with the lower TTRT value has precedence.
- Given equal values of TTRT, a frame with a 48-bit address has precedence over a frame with a 16-bit address.
- Given equal values of TTRT and equal address lengths, the frame with the address of larger numerical value has precedence.

The process is completed when one station receives its own claim frame, which has made a complete circuit of the ring without being preempted. At this point, the ring is filled with that station's claim frames, and all other stations have yielded. All stations store the value of TTRT contained in the latest received claim frame. The result is that the smallest requested value for TTRT is stored by all stations and will be used to allocate capacity.

The motivation for giving precedence to the lowest TTRT value is to make the LAN responsive to time-critical applications. If we define ring latency (RL) as the total overhead during one complete token circulation, then ring utilization can be expressed as:

$$\frac{TTRT - RL}{TTRT}$$

Low values of TTRT will provide a low guaranteed response time for synchronous traffic and thus support real-time applications. High values of TTRT allow very high ring use under heavy loads.

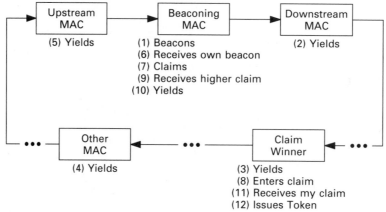

Source: K. Ocheltree and R. Montalvo, "FDDI Ring Management," *Proceedings, 14th Conference on Local Computer Networks* (Oct 1989).

Figure 10.8 Normal FDDI Ring Initialization

10.2.4.2   Initialization Process

The station that has won the claim-token process is responsible for initializing the ring. All the stations on the ring recognize the initialization process as a result of having seen one or more claim frames. The initializing station issues a nonrestricted token. On the first circulation of the token, it may not be captured. Rather, each station uses the appearance of the token for transition from an initialization state to an operational state and to reset its TRT.

Figure 10.8 illustrates the ring-initialization process.

10.2.4.3   Beacon Process

The beacon frame is used to isolate a serious ring failure such as a break in the ring. For example, when a station is attempting the claim-token process, it will eventually time out if it does not come to a resolution (winning or losing) and enter the beacon process.

Upon entering the beacon process, a station continuously transmits beacon frames. A station always yields to a beacon frame received from an upstream station. Consequently, if the logical break persists, the beacon frames of the station immediately downstream from the break will normally be propagated. If a station in the beacon process receives its own beacon frames, it assumes that the ring has been restored, and it initiates the claim-token process.

10.3   FDDI PHYSICAL-LAYER SPECIFICATION

The FDDI physical-layer specification includes a physical-layer protocol, a medium-dependent specification, and a definition of alternative configurations.

10.3.1   Physical-Layer Protocol

The medium-independent portion of the physical-layer specification is referred to as the physical-layer protocol. The key topics addressed are data encoding and timing jitter.

10.3.1.1   Data Encoding

As is the case with the IEEE 802.4 optical-fiber specification, the FDDI data-encoding scheme is based on the use of intensity-modulation. In the case of 802.4, the data to be transmitted are precoded in Manchester form before being submitted to the intensity-modulation process, in order to provide transitions for synchronization. The disadvantage of this approach is that the efficiency is only 50 percent. That is, because there can be as many as two transitions per bit time, a signaling rate of 200 million signal elements per second (200 Mbaud) is needed to achieve a data rate of 100 Mbps. At the high data rate of FDDI, this represents an unnecessary cost and technical burden.

To achieve greater efficiency, the FDDI standard specifies the use of a code referred to as 4B/5B. In this scheme, encoding is done 4 bits at a time; each 4 bits of data are encoded into a symbol with five *cells,* such that each cell contains a single signal element (presence or absence of light). In effect, each set of 4 bits is encoded as 5 bits. The efficiency is thus raised to 80 percent: 100 Mbps is achieved with 125 Mbaud.

To understand how the 4B/5B code achieves synchronization, the reader needs to know that there is actually a second stage of encoding: each cell of the 4B/5B stream is treated as a binary value and encoded using nonreturn to zero inverted (NRZI). In this code, a binary 1 is represented with a transition at the beginning of the bit interval, and a binary 0 is represented with no transition at the beginning of the bit interval; there are no other transitions. The advantage of NRZI is that it employs differential encoding. In differential encoding, the signal is decoded by comparing the polarity of adjacent signal elements rather than the absolute value of a signal element. A benefit of this scheme is that it is generally more reliable to detect a transition in the presence of noise and distortion than to compare a value to a threshold. This aids the ultimate decoding of the signal after it has been converted back from the optical to the electrical realm.[2]

Now we are in a position to describe the 4B/5B code and to understand the selections that were made. Table 10.2 shows the symbol encoding used in FDDI. Each possible five-cell pattern is shown, together with its NRZI realization. Since we are encoding 4 bits with a 5-bit pattern, only 16 of the 32 possible patterns are needed for data encoding. The codes selected to represent the sixteen 4-bit data blocks are such that a transition is present at least twice for each five-cell code. Given an NRZI format, no more than three 0s in a row are allowed.

The FDDI encoding scheme can be summarized as follows:

1. A simple intensity-modulation encoding is rejected because it does not provide synchronization; a string of 1s or 0s will have no transitions.

2. The data to be transmitted must first be encoded to assure transitions. The 4B/5B code is chosen over Manchester because it is more efficient.

3. The 4B/5B code is further encoded using NRZI so that the resulting differential signal will improve reception reliability.

4. The specific 5-bit patterns used for encoding the sixteen 4-bit data patterns are chosen to guarantee no more than three 0s in a row to provide for adequate synchronization.

Only 16 of the 32 possible cell patterns are required to represent the input data. The remaining cell patterns are either declared invalid or assigned special meaning as control symbols. These assignments are listed in Table 10.2. The nondata symbols fall into the following categories:

---

2.   See Appendix A for more details on NRZI.

Table 10.2 4B/5B Code

Code Group	Symbol	Assignment
	Line-State Symbols	
00000	Q	Quiet
11111	I	Idle
00100	H	Halt
	Starting Delimiter	
11000	J	1st of sequential SD pair
10001	K	2nd of sequential SD pair
	Data Symbols	
11110	0	0000
01001	1	0001
10100	2	0010
10101	3	0011
01010	4	0100
01011	5	0101
01110	6	0110
01111	7	0111
10010	8	1000
10011	9	1001
10110	A	1010
10111	B	1011
11010	C	1100
11011	D	1101
11100	E	1110
11101	F	1111
	Ending Delimiter	
01101	T	Used to terminate the data stream
	Control Indicators	
00111	R	Denoting logical 0 (reset)
11001	S	Denoting logical 1 (set)
	Invalid Code Assignments	
00001	V or H	Violation or halt
00010	V or H	Violation or halt
00011	V	Violation
00101	V	Violation
00110	V	Violation
01000	V or H	Violation or halt
01100	V	Violation
10000	V or H	Violation or halt

- *Line-state symbols:* Q indicates the absence of any transitions and loss of clock-recovery ability. H indicates a forced logical break in activity while maintaining DC balance and clock recovery. I indicates the normal condition between frame and token transmissions. The I symbol is used in frame absorption. When a frame returns to the originating station, it is stripped by that station by transmitting Is immediately following its recognition (following the source address field), instead of repeating the frame. Similarly, a token is absorbed by a station by transmitting Is after determining that the incoming frame is a token.

- *Starting delimiter:* The starting-delimiter field consists of a J and K symbol pair and is used to designate the beginning of a frame.

- *Ending delimiter:* The ending-delimiter field consists of one or two T symbols and is used to designate the end of the frame, except for the frame-status field, if present.

- *Control indicators:* The R and S symbols are used in the frame-status field to indicate the presence or absence of a condition, as explained in section 10.2.

- *Invalid code assignments:* The remaining symbol codes are designated as violation (V) symbols, some of which may be recognized as off-alignment H symbols.

10.3.1.2 Timing Jitter

In a ring LAN, an important concern involves the ability to keep all the repeaters around the ring synchronized. In essence, each repeater recovers clocking information from incoming signals by means of the transitions imposed by the encoding scheme (e.g., differential Manchester in 802.5 and 4B/5B in FDDI).[3] As data circulate around the ring, each repeater receives the data and recovers the clocking. The clocking enables the receiver to maintain bit synchronization so that it samples the incoming stream once per bit time. This clock recovery will deviate in a random fashion from the timing of the transmitter due to signal impairments in transmission and imperfections in the receiver circuitry. In addition, the repeater must either use the recovered clock information for its own transmissions or maintain its own clock. In the former case, the reception difficulties just mentioned cause clock deviation. In the latter case, there may be drift between clocks in adjacent repeaters. All of these problems result in timing errors that are referred to as *timing jitter*.

As each repeater receives incoming data, it issues a clean signal with no distortion. However, the timing error is not eliminated. The cumulative effect of the jitter is to cause the bit latency or "bit length" of the ring to vary. However, unless the latency of the ring remains constant, bits will be dropped (not retransmitted) as the latency of the ring decreases or added as the latency increases.

The approach taken by FDDI for dealing with timing jitter is to use a distributed clocking scheme with elastic buffers. Each repeater uses its own autonomous clock to transmit bits from its MAC layer onto the ring. For repeating incoming data, a buffer is imposed between the receiver and the transmitter. Data are clocked into the buffer at the clock rate recovered from the incoming stream but clocked out of the buffer at the station's own clock rate. The buffer has a capacity of 10 bits and expands and contracts as needed. At any time, the buffer contains a certain number of bits. As bits come in, they are placed in the buffer and thus experience a delay equal to the time

---

3.   See Appendix A for a discussion of encoding schemes and how clocking information is embedded in the encoding.

it takes to transmit the bits ahead of them in the buffer. If the received signal is slightly faster than the repeater's clock, the buffer will expand to avoid dropping bits. If the received signal is slow, the buffer will contract to avoid adding bits to the repeated bit stream.

The buffer in each repeater is initialized to its center position each time that it begins to receive a frame, during the preamble that begins the frame. This increases or decreases the length of the preamble, initially transmitted as 16 symbols, as it proceeds around the ring. Because the stability of the transmitter clock is specified as 0.005 percent, a buffer of 10 bits allows transmission of frames 4,500 octets in length without overrunning or underrunning the limits of the buffer.

10.3.2 Physical-Medium Specification

The FDDI standard specifies an optical-fiber ring with a data rate of 100 Mbps, using the NRZI-4B/5B encoding scheme described previously. The wavelength specified for data transmission is 1,300 nm.

The specification indicates the use of multimode fiber transmission. Although today's long-distance networks rely primarily on single-mode fiber, that technology generally requires the use of lasers as light sources rather than the cheaper and less-powerful light-emitting diodes (LEDs), which are adequate for FDDI requirements. The dimensions of the fiber cable are specified in terms of the diameter of the core of the fiber and the outer diameter of the cladding layer that surrounds the core. The combination specified in the standard is 62.5/125 μm. The standard lists as alternatives 50/125, 82/125, and 100/140 μm. In general, smaller diameters offer higher potential bandwidths but also higher connector loss.

10.3.3 Station and FDDI Network Configurations

Each FDDI station is composed of logical entities that conform to the FDDI standards. The role of a given station depends on the number of entities it has. Networks with different physical topologies may be constructed, depending on the types of stations used.

10.3.3.1 Dual Ring

To enhance the reliability of an FDDI ring, the standard provides for the construction of a dual ring, as illustrated in Figure 10.9. Stations participating in a dual ring are connected to their neighbors by two links that transmit in opposite directions. This creates two rings: a primary ring and a secondary ring on which data may circulate in the opposite direction. Under normal conditions, the secondary ring is idle. When a link failure occurs, the stations on either side of the link reconfigure as shown in Figure 10.9, part (b). This isolates the link fault and restores a closed ring. In this figure, a dark dot represents a MAC attachment within the station. Thus, in the counter direction, signals may be merely repeated while the MAC protocol is only involved in the primary direction. As an option, a station may contain two MAC entities and therefore execute that MAC protocol in both directions.

Should a station fail, as shown in Figure 10.9, part (c), then the stations on either side reconfigure to eliminate the failed station and both links to that station.

10.3.3.2 Station Types

The type of station just described is only one of four station types defined in the FDDI standard (Table 10.3). The use of four different station types allows for the creation of complex topologies and for designs with high levels of reliability.

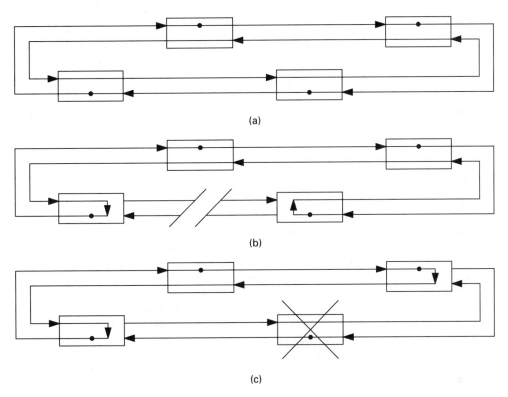

(a)

(b)

(c)

• = MAC attachment.

Source: F. Ross, "The Fiber Distributed Data Interface," in *Handbook of Local Area Networks*, ed. J. Slone and
A. Drinan (New York: Auerbach, 1991).

Figure 10.9 FDDI Dual-Ring Operation

The dual-attachment station, as just described, can be used to construct a dual ring. In some cases, this dual ring will constitute the entire FDDI LAN. In other cases, the dual ring can serve as the trunk ring for a more complex topology. In its most general form, the topology that can be achieved with FDDI is referred to as a *dual ring of trees*.

Figure 10.10 is an example that shows the use of all four station types. The main trunk is a dual ring consisting only of stations that are capable of supporting the two rings. Some of these stations are DASs, whose function is to provide an attachment point for end-user stations. Others are dual-attachment concentrators, which participate in the dual ring and may support an end-user station. In addition, each DAC may support stations that attach to a single ring. Each DAC therefore serves as the root of a tree. Single-attachment stations may attach to the DAC by means of a single ring. The SAS connection does not provide the reliability of the dual-ring configuration available to the DAS. However, FDDI constrains the topology so that an SAS must attach to a concentrator. In the event of a failure of the SAS or its connection to the concentrator, the concentrator may isolate the SAS. Therefore, the reliability of the dual ring is maintained. To achieve a tree structure of depth greater than two levels, single-attachment concentrators may be used. An SAC may attach to a DAC or another SAC and may support one or more SASs.

Table 10.3 FDDI Station Types

Station Type	Definition	Connects To
Dual-attachment station (DAS)	Has two pairs of PHY and PMD entities and one or more MAC entities; participates in the trunk dual ring.	DAS, DAC
Dual-attachment concentrator (DAC)	A DAS with additional PHY and PMD entities beyond those required for attachment to the dual ring. The additional entities permit attachment of additional stations that are logically part of the ring but are physically isolated from the trunk ring.	DAS, DAC, SAC, SAS
Single-attachment station (SAS)	Has one each PHY, PMD, and MAC entities and therefore cannot be attached into the trunk ring but must be attached by a concentrator.	DAC, SAC
Single-attachment concentrator (SAC)	An SAS with additional PHY and PMD entities beyond those required for attachment to a concentrator. The additional entities permit attachment of additional stations in a tree-structured fashion.	DAC, SAC, SAS

It is important to note that even with an elaborate tree structure, an FDDI configuration still maintains a ring topology. Figure 10.11 shows the circulation path for a simple configuration of a dual ring of two stations, one of which is a DAC. Note that the six stations form a single ring around which a single token will circulate. In addition, for reliability, a secondary ring is available that encompasses the DASs and DACs.

Figure 10.12 illustrates the architecture of the various station types. An SAS has one physical-layer protocol (PMD, PHY) and one MAC entity. A DAS has two PMD and PHY entities and one or two MAC entities. Finally, both types of concentrators have a similar architecture. Each consists of multiple PMD and PHY entities, with an optional MAC entity. In the case of the SAC, there are at least two sets of physical-layer entities: one for connection to a master and at least one for connection of slaves. In the case of a DAC, there are at least three sets: one for primary connection to the dual ring, one for secondary connection to the dual ring, and at least one for connection of slaves. For both kinds of concentrators, there needs to be something equivalent to a configuration switch that can switch pairs of physical-layer entities (PMD, PHY) into and out of the ring.

10.3.3.3 Port Types

The FDDI standard specifies connection rules to ensure against the construction of illegal topologies. These rules are expressed in terms of allowable connections between port types. Table 10.4 defines the four port types, and Figure 10.13 illustrates their use.

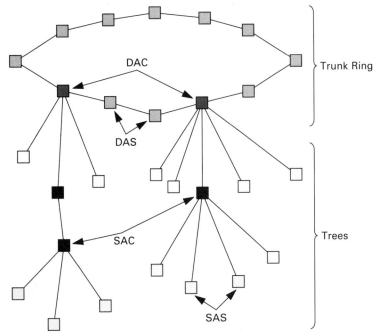

Source: M. Wolter, "Fiber Distributed Data Interface (FDDI) — A Tutorial,"
Connexions (Interop, Inc.: Oct. 1990).

Figure 10.10 General FDDI Topology

10.3.3.4   FDDI Topologies

The definition of four station types allows for the creation of a wide variety of topologies. The following are of particular interest:

- *Stand-alone concentrator with attached stations:* This consists of a single concentrator and its attached stations. Such a configuration could be used to connect multiple high-performance devices in a work group or multiple LANs, with each FDDI station being a bridge.

- *Dual ring:* This topology, which consists of a set of DASs connected to form a single dual ring, is useful when there are a limited number of users. It could also be employed to interconnect departmental LANs, with each FDDI station being a bridge.

- *Tree of concentrators:* This is a good choice for interconnecting large groups of user devices. Concentrators are wired in a hierarchical star arrangement with one concentrator serving as the root of the tree. This topology provides great flexibility for adding and removing concentrators and stations or changing their location without disrupting the LAN.

- *Dual ring of trees:* This is the most elaborate and flexible topology. Key stations can be incorporated into the dual ring for maximum availability, and the tree structure provides the flexibility described in the preceding item.

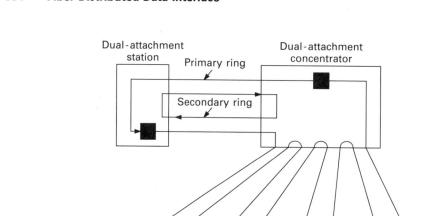

= MAC entity,

Figure 10.11 Star-Shaped Ring

10.3.3.5   Dual Homing

We have so far described the use of DACs and DASs in the dual ring, with SACs and SASs in the tree elements below the dual ring. This arrangement provides redundancy for the dual-ring stations only. In addition, the FDDI standard allows redundant paths in tree topologies as well as in the dual ring, by using DACs and DASs in the tree portion. The concept is referred to as dual homing.

Figure 10.14 illustrates a simple case of dual homing. A DAC or DAS is cascaded from two DACs that are part of the dual ring. Initially, the B port of the slave station and the corresponding M port of the master station are active, with the A port of the slave and the corresponding M port of another master station set up as backup links. The backup links are shown in Figure 10.14 as dashed lines. The backup connection (port A) becomes active only if the primary connection (port B) fails.

10.3.3.6   Optical Bypass

An additional degree of reliability can be provided by the use of an optical bypass switch, which can be installed in any DAC or DAS. The switch bypasses the station's receiver and transmitter connections so that the optical signal from the previous station is passed directly to the next station. Bypassing can be activated by the station itself, a neighboring station, or a human operator. It can be activated automatically upon the loss of power at the station or by means of a network-control function.

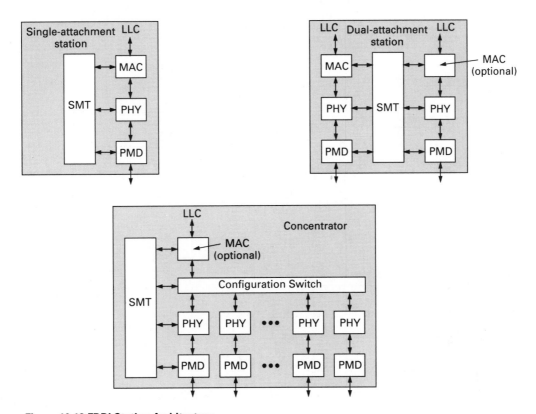

Figure 10.12 FDDI Station Architecture

However, optical bypass switches have a power penalty that may cause the maximum allowable loss between stations to be exceeded. Thus, only a limited number of stations in the dual ring can be equipped with such devices. Figure 10.15 shows the logical position of an optical bypass switch in the physical-layer block diagram.

Table 10.4 FDDI Port Types

Port Type	Definition	Part Of
Port A	Connects to the incoming primary ring and the outgoing secondary ring of a dual ring	DAS, DAC
Port B	Connects to the outgoing primary ring and the incoming secondary ring of a dual ring	DAS, DAC
Port M (master)	Connects a concentrator to an SAS, a DAS, or another concentrator	DAC, SAC
Port S (slave)	Connects an SAS or an SAC to a concentrator	SAS, SAC

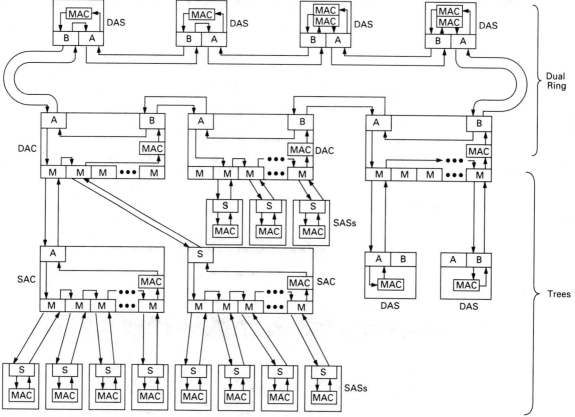

Source: K. Ocheltree, "Using Redundancy in FDDI Networks," *Proceedings, 15th Conference on Local Computer Networks* (Oct. 1990).

Figure 10.13 Ring-of-Trees Topology

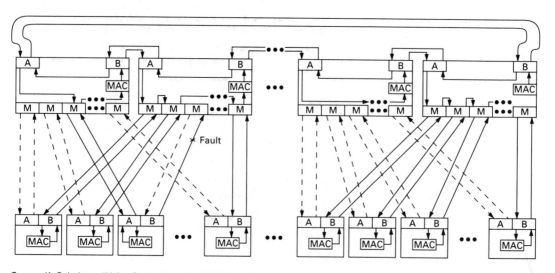

Source: K. Ocheltree, "Using Redundancy in FDDI Networks," *Proceedings, 15th Conference on Local Computer Networks* (Oct. 1990).

Figure 10.14 Concentrator Tree with Dual Homed Stations

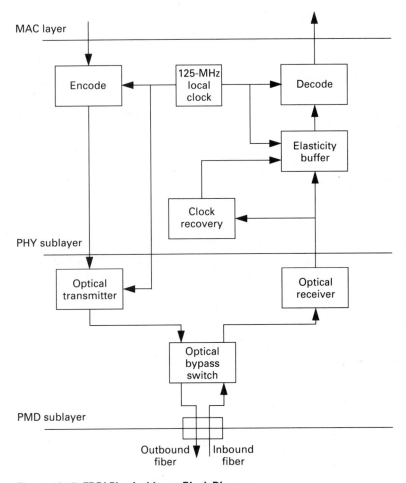

Figure 10.15 FDDI Physical-Layer Block Diagram

10.4   FDDI STATION MANAGEMENT

The FDDI station-management (SMT) specification defines three major functions:

1. Connection management (CMT)

2. Ring management (RMT)

3. SMT frame services

10.4.1   Connection Management

Connection management is concerned with the insertion of stations onto the ring and removal of stations from the ring. This involves establishing or terminating a physical link between adjacent ports and connecting ports to MAC entities. Connection management can be considered as comprising three subcomponents:

1. Entity-coordination management (ECM)
2. Physical-connection management (PCM)
3. Configuration management

10.4.1.1   Entity-Coordination Management

Entity-coordination management is responsible for the media interface to the FDDI ring, including the coordination of the activity of all the ports and the optional optical bypass switch associated with that station. For example, ECM coordinates the trace function, which is part of ring management.

10.4.1.2   Physical-Connection Management

Physical-connection management provides for managing the point-to-point physical links between adjacent PHY/PMD pairs. This includes initializing the links and testing the quality of the links (referred to as link confidence).

Initialization is accomplished by signaling between the adjacent ports. One port transmits a continuous stream of symbols until the neighbor responds with another stream of symbols. PCM sequences through a number of these request-response exchanges to communicate the following information:

- Port type (A, B, M, S)
- Willingness to establish a link
- Duration of the link-confidence test performed
- Availability of the MAC entity for a link-confidence test
- Outcome of the link-confidence test
- Availability of the MAC for a local-loop test
- Intent to place a MAC in the connection if established

Once the connection has been verified, configuration management is invoked.

10.4.1.3   Configuration Management

Configuration management provides for configuring PHY and MAC entities within a node. Essentially, configuration management is concerned with the internal organization of the station entities and may be thought of as controlling a configuration switch (Figure 10.12), which implements the desired interconnections.

10.4.2   Ring Management

Ring management receives status information from medium-access control (MAC) and from connection management. Services provided by ring management include:

- Stuck-beacon detection
- Resolution of problems through the trace process
- Detection of duplicate addresses

10.4.2.1   Stuck-Beacon Detection

As discussed in section 10.2, a beacon is a MAC control frame used to isolate a serious ring failure such as a break in the ring. A stuck beacon indicates that a station is locked into sending continuous beacon frames.

As described previously, a station that suspects a ring failure will transmit a continuous stream of beacons. Eventually, it should receive either a beacon from an upstream station or its own beacon. If neither event occurs, the station will continue to transmit its own beacon indefinitely, a condition known as a stuck beacon.

A stuck-beacon timer under the control of ring management measures the duration of beacon transmission. If a time limit is exceeded, ring management initiates a stuck-beacon recovery procedure. The procedure begins with the transmission of a *directed beacon,* which has a group address of all stations that implement ring management and informs the ring of the stuck condition. The directed beacons are sent for a sufficiently long time to assure that they are seen by all the MACs. If the stuck-beacon condition is still unresolved after the direct beacons are sent, a trace function is initiated.

10.4.2.2 Trace Function

The trace function uses PHY signaling of symbol streams to recover from a stuck-beacon condition. The result of the directed beacon is to localize the fault to the beaconing MAC and its nearest upstream neighbor.

10.4.2.3 Duplicate-Address Detection

If two or more MAC entities have the same address, then the ring cannot function properly. Duplicate-address detection is performed during ring initialization and consists of monitoring the ring for conditions that indicate the presence of duplicate addresses.

If two or more MACs have the same address, at least one of the MACs will experience one of the following conditions:

- It will receive its own beacon while issuing claim frames for longer than the maximum delay of the FDDI ring (DMax). This indicates that the other duplicate is sending beacon frames while this duplicate is sending claim frames.

- It will receive its own claim frames while issuing beacon frames for longer than DMax. This indicates that the other duplicate is sending claim frames while this duplicate is sending beacon frames.

- It will receive its own claim frames for a period of time greater than DMax after having "won" the claim-token contest. This indicates that the other duplicate is sending claim frames while this duplicate has stopped claiming and issued a token.

- It will receive its own claim frame with a different value of TTRT. This indicates that duplicates with different requested TTRT values are both claiming.

When a station detects the duplicate-address condition, it can respond by changing its MAC address, configuring the MAC to lose the claim process and disabling its LLC services, or removing the MAC from the ring.

10.4.3 SMT Frame Services

The frame-services portion of SMT deals with the management of the station after the ring has achieved an operational state. These services are implemented by a set of SMT frames. Table 10.5 lists the frames, and Figure 10.16 illustrates the frame format. The frames are:

- *Neighbor-information frame:* used to transmit a station's own address and basic station descriptor to downstream neighbors. Each station periodically issues the frame using next-station

Table 10.5 FDDI SMT Frames

Frame Class	Abbreviation	Frame Types in Class
Neighbor information	NIF	Announcement, request, response
Station information	SIF	
Configuration		Request,* response
Operation		Request,* response
Echo	ECF	Request,* response
Resource allocation	RAF	Announcement, request, response
Request denied	RDF	Response
Status report	SRF	Announcement*
Parameter management	PMF	
Get PMF		Request,* response*
Change PMF		Request,* response*
Add PMF		Request,* response*
Remove PMF		Request,* response*
Extended service	ESF	Announcement,* request,* response*

* = optional.

addressing (NSA). NSA is a special addressing mode that permits a station to send a frame to the next station in the token path without knowing the address of that station.

- *Station-information frame:* used to request and supply a station's configuration and operating information.
- *Echo frame:* used for SMT-to-SMT loopback testing.
- *Resource-allocation frame:* intended to support a variety of network policies for the allocation of resources. A typical use is the allocation of synchronous bandwidth to the stations within a ring.

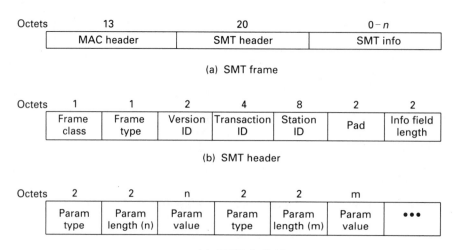

(a) SMT frame

(b) SMT header

(c) SMT info field

Figure 10.16 SMT Frame Format

- *Request-denied frame:* issued in response to an unsupported optional frame class or type request or an unsupported version ID.

- *Status-report frame:* used by stations to periodically announce station status, which may be of interest to the manager of an FDDI ring.

- *Parameter-management frame:* provides the means for remote management of station attributes via the parameter-management protocol.

- *Extended-service frame:* user-defined frames that extend or exercise new SMT services.

10.5 FDDI-II

FDDI-II is an upward-compatible extension to FDDI that adds the ability to support circuit-switched traffic, in addition to the packet-mode traffic supported by the original FDDI.

With FDDI, all data are transmitted in frames of variable length. Each frame includes delimiters to mark its beginning and end, as well as address information indicating source and destination MAC stations. FDDI is not suitable for maintaining a continuous, constant-data-rate connection between two stations. Even the so-called synchronous traffic class of FDDI only guarantees a minimum sustained data rate; it does not provide a uniform data stream with no variability. Such a continuous, constant data stream is typical of circuit-switched applications, such as digitized voice or video.

FDDI-II provides a circuit-switched service while maintaining the token-controlled packet-switched service of the original FDDI. With FDDI-II, it is possible to set up and maintain a constant-data-rate connection between two stations. Instead of using embedded addresses, the connection is established on the basis of a prior agreement, which may have been negotiated using packet messages or established by some other suitable convention known to the stations involved.

The technique used in FDDI-II for providing circuit-switched service is to impose a 125-μsec frame structure on the ring. A circuit-switched connection consists of regularly repeating time slots in the frame. This mode of transmission is sometimes referred to as *isochronous*. The term is used in the FDDI documents with the generally accepted meaning. Note, however, that the terms *synchronous* and *asynchronous* are used in FDDI with special meanings that relate to ring transmission (Table 10.6).

10.5.1 FDDI-II Architecture

Figure 10.17 is a block diagram of an FDDI-II station. The physical layer and the presence of station management are the same as for the original FDDI. At the MAC level, two new components, referred to collectively as hybrid ring control, are added: the hybrid multiplexer and isochronous MAC.

The IMAC module provides the interface between FDDI and the isochronous service, represented by the circuit-switched multiplexer.

The HMUX multiplexes the packet data from the MAC and the isochronous data from IMAC.

10.5.2 Hybrid Mode

An FDDI-II network can operate in either basic or hybrid mode. In *basic mode,* only the packet-switched service, controlled by a circulating token, is available. In this mode, the network operates in the same fashion as the original FDDI. In *hybrid mode,* both packet and circuit services are

Table 10.6 Definitions of Data-Transmission Modes

Term	FDDI Definition	CCITT Definition*	ISO Definition †
Asynchronous transmission	A class of data-transmission service whereby all requests for service contend for a pool of dynamically allocated ring bandwidth and response time.	The essential characteristic of time-scales or signals such that their corresponding significant instants do not necessarily occur at the same average rate.	Data transmission in which the time of occurrence of the start of each character, or block of characters, is arbitrary; once started, the time of occurrence of each signal representing a bit within the character, or block, has the same relationship to significant instants of a fixed time frame.
Synchronous transmission	A class of data-transmission service whereby each requester is preallocated a maximum bandwidth and guaranteed a maximum access time.	The essential characteristic of time-scales or signals such that their corresponding significant instants occur at precisely the same average rate.	Data transmission in which the time of occurrence of each signal representing a bit is related to a fixed time base.
Isochronous transmission	The essential characteristic of a time scale or a signal such that the time intervals between consecutive significant instants either have the same duration or durations that are integral multiples of the shortest duration.	The essential characteristic of a time-scale or a signal such that the time intervals between consecutive significant instants either have the same duration or durations that are integral multiples of the shortest duration.	A data transmission process in which there is always an integral number of unit intervals between any two significant instants.

*From CCITT G.701, Vocabulary of Digital Transmission and Multiplexing, and PCM Terms.
†From the ISO 2382: Information Technology—Vocabulary.

available. An FDDI-II network typically starts out in basic mode to set up the timers and parameters necessary for the timed token protocol, then switches to hybrid mode.

When operating in hybrid mode, FDDI-II employs a continuously repeating protocol data unit referred to as a *cycle*. The cycle is a framing structure similar in principle to that used in synchronous transmission systems (e.g., SONET/SDH [synchronous optical network/synchronous digital hierarchy]). The contents of the cycle are visible to all stations as it circulates around the ring. A station called the cycle master generates a new cycle 8,000 times per second, or once every 125 μsec. At 100 Mbps, this works out to a cycle size of 12,500 bits. As each cycle completes its circuit of the ring, it is stripped by the cycle master.

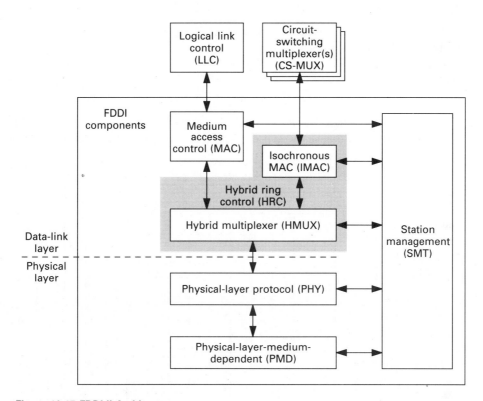

Figure 10.17 FDDI-II Architecture

10.5.2.1   Cycle Format and Channels

Figure 10.18 illustrates the format of the cycle, which consists of the following components:

- *Preamble:* This is a five-symbol (20-bit) nondata stream. The actual size of the preamble will vary from four to six symbols to maintain synchronization in the face of jitter.

- *Cycle header:* This 12-octet header contains information that defines the usage of the remainder of the cycle, as described in the following subsection.

- *Dedicated packet group (DPG):* These 12 octets are always available for token-controlled packet transfer.

- *Wideband channels (WBCs):* Each wideband channel consists of 96 octets per cycle.

Each of the wideband channels, at 96 octets, provides a capacity of 6.144 Mbps. Each channel may be set aside for circuit switching or packet switching. If the channel is used for packet switching, then it is merged with the dedicated packet-group octets and any other WBCs set aside for packet switching to form one large channel dedicated to packet switching. This channel, referred to as the *packet-data channel,* is controlled by a circulating token; capacity is allocated on this channel as indicated in Figure 10.7. Thus, the minimum capacity of the packet-data channel is 768 Kbps, and it can grow in increments of 6.144 Mbps, to a maximum of 99.072 Mbps. The capacity allocation of FDDI-II can be summarized as follows:

	Number of Bits per Cycle	Data rate (Mbps)
Overhead (cycle header + preamble)	116	0.928
N channels of circuit-switched data	$N \times 768$	$N \times 6.144$
Packet-data channel	$96 + (16 - N) \times 768$	$0.768 + (16 - N) \times 6.144$
TOTAL	12,500	100

The IMAC sublayer within the HRC controls the WBCs that are used for circuit-switched traffic. Each 6.144-Mbps wideband channel can support a single isochronous channel. Alterna-

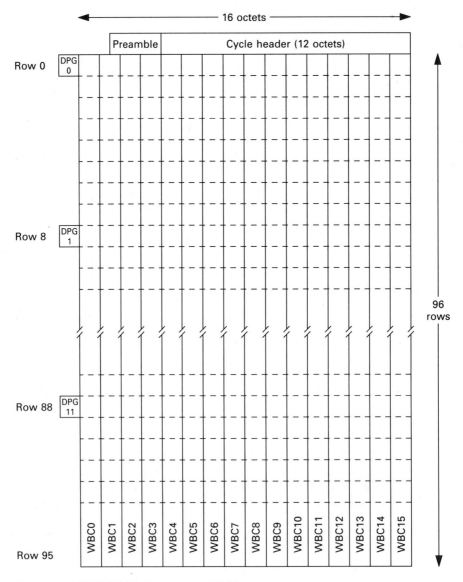

Figure 10.18 FDDI-II Cycle Structure at 100 Mbps

Table 10.7 Possible WBC Subchannel Sizes

Bits/Cycle	Channel Rate (Kbps)	Possible Application and/or Current Channel Equivalents
1	8	Compressed voice, data
2	16	Compressed voice, data
4	32	Compressed voice, data
8	64	Voice, ISDN B channel
48	384	6 B channels, ISDN H0 channel
192	1,536	24 B channels, ISDN H11 channel
192 + 1	1,544	T1 carrier
240	1,920	30 B channels, ISDN H12 channel
256	2,048	E1 carrier
768	6,144	FDDI-II WBC

tively, one WBC may be subdivided by IMAC into a number of subchannels. These separate subchannels permit simultaneous, independent, isochronous dialogues between different pairs of FDDI-II stations. Table 10.7 summarizes the possible subchannel sizes.

10.5.2.2 Cycle Header
The FDDI-II cycle header consists of the following fields (Figure 10.19):

- *Starting delimiter:* indicates the beginning of a cycle; it is represented by the JK symbol pair.

- *Synchronization control:* used to establish the synchronization state of the ring. A value of R indicates that synchronization has not yet been established and that the cycle may be legally interrupted by another cycle. The C1 field is set to R during hybrid-mode initialization or by any station that detects loss of cycle synchronization by not receiving a cycle within 125 μsec of the previous cycle. A value of S indicates that synchronization has been established; this value can only be set by the cycle master.

- *Sequence control:* indicates the status of cycle sequencing. A value of R indicates that either the cycle sequence has not yet been established or a cycle-sequence error has been detected; a value of S indicates that valid cycle sequence is established and stations can latch each CS value to compare to the CS value in the next cycle.

- *Cycle sequence:* takes the form NN, where N is a data symbol. If the C1 and C2 fields both contain R, then the CS field is interpreted as containing a monitor rank. The monitor rank can take on a value from 0 to 63 and is used during the monitor-contention process. During this

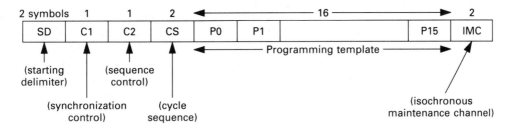

Figure 10.19 FDDI-II Cycle Header

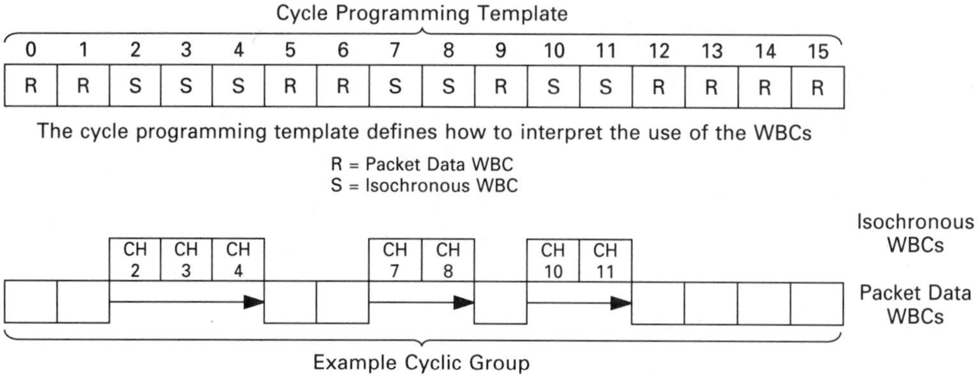

Cycle Programming Template

0	1	2	3	4	5	6	7	8	9	10	11	12	13	14	15
R	R	S	S	S	R	R	S	S	R	S	S	R	R	R	R

The cycle programming template defines how to interpret the use of the WBCs

R = Packet Data WBC
S = Isochronous WBC

Figure 10.20 Example of the Sorting of the Wideband Channels

process, monitor stations transmit their rank in the CS field, and the station with the highest rank becomes the new cycle master. During normal operation, both C1 and C2 contain S, and CS contains a value between 64 and 255, representing the cycle-sequence number. The cycle master increments this number by 1 for each new cycle, with 255 incremented to wrap around to 64.

- *Programming template:* consists of 16 symbols, 1 for each WBC. An R value indicates that the corresponding WBC is part of the packet-data channel, whereas an S indicates that the corresponding WBC is dedicated to isochronous traffic. Figure 10.20 illustrates this interpretation. The programming template is read by all stations but may only be modified by the cycle master.

- *Isochronous maintenance channel:* dedicated to carrying isochronous traffic for maintenance purposes. Its use is outside the scope of the present standard.

10.5.3   Operation

During normal operation, the activity on an FDDI-II network consists of a sequence of cycles generated by the cycle master. Stations communicate using circuit switching by sharing the use of a dedicated isochronous channel. Stations communicate using packet switching over the packet-data channel, observing the rules imposed by the token-ring protocol.

10.5.3.1   Initialization

Typically, the ring will be configured to initialize in basic mode. Once basic mode is established and operating, one or more stations may attempt to move the network to hybrid mode by issuing a cycle. One monitor station can be preassigned this task, or all monitor stations may compete. During the monitor-contention process, each contending monitor station continually issues cycles with an R value in the C1 and C2 fields and its monitor value in the CS field. If it sees an incoming frame with a higher monitor value, it ceases to transmit its own cycles and simply repeats incoming cycles. Eventually, the monitor with the highest rank sees its own rank. It then issues cycles with an S value in the C1 and C2 fields and a cycle sequence number in the CS field.

10.5.3.2 Programming-Template Maintenance

The cycle master maintains the programming template. The allocation of capacity between packet and circuit transmission may be modified dynamically by means of SMT requests to the cycle master. When a request for modification comes in, the cycle master waits until it receives the token on the packet-data channel, to ensure that no other station's packet data are circulating on the ring. It then generates a new cycle with the new programming template and issues a new token on the packet-data channel. Other FDDI-II stations will adjust to the new allocation as soon as they receive the new programming template.

10.6 SUMMARY

The fiber distributed data interface (FDDI) is a term that refers to a set of standards that specify a high-speed local and metropolitan area network. The FDDI uses a ring topology, operating at 100 Mbps over optical fiber. The medium-access control technique is the token ring technique. The FDDI token-ring algorithm is similar to that used in IEEE 802.5; the capacity allocation portions of the two standards differ.

The original specification, sometimes referred to as FDDI-I, supports a packet-mode data-transfer service. A more recent upwardly-compatible version is referred to as FDDI-II. FDDI-II supports both packet-mode and isochronous data transfer. The latter data-transfer service is suitable for circuit-switched applications.

11
MAN Standards

One of the newest sets of networking standards is those for metropolitan area networks (MANs). Although the IEEE (Institute of Electrical and Electronics Engineers) 802.6 committee was chartered in 1982, it was only after a number of false starts that the committee has defined a technical approach to MANs that has achieved widespread support. The result is the IEEE 802.6 standard, which has been adopted by ANSI (the American National Standards Institute).

As the name suggests, a MAN occupies a middle ground between local area networks (LANs) and wide area networks (WANs). Interest in MANs has come about as a result of a recognition that the traditional point-to-point and switched network techniques used in WANs may be inadequate for the growing needs of organizations. Although broadband ISDN (integrated services digital network), with ATM (asynchronous transfer mode), holds out promise for meeting a wide range of high-speed needs, there is a requirement now for both private and public networks that provide high capacity at low costs over a large area. The high-speed shared-medium approach of the LAN standards provides a number of benefits that can be realized on a metropolitan scale.

A useful way to view the 802.6 MAN standard is that it is an adaptation of the features of both LANs and ATM that is well-suited to the metropolitan area. Some of the key characteristics of the 802.6 MAN that can be compared to LANs and BISDN ATM are the following:

- *High speed:* The 802.6 MAN offers a variety of speeds. The initial standard specifies 44.7 Mbps. Work is ongoing on speeds ranging from 1.544 Mbps to 155 Mbps. These rates overlap the range of the ISO 8802 LANs and BISDN.

- *Shared medium:* Like LANs, the 802.6 MAN uses a shared medium with much greater capacity than the attached devices. This allows support of bursty, asynchronous traffic as well as isochronous traffic.

- *Support for LLC:* The 802.6 standard has been designed to support data traffic under unacknowledged connectionless 802.2 LLC (logical link control).

- *Addressing:* The 802.6 stations must be able to recognize the 48-bit and 16-bit addresses used by the other 802 LAN standards. In addition, the 60-bit CCITT format is an option; this enables ISDN compatibility.

- *Fixed-length packets:* Unlike the 802 LANs, and like ATM, 802.6 uses a fixed-length packet. For compatibility with ATM, the same 53-octet cell (called a slot in 802.6) with a 48-octet payload is used. The fixed-length format provides effective and efficient support for small and large packets (the latter handled by segmentation) and for isochronous data.

- *Dual bus:* The most obvious difference between 802.6 and 802 LANs is the use in 802.6 of two separate buses, both of which carry data at the same time.

The IEEE 802.6 standard is referred to as the distributed-queue dual-bus (DQDB) subnetwork standard. The term *DQDB* refers to the topology and access-control technique employed, and the term *subnetwork* suggests that a single DQDB network will be a component in a collection of networks to provide a service.

Recall from Chapter 9 the definition of LANs provided in IEEE (1990). The same document provides the following definition of a MAN:

A MAN is optimized for a larger geographical area than a LAN, ranging from several blocks of buildings to entire cities. As with local networks, MANs can also depend on communications channels of moderate-to-high data rates. Error rates and delay may be slightly higher than might be obtained on a LAN. A MAN might be owned and operated by a single organization, but usually will be used by many individuals and organizations. MANs might also be owned and operated as public utilities. They will often provide means for internetworking of local networks. Although not a requirement for all LANs, the capability to perform local

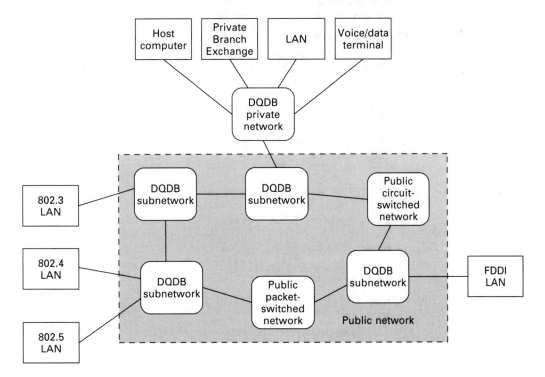

Figure 11.1 DQDB MAN Made Up of Subnetworks

networking of integrated voice and data (IVD) devices is considered an optional function for a LAN. Likewise, such capabilities in a network covering a metropolitan area are optional functions of a MAN. (page 9)

Figure 11.1, based on one in IEEE 802.6, suggests the use of DQDB subnetworks. A subnetwork or set of subnetworks can be used as a public network controlled by a Bell operating company or other public provider or as a private backbone network covering a building or group of buildings for a given user. To support services across a metropolitan area, a single DQDB network may range from a few kilometers to more than 50 km in extent. Subnetworks can operate at a variety of data rates.

DQDB subnetworks can be connected by bridges or routers. The links between a pair of bridges or routers can be point-to-point or a network such as a packet-switched network, a circuit-switched network, or ISDN.

11.1   TOPOLOGY

The topology chosen for the 802.6 MAN was in large part dictated by the assumption that the medium for the MAN would be optical fiber. Optical fiber provides the high data rates needed for the MAN application. On the other hand, optical fiber as a shared medium presents a number of problems. In particular, the use of multiple optical-fiber taps on a medium introduces significant losses and limits the range of the medium and the number of devices that can be supported.

Two approaches are possible to deal with the problems of optical fiber. One approach is the ring topology, which involves a set of point-to-point links between stations. This is the approach taken by FDDI. Another approach, which has been studied for many years, is the use of a dual-bus architecture. This is the approach taken by IEEE 802.6.

The dual-bus approach allows the use of unidirectional taps rather than bidirectional taps. A unidirectional tap is technically more feasible for optical fiber. Figure 11.2, part (a), shows the dual-bus topology using unidirectional taps. Each node attaches to both buses and has both transmit and receive taps on both buses. On each bus, a station may transmit only to those stations downstream from it. By using both buses, a station may transmit to and receive from all other stations. A given node, however, must know which bus to use to transmit to another node; if not, all data would have to be sent out on both buses. Transmissions on the two buses are independent; thus, the effective data rate of a DQDB network is twice the data rate of the bus.

For clarity in our discussion, we use the following terminology (not part of the 802.6 standard): upstream (A) refers to upstream on bus A; downstream (A) refers to downstream on bus A. The node that is upstream (A) of all other nodes is designated head of bus A, or head (A). The terms *upstream (B), downstream (B),* and *head (B)* have the obvious corresponding meanings.

11.1.1   Access-Unit Attachment

With an optical-fiber bus, either an active or a passive tap can be used; both are permissible with the 802.6 standard.

In the case of an active tap, the following steps occur:

1. Optical signal energy enters the tap from the bus.

2. Clocking information is recovered from the signal, and the signal is converted to an electrical signal.

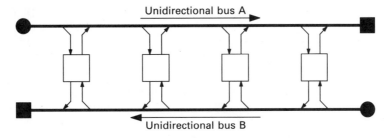

(a) Logical block diagram

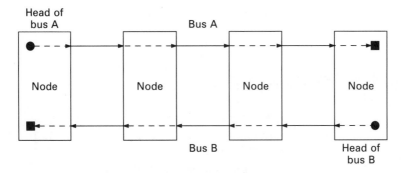

(b) Configuration diagram

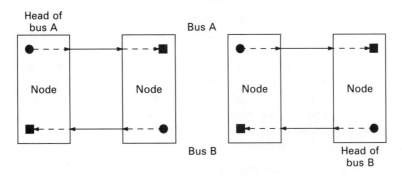

(c) Reconfiguration (broken link between two nodes)

Figure 11.2 Open-Bus Topology

3. The converted signal is presented to the node and perhaps modified by the latter.

4. The optical output (a light beam) is modulated according to the electrical signal and launched into the bus.

In effect, the bus consists of a chain of point-to-point links, and each node acts as a repeater.

In the case of a passive tap, the tap extracts a portion of the optical energy from the bus for reception, and it injects optical energy directly into the medium for transmission. Thus, there is a single run of cable rather than a chain of point-to-point links. This passive approach is equivalent to the type of taps typically used for twisted-pair and coaxial cable.

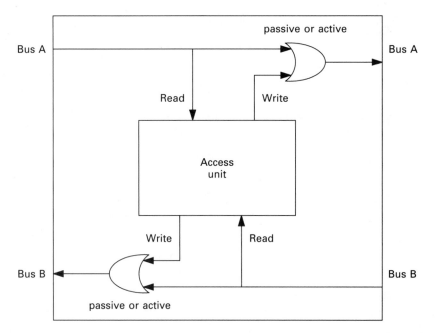

Figure 11.3 Example of Access-Unit Attachment (IEEE 802.6)

The electronic complexity and interface cost are drawbacks for the implementation of the active tap. Also, each tap will add some increment of delay, just as in the case of a ring. For passive taps, the lossy nature of pure optical taps limits the number of devices and the length of the medium.

Figure 11.3 depicts the access unit in functional terms. Access units attach to both buses via read and write connections. Writing on the bus is by logical OR of the data from upstream with the data from the unit: if the unit attempts to write a 0, the result is the value already on the bus; if the unit attempts to write a 1, the result is a 1 on the bus. The read connection is placed ahead of the write connection to allow all data to be copied from the bus unaffected by the unit's own writing.

11.1.2   Synchronization and Timing

Transmission on each bus consists of a steady stream of fixed-size slots with a length of 53 octets. Nodes read and copy data from the slots; they also gain access to the subnetwork by writing to the slots. Head (A) is responsible for generating the slots on bus A, while head (B) is responsible for generating the slots on bus B. The slot-generation function is indicated by a solid circle in Figure 11.2, part (b); the bus-termination function is indicated by a solid square.

Operation of the subnetwork is controlled by a 125-μsec. clock. The timing interval was chosen to provide support for isochronous services; it reflects the 8-kHz public-networking frequency required by voice services. The slot generators in head (A) and head (B) transmit multiple slots to the shared medium every 125 μsec.; the number of slots generated per clock cycle depends on the physical data rate.

Under normal conditions, the 125-μsec. timing is provided by a single source. If the DQDB subnetwork is connected to a public telecommunications network, the timing may be provided by that network. Indeed, if the subnetwork is supporting certain isochronous services and is connected to a public network, it may be required that the timing be derived from the public network.

The alternative source of timing is a node within the DQDB subnetwork. One node would be designated for this purpose.

11.1.3   Looped-Bus Topology

The topology depicted in Figure 11.2, part (a), is, for self-evident reasons, referred to as an open-bus topology. There is an alternative topology, depicted in Figure 11.4, part (a), known as the

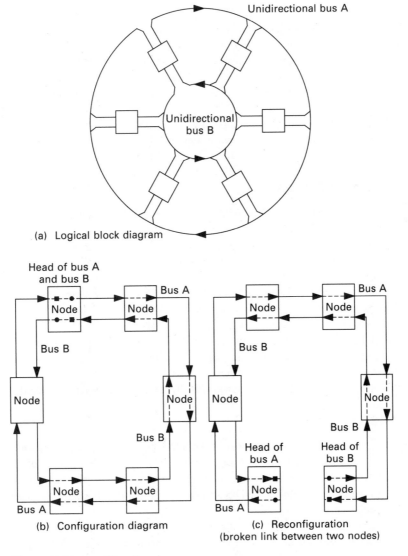

(a) Logical block diagram

(b) Configuration diagram

(c) Reconfiguration
(broken link between two nodes)

Figure 11.4 Looped-Bus Topology

looped-bus topology. In this topology, the nodes are attached to the two buses to form two closed loops. The head (A) and head (B) roles are both played by the same node.

Note that the looped-bus topology resembles a dual-ring topology. The two are different, however, since the head (A, B) node does not repeat incoming transmissions on the corresponding outgoing link.

11.1.4   Reconfiguration

The DQDB subnetwork includes a reconfiguration capability in the event of the failure of a link or node. This feature is particularly effective in the case of the looped-bus topology, since full connectivity can be maintained.

Figure 11.4, part (c), shows the effect of the loss of a link on the looped-bus topology. The head (A) and head (B) functions migrate from the original head (A, B) node to the two nodes adjacent to the fault. The result is a fully connected open-bus topology. If a node adjacent to a break is not capable of performing the head-of-bus functions, then the node on that side of the fault that is nearest the fault and capable of performing the head-of-bus functions is designated as head of one of the buses. The nodes that are passed over thus become isolated from the subnetwork.

When a fault occurs on an open-bus topology, the best that can be done is to reconfigure as two separate open-bus subnetworks, as shown in Figure 11.2, part (c).

11.2   PROTOCOL ARCHITECTURE

Figure 11.5 depicts the protocol architecture of the IEEE 802.6 DQDB standard. As with the IEEE 802 LAN standards, the DQDB standard is divided into three layers. The upper layer corresponds to the upper portion of the OSI (open systems interconnection) data-link layer. In the case of the 802 LAN standards, this is the LLC layer. In the case of 802.6, a number of different protocols can be supported at this layer.

The middle layer of 802.6 is referred to as the DQDB layer. This corresponds roughly to the MAC layer of the 802 LAN standards and, as with the MAC layer, regulates access to the shared medium. It corresponds to the lower portion of the OSI data-link layer.

The lowest layer of the 802.6 architecture is, of course, the physical layer. This layer is defined to support a variety of physical transmission schemes.

In this section, we look first at the services provided by the DQDB layer. Next, the functions and protocols of the DQDB layer are examined. Finally, the physical layer is covered.

11.2.1   DQDB Services

The layer above the DQDB layer is not part of the 802.6 protocol architecture as such. Rather, it serves to define the services that an 802.6 subnetwork must support. Three types of services have so far been defined: connectionless service, connection-oriented data service, and isochronous services. Convergence functions within the DQDB layer adapt the underlying medium-access service to provide a specific service to the user.

The *connectionless data service* provides support for connectionless communication via the LLC type-1 protocol (see Chapter 9). The connectionless medium-access service supports the trans-

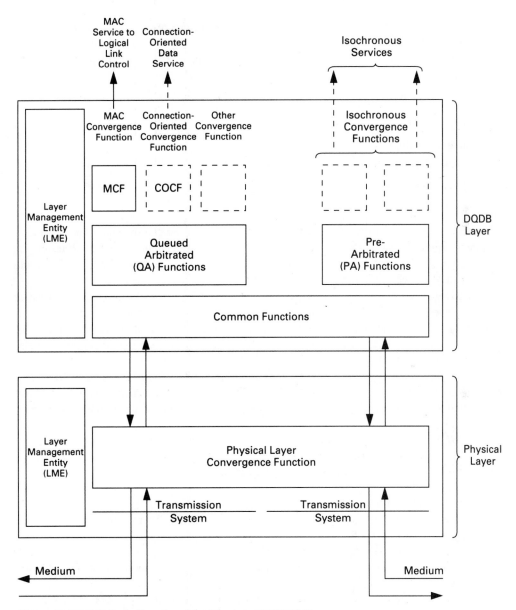

Figure 11.5 DQDB Node Functional Architecture (IEEE 802.6)

port of frames up to a length of 9,188 octets. Transmission is in the form of fixed-length 52-octet segments. Accordingly, the service must include a segmentation-and-reassembly function.

The *connection-oriented service* supports the transport of 52-octet segments between nodes sharing a virtual channel connection. Thus, as with the connectionless service, segmentation and reassembly are required. The control signaling required to establish, maintain, and clear a connection is outside the scope of the current 802.6 standard.

The *isochronous service* provides support for users that require a constant interarrival time. The service is provided over a logical isochronous connection. The control signaling required to establish, maintain, and clear a connection is outside the scope of the current 802.6 standard.

11.2.2   DQDB Layer

The DQDB layer can be viewed as being organized into three sublayers:

1.   Common functions
2.   Arbitrated functions
3.   Convergence functions

11.2.2.1   Common Functions

The common-functions module deals with the relay of slots in the two directions and provides a common platform for asynchronous and isochronous services. In addition to the basic transmission and reception of slots, the common-functions module is responsible for head-of-bus, configuration-control, and MID (message identification) page-allocation functions.

The *head-of-bus function* is performed only by the one or two nodes designated as head of bus. It includes generating and transmitting slots. Each slot is a formatted data unit. Included in the header is a bit to indicate the type of slot; this is marked by the head-of-bus function to indicate whether this is a slot for isochronous data or asynchronous data. In the former case, the head also inserts the virtual channel identifier into the slot header.

The *configuration-control function* is involved in the initialization of the subnetwork and its reconfiguration after a failure. An example of a configuration-control function is the activation and deactivation of the head-of-bus functions at appropriate nodes during the process of reconfiguration.

The *MID page-allocation function* participates in a distributed protocol with all nodes on the subnetwork to control the allocation of message-ID values to nodes. The message ID is used in the segmentation-and-reassembly function, as described in section 11.4.

11.2.2.2   Arbitrated Functions

The arbitrated functions are responsible for medium-access control. There are two functions, corresponding to the two kinds of slots carried on the bus.

All slots on the bus are 53 octets in length, consisting of a 1-octet access-control field and a 52-octet segment. The two types of slots generated on the network are queued-arbitrated (QA) and prearbitrated (PA) slots.

PA slots are used to carry isochronous data. The *PA function* provides access control for the connection-oriented transfer over a guaranteed bandwidth channel of octets that form part of an isochronous octet stream. The PA function assumes the previous establishment of a connection. As a result of connection establishment, the PA function will be informed of the virtual channel ID (VCI) associated with this connection. The VCI is part of the access-control field and is generated by the head-of-bus function. An isochronous connection may involve all of the segment octets in a slot; alternatively, a single segment may be shared by more than one isochronous connection. In the latter case, the PA will be informed of the VCI and the offset of the octets to be used for reading and writing within the multiple-user PA-segment payload.

QA slots are used to carry asynchronous data. The *QA function* provides access control for asynchronous data transfer of 48-octet segment payloads. The QA function accepts the segment payloads from a convergence function and adds the appropriate segment header to form a segment. A distributed reservation scheme known as distributed queueing is used to provide medium-access control. The MAC protocol is used to gain access to an available QA slot.

11.2.2.3   Convergence Functions

The DQDB layer is intended to provide a range of services. For each service, a convergence function is needed to map the data stream of the DQDB user into the 53-octet transmission scheme of the DQDB layer. The concept is the same as that of the ATM adaptation layer (AAL) used in BISDN. Three services have been identified so far:

1. *Connectionless data transfer:* The standard fully specifies the convergence function to support the connectionless MAC data service to LLC.

2. *Isochronous service:* The standard gives guidelines for the provision of an isochronous service.

3. *Connection-oriented data service:* The convergence function for this service is under study.

The *MAC convergence function (MCF)* adapts the connectionless MAC service to the QA function. The key task here is one of segmentation and reassembly. MAC service units of a length up to 9,188 octets must be transmitted in a sequence of slots. The MCF transmit process involves encapsulating the LLC PDU (MAC SDU) to form an initial MAC PDU (IMPDU). The IMPDU is segmented into segmentation units of 44 octets, each of which is carried in a QA slot. The segmentation-and-reassembly protocol is described in section 11.4.

The *isochronous convergence function (ICF)* adapts an isochronous octet-based service to the guaranteed-bandwidth octet-based service of the PA function. The ICF is analogous to the isochronous MAC service of FDDI-II (fiber-distributed data interface II). The primary function of the ICF is buffering to allow for instantaneous rate differences between the PA service and the provided isochronous service. This is because the PA function guarantees the average arrival and transmission rate of isochronous services but cannot guarantee that octets will be supplied at regular fixed intervals. The buffering ensures that a fixed interarrival time can be maintained.

A *connection-oriented convergence function (COCF)* is mentioned in the standard but not defined. The COCF would use the QA slots and the same segmentation-and-reassembly procedures as the MCF.

11.2.3   Physical Layer

The DQDB layer is independent of the physical layer. Therefore, a variety of DQDB networks can be implemented using the same access layer but operating at different data rates over different transmission systems. Three transmission systems are referenced in the standard:

1. *ANSI DS3:* transmits data at 44.736 Mbps over coaxial cable or optical fiber

2. *ANSI SONET (CCITT SDH):* transmits data at 155.52 Mbps and above over single-mode optical fiber

3. *CCITT G.703:* transmits data at 34.368 Mbps and 139.264 Mbps over a metallic medium

For each transmission system, a physical-layer convergence protocol is used to provide a consistent physical-layer service to the DQDB layer.

The only physical-layer convergence function defined in the current standard is for DS3. This is summarized in section 11.5.

11.3   DISTRIBUTED-QUEUE ACCESS PROTOCOL

Access to QA slots on the DQDB medium is provided by the distributed-queue access protocol. Although the basic mechanism of this protocol at any one node is straightforward, the resulting distributed activity is complex. In addition, the basic protocol is augmented by two features designed to optimize the protocol: bandwidth balancing and priorities. We begin with a general description of the basic protocol. This is followed by a more detailed discussion of the protocol mechanism and a worked-out example. Bandwidth balancing and priorities are covered in the final two subsections.

In discussing the distributed-queue protocol, we need to remember that there are actually two media: bus A and bus B. Since the access-control mechanisms are exactly the same with respect to bus A and bus B, we will generally confine ourselves to a discussion of access-control of bus A, unless otherwise noted.

11.3.1   Description of the Basic Protocol

The distributed-queue access protocol is a *distributed reservation* scheme. The two words suggest the key characteristics of the protocol:

- *Reservation:* For most reservation schemes, including this one, time on the medium is divided into slots, much as with synchronous TDM (time-division multiplexing). A node wishing to transmit reserves a future slot.

- *Distributed:* To accommodate changing requirements, the reservation scheme must be dynamic. That is, nodes make reservation requests when they have data to send. The function of granting requests can be either centralized at a single node or distributed. In the latter case, which is the one used by the 802.6 standard, the network nodes collectively determine the order in which slots are granted.

The distributed reservation scheme for the DQDB subnetwork must take into account the nature of the topology. The essence of the protocol can be summarized as follows. Node X wishes to transmit a block of data to node Y. X must choose the bus on which Y is downstream from X. Let us assume that the bus is A; that is, Y is downstream (A) from X. For X to transmit a block of data in a slot to Y, it must use an available block coming from upstream (A). If the upstream (A) stations monopolize the medium, X is prevented from transmitting. Therefore, X's reservation request must be made to its upstream (A) peers. This requires the use of bus B, since those stations upstream (A) from X are also downstream (B) from X and capable of receiving a reservation request from X on bus B.

The protocol requires that each station defer its own need to transmit to the needs of its downstream peers. As long as one or more downstream peers have outstanding reservation requests, a station will refrain from transmitting, allowing unused slots to continue downstream. The key requirement for the protocol, then, is a mechanism by which each station can keep track of the requests of all its downstream peers.

The actual behavior of a node will depend on its position on the bus. The four positions of significance (with respect to bus A) are illustrated in Figure 11.6, which shows a DQDB subnetwork with N nodes. Consider first *node* $(N-1)$, which is head (B). This node has no downstream (A) nodes and therefore does not transmit data on bus A and does not need to make reservations on bus B. The only data-transfer activity for node $(N-1)$ on bus A is reception. The node reads all passing slots. Any QA slot with a destination address matching node $(N-1)$ is copied.

Now consider the node closest to head (B), which in this case is labeled *node* $(N-2)$. Whenever this node needs to transmit a segment of data, it issues a request on bus B for an available slot on bus A. This is actually done by setting a request bit in a passing slot. Although node $(N-2)$ makes reservations on bus B, it never receives any reservation requests on bus B: its only upstream (B) peer is node $(N-1)$, which does not issue requests on bus B. On bus A, node $(N-2)$ receives segments of data addressed to it. In addition, when node $(N-2)$ has data to send and has issued a request, it may transmit its segment of data in the first free slot that passes. The first bit in the slot indicates whether the slot is free or busy.

A third node whose position is important is head (A), which is labeled *node 0* in the figure. As the head of bus A, this node is responsible for generating the stream of slots on bus A. Thus, there will be no QA slots on bus A with data addressed to this node, and all QA slots originate as free slots. When this node has data to send to any other node, it can simply insert that data in the next QA slot that it generates. Because there are no upstream (B) peers of node 0, it has no need to issue requests.

However, it is responsible for seeing that outstanding requests plus its own needs are satisfied on a round-robin, or first-come-first-served, basis. To do this, node 0 must keep a running count of how many requests have arrived on bus B that have not yet been satisfied. Table 11.1, part (a), summarizes the required behavior. Head (A) keeps track of the number of outstanding requests, which is simply the difference between incoming QA slots with a request and outgoing QA slots that are free. If head (A) has a segment of data to send at time T, it must wait until it has satisfied all of the requests outstanding at that time by issuing free QA slots. Once it has satisfied all those requests, it may transmit its own segment. Meanwhile, head (A) must keep track of additional requests that arrive after time T. To distinguish between requests that arrive before and after time T, they are referred to as preceding and following requests, respectively, in Table 11.1.

One way to visualize this operation is to think of it in terms of tickets. Each time that a request arrives, head (A) generates a ticket. Each time that head (A) issues a free QA slot, it discards the oldest ticket. When the node has its own data to send, it generates a ticket on its behalf and places it on the bottom of the stack. As additional tickets are generated by arriving requests, these are placed on the bottom of the stack. When head (A)'s ticket reaches the top of the stack, head (A) can issue a busy QA slot containing its data.

Finally, Figure 11.6 depicts the behavior of a node other than the three already discussed, labeled *node x*. Like node $(N-2)$, whenever node x needs to transmit a segment of data, it issues a request on bus B for an available slot on bus A. In addition, like node 0, node x must keep a count of requests that pass by on bus B so that its own requests are handled fairly. On bus A, node x receives segments of data addressed to it. In order to enforce a round-robin discipline, node x

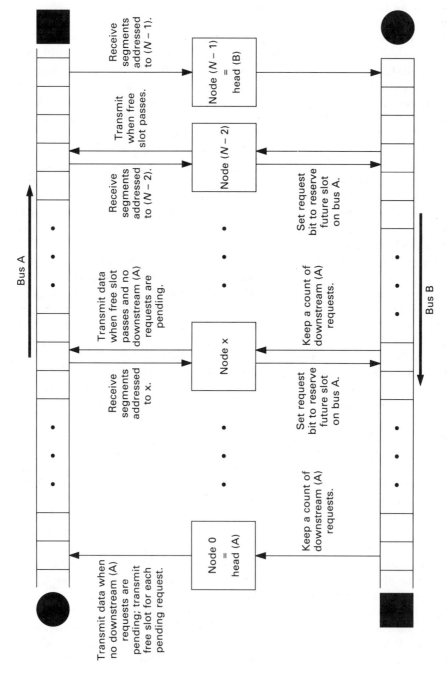

Figure 11.6 Basic Operation of the Distributed-Queue Protocol (Data Transmission on Bus A)

must keep track of incoming requests that precede and follow its own request, in a manner similar to the behavior of node 0. When node x has data to send and has issued a request, it may transmit its segment of data in a passing free slot only after all preceding requests have been satisfied. Table 11.1, part (b), which is quite similar to Table 11.1, part (a), summarizes the rules of behavior for node x.

11.3.2 Counter Mechanism

The DQDB protocol can be described in terms of a distributed collection of FIFO (first-in, first-out) queues. At each node, a queue is formed for each bus. For each request read in a passing slot, the node inserts one item in the queue. When the node itself issues a request, it adds an item to the queue for itself. When its own item is at the top of the queue, the node may transmit in the next free QA slot. A node may only have one item for itself in each queue (one for each bus) at any time.

This queueing mechanism can be simply implemented with a pair of counters for each queue, as illustrated in Figure 11.7, which shows the counters used for transmission on bus A; a corresponding pair of counters is used by the same node for transmission on bus B. When the node is not ready to send, it keeps track of requests on bus B from its downstream (A) neighbors in a request count. Each time a request is observed (the request bit is set), the count is increased by 1; each time a free slot passes on bus A, the count is decremented by 1 to a minimum count of 0.

At any time, the value of RQ represents the unmet need for free QA slots by the node's downstream (A) peers. The node is obligated to let this number of free slots pass before itself using a QA slot to transmit. Therefore, when the node does have data to transmit on bus A, it issues a request on bus B as soon as possible. The earliest opportunity will be the first slot to pass in which the request bit has not yet been set. Of course, while waiting for the opportunity to set the request bit, the node must continue to count passing requests in RQ. When the node does set the request bit on a passing slot on bus B, it immediately transfers the current value of RQ to a countdown count (CD) and resets RQ to 0. The node then decrements CD until it reaches 0, at which time, the node may transmit on bus A in the next free QA slot. Meanwhile, the node counts new requests on bus B in RQ. The effect of the preceding is to maintain a single FIFO queue into which the node may insert its own request.

Note that the queue formation is such that a slot is never wasted on the subnetwork if there is a segment queued for it. This is so because the CD count in the queued nodes represents the number of segments queued ahead. Since at any point in time, one segment must have queued first, then at least one node is guaranteed to have a CD count of 0. It is that node that will access the next passing free QA slot.

This is a remarkably effective protocol. Under conditions of light load, the value of CD will be small or 0 and free QA slots will be frequent. Thus, with a light load, delay is negligible—a property shared by CSMA/CD (carrier sense multiple access with collision detection) protocols. Under heavy loads, virtually every free QA slot will be utilized by one of the waiting nodes. Thus, with a heavy load, efficiency approaches 100 percent—a property shared by token-bus and token-ring protocols. This combination of quick access under light load and predictable queueing under heavy load makes the protocol suitable for a MAN of high data rate that will carry a mix of bursty traffic (e.g., interactive use) and more sustained streamlike traffic (e.g., file transfers).

Table 11.1 Behavior of Nodes in Figure 11.6

(a) Behavior of head (A)

At instant of time when it is ready to issue the next QA slot on bus A

	No preceding requests are outstanding.	**One or more preceding requests are outstanding.**
Head (A) has no data to send.	Issue a free QA slot (busy bit set to 0).	Issue a free QA slot and reduce by 1 the count of preceding requests.
Head (A) has a segment of QA data to send.	Issue a QA slot containing the data (busy bit set to 1; destination address and data inserted); following requests, if any, now become preceding requests.	Issue a free QA slot and reduce by 1 the count of preceding requests.

At instant of time when it receives the next QA slot on bus B

	Incoming slot contains a request.	**Incoming slot does not contain a request.**
Head (A) has no data to send.	Add 1 to count of preceding requests.	—
Head (A) has a segment of QA data to send.	Add 1 to count of following requests.	—

Table 11.1 (*Cont.*)

	(b) Behavior of node x **At instant of time when it observes** **a free QA slot on bus A**	
	No preceding requests are outstanding.	**One or more preceding requests are outstanding.**
Node x has no data to send.	Let free slot pass.	Let free slot pass and reduce by 1 the count of preceding requests.
Node x has a segment of QA data to send and has previously issued a request on bus B.	Set the busy bit to 1 on passing slot and insert data; following requests, if any, now become preceding requests.	Let free slot pass and reduce by 1 the count of preceding requests.

	At instant of time when it observes **a QA slot on bus B**	
	Incoming slot contains a request.	**Incoming slot does not contain a request.**
Node x does not have an outstanding request.	Add 1 to count of preceding requests.	—
Node x has a segment of QA data to send and has already issued a request for that segment.	Add 1 to count of following requests.	—
Node x has a segment of QA data to send and has not yet issued a request for that segment.	Add 1 to count of preceding requests.	Insert request into passing slot (set request bit to 1).

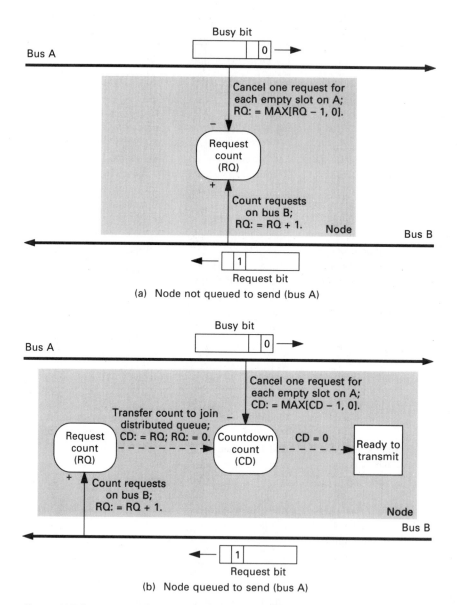

(a) Node not queued to send (bus A)

(b) Node queued to send (bus A)

Figure 11.7 Request and Countdown Counter Operation

11.3.3   A Simple Example

Figure 11.8, adapted from an example in the 802.6 document, provides a simple example of the operation of the basic protocol. The example is limited to transmission of data on bus A; none of the nodes is a head-of-bus node.

The example starts at a point when there are no outstanding requests. At that point, all nodes have an RQ value of 0. Then, the following events occur:

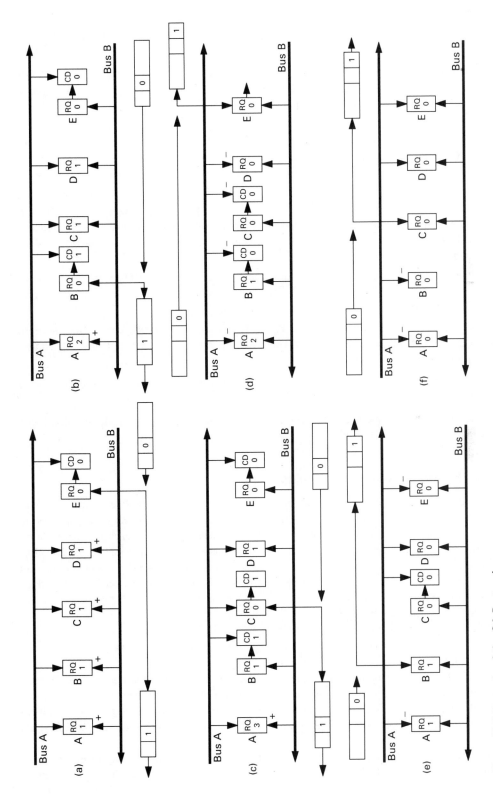

Figure 11.8 Example of the QA Protocol

415

(a) Node E issues a request on bus B by changing the busy bit in a passing slot from 0 to 1. Each downstream (B) node (nodes A–D) increments its RQ counter. At the same time, node E transfers its RQ count to its CD count. In this case, the count is 0, so node E can transmit on bus A as soon as it sees a free QA slot.

(b) Node B issues a request on bus B. The node transfers the value of RQ, which is 1, to CD and sets RQ to 0. This node will have to wait until one free QA slot passes on bus A before gaining access. Node A sees the request bit that has been set and increments its RQ value to 2.

(c) Node C issues a request on bus B. C sets its CD value to 1 and its RQ value to 0. Node B increments its RQ value to 1. Note that B's CD value is unchanged; the arrival of new requests after B has issued its own request does not affect the timing of B's access to bus A. Node A increments its RQ to 3.

(d) A free QA slot passes down bus A. Nodes A and D decrement their RQ counts. Nodes B and C decrement their CD counts. Node E has a CD of 0 and so can seize the free slot by changing the busy bit from 0 to 1 and inserting a QA segment.

(e) Another free QA slot passes down bus A. Node A decrements its RQ count. Both nodes B and C are eligible to seize the free slot. However, the free slot passes node B first, which uses it to transmit a QA segment.

(f) Node C uses the next passing free slot to transmit. The system returns to its original state, in which all nodes have an RQ value of 0.

Note that the three requests are satisfied in the order issued. Thus, the behavior of the network as a whole is that of a FIFO queue.

11.3.4   Priority Distributed Queueing

The distributed-queueing protocol supports three levels of priority. Priority access control is absolute in that QA segments with a higher priority will always gain access ahead of segments at all lower levels. This is achieved by operating separate distributed queues for each level of priority.

To support priority, several refinements need to be made to the access method described so far. Each segment includes 3 request bits, one for each level of priority. A node wishing to transmit on bus A at a particular priority level sets the appropriate bit on the next slot on bus B for which that bit is 0. To keep track of these requests, each node must maintain six RQ counters, one for each priority level in each direction, and six CD counters.

The operation of the RQ and CD counters is specified in such a way as to achieve absolute priority. We need to consider the two cases of a request pending and no request pending by a node at a particular priority level for one of the buses.

First, let us consider the case of a node that has no requests pending at a given priority level for bus A; the same description will also apply to bus B. The RQ count operating at that priority level will count requests at the same and higher priority levels. Thus, the RQ count records all queued segments at equal and higher priorities. As before, the RQ count is decremented for each passing QA slot on bus B.

Now suppose that the node has a QA segment queued at a particular priority level for bus A. In our original definition of the CD count, this variable is decremented with passing QA slots on one bus and unaffected by traffic on the other bus. To account for priorities, we continue to decrement CD with every passing free QA slot on one bus but increment CD for every request on the other bus that is of higher priority. This allows the higher-priority segments to claim access ahead of already-queued segments. To avoid double counting, the RQ count is incremented only for requests of the same priority level; the higher-priority requests are already being counted in the CD count.

At the present time, the use of the priority levels is unspecified in the standard. The standard dictates that connectionless data segments (carrying LLC PDUs) must operate at the lowest priority level (level 0). It is possible that control-signaling messages or connection-oriented data might be assigned to one of the two higher priority levels; this is a matter for further study.

11.3.5 Bandwidth Balancing

A problem can arise in the access-control mechanism so far described under conditions of heavy load and a network of large extent. To understand the problem, which is one of bandwidth unfairness, we first need to clarify the relationship between data that a node needs to send, the use of requests, and the use of free slots. This relationship is illustrated in Figure 11.9, taken from the 802.6 document. The relationship concerns data generated at a node to be transmitted in QA segments. The DQDB user (i.e., LLC) provides service data units to the DQDB layer. Each block of arriving data is broken up into one or more segments and placed in a FIFO segment queue awaiting transmission. There are six such queues, one for each of three levels of priority on each of the two buses.

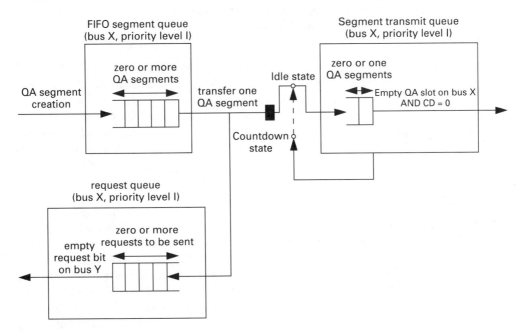

Figure 11.9 Relationship Between QA-Segment Queue, Request Queue, and Segment-Transmit Queue

The figure shows the relationships for one of the six segment queues. A segment-transmit queue is used to hold a segment that is awaiting a free slot on the bus. When a segment is transferred from the segment queue to the transmit queue, a request needs to be issued on the other bus. It may not be possible to issue the request immediately, since the node must wait for a passing slot in which the corresponding request bit has not yet been set. Therefore, a request queue is needed, which holds the requests until they can be issued. Each time that an empty request bit on a passing slot is set, one item is removed from the request queue.

The DQDB protocol dictates that once a node has issued a request for a free QA slot, it cannot issue another request until the first one is satisfied. To enforce this, the transmit queue can only hold one segment. If there is a segment in the transmit queue, it may be issued when the corresponding CD count is 0 and an empty QA slot passes. If there is no segment in the transmit queue, one item from the segment queue may be transferred to the transmit queue, accompanied by the insertion of an entry in the request queue.

We are now in a position to explain the bandwidth-unfairness problem, using an example in Hahne (1990). Consider two nodes that are transmitting very long messages on bus A; call the upstream (A) node 1 and the downstream (A) node 2. Assume that no other nodes require access to bus A. The following definitions apply:

D = the number of slots in transit between nodes 1 and 2; this is obviously a direct function of the physical length of the medium between the two nodes. Assume an integer value.

Δ = the difference in the arrival times of the messages from DQDB users to the DQDB entities. That is:

= (time that the first segment is placed in the segment queue of node 2) − (time that the first segment is placed in the segment queue of node 1).

$c(\Delta)$ = a function that clips its argument to the range $[-D, D]$.

P = number of requests plus idle slots circulating between the two nodes.

Once both nodes have received messages from their users (both nodes have begun filling their segment queues), node 1 leaves slots idle only in response to requests from node 2. Therefore, once node 2 begins to receive QA slots from node 1, the only idle slots node 2 receives are in response to its earlier requests. Each idle slot received by node 2 results in a segment being transmitted, a new segment being placed in the transmit queue, and a request being issued on bus B. Therefore, the value of P is constant; let us refer to these conserved entities as *permits*. This quantity determines the throughput of the downstream node. We can express P as follows:

$$P = 1 + D - c(\Delta)$$

To verify this equation, consider two extreme cases. First, assume that a message arrives from node 1's user more than D time units before node 2 has a message to send ($\Delta \geq D$). In that case, node 1 will fill the bus with data and will only allow a free slot to pass when it receives a request from node 2. When node 2 is ready to transmit, it must issue a request and then wait for that request to reach node 1 and for a free slot to return. In this instance, there is only one permit in the network: $P = 1$. At the other extreme is the case of $\Delta \leq -D$. Initially, only node 2 is active. It inserts its first segment in the transmit queue and sends its first reservation request. The first segment is transmitted immediately in a free slot. The node continues to transmit segments and issue requests in this fashion. By the time node 1 is ready to transmit, bus B is already carrying D

requests. In the time that it takes for node 1's first segment to reach node 2, node 2 injects another D requests, so that $P \approx 2D$.

Now let us define the following quantities:

$\gamma 1$ = steady-state throughput of node 1 (in segments per slot time).
$\gamma 2$ = steady-state throughput of node 2 (in segments per slot time).
Q = average value of CD at node 1.

Note that, at any instant in time, permits can be stored in the request channel (bus B between nodes 1 and 2), in the data channel (bus A between nodes 1 and 2), and in the counter CD at node 1. Some thought should convince the reader that the following relationships hold:

$$\gamma 1 + \gamma 2 = 1$$
$$\gamma 1 = 1/Q$$
$$\gamma 2 = P/T$$
$$T = 2D + Q$$

Solving these equations, we have:

$$\gamma 1 = \frac{2}{2 - D - c(\Delta) + \sqrt{(D - c(\Delta) + 2)^2 + 4Dc(\Delta)}}$$
$$\gamma 2 = 1 - \gamma 1$$

Note that if the nodes are very close together ($D \approx 0$), or if they start transmitting at about the same time ($\Delta \approx 0$), then each node gets about half of the capacity. However, if D is very large (large network) and the downstream node starts later, its predicted throughput rate is only about $1/2 D$. Node 1 also suffers a penalty if it starts later, though not as great; its worst-case rate is approximately $1/\sqrt{2D}$.

As Hahne (1990) points out, one way of explaining the bandwidth-unfairness phenomenon of DQDB is that the protocol pushes the system too hard. In its attempt to use every single slot on the bus, the protocol causes a buildup in the nodes of request queues that never recede. The refinement proposed in Hahne's paper, and subsequently adopted by IEEE 802.6, "leaks" some bandwidth to prevent the hogging of bandwidth in overload situations. The technique is known as *bandwidth balancing*.

In ordinary DQDB, a node may transmit a segment when its CD count is 0 and the current QA slot is free. Bandwidth balancing permits the node to transmit only a fraction α of that time. This is achieved by artificially incrementing RQ after every β segments transmitted; thus, $\alpha = \beta/(1 + \beta)$. This forces the node to send an extra free slot downstream after using β free slots. For example, if $\alpha = 0.9$ ($\beta = 9$), then after every 9 QA segments transmitted, the node lets an extra slot pass. To implement this scheme, one more counter, called the trigger counter, is needed for each direction at each node. The trigger counter is incremented by 1 every time a QA segment is transmitted. When the counter equals β, it is set to 0 and RQ is incremented by 1.

The parameter β—called bandwidth-balancing modulus, or BWB_MOD, in the standard— must be set in each node. The value may be set between 0 and 64, with a default value of 8. A value of 0 disables the bandwidth-balancing function.

To get a feel for the effect of BWB_MOD on performance, let us consider the following set of conditions, which yield maximum subnetwork throughput:

- No station has any PA traffic.

- Every station has QA traffic ready to transmit at all times.

- All QA segments have the same priority.

- All nodes have the same value for BWB_MOD.

The following definitions apply:

$$\gamma = \text{throughput of any one node.}$$
$$N = \text{number of nodes.}$$
$$\beta = \text{value of BWB\_MOD.}$$

Recall that the maximum throughput of a node is limited by $\beta/(1+\beta)$. We can express the throughput of a node as the amount of capacity not used by the other nodes, subject to the limitation. Therefore:

$$\gamma = \frac{\beta}{1+\beta} \times [1-(N-1)\times\gamma]$$

Solving for γ:

$$\gamma = \frac{1}{N+(1/\beta)}$$

One BWB_MOD is associated with each bus, but no distinction is made on the basis of priority. When BWB_MOD resets to 0, the RQ counts for that bus for all priority levels for which no QA segment is queued are incremented, and the CD counts for that bus for all priority levels for which a QA segment is queued are incremented.

The standard recommends that bandwidth balancing be enabled for a bus that spans a distance that is greater than the effective length of one 53-octet slot, which is approximately the following:

> 2 km at 44.376 Mbps (DS3 rate)
> 546 m at 155.520 Mbps (STM-1 rate)
> 137 m at 622.080 Mbps (STM-4 rate)

11.3.6   State Machine Description

The IEEE 802.6 standard contains a state machine description of the distributed-queue access protocol that helps to clarify the mechanism. Figure 11.10, which is adapted from a figure in the standard, shows the state machine for a station for one bus X (X = A or B; Y = the other bus) and one priority level I (I = 0, 1, 2). Each node has six such state machines operating simultaneously.

There are two states: A node is in the idle state when it has no QA segments to send. A node is in the countdown state when is has a QA segment to send.

First, consider the *idle state*. Three internal events can occur. If data arrive from the DQDB user at priority level I intended for a downstream (X) node, the node transitions to the countdown state. The node performs several actions as part of the transition:

1. It informs the other two bus X state machines within the node of this internal request with a signal, SELF_REQ_I.

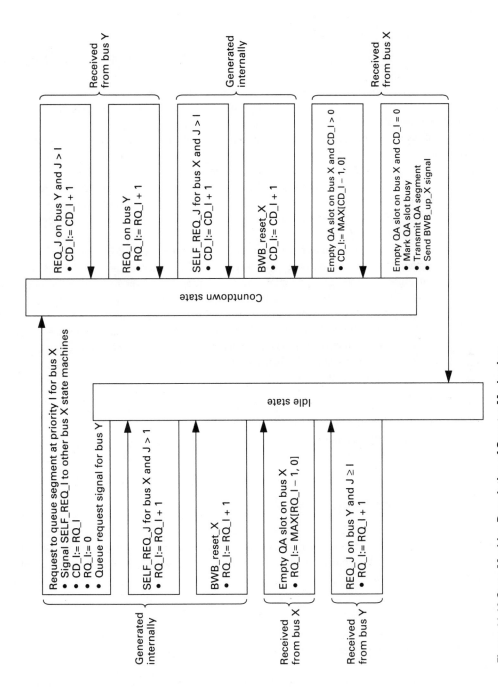

Figure 11.10 State Machine Description of Counter Mechanism

421

2. It transfers the value of its request count (RQ_I) to its countdown count (CD_I) and clears RQ_I.

3. It queues a request signal for bus Y.

Another internal event is the arrival of a SELF_REQ_J signal from one of the other bus X state machines. If the priority of the internal request is greater than I, then RQ_I must be incremented by 1 to give that request priority. The final internal event occurs when the bandwidth-balancing counter (BWB_MOD) for bus X is reset to 0. This is depicted as a signal, BWB_reset_X, sent to each bus X state machine. The resulting action is to increment RQ_I.

Two external events affect the machine in the idle state. When an empty QA slot passes on bus X, RQ_I is decremented by 1 to a minimum value of 0. If a slot passes on bus Y with the priority J bit set (REQ_J) and J ≥ I, then RQ_I is incremented by 1.

In the *countdown state,* external events related to the Y bus affect the machine. If a slot passes on bus Y with the REQ_J bit set and J > I, then CD_I is incremented by 1. If a slot passes on bus Y with the REQ_I bit set, then RQ_I is incremented by 1. These actions keep the machine's requests queued properly.

There are also two significant internal events. One is the arrival of a SELF_REQ_J signal from one of the other bus X state machines. If J > I, then CD_I is incremented, so that a new internal request of higher priority gets preference over a waiting QA segment of lower priority. The other internal event is the arrival of a BWB_reset_X signal. Again, this causes CD_I to be incremented: bandwidth balancing takes precedence over waiting QA segments.

Finally, two external events related to bus X affect the machine in the countdown state. If an empty QA slot passes and CD_I > 0, then CD_I is decremented by 1 to a minimum value of 0. If an empty QA slot passes and CD_I = 0, then the node transitions to the idle state. The node performs several actions as part of the transition:

1. It marks the passing QA slot as busy by setting the busy bit to 1.

2. It begins transmitting its QA segment in the QA slot.

3. It causes the BWB_MOD counter for bus X to be incremented (modulo its maximum value) by issuing a BWB_up_X signal.

11.4   DQDB PROTOCOL DATA UNITS

A rather complex set of protocol data unit formats is used to support the DQDB-layer functions. Table 11.2 lists the five PDU types and indicates their relationship to each other and the DQDB sublayer that is responsible for generating and reading each type. These PDU types are discussed in the balance of this section.

11.4.1   Slot

As we have already discussed, the basic unit of transfer on a DQDB subnetwork is the 53-octet slot. The slot consists of a 1-octet header and a 52-octet segment; its format is shown in Figure 11.11, part (a).

The slot header, referred to as the access-control field, contains the bits that control slot access. The fields are:

Table 11.2 IEEE 802.6 PDU Formats

PDU	Relative Position*	Sublayer	Description
Slot	Contains a QA segment, or PA segment	Common functions	Basic unit of data transfer.
QA segment	Contained in a slot; carries a DMPDU	Queued-arbitrated (QA) functions	Used to carry a portion of a MAC service data unit or other SDU.
PA segment	Contained in a slot	Prearbitrated (PA) functions	Used to carry isochronous service octets.
Initial MAC protocol data unit (IMPDU)	Carried in a sequence of DMPDUs	MAC convergence function (MCF)	Contains a MAC service data unit.
Derived MAC protocol data unit (DMPDU)	Carries a portion of an IMPDU; contained in a QA segment	MAC convergence function (MCF)	A sequence of DMPDUs carries a single IMPDU.

*   See Figure 11.13.

- *Busy:* indicates whether the slot contains information or is free.

- *Slot type:* indicates whether this is a QA slot or a PA slot. The combination of busy bit and slot-type bit is referred to as the slot access control field, with the assignments indicated in Table 11.3, part (a).

- *Previous slot reserved:* indicates whether the segment in the previous slot may be cleared or not. This bit is set by a node when the immediately preceding slot contained a QA segment destined only for that node. The use of this bit is for further study.

- *Reserved:* set to 00; reserved for future use.

- *Request:* 3 request bits for the three priority levels.

11.4.2 Segment

Each slot contains a 52-octet segment, which may be either a QA segment or a PA segment. Both types of segments consist of a 4-octet header followed by a 48-octet segment payload. The QA- and PA-segment headers have an identical format, with some differences in interpretation of the fields. The formats are shown in Figure 11.11, part (b). The header fields are:

- *Virtual channel identifier* (*VCI*): identifies the virtual channel, or logical connection, to which the segment belongs. The VCI value of all 1s corresponds to the connectionless MAC service. Other non-0 VCI values are available for use for the connection-oriented data service and isochronous services.

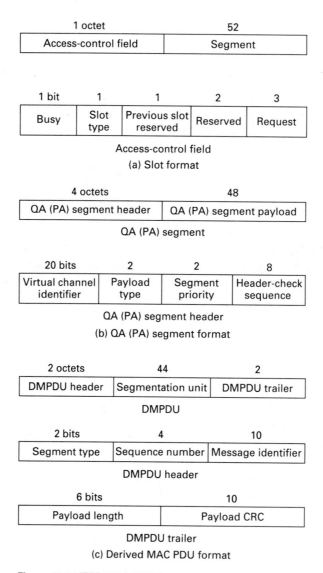

Figure 11.11 IEEE 802.6 PDU Formats

- *Payload type:* indicates the nature of the data to be transferred. The field could be used by DQDB subnetworks interconnected via bridges, where this value could differentiate between user data and network signaling and management data. The default value for both PA and QA segments is 00; all other values are for further study.

- *Segment priority:* this field is reserved for future use with multiport bridges. A multiport bridge is one that connects three or more subnetworks.

Table 11.3 Coding of Some IEEE 802.6 PDU Fields

(a) Slot access-control field

Busy	SL_Type	Slot State
0	0	Empty QA slot
0	1	Reserved
1	0	Busy QA slot
1	1	PA slot

(b) Address-type subfield

Address_Type	MSAP Address Structure
0010	16 bit
1000	48 bit
1100	Individual 60 bit, publicly administered
1101	Individual 60 bit, privately administered
1110	Group 60 bit, publicly administered
1111	Group 60 bit, privately administered
All other codes	Reserved for future standardization

(c) Protocol-identification (PI) field

PI Range	Protocol Entity
1	LLC
48–63	Available for use by local administration
Other values	Reserved for future standardization by IEEE 802.6

(d) Quality of service: delay (QOS_Delay)

Priority Requested	QOS_Delay Subfield	Relative Delay Requested
7	111	Shortest
6	110	
5	101	
4	100	
3	011	
2	010	
1	001	
0	000	Longest

(e) DMPDU Segment_Type field

Segment_Type	DMPDU Type
00	Continuation of message (COM)
01	End of message (EOM)
10	Beginning of message (BOM)
11	Single-segment message (SSM)

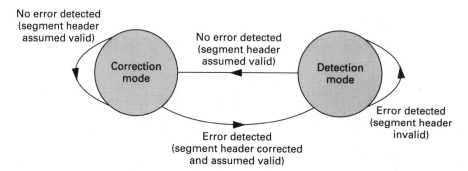

Figure 11.12 HCS Operation at Receiver

- *Header-check sequence (HCS):* covers the segment header and is used for the detection of errors and the correction of single-bit errors. It uses the same polynomial code as for ATM ($X^8 + X^2 + X + 1$). The operation of the error-control mechanism, shown in Figure 11.12, is almost identical to that specified for ATM (Figure 8.11). The only difference is that when the HCS decoder is in the correction state, there is a probability that multiple-bit errors will be corrected as if they were single-bit errors, allowing an erroneous header to pass as valid.

11.4.3   Transfer of MAC Service Data Units

The DQDB layer provides the MAC service by accepting MAC service data units (LLC PDUs) from a DQDB user and transmitting each to a destination DQDB user. Since the QA-segment format limits the protocol to a segment payload of 48 octets, it is clear that a segmentation-and-reassembly function must be performed. The approach that is taken to this function is depicted in Figure 11.13. An arriving MAC SDU is encapsulated into an initial MAC PDU (IMPDU), which includes an IMPDU header and trailer plus the entire MAC SDU. This IMPDU is then segmented into 44-octet *segmentation units,* each of which can be fit into a derived MAC PDU (DMPDU). The DMPDU includes the 44-octet segmentation unit plus a header and trailer, for a total length of 48 octets. Thus, each 48-octet DMPDU fits into a single QA segment, which, in turn, fits into a single QA slot.

11.4.3.1   Initial MAC Protocol Data Unit

A MAC SDU is transferred within an IMPDU. An IMPDU is transferred between peer MAC-convergence-function protocol entities. The format of an IMPDU is shown in Figure 11.14. The IMPDU is constructed by adding the following major elements to a variable-length MAC SDU, which is stored in the INFO field:

- *Common PDU header:* carried in all DQDB-layer PDUs supporting frame-based bursty data services.

- *MCP header:* specific to the MAC convergence protocol and therefore specific to the transfer of a MAC SDU.

- *Header extension:* provides the optional capability to convey additional IMPDU protocol-control information that may be standardized in the future. An example of its use would be to

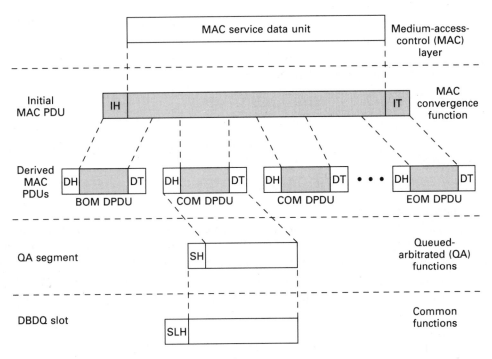

Figure 11.13 PDUs for Support of MAC Service

IMPDU header		Header extension	INFO	PAD	CRC 32	Common PDU trailer
Common PDU header	MAC-convergence-protocol header					
4 octets	20	+	*	#	!	4

+ = in the range 0 to 20 octets inclusive, in steps of 4 octets
* = contains the MAC SDU: up to and including 9,188 octets
# = 0, 1, 2, or 3 octets, as needed to make the total length of the INFO
plus PAD fields an integral multiple of 4 octets
! = absent (0 octets) or present (4 octets)

IMPDU

1 octet	1	2
Reserved	Beginning-end tag	Buffer-allocation size

Common PDU header

6 bit	2
Protocol identification	PAD length

PI/PL field

8 octets	8	1	1	2
Destination address	Sourse address	PI/PL	QOS/CIB/HEL	Bridging

MAC-convergence-protocol header

3 bits	1	1	3
Quality of service: delay	Quality of service: loss	CRC 32 indicator bit	Header-extension length

QOS/CIB/HEL field

4 bits	60 – N	N (= 16, 48, or 60)
Address type	Padding	MSAP address

Address field

1 octet	1	2
Reserved	Beginning-end tag	Length

Common PDU trailer

Figure 11.14 Initial MAC PDU Format

convey service-provider–specific information in cases where this protocol is used to access the services of a public network.

- *PAD:* contains the minimum number of octets so that the total length of the INFO field plus the PAD field is an integral multiple of 4 octets.
- *CRC 32:* Provides the optional capability for including a 32-bit CRC (cyclic-redundancy check), calculated over all the fields of the MCP header, the header extension field, the INFO field, and the PAD field.
- *Common PDU trailer:* carried in all DQDB-layer PDUs supporting frame-based bursty data services.

The *common PDU header* consists of three fields:

1. *Reserved:* reserved for future use.
2. *Beginning-end tag:* This is an 8-bit sequence number associated with an IMPDU and incremented by 1 (modulo 256) for successive IMPDUs sent by the node. This value is used in segmentation and reassembly, explained in the following subsection.
3. *Buffer-allocation size:* the total length of the IMPDU, exclusive of the common PDU header and trailer. This alerts the receiver to buffer space requirements. Again, this value is used in segmentation and reassembly.

The *MCP header* consists of the following fields:

- *Destination address:* the MAC address of the destination node.
- *Source address:* the MAC address of the source node.
- *PI/PL:* the protocol-identification subfield identifies the MAC service user to which the INFO field is to be sent. Valid values for this field are shown in Table 11.3, part (c). The pad-length subfield indicates the length of the PAD field in the IMPDU.
- *QOS/CIB/HEL:* the QOS delay subfield indicates the requested quality of service for an IMDPU with respect to delay in accessing the subnetwork. The value is based on the priority requested by the MAC user, and the coding is shown in Table 11.3, part (d). The QOS loss bit is currently reserved. It may be used for congestion control at bridges by indicating which IMPDUs are eligible for discard. The CRC 32 indicator bit indicates the presence or absence of the CRC 32 field in the IMPDU. The header-extension-length subfield gives the length of the header-extension field in the IMPDU, in units of 4 octets.
- *Bridging:* reserved for future use for MAC-level bridging. One use for this field would be a hop count: after an IMPDU has passed through a given number of bridges, it would be discarded.

The two address fields have the format shown in Figure 11.14. The first 4 bits indicate the address type, with the values listed in Table 11.3, part (b). Support for 48-bit addresses is mandatory. Support for 16-bit addresses is optional. Both of these address types conform to the MAC address format for IEEE 802 (Figure 9.3). Support is also optional for 60-bit addresses, which may be publicly administered (local MAN operator) or privately administered.

The *common PDU trailer* contains the same information in the same format as the common PDU header. The same value is inserted into the beginning-end tag field in both header and trailer, and the same value is inserted in the buffer-allocation size and length fields.

11.4.3.2   Derived MAC Protocol Data Unit

As Figure 11.13 illustrates, an IMPDU is segmented into one or more DMPDUs. Each DMPDU carries a 44-octet portion of the IMPDU, known as a *segmentation unit*. In addition, each DMPDU has a header and trailer.

The *DMPDU header* contains the following fields:

- *Segment type:* There are four types of DMPDUs. A single-segment message (SSM) contains an entire IMPDU. If the IMPDU is segmented into two or more DMPDUs (Figure 11.13), the first DMPDU is the beginning of message (BOM), the last DMPDU is the end of message (EOM), and any intermediate DMPDUs are continuation of message (COM). The coding is shown in Table 11.3, part (e).

- *Sequence number:* used in reassembling an IMPDU to verify that all of the DMPDU segmentation units have been received and concatenated properly. A value of the sequence number is set at BOM and incremented for each successive COM and the EOM for a single IMPDU.

- *Message identifier:* This is a unique identifier associated with the set of DMPDUs that carry a single IMPDU. Again, this number is needed to ensure proper reassembly.

The *DMPDU trailer* contains the following fields:

- *Payload length:* indicates the number of octets from the IMPDU that occupy the segmentation unit of the DMPDU. The number has a value between 4 and 44 octets, in multiples of 4. The value will always be 44 for BOM and COM DMPDUs. It is a lesser number in an SSM if the IMPDU is less than 44 octets in length. It is a lesser number in an EOM if the length of the IMPDU is not an integer multiple of 44 octets in length, necessitating the use of a partially filled EOM.

- *Payload CRC:* This is a 10-bit CRC on the entire DMPDU.

11.5   PHYSICAL-LAYER CONVERGENCE PROCEDURE FOR DS3

The physical-layer convergence procedure (PLCP) adapts the services of the transmission system to provide a uniform, generic physical-layer service to the DQDB layer. The PLCP maps DQDB timing information, slot octets, and management information octets into a format that is suitable for transfer by the associated transmission system. A different PLCP is needed for each transmission system.

To date, the only PLCP that has been standardized by IEEE 802.6 is for the DS3 transmission system. DS3 was chosen because it is the only commonly used signal in North America with adequate bandwidth for the services being defined. The DS3 PLCP frame format is defined for use over the standard public network and can be extended into the customer's premises.

11.5.1   DS3

The DS3 signal is one of the most difficult formats for adaption. Unlike SONET (synchronous optical network), DS1, and most other signaling schemes, DS3 is not based on a 125-μsec. frame duration.

Table 11.4 Construction of DQDB PLCP Frame for DS3

	DS3	DQDB PLCP
Frame size	595 octets	690–691 octets
Frame time	106.4 μsec.	125 μsec.
Signaling rate	44.736 Mbps	44.210 Mbps
Overhead	56 bits/frame	54.5–55 octets
Payload size	588 octets	636 octets
Payload data rate	44.210 Mbps	40.704 Mbps

The DS3 signal operates at a data rate of 44.736 Mbps and provides a frame duration that is nominally 106.4 μsec. Its payload is typically quantitized into nibbles (1 nibble = 4 bits) due to the nature of the format.

Table 11.4 lists the key characteristics of DS3. The DS3 frame of 595 octets is divided into seven subframes of 680 bits each. Each subframe, in turn, consists of eight blocks of 85 bits. The first bit in each block is for management and framing purposes; the remaining 84 bits, or 21 nibbles, is the payload. Since 1 bit in 85 is overhead, the nominal information rate is 84/85 × 44.736 Mbps = 44.21 Mbps.

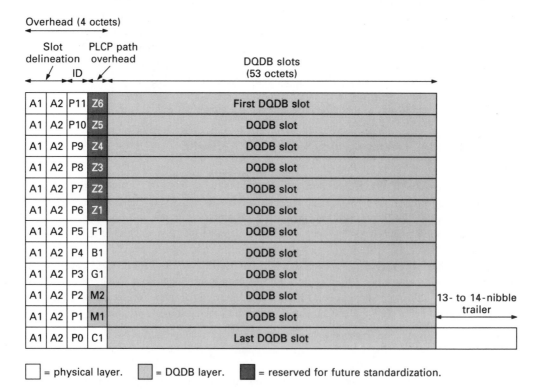

Figure 11.15 PLCP Frame Format for DS3 Transmission

11.5.2 PLCP Frame Format

The PLCP frame must be designed to accommodate DQDB, which uses 125-μsec. timing. The reader can observe that the DS3 signal contains exactly 699 octets over a 125-μsec. time period, which is an integral number of octets. However, the actual payload available from DS3 is at a rate of 44.21 Mbps, which yields 690.78 octets, or 1,381.56 nibbles, over a 125-μsec. frame. The PCLP must find a way of mapping the 53-octet slots into this DS3 payload. We must therefore assume a frame size of 690 octets, with bit stuffing used to smooth out the frame size to the actual transmission rate.

If we work with the numbers on Table 11.4, we can design a frame to hold the maximum number of DQDB slots. Each slot is 53 octets. The highest multiple of 53 octets that will fit into a frame of 690 octets is 13. However, since $53 \times 13 = 689$ octets, this leaves virtually no capacity for framing and management information. Accordingly, the PCLP frame for DS3 includes 12 DQDB slots, for a total payload of 636 octets.

Figure 11.15 shows the resulting frame format. The format can be depicted as 12 rows of 57 octets, with the last row containing a trailer of 13 or 14 nibbles. The first two columns (A1, A2) are used to provide slot delineation. Each A1 octet has the bit pattern 11110110, and each A2 octet has the bit pattern 00101000. These codes are the same as those used in the CCITT Synchronous Digital Hierarchy (SDH) Recommendations G.707-9.

Path-overhead identifier octet format

6 bits	1	1
Path-overhead label	Reserved	Parity

Path-status format

4 bits	1	1
Far-end block error	Yellow signal	Link-status signal

Path-overhead identifier codes

P11	001011	0	0
P10	001010	0	1
P9	001001	0	1
P8	001000	0	0
P7	000111	0	0
P6	000110	0	1
P5	000101	0	1
P4	000100	0	0
P3	000011	0	1
P2	000010	0	0
P1	000001	0	0
P0	000000	0	1

(a) Path-identifier octet (P11 − P0)

Link-status signal codes

LSS Code	LSS Name	Link Status
000	Connected	Received link connected
011	rx_link_dn	Received link down, no input or forced down
110	rx_link_up	Received link up

(b) Path-status octet (G1)

Cycle/stuff counter codes

C1 Code	Frame Phase of Cycle	Trailer Link
11111111	1	13
00000000	2	14
01100110	3 (no stuff)	13
10011001	3 (stuff)	14

(c) Cycle/stuff counter (C1)

Figure 11.16 Format and Coding of Some PLCP Frame Octets

The third column (P11–P0) identifies the PCLP overhead octets of the fourth column. That is, each Pi uniquely identifies one row of the PLCP and therefore uniquely identifies one of the octets from the fourth column. Figure 11.16, part (a). shows the convention used. The first 6 bits of octet Pi are set to the binary value of i. The seventh bit is reserved, and the eighth bit provides odd parity.

The fourth column is referred to as PLCP path overhead. The following octets make up the column:

- *Z6–Z1:* reserved for future use.

- *F1:* a 64-Kbps user channel. Use of this octet is outside the scope of the PLCP specification. One possible application is for assisting maintenance personnel.

- *B1:* a bit-interleaved parity octet allocated for PLCP path-error monitoring. Longitudinal parity is calculated over columns 4 through 57 of the previous PLCP frame and inserted into the B1 octet of the current frame. The code is calculated such that the first bit is even parity over the first bit of each octet in the 12 $\times$ 54 octet structure, and so on.

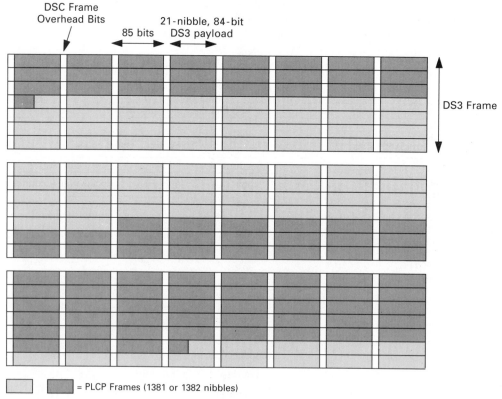

Source: R. Brandwein, T. Cox, and J. Dahl, "The IEEE 802.6 Physical Layer Convergence Procedures," *IEEE LCS Magazine* (May 1990).

Figure 11.17 Use of DS3 Frames to Carry PLCP Payload

- *G1:* This octet is allocated to convey the received PLCP status and performance to the transmitting PLCP (Figure 11.16, part [b]). The first 4 bits, the far-end block error, convey the count of interleaved-bit blocks that have been detected to be in error by the B1 code in the preceding frame. The yellow signal bit alerts the transmitting PLCP that a received failure indication has been declared along the PLCP path. When the failure has ceased, the bit is reset to 0 on subsequent frames. The link-status signal is used to communicate information about the status of the transmission link between the two adjacent PLCP entities.

- *M2–M1:* provided for the transport of DQDB-layer management information octets, which are not processed by the PLCP sublayer.

- *C1:* used to guide a nibble-stuffing function to maintain alignment and synchronization between the PLCP frame and the DS3 frame. As indicated in Figure 11.15, each PLCP frame ends with 13 or 14 nibbles. Frame transmission is organized into groups of three frames. The first frame in the group always ends with 13 nibbles; the second frame ends with 14 nibbles; and the third frame ends with either 13 or 14 nibbles as timing needs dictate. The C1 code (Figure 11.16, part [c]) indicates which phase of the three-frame cycle this frame is and, if it is the third frame, whether or not the fourteenth nibble is added.

11.5.3   Use of DS3 Frames to Carry PLCP Payload

Figure 11.17 illustrates the DS3 frame format and the way in which its payload nibbles are used to carry PLCP frames. Note that the PLCP frame "floats" inside the DS3 frame structure: there is no relationship between the start of the PLCP frame and the start of the DS3 frame.

11.6   SUMMARY

An important recent addition to the IEEE 802 family of standards is the IEEE 802.6 metropolitan area network (MAN) standard. The IEEE 802.6 standard uses a 53-octet cell as the fundamental unit of transmission. Thus, it can be readily integrated with the ATM-based broadband ISDN and other networks based on the use of ATM.

The IEEE 802.6 standard is also referred to as the distributed-queue, dual-bus (DQDB) specification. This refers to the use of a dual-bus topology and a medium-access-control technique based on the maintenance of distributed queues; that is each node maintains queues of outstanding requests that determine access to the MAN medium. The DQDB scheme supports both packet mode and isochronous mode data transfer.

The DQDB scheme is intended to be used with a variety of physical layers. A detailed specification has been produced for a DS3 physical layer; others are pending.

Part 4
Network Management
and Security

As the networks used in an organization, and the distributed applications they support, grow in scale and complexity, management issues become increasingly difficult and important. In this part, we explore the two most important areas for those responsible for the management of a distributed data-processing system.

Chapter 12 is devoted to the topic of network management. The task of network management involves setting up and running a network, monitoring network activity, and controlling the network to provide acceptable performance. In particular, the network manager must assure high availability (the network and its resources are available for use almost all the time) and low response time. The chapter summarizes the complex set of standards developed for OSI (open systems interconnection) network management.

Chapter 13 examines the issues related to network security. The use of a shared networking facility for business information communications creates a risk of unauthorized access. This chapter examines the threats that are present in a networking environment and the tools available to the manager to counter those threats.

12
OSI Network Management

Networks and distributed processing systems are of critical and growing importance in business, government, and other organizations. Within a given organization, the trend is toward larger, more complex networks supporting more applications and more users. As these networks grow in scale, two facts become painfully evident:

1. The network and its associated resources and distributed applications become indispensable to the organization.

2. More things can go wrong, disabling the network or a portion of the network or degrading performance to an unacceptable level.

A large network cannot be put together and managed by human effort alone. The complexity of such a system dictates the use of automated network-management tools. The urgency of the need for such tools is increased, as is the difficulty of supplying such tools, if the network includes equipment from multiple vendors. In response, ISO (the International Organization for Standardization) and CCITT have issued a set of standards that deal with network management, covering services, protocols, and management information base.

This chapter begins with an introduction to the overall concepts of standardized network management. Next, it examines the architecture and functional areas of OSI network management. This is followed by a more detailed look at OSI network-management functions and the management information base that supports OSI network management. Finally, the topics of network management services and protocols are discussed.

12.1 NETWORK-MANAGEMENT SYSTEMS

A network-management system is a collection of tools for network monitoring and control that is integrated in the sense that it involves:

- A single operator interface with a powerful but user-friendly set of commands for performing most or all network-management tasks.

- A minimal amount of separate equipment. That is, most of the hardware and software required for network management is incorporated into the existing user equipment.

A network-management system consists of incremental hardware and software additions implemented among existing network components. The software used in accomplishing the network-management tasks resides in the host computers and communications processors (e.g., front-end processors, terminal cluster controllers). A network-management system is designed to view the entire network as a unified architecture, with addresses and labels assigned to each point and the specific attributes of each element and link known to the system. The active elements of the network provide regular feedback of status information to the network-control center.

Figure 12.1 suggests the architecture of a network management system. Each network node contains a collection of software devoted to the network-management task, referred to in the diagram as a network-management entity. Each NME performs the following tasks:

- It collects statistics on communications and network-related activities.

- It stores statistics locally.

- It responds to commands from the network-control center, including commands to:

    Transmit collected statistics to the network-control center.
    Change a parameter (e.g., a timer used in a transport protocol).
    Provide status information (e.g., parameter values, active links).
    Generate artificial traffic to perform a test.

At least one host in the network is designated as the network-control center. In addition to the NME software, the network-control host includes a collection of software called the network-

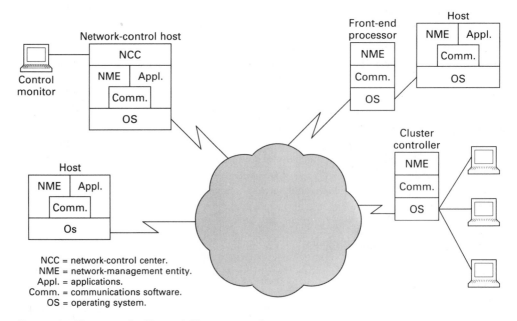

NCC = network-control center.
NME = network-management entity.
Appl. = applications.
Comm. = communications software.
OS = operating system.

Figure 12.1 Elements of a Network-Management System

control center. The NCC, which includes an operator interface to allow an authorized user to manage the network, responds to user commands by displaying information and/or by issuing commands to NMEs throughout the network. This communication is carried out via an application-level network-management protocol that uses the communications architecture in the same fashion as any other distributed application.

Several observations are in order:

- Since network-management software relies on the host operating system and on the communications architecture, most offerings to date are designed for use on a single vendor's equipment.

- As depicted in Figure 12.1, the network-control center communicates with and controls what are essentially software monitors in other systems. The architecture can be extended to include technical-control hardware and specialized performance-monitoring hardware as well.

- For maintaining high availability of the network-management function, two or more network-control centers may be used. In normal operation, one of the centers is idle or simply collecting statistics, while the other is used for control. If the primary network-control center fails, the backup system can be used.

12.2 OSI NETWORK-MANAGEMENT OVERVIEW

12.2.1 OSI Network-Management Standards

The first standard related to network management issued by the ISO was ISO 7498-4, which specifies the management framework for the OSI model. This document dictates that OSI management support user requirements for:

- Activities that enable managers to plan, organize, supervise, control, and account for the use of interconnection services

- The ability to respond to changing requirements

- Facilities to ensure predictable communications behavior

- Facilities that provide for the protection of information and for the authentication of sources of and destinations for transmitted data

Subsequently, ISO has issued a voluminous set of standards and draft standards for network management. CCITT is the joint sponsor of this effort and has set aside the X.700 series of numbers for its recommendations. Table 12.1 lists the current set of management standards documents. Figure 12.2, from ISO 10040, depicts the relationship among the various documents. The standards fall into five general categories:

1. *OSI management framework and overview:* includes ISO 7498-4, which provides a general introduction to management concepts, and ISO 10040, which is an overview of the remainder of the documents

2. *CMIS/CMIP:* defines the common management information service (CMIS), which provides OSI management services to management applications, and the common management information protocol (CMIP), which provides the information-exchange capability to support CMIS

Table 12.1 OSI Systems-Management Standards

Title	ISO	CCITT
OSI Management Framework and Overview		
OSI Basic Reference Model Part 4: Management Framework	7498-4	X.700
Systems Management Overview	10040	X.701
CMIS/CMIP		
Common Management Information Service Definition	9595	X.710
Amendment 4: Access Control	9595 DAM 4	X.710
Amendment X: Allomorphism	9595 PDAM X	X.710
Common Management Information Protocol Specification Part 1: Specification	9596-1	X.711
Amendment X: Allomorphism	9596 PDAM X	X.711
Part 2: Protocol Implementation Conformance Statement (PICS) Proforma	9596-2	X.712
Systems-Management Functions		
Part 1: Object Management Function	10164-1	X.730
Part 2: State Management Function	10164-2	X.732
Part 3: Attributes for Representing Relationships	10164-3	X.733
Part 4: Alarm Reporting Function	10164-4	X.734
Part 5: Event Report Management Function	10164-5	X.735
Part 6: Log Control Function	10164-6	X.736
Part 7: Security Alarm Reporting Function	10164-7	X.737
Part 8: Security Audit Trail Function	10164-8	X.740
Part 9: Objects and Attributes for Access Control	10164-9	X.741
Part 10: Accounting Meter Function	10164-10	X.742
Part 11: Workload Monitoring Function	10164-11	X.739
Part 12: Test Management Function	10164-12	
Part 13: Summarization Function	10164-13	
Accounting Management	SC 21 N 4971	
Part s: Scheduling Function	SC 21 N 6021	
OSI Software Management	SC 21 N 6040	
General Relationship Model	SC 21 N 6041	
Management Domains	SC 21 N 6047	
Management Knowledge	SC 21 N 6048	
Synchronization	SC 21 N 6049	
Performance Management	SC 21 N 6306	
Confidence and Diagnostic Test Classes	SC 21 N 6307	
Management Information Model		
Part 1: Management Information Model	10165-1	X.720
Part 2: Definition of Management Information	10165-2	X.721
Part 4: Guidelines for the Definition of Managed Objects	10165-4	X.722
Part 5: Generic Managed Information	10165-5	
Layer Management		
Elements of Management Information Related to OSI Network Layer Standards	10733	
Transport Layer Management	10737	

Set out the Structure

Management Framework

Systems Management
Overview

Explain the Requirements

Guide to Systems
Management

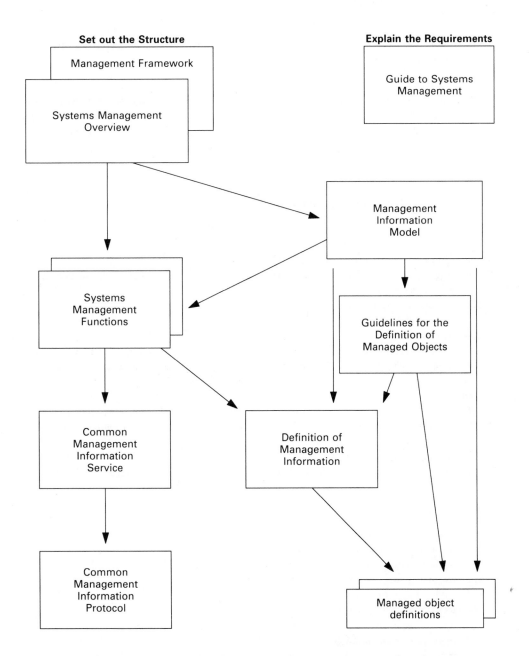

Management
Information
Model

Systems
Management
Functions

Guidelines for the
Definition of
Managed Objects

Common
Management
Information
Service

Definition of
Management
Information

Common
Management
Information
Protocol

Managed object
definitions

Figure 12.2 Relationship Between Standards (IS 10040)

3. *Systems-management functions:* defines the specific functions that are performed by OSI systems management

4. *Structure of management information:* defines the management information base (MIB), which contains a representation of all objects within the OSI environment subject to management

5. *Layer management:* defines management information, services, and functions related to specific OSI layers

As in any of the complex subject areas of OSI-related standardization, one key to understanding is the terminology employed. Table 12.2 provides a glossary of some of the most important terms used in OSI network-management documents. Note especially that the term *systems management* is used for what is generally referred to as network management in non-OSI literature.

Table 12.2 A Glossary of Terms for OSI Network Management

Attribute

A property of a managed object. An attribute has a value.

Common management information service element

An application-service element used to exchange information and commands for the purpose of systems management.

Common management information services

The set of services provided by the common management information service element.

Layer management

Functions related to the management of the (*N*) layer partly performed in the (*N*) layer itself according to the (*N*) protocol of the layer and partly performed as a subject of systems management.

Managed object

The OSI management view of a resource within the OSI environment that may be managed through the use of OSI management protocols. Examples include a layer entity, a connection, and an item of physical communications equipment.

Management information base (MIB)

The conceptual repository of management information within an open system. It consists of the set of managed objects, together with their attributes.

Systems management

Functions in the application layer related to the management of various OSI resources and their status across all layers of the OSI architecture.

Systems-management application entity (SMAE)

An application entity whose purpose is systems-management communication.

Systems-management application process (SMAP)

An application process participating in systems management.

Systems-management application-service element (SMASE)

An application-service element providing systems-management services.

Systems-management function

A part of systems-management activities that satisfies a set of logically related user requirements.

Systems-management protocol

An application-layer protocol supporting systems-management services.

Systems-management service

A named set of service primitives that provide a service for use in systems management.

12.2.2 OSI Management Framework

An architectural model of an OSI system participating in network management is shown in Figure 12.3. Key elements of this architecture include:

- *Systems-management application process* (*SMAP*): This is the local software within a system that is responsible for executing the network-management functions within a single system (host, front-end processor, router, etc.). It has access to system parameters and capabilities and can therefore manage all aspects of the system and coordinate with SMAPs on other systems.

- *Systems-management application entity* (*SMAE*): This application-level entity is responsible for communication with other nodes, especially with the system that exercises a network-control-center function. A standardized application-level protocol, common management information protocol is used for this purpose.

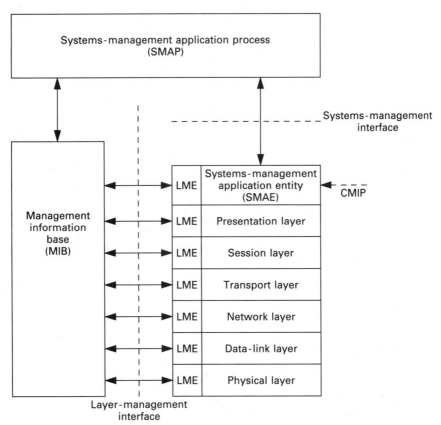

LME = layer-management entity.
CMIP = common management information protocol.

Figure 12.3 Architectural Model of OSI Management

- *Layer-management entity:* Logic is embedded into each layer of the OSI architecture to provide network-management functions specific to that layer.

- *Management information base:* the collection of information at each node pertaining to network management.

Figure 12.4 provides detail concerning the structure of the systems-management application entity. Like any other application-level entity, the SMAE can be logically defined as an interrelated set of application-service elements. In this case, two of the elements are ones that have been developed to be generally useful in a variety of applications: the association-control-service element and the remote-operations-service element.

Two ASEs that are specific to network management are the common management information service element and the systems-management application-service element. The SMASE provides various services that are available to the network manager and to applications (e.g., SMAP) that implement network-management functions. The SMASE implements basic management functions in the areas of fault management, accounting management, configuration management, performance management, and security management. For those functions that require communication with other systems, the SMASE relies on the CMISE. The CMISE provides the collection of basic network-management functions that supports the five functional areas visible to network managers via the SMASE.

In order to provide network management of a distributed system, all of the elements illustrated in Figures 12.3 and 12.4 must be implemented in a distributed fashion across all of the systems

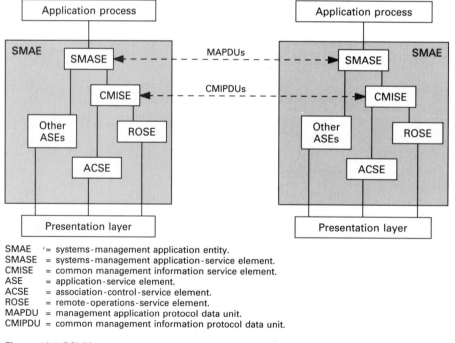

```
SMAE    '= systems-management application entity.
SMASE   = systems-management application-service element.
CMISE   = common management information service element.
ASE     = application-service element.
ACSE    = association-control-service element.
ROSE    = remote-operations-service element.
MAPDU   = management application protocol data unit.
CMIPDU  = common management information protocol data unit.
```

Figure 12.4 OSI Management in the Application Layer

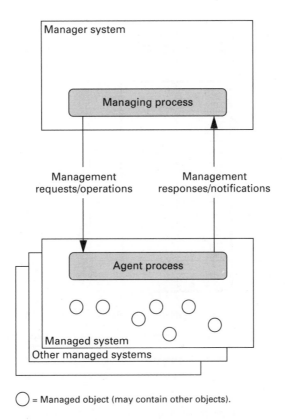

◯ = Managed object (may contain other objects).

Figure 12.5 Systems-Management Interactions

that are subject to network management. Interactions that take place among systems are depicted, in abstract fashion, in Figure 12.5. Management activities are effected through the manipulation of managed objects. Each system contains a number of such objects. Each object is a data structure that corresponds to an actual entity to be managed. The SMAP in a system is allowed to take on either an agent role or a manager role.

The manager role for an SMAP occurs in a system that acts as a network-control center. The agent role for an SMAP occurs in managed systems. The manager issues requests for information and operations commands for execution to the managed systems in the network. In each managed system, the agent interacts with the manager and is responsible for managing the objects within its system.

The way in which an agent represents and stores the data from which management information is derived is a local matter and not the subject of standardization. A local mapping function is used to map information concerning managed objects into a form that can be stored locally and used by local management software. However, for purposes of interaction with other systems, a standardized form of representation is required. Thus, the local representation must be mapped into a standardized form for agent-manager communication. These concepts are captured in Figure 12.6.

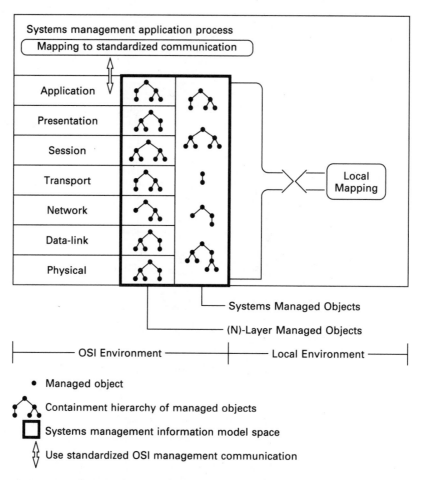

Figure 12.6 Relationship Between Information and Communication Aspects of the Systems-Management Model (IS 10040)

12.2.3   Management Functional Areas

The OSI management documents divide the task of network management into five functional areas (Table 12.3). These areas provide a useful checklist for assessing any network-management offering.

Fault-management facilities allow network managers to detect problems in the communications network and the OSI environment. These facilities include mechanisms for the detection, isolation, and correction of abnormal operation in any network component or in any of the OSI layers. Fault management provides procedures to:

1.   Detect and report the occurrence of faults. These procedures allow a managed system to notify its manager of the detection of a fault, using a standardized event-reporting protocol.

2.   Log the received event report. This log can then be examined and processed.

Table 12.3 OSI Management Functional Areas

Fault management	The facilities that enable the detection, isolation, and correction of abnormal operation of the OSI environment
Accounting management	The facilities that enable charges to be established for the use of managed objects and costs to be identified for the use of those managed objects
Configuration and name management	The facilities that exercise control over, identify, collect data from, and provide data to managed objects for the purpose of assisting in providing for continuous operation of interconnection services
Performance management	The facilities needed to evaluate the behavior of managed objects and the effectiveness of communication activities
Security management	Addresses those aspects of OSI security essential to operate OSI network management correctly and to protect managed objects

3. Schedule and execute diagnostic tests, trace faults, and initiate correction of faults. These procedures may be invoked as a result of analysis of the event log.

Accounting-management facilities allow a network manager to determine and allocate costs and charges for the use of network resources. Accounting management provides procedures to:

- Inform users of costs incurred, using event-reporting and data-manipulation software

- Enable accounting limits to be set for the use of managed resources

- Enable costs to be combined where multiple resources are used to achieve needed communication

Configuration- and name-management facilities allow network managers to exercise control over the configuration of the network components and OSI layer entities. Configurations may be changed to alleviate congestion, isolate faults, or meet changing user needs. Configuration management provides procedures to:

- Collect and disseminate data concerning the current state of resources. Locally initiated changes or changes occurring due to unpredicted events are communicated to management facilities by means of standardized protocols.

- Set and modify parameters related to network components and OSI layer software.

- Initialize and close down managed objects.

- Change the configuration.

- Associate names with objects and sets of objects.

Performance-management facilities provide the network manager with the ability to monitor and evaluate the performance of system and layer entities. Performance management provides procedures to:

- Collect and disseminate data concerning the current level of performance of resources
- Maintain and examine performance logs for such purposes as planning and analysis

Security-management facilities allow a network manager to manage those services that provide access protection of communications resources. Security management provides support for the management of:

- Authorization facilities
- Access control
- Encryption and key management
- Authentication
- Security logs

12.3   SYSTEMS-MANAGEMENT FUNCTIONS

A set of standards has been issued under the general category *systems-management functions* (SMF). Each SMF standard defines the functionality to support systems-management functional area (SMFA) requirements. A given SMF may support requirements in one or more of the five SMFAs; for example, the event-report-management function may be applicable to all SMFAs. Looked at the other way, each SMFA requires several SMFs.

Each of the SMF standards defines the functionality for the SMF and provides a mapping between the services provided by the SMF and CMIS. This relationship is depicted in Figure 12.7. In the remainder of this section, we summarize the SMFAs that are currently defined.

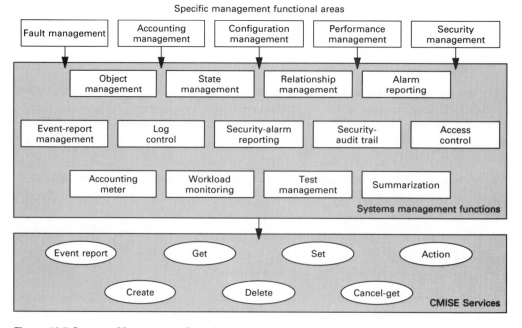

Figure 12.7 Systems Management Overview

12.3.1 Object-Management Function

Object management specifies how to create, delete, examine, and change the values of attributes of existing objects. It also specifies the notifications to be sent when the value of an attribute changes.

The object-management function is the most fundamental of all the systems-management functions. In essence, systems management deals with the management of managed objects. Each object represents some entity in the environment over which management control is desired. However, the actual mapping between real objects and their abstract representation as managed objects is beyond the scope of the standards. All that can be observed and controlled through systems management are the managed objects and their attributes.

Managed objects can be created and deleted, and the values of their attributes can be changed, in one of three distinct ways:

1. Through configuration processes in the local system environment that are outside the scope of OSI

2. Through (*N*)-layer operation or the (*N*)-layer management entity of an open system

3. Through the object-management function as part of the OSI systems-management services

The last method is dealt with in X.730/ISO 10164-1.

Table 12.4 lists the ten services provided by the object-management function. Six of these are referred to as pass-through services. These services do not require any independent functionality in the object-management-function module. Rather, requests from higher layers are simply mapped into requests to the common management information service (CMIS). The mapping is as follows:

Object-Management-Function-Service Primitive	**CMIS-Service Primitive**
PT-CREATE	M-CREATE
PT-DELETE	M-DELETE
PT-ACTION	M-ACTION
PT-SET	M-SET
PT-GET	M-GET
PT-EVENT-REPORT	M-EVENT-REPORT

The remaining four services may or may not involve the actions of CMIS. Each of these services involves notification to a higher layer of an event: object creation, object deletion, object-name change, or attribute-value change. Each primitive passes information that identifies the object and the change and indicates the source of the change. Possible sources of an event occurrence are:

- *Internal resource:* The event was effected through the internal operation of the resource that is represented by this managed object.

- *Local open system:* The event was effected by a create request from a higher layer that was initiated within the same open system.

- *Remote open system:* The event was effected by a create request from a higher layer that was initiated from another open system.

- *Unknown:* Cause of the event is unknown.

Table 12.4 Services Provided by the Object-Management Function

Direct Services	
Object-creation reporting	Allows an open system to keep other open systems aware of the creation of new managed objects, so that those other open systems can address and manage newly created objects
Object-deletion reporting	Allows an open system to keep other open systems aware of the deletion of existing managed objects, because those other open systems can no longer manage the deleted objects
Attribute-value-change reporting	Allows an open system to keep other open systems aware of changes in attributes of managed objects
Pass-Through Services	
PT-CREATE	Used to request that a peer service user create a new managed object, complete with its identification and the values of its associated management information, and simultaneously register its identification
PT-DELETE	Used to request that a peer service user delete a managed object and deregister its identification
PT-ACTION	Used to request that a peer service user perform an action on one or more managed objects
PT-SET	Used to request the modification of attribute values by a peer service user
PT-GET	Used to retrieve attribute values from a peer service user
PT-EVENT-REPORT	Used to report an event to a peer service user

12.3.2   State-Management Function

The state-management-function standard specifies a model for how the management state of an object is to be represented. The model allows the OSI management user to monitor the past state of managed objects and receive notices in response to changes in the state of managed objects. Services are defined for monitoring operability and usage of system resources and for administratively restricting their availability.

The management state of a managed object represents the instantaneous condition of availability and operability of the associated resource from the point of view of management. Different classes of managed objects may have different attributes that are relevant to the monitoring and operation of the associated resource. However, the management state is expected to be common to a large number of resources and has therefore been standardized in X.731/ISO 10164-2. The state-management function provides services for inquiring about and changing the management state and for reporting changes in management state that occur through some cause other than the state-management function.

Three state diagrams are defined in the standard, corresponding to the three primary factors that affect the management state of an object:

1. *Operability:* whether or not the resource is installed and operational
2. *Usage:* whether or not the resource is actively in use at a specific instant and, if so, whether or not it has spare capacity for additional users at that instant
3. *Administration:* whether or not an object may be used

   In each of these areas, there is a state attribute whose value is the current state of the object with respect to that area. For operability, the operational-state attribute takes on two values (Figure 12.8 part [a]): disabled and enabled. The state of the object is determined by the natural operation of the resource. Therefore, this attribute cannot be set by management but is read-only in nature.

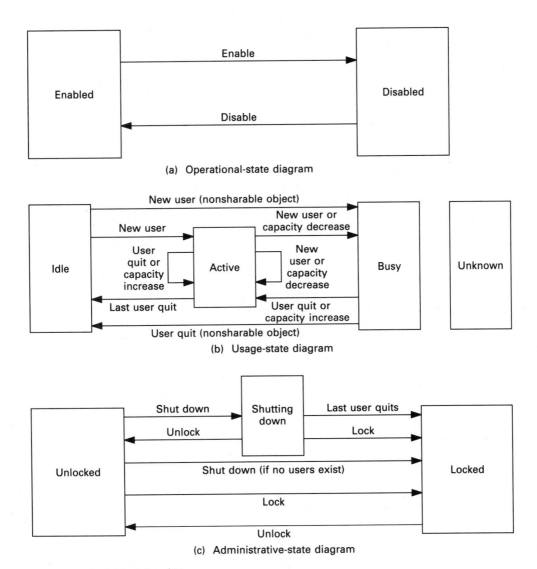

(a) Operational-state diagram

(b) Usage-state diagram

(c) Administrative-state diagram

Figure 12.8 Individual State Diagrams

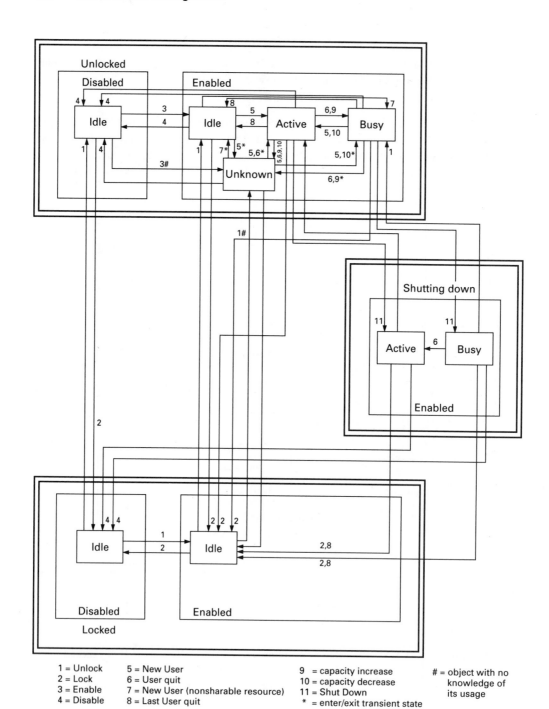

Figure 12.9 Combined State Diagram (IS 10164-2)

The usage-state attribute has four possible state values (Figure 12.8, part [b]): idle, active, busy, and unknown. A resource is said to be *in use* when it has received one or more requests for service that it has not yet completed or otherwise discharged or when some part of its capacity has been allocated, and not yet retrieved, as a result of a previous service request. Two states are needed to describe the concept of in use. If the object is in use but is able to accommodate one or more additional users, it is in the active state. If the object is in use and can accommodate no more additional users, then it is in the busy state. Thus, an object that can accommodate only one user does not exhibit the active state, and an object that can accommodate an unlimited number of users does not exhibit the busy state.

The usage-state diagram shows that the state of the object can change with the addition or deletion of a user and with a capacity increase or capacity decrease. As with the operational state, the usage state is determined by the operation of the resource, and therefore, the usage-state attribute is read-only.

The administrative-state attribute has three possible state values (Figure 12.8, part [c]): unlocked, locked, and shutting down. This state is under the control of management and allows a management user to lock or unlock access to a resource for purposes of enforcing a concurrency discipline. When a resource is locked, the resource is administratively prohibited from performing services for its users. If the resource can be locked gracefully, then locking involves the act of shutting down. When the shutting-down service is invoked, the resource will only be locked if there are no current users. If there is one or more current users, the resource enters the shutting-down state, which denies access to new users. As soon as the last user quits, the object's state becomes locked. If the resource can only be locked abruptly, then there is no shutting-down state.

Figure 12.9 is a combined state diagram, indicating the relationships among the various states.

12.3.3 Attributes for Representing Relationships

X.732/ISO 10164-1 models and identifies types of relationships that can exist among managed objects representing different parts of a system. Services are defined for establishing, examining, and monitoring the relationships among objects and therefore for observing how the operation of one part of a system depends on other parts.

In general, a relationship is a set of rules that describes how the operation of one managed object affects the operation of another managed object. For example, two managed objects may have a relationship in which one is activated in the event that the other fails as a result of a fault-management diagnostic.

12.3.3.1 Relationship Model

Figure 12.10 illustrates several concepts of the relationship model. A direct relationship exists between two objects if some portion of the management information associated with one managed object explicitly identifies the other managed object. An indirect relationship exists if the relationship can be deduced from the concatenation of two or more direct relationships.

Three categories of relationships are recognized by OSI management:

1. *Containment relationship:* This is a structuring relationship in which the existence of a managed object is dependent on the existence of a containing managed object.

2. *Reciprocal relationship:* This is a binding relationship between two objects that is represented by including, as one of a set of values of an attribute of each of the objects, the name of the other object.

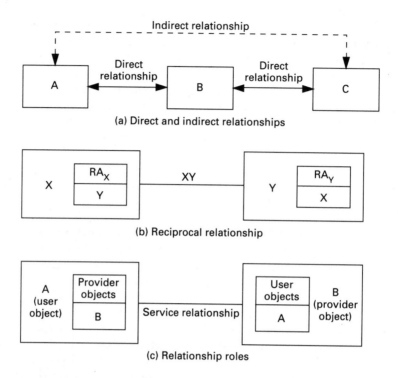

(a) Direct and indirect relationships

(b) Reciprocal relationship

(c) Relationship roles

Figure 12.10 Model for Relationship Attributes

3. *One-way relationship:* This is an asymmetric relationship between two objects in which the relationship is expressed in the value of the relationship attribute of only one member of the pair.

Relationships are defined by relationship attributes. For each particular type of relationship, called a *role,* there is a separate relationship attribute. A managed object may have multiple instances of any particular type of relationship. A relationship attribute is a set-valued attribute whose values are the names of other managed objects with which an object has a relationship. The use of sets supports one-to-one, one-to-many, many-to-one, and many-to-many relationships.

Figure 12.10, part (b), illustrates a reciprocal one-to-one relationship. The two objects, X and Y, have a direct reciprocal relationship XY that is expressed by the existence of the name of object Y as a value of X's relationship attribute RA_X and by the existence of the name of object X as a value of Y's relationship attribute RA_Y.

12.3.3.2 Relationship Type

The relationship type, which is implied by the name of the relationship attribute, describes the nature of the relationship between two or more objects. The relationship role describes the part played by each object that is in a particular relationship type. The following list describes relationship types and their corresponding relationship roles:

- *Service relationship:* This is an asymmetric relationship in which one of a pair of objects has the provider role and the other has the user role (Figure 12.10, part [c]).

- *Peer relationship:* This is a symmetric relationship between peers.

- *Fallback relationship:* This is an asymmetric relationship denoting that the second of a pair of managed objects (secondary role) is capable of service as a fallback, or "next preferred choice," to the first managed object (primary role).

- *Backup relationship:* This is an asymmetric relationship in which the object in the backup role is providing backup to the object in the backed-up role. The backed-up object is in the disabled state, defined earlier.

- *Group relationship:* This is a relationship between two objects in which one object (the member role) belongs to a group represented by the other object (the owner role).

12.3.4   Alarm-Reporting Function

X.733/ISO 10164-4 models alarm reporting. It specifies generic alarm notifications (events), together with their parameters and semantics. These notifications are associated primarily with fault management. The information provided includes error types, probable causes, and measures of severity. This type of functionality is essential in an environment with multiple open systems and multiple networks, where there is a requirement to locate the source of a fault.

Alarms are specific types of notifications concerning detected faults or abnormal conditions. The standard does not dictate the information that must be included in the alarm. Rather, the managed-object designer is encouraged to include in alarms information that will help with understanding the cause of the potentially abnormal situation and information related to side effects. An example of such diagnostic information is the current and past values of the configuration-management state of the object. The standard does provide a common set of notification types, with standardized parameters and parameter definitions, independent of particular managed objects (Table 12.5). These elements are available to the managed-object designer but may be supplemented by object-specific information.

Five basic categories of alarm are defined:

1. *Communications:* principally associated with the procedures and/or processes required to convey information from one point to another

2. *Quality of service:* principally associated with degradation in the quality of service

3. *Processing:* principally associated with a software or processing fault

4. *Equipment:* principally associated with an equipment fault

5. *Environmental:* principally associated with a condition relating to an enclosure in which the equipment resides

Error-reporting services for each type of error are defined in this SMF.

The ability to categorize alarms by severity helps the network manager decide quickly which alarms require an immediate response and which ones can wait. In order of decreasing severity, six levels are defined:

1. *Critical:* indicates that a service-affecting condition has occurred and an immediate corrective action is required. An example of this condition is when a resource defined by a managed object has gone out of service and that resource is required.

Table 12.5 Information Provided by the Alarm-Reporting Function

Alarm Type	Probable Cause		Perceived Severity
Communications	Loss of signal	Processor problem	Critical
Quality of service	Framing error	Terminal problem	Major
Processing	Local transmission error	External-interface-device	Minor
Equipment	Remote transmission error	problem	Warning
Enviromental	Call-establishment error	Dataset problem	Indeterminate
	Degraded signal	Multiplexor problem	Cleared
	Response time excessive	Receiver failure	
	Queue size excessive	Transmitter failure	
	Bandwidth reduced	Smoke detection	
	Retransmission rate excessive	Enclosure door open	
	Threshold crossed	High/flow ambient temperature	
	Storage-capacity problem	High/low humidity	
	Version mismatch	Intrusion detection	
	Corrupt data	Heating/cooling-system failure	
	CPU-cycles limit exceeded	Ventilation-system failure	
	Software error	Fire	
	Out of memory	Flood	
	Underlying resource	Toxic gas	
	unavailable	High/low pressure	
	Power problem	Air-compressor failure	
	Timing problem	Pump failure	
	Trunk-card problem	Engine failure	
	Line-card problem	Fuel problem	

2. *Major:* indicates that a service-affecting condition has developed and an urgent corrective action is required. An example of this condition is when a severe degradation in the capability of an object has occurred and the object needs to be restored to full capability.

3. *Minor:* indicates that a non–service-affecting fault condition has developed and corrective action should be taken in order to prevent a more serious fault.

4. *Warning:* indicates the detection of a potential or an impending service-affecting fault, before any significant effects have been felt. Action should be taken to further diagnose (if necessary) and correct the problem in order to prevent it from becoming a more serious service-affecting fault.

5. *Indeterminate:* indicates that the severity level of the service-affecting condition cannot be determined.

6. *Cleared:* indicates the clearing of one or more previously reported alarms. This alarm clears all alarms for this managed object that have the same alarm type, probable cause, and specific problems (if given).

12.3.5 Event-Report-Management Function

X.734/ISO 10164-5 provides a model for the control of event reporting. It specifies means for controlling the selection and distribution of events to manager-specifiable destinations. It specifies an event-forwarding discriminator managed object that defines manager-creatable/selectable criteria by which managed-object notification may be conveyed remotely as event reports, as well as time periods during which such event-forwarding discrimination can occur.

This function can play a key role in controlling the flow of management information. It is particularly important in WAN environments that have a limited bandwidth and in other real-time or bandwidth-constrained environments. As an example of its use, the network manager can specify which information can be exchanged between a managing process and individual agent processes (Figure 12.5).

The standard lists the following requirements that must be met by the event-report-management function:

- The definition of a flexible event-report-control service that will allow systems to select which event reports are to be sent to a particular managing system.
- Specification of the destination (e.g., the identities of managing systems) to which event reports are to be sent. One such possible destination is the local system.
- Specification of a mechanism to control the forwarding of event reports; for example, by suspending and resuming their forwarding.
- The ability for an external managing system to modify the conditions used in the reporting of events.
- The ability to designate a backup location to which event reports can be sent if the primary location is not available.

Figure 12.11 illustrates the event-report-management model, which describes the conceptual components that provide for remote event-reporting and local processing of potential events and describes the message flows for the control messages, event reporting messages, and retrieval messages. Notifications are issued by managed objects when events occur. Each notification triggers an event detection and processing function, which triggers a potential-event report. This report is distributed to event-forwarding discriminators within the local system. The discriminator determines which event reports are to be forwarded to a particular destination, following a particular time schedule. The discriminator contains a discriminator construct that specifies the characteristics a potential-event report must satisfy to be eligible for forwarding; this is, in effect, a filtering function. It also contains a scheduling capability that determines the intervals during which event reports will be selected for forwarding.

Event-report discriminators are managed objects and, like other managed objects, have states and attributes. Event-report management provides a service for reading and modifying the attributes of event-forwarding discriminators. Thus, event-report discrimination can be initiated, terminated, suspended, and resumed. The specific scheduling and filtering information can be read and modified. Event reports may be directed to the local system, the requesting system, or a third system.

The discriminator construct consists of a Boolean expression that defines the event or events to be reported. Tests on the following attributes of a potential-event report may be specified:

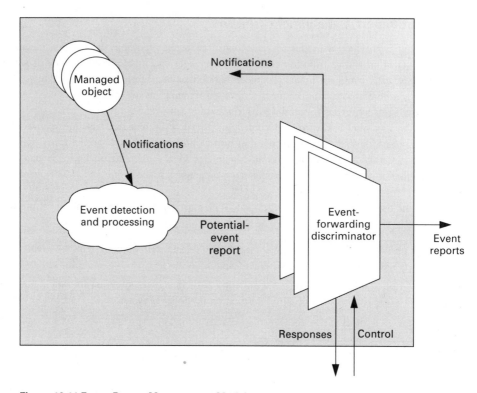

Figure 12.11 Event-Report-Management Model

- Managed-object class
- Managed-object instance
- Event type
- Event-type–specific attributes; e.g., for fault-related events, such attributes as severity, backed up-status, probable cause

The scheduling attributes include the following:

- *Start time:* defines the date and time at which the discriminator enters the phase of periodic behavior.

- *Stop time:* defines the date and time at which the discriminator stops exhibiting periodic behavior. If scheduling attributes are present, event reports are only issued between the start and stop times while the discriminator is unlocked.

- *Week mask:* This defaults to "always on." Otherwise, the week mask specifies the days of the week when the discriminator is active and a list of time intervals during the day when the discriminator is active.

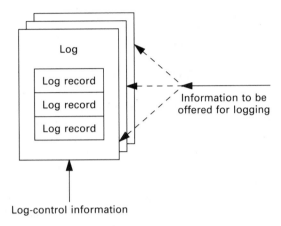

Figure 12.12 Log-Control Model

12.3.6   Log-Control Function

X.735/ISO 10164-6 specifies a model for how event logs can be controlled. A filter can be defined that specifies the events that are to be placed in the log. As with the event-report-management function, the log-control function provides for logging according to manager-settable schedules and manager-creatable logging criteria.

Figure 12.12 depicts a model of the log-control function. Each log consists of a set of records, one for each event logged. Information to be logged is derived from received event reports provided by the event-report function, incoming CMIP PDUs, and internal events. Records in a log are stored in order of arrival, and record identifiers are assigned in numerical sequence.

Each log is a managed object. Table 12.6 lists the attributes of the log object class. The key attributes that dictate the operation of the log are the scheduling information and the discriminator construct. The scheduling information dictates when the log is available to add new records. When information is presented for logging during the time when the log is available, a new record is added only if the information passes the discriminator-construct test.

To accommodate various levels of complexity in scheduling logging activity periods, three conditional packages[1] related to scheduling are defined for logging:

1. *Daily:* provides the capability of scheduling logging with a periodicity of 24 hours. The schedule either indicates that the logging function is on the entire day or lists the start and stop times of the intervals during the day when the logging function is on.

2. *Weekly:* provides the capability of scheduling logging with a periodicity of one week. The schedule specifies particular intervals of time on particular days when the logging function is on.

---

1.   A package is a collection of optional attributes, notifications, operations, and behavior that can be associated with a managed object. Packages are discussed in the next section.

Table 12.6 Log Object-Class Attributes

Attribute	Description
Log ID	Used to uniquely identify an instance of a log.
State	The administrative, operational, and usage states of the log.
Scheduling information	A description of the time during which logging is active.
Discriminator construct	A description of the type of information to be logged.
Maximum log size	The maximum size of the log in octets. When this attribute is set to 0, the log size is indeterminate.
Current log size	The current size of the log in octets.
Number of records	The number of records currently in the log.
Log-full action	The behavior of the log when its maximum capacity is reached. Options are: wrap—the earliest set of records in the log will be deleted to make room for new records, and halt—no more records will be logged.
Capacity-alarm threshold	Defined as percentages of the maximum log size. Used to generate events that will indicate that various levels of the log-full condition have been approached.
Notifications	Generated when the log is created, deleted, suspended, resumed, and modified.

3. *External scheduler:* provides the capability of scheduling logging based on a schedule defined in an external-scheduler-managed object. The logging function is controlled by messages exchanged between the scheduler-managed object and log-management objects.

12.3.7 Security-Alarm-Reporting Function

X.736/ISO 10164-7 models reporting of security-related events and misoperations in security services and mechanisms. It specifies generic security-alarm notifications, together with their parameters and semantics. It provides services for creating, deleting, and modifying event-forwarding discriminators for controlling the selection and distribution of security alarms to manager-specifiable destinations.

Security-related events are selected by an event-forwarding discriminator that sends them to a requesting security-management user through the use of the CMIS M-EVENT-REPORT service. These events, known as security alarms, carry a standard set of information as presented by the affected managed object.

Five types of security alarms are supported:

1. *Integrity violation:* an indication that a potential interruption in information flow has occurred, such that information may have been illegally modified, inserted, or deleted

2. *Operational violation:* an indication that the requested service could not be provided due to the unavailability, malfunction, or incorrect invocation of the service

3. *Physical violation:* an indication that a breach of the physical resource has been detected

Table 12.7 Security-Alarm Types and Causes

Security-Alarm Type	Security-Alarm Causes
Integrity violation	Duplicate information
	Information missing
	Information modification detected
	Information out of sequence
	Unexpected information
Operational violation	Denial of service
	Out of service
	Procedural error
	Other reason
Physical violation	Cable tamper
	Intrusion detection
	Other reason
Security service or mechanism violation	Authentication failure
	Breach of confidentiality
	Unauthorized access attempt
	Other reason
Time-domain violation	Delayed information
	Key expired
	Out-of-hours activity

4. *Security service or mechanism violation:* an indication that a security attack has been detected by a security service or mechanism

5. *Time-domain violation:* an indication that an event has occurred outside the permitted time period

Table 12.7 lists possible causes that have been defined for each security-alarm type. Additional values may be specified.

A security alarm is issued as a security-alarm-report record, which is a managed object. Each such object contains the following attributes:

- *Object class:* identifies the type of managed object

- *Object instance:* identifier for this particular managed object

- *Security-alarm type:* indicates one of the five types of security alarms

- *Event time:* time of the event that triggered the security alarm

- *Security-alarm cause:* indicates one of the causes defined for this alarm type

- *Security-alarm severity:* indicates critical, major, minor, warning, cleared, or indeterminate

- *Service user:* identity of the service user whose request for service led to the generation of the security alarm

- *Service provider:* identity of the intended provider of the service that led to the generation of the security alarm

- *Notification identifier:* identifies this notification
- *Correlated notifications:* lists other notifications that are associated with this notification
- *Security-alarm text:* allows a free-form text description relevant to the security alarm
- *Security-alarm data:* allows for the inclusion of additional information relevant to the security alarm

12.3.8   Security-Audit-Trail Function

X.740/ISO 10164-8 specifies the kinds of event reports that should be contained in a log that is to be used for evaluating the security of an open system as well as the performance of security mechanisms. Security-audit trails can be used to look for security attacks that are not detectable as they occur. This function is an extension of the log-control function.

12.3.9   Objects and Attributes for Access Control

X.741/ISO 10164-9 specifies a model for controlling access to management information and operations. It specifies managed objects and attributes to be used to grant or deny access according to the access-control policy represented by this access-control-management information.

Various levels of access control may be required. Some users may be given read and write access to specific attributes, whereas other users may have only read access or no access. Access control must prevent management notifications from being sent to unauthorized recipients, prevent unauthorized initiators from gaining access to management operations, and protect management information from unauthorized disclosure.

Figure 12.13 depicts the access-control model. A request for access to an object is validated by an access-control function that may grant or deny access according to the access-control policy that is represented by the access-control object associated with the object. Figure 12.13, part (a), shows the access-control aspects of establishing a management association, which is a logical connection at the application level. The association process passes the request to the access-control-enforcement function, which, in turn, passes the access-control information (ACI) to the access-control-decision function. The ADF compares the initiator ACI to ACI related to the target and examines contextual information (address of the requester time of day, etc.) and the relevant access-control-policy rules. The access decision is sent back to the AEF. If the decision is to grant access, the ACI is retained for future decisions.

Figure 12.13, part (b), provides an example of the access-control aspects of management operations. A request for access to a managed object triggered by a CMIP action results in a management request to the AEF. The AEF passes the required information to the ADF to enable it to make a decision: the ACI of the initiator, the management operation (action, create, delete, get, or set), ACI related to the data, and the identification of the target (object class and instance, action identifier, attribute identifiers). To make a decision, the ADF examines the retained ACI for the association that generated the request, as well as target ACI, contextual information, and access-control-policy rules. If permission is granted, the AEF allows the management request to be presented to the managed object.

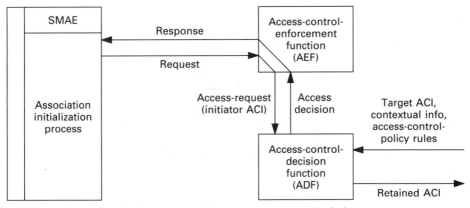

(a) Access control for a management association

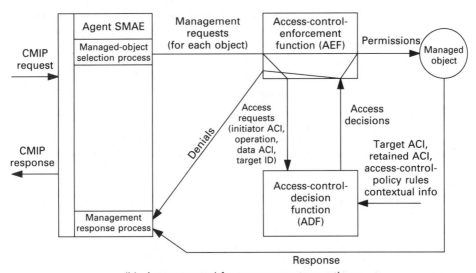

(b) Access control for management operations

Figure 12.13 Access-Control Model

12.3.10   Accounting-Meter Function

X.742/ISO 10164-10 specifies a model for accounting for the usage of system resources and a mechanism for enforcing account limits. The standard defines account meters and logs and specifies services for retrieving, reporting, and recording resource-usage data and for selecting which usage data are to be collected and under what conditions they are to be reported.

Table 12.8 lists the terminology employed in the standard. An accounting meter is an abstraction that represents the accounting-management function. There are two aspects to this function:

Table 12.8 Accounting-Meter-Function Terminology

Term	Definition
Accounting meter	The abstraction of activities, monitoring the utilization of resources, for the purpose of accounting and controlling the recording of accounting data
Accounting-meter control	Accounting-meter functionality dedicated to controlling the activities of gathering and providing data concerning the utilization of resources
Accounting-meter-control object	A managed object dedicated to the control of accounting management
Accounting-meter data	Data that account for the use of a resource and from which accounting records may be derived
Accounting-meter-data object	A managed object dedicated to the provision of management data
Accounting-record object	A data item containing accounting information relating to a specific period of resource utilization by a specific user

1. Control of the reporting of data associated with the usage of a resource
2. The specifics of the recorded data

To provide visibility of both aspects, three types of management objects are defined: accounting-meter-control object, accounting-meter-data object, and accounting-record object.

12.3.10.1 Accounting-Meter-Control Object

The accounting-meter-control object specifies the rules for the collection of accounting data as they relate to specific resources and their utilization. Accounting-management control allows a managing system to:

- Collect resource-usage data from a resource, as well as enable and disable the collection through operations upon an accounting-meter-control object

- Select, within the constraints imposed by a particular managed-object class, which resource-usage data are to be collected and under what circumstances they are to be reported

In order to collect resource-utilization data for a managed object or a set of managed objects, an accounting-meter-control object that specifies such collection must exist. The accounting-meter-control object can be generated as part of the creation of the resource-object instance, or it can be generated later, in response to a management request for the accounting function.

The attributes of an accounting-meter-control object are:

- *Units of usage:* specify the type of accounting unit being used. Possible units include SDUs, PDUs, seconds, minutes, bits, octets, characters, and blocks.

- *Recording triggers:* specify occurrences causing an update to the accounting-meter data. Events may be of three types: periodically scheduled, induced as a result of accounting-meter actions (e.g., upon the resumption of accounting for usage), and induced by an identified stimulus (e.g., completion of a service request).

- *Reporting triggers:* specify occurrences causing the accounting-meter-data object to emit an accounting-record notification.

- *Data-object reference:* specifies the set of related instances of accounting-meter data that are subject to accounting-meter control.

- *Resource name:* identifies the metered OSI resource.

12.3.10.2   Accounting-Meter-Data Object

Resource-usage data represent the use made of a resource by a user of that resource. An accounting-meter-data object contains information identifying the user of the resource and a measure of the quantity used, together with qualifying data.

The attributes of an accounting-meter-data object are:

- *Requester ID:* indicates the user of the service provided.

- *Responder ID:* indicates the service that provided the service used.

- *Subscriber ID:* indicates the subscriber having a contract with the authority providing the resource that is subject to accounting metering on behalf of the identified requester.

- *Meter info:* provides accounting data relating to the specific usage of a resource. Its parameters are: unit, which defines the class of unit used to measure usage; usage, which is the amount of units used; and tariff, which defines tariff-related information.

- *Service requested:* identifies the usage kind or quality of service required by the user of the resource being metered.

- *Service provided:* identifies the usage kind or quality of service provided.

- *Usage start time:* the time at which accounting started.

- *Usage meter time:* indicates whether the time is the current time (metering is still taking place) or the time at which metering was stopped.

- *Data-object state:* running or suspended.

- *Control-object reference:* identifies the accounting-meter-control object that controls this accounting-meter-data object.

- *Resource name:* identity of the metered OSI resource.

12.3.10.3   Accounting-Record Object

The data contained in accounting records may be derived either as a result of reading accounting data from an accounting-meter-data object or as a result of notifications generated by instances of accounting-meter data. They are logged according to the discriminator construct used by a log that contains accounting records.

12.3.11   Workload-Monitoring Function

X.739/ISO 10164-11 specifies a model for monitoring the attributes of managed objects. It defines managed objects that can report events based on the values of counters and gauges that reflect system performance. Service are provided for initiating, terminating, suspending, resuming, and modifying workload monitoring. A key use of workload monitoring is to recognize potential resource overload situations, which is an important fault-prevention function.

Table 12.9 lists the terminology employed in the standard. A key concept is that of capacity, which is the amount of a resource that can be supplied to users, consisting of already-allocated

Table 12.9 Workload-Monitoring-Function Terminology

Term	Definition
Capacity	Current amount of resources available to serve users, including resources already allocated for use as well as resources available for future allocation.
Resource utilization	The amount of capacity in use. It can be measured as instantaneous (amount in use at a point in time) or an estimate of the mean (mean resource utilization calculated over a period of time).
Resource-rejection rate	An estimate of the mean amount of service requests rejected per unit of time, calculated over a period of time.
Resource-request rate	An estimate of the mean amount of service requests per unit of time, calculated over a period of time.
Severe threshold	Indicates that a gauge value is close to or at capacity (for resource utilization) or that the maximum acceptable rate (for rejection rate or request rate) has been met or exceeded.
Severe-clear threshold	Indicates that the severe condition has cleared.
Early-warning threshold	Indicates that a gauge value is approaching capacity (for resource utilization) or the maximum rate (for rejection rate or request rate).
Early-warning-clear threshold	Indicates that the early-warning condition has cleared.
Gauge	An attribute whose value represents a dynamic variable in the system. The value of the gauge may be incremented or decremented. Changes that would take the gauge beyond its maximum or minimum leave the gauge value at its maximum or minimum, respectively.
Counter	An attribute whose integer value is associated with some internal event. The value is incremented by 1 when the event occurs. When it reaches its maximum value, it wraps around to 0.
Metric object	A managed object that contains at least one attribute whose value is calculated from the values of attributes observed in other managed objects.
Gauge-monitor metric object	Used for generating notifications based on the thresholds of a gauge for resource utilization, rejection rate, or request rate.
Mean-monitor metric object	Used for generating notifications related to a time-averaged value of the resource utilization, rejection rate, or request rate.

capacity and available capacity. The systems manager is concerned with monitoring the level of demand on the capacity of various resources. To support this requirement, the workload-monitoring function provides a service that can be characterized along several dimensions:

- *Resource-usage model:* resource utilization, resource-rejection rate, and resource-request rate
- *Managed-object attribute:* settable counter, nonsettable counter, and gauge
- *Metric object:* gauge-monitor metric object and mean-monitor metric object

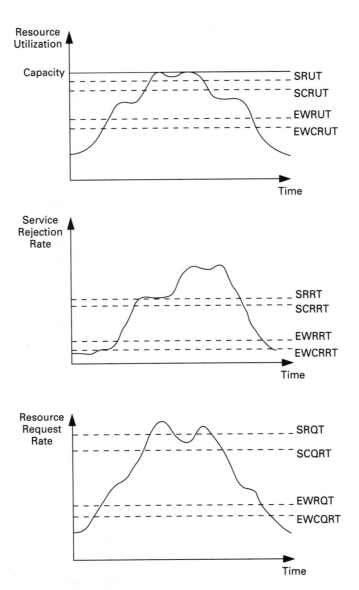

Figure 12.14 Resource Utilization, Service Rejection, and Resource-Request Rate (IS 10164-11)

Three models are defined to fulfill resource-usage-monitoring requirements. *Resource utilization* provides for monitoring the current demand on capacity. The *resource-rejection rate* is a measure of the rate at which resource requests are rejected due to overload. The *resource-request rate* is a measure of the demand on the resource. The workload-monitoring function enables managers to use one or more of these models to meet their requirements. If more than one model is used in monitoring a single resource, there is a relationship among the parameters measured. Figure 12.14 suggests the relationship between the three concepts for the same hypothetical resource.

Another dimension of the workload-monitoring function has to do with the nature of the attribute that reflects the performance of a resource. A *counter* is a management abstraction of an underlying counting process. Two types of counters are modeled to meet different needs. A nonsettable (simple) counter is not subject to change by management operation. It simply counts from 0 to some maximum value and then wraps around and begins again at 0. A settable counter exhibits the same behavior as a simple counter, but in addition, its value may be reset by management action. This allows management to reinitialize some resource and begin counting again from 0. Table 12.10 lists some examples of counters suggested in the ISO documents.

Table 12.10 Suggested Counter Types (X.721/DIS 10165-2)

Counter Type	Definition
Corrupted PDUs received	The total number of corrupted PDUs received
Incoming connection reject error	The total number of incoming connection requests that were received by the managed object but rejected due to protocol errors
Incoming connection requests	The total number of incoming connection requests
Incoming disconnect	The total number of incoming disconnect requests
Incoming disconnect error	The total number of incoming disconnect requests received by the managed object due to protocol errors
Incoming protocol error	The total number of error-report or reset PDUs that were received by the managed object due to protocol errors
Octets received	The total number of user data octets received
Octets retransmitted error	The total number of octets retransmitted
Octets sent	The total number of user data octets sent
Outgoing connection reject error	The total number of outgoing connection requests that were sent by the managed object but rejected due to protocol errors
Outgoing connection requests	The total number of outgoing connection requests
Outgoing disconnect	The total number of outgoing disconnect requests
Outgoing disconnect error	The total number of outgoing disconnect requests sent by the managed object due to protocol errors
Outgoing protocol error	The total number of error-report or reset PDUs that were sent by the managed object due to protocol errors
PDUs received	The total number of PDUs received
PDUs retransmitted error	The total number of PDUs retransmitted
PDUs sent	The total number of PDUs sent

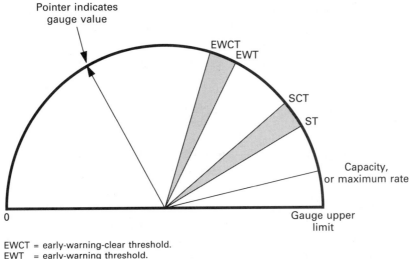

Pointer indicates
gauge value

EWCT
EWT
SCT
ST

Capacity,
or maximum rate

0

Gauge upper
limit

EWCT = early-warning-clear threshold.
EWT = early-warning threshold.
SCT = severe-clear threshold.
ST   = severe threshold.

Figure 12.15 Gauge Model

A *gauge* is a management abstraction of an underlying dynamic variable. Examples are the number of logical connections currently operated by a protocol machine or the rate of change of a traffic counter. As the dynamic variable changes, the gauge value increases and decreases.

12.3.11.1 Gauge-Monitor Metric Object

Two types of managed objects can be used for workload monitoring: the gauge-monitor metric object and the mean-monitor metric object. Each object can monitor any of the three performance-related resource attributes (simple counter, settable counter, gauge) and can support any of the three performance models (resource utilization, resource-rejection rate, resource-request rate).

A generic model of a gauge used for workload monitoring is illustrated in Figure 12.15. The gauge can theoretically take on any value between 0 and the upper limit of the gauge variable. For a specific resource attribute, the maximum value it can take on is the capacity of the resource. Associated with the gauge metric object are several pairs of thresholds, which are used to trigger notifications. The severe threshold indicates that the resource being monitored is at or near capacity; this might trigger some urgent action. The early-warning threshold indicates that the resource being monitored is approaching capacity; this might trigger some countermeasure to avoid saturation.

Two types of notification are associated with each threshold. When the threshold is reached or crossed in the positive direction, a notification that the condition exists is sent out. When the threshold is reached or crossed in the negative direction, a notification that the condition has cleared is sent out. To avoid the repeated triggering of event notifications when the gauge makes small oscillations around a threshold value, the threshold is specified in pairs: the higher value is used to trigger the positive-direction event, and the lower value is used to trigger the negative-direction event. Figure 12.14 illustrates the use of these thresholds for the three monitoring models.

The workload gauge is derived from the managed-object attribute according to the following rules:

- If the attribute is a gauge, then the workload gauge takes on the same value as the attribute.

- If the attribute is a simple counter, the gauge value is the difference between successive observations of the counter.

- If the attribute is a settable counter, the gauge value is the value of the counter just prior to its last reset.

For the simple counter, the gauge-value calculation must take into account the wrap-around feature of counters. Thus, the gauge value is defined as follows:

$$V(t) = [\text{counter}(t) - \text{counter}(t - DT) + CWV] \text{ modulo } CWV$$

where

$V(t)$	= gauge value
counter(t)	= value of the counter at current time t
counter(t $- DT$)	= previous value of the counter, at time $(t - DT)$
DT	= sampling interval
CWV	= modulus of the counter

12.3.11.2   Mean-Monitor Metric Object

The mean monitor metric object may be used for generating notification related to a time-averaged value of the resource utilization. As with the gauge monitor, the mean monitor derives a value from a counter or gauge using the rules outlined in the preceding subsection. The difference here is that this derived value is then used as input to a calculation for estimating a mean value. Again, thresholds are used to trigger notifications.

12.3.12   Test-Management Function

ISO 10164-12 specifies a model for managing confidence and diagnostic test procedures. It defines managed-object classes that are used to control the tests, which may be conducted either interactively or asynchronously, with results to be reported later.

The test-management function provides options for testing along several dimensions:

- Synchronous versus asynchronous test

- Solicited versus unsolicited report

- Implicit versus explicit termination

12.3.12.1   Test Model

Figure 12.16, part (a), gives a general model of the test-management function. The managing open system initiates a test on a remote open system by means of an exchange between application processes. An application process in the managing system, the test conductor, issues a test request to an application process in the managed system, the test performer. Each test involves some action on the managed system, making use of managed objects. In general, a configuration must be set up and a test workload processed. There may also be a need to indicate the scheduling of the test and the reporting of results. The test request may provoke a response, which either includes the

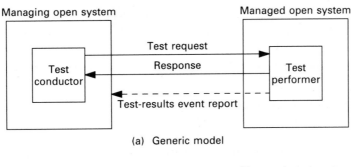

(a) Generic model

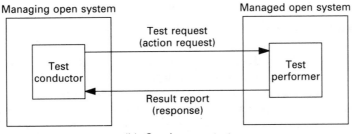

(b) Synchronous test

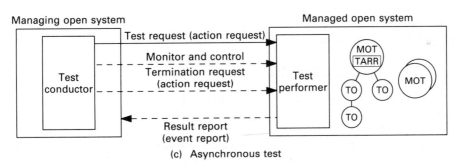

(c) Asynchronous test

Figure 12.16 Test-Management-Function Model

test results or simply acknowledges agreement to perform the test. In the later case, the test results may be issued at a later time in the form of an event report.

Tests may be defined as being synchronous or asynchronous. In a synchronous test (Figure 12.16, part [b]), the final results of the test are returned in the response to the test-initiation operation.

An asynchronous test is one in which the final results of the test are to be made available by some further management operation or via notification. Figure 12.16, part (c), illustrates an asynchronous test and indicates the key elements of the asynchronous-test model:

- *Test-action-request receiver (TARR):* refers to the ability of a managed object to act upon a test request. A managed object with TARR functionality may create an instance of a particular test-object class, representing a particular test invocation.

- *Test object (TO):* object required for the control and monitoring of tests and for the emission of notifications pertaining to tests. The TO holds state information and may hold intermediate and unreported test results.

- *Managed object under test (MOT):* an object that provides a management view of the subjects of tests.

12.3.12.2   Reporting of Test Results

For a synchronous test, the results of the test are reported in the confirmation to the test request. For an asynchronous test, the results may be reported in a solicited or an unsolicited manner. A solicited test result is reported when the test conductor issues a report request to a test object. An unsolicited test result is issued by a test object as a notification.

12.3.12.3   Test Termination

A test may be terminated in one of two ways: implicit and explicit. An explicit test termination occurs when the test conductor requests termination; this occurs for asynchronous tests. The termination may occur whether or not the test is completed. Upon receipt of a test-termination request, the test performer shall terminate the test in progress, perform any necessary cleanup, return available results in test-result reports, and acknowledge the termination request. A test conductor may also request an abnormal, or aborted, test termination by requesting deletion of the test objects participating in the test. In this case, the test performer terminates the test without issuing any additional test-result reports.

Implicit, or spontaneous, termination occurs in synchronous tests upon the fulfillment of predefined criteria, including completion of the test and error conditions.

12.3.13   Summarization Function

ISO 10164-13 defines a model and managed-object classes used to summarize and apply statistical analysis to management information. The summarization of values of attributes includes specific object instances across time (time averages) and a set of object instances at a particular time (ensemble averages). Services include specifying management objects and attributes that are to be included in summary reports, scheduling of observations upon these objects and attributes, and scheduling of summary reports.

The summarization function involves extracting information from managed objects and placing it in a summarization object. Information may be obtained from the attributes of managed objects representing underlying resources, metric objects, and log records. The summarization object specifies an algorithm to be used to calculate summary information from the observed attributes. Figure 12.17 depicts the summarization function.

All summarization functions are based on the concept of a scanner. Scanning is a sampling process of observing attribute values at specified points in time. A summarization object may be defined as one of three types of scanners:

1. *Homogeneous scanner:* scans a common set of attribute types across a selected set of object instances to calculate ensemble and time statistics

2. *Heterogeneous scanner:* collects statistics from a set of different attributes collected from different managed objects

3. *Heterogeneous buffered scanner:* the same as a heterogeneous scanner but includes the ability to buffer results so that the results of multiple periods can be reported together

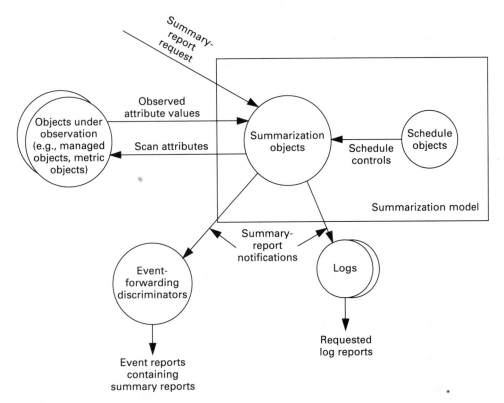

Figure 12.17 Summarization Function

12.3.14 Accounting Management

SC21 N 4971 is a working document that summarizes the accounting-management functional area. Accounting is provided by procedures that:

- Account for usage of resources
- Limit local use of a resource
- Control a user's use for all resources of a given type
- Maintain and report accounting records and accounting logs covering many instances of resource usage

  Figure 12.18 illustrates the key elements of accounting management:

- *Accounting meter:* accounts for the use of all resources.
- *User:* individual who consumes resources.
- *Subscriber:* represents the user of the resources, who may require information concerning the utilization of the communication service and who may be subject to accounting control.
- *Accounting-management activity:* controls the accounting information, generates accounting records, and may provide both accounting information for the current instances of resource utilization and historical accounting records.

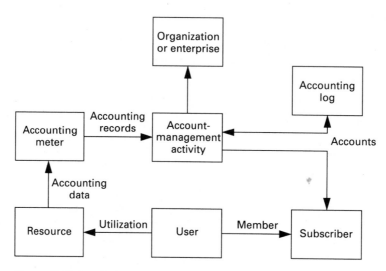

Figure 12.18 Accounting-Activity Model

- *Accounting logs:* maintained by a log-management activity and supplied with data by the accounting-management activity. Data, in the form of accounting records, may be retrieved from a log.

12.3.15 · Performance Management

SCX21 N 4981 is a working document that summarizes the performance-management functional area. The task of performance management is to monitor and control system performance, to provide statistical data concerning performance measurements and the definition of such statistical data. From the enduser's viewpoint, the output of performance management deals with reporting the quality of service, reflected by such measures as response time, rejection rates, and availability. From the system manager's viewpoint, performance management should provide:

- Information needed to determine how well actual performance compares with planned performance
- Information needed to determine how well user requirements are being met
- Guidance for improving system performance
- Tools for improving system performance

Thus, performance management is concerned with monitoring, analysis, and control. At this point, analysis is not a subject of OSI standardization. The OSI performance management standard deals with specifying the functions for monitoring system performance and the tools for setting and modifying performance-related parameters (e.g., threshold values).

Examples of questions that a system manager may wish to ask include:

- Is the system providing a required throughput?
- Is the system approaching an overload condition?

- Is adequate response time being provided?
- Is efficient use of communications resources being achieved?

Figure 12.19 provides a general model of the performance-management (PM) function. Key elements include:

- *Measurement points:* either passive points of observation, which are attributes of managed objects whose value may be solicited by performance management, or associated with a threshold mechanism that generates an event report

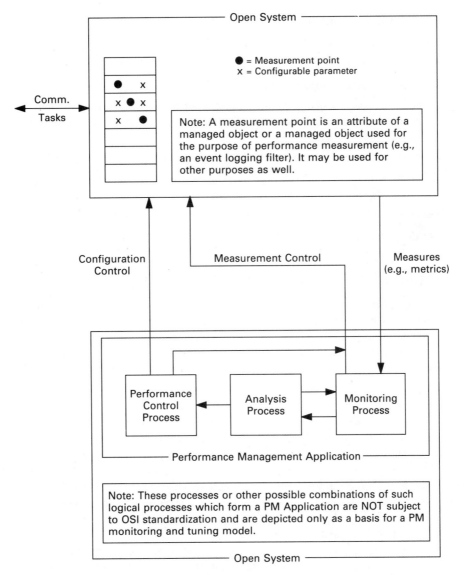

Figure 12.19 Performance-Management Monitoring and Tuning Model (SC 21 N 6306)

- *Configurable parameters:* settable attributes of managed objects, such as timers and threshold values, that may be set to adjust the configuration for performance-tuning purposes

- *Monitoring process:* collects measures from the open system under observation and modifies parameters associated with the monitoring process (e.g., schedules of data collection)

- *Analysis process:* analyzes data collected by the monitoring process and presents the results to both the monitoring process and the performance-control process

- *Performance-control process:* uses the results of performance monitoring and analysis to modify configurable parameters if necessary to adjust open system performance

12.3.16 Confidence and Diagnostic Test Classes

SC21 N 5518 is a working document that defines various types of confidence and diagnostic test procedures that may be conducted. These tests are required to investigate:

- The ability of a resource to perform its allotted function

- The ability of any part of the communication system to establish a connection between a number of open systems and to transfer data without alteration between a number of open systems

- The integrity of a protocol (i.e., to establish whether the correct series of correctly formed PDUs is used)

- The effect of increased utilization of a resource

- The ability to set up the necessary actions in order to identify the cause of a failure

  Table 12.11 summarizes the confidence and diagnostic tests that have been defined.

12.4 STRUCTURE OF MANAGEMENT INFORMATION

The foundation of the systems-management activity is the management information base (MIB), which contains a representation of all the resources under systems management. The structure of management information (SMI) defines the general framework within which an MIB can be defined and constructed. The SMI identifies the data types that can be used in the MIB and how resources within the MIB are represented and named.

12.4.1 Objects

OSI systems management relies heavily on the concepts of object-oriented design. Each resource that is monitored and controlled by OSI systems management is represented by a managed object. A managed object can be defined for any resource that an organization wishes to monitor and/or control. Examples of hardware resources are switches, work stations, PBXs, LAN port cards, and multiplexers. Examples of software resources are queuing programs, routing algorithms, and buffer-management routines. Managed objects that refer to resources specific to an individual layer are called (*N*)-layer managed objects. Managed objects that refer to resources that encompass more than one layer are called system managed objects.

A managed object is defined in terms of attributes it possesses, operations that may be performed upon it, notifications that it may issue, and its relationships with other managed objects. In

Table 12.11 Confidence and Diagnostic Tests

Test	Purpose	Input Parameters	Results
Internal resource	Exericise the function of a resource that is internal to the system under test.	Managed object under test	Test outcome: pass, fail, inconclusive Parameters specific to the resource
Connectivity	Verify that connectivity may be established between two entities within a specified time.	Managed objects under test Value of time-out period Effective time	Test outcome: pass, fail, inconclusive If pass, then establishment time If fail, then time-out period Result information specific to test
Data integrity	Determine whether two entities can exchange data without any corruption and measure, where applicable, the time taken for the connection establishment.	Managed objects under test Data to be transferred Value of time-out period	Test outcome: pass, fail due to time-out, fail due to corrupt data If pass, then time taken If fail due to time-out, then time taken If fail due to corrupt data, then original and corrupt data
Loopback	Verify that data may be sent and received over a specified communications path with an acceptable error rate.	Managed objects under test Loopback data units Value of test duration Value of time-out period Value of error threshold	Test outcome: pass, fail, inconclusive Elapsed time to send and receive loopback data Value of test duration If fail due to time-out, then time taken Data error rate Any problem data information specific to the test
Protocol integrity	Enable the control of the generation of PDUs. The order and temporal interval between PDUs may be defined. Actual responses may be compared with expected responses.	Managed objects under test Local initiation time Sequence of PDUs (type, parameters, sequencing, timing, expected responses)	Test outcome: pass, fail, inconclusive because interrupted If failed, then reason (wrong PDU received, PDU expected but not received)

order to structure the definition of an MIB, each managed object is an instance of a managed-object class. A managed-object class is a model or template for managed-object instances that share the same attributes, notifications, and management operations. The definition of a managed-object class, as specified by the template, consists of:

- Attributes visible at the managed-object boundary
- System-management operations that can be applied to the managed object

Table 12.12 Object Classes (X.721/DIS 10165-2)

Object Class	Description
Alarm record	Used to define the information stored in the log as a result of receiving alarm reports. Object classes are communicationAlarm, qualityofServiceAlarm, processingErrorAlarm, equipmentAlarm, and environmentalAlarm.
Attribute-value-change record	Used to define the information stored in the log as a result of receiving attribute-value-change notifications.
Discriminator	Used to define the criteria for controlling management services.
Event-forwarding discriminator	Used to define the conditions that shall be satisfied by a potential event report before the event report is forwarded to a particular destination.
Event-log record	Used to define the information stored in the log as a result of receiving event reports. This is a superclass, from which records for specific event types are derived.
Log	Used to define the criteria for controlling the logging of the information in the management APDUs.
Log record	Used to define the records in a log managed object.
Object-creation record	Used to define the information stored in the log as a result of receiving object-creation notifications.
Object-deletion record	Used to define the information stored in the log as a result of receiving object-deletion notifications.
Object-name-change record	Used to define the information stored in the log as a result of receiving object-name-change notifications.
Relationship-change record	Used to define the information stored in the log as a result of receiving relationship-change reports.
Security-alarm report	Used to define the information stored in the log as a result of receiving security-alarm reports.
State-change record	Used to define the information stored in the log as a result of receiving state-change reports.
System	Used to represent a set of hardware and software that forms an autonomous whole capable of performing information processing and/or information transfer.
Top	That class of which every other object class is a subclass.

- Behavior exhibited by the managed object in response to management operations
- Notifications that can be emitted by the managed object
- Conditional packages that can be encapsulated in the managed object
- Position of the managed object in the inheritance hierarchy

Table 12.12 lists the object classes that have so far been defined as part of the SMI.

12.4.1.1 Attributes

The actual data elements contained in a managed object are called attributes. Each attribute represents a property of the resource that the object represents, such as the operational characteristics, current state, or conditions of operation. The data type of an attribute may be integer, real, Boolean, character string, or some composite type constructed from the basic types. An attribute may have a single value or a set value. A set-valued attribute is one whose value is a set of members of a given data type.

In addition to a data type, each attribute has access rules (read, write, read/write) and the rules by which it can be located as the result of a filtered search (matching rules).

Table 12.13 lists the attribute types for which detailed definitions have been developed as part of the SMI. The counter and gauge attribute types and their related thresholds were discussed in section 12.3. The tide mark is a mechanism that records the maximum or minimum value reached by a gauge during a measurement period. A tide mark is set-valued with three components: the current value of the tide mark, the value of the tide mark immediately before the last reset, and the last reset time.

Table 12.14 shows additional attribute types that are contained in ISO 10165-2 but listed without detailed definitions.

12.4.1.2 Operations

Systems-management operations apply to the attributes of an object or to the managed object as a whole (Table 12.15). An operation performed on a managed object can succeed only if the invoking managing system has the access rights necessary to perform the operation and consistency constraints are not violated.

12.4.1.3 Behavior

A managed object exhibits certain behavioral characteristics, including how the object reacts to operations performed on it and the constraints placed on its behavior.

The behavior of a managed object occurs in response to either external or internal stimuli. External stimuli take the form of system-management operations delivered via CMIP messages. Internal stimuli are events internal to the managed object and its associated resource, such as timers.

12.4.1.4 Notifications

Managed objects are said to emit notifications when some internal or external occurrence affecting the object is detected. Notifications may be transmitted externally in a protocol or logged. A managing system may request that some or all of the notifications emitted by a managed object be sent to it. Notifications that are sent to a manager are contained in an event report.

Table 12.13 Definition of Attribute Types (X.721/DIS 10165-2)

Attribute Type	Value Type	Inherent Properties	Permitted Operations	Implicit Relations	Specification Properties
Counter	Single value	Current value is a non-negative integer. It has a maximum value. Counting direction is up, with increment 1. Current value wraps around when it reaches maximum. Initial value is 0.	Get Set to arbitrary value (within range) Set to default	Directly related to a single counter threshold. May trigger a defined event when it wraps or is set.	The internal event that is counted Maximum value Estimated wrap-around period, to indicate necessary reading rate
Gauge	Single value	Current value is a non-negative integer or real. It has a maximum and minimum value. It may increase or decrease by arbitrary amounts. It does not wrap around.	Get	Directly related to a tide mark or gauge threshold. Only one tide mark may be applied. Only one (possibly multi-level) threshold may be applied. Can be used to measure other management information.	The dynamic variable measured Maximum and minimum value

Attribute	Type	Definition	Operations	Relationship	Notes
Relative distinguished name	Single value	The value shall be unique within the scope of its superior managed-object instance.	Get	The object instance is contained in the superior managed-object instance.	Classes of object to which it may be applied
Counter threshold	Set-valued	Comparison levels are non-negative integers. Offset values are non-negative integers. Notifications switch is on or off.	Get, Set, Add, Remove	Directly related to a single count. Directly related to a defined notification.	Count to which it applies. Defined notificaton that may be triggered
Gauge threshold	Set-valued	NotifyHigh and notifyLow are integer or real. NotifyHigh switch and notifyLow switch are on or off.	Get, Set, Add, Remove	Directly related to a single gauge. Directly related to a defined notification.	Gauge to which it applies. Defined notification that may be triggered
Tide mark	Set-valued	Associated with a gauge. Has a direction (maximum or minimum). Current or former values are integer or real, depending on associated gauge.	Get, Derive	Directly related to a gauge. May be directly related to a defined event that is triggered when the current value changes.	Gauge to which it applies. Direction (maximum or minimum)

Table 12.14 Miscellaneous Attribute Types (X.721/DIS 10165-2)

Event-Related Attributes		Attribute Types for Relationship

Event-Related Attributes

Additional attribute-value-change info
Additional create info
Additional delete info
Additional name-change info
Additional relationship-change info
Additional state-change info
Attribute-value-change definition
Backed-up status
Correlated notifications
Event time
Event type
Generic state change
Monitored attributes
New administrative state
New availability status
New back-up object
New backed-up object
New control states
New installation status
New member
New name
New operational state
New owner
New peer
New primary
New provider object
New repair status
New secondary
New usage state
New user object
Notification ID
Old administrative state
Old availability status
Old back-up object
Old backed-up object

Old control status
Old installation status
Old member
Old operational state
Old owner
Old peer
Old primary
Old provider object
Old repair status
Old secondary
Old usage state
Old user object
Perceived severity
Probable cause
Problem data
Problem test
Proposed repair actions
Security-alarm cause
Security-alarm generator
Security-alarm severity
Service provider
Service user
Source indicator
Specific problems
Threshold info
Trend indication

State-Related Attributes

Administrative state
Availability status
Control status
Installation status
Management state
Operational state
Repair status
Usage state
State

Attribute Types for Relationship

Back-up object
Backed-up object
Member
Owner
Peer
Primary
Provider object
Relationships
Secondary
User object

Other Attribute Types

Active address
Allomorphs
Allomorphic list
Back-up address list
Capacity-alarm threshold
Current log size
Destination address
Discriminator construct
Intervals of data
Log-full action
Logging time
Managed-object class
Managed-object instance
Max log size
Name
Name bindings
Number of records
Object class
Packages
Scheduler name
Start time
Stop time
Week mask

12.4.1.5 Conditional Packages

A conditional package is a collection of optional attributes, notifications, operations, and behavior that are either all present or all absent in a managed object. The condition under which a package is present always reflects the capability of the underlying resource being modeled by the managed object.

Table 12.15 Systems-Management Operations (X.720/DIS 10165-1)

(a) Attribute-oriented operations			
Operation	**Scope**	**Semantics**	**Behavior**
Get attribute value	All attribute types, unless they are defined as not readable.	Read all attribute values or list of attribute values; return values that can be read and indicate an error for values that cannot be read.	Return error indications for those attributes that could not be read.
Replace attribute value	Does not apply to group attributes or attributes that are not writable.	Replace the values of specified attributes with supplied values.	Return error indications for those attributes whose values could not be re-placed because the attributes were non-writable.
Replace with default value	All attribute types, unless they are defined as not writable.	Replace the values of some attributes with the defaults defined as part of the object-class specification.	Return error indications for those attributes whose values could not be re-placed due to at-tribute not writable, no default defined, or general failure of the replace-with-default request.
Add member	Attributes whose val-ues are sets and whose values are writable.	Add supplied attribute members to the set that currently com-prises the attribute's value.	Return error indication for attribute to which members could not be added because attribute is not writable.
Remove mem-ber	Attributes whose val-ues are sets and whose values are writable.	Remove from the set that currently com-prises the attribute's value those mem-bers supplied by the operation.	Return error indication for attribute whose members could not be removed because attribute is not writ-able.

Table 12.5 (*Cont.*)

(b) Operations that apply to managed objects as a whole			
Operation	**Scope**	**Semantics**	**Behavior**
Create	All objects that are creatable as defined by the object-class definition.	Create and initialize a managed object. The operation has analogous effects on the resource, as defined by the managed-object-class definer.	The create request may specify explicit values for individual attributes and may specify a reference object from which values may be obtained. The managed-object-class definition may specify initial attribute values. An error indication is provided if the managed object cannot be created.
Delete	All managed objects that can be deleted remotely.	Delete the managed object. The operation has analogous effects on the resource, as defined by the managed-object-class definer.	The execution of the delete operation may depend on whether other managed objects are contained in this object and on relationships with other managed objects.
Action	All managed-object classes.	The managed object performs the specified action and indicates the result.	Action results and/or error indications are returned.

12.4.1.6   Inheritance Hierarchy

All managed objects that share the same attributes, management operations, behavior, notifications, and conditional packages belong to the same managed-object class. To provide for a convenient means of reusing definitions in the creation of new object classes, ISO 10165-1 introduces the concept of inheritance. A new object class can be defined by adding additional attributes, management operations, behavior, notifications, and/or conditional packages to an existing managed-object class. The new object class is referred to as a *subclass* of the old object class, and the old object class is referred to as a *superclass* of the new object class.

All object classes ultimately derive from a unique object class referred to as *top*. This is the ultimate superclass, and the other object classes form an inheritance hierarchy with top as the root. Figure 12.20 shows an example of a portion of an inheritance hierarchy.

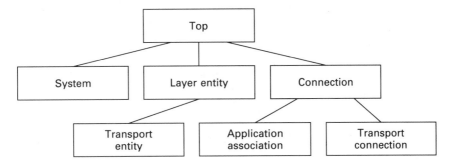

Figure 12.20 Inheritance Example

12.4.2   Containment and Naming

A managed object of a particular class can contain other managed objects of the same and/or different classes. The containing managed object is known as the superior managed object, and the contained managed objects are known as the subordinate managed objects. This relationship may be developed hierarchically to form a tree structure, with the subordinate objects at one level being viewed as the superior objects at the next lower level.

The containment relationship can be used to model real-world hierarchies of parts (e.g., assembly, subassemblies, components) or real-world data hierarchies (e.g., directory, files, records). The top level of the containment tree is referred to as the *root*, which is a null object that always exists. An example of a containment relationship is shown in Figure 12.21.

The containment relationship is used for naming managed objects. The unique path through the tree structure to a particular object gives a unique concatenation of names that identify a particular managed object. An example is given in Figure 12.22.

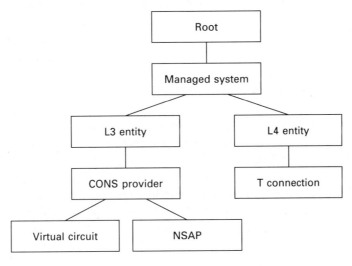

Figure 12.21 Containment Example

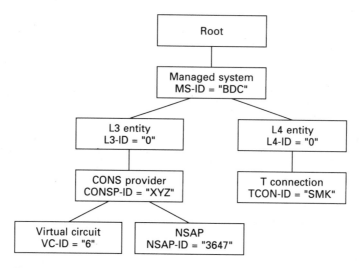

Figure 12.22 Naming Example

12.5   COMMON MANAGEMENT INFORMATION SERVICE

The common management information service (CMIS) defines the services provided for OSI systems management (ISO 9595). These services are invokable by management processes in order to communicate remotely.

Table 12.16 lists the CMIS services in terms of service primitives. CMIS services are of two types: confirmed services require that a remote management process send a response to indicate receipt and success or failure of the operation requested; nonconfirmed services do not use responses.

Three categories of service are relevant to CMIS:

1. *Association services:* The CMISE (common management information service element) user needs to establish an application association to communicate. The CMISE user relies on the association-control-service element (ACSE) for the control of application associations.

2. *Management-notification service:* This service is used to convey management information applicable to a notification. The definition of the notification and the consequent behavior of the communicating entities is dependent on the specification of the managed object that generated the notification and is outside the scope of CMIS.

3. *Management-operation services:* These six services are used to convey management information applicable to systems-management operations. The definition of the operation and the consequent behavior of the communicating entities is dependent on the specification of the managed object at which the operation is directed and is outside the scope of CMIS.

The CMIS provides several structuring facilities:

- Multiple responses to a confirmed operation can be linked to the operation by the use of a linked-identification parameter.

Table 12.16 CMISE Services

(a) Management-notification service		
Service	**Type**	**Definition**
M-EVENT-REPORT	Confirmed/nonconfirmed	Reports an event about a managed object to a peer CMISE-service user.

(b) Management-operation services		
Service	**Type**	**Definition**
M-GET	Confirmed	Requests the retrieval of management information from a peer CMISE-service user.
M-SET	Confirmed/nonconfirmed	Requests the modification of management information by a peer CMISE-service user.
M-ACTION	Confirmed/nonconfirmed	Requests that a peer CMISE-service user perform an action.
M-CREATE	Confirmed	Requests that a peer CMISE-service user create an instance of a managed object.
M-DELETE	Confirmed	Requests that a peer CMISE-service user delete an instance of a managed object.
M-CANCEL-GET	Confirmed	Requests that a peer CMISE-service user cancel a previously requested and currently outstanding invocation of the M-GET service.

- Operations can be performed on multiple managed objects, selected to satisfy some criteria and subject to a synchronizing condition.

Table 12.17 lists the seven CMIS services and the parameters of each service primitive. Table 12.18 defines the parameters.

12.5.1 Managed-Object Selection

The M-GET, M-SET, M-ACTION, and M-DELETE service primitives include a parameter to select the managed object or objects to be used in the given operation. Managed-object selection involves three concepts: scoping, filtering, and synchronization. These three facilities are provided as parameters.

12.5.1.1 Scoping

Scoping refers to the identification of an object or objects to which a filter is to be applied. Scoping is defined with reference to a specific managed-object instance referred to as the *base managed object*. The base managed object is the starting point for the selection of one or more objects to

Table 12.17 CMISE Services and Their Parameters

(a) M-EVENT-REPORT

Parameter Name	Request/Indication	Response/Confirm
Invoke identifier	M	M(=)
Mode	M	—
Managed-object class	M	U
Managed-object instance	M	U
Event type	M	C(=)
Event time	U	—
Event information	U	—
Current time	—	U
Event reply	—	C
Errors	—	C

(b) M-GET

Parameter Name	Request/Indication	Response/Confirm
Invoke identifier	M	M
Linked identifier	—	C
Base-object class	M	—
Base-object instance	M	—
Scope	U	—
Filter	U	—
Access control	U	—
Synchronization	U	—
Attribute identifier list	U	—
Managed-object class	—	C
Managed-object instance	—	C
Current time	—	U
Attribute list	—	C
Errors	—	C

(d) M-ACTION

Parameter Name	Request/Indication	Response/Confirm
Invoke identifier	M	M
Linked identifier	—	C
Mode	M	—
Base-object class	M	—
Base-object instance	M	—
Scope	U	—
Filter	U	—
Managed-object class	—	C
Managed-object instance	—	C
Access control	U	—
Synchronization	U	—
Action type	M	C(=)
Action information	U	—
Current time	—	U
Action reply	—	C
Errors	—	C

(e) M-CREATE

Parameter Name	Request/Indication	Response/Confirm
Invoke identifier	M	M(=)
Managed-object class	M	U
Managed-object instance	U	C
Superior-object instance	U	—
Access control	U	—
Reference-object instance	U	—
Attribute list	U	C
Current time	—	U
Errors	—	C

(c) M-SET

Parameter Name	Request/Indication	Response/Confirm
Invoke identifier	M	M
Linked identifier	—	C
Mode	M	—
Base-object class	M	—
Base-object instance	M	—
Scope	U	—
Filter	U	—
Access control	U	—
Synchronization	U	—
Managed-object class	—	C
Managed-object instance	—	C
Modification list	M	—
Attribute list	—	C
Current time	—	U
Errors	—	C

(f) M-DELETE

Parameter Name	Request/Indication	Response/Confirm
Invoke identifier	M	M
Linked identifier	—	C
Base-object class	M	—
Base-object instance	M	—
Scope	U	—
Filter	U	—
Access control	U	—
Synchronization	U	—
Managed-object class	—	C
Managed-object instance	—	C
Current time	—	U
Errors	—	C

(g) M-CANCEL-GET

Parameter Name	Request/Indication	Response/Confirm
Invoke identifier	M	M
Get invoke identifier	M	—
Errors	—	C

M = mandatory.

(=) = the value of the parameter is equal to the value of the parameter in the column to the left.

U = the use of the parameter is a service-user option.

— = the parameter is not present in the interaction described by the primitive concerned.

C = the parameter is conditional.

Table 12.18 Definition of CMIS Parameters

Access control

Information of unspecified form to be used as input to the access-control functions.

Action information

Specifies extra information when necessary to further define the nature, variations, or operands of the action to be performed.

Action reply

Contains the reply to the action.

Action type

Specifies a particular action that is to be performed.

Attribute identifier list

A set of attribute identifiers for which the attribute values are to be returned by the performing CMISE-service user.

Attribute list

The set of attribute identifiers and values that are returned by the performing CMISE-service user.

Base-object class

The class of the managed object that is to be used as the starting point for the selection of managed objects to which the filter is to be applied.

Base-object instance

The instance of the managed object that is to be used as the starting point for the selection of managed objects to which the filter is to be applied.

Current time

Time at which the response was generated.

Errors

Error notification for the operation.

Event information

Information that the invoking CMISE-service user is able to supply about the event.

Event reply

Reply to the event report.

Event time

Time of generation of event.

Event type

Type of event being reported.

Filter

Specifies the set of assertions that defines the filter test to be applied to the scoped managed object.

Get invoke identifier

Identifier assigned to the previously requested and currently outstanding M-GET operation.

Invoke identifier

The identifier assigned to this operation.

Linked identifier

If multiple replies are to be sent for this operation, this parameter specifies the identification that is provided by the performing CMISE-service user when those replies are returned. The linked identifier has the same value as that of the invoke identifier provided in the indication primitive.

Managed-object class

The class of the managed object referenced by the primitive.

Managed-object instance

The instance of the managed object referenced by the primitive.

Mode

Requested mode: confirmed or nonconfirmed.

Modification list

A set of attribute-modification specifications.

Reference-object instance

Specifies an existing instance of a managed object, called the reference object, of the same class as the managed object to be created. Attribute values associated with the reference-object instance become the default values for those not specified by the attribute-list parameter.

Scope

Indicates the subtree, rooted at the base managed object, that is to be searched.

Superior-object instance

Identifies the existing managed-object instance that is to be the superior of the new managed-object instance.

Synchronization

Indicates how the invoking CMISE-service user wants this operation synchronized across the selected object instances.

which a filter is to be applied. Recall from section 12.4 that, by the principles of containment and naming, managed objects form a hierarchy, or tree structure. Using the base object as the root, a subtree of the overall object tree is obtained. With this in mind, four specifications of scoping level are possible:

1. The base object alone
2. The nth level subordinates of the base object
3. The base object and all its subordinates down to and including the nth-level
4. The base object and all its subordinates; that is, the entire subtree

12.5.1.2 Filtering

A filter is a Boolean expression, consisting of one or more assertions about the presence or values of attributes in a scoped managed object. Each assertion may be a test for equality, ordering, presence, or set comparison. Attribute-value assertions can require that the following matching rules be met:

- *Equality:* Attribute value is equal to that asserted.

- *Greater or equal:* Attribute value supplied is greater than or equal to the value of the attribute.

- *Less or equal:* Attribute value supplied is less than or equal to the value of the attribute.

- *Present:* Attribute is present.

- *Substrings:* Attribute value includes the specified substrings in the given order.

- *Subset of:* All asserted members are present in the attribute.

- *Superset of:* All members of the attribute are presented in the asserted attribute.

- *Non–null-set intersection:* At least one of the asserted members is present in the attribute.

The filter test is applied to all the managed objects selected by the scoping parameter, and only those managed objects that match the filter are selected for the performance of the operation.

12.5.1.3 Synchronization

The scoping parameter may result in the selection of more than one managed object to be subject to filtering. In turn, if more than one object is scoped, the filtering parameter may result in the selection of more than one object for which the operation is to be performed. The question then arises as to the order in which objects will be processed. Since the order in which object instances are selected by the filter is not specified but is left as a local implementation matter, this order cannot be used. Instead, the CSIME-service user may request one of two types of synchronization:

1. *Atomic:* All managed objects selected for the operation are checked to ascertain whether they are able to successfully perform the operation. If one or more managed objects are not able to do so, then none performs it.

2. *Best effort:* All managed objects selected for the operation are requested to perform it.

12.5.2 Linkage

The M-GET, M-SET, M-ACTION, and M-DELETE service primitives, which are the primitives that can specify operation on multiple objects, also include a linkage parameter to provide for multiple replies to be sent for the operation. This is the linked-identifier parameter, which appears in each of the response and confirm primitives. The value of the parameter is the same as the invoke identifier that appears in the request and indication primitives. The invoke identifier is a unique identifier assigned to each operation.

12.5.3   Management-Notification Service

The only primitive defined for the management-notification service is M-EVENT-REPORT. This primitive is used to report a notification to a manager that has requested the notification. Unlike all other management operations, the event report is initiated by the agent process, and the managing process is the responder. The primitive may be of either the confirmed or the nonconfirmed variety.

12.5.4   Management-Operation Services

The M-GET primitive allows for the retrieval of data from the management information base. One management process, acting in the role of manager, will send a GET request to another management process, acting in an agent role. The request may be for information about a single managed object or a set of managed objects. For each managed object about which information is requested, the value of one, several, or all of its attributes may be requested.

The M-SET primitive allows for modification of data in the management information base. It is used to change the value or values of one or more attributes in one or more managed objects.

The M-ACTION primitive allows the invocation of a predefined action procedure specified as part of a managed object. The request specifies the type of the action and the input parameters.

The M-CREATE primitive is used to create a new instance of an object class. The conditional packages and attribute values that the managed object is to have may be specified as part of the request, or an existing instance can be referenced as a model.

The M-DELETE primitive is used to delete one or more objects from the management information base.

The M-CANCEL-GET primitive is used to stop a lengthy GET operation. The reason why only the GET operation may be canceled is that it is difficult to ensure the consistency of the MIB if an operation that alters the MIB is canceled after initiation.

12.6   COMMON MANAGEMENT INFORMATION PROTOCOL

The common management information protocol (CMIP) supports the services provided for OSI systems management by means of a set of protocol data units that implement the CMISE (common management information service element; ISO 9596). These PDUs are transmitted in response to CMISE-service primitives issued by CMISE-service users.

To understand the operation of CMIP, we need to see it in context with the CMISE-service user and the services that CMISE relies on. Figure 12.23 shows this relationship. As discussed in section 12.5, the CMIS provides seven services for performing management operations, in the form of service primitives. In addition, CMISE users need to be able to establish associations in order to perform management operations. These latter services are provided by the association-control-service element and are provided by CMISE as a pass-through; there is no CMIP involved. For the management-operation services, the CMISE employs a CMIP to exchange PDUs. The

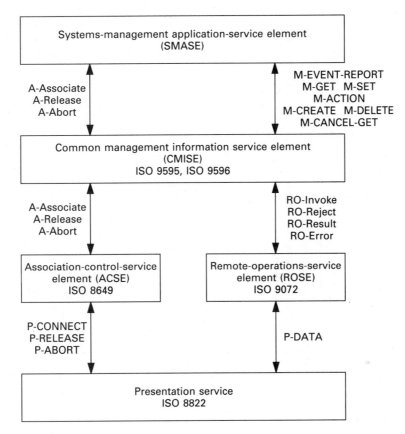

Figure 12.23 Services Provided by CMISE and Services Used by CMISE

CMIP, in turn, relies on the services of the remote-operations-service element.[2] Both ACSE and ROSE rely on the presentation service.

Table 12.19 lists the 11 PDUs that make up the CMIP. Up to three types of information are carried in each data unit. The argument entry defines the arguments, or parameters, carried in the data unit that are derived from the triggering CMISE-service primitive. The results and errors entries contain information from the performing entity about the result of the systems-management operation. These values are derived from the CMISE response primitive.

Table 12.20 shows the mapping between the CMIS primitives and the CMIP data units. Note that in carrying the response to M-GET, M-SET, M-ACTION, and M-DELETE service primitives, the CMIP data unit, in addition to its other parameters, includes a linked-ID parameter, in order to implement the linking facility discussed in section 12.5.

As an example of the use of CMIP to implement CMIS, Figure 12.24 illustrates the M-GET service. Implementations of the other services exhibit similar behavior. The following sequence of events occurs:

---

2.   See Chapter 5 for a description of ACSE and ROSE.

Table 12.19 CMIP Data Units

CMIP Data Unit	Argument	Result	Errors
m-EventReport	EventReportArgument	—	—
m-EventReport-Confirmed	EventReportArgument	EventReportResult	InvalidArgumentValue, noSuchArgument, noSuchEventType, noSuchObjectClass, noSuchObjectInstance, processingFailure
m-Get	GetArgument	GetResult	accessDenied, classInstanceConflict, complexityLimitation, getListError, invalidFilter, invalidScope, noSuchObjectClass, noSuchObjectInstance, operationCanceled, processingFailure, syncNotSupported
m-linked-Reply	LinkedReply-Argument	—	accessDenied, classInstanceConflict, complexityLimitation, invalidFilter, invalidScope, noSuchObjectClass, noSuch-ObjectInstance, processingFailure, setListError, syncNot-Supported
m-Set	SetArgument	—	—
m-Set-Confirmed	SetArgument	SetResult	—
m-Action	ActionArgument	—	—
m-Action-Confirmed	ActionArgument	ActionResult	accessDenied, classInstanceConflict, complexityLimitation, invalidScope, invalidArgumentValue, invalidFilter, noSuch-Action, noSuchArgument, noSuchObjectClass, noSuch-ObjectInstance, processingFailure, syncNotSupported
m-Create	CreateArgument	CreateResult	accessDenied, classInstanceConflict, duplicateManagedObject-Instance, invalidAttributeValue, invalidObjectInstance, missingAttribute, noSuchAttribute, noSuchObjectClass, noSuchObjectInstance, noSuchReferenceObject, processing-Failure
m-Delete	DeleteArgument	DeleteResult	accessDenied, classInstanceConflict, complexityLimitation, invalidFilter, invalidScope, noSuchObjectClass, noSuch-ObjectInstance, processingFailure, syncNotSupported
m-Cancel-Get-Confirmed	GetInvokedId, InvokeIdType	—	mistypedOperation, noSuchInvokeId, processingFailure

Table 12.20 Correspondence between CMISE Primitives and CMIP Data Units

CMIS Primitive	Mode	Linked ID	CMIP Data Unit
M-EVENT-REPORT.request/indication	Nonconfirmed	Not applicable	m-EventReport
M-EVENT-REPORT.request/indication	Confirmed	Not applicable	m-EventReport-Confirmed
M-EVENT-REPORT.response/confirm	Not applicable	Not applicable	m-EventReport-Confirmed
M-GET.request/indication	Confirmed	Not applicable	m-Get
M-GET.response/confirm	Not applicable	Absent	m-Get
M-GET.response/confirm	Not applicable	Present	m-linked-Reply
M-SET.request/indication	Nonconfirmed	Not applicable	m-Set
M-SET.request/indication	Confirmed	Not applicable	m-Set-Confirmed
M-SET.response/confirm	Not applicable	Absent	m-Set-Confirmed
M-SET.response/confirm	Not applicable	Present	m-linked-Reply
M-ACTION.request/indication	Nonconfirmed	Not applicable	m-Action
M-ACTION.request/indication	Confirmed	Not applicable	m-Action-Confirmed
M-ACTION.response/confirm	Not applicable	Absent	m-Action-Confirmed
M-ACTION.response/confirm	Not applicable	Present	m-linked-Reply
M-CREATE.request/indication	Confirmed	Not applicable	m-Create
M-CREATE.response/confirm	Not applicable	Not applicable	m-Create
M-DELETE.request/indication	Confirmed	Not applicable	m-Delete
M-DELETE.response/confirm	Not applicable	Absent	m-Delete
M-DELETE.response/confirm	Not applicable	Present	m-linked-Reply
M-CANCEL-GET.request/indication	Confirmed	Not applicable	m-Cancel-Get-Confirmed
M-CANCEL-GET.response/confirm	Not applicable	Not applicable	m-Cancel-Get-Confirmed

1. An M-GET.request primitive is received from a CMISE user. The parameters in the primitive identify this operation and distinguish it from others supported by CMISE, provide information about the managed object, and provide other relevant information (Figure 12.13, part [b]). The request is handled by the common management information protocol machine (CMIPM).

2. The CMIPM constructs an m-Get application protocol data unit (APDU) that contains the parameters in the M-GET.request primitive.

3. The CMIPM uses the RO-INVOKE.request service of the ROSE to send the APDU to the destination.

4. The ROSE delivers the APDU to the responding CMIPM in an RO-INVOKE.indication.

5. If the data unit is acceptable, the CMIPM issues an M-GET.indication to the destination CMISE user, containing the parameters from the original request primitive. This directs the peer service user to perform the requested GET operation and report the results.

6. The responding CMISE user issues an M-GET.response primitive back to the CMISE. The parameters in the primitive identify this operation and distinguish it from others supported by CMISE, provide the requested information from the managed object, and provide other relevant information (Figure 12.13, part [b]). If this operation failed, the primitive includes an error parameter to describe the nature of the error.

7. The CMIPM constructs an m-Get APDU that contains the parameters in the M-GET.response primitive.

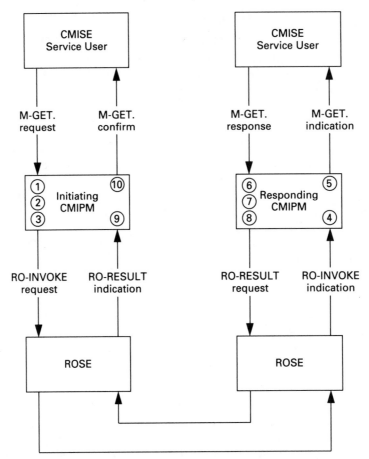

Source: U. Black, *OSI: A Model for Computer Communications Standards* (Englewood Cliffs, N.J.: Prentice-Hall, 1991).

Figure 12.24 CMIP GET Operation

8. If the operation was successful, the CMIPM uses the RO-RESULT.request service of the ROSE to send the APDU back to the initiating system.

9. The ROSE delivers the APDU to the initiating CMIPM in an RO-RESULT.indication.

10. The CMIPM issues an M-GET.confirm to the initiating CMISE user.

Figure 12.25, part (a), illustrates the sequence of events in terms of service primitives and APDUs. The figure also illustrates other possible outcomes of an M-GET.request. If the operation failed, the m-Get includes the error parameter obtained from the responding CMISE user, and the m-Get APDU is sent using the RO-ERROR service. Table 12.19 lists the possible error parameter values for all the CMIP APDUs.

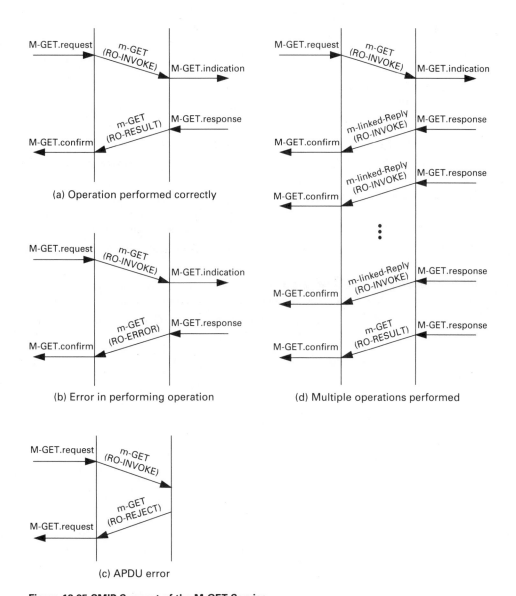

Figure 12.25 CMIP Support of the M-GET Service

If the arriving APDU from the requesting system is in error, then no indication is given to the destination CMISE user. Instead, the responding CMIPM issues an m-Get APDU using the RO-REJECT service.

Finally, if the M-GET operation specifies more than one managed object, each operation in the responding CSIME user results in the issuance of a separate M-GET.response. Each response includes the linked-ID parameter except the last. For each intermediate response, the responding CMIPM issues an m-linked-Reply APDU using the RO-INVOKE service.

12.7   SUMMARY

Of all the areas of OSI standardization, the set of standards developed for OSI systems management is the most voluminous and most complex. The first standard related to network management issued by ISO was ISO 7498-4, which specifies the management framework for the OSI model

Subsequently, ISO has issued a set of standards and draft standards for network management CCITT is the joint sponsor of this effort. The standards fall into five general categories:

1. *OSI management framework and overview:* includes ISO 7498-4, which provides a general introduction to management concepts, and ISO 10040, which is an overview of the remainder of the documents

2. *CMIS/CMIP:* defines the common management information service (CMIS), which provides OSI management services to management applications, and the common management information protocol (CMIP), which provides the information-exchange capability to support CMIS

3. *Systems-management functions:* defines the specific functions that are performed by OSI systems management

3. *Structure of management information:* defines the management information base (MIB), which contains a representation of all objects within the OSI environment subject to management

5. *Layer management:* defines management information, services, and functions related to specific OSI layers

13
OSI Security

The requirements of *information security* within an organization have undergone two major changes in the last several decades. Prior to the widespread use of data-processing equipment, the security of information felt to be valuable to an organization was provided primarily by physical and administrative means. An example of the former is the use of rugged filing cabinets with a combination lock for storing sensitive documents. An example of the latter is personnel-screening procedures used during the hiring process.

With the introduction of the computer, the need for automated tools for protecting files and other information stored on the computer became evident. This is especially the case for a shared system, such as a time-sharing system, and the need is even more acute for systems that can be accessed over a public telephone or data network. The generic name for the collection of tools designed to protect data and thwart hackers is *computer security*.

The second major change that affects security is the introduction of distributed systems and the use of networks and communications facilities for carrying data between terminal user and computer and between computer and computer. *Network security* measures are needed to protect data during their transmission.

To effectively assess the security needs of an organization, and to evaluate and choose various security products and policies, the manager responsible for security needs some systematic way of defining the requirements for security and characterizing the approaches to satisfying those requirements. This is difficult enough in a centralized data-processing environment; with the use of local area and wide area networks, the problems are compounded.

Such a systematic approach has been developed by the International Organization for Standardization (ISO), as part of its standard for an open systems interconnection (OSI) communications architecture. The standard is ISO 7498-2, OSI Basic Reference Model—Part 2: Security Architecture.

The OSI security architecture is useful to managers as a way of organizing the task of providing security. Furthermore, because this architecture was developed as an international standard, computer and communications vendors will begin to develop security features for their products and services that relate to this structured definition of services and mechanisms. In addition, the standard defines security features within the OSI framework, providing a functional assignment of security services and mechanisms to OSI layers. Thus, the architecture guides standards makers in developing enhancements of OSI-based standards.

The OSI security architecture addresses the issues of network security, as opposed to single-system security. Three concepts form the basis for the security architecture:

1. *Security threat:* any action that compromises the security of information owned by an organization.

2. *Security mechanism:* a communications mechanism that is designed to detect, prevent, or recover from a security threat.

3. *Security service:* a communications service that enhances the security of an organization's data-processing systems and information transfers. The services are intended to counter security threats.

Since the development of this abstract security architecture, ISO has been developing standards that elaborate on the concepts in 7498-2 and specify procedures and protocols for the implementation of security services. Table 13.1 lists the key ISO standards.

Table 13.1 Key OSI Security Standards

ISO 7498-2	OSI Basic Reference Model—Part 2: Security Architecture
ISO 8649 AM 1	Service Definition for the Association Control Service Element—Amendment 1: Authentication during Association Establishment
ISO 8650 AM 1	Protocol Specification for the Association Control Service Element—Amendment 1: Authentication during Association Establishment
ISO 9160	Data Encipherment—Physical Layer Interoperability Requirements
DIS 9796	Security Techniques: Digital Signature Scheme Giving Message Recovery
ISO 9797	Data Cryptographic Techniques: Data Integrity Mechanism Using a Cryptographic Check Function Employing a Block Cipher Algorithm
DIS 9798-1	Security Techniques: Entity Authentication Mechanisms—Part 1: General Model
CD 9798-2	Security Techniques: Entity Authentication Mechanisms—Part 2: Entity Authentication Using Symmetric Techniques
CD 9798-3	Security Techniques: Entity Authentication Mechanisms—Part 3: Entity Authentication Using Public Key Algorithms
DIS 10116	Mode Of Operation for an n-Bit Block Cipher
CD 10181-1	Security Frameworks—Part 1: Overview
CD 10181-2	Part 2: Authentication Framework
CD 10181-3	Part 3: Access Control
CD 10181-4	Part 4: Non-repudiation
CD 10181-5	Part 5: Integrity
CD 10181-6	Part 6: Confidentiality
CD 10181-7	Part 7: Security Audit Framework
DIS 10736	Transport Layer Security Protocol
CD 10745	OSI Upper Layers Security Model

13.1   SECURITY THREATS

A publication of the National Bureau of Standards identified some of the threats that stimulated the upsurge of interest in security:

- Organized and intentional attempts to obtain economic or market information from competitive organizations in the private sector
- Organized and intentional attempts to obtain economic information from government agencies
- Inadvertent acquisition of economic or market information
- Inadvertent acquisition of information about individuals
- Intentional fraud through illegal access to computer data banks with emphasis, in decreasing order of importance, on acquisition of funding data, economic data, law enforcement data, and data about individuals
- Government intrusion on the rights of individuals
- Invasion of individual rights by the intelligence community (Branstad 1978.)

These are examples of specific threats that an organization or an individual (or an organization on behalf of its employees) may feel the need to counter. The nature of the threat that concerns an organization will vary greatly from one set of circumstances to another. Fortunately, we can approach the problem from a different angle by looking at the generic types of threats that might be encountered. This is the approach taken in ISO 7498-2.

13.1.1   Security Requirements

In order to be able to understand the various types of threats to security, we need to have a definition of security requirements. Computer and network security addresses three requirements:

1. *Secrecy:* requires that the information in a computer system only be accessible for reading by authorized parties. This type of access includes printing, displaying, and other forms of disclosure, including simply revealing the existence of an object.
2. *Integrity:* requires that computer-system assets be modifiable only by authorized parties. Modification includes writing, changing, changing status, deleting, and creating.
3. *Availability:* requires that computer-system assets be available to authorized parties.

13.1.2   Types of Threats

The types of threats to the security of a computer system or network are best characterized by viewing the function of the computer system as that of providing information. In general, there is a flow of information from a source, such as a file or a region of main memory, to a destination, such as another file or a user. This normal flow is depicted in Figure 13.1, part (a). The remainder of the figure shows four general categories of threats:

1. *Interruption:* An asset of the system is destroyed or becomes unavailable or unusable. This is a threat to *availability*. Examples include destruction of a piece of hardware, such as a hard disk; the cutting of a communication line; or the disabling of the file-management system.

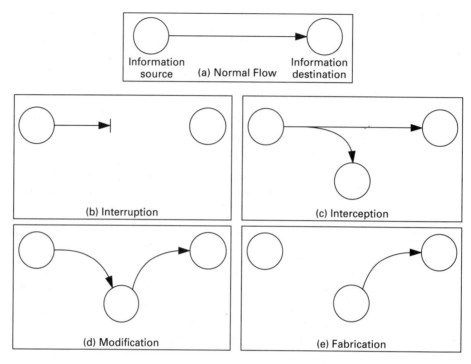

Figure 13.1 Security Threats

2. *Interception:* An unauthorized party gains access to an asset. This is a threat to *secrecy*. The unauthorized party could be a person, a program, or a computer. Examples include wiretapping to capture data in a network and the illicit copying of files or programs.

3. *Modification:* An unauthorized party not only gains access but tampers with an asset. This is a threat to *integrity*. Examples include changing values in a data file, altering a program so that it performs differently, and modifying the content of messages being transmitted in a network.

4. *Fabrication:* An unauthorized party inserts counterfeit objects into the system. This is also a threat to *integrity*. Examples include the insertion of spurious messages in a network or the addition of records to a file.

Table 13.2, consisting of definitions from ISO 7498-2, lists the types of threats that might be faced in the context of network security. One way of categorizing the threats is as either accidental or intentional. A more useful categorization is in terms of passive threats and active threats (Figure 13.2).

13.1.2.1   Passive Threats

Passive threats are in the nature of eavesdropping on or monitoring of the transmissions of an organization. The attacker's goal is to obtain information that is being transmitted. Two types of threats are involved here: release of message contents and traffic analysis.

Table 13.2 Security Threats

Threat

A potential violation of security. Threats may be classified as **accidental** or **intentional** and may be **passive** or **active.**

Accidental Threat

A threat with no premeditated intent. Examples include system malfunctions, operational blunders, and software bugs.

Intentional Threat

A threat with premeditated intent. An intentional threat, if realized, may be considered an attack.

Passive Threat

The threat of unauthorized disclosure of information without changing the state of the system. Examples of passive threats are **release of message contents** and **traffic analysis.**

Active Threat

The threat of a deliberate unauthorized change to the state of the system. Examples of active threats are **masquerade, replay, modification of messages,** and **denial of service.**

Release of Message Contents

Occurs when the content of a data transmission is read by an unauthorized user.

Traffic Analysis

The inference of information from observation of traffic flows (presence, absence, amount, direction, and frequency).

Masquerade

The pretence by an entity to be another entity. A masquerade is usually used with some other form of active attack.

Replay

Occurs when a message, or part of a message, is repeated to produce an unauthorized effect. For example, a valid message containing authentication information may be replayed by another entity in order to authenticate itself as something that it is not.

Modification of Messages

Occurs when the content of a data transmission is altered without detection and results in an unauthorized effect. Examples include modification of message contents, deletion, delay, and re-ordering of messages.

Denial of Service

The prevention of authorized access to resources or the delaying of time-critical operations.

The threat of *release of message contents* is clearly understood by most observers. A telephone conversation, an electronic-mail message, or a transferred file may contain sensitive or confidential information. We would like to prevent the attacker from learning the contents of these transmissions.

The second passive threat, *traffic analysis,* is more subtle. Suppose that we had a way of masking the contents of messages or other information traffic so that an attacker, even if he or she captured the message, would be unable to extract the information from the message. The common technique for doing this is encryption, discussed later in the chapter. If we had such protection in place, it might still be possible for an attacker to observe the pattern of these messages. The

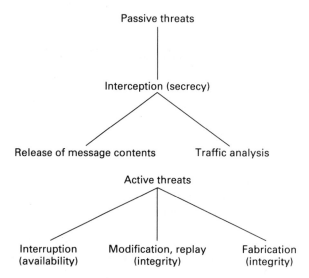

Figure 13.2 Active and Passive Network Security Threats

attacker can determine the location and identity of communicating hosts and can also observe the frequency and length of messages being exchanged. This information might be useful in guessing the nature of the communication that is taking place.

Passive threats are very difficult to detect, since they do not involve any alteration of the data. However, it is feasible to prevent these attacks from being successful. Thus, the emphasis in dealing with passive threats is on prevention rather than detection.

13.1.2.2 Active Threats

The second major category of threat is active threats. These involve some modification of the data stream or the creation of a false stream. We can subdivide these threats into four categories: masquerade, replay, modification of messages, and denial of service.

A *masquerade* takes place when one entity pretends to be a different entity. A masquerade attack usually includes one of the other forms of active attack. For example, authentication sequences can be captured and replayed after a valid authentication sequence has taken place. This may be done to enable an authorized entity with few privileges to obtain extra privileges by impersonating an entity that has those privileges.

Replay involves the passive capture of a data unit and its subsequent retransmission to produce an unauthorized effect.

Modification of messages simply means that some portion of a legitimate message is altered, or that messages are delayed or reordered, in order to produce an unauthorized effect. For example, a message meaning ''Allow John Smith to read confidential file *accounts*'' is modified to mean ''Allow Fred Brown to read confidential file *accounts*.''

The *denial of service* prevents or inhibits the normal use or management of communications facilities. This attack may have a specific target; for example, an entity may suppress all messages directed to a particular destination (e.g., the security-audit service). Another form of service denial is the disruption of an entire network, either by disabling the network or by overloading it with messages so as to degrade performance.

The characteristics of active threats are the opposite of those of passive threats. Whereas passive attacks are difficult to detect, measures are available to prevent their success. On the other hand, it is quite difficult to absolutely prevent active attacks, since this would require physical protection of all communications facilities and paths at all times. Instead, the goal with respect to active attacks is to detect these attacks and to recover from any disruption or delays they might cause. Because the detection has a deterrent effect, this may also contribute to prevention.

13.2 SECURITY MECHANISMS

Table 13.3 lists the security mechanisms defined in ISO 7498-2. As can be seen, the mechanisms are divided into those that are implemented in a specific layer of the OSI architecture and those that are not specific to any particular OSI layer or security service. In this section, we provide a brief summary of each mechanism.

13.2.1 Encipherment

One the most important automated tools for computer security is encryption.[1] Encryption is a process that conceals meaning by changing intelligible messages into unintelligible messages. Encryption can be by means of either a code or a cipher. A code system uses a predefined table or dictionary to substitute a meaningless word or phrase for each message or part of a message. The simplest code would substitute another letter for each letter of the alphabet. A cipher uses a computable algorithm that can translate any stream of message bits into an unintelligible cryptogram. Because cipher techniques lend themselves more readily to automation, it is these techniques that are used in contemporary computer and network security facilities. This subsection discusses only cipher techniques.

We begin by looking at the traditional approach to encryption, now known as conventional encryption. We then look at a new and quite useful technique known as public-key encryption.

13.2.1.1 Conventional Encryption

Figure 13.3, part (a), illustrates the conventional encryption process. The original intelligible message, referred to as *plaintext,* is converted into apparently random nonsense, referred to as *ciphertext.* The encryption process consists of an algorithm and a key. The key is a relatively short bit string that controls the algorithm. The algorithm will produce a different output depending on the specific key being used at the time. Changing the key radically changes the output of the algorithm.

Once the ciphertext is produced, it is transmitted. Upon reception, the ciphertext can be transformed back to the original plaintext by using a decryption algorithm and the same key that was used for encryption.

The security of conventional encryption depends on several factors. First, the encryption algorithm must be powerful enough so that it is impractical to decrypt a message on the basis of the ciphertext alone. Beyond that, the security of conventional encryption depends on the secrecy of the key, not the secrecy of the algorithm. That is, it is assumed that it is impractical to decrypt a

---

1. The terms *encipherment* and *encryption* are sometimes used interchangeably. Strictly speaking, *enciphering* is translating letters or symbols individually, *encoding* is translating entire words or phrases to other words or phrases, and *encryption* covers both encoding and encipherment.

Table 13.3 Security Mechanisms

Specific Security Mechanisms   May be incorporated into the appropriate (N) layer in order to provide some of the OSI security services.

Encipherment

The use of mathematical algorithms to transform data into a form that is not readily intelligible. The transformation and subsequent recovery of the data depend on an algorithm and one or more encryption keys.

Traffic padding

The insertion of bits into gaps in a data stream to frustrate traffic-analysis attempts.

Authentication exchange

A mechanism intended to ensure the identity of an entity by means of information exchange.

Digital signature

Data appended to, or a cryptographic transformation of, a data unit that allows a recipient of the data unit to prove the source and integrity of the data unit and protects against forgery (e.g., by the recipient).

Access control

A variety of mechanisms that enforce access rights to resources.

Data integrity

A variety of mechanisms used to assure the integrity of a data unit or stream of data units.

Routing control

Enables the selection of particular physically secure routes for certain data and allows routing changes, especially when a breach of security is suspected.

Notarization

The use of a trusted third party to assure certain properties of a data exchange.

Pervasive Security Mechanisms

Mechanisms that are not specific to any particular OSI security service or OSI layer.

Trusted functionality

That which is perceived to be correct with respect to some criteria; e.g., as established by a security policy.

Security label

A marking bound to a resource (which may be a data unit) that names or designates the security attributes of that resource.

Event detection

Detection of security-relevant events.

Security-audit trail

Data collected and potentially used to facilitate a security audit, which is an independent review and examination of system records and activities.

Security recovery

Deals with requests from mechanisms, such as event handling and management functions, and takes recovery actions.

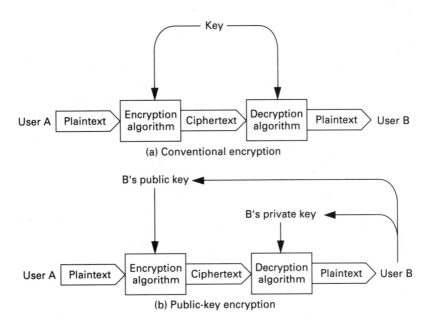

Figure 13.3 Encryption

message on the basis of the ciphertext *plus* knowledge of the encryption/decryption algorithm. In other words, we don't need to keep the algorithm secret; we only need to keep the key secret.

This feature of conventional encryption is what makes it feasible for widespread use. The fact that the algorithm need not be kept secret means that manufacturers can, and have, developed low-cost chip implementations of data-encryption algorithms. These chips are widely available and incorporated into a number of products. With the use of conventional encryption, the principal security problem is maintaining the secrecy of the key.

13.2.1.2 Public-Key Encryption

One of the major difficulties with conventional encryption schemes is the need to distribute the keys in a secure manner. A clever way around this requirement is an encryption scheme that, surprisingly, does not require key distribution. This scheme, known as public-key encryption, is illustrated in Figure 13.3, part (b).

For conventional encryption schemes, the keys used for encryption and decryption are the same. This is not a necessary condition. Instead, it is possible to develop an algorithm that uses one key for encryption and a companion but different key for decryption. Furthermore, it is possible to develop algorithms such that knowledge of the encryption algorithm plus the encryption key is not sufficient to determine the decryption key. Thus, the following technique will work:

1. Each end system in a network generates a pair of keys to be used for encryption and decryption of messages that it will receive.

2. Each system publishes its encryption key by placing it in a public register or file. This is the public key. The companion key is kept private.

3. If A wishes to send a message to B, it encrypts the message using B's public key.

4. When B receives the message, it decrypts it using B's private key. No other recipient can decrypt the message, since only B knows B's private key.

As you can see, public-key encryption solves the key-distribution problem, since there are no keys to distribute! All participants have access to public keys, and private keys are generated locally by each participant and therefore need never be distributed. As long as a system controls its private key, its incoming communication is secure. At any time, a system can change its private key and publish the companion public key to replace its old public key.

A further refinement is needed. Since anyone can transmit a message to A using A's public key, a means is needed to prevent impostors. To develop this scheme, it is necessary to know that public-key encryption algorithms are such that the two keys can be used in either order. That is, one can encrypt with the public key and decrypt with the matching private key, or encrypt with the private key and decrypt with the matching public key. Now consider the following scenario: B prepares a message and encrypts it with its own private key, and then encrypts the result with A's public key. On the other end, A first uses its private key and then uses B's public key in a double decryption. Since the message was encrypted with B's private key, it could only come from B. Since it was also encrypted with A's public key, it can only be read by A. With this technique, any two stations can at any time set up a secure connection without a prior secret distribution of keys.

A main disadvantage of public-key encryption compared to conventional encryption is that algorithms for the former are much more complex. Thus, for comparable size and cost of hardware, the public-key scheme will provide much lower throughput.

Table 13.4 summarizes some of the important aspects of conventional and public-key encryption.

Table 13.4 Coventional and Public-Key Encryption

Conventional Encryption	Public-Key Encryption
Needed to work:	**Needed to work:**
1. The same algorithm with the same key can be used for encryption and decryption.	1. One algorithm is used for encryption and decryption with a pair of keys, one for encryption and one for decryption.
2. The sender and receiver must share the algorithm and the key.	2. The sender and receiver must each have one of the matched pair of keys.
Needed for security:	**Needed for security:**
1. The key must be kept secret.	1. One of the two keys must be kept secret.
2. It must be impossible or at least impractical to decipher a message if no other information is available.	2. It must be impossible or at least impractical to decipher a message if no other information is available.
3. Knowledge of the algorithm plus samples of ciphertext must be insufficient to determine the key.	3. Knowledge of the algorithm plus one of the keys plus samples of ciphertext must be insufficient to determine the other key.

13.2.1.3   Location of Encryption Devices

In a networking environment, there are a number of locations at which security threats may occur. If encryption is to be used to counter these threats, then we need to decide what to encrypt and where the encryption gear should be located. As Figure 13.4 indicates, there are two fundamental alternatives: link encryption and end-to-end encryption.

With *link encryption,* each vulnerable communications link is equipped on both ends with an encryption device. Thus, all traffic over all communications links is secured. Although this requires a lot of encryption devices in a large network, the value of this approach is clear. One disadvantage of this approach is that the message must be decrypted each time it enters a packet switch; this is necessary because the switch must read the virtual circuit number in the packet header in order to route the packet. Thus, the message is vulnerable at each switch. If this is a public packet-switching network, the user has no control over the security of the nodes.

With *end-to-end encryption,* the encryption process is carried out at the two end systems. The source host or terminal encrypts the data. The data, in encrypted form, are then transmitted unaltered across the network to the destination terminal or host. The destination shares a key with the source and so is able to decrypt the data. This approach would seem to secure the transmission against attacks on the network links or switches. There is, however, still a weak spot.

Consider the following situation. A host connects to an X.25 packet-switching network, sets up a virtual circuit to another host, and is prepared to transfer data to that other host using end-to-end encryption. As you know, data are transmitted over such a network in the form of packets, consisting of a header and some user data. What part of each packet will the host encrypt? Suppose that the host encrypts the entire packet, including the header. This will not work because, remem-

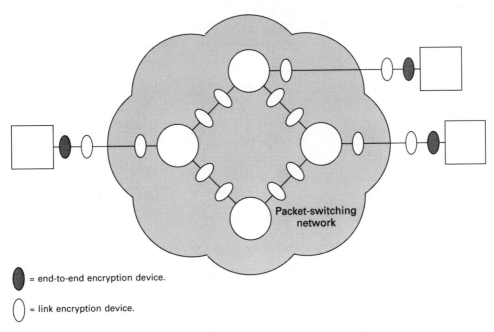

= end-to-end encryption device.

= link encryption device.

Figure 13.4 Encryption Across a Packet-Switching Network

ber, only the other host can perform the decryption. The packet-switching node will receive an encrypted packet and be unable to read the header. Therefore, it will not be able to route the packet! It follows that the host may only encrypt the user data portion of the packet and must leave the header in the clear, so that it can be read by the network.

Thus, with end-to-end encryption, the user data are secure. However, the traffic pattern is not, since packet headers are transmitted in the clear. To achieve greater security, both link and end-to-end encryption are needed, as is shown in Figure 13.4.

13.2.2   Traffic Padding

We mentioned that, in some cases, users are concerned about security from traffic analysis. With the use of link encryption, packet headers are encrypted, reducing the opportunity for traffic analysis. However, it is still possible in those circumstances for an attacker to assess the amount of traffic on a network and observe the amount of traffic entering and leaving each end system. An effective countermeasure to this attack is traffic padding, illustrated in Figure 13.5.

Traffic padding is a function that produces ciphertext output continuously, even in the absence of plaintext. A continuous random-data stream is generated. When plaintext is available, it is encrypted and transmitted. When input plaintext is not present, the random data are encrypted and transmitted. This makes it impossible for an attacker to distinguish between true data flow and noise and therefore impossible to deduce the amount of traffic.

13.2.3   Authentication Exchange

Encryption, as described earlier, protects against passive attack (eavesdropping). A different requirement is to protect against active attack (falsification of data and transactions). One particular form of such protection, which makes use of encryption, is known as message authentication.

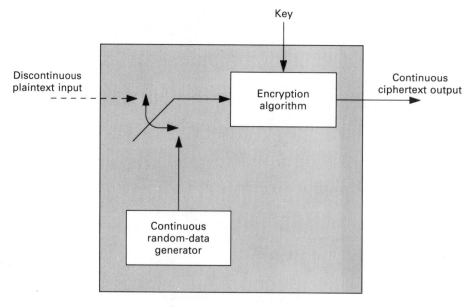

Figure 13.5 Traffic-Padding Encryption Device

A message, file, document, or other collection of data is said to be authentic when it is genuine and came from its alleged source. Message authentication is a procedure that allows communicating parties to verify that received messages are authentic. The two important aspects are to verify that the contents of the message have not been altered and that the source is authentic. We may also wish to verify a message's timeliness (that it has not been artificially delayed and replayed) and sequence relative to other messages flowing between two parties.

The method most commonly employed for message authentication involves the use of a message-authentication code. We will examine this technique and then look at the use of straightforward encryption as an alternative.

13.2.3.1 Message-Authentication Code

The use of a message-authentication code can be described as follows. The data to be sent, together with a secret key, are used to generate a message-authentication code. The data plus code are transmitted to the intended recipient. The recipient performs the same calculation on the data, using the same secret key, to generate a new message-authentication code. The received code is compared to the calculated code (Figure 13.6). If we assume that only the receiver and the sender know the identity of the secret key, and if the received code matches the calculated code, then:

- The receiver is assured that the message has not been altered. If an attacker alters the message but does not alter the code, then the receiver's calculation of the code will differ from the received code. Since the attacker is assumed not to know the secret key, the attacker cannot alter the code to correspond to the alterations in the message.

- The receiver is assured that the message is from the alleged sender. Since no one else knows the secret key, no one else could prepare a message with a proper code.

- If the message includes a sequence number (such as is used with X.25, HDLC [high-level data-link control], and the ISO transport protocol), then the receiver can be assured of the proper sequence, since an attacker cannot successfully alter the sequence number.

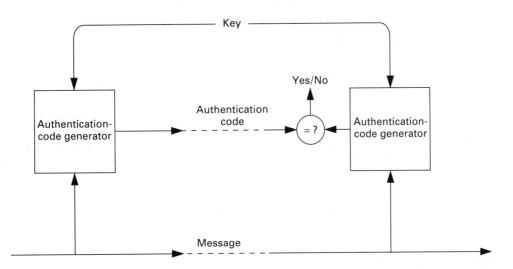

Figure 13.6 Principle of Message Authentication

A number of algorithms could be used to generate the code. The National Bureau of Standards, in its publication *DES Modes of Operation,* recommends the use of the DES (data encryption standard) algorithm. The DES algorithm is used to generate an encrypted version of the message, and the last number of bits of ciphertext are used as the code. A 16- or 32-bit code is typical.

The process just described is similar to encryption. One difference is that the authentication algorithm need not be reversible, as it must for decryption. It turns out that because of the mathematical properties of the authentication function, it is less vulnerable to being broken than encryption.

The most common practical use of authentication has been for financial messages, such as payments. For example, the Society for Worldwide Interbank Financial Telecommunications (SWIFT) uses an authentication function.

13.2.3.2   Message Authentication by Encryption

It is possible to perform authentication simply by the use of conventional encryption. If we assume that only the sender and receiver share a key (which is as it should be), then only the genuine sender would be able to successfully encrypt a message for the other participant. Furthermore, if the message includes an error-detection code and a sequence number, the receiver is assured that no alterations have been made and that sequencing is proper. Note that public-key encryption, as described earlier in this section, would not provide an authentication function, since anyone can use a device's public key to send a message, claiming to be someone else. However, the next subsection shows a use of public-key encryption that surmounts this problem.

Since conventional encryption will provide authentication, and since it is widely employed with readily available products, why not simply use this instead of a separate message-authentication code? Davies (1984) suggests three situations in which a message-authentication code is preferable:

1. There are a number of applications in which the same message is broadcast to a number of destinations. For example, notification to users that the network is now unavailable or an alarm signal in a military control center. It is cheaper and more reliable to have only one destination responsible for monitoring authenticity. Thus, the message must be broadcast in plaintext with an associated message-authentication code. The responsible system has the secret key and performs authentication. If a violation occurs, the other destination systems are alerted by a general alarm.

2. Another possible scenario is an exchange in which one side has a heavy load and cannot afford the time to decrypt all incoming messages. Authentication is carried out on a selective basis, with messages being chosen at random for checking.

3. Authentication of a computer program in plaintext is an attractive service. The computer program can be executed without having to decrypt it every time, which would be wasteful of processor resources. However, if a message-authentication code were attached to the program, it could be checked whenever assurance of the program's integrity is required.

Thus, there is a place for both authentication and encryption in meeting security requirements.

13.2.4   Digital Signature

Authentication, as just described, protects two parties exchanging messages from attack by any third party. However, it does not protect the two parties from each other. Several forms of dispute between the two are possible.

For example, suppose that John sends an authenticated message to Mary, using the scheme of Figure 13.6. Consider the following disputes that could arise:

- Mary may forge a different message and claim that it came from John. Mary would simply have to create a message and append an authentication code using the key that John and Mary share.

- John can deny sending the message. Since it is possible for Mary to forge a message, there is no way to prove that John did in fact send the message.

Both these scenarios are of legitimate concern. An example of the first scenario: An electronic funds transfer takes place, and the receiver increases the amount of funds transferred and claims that the larger amount had arrived from the sender. An example of the second scenario: An electronic-mail message contains instructions to a stockbroker for a transaction that subsequently turns out badly. The sender pretends that the message was never sent.

In situations where there is not complete trust between sender and receiver, something more than authentication is needed. The most attractive solution to this problem is the digital signature, which is analogous to the handwritten signature. It must have the following properties:

- It must be possible to verify the author and the date and time of the signature.

- It must be possible to authenticate the contents of the message at the time of the signature.

- The signature must be verifiable by third parties, to resolve disputes.

Thus, the digital-signature function includes the authentication function.

A variety of approaches has been proposed for the digital-signature function. They fall into two categories: direct and arbitrated. In the following subsections, we look at the most promising example from each category.

13.2.4.1 Direct Digital Signature

Earlier in this section, we pointed out that the public-key encryption scheme, as illustrated in Figure 13.3, part (b), is not useful for authentication. Surprisingly, there is a way of using public-key encryption to provide a digital signature, which, of course, includes authentication.

Figure 13.7, part (a), illustrates a simple direct digital-signature scheme using public-key encryption. For this scheme to work, it is necessary to know that, as indicated in subsection 13.2.1.2, public-key encryption algorithms are such that the two keys can be used in either order. That is, one can encrypt with the public key and decrypt with the matching private key, or encrypt with the private key and decrypt with the matching public key. Figure 13.7, part (a), illustrates the latter application. Note what is happening. A prepares a message to B and encrypts it using A's private key before transmitting it. B can decrypt the message using A's public key. Because the message was encrypted using A's private key, only A could have prepared the message. Therefore, the entire encrypted message serves as the signature. In addition, it is impossible to alter the message without access to A's private key, so the message is authenticated.

In the preceding scheme, the entire message is encrypted. Although this validates both author and contents, it would require a great deal of storage. Each document would have to be kept in plaintext to be used for practical purposes. A copy would also have to be keyed in ciphertext so the origin and contents could be verified in case of a dispute. A more efficient way of achieving the same results is to encrypt only a portion of the document. A minimal portion would include the sender's name, the receiver's name, a sequence number, and a checksum. If this portion of the

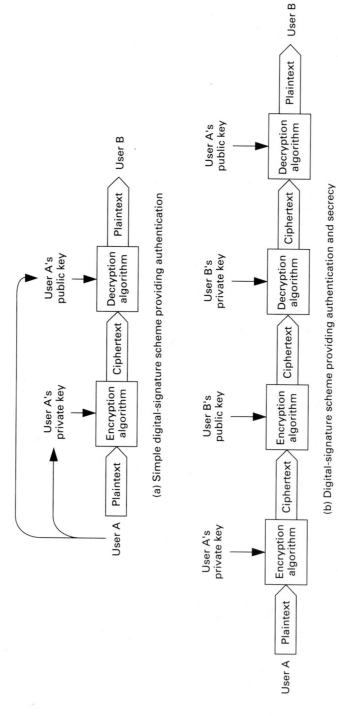

(a) Simple digital-signature scheme providing authentication

(b) Digital-signature scheme providing authentication and secrecy

Figure 13.7 Direct Digital Signature Using Public-Key System

message is encrypted with the sender's private key, it serves as a signature that verifies origin, content, and sequencing.

It is important to emphasize that the encryption process just described does not provide secrecy. That is, the message being sent is safe only from alteration, not from eavesdropping. This is obvious in the case of a signature based on a portion of the message, since the rest of the message is transmitted in the clear. Even in the case of complete encryption, as shown in Figure 13.7, part (a), there is no protection of secrecy, since any observer can decrypt the message using the sender's public key.

It is, however, possible to provide both the digital signature function, which includes authentication, and secrecy by a double use of the public-key scheme. This is illustrated in Figure 13.7, part (b). In this case, we begin, as before, by encrypting a message using the sender's private key. This provides the digital signature. Next, we encrypt again, using the receiver's public key. The final ciphertext can only be decrypted by the intended receiver, who alone possesses the matching private key. Thus, secrecy is provided. The disadvantage of this approach is that the public-key algorithm, which is complex, must be exercised four times rather than two in each communication.

13.2.4.2 Arbitrated Digital Signature

All of the schemes described so far share a common weakness: the validity of each scheme depends upon the security of the sender's private key. Now if a sender wishes to later deny sending a particular message, the sender can claim that the private key was lost or stolen and that someone else forged his or her signature. Administrative controls relating to the security of private keys can be employed to thwart or at least weaken this ploy, but the threat is still there, at least to some degree. This problem can be circumvented using an arbitrator.

As with direct signature schemes, there is a variety of arbitrated signature schemes. In general terms, they all operate as follows. Every signed message from a sender S to a receiver R goes first to an arbitrator A, who subjects the message and its signature to a number of tests to check its origin and content. The message is then dated and sent to R with an indication that it has been verified to the satisfaction of the arbitrator. The presence of A solves the problem inherent in direct signature schemes that S might disown the message.

The arbitrator plays a sensitive and crucial role in this sort of scheme, and all parties must have a great deal of trust that the arbitration mechanism is working properly. The use of a trusted system, described later in the chapter, might satisfy this requirement.

13.2.4.3 Digital Signature versus Authentication

All of the digital-signature schemes just described provide authentication plus the ability to resolve disputes between the communicating parties. Thus, on the face of it, these schemes would be superior to the "pure" authentication schemes discussed earlier. However, although authentication is becoming increasingly popular, the use of digital signatures is still rare. The principal reasons for this are:

- The digital-signature scheme is more complex and therefore more costly.

- All of the digital-signature schemes appear to be vulnerable in some way and require some administrative or other extra control mechanisms or procedures.

- In some circumstances, only pure authentication is required, and any additional functionality is superfluous.

13.2.5   Access Control

The purpose of access controls is to ensure that only authorized users have access to a particular system and its individual resources and that access to and modification of a particular portion of data are limited to authorized individuals and programs. Strictly speaking, access control is a computer security rather than a network security issue. That is, in most cases, access-control mechanisms are implemented within a single computer to control the access to that computer. However, since much of the access to a computer is by means of a networking or communications facility, access control is one of the areas of interest in OSI security.

13.2.5.1   User-Oriented Access Control

Figure 13.8 depicts, generically, the measures taken to control access in a data-processing system. They fall into two categories: those associated with the user and those associated with the data.

The control of access by user is, unfortunately, sometimes referred to as authentication. Since this term is now widely used in the sense of message authentication, we will refrain from applying it here. The reader is warned, however, that this usage may be encountered in the literature.

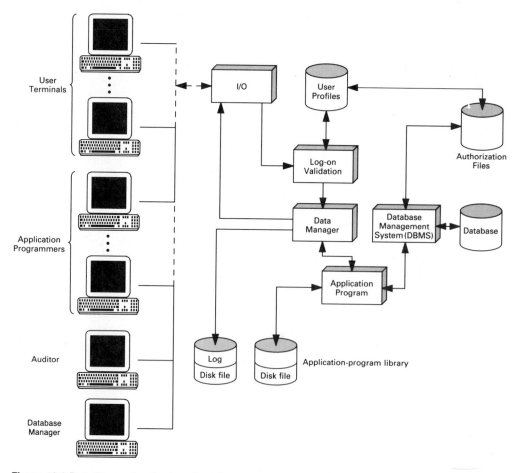

Figure 13.8 Data-Processing-System Security

A quite common example of user access control on a time-sharing system is the user log-on, which requires both a user identifier (ID) and a password. The system will only allow a user to log on if that user's ID is known to the system and if the user knows the password associated by the system with that ID. This ID/password system is a notoriously unreliable method of user access control. Users can forget their passwords and accidentally or intentionally reveal their passwords. Hackers have become very skillful at guessing IDs for special users, such as system-control and system-management personnel. Finally, the ID/password file is subject to penetration attempts.

There are a number of measures that can be taken to improve the security of the password scheme. Three requirements can be stated:

1. There should be a large number of possible password combinations. This reduces an outsider's chances of success in either guessing the codes or using a computer to make repetitive "brute-force" attempts under program control. It is useful to restrict the passwords to alphanumeric characters and to use pronounceable combinations of characters, so that users can easily remember them and avoid writing them down. A five-character password would have over 60 million possible combinations; even with the restriction to pronounceable combinations, this is a reasonably secure length, provided points 2 and 3 are met. One note of caution: Users should not be allowed to assign their own passwords. People tend to use personal names, dates, and other readily guessed information.

2. There should be automatic disconnection of the incoming terminal line after a small number of invalid password attempts have been made. The usual limit is three to five attempts. This means an attacker must hang up and redial after every few tries, increasing the time required to perform a brute-force penetration to a matter of years. The programmed attack favored by hackers is thus rendered useless. A related and very valuable feature is automatic deactivation of a user ID if it is employed in multiple invalid log-on attempts.

3. The operating system should log and report invalid sign-on attempts and other "events" with security implications. These could include, for example, an unauthorized person's attempting to run sensitive application programs, such as human resources systems, or using high-powered system utility programs to copy or modify files. This feature will reveal whether attempts at computer vandalism are taking place, so that further, more positive means can be used to report and apprehend the attackers. Security reports can also be used as evidence in police or FBI investigations and trials.

The problem of user access control is compounded over a communication network. The log-on dialogue must take place over the communication medium, and eavesdropping is a potential threat. One approach to this problem is to encrypt the ID/password. All of the paraphernalia of encryption, including key management, would then be required. If the messages themselves do not require encryption, this is an expensive means of protecting passwords.

User access control in a distributed environment, such as a LAN, can be either centralized or decentralized. In a centralized approach, the network provides a log-on service, determining who is allowed to use the network and to whom the user is allowed to connect.

Decentralized user access control treats the network as a transparent communication link, and the usual log-on procedure is carried out by the destination host. Of course, the security concerns for transmitting passwords over the network must still be addressed.

In many networks, two levels of access control may be used. Individual hosts may be provided with a log-on facility to protect host-specific resources and applications. In addition, the network as a whole may provide protection to restrict network access to authorized users. This two-level facility is desirable for the common case, currently, in which the network connects disparate hosts and simply provides a convenient means of terminal-host access. In a more uniform network of hosts, some centralized access policy could be enforced in a network-control center.

More elaborate techniques than a simple password/ID have been proposed for user identification. Exotic techniques such as voiceprints, fingerprints, and hand-geometry analysis may be foolproof but are at present considered too expensive.

13.2.5.2 Data-Oriented Access Control

Following successful log-on, the user has been granted access to one or a set of hosts and applications. This is generally not sufficient for a system that includes sensitive data in its database. Through the user-access-control procedure, a user can be identified to the system. Associated with each user, there can be a profile that specifies permissible operations and file accesses. The operating system can then enforce rules based on the user profile. The database-management system, however, must control access to specific records or even portions of records. For example, it may be permissible for anyone in administration to obtain a list of company personnel, but only selected individuals may have access to salary information. The issue involves more than just level of detail. Whereas the operating system may grant a user permission to access a file or use an application, following which there are no further security checks, the database-management system must make a decision on each individual access attempt. That decision will depend not only on the user's identity but also on the specific parts of the data being accessed and even on the information already divulged to the user.

A general model of access control as exercised by a database-management system takes the form of an access matrix (Figure 13.9). One axis of the matrix consists of identified subjects that may attempt data access. Typically, this list will consist of individual users or user groups, al-

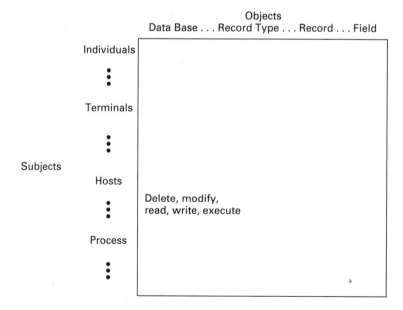

Figure 13.9 Database-Access Matrix

though access could be controlled for terminals, hosts, or applications instead of or in addition to users. The other axis lists the objects that may be accessed. At the greatest level of detail, objects may be individual data fields. More aggregate groupings—such as records, files, or even the entire database—may also be objects in the matrix. Each entry in the matrix indicates the access rights of that subject for that object.

In practice, an access matrix is usually sparse and is implemented by decomposition in one of two ways. The matrix may be decomposed by columns, yielding access-control lists. Thus, for each object, an access-control list lists users and their permitted access opportunities. Decomposition by rows yields capability tickets. A capability ticket specifies authorized objects and operations for a user. Each user has a number of tickets and may be authorized to lend or give them to others. Because tickets may be dispersed around the system, they present a greater security problem than access-control lists.

Network considerations for data-oriented access control parallel those for user-oriented access control. If only certain users are permitted to access certain items of data, then encryption may be needed to protect those items during transmission to authorized users. Typically, data access control is decentralized—that is, controlled by host-based database-management systems. If a network database server exists on a network, then data access control becomes a network function.

13.2.6   Data Integrity

In ISO 7498-2, a marked distinction is drawn between authentication and integrity. Authentication is viewed as the process of confirming the integrity of a peer communicator. However, when the the term *integrity* itself is used, it refers to the "correctness" of actual data. For integrity, techniques similar to error control are appropriate.

Data integrity is of central concern in virtually all communications protocols, and mechanisms exist to ensure that integrity. A common example of this is the use of a checksum to protect either the header or the entire protocol data unit (PDU); this technique can be used with both connection-less and connection-mode transmissions. In addition, for connection-mode techniques, sequence numbers are typically used to ensure that there are no losses, duplications, or misordering.

These protocol mechanisms can be exploited to provide data integrity as a security mechanism. For example, if the checksum of a PDU is encrypted, then an attacker may be able to modify the PDU but be unable to modify the checksum to hide the changes. The recipient would detect the mismatch between the received checksum and the calculated checksum and conclude that there had been either a transmission error or a security violation. Similarly, the use of encrypted sequence numbers protects against deletions, replay, and misordering.

13.2.7   Routing Control

Network-layer routes can be chosen either dynamically or by prearrangement to use only physically secure subnetworks, relays, or links. For dynamic routing techniques, a security label could be used to discriminate among different security classifications of PDUs during routing. Also, if persistent manipulation of data is detected, a different route may be requested.

13.2.8   Notarization

Properties about the data communication between two or more entities—such as its integrity, origin, time, and destination—can be assured by providing a notarization mechanism. The assurance is provided by a third-party notary, which is trusted by the communicating entities and which holds the information necessary to provide the required assurance.

13.2.9   Trusted Functionality

The techniques we have discussed so far have been concerned with protecting a given message or item from passive or active attack by a given user. A somewhat different but widely applicable requirement is to protect data or resources on the basis of levels of security. This is commonly found in the military, where information is categorized as unclassified (U), confidential (C), secret (S), top secret (TS), or beyond. This concept is equally applicable in other areas, where information can be organized into gross categories and users can be granted clearances to access certain categories of data. For example, the highest level of security might be for strategic corporate-planning documents and data, accessible only by corporate officers and their staff; next might come sensitive financial and personnel data, accessible only by administration personnel and corporate officers; and so on.

When multiple categories or levels of data are defined, the requirement is referred to as *multi-level security*. This requirement was first addressed in the context of a single computer system and was subsequently extended to networks. We examine the single-system concept in this subsection.

The general statement of the requirement for multilevel security is that a subject at a high level may not convey information to a subject at a lower or noncomparable level unless that flow accurately reflects the will of an authorized user. For implementation purposes, this requirement is in two parts and can be simply stated. A multilevel secure system must enforce:

1. *No read up:* A subject can only read an object of lower or equal security level. This is referred to in the literature as the *simple security property*.

2. *No write down:* A subject can only write into an object of higher or equal security level. This is referred to in the literature as the **-property*[2] (pronounced *star property*).

These two rules, if properly enforced, provide multilevel security. For a data-processing system, the approach that has been taken, and that has been the object of much research and development, is based on the *reference-monitor* concept. This approach is depicted in Figure 13.10. The reference monitor is a controlling element in the hardware and operating system of a computer that regulates the access of subjects to objects on the basis of security parameters of the subject and object. The reference monitor has access to a file, known as the *security-kernel database,* that lists the access privileges (security clearance) of each subject and the protection attributes (classification level) of each object. The reference monitor enforces the security rules (no read up, no write down) and has the following properties:

- *Complete mediation:* The security rules are enforced on every access, not just, for example, when a file is opened.

- *Isolation:* The reference monitor and database are protected from unauthorized modification.

---

2.   The "*" does not stand for anything. No one could think of an appropriate name for the property during the writing of the first report on the model. The asterisk was a dummy character entered in the draft so that a text editor could rapidly find and replace all instances of its use once the property was named. No name was ever devised, and so the report was published with the "*" intact.

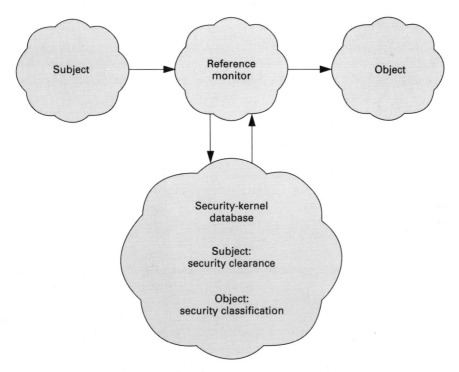

Figure 13.10 Reference-Monitor Concept

- *Verifiability:* The reference monitor's correctness must be provable. That is, it must be possible to mathematically demonstrate that the reference monitor enforces the security rules and provides complete mediation and isolation.

These are stiff requirements. The requirement for complete mediation means that every access to data within main memory and on disk and tape must be mediated. Pure software implementations impose too high a performance penalty to be practical; the solution must be at least partly in hardware. The requirement for isolation means that it must not be possible for an attacker, no matter how clever, to change the logic of the reference monitor or the contents of the security-kernel database. Finally, the requirement for mathematical proof is formidable for something as complex as a general-purpose computer. A system that can provide such verification is referred to as a *trusted system.*

In an effort to meet its own needs, and also as a service to the public, the U.S. Department of Defense in 1981 established the Computer Security Center within the National Security Agency with the goal of encouraging the widespread availability of trusted computer systems. This goal is realized through the center's Commercial Product Evaluation Program. In essence, the center attempts to apply mathematical techniques to verify commercially available products as meeting the security requirements just outlined. The center classifies verified products according to the range of security features they provide. These evaluations are needed for Department of Defense procurements but are published and freely available. Hence, they can serve as guidance to commercial customers for the purchase of commercially available, off-the-shelf equipment.

13.2.10   Security Label

Resources, including protocol data units (PDUs), may have security labels associated with them to indicate a security-classification level. A security label may be a distinct field in a PDU, or it may be implicit (e.g., implied by the use of a specific key to encrypt data or implied by the context of the data, such as the source or route).

13.2.11   Event Detection

Security-relevant event detection is a mechanism defined as part of OSI system management, specifically event-handling management. Examples of security-relevant events are:

- A specific security violation
- A specific selected event
- An overflow of a count of a number of occurrences (e.g., too many log-on attempts within a specified period of time)

  Detection of a security-relevant event could cause one or more of the following actions:

- Local reporting
- Remote reporting
- Logging
- Recovery action

13.2.12   Security-Audit Trail

A security-audit trail is a record of security-relevant information, such as a log of security-relevant events. Such a record permits detection and investigation of breaches of security by permitting a subsequent security audit. A security audit is an independent review and examination of system records and activities in order to test for adequacy of system controls, ensure compliance with established policy and operational procedures, detect breaches in security, and recommend any indicated changes in control, policy, and procedures.

The generation of a security-audit trail by logging and recording is classified as a security mechanism, whereas the actual security audit is a security-management function.

13.2.13   Security Recovery

Security recovery deals with requests from other mechanisms, such as event handling, and management functions and takes recovery actions by applying a set of rules. Recovery actions may be:

- *Immediate:* may create an immediate abort of operations, like disconnect
- *Temporary:* may produce temporary invalidation of an entity
- *Long-term:* may involve introducing an entity into a ``black list'' or changing a key

13.3   SECURITY SERVICES

The ISO 7498-2 standard defines a security service as a service provided by a layer of communicating open systems that ensures adequate security of the systems or of data transfers. These

Table 13.5 Security Services

Authentication The assurance that the communicating entity is the one that it claims to be.

Peer-entity authentication
Used in association with a logical connection to provide confidence in the identity of the entities connected.
Data-origin authentication
In connectionless transfer, provides assurance that the source of received data is as claimed.

Access Control The prevention of unauthorized use of a resource—i.e., this service controls who can have access to a resource, under what conditions access can occur, and what those accessing the resource are allowed to do.

Data confidentiality The protection of data from unauthorized disclosure.

Connection confidentiality
The protection of all (N)-user data on an (N) connection
Connectionless confidentiality
The protection of all (N)-user data in a single (N) SDU.
Selective-field confidentiality
The confidentiality of selected fields within the (N)-user data on an (N) connection or in a single connectionless (N) SDU.
Traffic-flow confidentiality
The protection of the information that might be derived from observation of traffic flows.

Data Integrity The assurance that data received are exactly as sent by an authorized entity—i.e., that they reflect no modification, insertion, deletion, or replay.

Connection integrity with recovery
Provides for the integrity of all (N)-user data on an (N) connection and detects any modification, insertion, deletion, or replay of any data within an entire SDU sequence, with recovery attempted.
Connection integrity without recovery
As for the preceding service, but provides only detection without recovery.
Selective-field connection integrity
Provides for the integrity of selected fields within the (N)-user data of an (N) SDU transferred over a connection and takes the form of determination of whether the selected fields have been modified, inserted, deleted, or replayed.
Connectionless integrity
Provides for the integrity of a single connectionless SDU and may take the form of detection of SDU modification. Additionally, a limited form of replay detection may be provided.
Selective-field connectionless integrity
Provides for the integrity of selected fields within a single connectionless SDU; takes the form of determination of whether the selected fields have been modified.

Nonrepudiation Provides protection against denial by one of the entities involved in a communication of having participated in all or part of the communication.

Nonrepudiation, origin
Provides proof that the message was sent by the specified party.
Nonrepudiation, destination
Provides proof that the message was received by the specified party.

services are broken down into five categories and 14 specific services (Table 13.5). The categories are:

1. Authentication
2. Access control
3. Data confidentiality
4. Data integrity
5. Nonrepudiation

13.3.1   Authentication

The authentication service is concerned with assuring that a communication is authentic. In the case of a single message, such as a warning or an alarm signal, the function of the authentication service is to assure the recipient that the message is from the source that it claims to be from. In the case of an ongoing interaction, such as the connection of a terminal to a host, two aspects are involved. First, at the time of connection initiation, the service assures that the two entities are authentic—that is, that each is the entity that it claims to be. Second, the service must assure that the connection is not interfered with in such a way that a third party can masquerade as one of the two legitimate parties for the purposes of unauthorized transmission or reception.

Two specific authentication services are defined in the standard:

1. *Peer-entity authentication:* provides for the corroboration of the identity of a peer entity in an association. It is provided for use at the establishment of, or at times during the data-transfer phase of, a connection. It attempts to provide confidence that an entity is not attempting either a masquerade or an unauthorized replay of a previous connection.

2. *Data-origin authentication:* provides for the corroboration of the source of a data unit. It does not provide protection against the duplication or modification of data units. This type of service supports applications like electronic mail, where there are no prior interactions between the communicating entities.

13.3.2   Access Control

In the context of network security, access control is the ability to limit and control the access to host systems and applications via communications links. To achieve this, each entity trying to gain access must first be identified, or authenticated, so that access rights can be tailored to the individual.

13.3.3   Data Confidentiality

Confidentiality is the protection of transmitted data from passive attacks. In terms of protecting against the release of message contents, several levels of protection can be identified. The broadest service is one that protects all user data transmitted between two users over a period of time. For example, if a virtual circuit is set up between two systems, this broad protection would prevent the release of any user data transmitted over the virtual circuit. Narrower forms of this service can also be defined, including the protection of a single message or even specific fields within a message. These refinements are less useful than the broad approach and may even be more complex and expensive to implement.

The other aspect of confidentiality is the protection of traffic flow from analysis. This requires that an attacker not be able to observe the source and destination, frequency, length, or other characteristics of the traffic on a communications facility.

Table 13.5 provides brief definitions of the four types of data confidentiality:

1. Connection confidentiality

2. Connectionless confidentiality

3. Selective-field confidentiality

4. Traffic-flow confidentiality

13.3.4 Data Integrity

The data-integrity service assures that messages are received as sent, with no duplication, insertion, modification, or replays. The destruction of data is also covered under this service. Thus, the data-integrity service addresses the threats of both message-stream modification and denial of service. As with confidentiality, integrity can apply to a stream of messages, a single message, or selected fields within a message. Again, the most useful and straightforward approach is total stream protection.

As Table 13.5 indicates, a distinction is made between the service with and without recovery. Since the integrity service relates to active threats, we are concerned with detection rather than prevention. If a violation of integrity is detected, then the service may simply report this violation, and some other portion of software or human intervention is required to recover from the violation. Alternatively, there are mechanisms available to recover from the loss of integrity of data, as we will review later in the chapter. The incorporation of automated recovery mechanisms is in general the more attractive alternative.

13.3.5 Nonrepudiation

The nonrepudiation service prevents either sender or receiver from denying a transmitted message. Table 13.5 briefly defines the two types of nonrepudiation:

1. Nonrepudiation with proof of origin

2. Nonrepudiation with proof of delivery

13.4 SECURITY SERVICES, MECHANISMS, AND THE OSI ARCHITECTURE

A security mechanism is any software or hardware means of implementing a security service. In the context of OSI, a security service is provided as part of an (N) service to (N) users. Each security service at the interface between layers (N) and (N + 1) is supported by one or more mechanisms incorporated into the (N) entity and its (N) protocol. Thus, the following questions can be posed:

- For each security service, what are the appropriate mechanisms?

- Which security services should be allocated to each OSI layer?

- What is the consequent placement of security mechanisms in the OSI layers?

All of these issues are addressed in ISO 7498–2. We begin with the first question.

13.4.1   Relationship of Security Services and Mechanisms

Table 13.6, from ISO 7498–2, shows the relationship between OSI security services and security mechanisms. Specifically, the table shows which mechanisms can be used to provide each service.

13.4.1.1   Authentication

Encryption is a key mechanism to be used for the authentication service. If two parties and two parties alone share the information needed for mutual exchange of encrypted data, then no third party can claim a false identity. A more explicit mechanism is the *digital-signature* technique. In effect, a sender must ''sign'' the message in such a way that the signature can be authenticated.

Another group of mechanisms that are relevant to authentication are referred to by ISO as the *authentication-exchange* mechanisms. These include the use of passwords or other means of identifying a user and the exchange of acknowledgment signals. Also included in this category is the use of an encrypted message-authentication code. These mechanisms can be used for peer-entity authentication.

13.4.1.2   Access Control

Various access-control techniques can be used to support the access-control service. Some of these techniques were discussed in section 13.2.

13.4.1.3   Confidentiality

By far, the most important technique for providing confidentiality is *encryption*. As we have seen, encryption can be used to protect against release of message contents by the use of an end-to-end technique. Link encryption provides traffic-flow confidentiality. Traffic-flow confidentiality is also supported by *traffic padding,* which involves filling in gaps in message traffic with meaningless ciphertext, so that the traffic pattern is not readily observable.

Another mechanism that may be relevant to confidentiality is *routing control*. For sensitive data, routes can be chosen so as to use only physically secure networks or links. For example, a user may employ both a private network and public telecommunications networks to interconnect offices. If the private network is equipped with an encryption mechanism, then all sensitive data should be routed through the private network only.

13.4.1.4   Integrity

A principal means of countering threats to integrity is the use of *encryption*. If an attacker is unable to decipher a message, then it becomes impossible for the attacker to successfully modify the message. A change made to the encrypted message will simply result in garble when it is deciphered by the intended receiver. For connectionless communication, *digital-signature mechanisms* may also be useful.

Encryption provides a means of detecting the modification of a message but does not, by itself, address other integrity concerns, such as replaying, reordering, or destroying messages. For this purpose, mechanisms that ISO refers to simply as *data-integrity mechanisms* are needed. In general, different mechanisms are used to provide integrity of selective fields or individual messages and integrity of a stream of messages. Typically, these mechanisms are based on the error-control mechanisms already present in the protocol.

13.4.1.5   Nonrepudiation

As we have seen, the principal mechanism for the nonrepudiation service is the *digital signature,* which involves the use of a private key applied to a portion of the data. To prevent the repudiation of the contents of a message, rather than the message itself, *data-integrity mechanisms*, such as encrypting an error-detecting code, are used as part of the digital signature. Finally, third-party *notarization* may enhance the nonrepudiation service.

13.4.2   Provision of Security Services at an OSI Layer

13.4.2.1   Determination of Services

Services at a particular layer may be provided either on request or automatically. In the former case, an $(N + 1)$ entity requests a desired target security protection from the (N) service. In the case of connection-mode communication, the protection services are usually requested/granted at connection-establishment time. The provision of a security service may involve a negotiation among the communicating $(N + 1)$ entities and the (N) service. This can be carried out either as a separate procedure or as an integral part of the connection-establishment protocol.

In the case of connectionless communication, the protection service is requested/granted for each instance of a UNITDATA.request. In either case, if the $(N + 1)$ entity does not specify a target security protection, the (N) layer will follow a security policy in accordance with the security portion of the management information base (MIB).

Once the level of security service to be provided by the (N) layer is decided, the (N) layer will attempt to achieve the target protection by either or both of the following methods:

- Invoking security mechanisms directly within the (N) layer
- Requesting protection services from the $(N - 1)$ layer

13.4.2.2   Establishment of a Protected (*N*) Connection

If one or more security services are to be provided for a connection-mode communication, the first step is to provide those services for connection establishment. In certain protocols, to achieve a satisfactory target protection, the sequence of operations is crucial. The following is the possible set of operations in the appropriate sequence:

1. *Outgoing access control:* The (N) layer must determine (from the MIB) whether the requested protected (N) connection is permitted.

2. *Peer-entity authentication:* If peer-entity authentication is requested, or dictated by the MIB, then an authentication exchange must take place, to provide unilateral or mutual authentication.

3. *Access-control service:* The destination (N) entity or intermediate systems may impose access-control restrictions.

4. *Confidentiality:* If a total or selective confidentiality has been chosen, a protected (N) connection must be established. This involves setting up an encryption scheme and distributing keys. This may be done by prearrangement, in the authentication protocol, or by a separate protocol.

5. *Data integrity:* If data integrity of all user data or selective field integrity has been chosen, a protected (N) connection must be established.

6. *Nonrepudiation services:* If a nonrepudiation service is selected, the (N) layer must provide the appropriate mechanisms.

Table 13.6 Summary Matrix of Security Services and Mechanisms

	Encipherment	Digital signature	Access control	Data integrity	Authentication exchange	Traffic padding	Routing control	Notarization
Authentication								
Peer entity authentication	Y	Y	•	•	Y	•	•	•
Data origin authentication	Y	Y	•	•	•	•	•	•
Access Control	•	•	Y	•	•	•	•	•
Data Confidentiality								
Connection confidentiality	Y	•	•	•	•	•	Y	•
Connectionless confidentiality	Y	•	•	•	•	•	Y	•
Selected field confidentiality	Y	•	•	•	•	•	•	•
Traffic flow confidentiality	Y	•	•	•	•	Y	Y	•

Data Integrity

Mechanism				Data Integrity				
Connection integrity with recovery	Y	•	•	Y	•	•	•	•
Connection integrity without recovery	Y	•	•	Y	•	•	•	•
Selective field connection integrity	Y	•	•	Y	•	•	•	•
Connectionless integrity	Y	Y	•	Y	•	•	•	•
Selective field connectionless integrity	Y	Y	•	Y	•	•	•	•

Nonrepudiation

Mechanism								
Nonrepudiation, origin	•	Y	•	Y	•	•	•	Y
Nonrepudiation, delivery	•	Y	•	Y	•	•	•	Y

Y = Yes: the mechanism is considered to be appropriate, either on its own or in combination with other mechanisms
• = The mechanism is considered not to be appropriate

13.4.2.3   Operation of a Protected (*N*) Connection

The operation of a protected (*N*) connection involves the following functions visible at the (*N*)-service boundary:

- Peer-entity authentication (at intervals)
- Protection of selected fields
- Reporting of active attack

  In addition, the following may be needed:

- Security-audit-trail recording
- Event detection and handling

13.4.2.4   Provision of Protected Connectionless Data Transmission

Not all of the services available in connection-mode protocols are available in connectionless protocols. Those that are appropriate are the following:

- Peer-entity authentication
- Data-origin authentication
- Access-control service
- Connectionless confidentiality
- Selective-field confidentiality
- Connectionless integrity
- Selective-field connectionless integrity
- Nonrepudiation, origin

13.4.3   Placement of Security Services and Mechanisms in OSI Layers

ISO 7498-2 lists the following principles used to allocate security services and mechanisms to OSI layers:

- The number of alternative ways of achieving a service should be minimized.
- It is acceptable to build secure systems by providing security services in more than one layer.
- Additional functionality required for security should not unnecessarily duplicate the existing OSI functions.
- Violation of layer independence should be avoided.
- The amount of trusted functionality should be minimized.
- Wherever possible, the additional security functions of a layer should be defined in such a way that implementation of one or more self-contained modules is not precluded.
- The OSI security architecture is assumed to apply to end systems containing all seven layers and to relay systems.

  Table 13.7, from ISO 7498-2, illustrates the layers of the reference model in which particular security services can be provided. Table 13.8, which can be derived from information in ISO 7498-2, shows the layers of the OSI model in which particular security mechanisms may be implemented. Let us consider each layer in turn.

Table 13.7 Placement of Security Services in OSI Layers

				Layer			
	1	**2**	**3**	**4**	**5**	**6**	**7**
Authentication							
Peer entity authentication			3	4			7
Data origin authentication			3	4			7
Access Control			3	4			7
Confidentiality							
Connection confidentiality	1	2	3	4			7
Connectionless confidentiality		2	3	4			7
Selective field confidentiality							7
Traffic flow confidentiality	1		3				7
Integrity							
Connection integrity with recovery				4			7
Connection integrity without recovery			3	4			7
Selective field connection integrity							7
Connectionless integrity			3	4			7
Selective field connectionless integrity							7
Nonrepudiation							
Nonrepudiation, origin							7
Nonrepudiation, delivery							7

13.4.3.1 Physical Layer

The only services provided at the physical layer are connection confidentiality and traffic-flow confidentiality, to be used across a physical link. Total encryption of the data stream is the principal security mechanism at the physical layer.

Table 13.8 Placement of Security Mechanisms in OSI Layers

				Layer			
	1	**2**	**3**	**4**	**5**	**6**	**7**
Encipherment	1	2	3	4		6	
Digital signature			3	4		6	7
Access control			3	4			7
Data integrity			3	4		6	
Authentication exchange			3	4			7
Traffic padding			3				7
Routing control			3				
Notarization						6	7

13.4.3.2   Data-Link Layer

Although ISO 7498-2 lists connection and connectionless confidentiality as potential data-link services, an annex to the standard states that encipherment at the data-link layer is not recommended. The encipherment can be done at the physical or network layer, depending on requirements. Thus, the provision of this service at the data-link layer is a duplication of effort.

13.4.3.3   Network Layer

Many of the defined services are suitable for provision at the network layer. In general, the network layer can provide simple bulk protection of all end-system to end-system communication. These services include:

- *Peer-entity authentication:* can be provided by authentication exchange or digital signature.
- *Data-origin authentication:* can be provided by encryption or signature mechanisms.
- *Access-control service:* provided through the appropriate access-control mechanisms. Access control can serve a number of purposes. For example, it allows an end system to control establishment of network connections and to reject unwanted calls. It also allows one or more subnetworks to control usage of network-layer resources.
- *Connection confidentiality:* provided by encryption and/or routing control.
- *Connectionless confidentiality:* provided by encryption and/or routing control.
- *Traffic-flow confidentiality:* This is achieved by a traffic-padding mechanism, in conjunction with a confidentiality service at or below the network layer, and/or routing control.
- *Connection integrity without recovery:* provided by using a data-integrity mechanism, sometimes in connection with an encryption mechanism.
- *Connectionless integrity:* provided by using a data-integrity mechanism, sometimes in connection with an encryption mechanism.

Identical security mechanisms need to be used by the protocol(s) that perform subnetwork access and by relaying and routing operations associated with providing the end-to-end network service.

13.4.3.4   Transport Layer

The list of services that can be provided at the transport layer is almost the same as for the network layer. The principal difference is that the network layer is principally concerned with supporting end-to-end communication between end systems, whereas the transport layer is concerned with supporting end-to-end communication between individual users in end systems. Thus, connection integrity with recovery is more properly implemented in the transport layer, which is managing the user-to-user connection. On the other hand, traffic-flow confidentiality applies to all user-to-user connections between a pair of end systems and so should be applied at the network level.

13.4.3.5   Session Layer

No security services are provided at the session layer. For end-to-end services between users, the transport layer is capable of providing the services. Furthermore, if encryption is done at the transport layer rather than the session layer, then the session header can be protected.

13.4.3.6   Presentation Layer

The presentation layer does not specifically provide security services, since these can be accomplished at the application layer. However, the presentation layer must provide those facilities that rely on mechanisms that can only operate on a transfer-syntax encoding of data; these facilities are provided on behalf of the application layer.

In particular, for application services that rely on encryption, the encryption is done at the presentation layer. Performing encryption at this layer, and providing the supported services at the application layer, provides a high granularity of protection compared to providing the services at lower layers. An example of the benefit of using the presentation layer for encryption is that only those fields that absolutely require encryption need be processed.

The only application service for which presentation mechanisms are never required is access control. Those application services that must rely on presentation mechanisms are:

- Connection confidentiality
- Connectionless confidentiality
- Selective-field confidentiality

All other application security services may be supported either by the presentation layer or by mechanisms in the application layer.

13.4.3.7   Application Layer

Each of the defined OSI security services may be provided at the application level. Indeed, it is only through the application-service interface that a user can request on-demand security services, regardless of the layer of the architecture at which the supporting mechanisms are placed.

13.5   AUTHENTICATION DURING ACSE ASSOCIATION ESTABLISHMENT

One of the first specifications of a security service and an associated security mechanism to be issued by ISO was the enhancement of the association-control-service element (ACSE) to support authentication during association establishment (ISO 8649 AM 1, ISO 8650 AM 1).

The objective of these amendments is to enable some simple forms of authentication. It was recognized that a generalized two-way handshake can support a very useful class of authentication methods. These methods include simple password mechanisms that are widely employed.

The approach taken by ISO is to define the original version of ACSE to be the mandatory kernel functional unit and to define the new capability as an optional authentication functional unit. The kernel is the default functional unit. An implementation that either explicitly or implicitly (i.e., by default) requests just the kernel functional unit only references the original ACSE functions and may not employ authentication. In this section, we look first at the ACSE service and then the supporting protocol.

13.5.1   ACSE Service

In the ACSE-service definition, the amendment simply adds three optional parameters to the A-ASSOCIATE service. Two of them carry authentication-related information, while the third may be used to negotiate the ACSE functional units for the association. An optional parameter is also

Table 13.9 Association-Control-Service Primitives and Parameters

Primitive	Functional Unit	Parameters Carried in APDU*
A-ASSOCIATE. request	Kernel	Application-context name, calling AP title, calling AE qualifier, calling AP invocation-identifier, calling AE invocation-identifier, called AP title, called AE qualifier, called AP invocation-identifier, called AE invocation-identifier, **ACSE requirements,** user information
	Authentication	**Authentication-mechanism name, authentication value**
A-ASSOCIATE. indication	Kernel	Application-context name, calling AP title, calling AE qualifier, calling AP invocation-identifier, calling AE invocation-identifier, called AP title, called AE qualifier, called AP invocation-identifier, called AE invocation-identifier, **ACSE requirements,** user information
	Authentication	**Authentication-mechanism name, authentication value**
A-ASSOCIATE. response	Kernel	Application-context name, responding AP title, responding AE qualifier, responding AP invocation-identifier, responding AE invocation-identifier, **ACSE requirements,** user information, result, diagnostic
	Authentication	**Authentication-mechanism name, authentication value**
A-ASSOCIATE. confirm	Kernel	Application-context name, responding AP title, responding AE qualifier, responding AP invocation-identifier, responding AE invocation-identifier, **ACSE requirements,** user information, result, result source, diagnostic
	Authentication	**Authentication-mechanism name, authentication value**
A-RELEASE. request/indication	Kernel	Reason, user information
A-RELEASE. response/confirm	Kernel	Reason, user information, result
A-ABORT. request	Kernel	User information
	Authentication	**Diagnostic**
A-ABORT. indication	Kernel	Abort source, user information
	Authentication	**Diagnostic**
A-P-ABORT. indication	Kernel	—

* For clarity, the ACSE-service parameters that are passed directly to the presentation or session layers are omitted. See Table 5.9 for a list of these parameters.

added to the A-ABORT service and may be used to express the authentication-related diagnostics. No new service primitives are introduced.

Table 13.9 updates Table 5.9 to show the new parameters (highlighted in bold). For the A-ASSOCIATE service, the following parameters are added:

- *ACSE requirements:* Used by the A-ASSOCIATE.request primitive to indicate the functional unit requested for the association. If not present, only the kernel functional unit is available for the association. If present, the parameter takes on the value *authentication*. If the ACSE does not support this functional unit, it simply removes the parameter. Otherwise, the parameter is delivered in an indication primitive. If the acceptor accepts the functional unit, it includes the parameter in the response primitive, which is delivered in the confirm primitive.

- *Authentication-mechanism name:* If the authentication functional unit is selected, then this parameter identifies the authentication mechanism in use. If this parameter is not in use, the communicating application entities (AEs) must implicitly know the mechanism in use (e.g., by prior understanding).

- *Authentication value:* The authentication value is used to transmit a password type of value between communicating application entities. The value may be issued by either or both entities for one-way or two-way authentication. The requesting entity issues its value in the request primitive, and it is delivered in the indication primitive. The accepting entity issues its value in the response primitive, and it is delivered in the confirm primitive.

The *diagnostic* parameter is added to the A-ABORT service. It takes on one of the following values when issued in an A-ABORT primitive:

- No reason given
- Protocol
- Authentication-mechanism name not recognized
- Authentication-mechanism name required
- Authentication failure
- Authentication required

In an annex to ISO 8650 AM 1, a simple authentication mechanism is specified, with the name *joint iso-ccitt association-control authentication mechanism*. It is intended both for general use and as an example of an authentication-mechanism specification. Figure 13.11 indicates the operation of the mechanism.

13.5.2   ACSE Protocol

In the ACSE-protocol specification, the amendment adds three optional fields to the A-ASSOCIATE-REQUEST and A-ASSOCIATE-RESPONSE APDUs. Two of them carry authentication-related information, while the third may be used to negotiate the ACSE functional units for the association. An optional field is also added to the A-ABORT APDU and may be used to express the authentication-related diagnostics. No new APDUs are introduced.

Table 13.10 updates Table 5.10 to show the new parameters (highlighted in bold). The new parameters in the ACSE authentication functional unit are mapped in a straightforward manner into the corresponding APDUs.

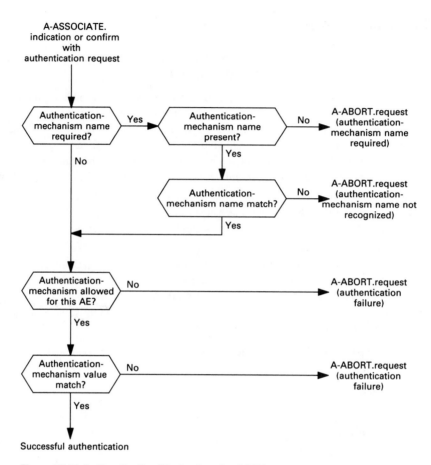

Figure 13.11 Authentication Mechanism for ACSE

Table 13.10 Association-Control Protocol Data Units and Parameters

APDU	Functional Unit	Parameters
A-ASSOCIATE-REQUEST (AARQ)	Kernel	Protocol version, application-context name, calling AP title, calling AE qualifier, calling AP invocation-identifier, calling AE invocation-identifier, called AP title, called AE qualifier, called AP invocation-identifier, called AE invocation-identifier, implementation information, user information
	Authentication	**ACSE requirements, authentication-mechanism name, authentication value**

Table 13.10 (*Cont.*)

APDU	Functional Unit	Parameters
A-ASSOCIATE-RESPONSE (AARE)	Kernel	Protocol version, application-context name, responding AP title, responding AE qualifier, responding AP invocation-identifier, responding AE invocation-identifier, result, result-souce diagnostic, implementation information, user information
	Authentication	**ACSE requirements, authentication-mechanism name, authentication value**
A-RELEASE-REQUEST (RLRQ)	Kernel	Reason, user information
A-RELEASE-RESPONSE (RLRE)	Kernel	Reason, user information
A-ABORT (ABRT)	Kernel	Abort source, user information
	Authentication	**Diagnostic**

13.6   EVOLVING ASPECTS OF OSI SECURITY

As Table 13.1 indicates, there is considerable activity in the development of standards related to OSI security. This section briefly surveys some of the areas not covered elsewhere in this chapter.

13.6.1   OSI Upper-Layers Security Model

CD 10745 is concerned with the development of an architectural model for OSI layers 6 and 7 to support application-independent security services and to minimize the need for application-specific application-service elements (ASEs) to contain internal security services. The model specifies:

- Security aspects of communication in the upper layers of OSI

- Upper-layer support of OSI security services

- Positioning of, and relationships among, security services in the upper layers

- Interactions among the upper layers, and between them and the lower layers, in providing and using security services

- Requirements for the management of security information in the upper layers, including audit

In other words, the emphasis in this document is to elaborate on the concepts in ISO 7498-2 with reference to layers 6 and 7. Because it is an architectural model, CD 10745 does not provide service definitions, protocol specifications, or specification of security mechanisms and techniques.

13.6.1.1   Secure-Communication Prerequisites

A key contribution of CD 10745 is to state the basic elements that are required for the provision of OSI security services. One of these elements is the *security state,* which is state information held in an open system that relates to the provision of security services. The exact nature of the state information will depend on the security services and mechanisms involved. In general, there are three categories of security-state information:

1. *System security state:* information established and maintained as part of the open system, independent of the existence or state of any communication activities

2. *Application-entity invocation security state:* information relating to application relationships between AEs, which have a lifetime beyond that of an association

3. *Association security state:* information that represents the net effect of security-related communications within the application association

   Examples of security-state information include:

- The set of security labels for information permitted to be exchanged on the association

- Keys or key IDs to be employed in the provision of security services in the upper layers

- Previously authenticated identities

- Sequence numbers, cryptographic synchronization variables, etc.

Another prerequisite element is a set of rules and guidelines to be used by application processes engaged in secure communications in an application context. Examples may include:

- The ASEs required to support the security protocols

- Rules for the negotiation and selection of security mechanisms in the upper layers

- Rules for the selection of underlying security services

- Rules for applying particular security services to particular categories of information to be exchanged

- Rules for reauthenticating relevant identities during the lifetime of an association

- Rules for changing keys throughout the lifetime of an association

- Rules to be followed in the event of communications failures or detected security violations

13.6.1.2   Architectural Placement of Security Functions

Secure communications are generally achieved by the generation, exchange, and processing of security information according to the procedures of the specific security mechanisms employed. Although the exchange of security information is governed by protocols or portions of protocols standardized under OSI, the generation and processing of security information is considered outside the scope of OSI. These functions are performed by what are referred to as *generic security functions (GSFs)*. GSFs can be invoked by OSI entities to provide the required security service.

Figure 13.12 shows a basic model for incorporating GSFs in the application and presentation layers. The basic structure for exchanging security information is provided by application entities, presentation entities (PEs), and supporting services implemented in OSI layers 1 to 5.

13.6.2   Security Frameworks

CD 10181-1 is an evolving document that defines a set of security frameworks covering:

- Authentication

- Access control

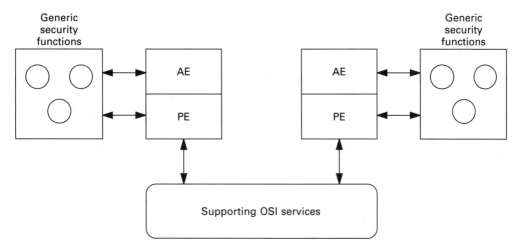

Figure 13.12 Basic Model for the Provision of Security Services in the OSI Upper Layers

- Nonrepudiation
- Integrity
- Confidentiality
- Audit

Each framework extends the concepts presented in ISO 7498-2 to provide a generic solution to a specific security requirement and can be used wherever that requirement exists. Thus, the intent of the frameworks is to ensure consistency in security enhancements to protocols when the same enhancement is needed in more than one protocol. The frameworks are concerned with defining means of providing protection for systems, objects within systems, and the interaction between systems. They do not deal with methodology for constructing systems or mechanisms.

13.7 SUMMARY

A framework for developing standards within the context of OSI has evolved, based on three key concepts: security threats, security mechanisms, and security services.

Potential security threats define the requirements that guide the design of a security system. Security threats may be broadly classified as either passive or active. Passive threats involve attempts by an attacker to obtain information relating to a communication. Active threats involve the modification or destruction of the contents, ordering, or timing of messages, as well as the creation of false transmissions.

A number of mechanisms have been developed to deal with these various threats. The most fundamental mechanism is encryption, which is a building block in the construction of more elaborate mechanisms.

The security mechanisms are the basic tools used to implement security services. The OSI-based security framework identifies five broad areas of security services:

- Authentication
- Access control
- Data confidentiality
- Data integrity
- Nonrepudiation

The area of OSI-based security is still evolving. We can expect to see a set of standards develop that provide broad coverage of this important function.

Part 5
OSI Implementation

For the large and growing body of OSI (open systems interconnection)-based standards to result in commercially accepted implementations, two key ingredients are needed. First, the vendor must be able to demonstrate objectively that the offered implementation conforms to the corresponding set of standards. Second, a standardized specification of the set of standards and options required for a particular application area is needed to guide both vendor and customer in the selection of a suite of protocols and options. Both these areas are in the process of standardization and are covered in this part.

Chapter 14 examines the standards for the conformance testing of OSI-based implementations. The chapter covers the basic methodology of conformance testing, the formal description technique developed for OSI conformance testing, and the conformance-test realization and assessment functions.

Chapter 15 begins with a discussion of the purposes of the international standardized profiles (ISPs). Then, the framework and taxonomy of ISPs are explained. The concepts that comprise a formal ISP document are explained, and the current status of ISP development is examined.

14
OSI Conformance Testing

A key element in the practical implementation of OSI (open systems interconnection) is conformance testing, which is intended to assure that a given implementation conforms to an OSI specification. Since 1983, ISO (the International Organization for Standardization) has been working on standards for conformance testing. The most important product of this effort is the five-part ISO 9646, issued in 1991 (Table 14.1). CCITT is participating in the effort; by mutual agreement, CCITT will adopt the technical work of ISO but publish it as CCITT recommendations.

We begin this chapter with a brief introduction to conformance. The remaining five sections of the chapter are devoted to the first five parts of ISO 9646. The last part of ISO 9646 is considered in Chapter 15.

14.1 PRINCIPLES OF PROTOCOL-CONFORMANCE TESTING

A conformance test is intended to determine whether a particular implementation of a protocol is equivalent to the specification of that protocol. Figure 14.1 indicates the role of conformance testing in the overall task of protocol design. Protocol design includes the following critical elements:

Table 14.1 OSI Conformance-Testing Standards

Title	ISO	CCITT
General Concepts	9646-1	X.290
Abstract Test Suite Specification	9646-2	X.291
The Tree and Tabular Combined Notation (TTCN)	9646-3	X.292
Test Realization	9646-4	X.293
Requirements on Test Laboratories and Clients for the Conformance Assessment Process	9646-5	X.294
Protocol Profile Test Specification	9646-6	

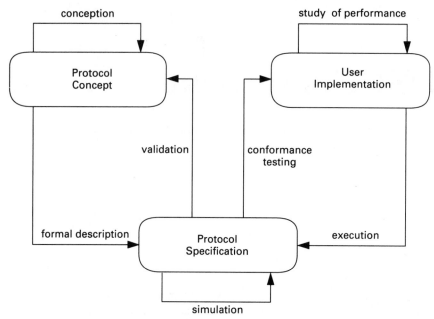

Source: R. Linn, "Conformance Evaluation Methodology and Protocol Testing," *IEEE Journal on Selected areas in Communications* (Sept.)

Figure 14.1 Design Aspects of Communication Protocols

- *Specification:* The protocol must be specified precisely and unambiguously. Formal description techniques, such as finite-state machines and protocol-description languages, are needed for this purpose.

- *Validation:* It must be determined that the protocol specification is logically consistent and complete, that it does not fail under unforeseen circumstances, and that it provides the intended services. This is one of the most difficult aspects of protocol design, for which mathematical and other formal tools are still evolving. Simulation using the protocol specification can help to uncover logical inconsistencies and gaps in the specification.

- *Implementation:* Based on the specification, an implementation of the protocol is produced. Performance studies may be used to make the implementation more efficient. Execution of the implementation may uncover flaws in the specification that had escaped notice.

- *Conformance testing:* The protocol must be executed against a series of inputs to determine whether the implementation in fact performs in the same way as the specification dictates under all circumstances and for all sets of inputs.

Conformance testing thus attempts to determine whether a given implementation matches a specification. If conformance testing could be done in a complete and correct manner, and if there were no flaws in the protocol specification, then two different implementations that passed the conformance test would be interoperable. That is, given the selection of the same set of options, two protocol implementations that conform to the same specification would be able to execute the

Source: G. Holzmann, *Design and Validation of Computer Protocols*, (Englewood Cliffs, N.J.: Prentice-Hall).

Figure 14.2 Conformance Testing

protocol between them with no errors. However, neither conformance testing nor protocol specification has reached that point of completeness and correctness. Consequently, another element must be added to the preceding list:

- *Interoperability testing:* Interoperability testing attempts to determine whether two or more implementations of a protocol will produce the expected behavior under actual operating conditions.

Figure 14.2 captures the essence of the conformance-testing function. Based on a known protocol specification, a series of tests is developed to determine conformance. The collection of tests is referred to as a test sequence or test suite. The implementation to be tested, referred to as the implementation under test (IUT), is treated as a black box, with a finite set of inputs and outputs. A separate piece of software, the tester, provides the IUT with inputs from the test suite and observes the resulting outputs. The IUT passes the test if it produces outputs that match those dictated by the protocol specification for all inputs of the test suite.

There are two key aspects to conformance testing:

1. *Test-suite design:* The test needs to be exhaustive, to cover all ordinary and extraordinary conditions with which the protocol must deal.

2. *Test method:* A method is needed for applying the test suite to an implementation.

14.1.1   Test-Suite Design

Traditional conformance-test design has focused on two aspects of the behavior of a protocol. First, the protocol must realize all functions of the specification, over the full range of parameter values. That is, the protocol must behave correctly for all possible sequences of correct inputs. Second, the protocol must react properly to erroneous inputs, behaving in a way that is consistent with the specification.

An example of the first type of test is the setting up of a connection. The test suite could cycle through a number of connection setups and terminations, using a different set of negotiable parameters for each instance. An example of the second type of test is delivering PDUs with various format errors to the protocol.

The difficulty with this approach to conformance testing is that being exhaustive is impractical. No matter how many sequences of inputs are tried, there is always the possibility that some untried sequence of inputs would reveal nonconformant behavior.

Given the constraint that the test suite must be finite, the problem just stated in principle admits of no solution. However, a different philosophy of testing may provide a greater degree of confidence in the outcome. More recent conformance-testing design has focused on the structure of the implementation rather than its behavior in the face of specific inputs. The intent is to show that the implementation and specification model equivalent sets of states and allow for the same state transitions. This approach encourages formal specification of the protocol in terms of state-transition models and lends itself to automatic test-suite generation. The ISO standards provide a base for this approach to conformance testing.

14.1.2   Test Methods

Once a test suite is designed, the actual task of applying the test to an implementation and observing the results may seem straightforward. Unfortunately, a number of difficulties must be addressed here.

Recall from Chapter 2 the following definitions:

- *Protocol specification:* Two entities at the same layer in different systems cooperate and interact by means of a protocol. Since two different open systems are involved, the protocol must be specified precisely. This includes the format of the protocol data units exchanged, the semantics of all fields, and the allowable sequence of PDUs (protocol data units).

- *Service definition:* In addition to the protocol or protocols that operate at a given layer, standards are needed for the services that each layer provides to the next higher layer. Typically, the definition of services is equivalent to a functional description that specifies *what* services are provided but not *how* the services are to be provided.

The distinction between a definition and a specification has to do with the issue of interoperability. PDUs are exchanged between protocol entities in different systems. These protocol entities may be instances of different implementations from different vendors. Therefore, it is critical that both implementations conform exactly to the same protocol specification. On the other hand, if two adjacent layers of the OSI architecture are executing within the same system, then the service interface betweeen those layers involves the exchange of information between two modules that are part of the same implementation. If this interface is never visible to other open systems, then we need not dictate that the interface be implemented in any particular way with any particular formats or procedure call/return conventions. Furthermore, it is best to leave this service definition in general functional terms so that the implementer can produce the most efficient implementation. The result is that virtually all OSI services are standardized as functional definitions rather than precise, detailed specifications.[1]

Now consider that we wish to treat a single protocol entity at layer (N) as a black box and perform a conformance test. We are interested in the behavior of the protocol, which is specified in terms of the input and output of PDUs. Unfortunately, the protocol entity, as a black box, does not actually issue PDUs. Instead, the protocol entity issues service requests and responses to the $(N-1)$ layer and service indications and confirms to the $(N+1)$ layer. So to observe the flow of

---

1.   Leaving aside considerations of testing, this style of standardization has drawbacks. For example, if a front-end processor is used to offload a lower portion of the OSI architecture from the main processor, then the service interface between the host and the front-end processor crosses a hardware boundary and may involve implementations from more than one vendor. Yet there is no standard, in most cases, for this host-to-front-end interface. See Stallings (1993) for a further discussion.

PDUs from an (*N*) entity and to provide PDUs as input to an (*N*) entity, it is necessary to interface to the (*N*) entity from below. The module that performs this task is referred to as the lower tester. The lower tester provides input to the (*N*)-layer IUT in the form of (*N* − 1) service indications and confirms and receives output from the IUT in the form of (*N* − 1) service requests and responses.

But the lower tester alone is inadequate. The lower tester, by itself, will only allow testing the protocol entity in a responding mode, reacting to incoming PDUs. The protocol entity is also providing service to the (*N* + 1) layer and acts as an initiator on behalf of its users. To fully test the (*N*) entity, it is necessary to use an upper tester that interfaces to the (*N*) entity as an (*N*) user. Furthermore, what is needed is for the upper tester to issue service requests and responses and then observe the resulting output of PDUs via the lower tester. Thus, there must be a set of test-coordination procedures that enable the upper and lower testers to cooperate in exercising the protocol implementation under test.

Typically, the lower and upper testers exhibit a master-slave relationship, with the lower tester playing the role of master and using test-coordination procedures to invoke the functions of the upper tester. The lower tester maintains the information about the test suite and issues instructions to the upper tester to perform certain actions as part of the test.

Figure 14.3 captures these concepts. One critical element in this architecture is whether the testing software is implemented on the same system as the (*N*) IUT or whether the testing is done from a remote system. A number of issues arise.

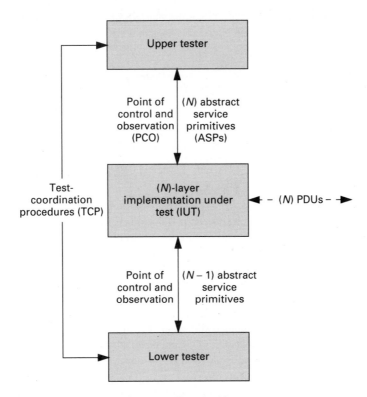

Figure 14.3 Basic Conformance-Test Architecture

If *local testing* is employed, both the upper and lower tester can be implemented and executed on the same system as the (N) IUT. Since the only points at which the behavior of the (N) entity can be observed are its interfaces to layers (N + 1) and (N), this is permissible. However, two practical issues arise. First, the lower and upper tester will have to be compiled and loaded onto a number of different types of equipment, raising the cost of implementing testing software. What is worse, there is no guarantee that different compilers and operating systems might not affect the operation of the testers in some subtle way. This makes it more difficult to have confidence in the validity of the testers themselves.

With *remote testing,* the IUT is tested via a network connection to a remote system. This works reasonably well for the lower tester. The lower tester can be implemented at layer (N) of the remote testing system and exchange PDUs with the (N)-entity IUT. These PDUs are carried over the network and result in (N − 1) service primitives' being exchanged with the (N)-entity IUT. The principal concern with this arrangement is the reliability of the exchange across the network. In contrast, the upper tester presents a more difficult problem. Some means must be found, from a remote system, of accessing the (N)-service interface to the IUT. We examine this issue in the next section.

14.2   GENERAL CONCEPTS

ISO 9646-1/X.290 provides a tutorial on OSI conformance testing, a definition of key terms, and an overview of the remainder of the standard. Table 14.2 lists some of the key definitions contained in this standard.

Table 14.2 OSI Conformance-Testing Terminology

Basic Terms

Implementation Under Test (IUT)
    An implementation of one or more OSI protocols in an adjacent user/provider relationship, being that part of a real open system which is to be studied by testing.
System Under Test (SUT)
    The real open system in which the IUT resides.
Dynamic Conformance Requirement
    One of the requirements which specifies what observable behavior is permitted by the relevant OSI International Standard(s) or CCITT Recommendation(s) in instances of communication.
Static Conformance Requirement
    One of the requirements that specify the limitations on the combinations of implemented capabilities permitted in a real open system which is claimed to conform to that OSI International Standard or CCITT Recommendation.
Protocol Implementation Conformance Statement (PICS)
    A statement made by the supplier of an OSI implementation or system, stating which capabilities have been implemented, for a given OSI protocol.
PICS Proforma
    A document, in the form of a questionnaire, designed by the protocol specifier or conformance test suite specifier, which when completed for an OSI implementation or system becomes the PICS.

Table 14.2 (*Cont.*)

Protocol Implementation Extra Information for Testing (PIXIT)

A statement made by a supplier or implementor of an IUT which contains or references all of the information (in addition to that given in the PICS) related to the IUT and its testing environment, which will enable the test laboratory to run an appropriate test suite against the IUT.

<hr>

Test Suite Terminology

<hr>

Abstract Test Method (ATM)

The description of how an IUT is to be tested, given at an appropriate level of abstraction to make the description independent of any particular realization of a means of testing, but with enough detail to enable tests to be specified for this test method.

Abstract Test Case

A complete and independent specification of the actions required to achieve a specific test purpose defined at the level of abstraction of a particular abstract test method, starting in a stable testing state and ending in a stable testing state.

Executable Test Case

A realization of an abstract test case.

<hr>

Test Method Terminology

<hr>

Point of Control and Observation (PCO)

A point within a testing environment where the occurrence of test events is to be controlled and observed, as defined in an abstract test method.

Lower Tester (LT)

The representation of the means of providing, during test execution, indirect control and observation of the lower service boundary of the IUT via the underlying service provider.

Upper Tester (UT)

The representation of the means of providing, during test execution, indirect control and observation of the upper service boundary of the IUT, as defined by the chosen abstract test method.

Abstract (N)-Service Primitive [(N)-ASP]

An implementation-independent description of an interaction between a service user and a service-provider, during test execution, control and observation of the upper service boundary of the IUT, as defined by the chosen abstract test method.

Test Management Protocol (TMP)

A protocol which is used in the test coordination procedures for a particular test suite.

Test System

The real system which includes the realization of the lower tester.

Local Test Method

An abstract test method in which both the lower and upper testers are located within the test system and there is a PCO at the upper service boundary of the IUT.

Distributed Test Method

An abstract test method in which the upper tester is within the SUT and there is a PCO at the upper service boundary of the IUT.

Coordinated Test Method

An abstract test method in which the upper tester is within the SUT and for which a standardized TMP is defined for the test coordination procedures, enabling the control and ob-

Table 14.2 *(Cont.)*

servation to be specified solely in terms of the lower tester activity, including the control and observation of test management PDUs.

Remote Test Method

An abstract test method in which the control and observation of test events is specified solely in terms of lower tester activity, and in which some requirements for test coordination procedures may be implied or informally expressed in the ATM, but in which no assumption is made regarding their feasibility or realization.

Embedded Testing

Testing specified for a single-protocol within a multi-protocol IUT including the specification of the protocol activity above the one being tested, but without specifying control or observation at service boundaries within the multi-protocol IUT.

14.2.1   The Conformance-Assessment Process

ISO 9646 distinguishes three types of standardized testing, in increasing order of ability to provide an indication of conformance:

1. Basic interconnection tests

2. Capability tests

3. Behavior tests

The purpose of a *basic interconnection test* is to determine whether or not there is sufficient conformance to the relevant protocol for interconnection to be possible, without trying to perform thorough testing. A basic interconnection test can act as an initial screening device. It will detect severe cases of nonconformance. If the basic interconnection test is passed, then more elaborate and detailed conformance tests may be attempted.

A *capability test* is used to verify the existence of one or more claimed capabilities of an IUT. Capability tests deal with what are referred to as static conformance requirements. Static conformance requirements, as the name suggests, deal with the presence or absence of features and capabilities, as opposed to whether a given capability operates in conformance with the specification. For example, five protocol classes have been defined for the OSI transport protocol. The list of PDUs and the formats of those PDUs for a particular class would be a static conformance requirement for an implementation that claims to provide that protocol class. Another example of a static conformance requirement is a range of values that have to be supported for specific parameters or timers. In general, there are two varieties of static conformance requirements:

1. Those that list the capabilities and options to be included in the implementation of a protocol

2. Those that list the services and capabilities that must be provided by the underlying layers of the OSI architecture to support the protocol implementation

Although the requirements here are referred to as static, the conformance test is dynamic, in the sense that the protocol is executed against some set of inputs. The goal of a capability test is to simply observe that the claimed set of capabilities is present.

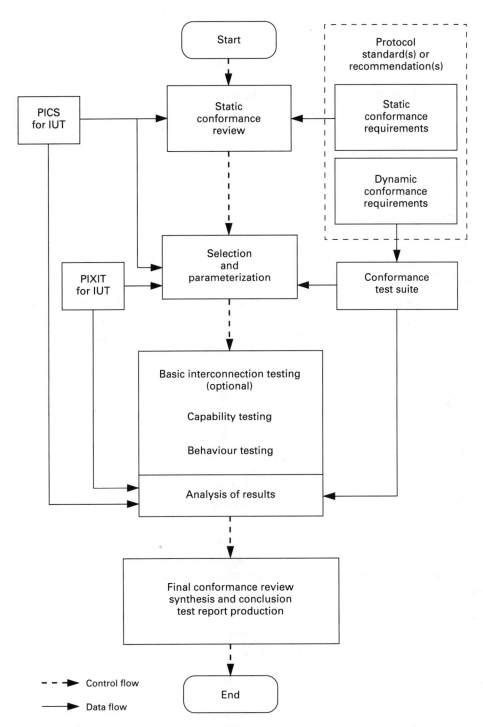

Figure 14.4 Conformance-Assessment-Process Overview

Behavior tests deal with dynamic conformance requirements, which specify the observable behavior of an implementation. These dynamic requirements form the bulk of any OSI-protocol specification and define the actual protocol: the use and format of its PDUs, state transitions, negotiation rules, and so on. Behavior tests include tests for valid behavior of the IUT for both valid and invalid protocol behavior by the lower tester.

Figure 14.4 depicts the conformance-assessment process. The protocol specification is a major input to this process, providing the static and dynamic conformance requirements. These are used to design the conformance-test suite. In addition, there are two other key inputs:

1. *Protocol-implementation conformance statement:* This is a statement of the capabilities and options that have been implemented. Conformance testing should be limited to, but thoroughly cover, those aspects of the protocol claimed in the PICS.

2. *Protocol information extra information for testing:* This is additional information that is needed to actually set up the test. An example is addressing information related to the realization of the upper tester.

14.2.2   Test Methods

The test methods described in ISO 9646 are referred to as abstract test methods. The corresponding test suites are referred to as abstract test suites. The test methods and suites are abstract in the sense of being independent of any particular implementation. They are therefore expressed in functional terms. Referring back to Figure 14.3, we see the key elements of an abstract test method:

- *Lower tester:* provides control and observation of the lower service boundary of the IUT.

- *Upper tester:* provides control and observation of the upper service boundary of the IUT.

- *Test-coordination procedures:* rules for cooperation between the lower and upper testers.

- *Abstract service primitives:* These are simply the service primitives defined in the service specification of an (*N*) entity.

- *Points of control and observation:* Each PCO is identified by the service boundary at which events are controlled and observed, the set of ASPs or PDUs that are controllable and observable at that point, and whether the control and observation occur in the system under test or in a remote testing system.

The standard defines four general configurations for testing. Each configuration is referred to as an abstract test method. Two of these methods use a PCO between the upper tester and the IUT, and two use only a single PCO between the lower tester and the IUT. The following subsections examine these four configurations.

14.2.2.1   Local Test Methods

In the local test method, the upper and lower testers are located within the same system. This allows the test-coordination procedures to be realized entirely within that system. Figure 14.3 shows one version of the local test method, in which the upper and lower testers are in the same system as the IUT. This is in some ways the simplest test configuration, but it has the drawbacks cited earlier.

Another version of the local test method is depicted in Figure 14.5, part (a). Here, the upper and lower testers are located in a test system that is distinct from the system under test. In this

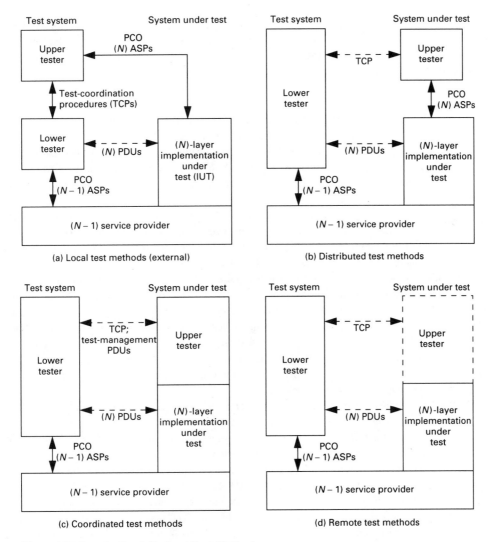

Figure 14.5 Standardized Abstract Test Methods

configuration, there must be a standardized hardware interface to the upper boundary of the IUT. Presumably, this means that the testing system must be colocated with the system under test so that a hardware link can be established between the upper tester and the IUT.

Note that even though the lower tester is considered to be below the IUT, functionally it is a peer protocol entity. The lower tester exchanges (N) PDUs with the (N)-layer IUT. Thus, the lower tester is emulating the protocol entity to be tested. The lower tester and the IUT are connected by an (N − 1) service composed of lower-layer protocols and the physical medium or network connecting the systems. One concern that arises when the lower tester is remote from the IUT is the reliability of the data exchange. If the IUT is in layer 5, 6, or 7, then the transport service can provide a reliable connection for the exchange of (N) PDUs. If the IUT is in layer 4 or below, then this reliability may not be provided. For example, if the connectionless network service is used, then a test of the transport protocol is complicated by the fact that the transport-protocol entity is dealing not only with errors created as part of the test suite but also with actual errors resulting from the use of the connectionless network protocol.

14.2.2.2   Coordinated Test Methods

The coordinated test method assumes that the test system is distinct and houses the lower tester but that the upper tester is implemented in the system under test.

In this configuration, the upper tester executes test events (service requests and responses) at the upper interface to the IUT but does not provide a means to externally observe test events (service indications and confirms) at that interface. Thus, there is only one PCO: beneath the lower tester.

In this configuration, as in other configurations, the lower and upper testers must coordinate their efforts: the same tests must be selected and executed concurrently, and the lower tester must be able to control the activities of the upper tester and receive reports of its observations. For this purpose, a standardized test-management protocol (TMP) is used.

The disadvantage of this method is that it requires a logical connection for the test-management protocol. This connection can be provided either in-band or out-of-band. *In-band communication* relies on the protocol being tested to carry the test-management protocol data units (TMPDUs). TMPDUs are exchanged between the lower and upper testers in the user data fields of the (N)-layer PDUs. Logically, this scheme is suspect, since one is relying on the protocol being tested to perform a function as part of the tester. Furthermore, if the protocol being tested is connectionless, even if it functions properly, it does not provide a reliable delivery mechanism for the ferry-protocol approach discussed below.

Out-of-band communication uses a lower-layer protocol, bypassing the (N)-entity IUT. It assumes that the lower-layer protocol is reliable enough to deliver the ferry-protocol data units. Again, if the IUT is at the transport layer or below, it may be difficult to provide a reliable bypass. In the standards work so far, the in-band communication approach is the one that is being pursued.

Whether in-band or out-of-band communication is used to support the TMP, the upper tester must access the upper service interface of the IUT to perform tests. The upper tester may be provided by the test laboratory in a high-level language for porting to the system under test. Alternatively, the upper tester can be implemented by the SUT's owner, since the TMP is standardized. In either case, a new user for the protocol under test is developed. This approach is best suited for testing general-purpose protocols that are likely to support a number of users. These protocols can be tested once, with the upper tester, rather than multiple times with different users. Examples of protocols in this category are the transport and session protocols and CMIP (common management information protocol).

14.2.2.3   Distributed Test Methods

In the distributed test scheme, as in the coordinated test method, the upper tester is implemented in the system under test. In this configuration, the upper tester executes test events (service requests and responses) at the upper interface to the IUT and also provides a means to externally observe test events (service indications and confirms) at that interface. Thus, there are two PCOs.

As with the coordinated test method, the distributed architecture does not address how coordination between upper and lower testers is to be achieved.

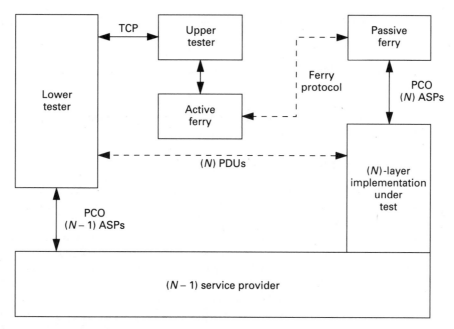

Figure 14.6 Ferry Method

One possibility for achieving coordination would require a human operator at the system under test and the test system. The operator of the lower tester in the test system verbally instructs the operator of the system under test to record and execute protocol events at the PCO above the IUT during test execution. In this case, the SUT operator acts as the upper tester.

A second way to configure the upper tester and test-configuration procedures is by using a ferry protocol (Zeng and Rayner 1986) to transfer the interaction at the IUT's upper boundary to an upper tester on the test system (Figure 14.6). The passive ferry accepts service indications and confirms from the IUT and transmits these in a ferry PDU to the active ferry, which unwraps the PDU and passes the service events to the upper tester. The upper tester issues service requests and responses to the active ferry, which transmits these to the passive ferry via the ferry protocol for delivery to the IUT. This configuration allows for effective coordination of the upper and lower testers via interprocess communication mechanisms on the test system, minimizing timing problems. But the ferry method does not resolve the in-band/out-of-band issues described earlier.

Because the distributed test method requires an exposed service interface, it has been limited to testing application-layer protocols (embodied in application-service entities) that normally provide such interfaces.

14.2.2.4 Remote Test Methods

In the remote test method, there is no upper tester as such, but some upper-tester functions may be performed by the system under test. In Figure 14.5, part (d), the depiction of an upper tester with a dotted line indicates that only the minimal test-coordination procedures are used to drive the IUT. For example, to establish a connection between the lower tester and the IUT, a user of the IUT may have to respond to a connection-indication service primitive issued by the IUT.

The focus of this method is on the protocol behavior of the IUT and not on the services that it provides to the next higher layer. The only means of control and observation is the exchange of (*N*) PDUs between the lower tester and the IUT via the (*N* − 1) service.

Because this method is limited in its control and observation, it cannot test all states of the protocol and is not as complete as the other test methods. It is best suited to protocols that do not need many user-initiated events executed during testing. One example of a protocol suited to this test method is X.25. The method has also been used to test the responder mode of the file-transfer, access, and management (FTAM) application-service element.

14.2.3   Embedded Testing

The test methods discussed so far are directed at the testing of a protocol entity within a single layer. Clearly, the end user is interested in an open system that implements the protocols at all layers of the OSI model. Therefore, some means is needed for testing a multilayer implementation. The approach suggested by ISO is to incrementally apply single-layer testing methods to each layer of a multilayer implementation. This approach makes use of the concept of embedding.

Embedded testing allows a protocol implementation to be tested while embedded under one or more higher-layer protocols. The upper tester resides at a service interface one or more layers above the protocol being tested. Embedded versions of the coordinated, distributed, and remote test methods have been defined by ISO. Figure 14.7 illustrates this scheme using the coordinated test method.

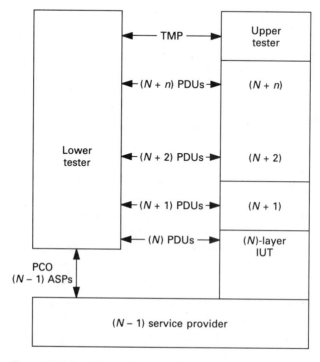

Figure 14.7 Coordinated Single-Layer Embedded Test Method

In this scheme, the upper tester indirectly controls the IUT's upper service interface. The intervening layers are not tested. Note that the lower tester must serve as a peer entity to all of the layers from the IUT to the upper tester. With this approach, a full seven-layer implementation can be tested by successively testing individual layers, assuming that the other layers are correct.

The primary advantage of this approach is that it does not require an exposed interface at every level of the architecture. There are two principal disadvantages. First, the test suite becomes more complex, since it must account for the behavior of the IUT and all the layers above it. Second, the test suite for a layer-(N) protocol is defined assuming a particular set of protocols at layers ($N+1$) through ($N+n$). A new test suite must be written if the combination of protocols changes.

14.2.4 System Configurations

The conformance-test standards are designed to be usable for protocols in a variety of system configurations. Figure 14.8 illustrates the basic configurations; other configurations can be derived from these basic configurations.

The full seven-layer open system implements standardized protocols at all layers of the OSI model. A partial open system implements standardized protocols in layers 1 to (N). An example of a partial open system would be a front-end processor to a host, in which protocols up through transport are implemented. Both of these configurations can be tested using the test methods discussed so far.

The final basic configuration is the open-relay system. These systems use OSI protocols in layers 1 to 3 (network relay) or 1 to 7 (application relay). An example of the former is an intermediate system (IS), as defined in Chapter 4.

ISO proposes two methods for testing relay systems (Figure 14.9). The *loopback method* requires only a single test system, located on one of the subnetworks to which the relay system is attached. For a connection-oriented relay, there are two test connections from the test system to the system under test. These must be looped together either within the relay or in the second subnetwork. For connectionless protocols, PDUs from the test system, issued through one PCO, are looped back within the second subnetwork and addressed to return to the second PCO.

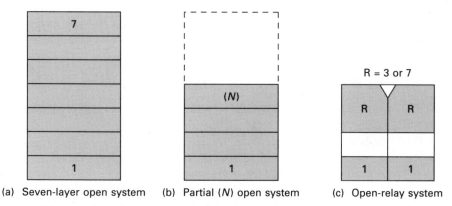

(a) Seven-layer open system   (b) Partial (N) open system   (c) Open-relay system

Figure 14.8 Basic Configurations for a System under Test

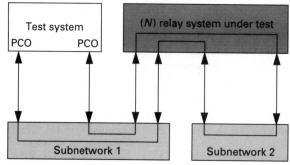

(a) Loopback test method

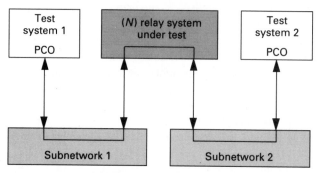

(b) Transverse test method

Figure 14.9 Test Methods for Relay Systems

The advantage of the loopback method is the need for only one tester and therefore the lack of any coordination requirements. The disadvantage is that the behavior of the relay is observed on only one of its sides, and its behavior on the second subnetwork cannot be properly assessed.

The *transverse test method* requires two testers, one on each subnetwork. This method enables a relay to be tested in its normal mode of operation, with its behavior on each subnetwork observed. A certain amount of coordination between the two testers must be implemented in some fashion.

14.2.5 Structure of the OSI Conformance-Test Standard

Following ISO 9646-1, there are four additional parts to the standard. Figure 14.10 indicates the relationship between the various parts of the standard and the conformance-testing concepts and activities. Part 2 deals with the specification of test suites based on given protocol and service specifications. Part 3 provides a standardized notation for implementation-independent test-suite specification. Part 4 deals with converting the abstract test-suite into an executable test suite. Part 5 concerns the roles of a test laboratory and its client in the conformance-assessment process.

The OSI standards do not include test-generation methodology or techniques. The charitable view is that it is assumed that the tester has already developed a set of tests. It can also be said that test generation is not addressed because no agreement has been reached on a formal method.

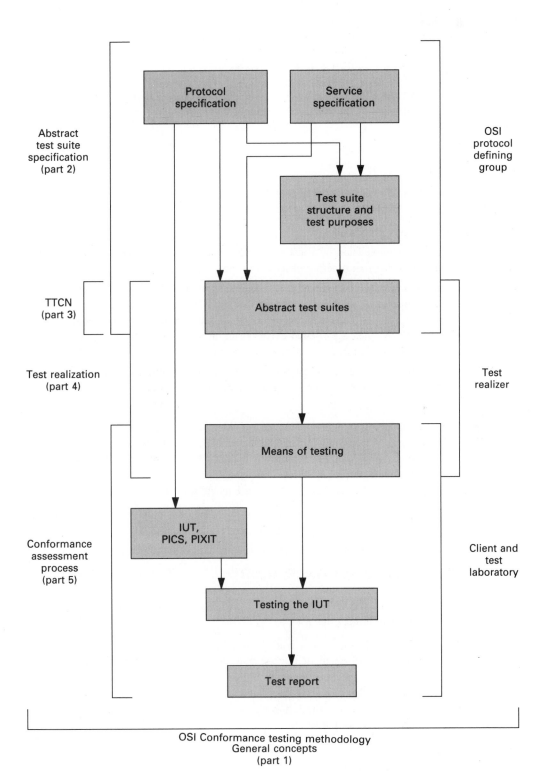

Figure 14.10 Relationships Between Parts, Concepts, and Activities

14.3   ABSTRACT TEST-SUITE SPECIFICATION

ISO 9646-2/X.291 provides a common approach to the specification of OSI conformance-test suites at a level that is independent of the means of executing those test suites; these are referred to as abstract test suites.

14.3.1   Structure

A test suite has a hierarchical structure (Figure 14.11), consisting of the following components:

- *Test event:* an indivisible unit of test specification at the level of abstraction of the specification (e.g., sending or receiving a single PDU).

- *Test step:* a named subdivision of a test case, constructed from test events and/or other test steps. A test step dictates an ordering of its test events.

- *Test case:* the actions required to achieve a specific test purpose. Each test case normally has a single test purpose, such as that of verifying that the IUT has a certain required capability (e.g., the ability to support certain packet sizes) or exhibits a certain required behavior (e.g., it behaves as required when a particular event occurs in a particular state). A test case may involve one or more consecutive or concurrent connections.

- *Test group:* a named, related set of test cases. A test group provides a logical ordering of its test cases. Nested test groups provide a logical ordering of the test cases in the test suite as a whole.

The key element in the test suite is the abstract test case. Each test case is a formal description of a test purpose, capable of being mapped into an executable form. A test purpose, on the other hand, is an informal prose description of a narrowly defined objective of testing. A test purpose, and therefore the corresponding test case, focuses on a single conformance requirement as specified in the appropriate ISO or CCITT standard. The test case includes the following key elements:

- *Test preamble:* a sequence of test events to put the IUT into the initial testing state required by the test body from the desired stable starting state of the test case

- *Test body:* specifies all sequences of test events necessary in order to achieve the test purpose

- *Test postamble:* a sequence of test events to return the IUT to the desired stable starting state of the test case

- *Verdict specification:* the verdict to be assigned to each possible sequence of test events comprising a complete path through the test case

The development of a test suite from a protocol specification is not an automated process but requires skill and judgment on the part of the test-suite designer. There are essentially two key elements: a need to test all the aspects of the protocol that are relevant to conformance and a need to design test-event sequences that will drive the protocol through a series of states in order to test each relevant aspect. ISO 9646-2 lists the following aspects of the protocol as needing attention, without claiming that the list is exhaustive:

- Capability tests (for static conformance requirements)

- Behavior tests for valid behavior

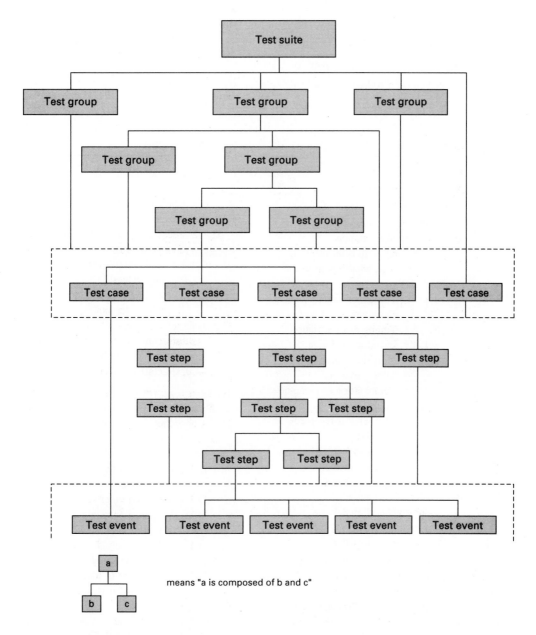

Figure 14-11 Test-Suite Structure

- Behavior tests that investigate the reaction of the IUT to invalid events, including syntactic, semantic, and procedural errors
- Tests focusing on PDUs sent to the IUT
- Tests focusing on PDUs received from the IUT

- Tests focusing on interaction between PDUs sent and received
- Tests related to each mandatory capability
- Tests related to each optional capability
- Tests related to each protocol phase
- Variations in the test event occurring in a particular state

Table 14.3 Example Description of a Single-Layer Test Suite

A. Capability tests
   A.1 Mandatory capabilities
   A.2 Optional capabilities

B. Behavior tests: response to valid behavior by peer implementation
   B.1 Connection establishment phase
     B.1.1 Focus on what is sent to the IUT
      B.1.1.1 Test event variation in each state
      B.1.1.2 Timing/timer variation
      B.1.1.3 Encoding variation
      B.1.1.4 Individual parameter value variation
      B.1.1.5 Combination of parameter values
     B.1.2 Focus on what is received from the IUT
     —substructured as B.1.1
     B.1.3 Focus on interactions
     —substructured as B.1.1
   B.2 Data transfer phase
   —substructured as B.1
   B.3 Connection release phase
   —substructured as B.1

C. Behavior tests: response to syntactically or semantically invalid behavior by peer implementation
   C.1 Connection establishment phase
     C.1.1 Focus on what is sent to the IUT
      C.1.1.1 Test event variation in each state
      C.1.1.2 Encoding variation of the invalid event
      C.1.1.3 Encoding variation

      C.1.1.4 Individual invalid parameter value variation
      C.1.1.5 Invalid parameter value combination variation
     C.1.2 Focus on what the IUT is requested to send
      C.1.2.1 Individual invalid parameter values
      C.1.2.2 Invalid combinations of parameter values
   C.2 Data transfer phase
   —substructured as C.1
   C.3 Connection release phase
   —substructured as C.1

D. Behavior tests: response to inopportune events by peer implementation
   D.1 Connection establishment phase
     D.1.1 Focus on what is sent to the IUT
      D.1.1.1 Test event variation in each state
      D.1.1.2 Timing/timer variation
      D.1.1.3 Special encoding variations
      D.1.1.4 Major individual parameter value variations
      D.1.1.5 Variation in major combination of parameter values
     D.1.2 Focus on what is requested to be sent by the IUT
     —substructured as D.1.1
   D.2 Data transfer phase
   —substructured as D.1
   D.3 Connection release phase
   —substructured as D.1

- Timing and timer variations
- PDU-encoding variations
- Variations in the values of individual parameters
- Variations in combinations of parameter values

The designer might begin by developing the structure of the test suite in terms of test purposes, without yet specifying specific values to be tested or event sequences to achieve testing. Table 14.3, from ISO 9694-2, is an example of a single-layer test suite for a connection-oriented protocol. Based on this structure, it is then possible to develop a set of test cases to provide coverage. Table 14.4 suggests a minimum coverage for the example shown in Table 14.3.

Table 14.4 Minimum Adequate Coverage for the Example Shown in Table 14.3

a.   For capability-test groups (A.1, A.2):
    1.   At least one test purpose per relevant capability
    2.   At least one test purpose per relevant PDU type and each major variation of each such type, using "normal" or default values for each parameter
b.   For test groups concerned with test-event variation in each state (B.x.y.1, C.x.1.1, D.x.y.1), at least one test purpose per relevant state/event combination
c.   For test groups concerned with timers and timing (B.x.y.2, D.x.y.2), at least one test purpose concerned with the expiry of each defined timer
d.   For test groups concerned with coding variations (B.x.y.3, C.x.1.2, D.x.y.3), at least one test purpose for each relevant kind of encoding variation per relevant PDU type
e.   For test groups concerned with valid individual parameter values (B.x.y.4, D.x.y.4):
    1.   For each relevant integer parameter, test purposes concerned with boundary values and one randomly selected midrange value
    2.   For each relevant bitwise parameter, test purposes for as many values as practical, but no less than all the "normal" or common values
    3.   For other relevant parameters, at least one test purpose concerned with a value different from what is considered "normal" or default in other test groups
f.   For test groups concerned with syntactically or semantically invalid individual parameter values (C.x.1.3, C.x.2.1):
    1.   For each relevant integer parameter, test purposes concerned with invalid values adjacent to the allowed boundary values defined in the protocol specification, plus one other randomly selected value
    2.   For each relevant bitwise parameter, test purposes for as many invalid values as practical
    3.   For other relevant types of parameters, at least one test purpose per parameter
g.   For test groups concerned with combinations of parameter values (B.x.y.5, C.x.1.4, C.x.2.2, D.x.y.5):
    1.   At least one test purpose for each important combination of specific values (e.g., boundary values)
    2.   At least one test purpose per set of interrelated parameters to test a random combination of relevant values

Notation: The letters x and y represent all appropriate values for the first and second digits in the test-group identifier, respectively, so that B.x.1.1 stands for B.1.1.1, B.2.1.1, and B.3.1.1.

14.3.2   PICS Proforma

The design of the test suite for a protocol is heavily dependent on a statement of the conformance requirements for that protocol. A key element of any protocol standard is the PICS (protocol-implementation conformance statement) proforma, which is a document that serves two purposes:

1. It enumerates all the mandatory and optional capabilities and features of the protocol, and the relationship among various options. It also provides the legitimate range of variation of the global parameters controlling the implementation of the functions.

2. It serves as a fill-in-the-blanks questionnaire for an implementer, to indicate which features of the protocol are supported. The filled-in document serves as the PICS for that implementation.

A conformance-test designer can use the PICS to design an abstract test suite for a given protocol. Faced with a specific implementation and its PICS claims, a subset of the test suite can be prepared that is intended to test the specific implementation.

Given the wide variety of protocol standards, there is no unique PICS proforma structure. In general, the proforma consists of a set of tables that address the various aspects of the protocol specification. Each table entry indicates a status for a capability:

- *Mandatory:* The capability is required in all implementations.

- *Optional:* The capability may be implemented as an option. The option may be Boolean (capability is present or absent), mutually exclusive (one of two or more actions or alternatives may be supported), or selectable (*m* out of *n* actions or alternatives may be supported).

- *Prohibited:* There is a requirement that this capability not be used in a given context.

- *Not applicable:* No requirement can be expressed in a given context.

- *Conditional:* The requirement depends on the selection of other optional or conditional items.

Figure 14.12 gives examples of possible PICS proforma tables for the OSI transport-protocol specification.

14.4   THE TREE AND TABULAR COMBINED NOTATION

ISO 9646-3/X.292 defines an informal notation with the following objectives:

- Can be used to express abstract test suites

- Is independent of test methods, layers, and protocols

- Reflects the abstract-testing methodology defined in ISO 9646

The tree and tabular combined notation (TTCN) is defined in two forms:

1. A graphical form (TTCN.GR) suitable for human readability

2. A machine-processable form (TTCN.MP) suitable for transmission of TTCN descriptions between machines and possibly suitable for input into an automated executable test-generation function

TTCN.GR is defined in terms of a set of table formats, called tabular proforma. TTCN.MP differs from TTCN.GR only in syntax: keywords are used instead of boxes to structure the information. This section describes TTCN.GR.

D.5.1 Classes implemented

Classes implemented				
Item no.	Class	Reference	Status	Support
0	Class 0	14.1	o.1	
1	Class 1	14.2	c1	
2	Class 2	14.3	o.1	
3	Class 3	14.4	c2	
4	Class 4	14.5	c2	

o.1: at least one of these classes shall be supported
c1: IF cls0 THEN o ELSE x
c2: IF cls2 THEN o ELSE x
cls0 = D.5.1/0
cls2 = D.5.1/2

D.6.1 PDU support

Supported PDUS			Sending		Receipt	
Item no.	PDU	Ref.	Status	Support	Status	Support
1	CR	15.1	o		m	
2	CC	15.1	m		c3	
3	DT	15.2	m		m	
...	...	...	...		...	

c3: IF sendCR THEN m ELSE n/a
sendCR = D.6.1/1a

D.6.3.1 Parameters of the XY-PDU

Supported parameters					Values	
Item no.	Parameter	Ref.	Status	Support	Allowed	Supported
1	data size	15.6	m		128, 256, 512	
2	timeout	15.7	o		1-3600 secs	secs
3	class	15.8	m		0–4	
...	...	...	...		...	

Figure 14.12 Examples of PICS Proforma Tables

14.4.1   TTCN Principles

TTCN is designed to be a universal language for specifying the behavior of test systems and the protocol entity being tested. It contains sufficient features to describe all the tests that could be designed for all OSI protocols.

TTCN must therefore express the dynamic behavior and the exchange of messages between a test system and a protocol entity. We have seen that the overall test suite can be defined as a tree-structured collection of test cases and test events. At the primitive level of a test case or test event, the behavior of the protocol entity in response to a certain event may be depicted as a tree, with the nodes of the tree labeled with inputs and edges labeled as outputs. In effect, such a tree shows the specific behavior of the protocol entity, which may be modeled as a finite-state machine, in response to one or a sequence of inputs. TTCN, then, is a language for describing the tree of behavior and actions associated with the events of a test suite and the possible behavior of the protocol entity in response to the test events.

The name of the notation is derived from the fact that the TTCN definition of a test suite consists of a tree of tables. Each table defines one aspect of the test suite, and the tree is a structure that orders the elements of the test suite.

The basic assumption underlying the definition of abstract test suites and of the TTCN is that a protocol IUT can be driven into a known stable state (i.e., a desired state for testing) by a sequence of inputs and outputs. Once it has reached that state, a sequence of test steps is used to exercise a particular aspect of the protocol. Finally, the protocol entity is driven back to a stable initial state by a sequence specified as part of this test case. Thus, the sequence for a particular test case consists of a preamble, body, and postamble.

An abstract test suite composed in TTCN consists of four sections:

1. *Suite overview:* the information needed for the general presentation and understanding of the test suite

2. *Declaration part:* describes the set of components that comprise the test suite

3. *Constraints part:* the set of values for ASPs, PDUs, and their parameters used in the dynamic part

4. *Dynamic part:* specifies the test behavior, expressed mainly in terms of the occurrence of ASPs and PCOs

14.4.2   Suite Overview

Table 14.5 is the proforma for the test-suite-overview portion of a TTCN-defined test suite.[2] The suite overview includes the following key elements:

- The name of the test suite.

- Reference to the relevant base standards.

- Reference to the PICS proforma.

- Reference to the PIXIT proforma.

- Reference to where in the abstract test-suite specification the mapping of the PICS and PIXIT entries used in test-case selection is specified.

- An indication of the test method or methods to which the test suite applies. In the case of coordinated methods, a reference is provided to where the test-management protocol is specified.

---

2.   The following conventions are used in the proforma tables: Bold text (**like this**) shall appear verbatim in the actual text. Italic text (*like this*) is used to indicate that actual text must be substituted for the italicized phrase. A vertical line (|) is used to delimit alternatives.

Table 14.5 Test-Suite-Overview Proforma

Test-Suite Overview	
Suite Name:	*SuiteIdentifier*
Standards ref:	*Reference*
PICS proforma ref:	*Reference*
PIXIT proforma ref:	*Reference*
PICS/PIXIT use:	*Reference*
Test Method(s):	*FreeText*
Comments:	*FreeText*

Test-Group or Case Identifier	**Test-Group or Case Reference**	**Page**	**Description**
•	•	•	•
•	•	•	•
TestCaseIdentifier | *TestGroupIdentifier*	*TestCaseReference |* *TestGroupReference*	*Number* •	*FreeText* •
•	•	•	•
Test-Step Identifier	**Test-Step Reference**	**Page**	**Description**
•	•	•	•
•	•	•	•
TestStepIdentifier	*TestStepReference*	*Number*	*FreeText*
•	•	•	•
•	•	•	•
Default Identifier	**Default Reference**	**Page**	**Description**
•	•	•	•
•	•	•	•
DefaultIdentifier	*DefaultReference*	*Number*	*FreeText*
•	•	•	•
•	•	•	•

- A test-case index, which lists, for each test case and test group:
  - Identifier, which is a short name for the test case or group
  - Reference, which is a full name for the test-group or case behavior description and which serves to define its conceptual location in the test-suite structure
  - Number of the page on which the table is located
  - Description of the test purpose or test-group objective
- A test-step index, providing the information for each test step in the step group.
- A default index, providing information about default behavior, which can occur at various points in the test suite.

14.4.3   Declarations Part

The purpose of the declarations part is to describe all the components of the test suite referenced in the dynamic part. Table 14.6 shows the proformas for all the declarations, and Table 14.7 gives

Table 14.6 Declaration Proformas

User-Type Definitions

Name	Base Type	Definition	Comments
UserTypeIdentifier	BaseType	TypeDefinition	FreeText

User-Operation Definition

Operation Name: OPidentifier [FormalPARlist]
Result Type: Type

Description

FreeText

Test-Suite Parameters

Name	Type	PICS/PIXIT Ref	Comments
TS_PARidentifier	Type | ReferenceType	Reference	FreeText

Test-Suite Constants

Name	Type	Value	Comments
TS_CONSTidentifier	Type	Value	FreeText

Test-Suite Variables

Name	Type	Value	Comments
TS_VARidentifier	Type | ReferenceType	Value	FreeText

Test-Case Variables

Name	Type	Value	Comments
TS_VARidentifier	Type | ReferenceType	Value	FreeText

PCO-Type Declarations

Name	Type	Role	Comments
PCOidentifier	PCOtypeIdentifier	UT | LT	FreeText

Timer Declarations

Timer Name	Duration	Units	Comments
TimerIdentifier	TimerDuration	TimeUnit	FreeText

Abbreviation Declarations

Abbreviation	Expansion	Comments
AbbreviationIdentifier	FreeText	FreeText

ASP-Type Declaration

ASP Name: ASPid&FullId **PCO Type:** PCOtypeIdentifier **Comments:** FreeText

Service-Parameter Information

Parameter Name	Type	Comments
ASP_PARid&FullId	Type	GROUP	PDU	FreeText

ASP-Parameter Group-Type Declaration

Parameter Group Name: ASP_PARgroupIdentifier **Comments:** FreeText

Service-Parameter Information

Parameter Name	Type	Comments
ASP_PARid&FullId	Type	GROUP	PDU	FreeText

PDU-Type Declaration

PDU Name: PDUid&FullId **PCO Type:** PCOtypeIdentifier **Comments:** FreeText

PDU-Field Information

Field Name	Type	Comments
FIELDid&FullId	Type&Length	GROUP	PDU	FreeText

PDU-Field Group-Type Declaration

Field Group Name: FIELDgroupIdentifier **Comments:** FreeText

PDU-Field Information

Field Name	Type	Comments
FIELDid&FullId	TypeWithLength	GROUP	PDU	FreeText

Table 14.7 Examples of TTCN Declarations

User-Type Definitions

Name	Base Type	Definition	Comments
Transport Classes	INTEGER	(0, 1, 2, 3, 4)	Classes that may be used for transport-layer connection
Class_Number	INTEGER	(0 . . . 4)	

Test-Suite Constants

Name	Type	Value	Comments
TS_CONST1	BOOLEAN	TRUE	
TS_CONST2	IA5String	"A string"	

Test-Suite Variables

Name	Type	Value	Comments
state	IA5STRING	"idle"	Used to indicate the final stable state of the previous test case, if any, in order to help determine which preamble to use

User-Operation Definition

Operation Name: substr(source:IA5STRING; start_index, length:INTEGER)
Result Type: IA5STRING

Description

substr(source, start_index, length) is the string of length *length* starting from *start_index* of the source string source.
For example:
substr("abcde",3,2) = "cd"

PCO-Type Declarations

Name	Type	Role	Comments
L	TSAP	LT	Transport-service access point at the lower tester
U	SSAP	UT	Session-service access point at the upper tester

Test-Suite Parameters

Name	Type	PICS/PIXIT Ref	Comments
PAR1	INTEGER	PICS question xx	
PAR2	INTEGER	PICS question yy	
PAR3	INTEGER	PIXIT question zz	

Timer Declarations

Timer Name	Duration	Units	Comments
wait	15	sec.	General-purpose wait.
no_response	A	min.	Used to wait for IUT to connect or react to connection establishment; longer duration than general-purpose wait. Gets value from PIXIT.
delay_timer		ms	Duration to be established during execution of the test suite.

Abbreviation Declarations

Abbreviation	Expansion	Comments
CR	N_DATAind<NSDU ~CR_TPDU	CR denotes any N_DATA indication whose NSDU is the encoding of a connect-request TPDU.
CC	N_DATAind<NSDU ~CC_TPDU	CC denotes any N_DATA indication whose NSDU is the encoding of a connect-confirm TPDU.

ASP-Type Declaration

ASP Name: CONreq(T_CONNECTrequest)	PCO Type: TSAP	Comments:

Service-Parameter Information

Parameter Name	Type	Comments
Cda (Called Address)	CDA	. . . of upper tester
Cga (Calling Address)	CGA	. . . of lower tester
QoS (Quality of Service)	QOS	Should ensure class 0 is used

PDU-Type Declaration

PDU Name: INTC (Interrupt Confirm)	PCO Type: NSAP	Comments:

PDU-Field Information

Field Name	Type	Comments
GFI	BITSTRING	General format identifier
LCGN	BITSTRING	Logical channel group number
LCI	BITSTRING	Logical channel identifier
PTI	OCTETSTRING	Packet type identifier
EXTRA	OCTETSTRING	To create long INTC packets

examples of some of these. There are 13 categories of test-suite components that require declarations:

1. *User-defined types:* New types may be defined that are derived from the predefined base types, which are:
   - Integer
   - Boolean
   - Bitstring
   - Hexstring (string of 4-bit hexadecimal digits)
   - Octet string
   - Character string, which may be:
     - NumericString
     - PrintableString
     - TeletexString
     - VideotexString
     - VisibleString
     - IA5String
     - GraphicString
     - GeneralString

   Each new type is defined either as an enumeration of values of a predefined type or by specifying a subrange of values.

2. *User-defined operations:* TTCN makes use of predefined arithmetic ($+$, $-$, $*$, $/$, MOD), relational ($=$, $<$, $>$, $<>$, $>=$, $<=$), and Boolean operators (AND, OR, NOT). A user-defined operation is defined with a name, a list of input parameters and their types, the type of the result parameter, and a description of the operation.

3. *Test-suite parameters:* These are constants derived from the PICS and/or PIXIT that globally parameterize the test suite.

4. *Test-suite constants:* declare a set of names for values not derived from the PICS or PIXIT that will be constant throughout the test suite.

5. *Test-suite variables:* These are global variables used to pass information from one test case to another. Each declared variable may be assigned an initial value.

6. *Test-case variables:* These are variables that are declared globally but whose scope is defined to be local to the test case.

7. *PCO declarations:* list the points of control and observation (PCOs) to be used in the test suite and explain where in the testing environment these PCOs exist.

8. *Timer declarations:* list the timers used by the test suite. The duration of each timer may be a test-suite parameter, a test-suite constant, an explicit value, or undefined at the time of test initiation.

9. *Abbreviations:* define any abbreviations used in the TTCN definition of the test suite.

10. *ASP-type declaration:* declares the types of ASPs that may be sent or received at the declared PCOs. Normally, the declared information is that found in the corresponding ISO or CCITT service definition. Inclusion in the declaration allows the addition of commentary specific to testing and the test suite and provides for cases in which there is no corresponding OSI service definition (e.g., X.25). Each ASP declaration also declares the parameters for the primitive.

11. *ASP-parameter group-type declarations:* One or more parameters of an ASP may be declared separately. This may be a convenient way to structure an ASP declaration for a primitive with many parameters. It also allows reuse of a group of parameters common to several primitives (e.g., a request and its corresponding indication).

12. *PDU-type declaration:* lists the PDUs that may be sent or received either directly or embedded in ASPs at the declared PCOs. Each PDU declaration includes a list of the fields and field groups associated with the PDU.

13. *PDU-field group-type declarations:* One or more contiguous fields of a PDU may be declared separately.

14.4.4 Constraints Part

The purpose of the constraints part is to define constraints on the values of ASP parameters and parameter groups and on the values of PDU fields and field groups. The constraint may dictate that a parameter or field must have a certain value or be within a certain range of values. A constraint may also specify that a group of fields or parameters must satisfy a set of constraints at the same time.

As an example, Table 14.8 shows a PDU-type declaration and a corresponding PDU-constraints declaration. The constraints have the following interpretations:

- *CN1:* FLD1 must have a value greater than 3; FLD2 must be TRUE; FLD3 may be any string.

- *CN2:* FLD1 must have the value 4 or 5 or 6; FLD2 must be FALSE; FLD3 may be any string.

- *CN3:* FLD1 must have the value 0; if this is a received PDU, FLD2 must be present and take on any value; FLD3 must be absent.

Table 14.8 Example of a PDU-Type Declaration and an Associated PDU-Constraints Declaration

PDU Type-Declaration		
PDU Name: PDU_B	**PCO Type:**	**Comments:** This is the declaration of the PDU named PDU_B

PDU-Field Information		
Field Name	**Type**	**Comments**
FLD1	INTEGER	
FLD2	BOOLEAN	
FLD3	IA5STRING	

PDU-Constraints Declaration

PDU Name: PDU_B

	Field Name			
Constraint Name	**FLD1**	**FLD2**	**FLD3**	**Comments**
CN1	>3	TRUE	"A string"	
CN2	(4, 5, 6)	FALSE	"A string"	
CN3	0	?	—	

The symbol *?* refers to received PDUs and ASPs.

Once a constraint has been defined and named, it may then be used in the dynamic part of the test suite.

14.4.5   Dynamic Part

The dynamic part contains the main body of the test suite: the test-case, test-step, and default-behavior descriptions.

14.4.5.1   Test-Case Dynamic Behavior

The first part of Table 14.9 shows the proforma for a test-case dynamic-behavior table. The table consists of the following entries:

- *Reference:* a full name for this test case behavior description, which defines its location in the test-suite structure. In effect, the name is a path name through the tree from the test-suite root.

- *Identifier:* a shorter name for the test case.

- *Purpose:* an informal statement of the purpose of the test case.

- *Default:* an identifier of a default-behavior description, if any, that applies to this test-case behavior description.

- *Behavior description:* describes the behavior of the lower and/or upper tester in terms of test events, using the tree notation described later in this subsection.

- *Label:* used to identify statements in the behavior-description column for statement line numbering and/or to allow jumps using the GOTO statement.

- *Constraints reference:* associates a statement in the behavior-description column with a reference to specific ASP and/or PDU values defined in the constraints part.

- *Verdict:* associates a verdict with a statement in the statement tree of the behavior-description column.

- *Comments:* comments provided for individual TTCN statements in the behavior-description column.

- *Extended comments:* general comments that apply to the test case as a whole and/or longer comments on individual statements.

The heart of a test case table is the four columns: behavior description, label, constraints reference, and verdict. The behavior description is a precise description of sequences of events initiated by the upper and lower tester and anticipated events initiated by the IUT. These statements are in the TTCN language, which is in the style of a programming language. Each statement may have an associated label, which can be used as the target for a GOTO statement. Each statement may have associated constraints, which serve two purposes:

1. For a tester-initiated event, the constraints dictate exact values or allow values to be selected from a set for the parameters of an ASP or a PDU.

2. For an IUT-initiated event, the constraints dictate acceptable parameter values. If the incoming PDU or ASP does not satisfy the constraints, then the event indicated by that statement is not satisfied.

Finally, those statements that complete a test sequence will have an associated verdict.

Table 14.9 TTCN Dynamic-Part Proformas

Test-Case Dynamic Behavior

Reference: *TestCaseReference*
Identifier: *TestCaseIdentifier*
Purpose: *FreeText*
Default: *DefaultsReference*

Behavior Description		Label	Constraints Reference	Verdict	Comments
	StatementLine	•			
	•	•	•	•	•
	•	•	•	•	•
TreeHeader	•	*Label*	*Constraints Reference*	*Verdict*	*FreeText*
	•	•		•	•
	•	•	•	•	•
	StatementLine	•	•	•	•

Extended Comments: *FreeText*

Test-Step Dynamic Behavior

Reference: *TestStepReference*
Identifier: *TestStepIdentifier [FormalPARlist]*
Objective: *FreeText*
Default: *DefaultsReference*

Behavior Description		Label	Constraints Reference	Verdict	Comments
	StatementLine	•			
	•	•	•	•	•
	•	•	•	•	•
TreeHeader	•	*Label*	*Constraints Reference*	*Verdict*	*FreeText*
	•	•		•	•
	•	•	•	•	•
	StatementLine	•	•	•	•

Extended Comments: *FreeText*

Default Dynamic Behavior

Reference: *DefaultReference*
Identifier: *DefaultIdentifier [FormalPARlist]*
Objective: *FreeText*

Behavior Description		Label	Constraints Reference	Verdict	Comments
	StatementLine	•			
	•	•	•	•	•
	•	•	•	•	•
	•	*Label*	*Constraints Reference*	*Verdict*	*FreeText*
	•	•		•	•
	•	•	•	•	•
	StatementLine	•	•	•	•

Extended Comments: *FreeText*

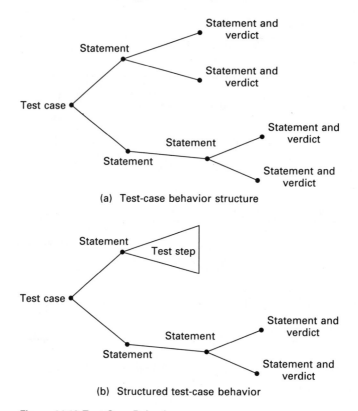

(a) Test-case behavior structure

(b) Structured test-case behavior

Figure 14.13 Test-Case Behavior

The behavior-description portion of a test case is structured as a tree, as indicated in Figure 14.13, part (a). The nodes of the tree are statements, with each statement corresponding to either a tester action or an IUT action. A node has more than one branch emanating from it to the next lower level if there is more than one possible course of action at that point. At the leaves of the tree are the statements that end a test sequence; associated with each of these is a verdict.

TTCN statements are of four kinds: test events initiated by the tester, test events received by the tester from the IUT, pseudoevents, and constructs. The TTCN behavior-description language obeys the following syntax:

Statement   :: = Event | PseudoEvent | Construct
Event   :: = Send | ImplicitSend | Receive | Otherwise | Timeout
Construct   :: = GoTo | Attach | Repeat
PseudoEvent   :: = [TTCNExpression] | [TimerOperation]

Table 14.10 defines the terms in the syntax description.

Each TTCN statement in a behavior description is shown on a separate line. Statements can be related to one another as a sequence or as alternatives. A sequence of statements indicates that the statements are to be executed one after the other and is depicted by indenting each successive statement from the previous one. For example:

Table 14.10 TTCN Statement Elements

___

Event

The ASPs or PDUs to be initiated or received by the lower or upper tester, the OTHERWISE event, or the TIMEOUT event.

Send

The ASPs or PDUs to be initiated by the lower or upper tester. Each event name is prefixed by an exclamation mark (!). The name may be further prefixed by a PCO identifier if more than one PCO exists in the test configuration.

ImplicitSend

In the remote test methods, there is no explicit PCO above the IUT; it is necessary to have a means of specifying, at a given point in the description of the behavior of the lower tester, that the IUT should be made to initiate a particular PDU or ASP. The event name is preceded by <IUT! to indicate an implicit send. The way in which the implicit send is effected should be specified in the PIXIT.

Receive

The ASPs or PDUs to be received by the lower or upper tester. Each event name is prefixed by an exclamation mark (!). The name may be further prefixed by a PCO identifier if more than one PCO exists in the test configuration.

Otherwise

The TTCN mechanism for dealing with unforeseen test events in a controlled way. It is used to denote that the appropriate tester shall accept *any* incoming event that has not previously matched one of the alternatives to the OTHERWISE.

Timeout

Allows expiration of a timer or all timers to be checked in a test case. The event succeeds if the corresponding timer has expired.

PseudoEvent

An expression or timer operation. These are termed pseudoevents because they cause some action to be taken but do not generate an event at a PCO.

TTCNExpression

A TTCN expression may be a Boolean expression or an assignment. It provides some of the basic mechanisms of a programming language.

TimerOperation

The timer operations are StartTimer, CancelTimer, and ReadTimer.

Construct

A goto, attach, or repeat statement. These constructs allow for the imposition of a structure on the sequence of statements but do not themselves generate any events or pseudoevents.

GoTo

Jump to the statement corresponding to the label specified in the GoTo statement.

Attach

Allows a subtree to be attached to a tree. In effect, this is a macro facility.

Repeat

The iteration statement in TTCN. It allows a tree step to be iterated until a Boolean expression is true.

___

EVENT_A
CONSTRUCT_B
EVENT_C

Statements at the same level of indentation subordinate to the same preceding statement represent possible alternative TTCN statements that may occur at that time. Alternative statements are listed in the order in which the tester shall repeatedly attempt them until one occurs. An example that combines sequences and alternatives:

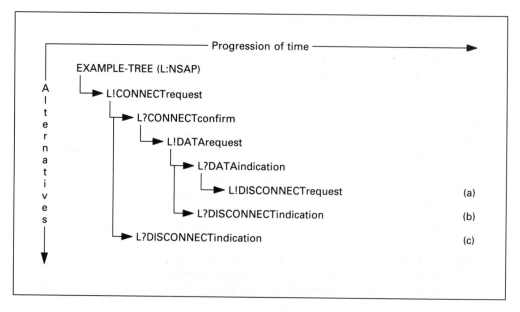

(a) Depiction of a behavior tree

Test-case Dynamic Behavior				
Reference: TTCN_EXAMPLES/TREE_EXAMPLE_1 Identifier: TREE_EX_1(L:NSAP) Purpose: To illustrate the use of trees Default:				
Behavior Description	**Label**	**Constraints Reference**	**Verdict**	**Comments**

L!CONNECTrequest
    L?CONNECTconfirm
        L!DATArequest
            L?DATAindication
                L!DISCONNECTrequest
            L?DISCONNECTindication
    L?DISCONNECTindication
		CR1
		C1
		DTR1
		DTI1
		DSCR1
		DSCI1
		DSCR1
			pass
			inconc
			inconc
				Request. . .
				. . .Confirm
				Send data
				Receive data
				Accept
				Premature
				Premature

(b) TTCN description

Figure 14.14 Example of Test-Case Dynamic-Behavior Table

EVENT_A
CONSTRUCT_B1
STATEMENT_B2
EVENT_B3
EVENT_C

Figure 14.14 gives an example of a behavior description. The upper part is a graphic description of the behavior to be described. The behavior describes the events at a lower tester during an attempt to establish a connection, exchange data, and terminate the connection. If the behavior succeeds, the following events occur at the lower-tester PCO:

(a) CONNECTrequest, CONNECTconfirm, DATArequest, DATAindication, DISCONNECT-request

Progress can be thwarted by the IUT or the service provider. This generates two alternative sequences:

(b) CONNECTrequest, CONNECTconfirm, DATArequest, DISCONNECTindication

(c) CONNECTrequest, DISCONNECTindication

Figure 14.14, part (b), shows the corresponding TTCN description. For each leaf of the tree, a verdict is recorded. Possible verdict values are pass, fail, and inconclusive.

14.4.5.2 Test-Step Dynamic Behavior

The second part of Table 14.9 shows the proforma for a test-step dynamic-behavior table. Test steps can be used for substructuring a behavior tree, as indicated in Figure 14.13, part (b). The test step allows for modular construction of a test-behavior description. The test step is attached to a test case by means of the ATTACH statement, which functions as a macro call. The REPEAT statement can be used to iterate a test step.

14.4.5.3 Default Dynamic Behavior

The third part of Table 14.9 shows the proforma for a default dynamic-behavior table.

A TTCN test specification must specify alternative behavior for every possible event. It often happens in a behavior tree that every sequence of alternatives ends in the same behavior. This behavior may be "factored out" as default behavior to this tree and declared in a default dynamic-behavior table, which is referenced in a test-case dynamic-behavior table.

The default mechanism can improve the readability of a test case. Consider this example:

MAIN_TREE

A
  A1
    A11
    C
      D
  A2
    C
      D
B
  B1
    C
      D
C
  D

is equivalent to

MAIN_TREE   with default   **DEFAULT**

A   C
  A1   D
    A11
  A2
B
  B1

The same effect, less concisely, can be achieved with subtree attachment using a test-step table.

14.5   TEST REALIZATION

ISO 9646-4/X.293 specifies requirements and gives guidance concerning the realization of a means of testing IUTs, in conformance with a reference OSI standard abstract test suite specified in compliance with ISO 9646-2.

14.5.1   Means of Testing

Test realization involves producing a means of testing an IUT based on an abstract test specification. Figure 14.15 illustrates the process that is involved. There are essentially two complementary processes that result in the development of a means of testing: selection/parameterization and derivation.

Let us first consider an abstract test suite (ATS) that has been designed for a particular protocol. In the *selection process*, the appropriate abstract test cases of the ATS are selected for the

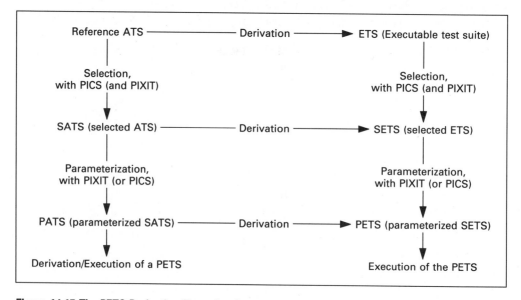

Figure 14.15 The PETS Derivation/Execution Process

particular IUT. The selection is determined by the PICS and PIXIT, which indicate the portion of the protocol specification supported by this particular implementation. Only the subset of test cases from the ATS that test the implemented features of the protocol are selected. In the *parameterization process,* the parameters in the selected abstract test cases are given appropriate values—again, according to the PICS and PIXIT. The result is a set of test cases that are appropriate for the IUT and for which all parameters have been assigned values appropriate for this test.

A separate process is the *derivation process,* which converts from an abstract specification to an executable specification. As indicated in Figure 14.15, the derivation can be done at several points. The original ATS could be converted to an executable test suite (ETS). The ETS is a base for tests of a family of implementations. For a specific implementation, the selection and parameterization processes must be performed on the ETS.

As an alternative, the derivation process could be applied to the abstract test cases after selection or parameterization. Either of these alternatives may be more efficient if only one or a small number of implementations are to be tested in a given test configuration.

14.5.2 Realization Requirements

Test realization requires the realization of the three abstract testing functions: lower-tester, upper-tester, and test-coordination procedures.

14.5.2.1 Realization of the Lower Tester

An essential element of any abstract test method is the lower tester. An implementation of the lower tester must provide the following functions:

- Run executable test cases, which are derived from abstract test cases
- Produce verdict indications in accordance with the reference standardized ATS
- Control and observe the test events that are included in abstract test cases

  ISO 9646-4 suggests two techniques for implementing the lower tester:

1. *Encoder/decoder:* The tester encodes and decodes the ASPs (abstract service primitives) and PDUs (protocol data units) as required for the test case being run, without itself being an implementation of the protocol in question.

2. *Enhanced implementation:* The tester is an actual conformant implementation of the protocol concerned, modified by the addition of an error generator, a configuration module, or a similar device to ensure that invalid or unusual ASPs or PDUs can be generated as requested by the test case being run.

  The latter approach will generally involve less software development. However, the testing authority must be assured that the implementation being used as the base for the lower tester is itself in conformance with the protocol.

14.5.2.2 Realization of the Upper Tester

ISO 9646-4 suggests three techniques for implementing the upper tester:

1. *Software implementation:* This may or may not be independent of the design of the system under test (SUT) and the protocol implementation under test (IUT). It is installed in the SUT above the IUT, with a mapping region that interfaces with the local realization of the ASPs.

2. *Human operator:* The functions of the upper tester are performed by a person having access to a user interface that maps onto the IUT service boundary and accesses and manipulates the realization of the appropriate ASPs.

3. *Notional:* The upper layers of the SUT are used to realize the functions of the upper tester, without any additional mechanism's being installed. This method can be used only to realize the remote abstract test method.

14.5.2.3   Realization of the Test-Coordination Procedures

ISO 9646-4 suggests three techniques for implementing the test-coordination procedures:

1. *Scenario interpreter:* The upper tester is a software implementation that takes its instructions from files generated in conjunction with the lower-tester installation.

2. *Human operator:* When a human operator is used to implement the upper tester, the operator synchronizes with the lower tester. One method of communication would be a set of prompting messages from a user interface of the lower tester.

3. *Test-management protocol:* A protocol exists between the upper and lower testers by which the lower tester can control and observe the upper tester.

14.5.3   Documentation

A key element of the documentation that must be produced by the conformance test is a conformance log. A conformance log is a human-readable record of information produced as a result of a test execution, sufficient to record the observed test outcomes and verify the assignment of test verdicts. The information relates the observations of actual test events that occur during test execution to the abstract test cases documented in TTCN. The conformance log should contain the following elements:

-   A unique identifier of the log that includes the time and date of the start of test execution
-   An identification of the means of testing
-   An indication of the start and end of run of each test case, including a reference to the corresponding abstract test case
-   A record of the PDUs and their parameters exchanged between the lower tester and the IUT
-   A record of all the abstract test events that occur
-   An indication of the result of each test case, which will be a verdict assignment, an abstract or executable test-case error, or an abnormal test-case termination
-   A time stamp or ordering sequence for all test events logged by the lower tester

The conformance log is the "raw data" of the test execution. It is useful to designers for uncovering and identifying errors in the test implementation and in the protocol IUT. It is less useful to the end user. Beyond the conformance log, the conformance-testing process should produce a set of documentation that includes the following:

- Identification of the means of testing

- Name and version number of the standard for the protocol specification and name and version number of the abstract test suite

- Description of the means of testing

- Specifications of the test-coordination procedures and of the upper tester, when required

- The test cases, if any, that cannot be executed due to limitations in the means of testing

- Description of those procedures for test execution that are to be performed by the test laboratory and/or the client and that are specific to the means of testing

- Statement of conformance to the reference standard

- Statement of compliance with ISO 9646-4

- Guidance for interpreting the conformance logs

14.6 CONFORMANCE ASSESSMENT

ISO 9646-5/X.294 addresses the roles of both the test laboratory and the client during the conformance-assessment process, the need to reach mutual agreement between them, and the requirements that apply to each of them. Having standardized many aspects of the conformance-testing process, it is important for ISO 9646 to deal with the issue of the comparability of results of conformance assessments of similar implementations. If results are to be consistently produced, not only should the same source of tests be used, but also the methods of selecting and parameterizing these tests and presenting their results should be as similar as possible.

The test laboratory is responsible for conducting the conformance assessment for a client. Categories of test laboratories include:

1. *First-party test laboratories:* organizations developing or supplying OSI implementations

2. *Second-party test laboratories:* organizations willing to verify OSI implementations themselves before using them

3. *Third-party test laboratories:* organizations independent of suppliers and users of OSI implementations whose business is the testing of such implementations

During the conformance-assessment process, the client is responsible for the conformance statements accompanying the system under test and for the configuration of the SUT. Examples of clients include:

- Implementers or suppliers of real open systems that are applying for their own implementation to be tested

- Procurers of those implementations

ISO 9646-5 specifically addresses the following requirements:

- Requirements for the testability of the implementation with respect to abstract test methods

- General requirements applicable to the test laboratory and the client relevant to any conformance-test process

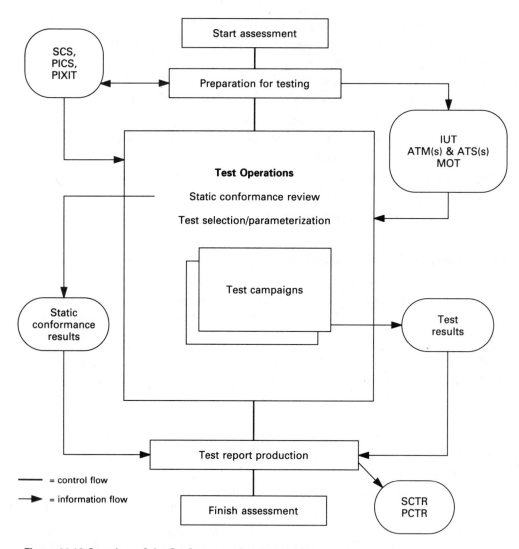

Figure 14.16 Overview of the Conformance-Assessment Process

- Exchange of technical and administrative information
- Cooperation between the test laboratory and the client to reach an agreement on the definition of the IUT, the abstract test methods and abstract test suites to be used, and the conditions under which testing will be performed
- Requirements for the structure and content of the conformance-test reports that document the results of the conformance assessment

Table 14.11 Use of Conformance-Testing Documents by Client and Test Laboratory

Document	Provided By	Partly Completed By	Completed By	Held By
PICS proforma	Protocol standard		Client	
PICS				Test lab
PIXIT proforma	ISO 9646-5	Test lab	Client	
PIXIT				Test lab
SCS	Client		Client	Test lab
SCTR proforma	ISO 9646-5		Test lab	
SCTR				Test lab
PCTR proforma	ISO 9646-5		Test lab	
PCTR				Test lab
Conformance log	Test lab		Test lab	Test lab

PICS = protocol-implementation conformance statement.
PIXIT = protocol implementation extra information for testing.
SCS = system-conformance statement.
SCTR = system-conformance test report.
PCTR = protocol-conformance test report.

Figure 14.16, from ISO 9646-5, is another view of the conformance-assessment process (compare this with Figure 14.4, from ISO 9646-1). The bulk of 9646-5 is a discussion of each of the steps in this process, listing the responsibilities of both client and test laboratory.

Figure 14.16 emphasizes the documents required to conduct a conformance assessment. The PICS and PIXIT were defined earlier. In addition, the following documents are part of the conformance-assessment process:

- *System-conformance statement (SCS)*: summarizes which OSI standards or CCITT recommendations are implemented and to which ones conformance is claimed.

- *System-conformance test report (SCTR)*: gives an overall summary of the conformance of the system or implementation to the set of protocols for which conformance testing was carried out.

- *Protocol-conformance test report (PCTR)*: gives details of the testing carried out for a particular protocol. It lists all the abstract test cases and identifies those for which corresponding executable test cases were run, together with the verdicts assigned to each test case executed.

Table 14.11 summarizes the key documents related to conformance assessment, indicating their use by the client and the test laboratory.

14.7 SUMMARY

A prerequisite for the development of interoperable open systems implementations is that the implemented protocols and services conform to the published standards. The goal of conformance testing is to assure that this conformance is verified.

The set of standards that have been developed for OSI-based conformance testing provide a framework for designing and performing tests, and for evaluating the results. A variety of test methods have been defined that allow various configurations of local and remote elements to be used in performing the test. A notation for defining the tests, the tree, and tabular combined notation (TTCN), has been standardized. With the aid of TTCN, test suites and test methods may be specified. The standards also address the issues of actual test realization and the standardized procedures for assessing test results.

15
International Standardized Profiles

The practical use of the OSI (open systems interconnection) protocols and services rests on two requirements. First, any implementation of OSI protocols and services must in fact conform to the relevant standards. Verifying that this requirement is satisfied is the task of conformance assessment, which was addressed in the preceding chapter. Second, two separate implementations, if they are to participate in a cooperative application, must interwork and interoperate correctly. Even if the conformance-assessment process were complete and error-free, the second requirement is not met simply by determining that the two implementations conform to the same set of standards. In addition, the two implementations must support compatible sets of options and parameters associated with the protocols at each layer of the OSI architecture. It is to address this issue of compatibility that ISO (the International Organization for Standardization) has developed the concept of international standardized profiles (ISPs), which is the subject of this chapter.

15.1 FUNCTIONAL STANDARDS AND PROFILES

Although the OSI model was first defined almost 20 years ago and has been an international standard for over a decade, OSI implementations have been slow to come to market. A key reason for this has to do with the magnitude of the task of transitioning from another communication suite to OSI. With well-established proprietary architectures, such as IBM's SNA (Systems Network Architecture), and a limited but widely used multivendor architecture—namely, the TCP/IP (Transmission Control Protocol/Internet Protocol)-protocol suite—it was inevitable that there would be inertia to overcome. But the pace of development and adoption of OSI has also been hampered by some practical problems relating to the standards themselves:

1. Most of the ISO and CCITT standards relating to OSI are based on paper designs, usually prepared by committee. That is, a functional requirement, such as for a connection-oriented transport protocol, is developed and then a specification for the protocol is drawn up. It is only after the specification has solidified that serious implementation efforts begin. It is pos-

sible—indeed, likely—that there will be some subtle logical flaws in such specifications that will only show up after field experience with the implementation.

2. The protocol specifications are essentially prose descriptions. Although they are often accompanied by some formal methods, such as state-machine definitions, the protocol specifications are not amenable to mathematical proof, nor is it possible to mathematically verify an implementation. Thus, there is opportunity for ambiguity and the risk that two different implementations will not interoperate.

3. A standard typically contains a number of options and parameters with undefined value ranges. This allows a single protocol specification to satisfy, in a consistent manner, a range of requirements that are similar but not identical. However, two implementations that choose different options and parameters may not be able to interoperate.

Problem 1 is dealt with by experience. Many of the ISO and CCITT standards have now been around for a number of years, and as the body of experience grows, so does confidence in the correctness of the specifications. For newer protocols, the amount of experience is less but growing.

Problem 2, and to a certain extent problem 3, are dealt with by the OSI conformance-testing process. The development of an abstract test suite for a protocol involves defining for various possible events the correct response of the protocol. Thus, the abstract test suite clarifies ambiguities in the original defining document. Also, when an implementation is subjected to a conformance test, the selection and parameterization functions (Figure 14.15) require that the implementation's choices with regard to options and parameters be made specific. Thus, to the extent that the conformance-assessment process is robust and correct, we can have a degree of confidence that the implementation under test (IUT) conforms to the protocol specification and that the options and parameters chosen by the protocol IUT are clearly documented.

Problem 3 is more significant than it might first appear. With virtually all of the protocol standards, there are a substantial number of options and adjustable parameters. As an example, consider ISO 9542, the connectionless ES-IS protocol discussed in Chapter 4. This is one of the simplest of the OSI protocols; the actual specification of the protocol takes just ten pages; however, the PICS proforma (reproduced in the Appendix 15A to this chapter), which defines the options and parameters for the protocol, takes an additional five pages. The PICS proformas for more complex protocols are correspondingly longer.

15.1.1   Functional Standards

Problem 3 becomes even more significant when we consider that no user is interested in a single protocol at a single layer of the OSI architecture. Rather, the user is interested a full 7-layer implementation that will support one or more distributed applications (e.g., file transfer). In order to specify the OSI requirements to satisfy a particular application, it is necessary to reference a set of standards and specify, for each standard referenced, the valid options and parameter settings within that standard that are needed to achieve the required function. Considering that collectively, across 7 layers, there will be a large number of options and parameters, it is not unlikely that two different implementations that claim to support a given application may make different choices and not be interoperable.

To address this problem, a number of organizations have created documents that identify preferred combinations of standards and options for various application areas. The resulting documents have been termed **functional standards.** Let us briefly consider two of these.

15.1.1.1 MAP/TOP Users' Group

The Manufacturing Automation Protocol (MAP) is an effort begun by General Motors in 1982; since then it has been taken over by the MAP/TOP Users' Group, administered by the Society of Manufacturing Engineers. The objective of MAP is to define a local area network and associated protocols for terminals, computing resources, programmable devices, and robots within a plant or a factory. It sets standards for procurement and provides a specification for use by vendors who want to build networking products for factory use that are acceptable to MAP participants. The strategy has three parts:

1. For cases in which international standards exist, select those alternatives and options that best suit the needs of the MAP participants.

2. For standards currently under development, participate in the standards-making process to represent the requirements of the MAP participants.

3. In those cases where no appropriate standard exists, devise interim MAP standards until the international standards are developed.

Thus, MAP is intended to specify those standards and options within standards appropriate for the factory environment. Because of the widespread support for MAP among manufacturing companies, this guarantees a large market for products that conform to those standards.

A similar effort, called Technical and Office Protocols (TOP), addresses the needs of the office and engineering environments. Like MAP, TOP specifies standards and options within standards and has received widespread support. TOP was begun by Boeing and is now, together with MAP, part of the MAP/TOP Users' Group.

15.1.1.2 U.S. Government OSI Users' Committee

A significant milestone in the development of functional standards was the creation of the U.S. Government OSI Users' Committee in 1986. The U.S. government is the world's largest user of computers and thus has a profound impact on the product plans of many of the vendors. The objectives of the committee are to:

- Develop implementable OSI specifications

- Coordinate cooperative efforts between government agencies and industry to introduce products that meet government needs and comply with international standards

- Define unique agency requirements and work for OSI incorporation of those requirements

The most important outcome of this committee's efforts has been a document initially referred to as the government OSI procurement specification (GOSIP) and now called the government OSI profile (GOSIP). GOSIP is published by the National Institute of Standards and Technology (NIST). Like MAP and TOP, GOSIP specifies standards and options within standards that are suitable for government use. Furthermore, GOSIP provides detailed implementation guidelines that should help assure that products from different vendors do in fact work together. GOSIP is now a federal information-processing standard (FIPS PUB 146) and is mandatory for use on government procurements.

15.1.2   International Standardized Profiles

In addition to MAP/TOP and GOSIP, a number of other efforts at functional standardization are under way. Other notable examples include the Standards Promotion and Application Group (SPAG) in Europe, operated by the European Commission, and the Promoting Conference for OSI (POSI) in Japan. All of these regional and special-purpose efforts represent an improvement over an ad hoc attempt to specify application-based requirements. However, these same efforts run the risk of fragmenting what should be a global market and adding further confusion to that already facing customers and end users.

In an effort to manage the development of functional standards in an orderly and consistent manner, ISO/IEC JTC1 (International Organization for Standardization/International Electrotechnical Commission Joint Technical Committee 1) established the Special Group on Functional Standardization (SGFS) to bring these regional and special-purpose activities together into a single program to provide functional standards of global significance. To achieve its purpose, SGFS created a new type of publication called the international standardized profile. In mid-1990, ISO published TR 10000, *Framework and Taxonomy of International Standardized Profiles,* and since then has published a number of ISPs. A key objective of this effort is to minimize the confusion on the part of users and suppliers by developing a common classification scheme, document scope,

Table 15.1 Terms Defined in ISO TR 10000

International Standardized Profile (ISP)

An internationally-agreed-to, harmonized document that identifies a standard or group of standards, together with options and parameters, necessary to accomplish a function or set of functions.

Profile

A set of one or more base standards and, where applicable, the identification of chosen classes, subsets, options, and parameters of those base standards, necessary for accomplishing a particular function. An ISP includes the specification of one or more profiles.

ISP Implementation Conformance Statement (ISPICS)

A statement made by the supplier of a system that claims to conform to an ISP, stating the capabilities and options that have been implemented, and all optional features that have been omitted.

Group

A set of profiles that are compatible, in the sense that a system implementing one profile from a group can interwork, according to OSI, with another system implementing a different profile from the same group, in terms of the operation of the protocols specified within those profiles.

Base Standard

An approved ISO international standard or technical report or CCITT recommendation that is used in the definition of a profile.

Table 15.2 International Standardized Profiles

ISO TR 10000-1	International Standardized Profiles, Part 1: Framework
ISO TR 10000-2	Part 2: Taxonomy of Profiles
DISP 10607-1	ISP AFTnn—FTAM, Part 1, Specification of ACSE, Presentation, and Session Protocols for use by FTAM
DISP 10607-2	Part 2: Definition of Document Types, Constraint Sets, and Syntaxes
DISP 10607-2 DAD 1	Addendum 1: Additional Definitions
DISP 10607-3	Part 3: AFT11—Simple File Transfer Service
DISP 10607-4	Part 4: AFT12—Positional File Transfer Service (Flat)
DISP 10607-5	Part 5: AFT22—Positional File Access Service (Flat)
DISP 10607-6	Part 6: AFT3—File Management Service
DISP 10608-1	Connection-mode Transport Service over Connectionless Network Service, Part 1: General Overview and Subnetwork-Independent Requirements
DISP 10608-2	Part 2: TA51 Profile Including Subnetwork-Dependent Requirements for CSMA/CD LANs
DISP 10608-5	Part 5: TA1111/TA1121 Profiles Including Subnetwork-Dependent Requirements for X.25 Packet Switched Data Networks Using Switched Virtual Circuits
DISP 10609-1	ISPs TB, TC, TD, and TE—Connection-mode Transport Service over Connection-mode Network Service, Part 1: Subnetwork-type Independent Requirements for Group TB
DISP 10609-2	Part 2: Subnetwork-type Independent Requirements for Group TC
DISP 10609-3	Part 3: Subnetwork-type Independent Requirements for Group TD
DISP 10609-4	Part 4: Subnetwork-type Independent Requirements for Group TE
DISP 10609-5	Part 5: Definition of Profile TB 1111/TB 1121
DISP 10609-6	Part 6: Definition of Profile TC 1111/TC 1121
DISP 10609-7	Part 7: Definition of Profile TD 1111/TD 1121
DISP 10609-8	Part 8: Definition of Profile TE 1111/TE 1121
DISP 10609-9	Part 9: Subnetwork-type Depedent Requirements for Network Layer, Data Link Layer, and Physical Layer Concerning Permanent Access to a Packet Switched Data Network Using Virtual Call

and document style for functional standards. Table 15.1 lists some key terms defined in TR 10000, and Table 15.2 lists the currently published ISPs.

The remainder of this chapter deals with the concepts introduced in TR 10000 and CD 9646-6, a related document that deals with conformance assessment for ISPs. In the remainder of this section, we provide some background that serves to explain the approach taken by ISO.

If a customer or user wishes to make use of a distributed application based on OSI, then all the systems that support the application must be interoperable at all seven layers of the OSI architecture. Thus, for a given application, options and parameter settings at all seven layers must be considered. The task can be made more manageable by organizing the OSI architecture into four relatively independent components, as illustrated in Figure 15.1. For a given application, a func-

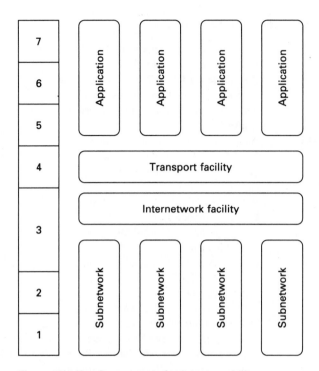

Figure 15.1 Key Components for Interoperability

tional standard, or profile, is needed for each component: application, transport protocol, internetwork protocol, and subnetwork.

The choices that need to be made for each are best described in the following order:

1. *Application suite:*[1] A given application suite will consist of a set of application-service entities (ASEs) plus the presentation functional units and session functional units specifically needed to support the application.

2. *Subnetwork:* A subnetwork or subnetworks interconnect the distributed systems. The set of subnetworks may be imposed; that is, a new application and perhaps new systems are added to an existing network facility. Alternatively, the subnetwork or subnetworks may be chosen for one or more applications. In this latter case, the choice is likely to be based on network technology, capacity requirements, and a variety of other factors that do not necessarily reflect the particular characteristics of the application.

3. *Internetworking facility:* Given a collection of subnetworks, an internetworking protocol and the associated ES-IS (end system to intermediate system) and IS-IS routing protocols must be selected. The choice of either connection mode or connectionless mode will depend on the nature of the subnetworks.

4. *Transport facility:* Either the connection-mode or connectionless-mode transport service is chosen, to match the mode of the application. Then, the appropriate class of transport protocol is

---

1. This is not an official OSI term but is a useful concept.

chosen, to match the characteristics of the internetworking facility and the underlying subnetworks.

For all four components, the appropriate options and parameter settings to support the given application must be selected.

The advantage of viewing the profiling process in this fashion is the potential for the reuse of profiles. For the application suite, a different profile will be defined for each separate application. A small number of general-purpose profiles can be defined for the transport facility, internetworking facility, and subnetworks. A total profile for an application then consists of a profile for the application suite together with a selection of the appropriate general-purpose profiles for each of the other three components.

One final point concerns the relationship between connection mode and connectionless mode. As was discussed in Chapter 2, a conversion from one mode to another can occur between layers. The allowable conversions are from the transport service to the network service and from the network service to the subnetwork capability. Both of these types of conversions need to be considered in developing a full profile to support an application.

15.2 FRAMEWORK AND TAXONOMY FOR ISPs

TR 10000-1 defines the concept of profiles and the way in which they are documented in international standardized profiles (ISPs). It also sets out the nature and content of the documentation required for an ISP. The document begins by listing the purposes for defining profiles:

- To identify base standards, together with appropriate classes, subsets, options, and parameters that are necessary to accomplish identified functions

- To provide a system of referencing the various uses of base standards that is meaningful to both users and suppliers

- To provide a means of enhancing the availability for procurement of consistent implementations of functionally defined groups of base standards, which are expected to be the major components of real application systems

- To promote uniformity in the development of conformance tests for systems that implement the functions associated with the profiles

15.2.1 Relationship of Profile to Base Standards

The relationship between a profile and the base standards to which it refers can be defined in terms of three concepts: selection, limitation, and conformance.

A profile is a *selection* of base standards that, in combination, can be used to provide a given function in a given environment. For each base standard selected, a choice is made of options permitted within that standard. In addition, suitable values for parameters that are left unspecified[2] in the base standard are provided.

A profile is also a *limitation* of the base standards for the given application. The choice of options and ranges of values is restricted so as to maximize the probability of interworking between

---

2.   In some cases, a parameter is completely unspecified in the base standard. In other cases, a default or recommended value is provided, but other values may be selected for implementation.

Table 15.3 Taxonomy of Profiles

Transport Profiles: Subnetworks

1	Packet-switched data networks (PSDNs)
11	Permanent access to a PSDN
111	PSTN leased line
1111	Virtual call
1112	Permanent virtual circuit
112	Digital data circuit/CSDN leased line
1121	Virtual call
1122	Permanent virtual circuit
113	ISDN B channel, semipermanent
1131	Virtual call
1132	Permanent virtual circuit
12	Switched access to a PSDN
121	PSTN case
1211	Virtual call
122	CSDN case
1221	Virtual call
123	ISDN B-channel case
1231	Virtual call
2	Digital data circuit
21	Leased (permanent) service
22	Dial-up (CSDN)
3	Analog telephone circuit
31	Leased (permanent) service
32	Dial-up (PSTN)
4	Integrated services digital network (ISDN)
41	Semipermanent service
411	B channel
4111	X.25 DTE-to-DTE operation
42	Circuit-mode service
421	B channel
4211	X.25 DTE-to-DTE operation
43	Packet-mode service
431	D-channel access
4311	Virtual call
4312	Permanent virtual circuit
432	B-channel semipermanent access
4321	Virtual call
4322	Permanent virtual circuit
433	B-channel demand access
4331	Virtual call

Transport Profiles: Subnetworks (*cont.*)

5	Local area networks
51	CSMA/CD
52	Token bus
53	Token ring
54	FDDI

Transport Profiles: Transport Groups

TA	COTS over CLNS*
TB	COTS over CONS with mandatory protocol classes 0, 2, and 4
TC	COTS over CONS with mandatory protocol classes 0 and 2
TD	COTS over CONS with mandatory protocol class 0
TE	COTS over CONS with mandatory protocol class 2
UA	CLTS over CLNS
UB	CLTS over CONS

Relay Profiles

RA	Relaying the CLNS
RB	Relaying the CONS
RC	X.25 protocol relaying †
RD	Relaying the MAC service using transparent bridging ‡
RE	Relaying the MAC service using source routing §
RZ	Relaying between CLNS and CONS

Application Profiles: FTAM (AFT)

1	File-transfer service
11	Simple (unstructured)
12	Positional (flat)
13	Full (hierarchical)
2	File-access service
22	Position (flat)
23	Full (hierarchical)
3	File-management service

Application Profiles: Message Handling (AMH)

1	Common facilities
11	MTA and MTS‖
12	UA to MS (P7)
13	UA or MS to MTA (P3)
2	IPMS

Table 15.3 (*Cont.*)

Application Profiles: Message Handling (AMH) (*cont.*)

21	IPM end system to IPM end system (P2 over P1)
22	IPM UA to IPM MS (P2 over P7)
23	IPM UA or IPM MS to MTA (P2 over P3)
24	IPM end system to IPM end system (P2-1984 over P1-1984)
3	EDIMS #
31	EDIM end system to EDIM end system (P$_{EDI}$ over P1)
32	EDIM UA ot EDIM MS (P$_{EDI}$ over P7)
33	EDIM UA or EDIM MS to MTA (P$_{EDI}$ over P3)

Application Profiles: Virtual Terminal (AVT)

1	Basic class (A mode)
11	A-mode default
12	TELNET
13	Line scroll
14	Paged
15	CCITT X.3 PAD interworking
16	Transparent
17	Enhanced line scroll
18	Enhanced paged
2	Basic class (S mode)
21	S-mode default
22	Forms
23	Paged
24	Enhanced forms
25	Enhanced paged

Application Profiles: Transaction Processing (ATP)

Substructure to be studied

Application Profiles: Remote Database Access (ARD)

Substructure to be studied

Application Profiles: OSI Management (AOM)

Substructure to be studied

Application Profiles: Directory (ADI)

| 1 | Directory-access protocol (DAP) |
| 2 | Directory-system protocol (DSP) |

Interchange Format and Representation Profiles: Office-Document Format (FOD)

1	Simple document structure
11	Character-content architecture only
2	Enhanced document structure
26	Character, raster-graphics, and geometric-graphics content architecture
3	Extended document structure
36	Character, raster-graphics, and geometric-graphics content architecture

Interchange Format and Representation Profiles: Computer-Graphics Metafile Interchange Format (FCG)

Substructure to be studied

Interchange Format and Representation Profiles: SGML Interchange Format (FSG)

Substructure to be studied

Interchange Format and Representation Profiles: Directory Data Definitions (FDI)

Substructure to be studied

---

* Subnetwork taxonomy applies within this group, with the exception that subnetworks of type ISDN (TA 4xxx) are for further study.

† Only the following subnetwork-type identifiers are valid: 11n, 21n, 31n, 41n, 431n, 432n, 5n.

‡ Only the following subnetwork-type identifier is valid: 5n.

§ Only the following subnetwork-type identifiers are valid: 53, 54.

‖ Deals with both X.410 mode and normal mode.

\# Profiles in this category should be structured to refer to the ones identified in the AMH 1 category plus specific text.

different systems that conform to the profile and make selections among the options and parameter ranges remaining in the profile. Of course, the choices made in the profile must not contradict the base standards. In particular, if certain combinations of options and/or parameter values are forbidden in the base standard, then they must also be forbidden in the profile. If the development of the profile indicates the need to modify or add to the requirements specified in the base standard, these changes must be made in the base standard and not simply incorporated in the profile.

A profile may contain *conformance* requirements that are more specific and limited in scope than those of the base standards to which the profile refers. Although conformance to a profile always implies conformance to the set of base standards that the profile references, the opposite is not always true. Thus, we need to deal separately with the issue of profile conformance.

15.2.2   Taxonomy

TR 10000-2 defines a system of labels (called a taxonomy) for the profiles, which provides a structure and classification within which the profiles will fit. These labels reflect the applicability of the profile and its constraints. There are two reasons for developing a taxonomy:

1. It provides a technical framework for the development of ISPs. The taxonomy reflects the structure of real systems (as suggested by Figure 15.1) and hence guides the development of ISPs in a way that is most useful for actually defining practical implementations. The framework thus serves to coordinate the work of the various groups interested in developing ISPs.

2. It helps users identify the particular profile or profiles that address their requirements.

The taxonomy provides a hierarchical structure. At a top level, profiles are divided into classes, with each class representing a category of functionality or reasonable independence from other classes. Each class is further subdivided recursively. Each leaf of the tree represents a profile, and the path to that leaf is the identifier of the profile.

Table 15.3 shows the taxonomy at its current stage of development.

15.2.2.1   Profile Classes

Six profile classes are defined in TR 10000-2:

1. *F:* interchange format and representation profiles
2. *A:* application profiles requiring the connection-mode transport service (COTS)
3. *B:* application profiles requiring the connectionless-mode transport service (CLTS)
4. *T:* transport profiles that provide the connection-mode transport service
5. *U:* transport profiles that provide the connectionless-mode transport service
6. *R:* relay profiles that define relay functions between T or U profiles

Thus, the profile classes divide OSI functionality into profiles that deal with the structuring and coding of information, profiles that deal with the application and its communication needs, and profiles that are concerned with the use of a network technology to achieve the interconnection requirements. To provide a full implementation of a given function or application, a combination of profiles will be needed. Figure 15.2 illustrates the relationships among classes and indicates the allowable combinations. A and T profiles can be combined, since the T profile provides the service required by the A profile. Similarly, B and U profiles can be combined. Conversely, combinations of A and U profiles or B and T profiles are not possible.

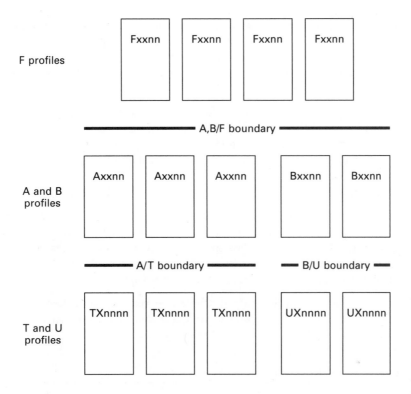

Figure 15.2 Relationships Between Profiles in the OSI Taxonomy

Since there is no single service definition that characterizes the A/F and B/F boundaries, there is no restriction on combining F profiles with A or B profiles at this level of the taxonomy. However, restrictions may exist in the base standards or in the profiles to limit the number of possible combinations.

15.2.2.2   Transport Profiles

Transport profiles specify how the two modes of transport service are provided over the two modes of network service and over specific subnetwork types. The transport profiles are subdivided into seven *groups:* five groups for class T and two groups for class U. The group concept is defined such that the profiles within a single group are compatible, in the sense that a system implementing one profile from a group can interwork with another system implementing another profile from the same group.

There are three factors that guarantee interworking between two transport profiles:

1. They provide the same mode of transport service.

2. They utilize the same mode of network service.

3. In the case of COTS over CONS, different protocol classes (0, 1, 2, 3, 4) may be implemented. As a result, it is possible for two implementations of COTS over CONS to be unable to agree on a protocol class. Thus, the requirement is for support of the same subset of transport-protocol classes.

With these requirements satisfied, a group can contain profiles that correspond to different subnetwork technologies; interworking between systems in the group is made possible by LAN bridges and/or network-layer relays (intermediate systems).

Based on the preceding line of reasoning, the following groups are identified:

- *TA:* COTS over CLNS (Transport class 4 is mandatory.)
- *TB:* COTS over CONS (Transport classes 0, 2, and 4 are mandatory.)
- *TC:* COTS over CONS (Transport classes 0 and 2 are mandatory.)
- *TD:* COTS over CONS (Transport class 0 is mandatory.)
- *TE:* COTS over CONS (Transport class 2 is mandatory.)
- *UA:* CLTS over CLNS
- *UB:* CLTS over CONS

Within each group, a number of subnetworks are identified. Table 15.3 lists all of the subnetworks so far identified, together with the restrictions that apply. Accordingly, the identifier for a particular transport profile indicates the class and group with two leading capital letters, followed by one or more digits to indicate the subnetwork (Table 15.4). A small letter in place of a digit indicates that all members of a subgroup are covered. For example:

- *Profile TA 51:* connection-mode transport service over connectionless-mode network service supporting a CSMA/CD (carrier sense multiple access with collision detection) local network

Table 15.4 Summary of Profile Label Formats

Transport profiles: CXabcd
   where:
      C   = transport-class designator (T or U).
      X   = a letter that identifies the group within the class.
      abcd = numberical identifier of the subnetwork type supported in this profile.

Relay profiles: RXp.q
   where
      R   = relay function.
      X   = relay-type identifier.
      p, q = subnetwork identifiers.

Application profiles: CXYabc
   where
      C   = application-class designator (A or B).
      XY = two letters that identify the primary subdivision, taken from the main categories of application functions and OSI managment.
      abc = numerical identifier for the member(s) of the subdivision.

Interchange format and representation profiles: FXYabc
   where
      F   = interchange format class designator.
      XY = two letters that identify the primary subdivision.
      abc = numerical identifier for the member(s) of the subdivision.

Table 15.5 Interworking Between Groups

(a) Interworking between groups in class T

Responder in Group	Network-Service Module	Initiator in Group				
		TA	TB	TC	TD	TE
TA	CL	Full	Special 1	Special 1	Special 1	Special 1
TB	CO	Special 1	Full	Full	Full	Full
TC	CO	Special 1	Restricted	Full	Full	Full
TD	CO	Special 1	Restricted	Restricted	Full	Special 2
TE	CO	Special 1	Restricted	Restricted	Special 2	Full

(b) Interworking between groups in class U

Responder in Group	Initiator in Group	
	UA	UB
UA	Full	Special 2
UB	Special 2	Full

Key:
Full: Full interworking is possible (one or more OSI relays may be required).
Restricted: Interworking is restricted, in that it may not be possible to use the class of transport protocol preferred by the initiator.
Special 1: Non-OSI relay required for interworking; special restrictions for interworking exist.
Special 2: Non-OSI relay required for interworking; interworking between these profile types is not contemplated.

- *Profile TC 112x:* connection-mode transport service over connection-mode network service with mandatory protocol classes 0 and 2, supporting a PSDN with permanent access via a digital data circuit or CSDN leased line

The group concept dictates that interworking is possible between systems using profiles in the same group. It is also possible to consider interworking between systems in different groups, but care must be taken. In some cases, the normal transport-protocol-class negotiation mechanism will allow the systems to achieve a level of communication via OSI relays. In other cases, a non-OSI relay will be required that performs some sort of protocol conversion.

At a top level, we can say that no interworking is possible between a group in class T and a group in class U because of the different mode of transport service provided. Table 15.5, parts (a) and (b), shows the interworking possibilities among groups within the same class. This table gives some indication of the difficulty providing interworking between profiles in different groups.

15.2.2.3 Relay Profiles

Relay profiles define the use of standards from OSI layers 1 to 4 to provide relaying functions between OSI transport profiles. At a top level, the following subclasses of relays have been identified:

- *RA:* relaying the CLNS
- *RB:* relaying the CONS
- *RC:* X.25 protocol relaying
- *RD:* relaying the MAC (medium-access control) service using transparent bridging
- *RE:* relaying the MAC service using source routing
- *RZ: relaying between CLNS and CONS*

A relay links two subnetworks. Hence, such subnetworks are used as a next level of distinction for relay profiles. For example:

- *Profile RA 51.53:* relays the connectionless-mode network service between a CSMA/CD LAN and a token-ring LAN
- *Profile RC 22.51:* relays the X.25 protocol between a CSDN and a CSMA/CD LAN

15.2.2.4   Application Profiles

Application profiles define the use of protocol standards encompassing OSI layers 5 through 7, to provide for the structured transfer of information between end systems. As with transport profiles, application profiles are divided into two classes: class-A application profiles are connection-mode and therefore require COTS; class-B application profiles are connectionless-mode and therefore require CLTS.

Each application profile is a complete definition of the use of protocol standards from layers 5 through 7, including a selection of application service elements, session functional units, and presentation functional units.

Currently, only class-A profiles have been defined:

- *AFT:* file transfer, access, and management (FTAM)
- *AMH:* message handling (based on X.400)
- *AVT:* virtual terminal
- *ATP:* transaction processing
- *ARD:* remote database access
- *AOM:* OSI management
- *ADI:* directory

15.2.2.5   Interchange Format and Representation Profiles

Interchange format and representation profiles define the structure and/or content of the information being interchanged by application profiles. Hence, the main feature that distinguishes them from application profiles is the absence of a transfer function.

The following profiles have been defined:

- *FOD:* office-document format
- *FCG:* computer-graphics metafile interchange format
- *FSG:* standard generalized markup language interchange format
- *FDI:* directory data definitions

15.2.3 The ISP Document

The definition of a profile must include the following elements:

- A concise definition of the scope and purpose of the function for which the profile is defined
- An illustration of the scenario within which the function is applicable
- Reference to a set of base standards
- Informative reference to other relevant source documents
- Specification of the application of each referenced base standard, which covers the following:

  Choice of classes or subsets of the overall specification
  Selection of options
  Selection of a range of parameter values
  Reference to registered objects (e.g., addresses)

- Statement of conformance requirements

In TR 10000-1, ISO dictates a specific structure for an ISP document; this structure is reproduced in Table 15.6. The document begins with several *preliminary elements,* which provide an informal description of the ISP:

- *Foreword:* indicates the organization or committee that prepared the ISP and information concerning whether this ISP replaces or amends a previous ISP
- *Introduction:* describes the process used to draft the ISP and the degree of international harmonization that it has received

The key portion of the document is the *normative elements,* which set out the provisions with which it is necessary to comply in order to be able to claim conformity with the ISP:

- *Scope:* defines the purpose and subject matter of the ISP, relates the ISP to the taxonomy published in TR 10000-2 (discussed in subsection 15.2.2), and includes the scenario of the profile. This latter is an illustration of the environment within which the ISP is applicable.

Table 15.6 Outline Structure of an ISP

	FOREWORD
	INTRODUCTION
1.	SCOPE
2.	NORMATIVE REFERENCES
3.	DEFINITIONS
4.	ABBREVIATIONS
5. . . .	Clauses defining requirements related to each base standard*
	INFORMATIVE ANNEX A. ISPICS Requirements List
	INFORMATIVE ANNEXES containing explanatory and/or tutorial material, as required.

* Where possible, these details shall be presented in a tabular form, consistent with the layout of the referenced standard, and not duplicating the representation required by the ISPICS Requirements List.

- *Normative references:* a list of normative documents (international standards, technical reports, ISPs, and CCITT recommendations) to which reference is made in the text.

- *Definitions:* definitions necessary to understand certain terms used in the ISP.

- *Abbreviations:* a list of the symbols and abbreviations used in the ISP.

- *Requirements:* includes clauses relating to the use made of each of the base standards referenced in the profile definition. Although the exact format is not dictated, it shall be in the

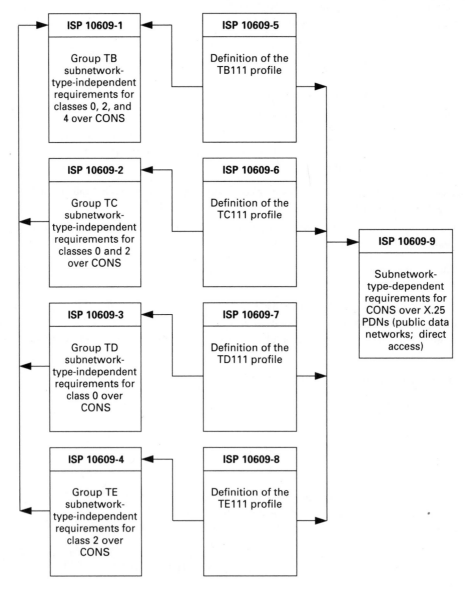

Figure 15.3 Multipart Structure of ISP 10609

form of static and dynamic conformance requirements. This section may be quite brief, with most of the detail concerning choices made of classes, subsets, options, and ranges of parameter values recorded in an annex containing the ISPICS (ISP implementation-conformance statement) requirements list (discussed in section 15.3).

- *Normative annexes:* integral sections of the ISP that, for reasons of convenience, are not included in the main body of the document. The first normative annex is always the ISPICS requirements list.

Finally, the document contains *supplementary elements,* which provide additional information intended to assist in understanding or using the ISP.

For similar profiles that cover several layers, there will be many cases in which the same set of options from a particular standard is called up by different profiles. To handle this situation efficiently, an ISP may be published as a set of related parts (multipart ISP) rather than a single document. A multipart ISP will encompass a number of related profiles.

One example of this structure is ISP 10609, which covers profiles TB, TC, TD, and TE, all of which provide COTS over CONS. Figure 15.3 shows how the group structure leads to a modular structure for the definition of the profiles within a group, with references to common elements of text. Parts 1 through 4 of the ISP provide the requirements that are independent of subnetwork type for the four COTS-over-CONS groups. The only difference between the groups is which transport-protocol classes are mandatory. Each group references the connection-mode transport-protocol (8073) and service (8072) standards and the connection-mode network-service (8348) definition. Since the four groups are so similar, many of their requirements are the same and are therefore independent of group. These group-independent and subnetwork-type-independent requirements are listed only once in part 1. Parts 2 through 4 reference part 1 for these requirements.

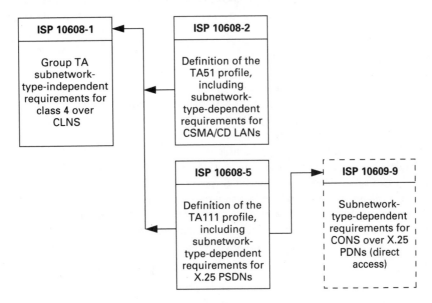

Figure 15.4 Multipart Structure of ISP 10608

The next four parts of 10609 correspond one for one with the first four parts and deal with a particular subnetwork type: 111, which is leased-line access via a public switched telephone network (PSTN) to a packet-switched data network (PSDN). Each part specifies the use of the X.25 protocol stack (layers 1, 2, and 3) to support the OSI connection-mode network service. Thus, each references various physical-layer standards, LAPB (7776), and the X.25 layer 3 (8208 and 8878). None of these parts contains any technical specification but references other ISP parts. Thus, part 5 references part 1, part 6 references part 2, and so on. In addition, all four parts reference part 9, which provides the subnetwork-type-dependent requirements. In this case, these requirements are for support of CONS over an X.25 PSDN.

The use of a multipart structure reduces the amount of duplicated text and the risk of unintentional differences between profiles. In this case, the number of documents required to specify a single profile is large, but as more profiles are defined, there will be more reuse of modules. As an example, ISO 10608 includes a cross-reference to a part of 10609.

Figure 15.4 shows the structure of 10608, which specifies CLTS over CONS (group TA). Note that part 2 includes the subnetwork-dependent part (ISO 8802-2 and 8802-3 for CSMA/CD access) instead of referencing it as a separate part. It was felt that the base standards in this case are used in a manner unique to the profile. Part 5 references part 9 of ISP 10609; this illustrates that cross-referencing is not restricted to ISP parts within a single ISP.

15.3   CONFORMANCE

As with the implementation of a base standard, the implementation of a profile raises the issue of conformance. Indeed, with the development and standardization of the ISP approach, it is likely that most customers will primarily be concerned with the conformance of a profile implementation, since it is the profile that defines a set of protocols implemented to support a specific function. ISO addresses the issue of profile conformance in ISO 10000-1 and deals with profile conformance testing in CD 9646-6.

15.3.1   Profile Conformance

As was mentioned in section 15.2, a profile may contain conformance requirements that are more specific and limited in scope than those of the base standards to which it refers. For example, when a feature is associated with an allowed parameter-value range, the profile can only adopt the same value range as that allowed by the base standard or a subset of that range.

The key document used to define the conformance characteristics of a specific implementation is the ISP implementation-conformance statement (ISPICS). The ISPICS is, in turn, related to and derived from two sets of documents: the PICS (protocol-implementation conformance statement) proformas of the base standards and the ISP requirements list (IPRL), which is part of the ISP.

The purpose of the IPRL is to provide a revised version of the conformance requirements of the constituent base standards of the profile. The conformance requirements in the base standards (defined in the PICS proformas) relate to the conformance requirements in the profile (defined in the IPRL) in the following ways:

- *Mandatory requirements in the base standards:* remain mandatory in the profile.

- *Conditional requirements in the base standards:* remain conditional in the profile.

- *Optional requirements in the base standards:* may be changed in various ways in the profile:

Mandatory: Support may be made mandatory.

Optional: Support may remain optional.

Conditional: Optional requirements may be made conditional within the profile.

Out of scope: optional requirements that are not relevant to the profile—for example, functional units of layer $(N-1)$ that are unused by layer (N) in the context of the profile.

Excluded: The use of an optional feature may be prohibited in the context of the profile. This should only be used to restrict the dynamic behavior in terms of the transmission of protocol elements.

- *Nonapplicable features in the base standards:* These are features that are logically impossible according to the base standards. They remain nonapplicable in the profile.

- *Excluded requirements in the base standards:* remain excluded in the profile.

Figure 15.5 illustrates this mapping. The only difference between static and dynamic conformance requirements is the ability to exclude optional dynamic requirements.

Figure 15.6 illustrates the relationships between the various documents. ISO 9646-2 specifies the format for creating PICS proformas. A specific PICS proforma is associated with a specific base standard; it states the conformance requirements for the base standard in terms of mandatory, optional, conditional, and excluded features. The PICS proforma serves as a questionnaire to be filled out by the supplier of a specific implementation of the base standard. The filled-out questionnaire is the PICS; it states the features supported by the implementation and the parameter ranges supported. An example of a PICS proforma is provided in Appendix 15A.

In a similar fashion, ISO 10000-1 specifies the format for creating IPRLs. A specific IPRL is associated with a profile; it states the conformance requirements for the profile in terms of mandatory, optional, conditional, and excluded features. An IPRL is provided for each profile in an ISP that contains multiple profiles. The IPRL specifies the profile constraints on the supported features listed in the PICS proformas of the relevant base standards (Figure 15.5). The ISPICS consists of the set of PICSs produced in accordance with the IPRL. For each base standard, the ISPICS states the features supported by the implementation and the parameter ranges supported.

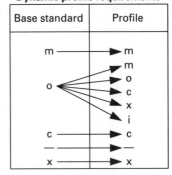

m = mandatory.
o = optional.
c = conditional.
i = out of scope.
x = excluded.
— = not applicable.

Figure 15.5 Static and Dynamic Profile Requirements

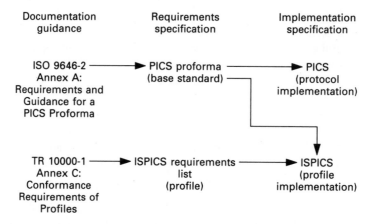

Figure 15.6 Conformance Documents

An example of an IPRL is provided in Appendix 15B. This is the portion of the IPRL for ISP 10607 (FTAM) that deals with the association-control-service element. The remainder of the IPRL covers the presentation and session protocols.

15.3.2   Profile Test Specification

The development of conformance tests for a profile is based on the conformance-test methodology for base standards. All test methods defined for testing base standards apply to profiles.

As with individual base standards, a preliminary step in testing a profile is to develop an abstract test suite. In the main, all that is required is to select the relevant test cases from the

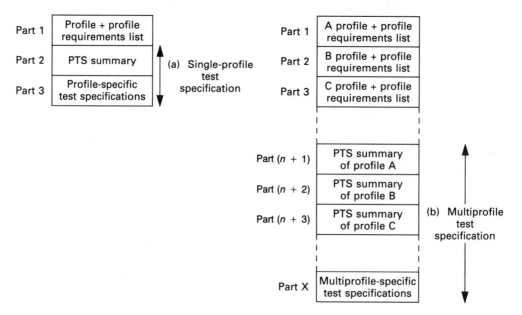

Figure 15.7 Structure of Profile Test Specifications

standardized abstract test suites for the base standards. A new test case is created for any profile-specific conformance requirement for which a testable test purpose is defined.

The defining document for profile testing is the profile test specification (PTS). The PTS is applicable to only one profile; an ISP containing more than one profile will require a corresponding number of PTS documents.

Figure 15.7, part (a), indicates the structure of a single-profile test specification. The profile description and its profile requirements list form the first part of the document. The PTS summary provides an overview of the test specification, with references to the base standards. The profile-specific test specifications is an optional part that holds additional test purposes and test cases beyond those defined for the base standards.

```
Section 1 - General Information

        Profile identifier:
        Profile RL ref:
        Profile IXIT ref:
        Profile IXRL ref:
        SCS proforma:
        SCTR proforma:

    Section 2.1 - Protocol 1

        Protocol identifier:
        PICS proforma ref:
        TSS & TP - Base standard ref:
                - Technical corrigenda
                - Additional TSS & TP

    Section 2.1.1 Conformance Testing Specification 1

        Testing method type:
        PCTR proforma ref:
        ATS - Base standard ref:
                - Technical corrigenda
                - Additional test cases
        Untestable TP:

    Section 2.1.m Conformance Testing Specification "m"



    Section 2.N - Protocol "N"

        Protocol indentifier:
        PICS proforma ref:
        TSS & TP - Base standard ref:
                - Technical corrigenda
                - Additional TSS & TP

    Section 2.N.1  Conformance Testing Specification 1



    Section 3 - Additional Profile(s) Specifics

        Additional TSS and TP
        Additional test cases
```

Figure 15.8 PTS Summary Proforma

In the case of an ISP with multiple parts and multiple profiles, Figure 15.7, part (b), describes the structure of the PTS document. Each profile description/IPRL is a separate part, as is each PTS summary and each profile-specific test specification.

Figure 15.8 illustrates the format for a PTS summary. Section 1 applies to the profile and the PTS as a whole and contains general information relative to the profile. Sections numbered 2.1– 2.N each apply to one protocol of the profile. They identify the protocol and its PICS proforma, as well as the abstract test-suite structure (TSS) and test purposes (TPS). Each abstract test suite for a protocol is referenced in a subsection, numbered 2.N.m. Section 3 provides information beyond that provided in the base standards; these are the additional test cases unique to the profile.

15.4   SUMMARY

Taken together, the collection of OSI-related standards presents an overwhelming combination of services, protocols, and options to be implemented. For any given application or environment, only a limited subset of these services, protocols, and options are required, or even appropriate. The lack of a uniform specification of what needs to be implemented for a particular application or environment has hampered the success of OSI in the marketplace.

To address this problem, the concept of functional standards, or functional profiles, was developed. A set of functional standards defines a specific subset of OSI-based standards, with specific options, for a given application area or functional environment. A number of organizations have pursued the development of functional standards.

To assure that the process of functional standardization is orderly, and to prevent the proliferation of competing functional standards, ISO has begun the development of international standardized profiles (ISPs), which are official, OSI-based functional standards. An overall framework and taxonomy has been defined, and the work of developing specific ISPs is ongoing.

APPENDIX 15A   PICS Proforma for Connectionless-Mode ES-IS Protocol (ISO 9542)

INTRODUCTION

The supplier of a protocol implementation which is claimed to conform to International Standard ISO 9542, whether as an End System or Intermediate System implementation, shall complete the applicable Protocol Implementation Conformance Statement (PICS) proforma following, and accompany it by the information necessary to identify fully both the supplier and the implementation.

ABBREVIATIONS AND SPECIAL SYMBOLS

General

N/A	Not Applicable
\<r\>	receive (PDU, or field of PDU)
\<s\>	send (PDU, or field of PDU)

Option-status and Predicate Symbols

M	mandatory
O	optional
P	prohibited
CI:	the status following this stymbol applies only when the PICS states that configurtion information is supported.
RI:	the status following this symbol applies only when the PICS states that redirection information is supported.
(CI∨RI):	the status following this symbol applies only when the PICS states that either configuration information or redirection information (or both) is supported.

INSTRUCTIONS FOR COMPLETING THE PICS PROFORMAS

The main part of each PICS proforma is a fixed-format questionnaire. A supplier may also provide, or be required to provide, additional information, categorized as either Exception Information or Supplementary Information. When present, each kind of additional information is to be provided as items labelled respectively X.<i> or S.<i> for cross-referencing purposes, where <i> is any unambiguous identification for the item (e.g. simply a number): there are no other restrictions on its format and presentation.

A completed PICS proforma is the Protocol Implementation Conformance Statement for the implementation in question.

Answers to the questionnaires are to be provided in the rightmost column, either by simply marking an answer to indicate a restricted choice (such as *Yes* or *No*), or by entering a value or a set or range of values.

Items of Exception Information are required by certain answers in the questionnaire: this is indicated by an "X . . ." cross-reference to be completed. This occurs when, for example, an answer indicates that a feature classified as Mandatory has not been implemented: the Exception item should contain the appropriate rationale.

The final section of the PICS, for Supplementary Information, allows a supplier to provide additional information intended to assist the interpretation of the PICS. It is not intended or expected that a large quantity will be supplied, and a PICS can be considered complete without any such information. An example might be an outline of the ways in which a (single) implementation can be set up to operate in a variety of environments and configurations.

References to items of Supplementary Information may be entered next to any answer in the questionnaire, and may be included in items of Exception Information.

PICS PROFORMAS

PICS Proforma: ISO 9542(1988)—End System

Item	Protocol Function	Clauses	Status	Support	
CI	Is configuration information supported?		O	Yes	No
RI	Is redirection information supported?		O	Yes	No

PICS Proforma: ISO 9542(1988)—End System (*cont.*)

Item	Protocol Function	Clauses	Status	Support		
Are the Following Functions Supported?						
CfRs	Configuration Response	6.6	M		Yes	No:X...
ErrP	Protocol Error Processing	6.13	(CI∨RI):M	N/A	Yes	No:X...
HCsV	PDU Header Checksum Validation	6.12	(CI∨RI):M	N/A	Yes	No:X...
HCsG	PDU Header Checksum Generation	6.12	O		Yes	No
RpCf	Report Configuration	6.2, 6.2.1	CI:M	N/A	Yes	No:X...
RcCf	Record Configuration	6.3, 6.3.2	CI:M	N/A	Yes	No:X...
FlCf	Flush Old Configuration	6.4	CI:M	N/A	Yes	No:X...
QyCf	Query Configuration	6.5	CI:M	N/A	Yes	No:X...
RcRd	Record Redirect	6.9	RI:M	N/A	Yes	No:X...
FlRd	Flush Old Redirect	6.11	RI:M	N/A	Yes	No:X...
RfRd	Refresh Redirect	6.10	RI:O	N/A	Yes	No
CfNt	Configuration Notification	6.7	CI:O	N/A	Yes	No
CTPr	ESCT Processing	6.3.2	CI:O	N/A	Yes	No
AMPr	Address Mask (only) Processing	7.4.5	RI:O	N/A	Yes	No
SMPr	Address Mask and SNPA Mask Processing	7.4.5, 7.4.6	RI:O	N/A	Yes	No

Item	**Are the Following PDUs Supported?**	Clauses	Status	Support		
ESH-s	\<s\> End System Hello	7.1, 7.5	M		Yes	No:X...
ESH-r	\<r\> End System Hello	7.1, 7.5	CI:M	N/A	Yes	No:X...
ISH-r	\<r\> Intermediate System Hello	7.1, 7.6	CI:M	N/A	Yes	No:X...
RD-r	\<r\> Redirect	7.1, 7.7	RI:M	N/A	Yes	No:X...

Item	**Are the Following PDU Fields Supported?**	Clauses	Status	Support		
FxPt	\<s\> Fixed Part	7.2.1–7.2.7	M		Yes	No:X...
	\<r\> Fixed Part	7.2.1–7.2.7	(CI∨RI):M		Yes	No:X...
SA-s1	\<s\> Source Address,	7.3.1,	M	N/A	Yes	No:X...
SA-rl	\<r\> one NSAP only	7.3.2,	CI:M	N/A	Yes	No:X...
SA-sm	\<s\> Source Address,	7.3.3	O		Yes	No
SA-rm	\<r\> two or more NSAPS		CI:M	N/A	Yes	No:X...
NET-r	\<r\> Network Entity Title	7.3.1/2/4	(CI∨RI):M	N/A	Yes	No:X...
DA-r	\<r\> Destination Address	7.3.1/2/5	RI:M	N/A	Yes	No:X...
BSNPA-r	\<r\> Subnetwork Address	7.3.1/2/6	RI:M	N/A	Yes	No:X...
Scty-s	\<s\> Security	7.4.2	O		Yes	No
Scty-r	\<r\> Security	7.4.2	O		Yes	No
Pty-s	\<s\> Priority	7.4.3	O		Yes	No
Pty-r	\<r\> Priority	7.4.3	O		Yes	No
QoSM-r	\<r\> QoS Maintenance	7.4.4	RI:O	N/A	Yes	No
AdMk-r	\<r\> Address Mask	7.4.5	RI:O	N/A	Yes	No
SNMk-r	\<r\> SNPA Mask	7.4.6	RI:O	N/A	Yes	No

ESCT-r	\<r\> Suggested ES Configuration Timer	7.4.7	CI:O	N/A	Yes	No
OOpt-r	\<r\> (ignore) unsupported or unknown options	7.4.1	M		Yes	No:X...
OOpt-s	\<s\> Other options		P		No/Yes:X...	

Parameter Ranges

HTv	What range of values can be set for the Holding Time field in transmitted PDUs?	6.1, 6.1.2	M	From: seconds To: seconds by increments of†: (other—specify)†: with a tolerance of:
CTv	If configuration information is supported, what range of values can be set for the Configuration Timer?	6.1, 6.1.1	CI:M	From: seconds To: seconds by increments of†: (other—specify)†: with a tolerance of:

† delete if inapplicable

PICS Proforma: ISO 9542 (1988)—Intermediate System

Item	Protocol Function	Clauses	Status	Support		
CI	Is configuration information supported?		O		Yes	No
RI	Is redirection information supported?		O		Yes	No

Are the Following Functions Supported?

Item	Protocol Function	Clauses	Status	Support		
ErrP	Protocol Error Processing	6.13	M		Yes	No:X...
HCsV	PDU Header Checksum Validation	6.12	M		Yes	No:X...
HCsG	PDU Header Checksum Generation	6.12	O		Yes	No
RpCf	Report Configuration	6.2, 6.2.2	CI:M	N/A	Yes	No:X...
RcCf	Record Configuration	6.3, 6.3.1	CI:M	N/A	Yes	No:X...
FlCf	Flush Old Configuration	6.4	CI:M	N/A	Yes	No:X...
RqRd	Request Redirect	6.8	RI:M	N/A	Yes	No:X...
CfNt	Configuration Notification	6.7	CI:O	N/A	Yes	No
CTGn	ESCT Generation	6.3.2	CI:O	N/A	Yes	No
AMGn	Address Mask (only) Generation	6.8	RI:O	N/A	Yes	No
SMGn	Address Mask and SNPA Mask Generation	6.8	RI:O	N/A	Yes	No

Item	Are the Following PDUs Supported?	Clauses	Status	Support		
ESH-r	\<r\> End System Hello	7.1, 7.5	CI:M	N/A	Yes	No:X...
ISH-r	\<r\> Intermediate System Hello	7.1, 7.6	CI:O	N/A	Yes	No

PICS Proforma: ISO 9542 (1988)—Intermediate System (*Cont.*)

Item	Protocol Function	Clauses	Status	Support			
ISH-s	\<s\> Intermediate System Hello	7.1, 7.6	CI:M	N/A	Yes	No:X...	
RD-s	\<s\> Redirect	7.1, 7.7	RI:M	N/A	Yes	No:X...	
RD-r	\<r\> (ignore) Redirect	6.9, 7.1, 7.7	M		Yes	No:X...	

Are the Following PDU Fields Supported?

Item	Protocol Function	Clauses	Status	Support			
FxPt	\<s\> Fixed Part	7.2.1–7.2.7	M		Yes	No:X...	
	\<r\> Fixed Part	7.2.1–7.2.7	M		Yes	No:X...	
SA-r	\<r\> Source Address, one or more NSAPS	7.3.1/2/3	CI:M	N/A	Yes	No:X...	
NET-s	\<s\> Network Entity Title	7.3.1/2/4	M	N/A	Yes	No:X...	
NET-r	\<r\> Network Entity Title	7.3.1/2/4	ISH-r:M	N/A	Yes	No:X...	
DA-s	\<s\> Destination Address	7.3.1/2/5	RI:M	N/A	Yes	No:X...	
BSNPA-s	\<s\> Subnetwork Address	7.3.1/2/6	RI:M	N/A	Yes	No:X...	
Scty-s	\<s\> Security	7.4.2	O		Yes	No	
Scty-r	\<r\> Security	7.4.2	O		Yes	No	
Pty-s	\<s\> Priority	7.4.3	O		Yes	No	
Pty-r	\<r\> Priority	7.4.3	O		Yes	No	
QoSM-s	\<s\> QoS Maintenance	7.4.4	RI:O	N/A	Yes	No	
AdMk-s	\<s\> Address Mask	7.4.5	RI:O	N/A	Yes	No	
SNMk-s	\<s\> SNPA Mask	7.4.6	RI:O	N/A	Yes	No	
ESCT-s	\<s\> Suggested ES Configuration Timer	7.4.7	CI:O	N/A	Yes	No	
ESCT-r	\<r\> (ignore) Suggested ES Configuration Timer	7.4.7	ISH-r:M	N/A	Yes	No:X...	
OOpt-r	\<r\> (ignore) unsupported or unknown options	7.4.1	M		Yes	No:X...	
OOpt-s	\<s\> Other options		P		No	Yes:X...	

Parameter Ranges

Item	Protocol Function	Clauses	Status	Support			
HTv	What range of values can be set for the Holding Time field in transmitted PDUs?	6.1, 6.1.2	M	From: seconds To: seconds by increments of†: (other—specify)†: with a tolerance of:			
CTv	If configuration information is supported, what range of values can be set for the Configuration Timer?	6.1, 6.1.1	CI:M	From: seconds To: seconds by increments of†: (other—specify)†: with a tolerance of:			

†   delete if inapplicable

APPENDIX 15B   ISPICS Requirements List for ACSE

In the event of a discrepancy becoming apparent in the body of this part of ISO/IEC ISP 10607 and the tables in this annex, this annex is to take precedence.

The tables summarize the characteristics of the ACSE, Presentation and Session protocols as required by the FTAM International Standardized Profiles ISO/IEC ISP 10607. The level of support for each feature of these protocols is specified in the tables.

The abbreviations as used in the headings of the tables are

D   conformance requirement as defined in the base standard
P   conformance requirement for this part of ISO/IEC ISP 10607.

When the level of support in the tables specifies two values, separated by a space, the left value applies to the Initiator role of the implementation and the right value applies to the Responder role of the implementation.

ASSOCIATION CONTROL SERVICE ELEMENT

Association Control Service Element Protocol

Protocol Element/Parameter	D	P	Range of Values or Reference
Defect Solutions and Amendments			see annex B
These defect reports to ISO 8650 have been resolved. They are, therefore, considered as part of ISO 8650 on which this part of ISO/IEC ISP 10607 is based.			
Association Establishment:			
A-ASSOCIATE-REQUEST	m	m	see 6.1
protocol version	o	m	"version-1"
application context name	m	m	see 6.2
calling AP title	o	m o	
calling AP invocation-identifier	o	l	
calling AE qualifier	o	m o	
calling AE invocation-identifier	o	l	
called AP title	o	m	
called AP invocation-identifier	o	l	
called AE qualifier	o	m	
called AE invocation-identifier	o	l	
implementation information	o	l	
user information	o	m	
A-ASSOCIATE RESPONSE	m	m	see 6.1
protocol version	o	m	"version-1"
application context name	m	m	see 6.2
responding AP title	o	m	
responding AP invocation-identifier	o	l	

Association Control Service Element Protocol *(Cont.)*

Protocol Element/Parameter	D	P	Range of Values or Reference
responding AE qualifier	o	m	
responding AE invocation-identifier	o	l	
result	m	m	
result source-diagnostic	m	m	
implementation information	o	l	
user information	o	m	
Association Release:			
A-RELEASE-REQUEST	m	m	
reason	o	l	
user information	o	m	
A-RELEASE-RESPONSE	m	m	
reason	o	l	
user information	o	m	
A-ABORT	m	m	see 6.3
abort source	m	m	
user information	o	m	

Appendix A
Digital Signaling

Many of the data-transmission specifications discussed in this book make use of digital signaling. That is, the data are transmitted as a sequence of discrete signals. For this purpose, the data (binary 1s and 0s) must be represented by signal elements that are suitable for transmission over the given medium and that can be recognized by the receiver and decoded to reproduce the transmitted data. Typically, the form of the encoding is chosen to optimize the transmission, in terms of reliability, performance, and/or cost. This appendix provides a brief survey of some of the more common encoding techniques; they are defined in Table A.1 and depicted in Figure A.1.

A.1 EVALUATION CRITERIA

There are two important tasks involved in interpreting digital signals at the receiver. First, the receiver must know the timing of each bit. That is, the receiver must be able to determine with some accuracy when a bit begins and ends. Second, the receiver must determine whether the signal level for each voltage pulse is high or low.

A number of factors determine how successful the receiver will be in interpreting the incoming signal: the signal-to-noise ratio (S/N), the data rate, and the bandwidth of the signal. With other factors held constant, the following statements are true:

- An increase in the data rate increases the bit-error rate (the probability of a bit's being received in error).

- An increase in S/N decreases the bit-error rate.

- Increased bandwidth allows increased data rate.

There is another factor that can be used to improve performance—the encoding scheme— which is simply the mapping from data bits to signal elements. A variety of approaches have been tried. Before describing some of these approaches, let us consider the ways of evaluating or comparing the various techniques. Among the important factors:

Table A.1 Definition of Digital-Signal-Encoding Formats

Nonreturn to zero—level (NRZ-L)
  0 = high level.
  1 = low level.

Nonreturn to zero inverted (NRZI)
  0 = no transition at beginning of interval (one bit time).
  1 = transition at beginning of interval.

Bipolar-AMI (alternate mark inversion)
  0 = no line signal.
  1 = positive or negative level, alternating for successive 1s.

Pseudoternary
  0 = positive or negative level, alternating for successive 0s.
  1 = no line signal.

Manchester
  0 = transition from high to low in middle of interval.
  1 = transition from low to high in middle of interval.

Differential Manchester
  Always a transition in middle of interval.
  0 = transition at beginning of interval.
  1 = no transition at beginning of interval.

B8ZS
  Same at bipolar-AMI, except that any string of eight 0s is replaced by a string with two code violations.

HDB3
  Same as bipolar AMI, except that any string of four 0s is replaced by a string with one code violation.

- Signal spectrum
- Signal-synchronization capability
- Error-detection capability
- Cost and complexity

Several aspects of the *signal spectrum* are important. A lack of high-frequency components means that less bandwidth is required for transmission. On the other hand, lack of a direct-current (dc) component is also desirable. With a dc component to the signal, there must be direct physical attachment of transmission components; with no dc component, alternating-current (ac) coupling via transformer is possible. This provides excellent electrical isolation, reducing interference. Finally, the magnitude of the effects of signal distortion and interference depends on the spectral properties of the transmitted signal. In practice, the transmission fidelity of a channel is usually worse near the band edges. Therefore, a good signal design should concentrate the transmitted power in the middle of the transmission bandwidth. In such a case, a smaller distortion should be present in the received signal. To meet this objective, codes can be designed with the aim of shaping the spectrum of the transmitted signal.

For successful reception of digital data, as noted earlier, the receiver must know the timing of each bit. That is, the receiver must know with some accuracy when a bit begins and ends, so that

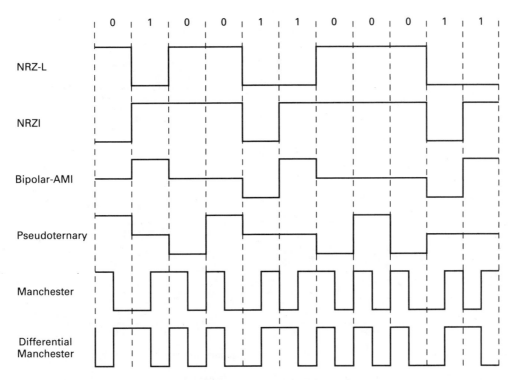

Figure A.1 Digital-Signal-Encoding Formats

the receiver may sample the incoming signal once per bit time to recognize the value of each bit. Thus, there must be some *signal-synchronization capability* between transmitter and receiver. It is inevitable that there will be some drift between the clocks of the transmitter and receiver, and so some separate synchronization mechanism is needed. One approach is to provide a separate clock lead to synchronize the transmitter and receiver. This approach is rather expensive, since it requires an extra line plus an extra transmitter and receiver. The alternative is to provide some synchronization mechanism that is based on the transmitted signal. This can be achieved with suitable encoding.

Error detection is the responsibility of a data-link protocol that is executed on top of the physical signaling level. However, it is useful to have some *error-detection capability* built into the physical signaling scheme. This permits errors to be detected more quickly. Many signaling schemes have an inherent error-detection capability.

Finally, although digital logic continues to drop in price, the *cost and complexity* of the signaling scheme are a factor that should not be ignored.

A.2   NONRETURN TO ZERO (NRZ)

The most common, and easiest, way to transmit digital signals is to use two different voltage levels for the two binary digits. Codes that follow this strategy share the property that the voltage level is constant during a bit interval; there is no transition (no return to a zero voltage level). For

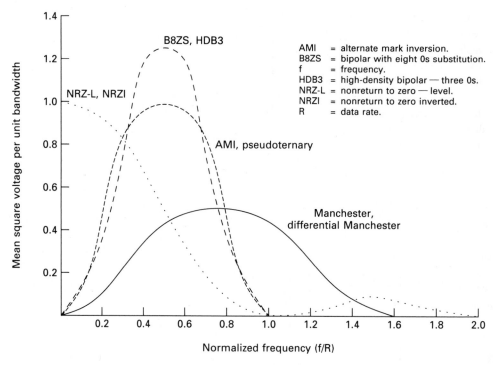

Figure A.2 Spectral Density of Various Signal-Encoding Schemes

example, the absence of voltage can be used to represent binary 0, with a constant positive voltage used to represent binary 1. More commonly, a negative voltage is used to represent one binary value and a positive voltage is used to represent the other. This latter code, known as *nonreturn to zero—level* (*NRZ-L*), is illustrated in Figure A.1.[1] NRZ-L is generally the code used to generate or interpret digital data by terminals and other devices. If a different code is to be used for transmission, it is typically generated from an NRZ-L signal by the transmission system.

A variation of NRZ is known as *NRZI* (*nonreturn to zero, inverted*). As with NRZ-L, NRZI maintains a constant voltage pulse for the duration of a bit time. The data themselves are encoded as the presence or absence of a signal transition at the beginning of the bit time. A transition (low to high or high to low) at the beginning of a bit time denotes a binary 1 for that bit time; no transition indicates a binary 0. NRZI is an element of the encoding scheme for FDDI (fiber-distributed data interface).

NRZI is an example of *differential encoding*. In differential encoding, the signal is decoded by comparing the polarity of adjacent signal elements rather than by determining the absolute value of a signal element. One benefit of this scheme is that it may be more reliable to detect a transition

---

1.   In this figure, a negative voltage is equated with binary 1 and a positive voltage with binary 0. This is the opposite of the definition used in virtually all other textbooks. However, there is no "standard" definition of NRZ-L, and the definition here conforms to the use of NRZ-L in data-communications interfaces and the standards that govern those interfaces.

in the presence of noise than to compare a value to a threshold. Another benefit is that with a complex transmission layout, it is easy to lose the sense of the polarity of the signal. For example, on a multidrop twisted-pair line, if the leads from an attached device to the twisted pair are accidentally inverted, all 1s and 0s for NRZ-L will be inverted. This cannot happen with differential encoding.

The NRZ codes are the easiest to engineer and, in addition, make efficient use of bandwidth. This latter property is illustrated in Figure A.2, which compares the spectral density of various encoding schemes. In the figure, frequency is normalized to the data rate. As can be seen, most of the energy in an NRZ signal is between dc and half the bit rate. For example, if an NRZ code is used to generate a signal with a data rate of 9,600 bps, most of the energy in the signal is concentrated between dc and 4,800 Hz.

The main limitations of NRZ signals are the presence of a dc component and the lack of synchronization capability. To picture the latter problem, consider that with a long string of 1s or 0s for NRZ-L, the output is a constant voltage over a long period of time. Under these circumstances, any drift between the timing of transmitter and receiver will result in the loss of synchronization between the two.

Because of their simplicity and relatively low-frequency response characteristics, NRZ codes are commonly used for digital magnetic recording. However, their limitations make these codes unattractive for signal-transmission applications.

A.3   MULTILEVEL BINARY

A category of encoding techniques known as multilevel binary addresses some of the deficiencies of the NRZ codes. These codes use more than two signal levels. Two examples of this scheme are illustrated in Figure A.1: bipolar-AMI (alternate mark inversion) and pseudoternary.[2]

In the case of the *bipolar-AMI* scheme, a binary 0 is represented by no line signal, and a binary 1 is represented by a positive or negative pulse. The binary-1 pulses must alternate in polarity. There are several advantages to this approach. First, there will be no loss of synchronization if a long string of 1s occurs. Each 1 introduces a transition, and the receiver can resynchronize on that transition. A long string of 0s would still be a problem. Second, since the 1 signals alternate in voltage from positive to negative, there is no net dc component. Also, the bandwidth of the resulting signal is considerably less than the bandwidth for NRZ (Figure A.2). Finally, the pulse-alternation property provides a simple means of error detection. Any isolated error, whether it deletes a pulse or adds a pulse, causes a violation of this property.

The comments in the previous paragraph also apply to *pseudoternary*. In this case, it is the binary 1 that is represented by the absence of a line signal and the binary 0 by alternating positive and negative pulses. There is no particular advantage of one technique versus the other, and each is the basis of some applications.

---

2.   These terms are not consistently used in the literature. In some books, these two terms are used for different encoding schemes than those defined here, and a variety of terms have been used for the two schemes illustrated in Figure A.1. The nomenclature used here corresponds to the usage in various CCITT standards documents.

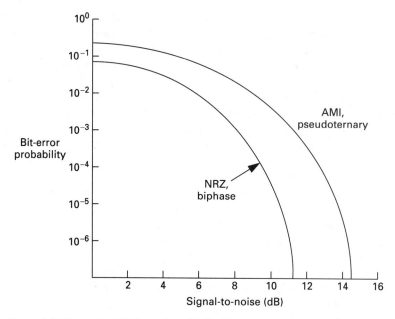

Figure A.3 Theoretical Bit-Error Rate for Various Digital-Encoding Schemes

Although a degree of synchronization is provided with these codes, a long string of 0s in the case of AMI or 1s in the case of pseudoternary still presents a problem. Several techniques have been used to address this deficiency. One approach is to insert additional bits that force transitions. This technique is used in ISDN (integrated services digital network) for relatively low-data-rate transmission. Of course, at a high data rate, this scheme is expensive, since it results in an increase in an already high signal-transmission rate. To deal with this problem at high data rates, a technique that involves scrambling the data is used. We examine two examples of this technique later in this appendix.

Thus, with suitable modification, multilevel binary schemes overcome the problems of NRZ codes. Of course, as with any engineering design decision, there is a trade-off. With multilevel binary coding, the line signal may take on one of three levels, but each signal element, which could represent $\log_2 3 = 1.58$ bits of information, bears only 1 bit of information. Thus, multilevel binary is not as efficient as NRZ coding. Another way to state this is that the receiver of multilevel binary signals has to distinguish between three levels ($+A$, $-A$, and 0) instead of just two levels in the other signaling formats previously discussed. Because of this, the multilevel binary signal requires approximately 3 dB more signal power than a two-valued signal for the same probability of bit error. This is illustrated in Figure A.3. Put another way, the bit-error rate for NRZ codes, at a given signal-to-noise ratio, is significantly less than that for multilevel binary.

A.4 BIPHASE

There is another a set of alternative coding techniques, grouped under the term *biphase,* which overcomes the limitations of NRZ codes. Two of these techniques, Manchester and differential Manchester, are in common use.

In the *Manchester* code, there is a transition at the middle of each bit period. The midbit transition serves as a clocking mechanism and also as data: a low-to-high transition represents a 1, and a high-to-low transition represents a 0.[3] In *differential Manchester,* the midbit transition is used only to provide clocking. The encoding of a 0 is represented by the presence of a transition at the beginning of a bit period, and a 1 is represented by the absence of a transition at the beginning of a bit period. Differential Manchester has the added advantage of employing differential encoding.

All of the biphase techniques require at least one transition per bit time and may have as many as two transitions. Thus, the maximum modulation rate is twice that for NRZ; this means that the bandwidth required is correspondingly greater. To compensate for this, the biphase schemes have several advantages:

- *Synchronization:* Because there is a predictable transition during each bit time, the receiver can synchronize on that transition. For this reason, the biphase codes are known as self-clocking codes.

- *No dc component:* Biphase codes have no dc component, yielding the benefits described earlier.

- *Error detection:* The absence of an expected transition can be used to detect errors. Noise on the line would have to invert the signal both before and after the expected transition to cause an undetected error.

As can be seen from Figure A.2, the bulk of the energy in biphase codes is between one-half and one times the bit rate. Thus, the bandwidth is reasonably narrow and contains no dc component. However, it is wider than the bandwidth for the multilevel binary codes.

Biphase codes are popular techniques for data transmission. The more common Manchester code has been specified for the IEEE 802.3 standard for baseband coaxial cable and twisted-pair CSMA/CD (carrier sense multiple access with collision detection) bus LANs (local area networks). Differential Manchester has been specified for the IEEE 802.5 token-ring LAN, using shielded twisted pair.

A.5   SCRAMBLING TECHNIQUES

As was mentioned, one way to deal with the synchronization deficiency of multilevel binary codes is to force transitions by including additional bits. This approach is not attractive at high data rates because of the many additional but superfluous bits that would need to be transmitted, reducing efficiency.

Another approach is to make use of some sort of scrambling scheme. The idea behind this approach is simple: sequences that would result in a constant voltage level on the line are replaced by filling sequences that will provide sufficient transitions for the receiver's clock to maintain synchronization. The filling sequence must be recognized by the receiver and replaced with the

---

3.   In the definition of Manchester used in LAN standards and products, a binary 1 corresponds to a low-to-high transition and a binary 0 to a high-to-low transition. Unfortunately, there is no official standard for Manchester, and a number of books use the inverse, in which a low-to-high transition defines a binary 0 and a high-to-low transition defines a binary 1. Here, we conform to industry practice and to the definition used in the various LAN standards.

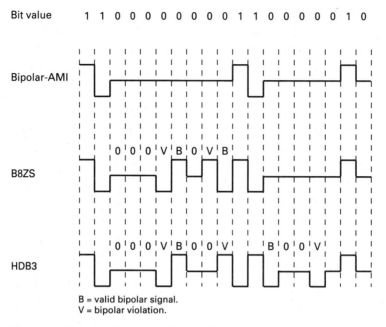

Figure A.4 Encoding Rules for B8ZS and HDB3

original data sequence. The filling sequence is the same length as the original sequence, so there is no data-rate increase. The design goals for this approach can be summarized as follows:

- No dc component
- No long sequences of zero-level line signals
- No reduction in data rate
- Error-detection capability

Two techniques are in use in ISDN; these are illustrated in Figure A.4.

A coding scheme that is commonly used in North America is known as *bipolar with eight 0s substitution (B8ZS)*. The coding scheme is based on bipolar-AMI. We have seen that the drawback of the AMI code is that a long string of 0s may result in loss of synchronization. To overcome this problem, the encoding is amended with the following rules:

- If an octet of all 0s occurs and the last voltage pulse preceding this octet was positive, then the eight 0s of the octet are encoded as $000+-0-+$.
- If an octet of all 0s occurs and the last voltage pulse preceding this octet was negative, then the eight 0s of the octet are encoded as $000-+0+-$.

This technique forces two code violations of the AMI code, an event unlikely to be caused by noise or other transmission impairment. The receiver recognizes the pattern and interprets the octet as consisting of all 0s.

A coding scheme that is commonly used in Europe and Japan is known as the *high-density bipolar—three 0s (HDB3)* code (Table A.2). As before, it is based on the use of AMI encoding.

Table A.2 HDB3 Substitution Rules

Polarity of Preceding Pulse	Number of Bipolar Pulses (1s) Since Last Substitution	
	Odd	Even
−	000 −	+ 00 +
+	000 +	− 00 −

In this case, the scheme replaces strings of four 0s with sequences containing one or two pulses. In each case, the fourth 0 is replaced with a code violation. In addition, a rule is needed to ensure that successive violations are of alternate polarity so that no dc component is introduced. Thus, if the last violation was positive, this violation must be negative and vice versa. The table shows that this condition is tested for by knowing whether the number of pulses since the last violation is even or odd and the polarity of the last pulse before the occurrence of the four 0s.

Figure A.2 shows the spectral properties of these two codes. As can be seen, neither has a dc component. Most of the energy is concentrated in a relatively sharp spectrum around a frequency equal to one-half the data rate. Thus, these codes are well-suited to high-data-rate transmission.

References

Bae, J., and Suda, T. 1991. "Survey of Traffic Control Schemes and Protocols in ATM Networks." *Proceedings of the IEEE*, February.

Bellamy, J. 1991. *Digital Telephony*. 2d ed. New York: Wiley.

Black, U. 1991. *OSI: A Model for Computer Communications Standards*. Englewood Cliffs, N.J.: Prentice-Hall.

Brandwein, R.; Cox, T.; and Dahl, J. 1990. "The IEEE 802.6 Physical Layer Convergence Procedures." *IEEE LCS Magazine*, May.

Branstad, D., ed. 1978. *Computer Security and the Data Encryption Standard*. Gaithersburg, Md.: National Bureau of Standards, Special Publication No. 500–27, February.

Burg, F., and Iorio, N. 1989. "Networking of Networks: Interworking According to OSI." *IEEE Journal on Selected Areas in Communications*, September.

Burg, J., and Dorman, D. 1991. "Broadband ISDN Resource Management: The Role of Virtual Paths." *IEEE Communications Magazine*, September.

Bush, J. 1989. "Frame-Relay Services Promise WAN Bandwidth on Demand." *Data Communications*, July.

Cargill, C. 1989. *Information Technology Standardization: Theory, Process, and Organizations*. Bedford, Mass.: Digital Press.

Cerni, D. 1984. *Standards in Process: Foundations and Profiles of ISDN and OSI Studies*. Washington, D.C.: National Telecommunications and Information Administration, Report 84–170, December.

Chen, K., and Rege, K. 1989. "A Comparative Performance Study of Various Congestion Controls for ISDN Frame-Relay Networks." *Proceedings, IEEE INFOCOM '89*, April.

Davies, D., and Price, W. 1984. *Security for Computer Networks*. New York: Wiley.

Day, A. 1991. "International Standardization of BISDN." *IEEE LTS*, August.

Dijkstra, E. 1959. "A Note on Two Problems in Connection with Graphs." *Numerical Mathematics*, October.

625

Doshi, B., and Nguyen, H. 1988. "Congestion Control in ISDN Frame-Relay Networks." *AT&T Technical Journal,* November/December.

Fletcher, J. 1982. "An Arithmetic Checksum for Serial Transmissions." *IEEE Transactions on Communications,* January.

Hagens, R. 1989. "Components of OSI: ES-IS Routing." Interop, Inc. *Connexions,* August.

Hahne, E.; Choudhury, A.; and Maxemchuk, N. 1990. "Improving the Fairness of Distributed-Queue-Dual-Bus Networks." *Proceedings, IEEE INFOCOM '90,* June.

Handel, R., and Huber, M. 1991. *Integrated Broadband Networks: An Introduction to ATM-Based Networks.* Reading, Mass: Addison-Wesley.

Holzmann, G. 1991. *Design and Validation of Computer Protocols.* Englewood Cliffs, N.J.: Prentice-Hall.

Institute of Electrical and Electronics Engineers. 1990. *IEEE Standard 802: Overview and Architecture.* IEEE Std 802-1990, December.

Jayasumana, A. 1987. "Performance Analysis of Token Bus Priority Schemes." *Proceedings, IEEE INFOCOM '87,* March.

Johnson, M. 1987. "Proof That Timing Requirements of the FDDI Token Ring Protocol are Satisfied." *IEEE Transactions on Communications,* June.

Jones, T.; Rehbehn, K.; and Jennings, E. 1991. *The Buyer's Guide to Frame Relay Networking.* Herndon, Va.: Netrix Corporation.

Kessler, G. 1988. "A Comparison Between CCITT Recommendation X.25 and International Standards 8208 and 7776." *IEEE Transactions on Communications,* April.

———. 1991. "Inside FDDI-II." *LAN Magazine,* March.

Kim, B. 1989. *Current Advances in LANs, MANs, and ISDN.* Norwood, Mass.: Artech House.

Lai, W. 1988. "Packet Forwarding." *IEEE Communications Magazine,* July.

Linn, R. 1989. "Conformance Evaluation Methodology and Protocol Testing." *IEEE Journal on Selected Areas in Communications,* September.

McConnell, J. 1991. "OSI Internetwork Routing." *Open Systems Data Transfer,* Omnicom, Inc., February.

McCool, J. 1988. "FDDI: Getting to Know the Inside of the Ring." *Data Communications,* March.

Minzer, S. 1989. "Broadband ISDN and Asynchronous Transfer Mode (ATM)." *IEEE Communications Magazine,* September.

National Standards Policy Advisory Committee. 1979. *National Policy on Standards for the United States.* 1979. Reprinted in Cerni (1984).

Ocheltree, K. 1990. "Using Redundancy in FDDI Networks." *Proceedings, 15th Conference on Local Computer Networks,* October.

Ocheltree, K., and Montalvo, R. 1989. "FDDI Ring Management." *Proceedings, 14th Conference on Local Computer Networks,* October.

Parekh, S., and Sohraby, K. 1988. "Some Performance Trade-offs Associated with ATM Fixed-Length vs. Variable-Length Cell Formats." *Proceedings, GlobeCom* November. Reprinted in Kim (1989).

Prycker, M. 1991. *Asynchronous Transfer Mode: Solution for Broadband ISDN.* New York: Ellis Horwood.

Ross, F. 1991. "The Fiber Distributed Data Interface." In *Handbook of Local Area Networks,* edited by J. Slone and A. Drinan. New York: Auerbach.

Slone, J., and Drinan, A., eds. 1991. *Handbook of Local Area Networks*. New York: Auerbach.

Stallings, W. 1991. *Data and Computer Communications*. 3d ed. New York: Macmillan.

————. 1993. *Local and Metropolitan Area Networks*. 4th ed. New York: Macmillan.

Tsuchiya, P. 1989. "Components of OSI: IS-IS Intra-Domain Routing." Interop, Inc. *Connexions*, August.

Valenzano, A.; DeMartini, C.; and Ciminiera, L. 1992. *MAP and TOP Communications: Standards and Applications*. Reading, Mass.: Addison-Wesley.

Wolter, M. 1990. "Fiber Distributed Data Interface (FDDI)—A Tutorial." Interop, Inc. *Connexions*, October.

Zeng, H., and Rayner, D. 1986. "The Impact of the Ferry Concept on Protocol Testing." *Proceedings, Protocol Specification, Testing, and Verification* 5.

Index

List of Acronyms

AAL	ATM adaptation layer
ACSE	association-control-service element
AMI	alternate mark inversion
ANSI	American National Standards Institute
ASCII	American Standard Code for Information Interchange
ASE	application-service entity
ASN.1	Abstract Syntax Notation One
ATM	asynchronous transfer mode
B8ZS	bipolar with eight 0s substitution
BISDN	broadband ISDN
CCITT	International Consultative Committee on Telegraphy and Telephony
CLNP	connectionless network protocol
CMIP	common management information protocol
CMIS	common management information service
CMISE	common management information service element
CONS	connection-mode network service
CRC	cyclic-redundancy check
CSMA/CD	carrier sense multiple access with collision detection
DAC	dual-attachment concentrator
DAS	dual-attachment station
DCE	data circuit-terminating equipment
DES	data encryption standard
DLCI	data-link connection identifier
DMPDU	derived MAC protocol data unit
DQDB	distributed-queue dual-bus
DTE	data terminal equipment
ES	end system
FCS	frame-check sequence
FDDI	fiber-distributed data interface
FMBS	frame-mode bearer service
GOSIP	government OSI profile
HDB3	high-density bipolar—three 0s
HDLC	high-level data-link control
IA5	International Alphabet 5
IEEE	Institute of Electrical and Electronics Engineers
IEC	International Electrotechnical Commission
IONL	internal organization of the network layer
IS	intermediate system
ISDN	integrated services digital network
ISO	International Organization for Standardization
ISP	international standardized profile